*Charles Stewart Parnell:*
*the man and his family*

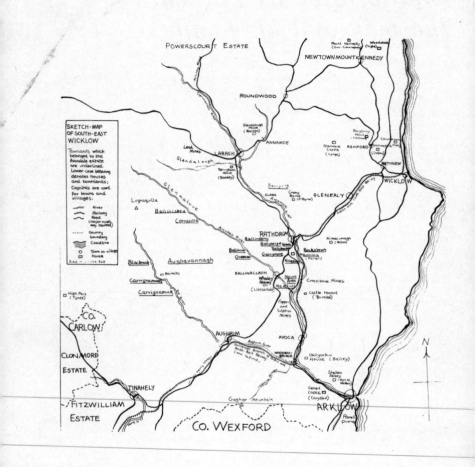

# CHARLES STEWART PARNELL:

*The Man and his Family*

R. F. FOSTER

*Lecturer in History,*
*Birkbeck College,*
*University of London*

THE HARVESTER PRESS LIMITED
HUMANITIES PRESS INC

First published in 1976 by
THE HARVESTER PRESS LIMITED
*Publisher: John Spiers*
2 Stanford Terrace, Hassocks, Sussex
and in the USA 1976 by
Humanities Press Inc.,
Atlantic Highlands, NJ 07716

© 1976 R. F. Foster

Harvester Press
**British Library Cataloguing in Publication Data**
Foster, Robert Fitzroy
    Charles Stewart Parnell.
    Bibl. – Index.
    ISBN 0–85527–044–6
    941.5081'0924   DA958.P2
    Parnell, Charles Stewart

Humanities Press
**Library of Congress Cataloging in Publication Data**

Foster, Robert Fitzroy.
    Charles Stewart Parnell: the man and his family.

    Bibliography:  p.
    Includes index.
    1.   Parnell, Charles Stewart, 1846–1891.  2.  Parnell
family.
DA958. P2F67  1976    941.5081'092'4  [B] 76–20633

ISBN 0-391-00646-0

Printed in Great Britain by
Redwood Burn Ltd.,
Trowbridge, Wiltshire

To Aisling

Thus Parnell, of the seventh generation of his family in Ireland, was the logical outcome of his ancestry, of his family traditions and environment, and of the political circumstances of his native Ireland alike in his own day and in the preceding century. That is the sole clue that is needed to what he himself was and to what he did and tried to do.

— Henry Harrison, *Parnell Vindicated*
(London, 1931), p. 56

# Contents

*Plates appear between pages 76 and 77*

Plate 1 Avondale in the time of the Parnells.

Plate 2 Charles Stewart Parnell aged twenty.

Plate 3 Delia Tudor Stewart Parnell.

Plate 4 Charles Stewart Parnell aged eight.

Plate 5 Fanny Parnell.

Plate 6 Theodosia Parnell.

Plate 7 Emily Dickinson on a favourite horse.

*By courtesy of the National Library of
Ireland and British Library Board*

# *Foreword*

Parnell as a political phenomenon has been a historical preoccupation for nearly a hundred years; but his personal life has invariably been seen merely in apposition to his extraordinary position in late nineteenth-century Irish and British politics. There is at least one very good reason for this: the complete dearth of Parnell family papers. The result has been a tendency to inaccurate hagiography wherever his background and his family are concerned – a heavy reliance on the patriotic myths surrounding his ancestors, and great emphasis on the supposedly anti-British influence of his American mother. Accompanying this interpretation there has been a tendency to ignore the background which produced the man, and with which he retained links until the end of his life: the Anglo-Irish ascendancy of county Wicklow.

In this book I have attempted to redress the balance in emphasis. The shortage of specific family material has led to an approach which involves beginning with the general picture and then finding Parnell's place in it. Thus my study commences with a view of nineteenth-century Wicklow and its society; then surveys the Parnell family background; and finally deals with the man himself. The emphases that emerge are new. Nineteenth-century Wicklow had a special character of its own, and seen against its background the public Parnell appears as a more logical product of his environment than has been thought. Nor do the family traditions which influenced him most seem to have been connected with his celebrated great-grandfather Sir John, or with his erratic mother. The neglected figure of his paternal grandfather, a radical pamphleteer and improving landlord, provides a more interesting link; and the political involvements of his sisters Fanny and Anna deserve far more serious consideration than they have had before. On a wider scale, the way that Parnell's connection with Wicklow and his involvements there continued throughout his life deserves specific examination; his financial, personal and political life were constantly affected by these factors. I have recapitulated briefly on the significance of these reassessments and evaluations in the conclusion to this book.

Throughout, I have avoided discussing Parnell's political life; it is not part of my study here. But I believe this necessarily limited view of his background and personal life sheds light on the traditionally 'enigmatic' figure he became; and that such an essay in contextual biography has its own value. For, if primarily a study of Parnell himself, this book is nearly as much concerned with examining one nineteenth-century Irish family (albeit an extraordinary one, living through an extraordinary era): their property, their background, their social context, and the forces that made them what they were.

# Acknowledgements

I owe thanks to many people for various kinds of help over the past four years with regard to this book. The following acknowledgements are the most important; but there should be, I know, many more. For permission to quote from collections of papers I am grateful to the following: the Director and Trustees of the National Library, Dublin; the Keeper of the State Papers, Dublin Castle; the Registrar of Deeds, Dublin; the Minister of Lands (for the papers at Avondale House, Rathdrum, Co. Wicklow); Dr Leon O Broin (for quotations from the Doran Papers); and the present (eighth) Lord Congleton. The extracts from Katherine Parnell's *Charles Stewart Parnell* appear by courtesy of Cassell and Company. I am grateful to Mr James Cusack of Clonmel for allowing me to use a letter from C. J. Kickham in his possession. My thanks also to Mr Hubert Poole of Cahir, Co Tipperary, for permission to quote from the manuscript diary of his relative, Alfred Webb. I am grateful to the Library of Trinity College, Dublin, for making available to me manuscripts in their possession. Every effort has been made to get in touch with the owners of copyright material; if there is any instance where this has failed, I hope this general acknowledgement will be accepted as adequate.

My knowledge of the Parnells and Wicklow was increased, and my enthusiasm stimulated, by conversations with Captain A. J. P. Mateer (John Howard Parnell's stepson), the late Mr R. C. Barton of Glendalough House, and Mr Hugh Gaffney of Roundwood; I have referred to the recollections of all three in notes, but should like to record my gratitude here. I also enjoyed helpful conversations about Wicklow and the Parnells with Dr Charles Dickson and Colonel C. N. Paget.

Denis McCullough helped me with some legal enquiries; Richard Comerford, Kevin Mellyn and Sally Fawcus kindly provided and checked references for me. The staff of the National Library of Ireland, the Registry of Deeds, and the British Museum were uniformly helpful. I also owe thanks to Mrs Eva Laide, ex-curator of Avondale, for helping me with the material there. Lord Congleton helpfully provided quotations from family papers. Beryl Cunningham drove me tirelessly on field-work expeditions round Wicklow. Valerie Elliott and Patricia Capel did vast amounts of typing with short notice and at high speed.

Dr Anthony Malcomson of the Belfast Public Record Office both added to my knowledge of eighteenth-century Irish politics and steered me out of several errors. The Provost of Trinity College, Dublin, Dr F. S. L. Lyons, who was at the time writing his own book about Parnell, unstintingly provided enlightening references and encouraging discussions. Finally, any Irish historian working on this period owes a large debt to Professor T. W. Moody; and in my case the obligation is enormous. He initiated the subject as a thesis, gave unsparingly of his time and advice, and provided invaluable references from manuscripts and other unpublished material which would never have otherwise come my way.

My most heartfelt thanks of all go to my wife: to whom this book is dedicated as a small recompense for her aid, encouragement, advice and unfailing forbearance while I was writing it.

*Birkbeck College,*                                                    R. F. Foster
*London University*
*June 1975*

# Introduction: The 'special case' of nineteenth-century Wicklow

It is by now a truism that Parnell's life and politics constitute an enigma. Why a Protestant landowner from the conservative country gentry should have taken up the cause of nationalist politics and radical land reform is still debated; the picture is further distorted by the evidence that he disliked politics and the life he was constrained to lead, and his later years were marked by a sporadic desire to retire altogether into the obscure private life he had fashioned for himself at Eltham. An understanding of this can only be achieved by considering what he left behind him when he entered politics, and its continuing influence upon him throughout his career: his family and social background.

A study of Parnell and his background must begin by defining that background: the social context from which, in a sense, he migrated. Before considering the details of family history and local environment, I propose to outline a more general picture as an introduction: the peculiarities of county Wicklow, always so important to him, based on a survey roughly covering the years from 1820 to 1870. Many of the special features thus outlined survive to this day; those that do not were no less important in their influence upon the character and fortunes of the Parnell family. And several of the issues that such a study raises will recur throughout this book.

To begin on the widest level: Wicklow, immediately south of Dublin, is wooded and fertile in the east where it is bordered by the sea, and more bare and mountainous to the west; the whole county comprises some of the loveliest countryside in Ireland. It has increasingly today the character of a dormitory for those with business interests in the capital or elsewhere but an inclination towards country life; and this process is not one of recent development. In 1883 there were twenty landowners of over 3,000 acres resident in the county, and nine of them had far larger estates elsewhere; fourteen more great landowners had secondary residences in Wicklow.[1] Wealthy commercial families like the Guinnesses, Latouches and Jamesons lived there as well as those whose investment was in land on the other side of Ireland. The median size of estates in Wicklow was larger than in most other counties, and the number of absentee owners lower. [2] The social composition of the county reflected this general picture: it showed an extremely high incidence of Protestants. By the 1861 census only two other counties outside Ulster had a larger number of Established Church members, and they were special cases – Cork and Dublin. [3]

There was, therefore, a large number of well-off gentry on medium–size estates, most of these concentrated on the far more fertile eastern side of the county. There were, of course, several enormous holdings; the Fitzwilliams owned 90,000 acres, the Powerscourts 41,000; the Carysforts, Cunninghams, Downshires, Beresfords and Wicklows all had estates exceeding 10,000 acres. But there was also a large representation of what can be called 'middling gentry': families like the Humes, Actons, Tottenhams, Synges, Tighes, Westbys, Grattans, Truells, and Parnells, who constituted the J.P. class of the county. They held more than one county office, owned estates of several thousand acres, and often maintained a Dublin or London house as well as a Wicklow seat. It is a class not usually considered characteristic of nineteenth-century Ireland; but the high incidence of this element in Wicklow is indicated even today by the large number of Victorian country houses in the county. Their owners were on the next level to the Carysforts, Powerscourts or Fitzwilliams, who might spend only half the year in Wicklow; it was the *agent* of the great landowning absentee whose position approximated more closely to the middling gentry. (Thus Robert Chaloner, who ran the Fitzwilliam estates in this period, held the offices of Deputy Lieutenant and J.P., was involved in county politics, and had daughters married into Wicklow families; his invaluable letter-book and notebooks provide as much insight into general county life as into the handling of the gigantic Coolattin estate.) [3]

The fortunes and characteristics of this class must be what will preoccupy us here. But one more area should be surveyed, in which Wicklow was also a special case: the Famine, which bisects the period under consideration. While affected severely, like everywhere else, Wicklow was nonetheless considerably less hard hit than other counties and recovery was at a faster rate than elsewhere. Agriculturally, only the number of horses and pigs decreased between 1841 and 1848; cattle increased by over 21,000 head, sheep by nearly 20,000, and the gross value of livestock by over £180,000. [4] Most crops steadily increased in acreage from 1848 on, after a drop in yield during 1847–8. The accounts for a large dairy farm like the Tottenhams' near Ashford show little variance for the period. [5] Moreover, rental arrears on the Fitzwilliam estate, while increasing in the 1840s, never reached the level of the 1820s, and decreased rapidly in the 1850s.[6] On the overall level, population density in Wicklow decreased far less than elsewhere;[7] the county escaped famine fever until 1847.[8] To take a local sample, an analysis of the population records on the Fitzwilliam estate shows that over these years, while the population dropped dramatically, the proportionate decrease in numbers of adults was far smaller than in that of children; thus the decline seems due more to emigration and the later marrying age than to the direct depradations of the famine.[9] Moreover, by 1856–7 no county in Ireland recorded a smaller number of emigrants than Wicklow; for the following decade, her percentage of emigrants was half the national average.[10] During the worst of the Famine, people migrated *into* Wicklow, even from usually prosperous Kildare, in search of a means of subsistence.[11]

The Wicklow landlords, in any case, reacted more actively than those elsewhere. In November 1845 Chaloner ordered several tons of Indian rice for safety's sake; he went on to order many more, as well as vast stocks of corn and oatmeal.[12] By 1848 he was referring to 'fast recovery' and the fact that there was no resistance to rents,[13] a judgement repeated by the records of his neighbours James Grattan and Lord Powerscourt.[14] The Powerscourts served no eviction notices; Lord Fitzwilliam did, but a good proportion of these was dismissed before being served, and the estate records show notices being presented year after year without any direct action being taken. Evictions served were a tiny proportion of those entered, and even this could mean nothing at all. Eviction was used by the late 1850s only as a paper tiger; the small proportion of recalcitrants in the Fitzwilliam eviction records are marked, significantly, '*try* ejectment'.

Still considering the enormous Fitzwilliam estate, although Chaloner did not encourage emigration in the early period he aided it during the famine, and wrote frequently to the Canadian agent who received people from the estate to find out what had become of them. Other landlords acted similarly. In a more positive fashion, James Grattan and William Parnell experimented with different methods of food production and slaughtered stock cattle on their farms for the tenantry.[15] The Powerscourts and Fitzwilliams arranged relief works, though paternalism was dealt out from Coolattin in careful measure; it is significant that in the early 1850s some tenants appealed over Chaloner's head to Lord Fitzwilliam about rent abatements, and yet more significant that they got their way. Bad landlords certainly existed; indeed, those estates whose records *can* be examined are by definition those that were well managed. The striking thing is that they account for such a large proportion of the county. But during the famine the Crony Byrne landlord evicted without compassion at

Knockananna;[16] there were probably several more who did likewise.

However, even James Grattan, most liberal of landlords, decided by 1849 that his tenants had recovered enough to use the situation for their own advantage as regarded rent arrears and emigration assistance.[17] More general data bear out the picture of a comparatively light visitation and speedy recovery. Life for the landlords had been little affected at any time; Lady Caroline Howard of Shelton Abbey 'wondered why others are all so prosperous' in the early 1850s [18] and even in 1847, when Mrs Airey wrote to her daughter Mrs Tottenham of Ashford that they would all have to emigrate, it was in a highly facetious spirit. [19] But even for their unfortunate dependants, the holocaust had been of comparatively short duration; and of its inheritances, emigration continued only at an exceptionally low rate while the arrears situation became a new *status quo* and non-payment of rent, as James Grattan sensed, was the genesis of a later, deliberate, mode of agitation.

This consideration of Wicklow and the famine has led on, inevitably, to the question of the way the Wicklow gentry ran their estates – and, for that matter, how they lived in the context of county affairs. Here there is evidence that they devoted more attention than was common to social duties. The record of a Resident Magistrate at Baltinglass shows that attendance of J.P.s. at petty sessions was exceptionally regular; the same diary records the general peacability of the county, with a high incidence of property crimes compared to those of violence[20] (as well as the astounding intelligence that on 12 May 1841 'there was *no-one drunk* at Baltinglass fair'). Wages on the Crofton and Proby estates were far above national averages. [21] Throughout the county relations between landlords and tenantry were generally good – though on this level as at every other, the way an estate was run depended upon the men running it. Thus the Coolattin administration was continually criticised by Grattan in the 1820s, when it was under the supervision of Mr Haigh, whereas Chaloner's régime was totally different; and even the powers that Chaloner delegated could in turn be exercised within a wide sphere of discretion. [22] In general terms, while I am by no means prepared to argue that the Wicklow gentry constituted anything like the 'backbone class' of their English counterparts, a certain spirit of *noblesse oblige* can be discerned. Charitable efforts were made, though often on an unrealistic basis; the Coolattin Poor Shop was little patronised, and this probably means that relief on a cut-price money basis was irrelevant, rather than that there was a low level of neediness. [23] James Grattan, always a trenchant critic of his well-intentioned but less committed neighbours, gives an ironic description of the gentry meeting over tea at Mrs Latouche's orphanage at Delgany. [24] Men like Daniel Tighe and Lord Powerscourt subscribed to a long list of charitable organisations; and as regards charity that began nearer home, a fair amount was done in the area of education. Robert Truell of Clonmannin compiled tables to estimate the state of education in the county; Grattan called for 'schools to be built before gaols'; the Fitzwilliam estate supported large schools at Shillelagh, Carnew and Ballard, and gave assistance to individuals who founded 'classical schools'. The Powerscourt school expenses rose 150 per cent in the 1850s. [25] Ladies like Caroline and Alicia Howard, sisters of the Earl of Wicklow, taught classes in the local schools, albeit without much enjoyment. [26] Later in the century John Synge of Glanmore Castle, near Ashford, was known as 'Peztalozzi John' for his constant advocacy of that method of teaching. The stress laid on education took, of course, a different form where the landlords' own children were concerned, and the Tighes, Loftuses, Probys and the rest sent their sons to Eton, Winchester, Harrow and other English schools: a routine that Mrs John Henry Parnell, for all her well‑publicised patriotism, did not choose to break.

As always in Ireland, considerations of education lead on to those of religion; and in this connection a particularly interesting situation arose in 1840, when two Protestant clergymen on the Fitzwilliam estate attempted to keep their flock separate from Roman Catholics in the local schools and met with firm opposition from both Chaloner and the Earl, grounded on a basis of non-sectarianism and appealing to the broadest tenets of religious tolerance. The Fitzwilliams favoured non‑sectarian schools with children of either religion receiving instruction in their separate faiths at a set hour each day; the Reverends Moore and Dowse and the Church Education Society attempted first of all to withdraw their parishioners' children to the vestry for religious in‑struction, and then to set up an exclusively Protestant school in the churchyard. They eventually got their way, though the Earl resorted to legal advice in an attempt to stop them; all he could do was eject the Reverend Moore from his living. [27] Both this affair and Chaloner's correspondence show an extremely good relationship between landlord and Roman Catholic clergy. James Grattan also organised non-sec‑tarian schools and preferred 'to attend in the first instance to their minds . . . rather than to their religious education'. [28] The Powerscourt estate treated its parish clergy well, and the priest reciprocated by for‑bidding rioters to storm the house in an attempted local rising of 1867. [29] There were Orange lodges in various parts of the county but where Drought, the R.M. mentioned above, records breaking up such meetings it is clear that the membership was not of the gentry class.

Religious tolerance and an interest in education imply a certain standard of intellectual life among the gentry; at the very beginning of the century the Tighes had a printing-press at Rossanna, and George Ball had another nearby at Roundwood. The influence of Mary Tighe, author of *Cupid and Psyche,* permeated from Woodstock in Co.

Kilkenny; her Wicklow relatives wrote less publicised verse and painstaking literary translations. [30] James Grattan and William Parnell were cultivated men, as is shown both by their writings and the catalogues of their sizeable libraries. [31] As in other circles of the Irish gentry, religious revival coloured intellectual life in the early part of the century; the 'Plymouth' Brethren met in the drawing-room of Powerscourt House and Mrs Francis Howard, who often visited Wicklow from her home in Swords, wrote enthusiastically in 1839 of 'the stride religion has taken into the fashionable world'. [32] Revivalism alone, however, did not dictate the intellectual tone of county life. Nor was culture restricted to those like the Powerscourts who lived among Breughels and Tintorettos and travelled as far afield as St Petersburg in search of art treasures. In Lord Fitzwilliam's dictum that a parish priest must have a comfortable house; in his agent's statement to the bigoted Reverend Dowse that 'if one had to wait for a perfect Christian to say grace I believe the ceremony would have to be omitted'; in Grattan's and Parnell's denunciations of the ignorance and viciousness of the Irish *status quo;* in the Tighes' literary allusions and anecdotes – in all this, a quality of intellectual life above the norm as well as an uncharacteristically broad-minded religious attitude among the Wicklow gentry is strongly indicated.

There was, moreover, a certain *esprit de corps* which bound the Wicklow families together. Social life took the form of its time, the lengthy Victorian 'visit', with the purpose, as Lady Caroline Howard defined it, of 'cheering each other up'. Tighes, Hamiltons, Westbys, Howards, Parnells and Croftons not only lived in and out of each other's houses; they visited Bath, Harrogate, Weymouth or the Riviera only to encounter each other yet again. A liberal like James Grattan might describe the Irish gentry as 'ignorant, prejudiced, vulgar and brutal' and decide to keep aloof from them; [33] but, significantly, he still made the funeral arrangements for the very neighbour whose death through dissipation had prompted the reflection. Much of the spirit which united the gentry was that common to all Irish landlords with regard to the people who supported them: the kinship of a beleagured garrison. Grattan himself, while he believed in the importance of preserving the Irish language and approaching Irish history with a new attitude, still contributed to the governing syndrome by collecting 'Irish Bulls' – much as across the Atlantic Southern gentlemen swapped stories about their own alien, inscrutable dependants. The impression remains of a closed circuit in Wicklow society, where the resident middling gentry visited each other, travelled abroad with each other, and married each other.

What emerges overall, nonetheless, is a picture of an idiosyncratic upper class, more like English Tories than figments from Maria Edgeworth or Charles Lever – no less arrogant, probably, than their contemporaries elsewhere in Ireland but more enlightened and more tolerant, and running their estates with a different kind of approach. The phrase 'model estate' rings oddly in nineteenth-century Ireland; but in Wicklow one can instance not only the pleasant planning of villages like Enniskerry or Kiltegan, but also the stock-books of the Tottenham dairy farm, where every beast was entered by name, and the Grattan plantations, recorded tree by tree, not to mention the wealth of 'estate cottages' still to be noticed all over the county. Model estates, of course, constituted an anomaly considering the Irish *status quo;* a reformer like Grattan was, in fact, trying hard to be a 'godly squire' in a situation that did not allow such phenomena. Nonetheless, a look into Wicklow society provides a different impression from what might be expected of nineteenth-century Ireland.

Nineteenth-century Ireland, however, it still was; and thus, liberalism on other levels notwithstanding, it should come as no surprise to find the Wicklow gentry politically conservative. Tory members were generally returned for the county. Though James Grattan represented it from 1827 to 1841, he was something of a maverick in county politics; and when in 1832 he ran as a Liberal calling for Tithe reform, with Catholic support (though he distrusted O'Connell), he had to face immense and united opposition from his own class. 'None of the gentry acted well', he recorded gloomily. When he was returned despite the powerful countering influence of Lord Fitzwilliam and Lord Wicklow, he saw it as being 'brought in by the people' in defiance of the gentry: 'the county was illuminated on the night of my return *in spite of them all*'.[34] The Wicklow gentry exercised considerable control over their tenants' votes, as numerous references in the papers of the Fitzwilliams, Tottenhams and Howards show. It is to be wondered at, not that Grattan's stand alienated his neighbours, but that with their opposition he managed to get elected at all.

There were, nonetheless, those among the gentry who, nurtured in the special atmosphere of Wicklow, reacted against the political tenets of their class. James Grattan was one; William Parnell another; Charles Stewart Parnell was to be a third. For the Parnell family was worked closely into the fabric of county life that I have described. Like the Tighes of Rossanna or the Grattans of Tinnehinch, their ancestors were the prominent figures of late eighteenth-century politics.[35] Like Westaston, Humewood, Glenmore and Clonabraney their estate ran from four to five thousand acres and included a large house of some architectural merit. They were J.P.s and Deputy Lieutenants for the county. Charles Stewart Parnell's grandfather, William Parnell, and his uncle, Sir Ralph Howard, were M.P.s for the county. The family was related to the Howards, Powerscourts and Carysforts. They partook fully in county life, visiting Shelton Abbey for shooting-parties and entertaining the county to cricket at Avondale, their home near

Rathdrum. Charles Stewart Parnell has too often been seen as a phenomenon, a man removed from and transcending his background; this book comprises a study of that background, on the level of local environment as well as family, and an attempt to fix him more firmly in this context. To any study like this, an introductory survey of the idiosyncratic background of Wicklow 'county' life in the nineteenth century has seemed a necessary prelude.

# Part I

## *The Avondale inheritance*

# 1   *Sir John Parnell and his family*

There was a vein of talent that ran through the entire family in their several generations – serviceable to their country in some – agreeable in others – singular and eccentric in all ... on the whole they were a race that deserve notice in the history of Ireland. H. Grattan on the Parnell family in *Memoirs of the life and times of the rt hon. Henry Grattan* (5 vols., London, 1839–46), v, 145 (n.).

## I

It may seem ironic that the remark quoted above was made in the year of the birth of Charles Stewart Parnell, who was to bring more fame to the family than all his ancestors put together, but it raised a point essential to any consideration of the forces that shaped him as a man and as a politician – the distinguished history of the Parnell family in public life and the considerable mystique connected with the name. In this chapter the career and influence of 'the great' Sir John Parnell, great-grandfather of Charles Stewart Parnell, will primarily be considered, since it was his name and reputation which were so often invoked in philippics about his great-grandson; but he was, essentially, one of a distinguished clan.

The family history of the first Parnells in Ireland has been condensed and served up many times in the early pages of studies of Charles Stewart Parnell.[1] I pretend to offer nothing new; the following facts are presented merely as introduction. Thomas Parnell, son of a mercer and mayor of Congleton in Cheshire, came to Ireland at the time of the Restoration; it has been conjectured that he was a Cromwellian sympathiser. Whatever his politics, his fortune enabled him to purchase a house in Dawson Street, Dublin, and an estate called Rathleague in the Queen's County. He died in 1685; his two sons were

Thomas the poet, Archdeacon of Clogher, who died in 1718, leaving only short-lived issue, and his brother John, who thus in time inherited all the family property. Thomas had achieved some fame as a poet, and is recorded in the copious memoirs and correspondence of the age of Swift and Pope. John became a barrister, M.P., and judge, married a daughter of Lord Chief Justice Whitshed, and died in 1727. He had one son, John, who became M.P. for Bangor and was created first baronet of Rathleague in 1766; he died in 1782.

Sir John married Anne Ward, daughter of Michael Ward of Castleward, Co. Down, and sister of the first Lord Bangor. Their only son, the second Sir John Parnell, became Chancellor of the Irish Exchequer, an important Privy Councillor, and one of the most important Irishmen of his day. Dismissed from office for refusing to support the Union, Sir Jonah Barrington awarded Parnell the sobriquet of 'Incorruptible'; this view was amplified by the hagiographical references of nationalist posterity.[2] Contemporaries were a good deal more restrained in their judgement;[3] and, as can be expected, references to him in the correspondence of English politicians of the time are remarkable for their asperity. An examination of his career and political history is in itself instructive, and can help redeem the balance on both sides.

The future second baronet was born on 25 December 1744. In June 1766 he entered Lincoln's Inn; from 1776 to 1783 he represented Inistiogue in parliament, sitting for the Queen's County after that. On 19 July 1774 he married Letitia Charlotte, daughter of Sir Arthur Brooke of Colebrooke in Co. Fermanagh. In December 1780 he became a Commissioner of the Revenue; in April 1782 he succeeded to the baronetcy which had been conferred upon his father in 1766; in September 1785 he became Chancellor of the Irish Exchequer. On 27 October 1786 he was sworn a member of the British Privy Council, and in February of the same year elected a bencher of King's Inns, Dublin, though he was never called to either bar. In 1793 he became, virtually *ex officio*, a member of the newly constituted Board of Treasury. Dismissed from office for opposition to the Union, he sat for Queen's County in the first parliament of the United Kingdom at Westminster in January 1801, his seat having been transferred there from College Green. He died on 5 December that year, aged 57.

It is a remarkable career; a steady advancement in power and influence, honourable loss of office over a matter of principle, and a sudden death at the height of his exaltation. His history, however, is not without its anomalies. Sir Jonah Barrington's picture of him is of a man pushed to success almost against himself: 'cheerful and confident, he generally preferred society to trouble and seemed to have rid himself of a weight when he had performed a duty'. Parnell is pictured, by Barrington and others, as a large, casual, untidy kind of man; his father, by contrast, was 'a crafty, prudent minor politician' who intended his son for a diplomatic career and had him educated with a view to this pursuit; but since the future Chancellor lacked 'the necessary attainments of evasion and duplicity, his talents became destined for home consumption' and he soon advanced 'by the intrigues of his father and the forced exertion of his own abilities'. [4]

Much of Barrington is pure gossip, and this may be little different, though he knew Parnell well. It is, however, certain that whatever about the path he followed or was led along, the political principles that he usually embraced tended rather to reflect faithfully the line laid down by government than to express the strongly independent opinions later attributed to him. His views on the Catholic question, for instance, are illuminating. Lecky points out that he was ambivalent about the 1792 Relief Bill; [5] Parnell was not, in fact, prepared to advocate the Catholic cause until after 1793, when they were admitted to the franchise. Froude also emphasises Parnell's conservative attitude over the Catholics; [6] but one does not have to depend upon secondary sources for Parnell's strongly Protestant viewpoint. Time and again he spoke on behalf of the Protestant interest in Irish society; during the debate on Catholic relief in 1792 he went so far as to defend the Penal Laws.

> I rise to rescue the Protestants of Ireland from the calumnies which have been thrown upon them; I rise to rescue the memory of our forefathers from the unjust and unfounded aspersions that have been cast upon them. They have been described as cruel tyrants for enacting laws to which they were compelled by self-defence and the necessity of the times and which laws we, their posterity, relaxed in the most essential points the moment a favourable opportunity arrived. Was this tyranny in the Protestant gentlemen of Ireland? No, Sir, the Protestant gentlemen of Ireland are as liberal as they are brave. Sir, I cannot forget that I am a Protestant myself; that I am born of Protestant parents; and that I am a member of the Protestant establishment; and therefore I will not hear Protestants degraded under colour of an invective against laws that we have repealed. [7]

When questions of Catholic rights came up, Parnell could be counted on to stand against 'speaking to the passions of the people'; even when supporting a government bill enfranchising Catholics and removing distinctions against them he contrived to imply his personal disagreement with the principle, [8] and he only abstained from opposing it after British government pressure. This is not to say he was hysterically anti-Catholic; his views of the religion were described approvingly by Henry Dundas as 'sound and dispassionate'. [9] Indeed, Parnell was so dispassionate that he quickly abandoned even his equivocal support of

Catholics when there were bigger fish to fry. In 1799 a letter of Buckingham's describing the machinations of anti-Unionists told how, after Catholic opinion had been induced to hold off opposing the measure, a meeting was held at Speaker Foster's house. Here 'Ponsonby at length yielded to the earnest solicitations of Parnell and Foster and engaged to abandon the Catholics and support the Orange Party' – in a resolution calling for active exertions by the militia against rebellious elements in the country and decisive support for maintaining 'the Protestant ascendancy' threatened by the Union. [10] The consciousness of being part of the ascendancy which Parnell emphasised so strongly, even while nominally supporting the recognition of Catholic rights, was a guiding principle of his politics; when the organ of the Protestant ascendancy – their parliament – was threatened, the Irish Catholics were seen by Parnell purely in the terms of their political usefulness and when they were cast as potential opponents on the issue he had no hesitation in trying to play the Orange card instead.

The Catholic question was not the only sphere of reform to which Sir John Parnell showed himself at best a fair-weather friend and more often a whole-hearted enemy. Social reform was an issue that preoccupied few of the legislators at College Green; but one attempted instance was Grattan's suggestion in 1792 that, owing to the national prosperity proudly declared by Parnell as Chancellor, cottagers could be exempted from the hearth tax. This was firmly opposed by Parnell 'until the unfunded debt accrued in previous years was paid off'. [11] An unsigned state paper of the time is more explicit about his attitude, recording that 'he admitted the distress occasioned by the tax and that nothing would contribute more effectively to the relief of the people than its repeal or modification; but justified it by this extraordinary position, that it was necessary to make them *feel* there was a government over them'. [12] Parnell was constrained to accept exemption of the cottagers in 1795, but similar measures introduced later by Grattan, as well as suggestions for franchise extension, received his uncompromising opposition. Despite the fact that he held the rank of colonel in the Volunteers, he attacked 'parliamentary dictation' by that body over constituency and franchise reform; [13] he also opposed any idea of administrative reorganisation with regard to public money. [14] Parnell's grounds for upholding the status quo were invariably the iniquity of the French example, the country's prosperity under the present system, and the absence of reforming legislation in England. In the condition of parliament and government as in the system of taxation Sir John Parnell was a man who liked things as they were and wanted them kept that way.

This bias is clearly shown in the question of government sinecures and pensions, a long drawn-out controversy which shows him consistently aligned against Grattan, Forbes and all the comparatively progressive elements in the Irish parliament. [15] Again, pensions were defended by Parnell on rather flimsy grounds, such as that 'the ancient and illustrious families of this country' must be maintained, and that every government had increased the list since 1726. On questions like the sale of peerages, Parnell's only line of defence against Grattan's impassioned attacks in 1790 was to ask his opponent if he felt he could do the job of Chancellor better himself. [16] The opposition campaign carried over into the next session, becoming concentrated upon the expenditure of public money mentioned above; Parnell's answer was a classic statement of the conservative case. [17] He was capable of presenting the government policy of retrenchment on public works expenditure in 1787 as a measure against 'jobbing parliamentary grants'; [18] when it came to restricting the pension list or the controversy over the administration of public money, however, he refused any change. And on the rare occasions when he backed popular measures, he did so under duress from the British administration.

An additional anomaly, also pointed out to him, was that at the same time as cutting back heavily on public works he was extravagantly extolling the wealth of Ireland under his chancellorship: 'it would be difficult in the history of the world to show a nation rising faster in prosperity'. [19] This raises the question of his ability as Chancellor. The Irish revenue was divided into two parts, hereditary and additional; the hereditary revenue (outside Parliament's control) was inadequate, and loans were raised from 1715 on, resulting in an increasing National Debt and the occasional embarrassment of government by parliament's threatening a short money bill. Despite reorganisation in 1793, national finances were chaotic by 1800: for which the financial effects of the war may have largely been to blame. However, Ireland in the late eighteenth century is usually considered to have been enjoying an economic – especially a commercial – boom; Parnell's statements in the Irish House of Commons testified to this, and he repeatedly spoke of a steady reduction in the National Debt. These statements were not, however, necessarily the last word. At the end of Parnell's administration, Castlereagh wrote to Pitt explaining why Irish finance had been doubly confused of late, and why Irish demands on the English treasury, a new development dating from 1796, had been so much beyond Parnell's estimates. The Irish Chancellor had miscalculated quit-rent proceeds, underestimated government costs, forgotten the deficiencies of the previous years, and ignored the extraordinary militia charge following the 1798 Rising. [20] Attention was frequently drawn to similar inefficiency by political opponents during Parnell's term of office – notably by Isaac Corry, who was to succeed him as Chancellor after his fall, [21] but also by Grattan, Flood, Griffith, Conolly and others; one accusation neatly sums up Parnell's evasiveness in debate, that 'he boasted of a redundancy till some plan was proposed to employ it usefully, and then explained away all the boasts he had made'.[22] Expenditure remained grossly in excess of revenue, while at the same time no public works were undertaken and taxation on trade increased; Parnell's chief innovation was repeatedly to introduce state lotteries. He was also capable of explaining deficits by such ingenious hypotheses as 'a sudden drop in trade owing to the disturbed state of the public mind which has been agitated by inflammatory writings'.[23] Parnell eventually introduced legislation regulating issue of public money, the granting of a civil list in lieu of hereditary revenue, and a fixed pension list, but he always refused any suggestions of an absentee tax. He was, after all, a servant of the administration; his business was to pilot through unpopular measures like the one whereby in 1791 an English import tax on Irish beer was to be left unaltered. Westmorland admitted in a letter to Grenville that the principle was indefensible; all he could hope was that 'as there is some difficulty in understanding the duties, patriotism will be silent; should it be warmly contested, it will be too unreasonable to desire Parnell or Beresford to expose themselves and to be abused, with the argument so plain against them'.[24] Parnell's own inclinations were towards lotteries and theories like 'following the example of the Roman State where the government act the part of pawnbroker and lend money on pledges at a reasonable interest'.[25] The more practical nature of his work as Chancellor, however, was to engineer such measures as that described in Westmorland's cynical letter. Little wonder that here as in other areas the 'Patriots' were so firmly aligned against him; nor, perhaps, bearing in mind his miscalculations and evasions in office, that a colleague described him as 'the most, brutal, blundering, inefficient financier in the habitable world'.[26]

The picture that is built up is not that of a man who would readily be grouped with the 'Patriots'; the tradition that Parnell and Grattan, for instance, were particularly close friends seems to date from their struggle against the Union rather than earlier – though they were on good enough terms in 1785 for Grattan to write to Parnell congratulating him on his appointment,[27] and were friendly in 1794–5. Lecky believed it was due to 'intimate friendship' that Grattan wanted Parnell to continue in office when the appointment of the progressive Fitzwilliam seemed to threaten his position;[28] but the real reason for this was that Denis Bowes Daly and others desired Parnell's removal so that Grattan could take over the post – and Grattan did not want this situation to arise.[29] Moreover, Grattan at this time wrote anonymously to Parnell, 'apprising him that his place was in danger and recommending him to look to it':[30] hardly the action of an 'intimate'. Certainly the two men were politically alienated in the early nineties; on occasion Parnell was even driven to abandon his habitual courtesy.[31] After 1794 there was some sort of *modus vivendi*, with Grattan abstaining from 'vexatious opposition' once the place and pension bills were conceded;[32] but the two men still clashed over tariffs and duties in 1795 and 1796.[33] Grattan outlived Parnell by many years, and probably recalled him best as a friend and ally at the time of the great Union fight; but the evidence points to a relationship before that which was distinguished by political animosity.

It is for his opposition to the Union, in fact, that Parnell is chiefly remembered. Yet up to 1799 his policy had been, in a sense, firmly 'unionist'. Time and again he proclaimed the identity of economic and political interest between the two countries.[34] His unionism went no less deep for being based on an opportunistic recognition of the advantages of a close identification with England. Yet he became one of the most fervent opponents of legislative union. In 1798 Pitt personally informed him of his intention, and Parnell after an interval declared his opposition. In January 1799 he was removed from office; on the 22nd of that month he announced his stand in parliament. He supported Parsons' amendment in the debate of January 1800, attacked the Union in a speech of 5 February, and attempted to move a general referendum on the question on 13 March. 26 May found him defending his old opponent, Grattan, against Castlereagh, his old colleague, and the wheel had come full circle.

His opposition had not, however, been unequivocal from the beginning. In November 1798 government opinion felt he was 'certainly to be gained';[35] but he was 'not at all conclusive', and by Christmas Portland felt his attitude must be more clearly defined.[36] When he finally declared himself, it was on the grounds of the unconstitutional nature of the measure and its potential danger to security; he never appealed to high-souled patriotic fervour, as did Grattan and his associates.[37] From January 1799 Parnell, Speaker Foster and William Ponsonby formed a nucleus of opposition to the measure.[38] Referring to this triumvirate, Cooke remarked suggestively in April that 'the Protestants think the Union will diminish their power, however it may secure their property';[39] these three certainly had the sort of parliamentary and administrative influence that no Union peerage or sinecure could make up for. Parnell's position nonetheless remained fairly moderate at first, as Cooke thankfully wrote to Lord Auckland;[40] but he resented the fact that he received no thanks from Castlereagh when he promised to support the government on everything except the Union.[41] More than one overture was made by government spokesmen to Parnell during 1799, suggesting that he should back down;[42] though he refused, his speeches against the measure as late as February 1800 were subdued, and restricted to questions of commercial disadvantage and the *weakening* of the British link by removing the parliament.[43] His alienation from the

government did not mean a redirection towards the philosophy of the
Patriot camp.

Several references in the government correspondence of the time,
moreover, show a general belief that Parnell was not entirely happy in
his new position. Buckingham wrote to Grenville in January 1799,
when Parnell lost office: '*I know for certain* that he was convinced as
late as yesterday morning that Government would not dare to remove
him; and consequently he is completely duped into his patriotism by
the Speaker, who has thrown away his scabbard'.[44] This would
certainly be compatible with Parnell's subdued behaviour at the time;
Carysfort referred to Parnell's 'manoeuvring to regain his post',[45] and
Buckingham made the same suggestion the next month.[46] This general
opinion was subscribed to by Cooke, writing to Grenville: 'Parnell's
[conduct] has been timidity; he is, I know, disgusted with opposition,
but so pledged he dare not retreat'.[47] The government believed that he
had overplayed his hand, been seduced into open opposition by Foster,
and once there was unhappy with such a position. Certainly, while the
Union was against his personal interests, many of the political principles appealed to by its opponents must have been anathema to all he
had ever advocated. It would have been interesting to see what course
his career took after 1800; but he barely outlived his parliament, dying
suddenly in December 1801.[48] An unkind comment from Cornwallis
on one of Parnell's last appearances at College Green stated that 'he
was apparently so much intoxicated that it is impossible to say whether
he was serious in the declarations he made' (about taking the sense of
the people on the subject of the Union);[49] but, whatever the view of
the government on his political position, his stand had already made
him something of a popular hero. Addresses praising his integrity had
been presented by his constituents, by Dublin corporation, and by two
Dublin guilds – to whom he modestly replied that 'the regards of the
most respectable and most honourable members of the community are
a better foundation of honest pride than rank or emolument'. The
Maryborough Volunteers, a local yeomanry corps, also presented him
with a tribute and a sword of honour; and in the last few months of his
life his health was proposed at so many dinner-tables that it was
remarked (by Joseph Atkinson, Treasurer of the Ordance for Ireland)
that if Parnell had lost his bread and butter by the Union, it had been
amply made up to him '*in toast*'.[50]

## II

Whatever about the integrity of Parnell's reasons for breaking with the
government, his reputation for probity extended further than this issue
alone; both Barrington and Addington referred to the fact that Parnell
never used his official position to provide for his relatives,[51] and he

himself wrote bitterly when he lost his post: 'I have not saved money nor made charges as Beresford did for my frequent journeys by order of government; I shall seek refuge in economy'.[52] This leads on to the interesting and relevant question of what exactly his fortunes were. As an only son, he had inherited the estate of Rathleague in the Queen's County; maps of the property show that in 1789 this comprised 3,683 acres, to which were added 173 acres in Cheshire, as well as lands near Bangor.[53] The first baronet also owned land in Armagh, Tipperary, and King's County, totalling 671 acres;[54] and there was, besides, an estate in Armagh called Collure and held on a long lease from Trinity College.[55] About 1780 a statement of the first baronet's property gave the gross rental of the land in Queen's County as £1,597, in Armagh as £1,157, and an additional holding near Killincarrick in Co. Wicklow as £20.[56] The second baronet, as an only son, inherited all of this; he later acquired 186 acres in Kildare as well, realising £352 p.a.[57] There were also several houses in Maryborough; and even more significant was the large amount of Dublin property owned by the first baronet, Barrington's 'crafty and prudent minor politician'. This comprised at least ten sizeable houses round the centre of the city, certainly producing several hundred pounds a year in rent.[58] After his father's death the second Sir John Parnell added some properties round George's Street which must have been extensive, as they are recorded as having an almost incredible '£6,000 expended recently on building and improvements';[59] he also bought a house in Merrion Square which was later rented out at £300 a year. There was also the Parnell family's interest in the lands of Ballytrasna, Co. Wicklow, which – under the name of Avondale – were deeded to Sir John by Samuel Hayes in 1795. This estate was not, however, in Parnell's possession for the greater part of his life and I shall deal with it separately.

Parnell's wealth was further augmented by marriage; Letitia Charlotte was co-heiress of Sir Arthur Brooke of Colebrooke, and by her marriage settlement brought him £5,000, the income of the manor of Brookeborough, several farms in Fermanagh, and an annuity of £300, paid to Parnell's father.[60] A man of extensive property, Parnell seems rarely to have parted with any of it.[61] Bearing in mind that what I have detailed was merely his private landed fortune, irrespective of other investments, he must have died a wealthy man – made all the richer by being reimbursed just before his death with £7,500 for the loss of half the Maryborough representation following the Union. I have not mentioned the emoluments from his several offices, since the likelihood is that these were more than balanced by the considerable expense incurred by holding office in the eighteenth century.

Lady Parnell had died in 1783, after having six children. The eldest son, John Augustus, was born deaf and blind, so the second son, Henry

Brooke, was enabled to succeed by a special act of Parliament passed
in 1789; on John Augustus's death in 1812 Henry succeeded to the
baronetcy and was later created Lord Congleton. Another son,
William, inherited the Wicklow estate and was M.P. for the county. A
daughter, Sophia, married George Evans of Portrane, M.P. for
Dublin.[62] Two more sons, Thomas and Arthur, are scantily recorded;
though Thomas designed the roads on the Powerscourt estate, and was
known as an evangelist in Dublin; he influenced his nephew John
Vesey Parnell, the second Lord Congleton, in his adoption of the
'Plymouth' Brethren faith.[63]

The Congleton branch of the family became settled more in
England than in Ireland, and seems to have grown apart from the
others; I shall deal briefly with it before returning to William Parnell,
Charles Stewart Parnell's grandfather. Henry Brooke Parnell, was
born in 1776 and became M.P. for Maryborough from 1797 to 1800;
after the union he represented Queen's County, with an interlude as
M.P. for Portarlington in 1802; he sat for Dundee from 1833 to 1841.
Prominent in government as a Liberal, he became a Lord of the
Treasury in 1806, chaired various finance committees, and was
Secretary of War, Treasurer of the Navy and Paymaster-General, with
varying success. On 18 August 1841 he was created Baron Congleton;
a year later, he committed suicide. His political record, which can be
summed up as that of an advanced Liberal who was rarely listened
to,[64] cannot have been very satisfying to him; and in his last days he
was a prey to suicidal depression.[65]

He had married Lady Caroline Elizabeth Dawson, the eldest
daughter of the first Earl of Portarlington, in 1801. They separated in
1815 and she survived her husband by many years, dying in Paris in
1861. They had six children: John Vesey, the second Lord Congleton;
Henry William, who succeeded him in 1883; George Damer, vicar of
Long Cross, Chertsey, who died in 1882; Caroline Sophia, who
married C. T. Longley, later Archbishop of Canterbury, and died in
1858; Mary Letitia, who first married Lord Henry Seymour Moore
and then Edward Henry Cole and died in 1885; and Emma Jane, who
married the fifth Earl of Darnley and died in 1885.[66] Thus most of
this generation lived to see their Irish cousin achieve great
prominence; but there seems to have been no connection between the
two branches of the family at this time.[67] The Congletons had their
own celebrity; the second baron was a founder of the religious movement known as 'the Brethren', (later the 'Plymouth Brethren'), and
led a remarkable life. He travelled on an evangelical mission to
Baghdad in the unlikely company of Francis Newman (John Henry
Newman's brother), married an Armenian merchant's widow who had
been cast out by her family when she joined the Brethren, sailed on a
raft down the river Tigris, and proselytised in India among the polite

but uninterested native population until he became depressed by 'the hopelessness which he thought the want of miraculous power in the Church cast around labour among the heathen'.[68] When he returned to England he founded a meeting-house for the Brethren in Islington; at Sunday gatherings here both Lord Congleton and his wife made a deep impression of the youthful Edmund Gosse, the dark-skinned Lady Congleton being 'an object of helpless terror to me; I shrank from her aimable caresses and vaguely identified her with a personage much spoken of in our family circle, the "Personal Devil" '.[69] While sitting in the House of Lords and living in Great Cumberland Place, Lord Congleton remained devoted to the spartan life-style of a missionary; and he combined with his belief in 'the exceeding sinfulness of sin and the utter worthlessness of the flesh' an attractive insouciance of manner and a total disregard of money.

His brother, who inherited the title, was a Liberal Unionist in politics and died in 1896. It is unlikely that he knew his cousin and political opponent from Wicklow; two entries in the third Lord Congleton's diary for 7 and 8 October 1891 read 'Heard of the death of Charles Stewart Parnell, the Homerule agitator?!' and 'Charles S. Parnell's death . . . Wretched Man?!'[70] However, in his lifetime the Congletons renewed their Irish connection, living at Anneville near Mullinger; and by 1914 C. S. Parnell's brother, John Howard Parnell, had made the acquaintance of the fifth Lord Congleton and visited him there.[71] But in the nineteenth century the Wicklow Parnells stayed with a Howard relative on their visits to London, and their reminiscences never mentioned Congleton relations – even before politics estranged them. To trace the direct influence on Charles Stewart Parnell's background we have to turn back to the Wicklow branch of Sir John Parnell's family.

# 2 The Avondale tradition: Samuel Hayes and William Parnell

Avondale, centred round Rathdrum, Co. Wicklow, came into the Parnell family in 1795 on the death of its previous owner, Samuel Hayes. Under him it ran at about 4,500 acres; the Parnells reduced it to just over 3,800.[1] The demesne was noted for its trees, and for the beautiful siting of the house above a deep river gorge. Its owner, Samuel Hayes, is an elusive figure; but he seems to have been born in 1743,[2] attended Oxford, was a barrister-at-law, M.P. for Wicklow (1783–90), and Maryborough (1791–5), a J.P., and Colonel in the Volunteers; he was also an active member of the Dublin Society (later the R.D.S.) and the Royal Irish Academy.[3]

Both in parliament and in private life his interests were primarily agricultural, and in this sphere his chief preoccupation was forestry; in 1768 he received a Dublin Society medal for planting 2,550 beech trees; in 1788 he presented a bill to encourage forestation;[4] in 1794 he published *A practical treatise on planting and the treatment of woods and coppices*. He was also something of an antiquarian, being responsible for the discovery of the most easterly of the early Christian churches at Glendalough, Co. Wicklow, and supervising its restoration. Hayes's interest in agriculture extended to introducing a bill 'for speedy detection of sheep-stealers'; he believed, with some naïveté, that the high price of wool was caused only by the small numbers of 'that useful creature' kept by farmers owing to the ease with which they could be stolen.[5] He also introduced a bill to improve fisheries, and spoke at length in parliament on everything from lighting Dublin streets to parliamentary reform. His opinions often reveal a simplicity amounting to naïveté; during a time of rural unrest in 1790 he spoke at the quarter sessions advising malcontents to give up arms in favour of 'the implements of domestic sciences',[6] and he was given to such cheerful assumptions as that in Wicklow 'a dispute for tithe was unknown and a non-resident beneficed clergyman equally unheard-of'.[7] Politically he was described as 'entirely uninfluenced, but very friendly

to government' and 'an independent, honourable man . . . much connected with Sir. J. Parnell'.[8] His speeches embody a heavy-footed
whimsy, in accordance with the taste of the age, and a similarly
'period' wealth of classical allusion, often bewilderingly eclectic; in a
speech on the paving and lighting of Dublin he remarked that 'the
Commissioners had not only cleaned an Augean stable, but given light
to drag Caucus from his den; and he hoped they would go on till they
discovered the lamp of Aladdin'.[9] The picture that emerges of Colonel
Hayes is of an educated, optimistic, improving landlord, influenced by
the scientific progressivism and intellectual classicism of the late
eighteenth century: a specimen that might have been sketched to
perfection by Addison or Steele.

A characteristic of this type was the possession of some solid property, and in this Samuel Hayes was no exception. He owned a town
house in Nassau Street, several farms in Glenmalure, and the Wicklow
estate known as 'Hayesville' until 1770, when he began to build the
sizeable Palladian house called Avondale. Through his wife he had an
interest in property in Limerick, Wexford and Dublin.[10] However, the
demesne of Avondale and in particular its plantations remained his
chief interest and constitute his chief monument. A description of these
written a year before his death reads:

> On the front and side of the house spreads a smooth lawn spotted
> with clumps and single trees, gently rising to a hill crowned with
> large beech and uncommonly thriving fir, particularly spruce,
> whose feathered branches hang to the ground. On the back of
> the house the ground in some parts slopes down with a gentle
> declivity, in others falls in steep and abrupt precipices covered
> with ancient oaks, the roots of many of which are a hundred feet
> perpendicular over the topmost summit of others . . . The vale
> extends above four miles . . . where the natural growth of wood
> has been too thin Mr Hayes has not spared any expense to supply
> the defect with every foreign and domestic tree suited to the soil
> and climate, and perhaps no part of the country admits a greater
> variety than this part of Wicklow.[11]

Six years later Frazer's *Survey of Wicklow* drew especial attention to
'the elegant improvements of Avondale', emphasising the romantic
nature of the scenery.[12]

Where the coming of this idyllic demesne into the Parnell family is
mentioned, it is usually assumed that Hayes left it to Sir John Parnell
because he was a political admirer of his – occasionally even because
he admired his stand over the Union, a contention easily disproved by
the date of Hayes's death (1795). His will, moreover, was made in
1783;[13] and it embodied what was in essence a family agreement, not a
political gift. Hayes married Alice Le Hunte in 1766,[14] and the

Parnells' connection with the estate dates from then – when the future Chancellor was twenty-two years old and several years before he entered politics. A memorial in the Registry of Deeds [15] shows that trustees for the estate on the occasion of Hayes's marriage were Richard Le Hunte, his wife's uncle, and John Parnell – the future first baronet. Moreover, mention is made elsewhere of Mrs Anne Hayes, *née* Parnell, sister of the first Sir John and widow of John Hayes in 1776; [16] it seems clear that she was Samuel Hayes's mother, so he and the second baronet were first cousins. [17] The full deed of the marriage settlement is untraceable, but since John Parnell was a trustee for Hayes's property and a close relation besides, it seems likely that the estate was to revert to him if Samuel and Alice Hayes died without issue – as came to be the case. Hayes and the second Sir John *were* politically linked; Hayes sat for Maryborough, a borough in the control of Sir John, and it was probably due to his cousin that he became a Commissioner for Stamp Duties. But the advent of Avondale into the Parnell family can be seen as a family arrangement, or even as one of the 'crafty and prudent' first baronet's property interests coming home to roost; since it was the outcome of a will made in his favour by Sir John's first cousin, years before the future Chancellor became prominent, it can by no stretch of the imagination be said to have been a free gift from a political admirer.

## II

Little enough has been written about Parnell's family in general, and next to nothing about his paternal grandfather William Parnell-Hayes (he adopted the suffix when he inherited Avondale, but rarely used it.) However, as well as being a man worth studying in his own right, I believe William Parnell was an ancestor of Charles Stewart Parnell's who exercised a great influence on him, albeit indirectly; those who return to his 'patriotic' great-grandfather or even his martial American grandfather to explain Parnell's analysis of the Irish situation have never taken into account that his grandfather was as radical a theorist as it was possible for an Irish Protestant landlord to be and that, though he died long before his grandson was born, he left behind several provocative pamphlets, an absorbing propagandist novel about Irish rural life, and a considerable reputation as a controversialist.

William was born in 1777, the third son of Sir John Parnell. He attended Cambridge, where he did well. [18] Inheriting Avondale and living there most of his life, he married in 1810 Frances, the daughter of a prominent neighbour, Hugh Howard of Bushy Park. He was a J.P., Deputy Lieutenant of the county, and M.P. for Wicklow from 1817 to 1820. In 1805 he anonymously published *An enquiry into the causes of popular discontents in Ireland* and in 1807, under his own name, *An historical apology for the Irish Catholics.* A book of educational sermons for Irish country schools followed in 1816, [19] and in 1818 Parnell's anonymous novel *Maurice and Berghetta, or The priest of Rahery* aroused such a storm that he had to write a pamphlet defending it. This *Letter to the editor of the Quarterly Review* [20] was his last production; in January 1821 he died, aged only 44. His wife had predeceased him, leaving two children, Catherine and John Henry. The loss of his wife had depressed him deeply, but he had found solace in devoting himself to the education of his children; 'he was a good man in all his courses', said an obituary, 'but as a father he excelled inimitably'. [21]

Between writing and politics, he had occupied himself with the Avondale estate. He sold off some lands, [22] amounting to a few hundred acres, but did not diminish the demesne, except to exchange some property with a neighbour to unify his holdings. [23] In 1815 he leased the estate in trust to two relatives to provide £5,000 for his daughter's portion, over and above the £5,000 already due to her; thus the estate was, like so many others, charged heavily from this period on – an arrangement which was to influence the fortunes of his grandson Charles throughout his life.

From 1817 Parnell spent most of his time in London, as an M.P.; in 1820 a visitor touring Wicklow found Avondale deserted, though still 'enchanting'. [24] William had also been absent from the house for a long time in 1805, when it was rented out. [25] When he did live there, however, he seems to have been as good a landlord as the age had to offer; all contemporary accounts emphasise his preoccupation with the wellbeing of his tenantry, whose company he preferred to the 'exalted' society in which he moved. [26] During the 1817 famine he saw to it that store cattle were brought up and slaughtered at Rathdrum, and meat and soup provided twice a week for four months, at the parish expense. [27] His close connection with country life round Rathdrum, as well as his own particular view of the Irish ethos, is shown in many anecdotes through his writings: as where he laments how a Wicklow neighbour, a kind and good landlord, yet 'invariably prefaces a remark to a labourer with "You villain, you! I'll blow your bloody soul in a blaze of gunpowder to hell!" '. [28] Such criticism must have made his neighbours look on him with some suspicion; in 1801 a mere reference to rural conditions in Wicklow had been stigmatised as 'incendiary', [29] and Parnell's attacks on the *status quo* were far more than a bare recital of facts. In his *Enquiry* he violently attacked middlemen and agents for extending the insolence they themselves received from their superiors to 'those unfortunate beings who are placed at the extremity of the scale of degradation, the Irish Peasantry'; even this stricture was heavily criticised by the editor of the work. [30] Like his neighbour James Grattan, William Parnell was an enlightened squire placed in an incongruous format. He wrote bitterly of the way visitors to Ireland were beguiled from their initial horror at the condition of the peasantry 'by the unfeeling society in whose narrow circle they pass their time; they eat pineapples, drink champaign, and, feeling themselves very well off, forget how other people suffer'.[31] He himself, he added, found residence in Ireland almost unbearable because of all the misery around him; he 'seemed forced on to a study of these details of wretchedness till so pained with the idea of the recurrence of suffering that any exertion with a chance of mitigating it becomes a relief'.[32] In these and many other passages dealing with the life close at hand to him, Parnell manifests a marked degree of alienation from it; and here again there is an echo of his grandson.

Though William Parnell's political attitudes are best seen in his writings, where he expressed himself forcefully and unequivocally, it is worth looking first at his political record. He was first and foremost against the Union, in his speeches as in his writings; but his radicalism was not as evident in Westminster, where he defended increases in royal Dukes' settlements,[33] and was reticent about parliamentary reform.[34] Here there were echoes of the early conservatism which led him to advise his brother in 1802 not to 'generally abuse' his Majesty's ministers and to be an '*aristocratical* opportunist'.[35] There were, moreover, some direct contradictions in his attitudes in and out of parliament; at Westminster he spoke unequivocally against protectionism in trade and 'forcing manufactures';[36] but in his writings about Ireland he advocated these very measures. Where specifically Irish matters arose in parliament, however, he was tireless in advocating reform.[37] Besides speaking strongly on every Irish issue he moved two bills, neither of which came to fruition. One was for the protection of children employed in Irish cotton factories, the other to amend the Poor Law provisions whereby Irish paupers were shipped arbitrarily from England.[38] Both bills pinpointed abuses, but like many of Parnell's projected reforms, hampered a sound idea by complex and impracticable machinery.

His reforming efforts, however, were not restricted to Westminster. In his diary James Grattan described his neighbour's attempts to unite Liberal and Conservative gentry on the education issue,[39] and his criticism of local justice.[40] On several issues the two men disagreed; Grattan felt Parnell overstated the case of Catholic disabilities, and he felt differently about protectionism. But despite these differences, they shared common interests; their opinions and preoccupations cannot have been typical of Wicklow squires in the early nineteenth century, and the sort of unpopularity which Grattan later earned among his social equals for his liberal political stance must also have been felt by his neighbour at Avondale.

To the end of his life William Parnell was involved in attempts at practical reform; in December 1820 he published at his own expense five thousand copies of *Notes* on the need for a government grant towards educating the Catholic poor, and on the 20th of that month he succeeded in procuring an annual grant of £3,000 for this purpose. It was while in Dublin on this business that he caught the chill which led to his death.

## III

The essence of William Parnell's thought, however, and the intellectual heritage which he left behind him, is contained in his writings. Despite a polite reference to them in the *Gentleman's Magazine* in 1842,[41] these were generally forgotten after his death; none were reprinted after 1825, and the mistake is often made of attributing his *Historical Apology for the Irish Catholics* to his brother Henry, author of the far more restrained *History of the Penal Laws*. Even R. B. O'Brien, when listing his works, omits the interesting and controversial *Priest of Rahery*. Parnell was friendly with the *literati* of his day; Mary Tighe dedicated as attractive sonnet to him, and an often-repeated anecdote in Thomas Moore's *Journal* about his poem 'The Meeting of the Waters' shows he and Parnell were close friends.[42] But Parnell's concerns in his own writings were of a very different order; his work repays a close examination.

Parnell's first publication, in 1805, was his *Enquiry into the causes of popular discontent in Ireland* by 'An Irish Country Gentleman'. The *nom-de-plume* is significant: the analysis throughout is that of someone close to rural life, but whose ideal is an Ireland where the country gentry can rely on a contented, industrious and healthy peasantry. This aim was not remarkably radical or audacious; but Parnell's reasoning and his language must have appeared to many contemporaries to be both.

The germ of the pamphlet is causality. Land, Parnell begins, is drained by finding the source of the water; he examines the frequency of Irish rebellions and concludes that the causes must be like the risings themselves, 'active, constant and uniform'. Nor are they due to natural Irish propensities, or even the Roman Catholic religion, which in Parnell's view *suppresses* the desire for independence. Instead, he emphasises the initial nature of the conquest of Ireland; the maintenance of religious distinctions; confiscation; tithes; rural demoralisation; republicanism; and the Union.

With regard to the conquest, his case is that the English mismanaged it by neither treating the natives fairly, absorbing them, nor exterminating them: the only viable alternatives. Land confiscation set the seal on the Irish decline, since insecurity of property caused the decay of individual enterprise (a basic tenet of Parnell's belief); here as elsewhere, the English acted against their own long-term interests. Confiscation cannot be undone; but religious discrimination, which is part of the same policy, still persists. There is no doubt about Parnell's repugnance regarding this principle, but again he attacks it on the grounds of its foolishness: 'the height of infatuation was to rob a man, to spare his life, and yet to load him with every injury and insult'. [43] He also attacks Orange Lodges as 'the great political *blunders* of the Irish gentry'. [44] His case is essentially that the governing class by their own obtuseness create the nominal justification for Irish rebellion.

On religion, Parnell's stance is provocative. He is at pains to declare that he 'considers the Popish religion as the most formidable source of slavery and superstition that has sprung from the abuse of religion', but in view of other writings of his this seems at least partially intended as a precaution against being dismissed as just another Papist rebel. And here as elsewhere his emphasis is on expediency: discriminatory laws invariably strengthen a religion. Thus he would abolish all distinctions and opposes a church Establishment; in a passage Voltaire would have subscribed to, Parnell wrote: 'If we give these honeyed cakes to only one head of Cerberus it will increase the fury of all the rest; feed them all and we may go quietly to heaven above or to the shades below in our own way.' Other aspects of Irish life are dealt with trenchantly and perceptibly. He contrasts Ulster wealth, intellect and *moeurs* with those of the south of Ireland, and remarks on 'the great political importance' of Northern Presbyterians; the tithe situation provokes a detailed comparison between Irish and English landholders; and in his comments on 'the degraded state of the peasantry' (perhaps his chief preoccupation), Parnell is at his most impressive. His treatment recurs to the accumulation of grievances, and the arrogance of his own class of landlords; in places he almost idealises the rebels of 1798. [45] As regards ameliorative measures in rural life, he dismisses jury reform for the sapient reason that juries are composed of landlords in any case; a religious approach is equally pointless, since Roman Catholic landlords are as bad as the rest. Parnell's solution was to raise the peasantry in their own estimation by making municipal offices elective and salaried, and encouraging open competition for them. Thus the gentry would become reliant on their local reputation to gain office, and by the creation of a system of county administration the peasantry themselves would aspire to local office. [46]

The reasons to which most contemporaries would have attributed Irish rebellions are dealt with shortly by Parnell; he believed republicanism was a minor cause, magnified by governments to obscure their own shortcomings. The Union is dealt with at length, as might be expected; to the normal current criticisms, he added an interesting psychological view of the disunited elements in Irish society each disliking the measure, but not combating it because it penalised their enemies as well as themselves. On the question of union Parnell comes closer than anywhere else to referring to an indigenous national identity; but his eventual reasoning relies upon utility rather than principle. Again and again he returns to the equation which was to seem so obvious to reformers of a later age: an incentive to material industry means an accompanying increase in self-respect which in turn produces the progress of intellectual civilisation hand in hand with material wealth. [47]

A long quotation will give the best idea possible of Parnell's peculiar combination of embryonic national identity with the values of a country gentleman. The address is to the English nation:

> Why extract from her [Ireland] so galling a sacrifice as her independence: a sacrifice which under similar circumstances no Englishman would endure to make to France? Are the English to be the sole possessors of national honour? And yet Irishmen must be supposed to be blind to their interests, when the very fountain of their national honour is forever drained, if they are heard to murmur.
>
> You tell us to interest ourselves in the glory of the English government; we tell you we cannot. Why? Because we cannot love our stepmother as our mother. Could you under the same circumstances feel what you require for France? On the contrary in spite of yourselves, you despise us; we despise one another; as Irishmen we are the contempt of the world. You told us we should be rich, we are far poorer. You said we should be tranquil but our civil commotions are greater than ever. You said our religious distinctions should cease, they have acquired new rancour. You said English capital should go to Ireland, on the contrary all the capital of Ireland is drawn to England. Give us, then, back our independence; hunt our trade from your ports; that national spirit which lightened its shackles can assert its freedom; leave us to our rebellions, the courage that repressed them once can repress them again; take back the lenitives you would apply to our religious distinctions, we shall not always be bigots but shall one day acknowledge the maxim that by removing religious distinctions we remove religious animosities. These are evils that time and experience will remedy and we might yet be a happy and wealthy people; but if you destroy the principle of national honour you destroy the very principle of wealth and happiness and our misery will be such as our baseness deserves, our poverty as complete as your narrow jealousy could desire.
>
> I am aware that this language will be thought the exaggerated optimism of mistaken patriotism. It is not. The present situation

in Ireland amply justifies it . . . A sensible change has taken place
in the national character; from being patriotic, high-spirited and
generous the Irish are become abject, selfish and mercenary; they
have no longer a respect for each other; their homes are no
longer homes; that respectability of character which attaches importance and content to the idea of what is our own, is entirely
unknown to them; and they prefer a paltry lodging in London
and a transient glance at the refuse of London society to the noble mansions where their fathers were the centre of hospitality
and the objects of gratitude and esteem. The finest seats in
Ireland are now laid waste, the houses deserted, the trees felled.
Why? Because what is thought of these things in Ireland is no
longer of any consequence as long as it is not known at a London
*route*. To be praised by men devoid of importance is of little
moment; and hence the great stimulus to national importance is
done away.

When Ireland acquired its independence under Mr Fox the
Irish learnt to respect each other; public applause became the
great spur to patriotic efforts. It is an un-noticed, but it is a very
striking and important effect, which was produced on the
declaration of independence: the great capitalists seemed inspired with a new character; every gentleman built a palace and
surrounded it with a paradise; the before-forgotten peasantry
became objects of benevolence; their houses were made more
convenient, their wages raised; agriculture was created [i.e., en-
couraged] and new enterprise given to commerce. No expression
can give an idea of the improvement which took place in Ireland
immediately on the development of its national dignity. [48]

This passage gives a sample of Parnell's ostensibly radical language;
but it also shows that in his appeal to 'nationalism' he had by no
means forsaken the interests of his own class. However, practically
oriented as such appeals were, he remained in essence an idealist. In
parliament he confessed that 'nothing had given him greater pain since
the short time that he had sat in parliament than the seeing how frequently great questions of justice and morality were sacrificed to
expediency'; [49] and in his *Enquiry* he remarked sadly that every example in public life testified that 'the slightest private convenience over-
balances the greatest public interest'. [50] And when he attacked English
rule in Ireland as 'a long unbroken tissue of outrage' it was on the
grounds of this idealism rather than from a nationalist standpoint – or
from a radical one. A second edition of Parnell's pamphlet was produced with a preface and notes by an enraged 'Friend to the Constitution'
with the avowed intent of disproving Parnell's contentions by a running commentary in footnotes. This editor accused him of Jacobinism

and incendiary intent, but another long quotation shows to whom Parnell was in fact appealing:

> But I would repeat again to the remnant of that once important class of men, the Irish country gentlemen, that neither their dignity, nor their interest, nor their happiness can ever consist in setting themselves up as a party opposed to the mass of the peasantry and the majority of the nation. Their true and natural station is to be the protectors of their tenantry and peasantry; to enlighten their ignorance; to soften their prejudices; to repress but not to persecute either their civil or their political offences. But above all situations the situation of a country gentleman is most dignified and respectable when he stands forward incapable of a bribe and above the influence of any minister or party; a sure and immoveable defence of liberty and property, a guarantee of public right, the pride and local protector of his own immediate neighbourhood. But when country gentlemen, by any unnatural bias, are led to quit their true station, when instead of being the security of the peasantry they become their terror; when instead of a barrier to the ambitious views of government they are reduced to throw themselves upon its direction and become its instruments – such a reverse might have been unavoidable, may have been necessary, but still it is a reverse; still it is pregnant with insecurity, with incomparable degradation. Oh! do not lightly acquiesce in it, but examine what are the causes, what the circumstances, that led to it; and if more enlightened views, more prudent counsels, more temperate measures can make this unnatural thraldom dispensable, make such views, such counsels, such measures all your own; they must, they will, reconcile all interests; religious rancours will cease, political animosities will be composed, the poor man will be contented in his cabin, the rich man will be secure and respected in his palace.

It is not over-imaginative to see his grandson both sharing this ideal and responding to the appeal.

The analysis so evident in Parnell's *Enquiry* is also the basis for his *Historical apology for the Irish Catholics* – unlike the first work, published under Parnell's own name. Security of property is emphasised as the pressing reason for removal of Catholic disabilities; but with this Parnell presents a strong historical argument against their treatment, incidentally defining an approach to history that was well ahead of its time in condemning secondary sources and working entirely from contemporary accounts. Despite occasional bouquets to the current government, the English record in Ireland was indicted as damningly as before; Parnell also reiterated the argument that it was English

policy which made Catholics bad subjects. He also used the terms of
the loyalty oath to substantiate his case that Irish rebels were not
'traitors'; and he anticipates a later view of Irish history by seeing
events since the Plantagenet era as the wanton rejection of a great opportunity to make a solid and productive colony in favour of quick
gains from an avaricious economic policy.[51] His grasp of the detail of
Irish history is lucid and exact, enabling him to deal with 'the extinc-
tion of the principality of Thomond' as a case in point, and to discuss
the invasion of Gaelic rights by English officialdom. Parnell rejects the
idea of Catholic zeal as being influential in Elizabethan rebellions, finding confirmation in Cox and Moryson. A powerful government il-
legally invaded the rights of 'feeble but lawful princes'. We may agree
with him; but it was not a commonly acceptable thesis at the beginning
of the nineteenth century.

Parnell's eulogies of the humaneness and civilised intelligence of
leaders like O'Neill compared to their English adversaries must have
been similarly controversial. Against Elizabeth's rapaciousness the
Irish had no legal resort, 'having to go to law with the Devil when the
court was held in Hell'; the rebellions were inevitable and the Nine
Years' War was an attempted revolution of underestimated importance. Only after this era did Catholic bigotry become an appreciable
factor. Elizabeth was 'an oppressive and vindictive tyrant'; James's
record was, however, admirable except for the great mistake of land
confiscation. Parnell's point is that the first anti-Catholic legislation
*implanted* disaffection; this process, and longstanding grievances,
caused rebellion, which only took on a Catholic character after the
Government threw over the Catholics of the Pale.

Moving the argument to the present day, Parnell's final appeal was
to the expediency of abolishing current restrictions, which were a losing speculation for English interests; they alienated potential military
manpower and weakened commerce. The aims of security, peace and
tolerance appealed to by the discriminatory measures would in fact be
realised by the opposite policy. This great and simple truth, according
to Parnell, is missed by 'vulgar opinion' – one of the instances where
he manifests a distinct intellectural élitism. Concluding, he praises
Catholic loyalty and mounts his most bitter attack yet upon his
co-religionists:

> O hearts of barbarians, of zealots, of Protestants!
> The flames which made the name of Bonner accursed, the
> hideous night of St Bartholomew, are not so great a disgrace to
> the character of man as your cold conniving bigotry . . .
>   They at least had the excuse, the warmth of religious feeling;
> they sprang not from selfishness, but from a vision of fanaticism
> as inscrutable as physical insanity. These men merely made a

mistake; they worshipped a demon and thought him God.

But you, with perfect possession of your faculties, with a calm pulse and minds unaffected by the slightest emotion, perpetuate statutes to gall the best and most honourable feelings of many millions of men whose sensations of pleasure and pain are exactly of the same nature as those from which your own happiness or misery is derived.[52]

This classical liberalism is adulterated with the intellectual arrogance already referred to; Parnell finds it incredible that the English government should listen to 'Dublin guilds, common councilmen, aldermen, corporations; fat fools that have been hitherto nondescripts in the classes of science, literature and good sense'.[53] In conclusion he tells the fable of the wolf and the lamb, wherein the wolf makes the supposed excesses of the lamb and the lamb's parents the rationalisation for eating him: 'As to the business of this world, when Lambs are the accused and Wolves the judges, the injured must expect no better quarter; especially when the heart's blood of the one is the nourishment and entertainment of the other.'[54] Parnell's eloquent pamphlet was given at least one favourable review; Sydney Smith in the *Edinburgh Review* 'agreed entirely' and recommended the pamphlet's 'truth, good sense, and political courage'. Irish opinion, even among liberals, was hardly as sympathetic; but it was Parnell's next work which aroused most opposition.

This was *Maurice and Berghetta, or The priest of Rahery,* described not unfairly by Allibone's literary dictionary as 'a political novel'.[55] As a period piece it has considerable interest, and its intrinsic qualities are far greater than this. Moreover, its polemical purpose witnesses once again Parnell's two major interests: recognition of Catholic civil rights and the improvement of Irish rural life. The book is dedicated to 'the priesthood of Ireland', of whom in their social function Parnell declares himself a staunch admirer – although he holds no brief for Roman Catholicism. In a long introduction to the novel he occupies himself with the sad state of rural Ireland, attacking *laissez-faire* economics and the government policy towards famines.[56] New attitudes both towards the country and within it are needed; Parnell optimistically infers that these would automatically follow civil rights for Catholics and an improvement in peasant life. There is much in his introduction, however, which is of more original interest; an approach to social psychology again comes through, as where he compares the 'domestic' virtues of the English to the 'anti-domestic' virtues of the Irish peasantry, whose traditional vivacity and sociability he attributes to the miserable state of their own homes, where improvement is discouraged. As well as accounting for rowdy wakes and frequent faction fights, this has led to the compassionate and generous nature of the

Irish country people compared to the English.

The introduction to *Maurice and Berghetta* can be read individually as a literate and analytical tract on rural Irish problems, and this is the approach Parnell wished readers to take to the novel itself; nonetheless, the story is worth a brief treatment. It deals with the fortunes of Maurice O'Neal, a peasant orphan who by industry and intelligence improves his lot beyond recognition; his story is told by his guardian, the priest of Rahery. Maurice's life is, however, not all happiness. His young wife dies; he becomes involved with a well-intentioned but hasty Gaelic aristocrat who has fallen upon hard times and attempts to right his lot by rebellion. After this failure Maurice's sister Una emigrates to Spain, where her ancient descent from the O'Neills is recognised; his children follow and settle there, equally recognised and respected.

Accompanying this Gothic story-line is a strong current of sociological didacticism. Parnell's first emphasis is on what the Irish could achieve by industry; his second preoccupation is with what the Irish can learn from the English. Arguably the most important part of the book deals with Maurice's visit to England and his ensuing introduction of new agricultural methods to Rahery. Thirdly, Parnell attacks the uselessness and viciousness of 'old Irish' ways. Even attractive figures like Maurice's aristocratic friends the O'Sullivan Beeres are mentally crippled by nostalgia; Merrit McCormick, villain of the piece, embodies garrulity and vituperativeness to a bewildering degree and becomes prematurely senile as a result. Nonetheless, the kingly descent of the O'Neills is never forgotten, and heavily emphasised at the end, as a microcosm of the Irish identity so long suppressed by England; while Rory Oge, the Hi Sullivans' resourceful retainer, epitomises all the best Irish qualities of ingenuity and intelligence.

Parnell, if self-confessedly no novelist, had a more than capable way with a story. A clever ambivalence runs through his characterisation: Una is beautiful and gentle, but susceptible to pride; Headcroft, an English farmer, is likeable but lumpish; James Hi Sullivan is a hero, but an unreasonable one. Parnell's sharper observations are stated with economy and wit – though his didacticism can lead to some strange effects, as where the priest delivers a long homily to a Spanish visitor on the desirability of encouraging a diversity of sects. This is couched in the language of an eighteenth-century *philosophe,* and sounds strangely in the mouth of a rural curate. Other familiar biases come through strongly; Maurice's priority is to have a secure piece of property, and his ambitions go little further. Moreover, the grandiose ambitions of the Continental Irish damn them as surely as Merrit is condemned by his levity.

Through *Maurice and Berghetta* Parnell proclaims himself in favour of a simple and godly life among an Irish yeomanry whose Catholicism responds to benevolent patriarchs of priests; whose best qualities are intelligence and perspicacity, though these need to be guided; and who could learn greatly from English ways instead of merely defaming that country, richly though she may deserve it. Parnell's Irish characters, it should be noted, never speak in brogue, or with any of the idiosyncrasies of Samuel Lover's. The cadences, humour and subtleties of rural speech are faultlessly caught. Though Una and Maurice shine because their English was taught them by an English widow 'with a good accent', Parnell shows a real appreciation of the richly Irish use of English among country people that far exceeds the contemporary taste of his class for 'Irish Bulls'.

Whatever impact *Maurice and Berghetta* made upon the reading public must have been considerably increased by a long and vitriolic notice in the *Quarterly Review* of April 1819.[57] Though the novel was officially anonymous, it is on Parnell himself that the reviewer directs most of his fury, after briefly satirising 'an Ultonian Utopia . . . where everything which use could require or taste wish for is provided, down to a *fashionable accent*'. The synopsis of the plot is garbled and much of the sneering at 'royal peasants' is pure spleen; but some of the criticisms are apt enough, such as the point that the priests to whom the book is dedicated would not be much enamoured of the clerical narrator, self-confessedly inadequate, who regains his faith through reading books by Protestants. Most of Parnell's arguments, however, are not properly grasped; the novelist's own Anglo-Irish background is triumphantly adduced as a contradiction of his position; and in conclusion the reviewer aimed a shaft at Parnell's political career, drawing an analogy between the opinions expressed in the introduction and the unsuccessful history of Parnell's attempted legislation on behalf of factory children and paupers.

This indictment produced another pamphlet from Parnell, the last he was to write.[58] It was not, as might be expected, a defence of the novel itself; he professed to welcome both the criticism and the attendant publicity. What he took issue with was the reviewer's ignorance of agriculture, and most of the pamphlet is a restatement of his case for the introduction of English methods of cultivation into Ireland, and also a reiteration of the Irish faults of apathy and complacency – the feeling among the Irish peasantry, as Parnell dryly put it, that 'whatever failings they may have are to be excused in consideration of their wit'.[59] In his own extenuation he quotes a review from the *Irish Farmer's Journal*, which gives an interesting contemporary view and implies that controversy over the novel was widespread; the reviewer had 'heard a great deal' about it, and expected to be incensed by Parnell's criticisms but ended by agreeing wholeheartedly with him.[60] After patiently reiterating his own religious position (the *Quarterly* had roundly accused him of apostasy), Parnell announced that he intended to make some changes in the next edition of the work; he would

excise some of the ambivalent characteristics criticised as unconvin-
cing and, since the Spanish scenes were only relevant to Irish readers,
he would drop them from the English edition. He added defensively
that the book was 'read and liked' by the peasantry, and might have
some influence among them: which was, after all, his prime intention.

The reviewer had also criticised the novel's attack on the Irish
reliance upon the potato; when re-stating his case for a varied diet
Parnell underestimated the high nutritional value of the potato
(especially combined with milk), but he accurately prophesied dire
results from the next wholesale crop failure. In concluding this short
but forceful pamphlet, Parnell quoted agricultural statistics to back up
his case for agricultural innovations, and recapitulated upon the iniquities of successive British governments in Ireland; he also aimed a
last shaft at the Establishment of the Church of Ireland. The *Quarterly* did not let matters rest there, but answered with a further
broadside,[61] saying nothing new and including many mis-spellings and
inaccuracies where Parnell's novel was concerned. The only relevant
point raised was the question of different Irish and English editions;
perhaps reasonably, the *Quarterly* attacked the retention of 'all the
nonsense for the Irish'. As for Parnell:

> Whether advanced in a bill or in a novel, in sad reality or in fan-
> tastic fiction, his theories are the wildest yet the meanest, the
> most impracticable and the most idle, even if they could be put
> into practice, that we have ever witnessed . . . He is an amiable
> but weak, well-intentioned but extravagant gentleman, who ever
> hoped by the agency of a novel to eradicate sedition and potatoes
> out of Ireland and who thinks that the example of his hero is on
> the whole beneficial to his countrymen because, with the little
> faults of high treason and suicide, he combined a high and ar-
> dent love for short-handled spades and long-handled scythes. [62]

This last gibe showed an imperfect grasp of the novel, (confusing the
characters of Maurice and Hi Sullivan), but it remained the last word.
William Parnell died before he could answer. In retrospect, he did not
need to. The record of his life, and a close reading of his remarkably
interesting works, show him a man of intelligence, foresight and
dedication, and history in the long run was not to bear out his crabbed
and censorious reviewers, but to vindicate men of his minority
opinions.


In this section I have attempted to give a picture of the Parnell family
before Charles Stewart Parnell, emphasising not the contemporary
aspects of their lives but rather what they left behind them to shape
the lives of their descendants, whether in the form of money, property

or reputation. In the case of Sir John Parnell, his reputation can be seen to have been based largely on misapprehension of the real nature of his politics, though its influence was nonetheless potent for that. The Congletons are interesting mainly in being fairly close relations of Charles Stewart Parnell who pursued parliamentary careers and lived in London at almost the same time that he did, but with whom there is no evidence that he maintained contact. In Avondale Samuel Hayes bequeathed a tangible inheritance to Charles Stewart Parnell, and with it, the tradition of a showpiece estate as well as that of an improving landlord. The shade of William Parnell, however, seems most directly influential. It was often said, with questionable accuracy, that Parnell knew nothing of Irish history;[63] but one thing which is certain is that he must have read the works of his grandfather, and that his father did so before him. What one absorbs from these books is a strong sense of the criminal inefficiency as well as the ethical injustice of the British way of ruling Ireland, in a historical as well as a contemporary context; this is coupled with a forceful appeal to the country gentry to enter politics in this spirit and work for a change. Though warmly sympathetic to country people, there is a strong bias against urban middle-class interests in politics which is again as characteristic of the grandson as of the grandfather. I have yet to discuss the background of Parnell's mother, with its well-publicised anti-British flavour; but in the life and works of his paternal grandfather must lie a great influence on Parnell's political development. The same heritage that brought him Avondale must have carried with it an idea of the political duties inherent in such a position, cast in a strongly anti-British though not purely radical mould. These influences would have acted no less strongly on Parnell for being imbibed in the surroundings of the mid-nineteenth century Wicklow which I have profiled in my introduction.

# Part II

## *The family of John Henry Parnell, 1811–59*

# Part of the PARNELL FAMILY TREE

THOMAS PARNELL
(1625-86)

ANNE = THOMAS (1679-1717)
dau. of Thomas Minchin

JOHN = MARY dau. of Lord Chief Justice Whitshed
(?-1727)

ANNE = JOHN HAYES

THEOBALD TOBIAS (1711-36) d. unm.

JANE = CHARLES BROUGHTON (1734)

JOHN = ANNE (1744)
(?-1782) dau. of hon. Michael Ward of Castleward
M.P. for Maryborough. 1st Bt.

SAMUEL (of Avondale) = ALICE dau. of Thos. le Hunte (1743-95) (1805) No issue

LETITIA = JOHN (?-1783) (1744-1801) Chancellor of Irish Exchequer. 2nd Bt.

JOHN AUGUSTUS (1775-1812) d. unm.

HENRY BROOKE = LADY CAROLINE ELIZABETH DAWSON (1776-1842) dau. of 1st Earl of Portarlington
4th Bt. 1st Baron Congleton
(1801)
WITH ISSUE
dau. of Sir Arthur Brooke of Colebrooke

WILLIAM = FRANCES (1780-1814) dau. of hon. Hugh Howard (1811)

THOMAS ARTHUR d. unm.

SOPHIA = GEORGE HAMPDEN EVANS (?-1853) s. of Eyre Evans (1835) No issue

CATHERINE = GEORGE VICESIMUS WIGRAM (1805-79) s. of Sir Robert Wigram No issue

DELIA TUDOR = JOHN HENRY (1816-98) (1811-59)
dau. of Admiral Charles Stewart

WILLIAM (1837-42)

HAYES (1839-54)

EMILY = (1) CAPTAIN ARTHUR MONROE DICKINSON (1864) (1841-1918)
=(2) CUTHBERT S. BENGOUGH RICKETTS

JOHN = OLIVIA ISABELLA MATEER (1907) HOWARD (1843-1923) dau. of Col. James Smythe and widow of Archibald Mateer No issue

SOPHIA = ALFRED MacDERMOTT (1845-77)

DELIA = (1) JAMES LIVINGSTON THOMPSON (1859) (1838-82)

FANNY (1849-82) d. unm.

CHARLES STEWART = KATHARINE (1846-91) (d. 1921) dau. of Rev. Sir Matthew Page Wood and ex-wife of Captain W.H. O'Shea (1891)

ANNA (1851-1911) d. unm.

HENRY = PENELOPE (1850-1915) dau. of Rev. Thomas Luby

THEODOSIA = CLAUDE (d. 1917) (1853-1920) s. of Capt. Leopold Grimston Paget

HENRY (1861-82) d. unm.

TUDOR

DELIA

ALFREDA

DELIA = (1) O'CLERY =(2) WRIGHT

SOPHIE CLAUDE [O'SHEA] b. and d. 1882

CLARE = BERTRAM [O'SHEA] MAUNSELL (1883-1909)

KATHARINE = ARTHUR [O'SHEA] MOULE

ASSHETON CLARE BOWYER-LANE (1909-34) d. unm.

HAROLD DE MOWBRAY (1889-?)

MAUDE YOLAN HOWARD (1886-?)

MAURICE STEWART (1884-1934)

EVELEEN = CYRIL NEVIL (1928) (1891-)
dau. of Barnaby Lanktree
WITH ISSUE →

# 1   *The country gentleman:*
##      *John Henry Parnell*

There is little that is concrete known about Charles Stewart Parnell's father. Unlike his son, he created no stir in the world, and unlike his own father, he left no literary bequest behind him. The one personal record available is the absorbing journal he kept during his tour of North America and its incompleteness, as well as its many excisions, make this less valuable than it might otherwise be. The picture that emerges from a synthesis of this and secondary sources is, quite simply, of a country gentleman with little that is unpredictable about his make-up. John Henry Parnell fits smoothly into the Wicklow profiled in my first chapter: except in one all-important particular. He did not marry, as might have been expected, into one of the neighbouring county families, an Acton or a Truell, nor did he choose one of his relatives among the Wicklow Howards; but during his extended Grand Tour of North America he met and married (with uncharacteristic haste) an eighteen-year-old girl, Delia Tudor Stewart. She outlived him by nearly forty years, and brought up their many children with a new slant to their Wicklow county conditioning. It was not, as St John Ervine dismissed it, a childhood in a milieu 'out of the novels of Lever'; it was something much more complex.

Before dealing with Charles Stewart Parnell's youth, it is worth examining the life of John Henry Parnell, his marriage, and Delia Tudor Stewart Parnell's life up to the time of her husband's death in 1859. This event meant a total change for the family both in their way of life and in the influences which surrounded the upbringing of the children.

This section also deals briefly with the children of the marriage, up to 1859, and with the childhood of Charles Stewart as far as the same year. The really formative years of his youth were probably those of his rather haphazardly organised adolescence, following his father's death, which occurred when he was just thirteen; this period will form the next part of my study, and I shall also reserve for this a detailed treatment of Avondale as it was when Charles Stewart inherited it.

What follows is the background to Parnell's youth and, in a sense, to his later life.

## I

William Parnell-Hayes and Frances Howard had only two children: Catherine, born in 1810, and John Henry, born in 1811. Tradition has it that William left Avondale to Catherine, as it was always to pass to a younger child, and that she deeded it to her brother in return for £10,-000 in order that he might be better endowed when competing for the hand of Delia Tudor Stewart; this seems completely unfounded in fact.[1] Catherine *was* endowed with £10,000 drawn on the Avondale estate, but this was a marriage portion and came from an arrangement made by her father in 1815.[2] Moreover, memorials for deeds dated as early as 1823 refer unequivocally to John Henry Parnell (still a minor) as the heir of Avondale and the other lands that came to the Parnells through Samuel Hayes.[3] It would have been strange if the arrangement had been otherwise, for the only other property William Parnell had to bequeath was the much-mortgaged Parnell estate in Armagh, of which the head landlord was Trinity College. The idea that John Henry Parnell came into the Avondale estate only in 1834 is completely inaccurate. It may have originated from a fancy of Delia Tudor Stewart Parnell's or Emily Dickinson's; neither lady was a stickler for accuracy. It is true that Avondale twice passed to a younger son, but in the many recapitulations of Samuel Hayes's celebrated will that are to be found in Memorials in the Registry of Deeds, there is no mention of such a stipulation. When William Parnell inherited the estate, it was because his elder brother was left the larger family seat in the Queen's County; Avondale was a comparatively minor holding. When Charles Stewart Parnell inherited it before his elder brother, John Howard, the explanation was that the latter was to be provided for by his father's relative, Sir Ralph Howard. In 1821 John Henry Parnell inherited his father's estate at the Meeting of the Waters, and his sister a considerable fortune; any other arrangement would have been unexpected, and need not be looked for.

After their father's unexpected death John and Catherine were put in the charge of the Chancery Court. The adults who represented them legally and are described as 'next friends' (though not as legal guardians) were Thomas Parnell, William's evangelist brother, the Hon. Hugh Howard, their uncle on the maternal side; and the Hon. Granville Leveson Proby (later Lord Carysfort), who married another Howard aunt, Hugh's and Frances's sister.[4] At the time of her marriage in 1835 Catherine was living at Bushy Park, the home of her uncle Ralph Howard (Hugh's son).[5] Her brother's upbringing and later life reflect the same sort of background.[6] John went to school at

Eton and was admitted to Trinity College, Cambridge, on 30 April 1831 (mistakenly entered as 'Richard'); he matriculated at the end of that year.[7] His tour of America was during 1834–5; after his return to Wicklow he became a Justice of the Peace, Deputy Lieutenant of the county, and Chairman of the Rathdrum Board of Guardians, as well as M.F.H. of the Rathdrum Hunt. The date of his marriage is generally given as May 1834, but was actually 31 May 1835. His premature death took place on 3 July 1859.

The only first-hand account of John Henry Parnell's life is in the period from October 1834 to April 1835; a diary kept while travelling in Canada, the United States and Mexico.[8] This journal begins at Frederickton, Canada, on 7 October 1834, when Parnell and his travelling-companion, Lord Powerscourt (his neighbour and cousin), were staying at Government House there; parties, snipe-shooting and flirtations are vividly recorded, along with impressions of Canadian life and manners. Always critical and discriminating, the journal appears written to be read, often adopting a didactic tone;[9] the numerous expurgations in the text are further evidence of this.

Parnell and Powerscourt travelled to Montreal via Quebec, and thence to Albany and New York. Constantly on the look-out for 'Yankeeism' and 'American impertinence', it is not surprising that he found them; but he quickly learnt to appreciate the style and vivacity of American women. Nonetheless, on 4 December he moved on to Philadelphia, 'hoping never again to see New York except for the purpose of leaving it for Liverpool'.[10] Here the parties continued, as did Parnell's criticism of American manners in society.[11] Baltimore was his next stop, where he visited a country house in Maryland that reminded him of Shelton Abbey. On 22 December Parnell went to Washington, where he had been in the spring.

Prevented by the cold weather from leaving Washington for Cuba, he returned to New York and sailed from there with some friends on 22 January 1835. He had been ill at ease in the New York social round – 'but that is perhaps my fault'[12] – and wished he were travelling home. However, the 25 days' journey to Vera Cruz is described by him with wit and enjoyment. Mexico, however, horrified the travellers (now a party of 5: Powerscourt, Parnell, Kertchikoff (?) – a Russian diplomat – Worral, an American friend, and McCracken, an English officer): encounters with banditti in the Mexican hills en route to Mexico City are described with relish. In early March Parnell left Mexico City by horse for Tampico, guided by a villainous muleteer. He visited some silver mines belonging to an English company on the way, and was reminded again of Wicklow. At Tampico Powerscourt was tempted to set off to Buenos Aires; Parnell, on the other hand, felt nothing but revulsion for 'the barbarous and quarrelsome republics of South America, which must after all both in language and manners

very much resemble that of Mexico'. Here the diary ends, though there
were evidently some further entries. The date Parnell reached Tampico was some time about the middle of March; inside the back cover
of the journal is written 'libro hui finem posui hac die 12th April –
deck of the schooner *Comet* anchored within 18 miles of the Bellisle
with a contrary wind and close to shore'. He therefore spent little time
in New York on his return journey; but he was to come back the
following month for his marriage.

Parnell's American diary is characterised throughout by a deliberate
circumspectness; and most of the few passages with some personal
bearing – flirtations, gossip and the like – are scored out by a later
pen. The journal remains of great interest, and helps to build up a
definite picture of the man. He was, for a start, very much the young
gentleman. He was travelling with Lord Powerscourt (Richard
Wingfield, the 6th viscount), who was his first cousin, being the son of
his mother's sister. Their association meant that the travellers were
received with a flourish almost everywhere. At the beginning of their
Canadian visit Parnell records that 'all the grandees of the Province
were invited to meet us' [13] and this remained the tone of their stay.
Arrival in any town from Quebec to Mexico City immediately resulted
in a flow of invitations from the Governor and polite society. [14] It is
hard to know whether Parnell would have been similarly fêted if he
had been alone; he recorded that Powerscourt attended more parties
than he did, but only occasionally because 'they had not the civility to
ask me'; [15] he was, in fact, inclined to be anti-social. [16] Still, his
companion tended to create rather a splash in foreign society; in Vera
Cruz 'Mr. Gifford, the British Consul, *who had heard of the titled personage on board*, made his appearance and very politely took us ashore
in his own boat'; [17] and at the New Year's Day levée in the White
House Powerscourt withered a patronising Congressman:

> One of the members asked P[Powerscourt] – 'I guess you have
> not often been in a larger room than this' – P looked at him with
> sovereign contempt as he replied 'I have got a room in my own
> house which would hold two of this'. Mr. Willis, the Member,
> looked incredulous. [18]

Parnell himself, however, was capable of an equal hauteur in his attitudes. Some of his opinions reflect those of the age rather than an individual reaction, as where he expresses his shock that in America a
bride on honeymoon should travel unabashedly on a public steamer, [19]
and his dismissal of anybody with Indian blood as *ipso facto* both
debauched and idle. [20] But a more deep-rooted attitude is evident in his
summing-up of Canada:

> *Il faut avouer* that they [the Provinces] are pleasanter for

gentlemen than any part of the States, that is to say the society is more agreeable and their ideas are more suitable to an Aristocratic education and feelings – no vulgar fellow came up to shake our hands off against our inclination and more deference and real respect was shown altogether; but I must add that our colonies in America are far, far behind the United States in civilisation. [21]

He did not, however, do without 'deference and real respect' in the United States. At the Atlantic Hotel in New York, he was pleased that the public sitting room was partitioned for the Irish gentlemen's convenience, despite many complaints from 'the democracy', [22] and again, in a controversy about private boxes at the New York Opera he declared himself firmly for privilege [23] Parnell's social attitudes were those of the class he came from and amongst whom he lived. The contacts of Irish society, indeed, reached as far as Quebec, where the Irish travellers were looked up by a relative of the Hamiltons of Hamwood. [24] Parnell was closely involved in Wicklow 'society'. As well as being related to them, he was a close friend of the Powerscourts and was a trustee in the deed drawn up for his friend's marriage to Lady Margaret Jocelyn a year after their return. [25]

The picture of John Henry Parnell from other sources adds to the impression of an average young gentleman of his time. His son John Howard wrote:

> After his marriage he settled at Avondale as a quiet country gentleman, keeping fine horses and hounds and hunting with all the Wicklow gentry. He was very fond of agriculture, at which he was recognised as an expert, and gave great employment to the people in reclaiming the land at Avondale. He was a prominent magistrate and D.L. for Wicklow. High-tempered when aroused, he was of a quiet disposition as a rule. He was fond of shooting and preserving the game all over the country and had his shooting-lodge at Aughavannagh, an old military barracks in the mountains of Wicklow, where he often went to shoot. He was a very fine cricketer and maintained a first-rate cricket club. [26]

John Howard Parnell here, as often elsewhere, extracts the pith of the matter in a few words; his sister Emily's statements about their father's 'rare knowledge' of horses and 'courteousness as Master of the Hounds' [27] are little more than additional frills. R. B. O'Brien enlarged slightly on the picture, probably from conversations with both John and Emily; adding that he was 'a staunch Liberal'. [28] Charles Stewart Parnell said little more about his father when giving evidence before the Special Commission in 1889, except to say that 'he took a very extensive interest in local affairs'. [29] His local popularity was attested to

by the tribute paid to him by a fellow-member of the Rathdrum Board
of Guardians, that he was 'a patrician in feeling and descent, and yet
accessible even to the humblest peasant'; [30] long after his death, a
correspondent of his eldest son's recalled John Henry Parnell's reputation for 'espousing the popular side in local contests', which could be a
reference to his expressed indignation during the famine at landlords
who 'appropriated for their own benefit money voted by Parliament
for "public works" with the ostensible object of providing employment
for the starving people'. [31]

Evidence of John Henry Parnell's agricultural interests is to be
found in his diary; he describes in detail foreign phenomena like the
Canadian method of conserving root-crops [32] and in his travels round
Pennsylvania notes almost automatically facts like 'the cows can still
pick up some grass in the fields . . . I saw some wheat about 4 inches
high.' [33] His love of country-house life is amply demonstrated in his
delight at a visit to a country estate outside Baltimore: 'I mentioned to
him [Gilmour, the owner] what a pleasant life it is to have a country
house and farm if a man has sufficient income to support it'. [34] With a
predilection for this sort of life went an enjoyment of hunting; his disgust at a Mexican shooting-party where ladders were used to obtain a
better vantage point is almost comical: [35] 'I longed for my dog Rory'. [36]
The Mexicans, furthermore, 'annoyed me very much by showing that
they were afraid I should shoot them – as if I had not seen more of
shooting than the whole set put together'. [37]

The life of a nineteenth-century country gentleman presupposes
some involvement in local affairs; here John Parnell was as active as
might be expected, but no more. He was a J.P. from 1837 until his
death, a Deputy Lieutenant for Wicklow from 1835, and High Sheriff
of the county for the year 1837. [38] As such, he was involved with the
running of the county; letters to him from Robert Chaloner, Lord
Fitzwilliam's industrious agent at Coolattin, make such requests as
that 'Mr Newton would make a particularly good coroner; if you can
procure any support for him, you would oblige'. [39] Parnell also helped
the political interests of Chaloner's employer; in 1852 Chaloner
recorded that 'Lord M. [Milton – the Earl's eldest son] will write to ask
Tynte to propose him and to Parnell to second him. He is anxious to
have the election as early as possible'. [40]

Parnell was deputy vice-chairman of the Rathdrum Poor Law
Union in 1849, [41] vice-chairman in 1850 [42] and 1851 [43] and chairman
for 1852 until his death. [44] The workhouse of the Rathdrum Union was
opened in March 1842, accommodating 780 persons, and two aux-
iliary buildings eventually housed 460 more. [45] Parnell would evidently
have increased accommodation still further, but the Fitzwilliam interest was against this policy; in April 1849 Chaloner wrote to Parnell
refusing to agree to an enlarged establishment. [46] Parnell's close

involvement with the Poor Law union leads to the question of his own policy to tenants during the 1840s, but in the absence of account books for Avondale it is impossible to know how the estate was run during the famine. Chaloner's voluminous correspondence for the period does not mention any relief centre on the Parnell demesne, and Parnell does not appear on the Board of Guardians until 1849, when the worst was well over.[47]

He was indubitably a concerned and improving landlord; a memorial in the Registry of Deeds records his application for a loan under the Landed Estates Improvement Act (10th Victoria), under which a Commission 'approved of certain necessary works' at Ballyknockan (possibly the land reclamation scheme mentioned by John Howard Parnell) and granted a loan of £300.[48] On the lands John Henry Parnell held from Lord Fitzwilliam (about 130 acres at Corballis) he 'erected four cottages which must have cost beyond £100, and he levelled fences and drained part of the land'.[49] Another source reckoned that 'Mr Parnell laid out over £600' on the Corballis farms.[50] A letter of Chaloner's shows him referring a tenant who was 'a respectable man and an improving tenant' though under sentence of ejectment, to Parnell's estate in search of work – a significant incident. Parnell was preoccupied with improving the estate, and was responsible for creating a by-pass at the demesne entrance, where the public road originally ran through part of the estate; he shut this off and built a new road which skirted the boundary of his lands. This required renting more land from Lord Fitzwilliam – the portion between the gate off the main road, and the inner gate, still clearly demarcated today. When the estate came to be sold in 1899, this arrangement had to be revised.[51]

Outside Rathdrum, however, John Henry Parnell's public involvements seem to have been minimal. Many of the Wicklow gentry – not only those from the great commercial families such as Arthur Guinness and David Latouche, but also men such as Sir Ralph Howard, Colonel Acton and John Wall of Knockrig – were involved in Dublin charitable organisations;[52] Parnell's name never occurs in similar circumstances. Nor does he seem to have been involved in business ventures based in the capital, as many of the same men were. In his American journal he wrote prophetically 'these railroads pay so well that we must get them up in the Co. Wicklow, for instance from Bray to Wexford',[53] and in 1841 he was a director of the short-lived Munster and Leinster Railway Company;[54] but he was not involved with its successor, the Waterford, Wexford, Wicklow and Dublin Railway Company, although neighbours of his such as Daniel Tighe of Rossanna and Colonel Acton of Westaston were.[55] His involvements seem to have been local, and his interests domestic.

Secondary sources have recorded Parnell as a book-lover; an article in *Truth* on Anna Parnell stated that he 'read and thought a good deal',[56] and St John Ervine portrayed him as 'a clever man who drifted along', absorbed in his library. Both these authorities, however, were concerned with presenting John Henry Parnell as an abstracted and intellectual figure, too ineffectual to instil sense into his women-folk. Neither Emily Dickinson nor John Howard Parnell recalled their father as a reader. Nor does his journal contain any notable literary allusions; and the Avondale library catalogue (which I shall deal with in detail elsewhere) gives the impression of having been little added to after William Parnell's death. In his leisure, John Parnell certainly enjoyed chess; a typical entry in his diary, after an evening at tournament, is 'lost 8 dollars and dreamt of chess all night long'.[57] This interest was inherited by his son John Howard; John Henry Parnell's other chief pastime was bequeathed to Charles Stewart, who like his father always remained devoted to cricket. The very first page of John Henry Parnell's journal contains a reference to his disappointed hopes of playing cricket at Frederickton; he even attempts to organise 'a sort of a game of cricket' aboard ship en route to Vera Cruz;[58] and in Mexico he could again enjoy 'my old well-beloved game'.[59] His fondness for cricket eventually proved, in a sense, fatal; his death was occasioned by his insistence on playing for Leinster against Phoenix while suffering from a rheumatic fever.[60]

An important aspect of Parnell's character is his religious attitude. The doctrine of the Brethren which the second Lord Congleton imbibed from John Henry's uncle, Thomas Parnell, was not adopted by John; but it is notable that his sister Catherine married one of their number, George Vicesimus Wigram,[61] and that meetings of the Brethren were patronised by his aunt, Lady Powerscourt. A staunch Protestant, John Henry Parnell shows in his journal a leaning towards the strictness of 'left-wing' Protestantism rather than the happy-go-lucky religious attitudes of the majority of Church of Ireland squires in this period. In Mexico he 'did not think it altogether proper to spend Sunday shooting';[62] the average Irish country gentleman would probably have thought it improper to spend it any other way. In Philadelphia he 'was rather shocked to see Mrs W [his hostess] introduce cards on a Sunday evening . . . I mentioned my horror to one of the girls, who did not seem to enter into my feelings at all'.[63] He remained a regular churchgoer in America, in contrast to most of his acquaintances, and was constantly interested in the religious attitudes he found: the laxity of fashionable Philadelphia about professing any religion made him feel that an established State Church was essential.[64]

Parnell's attitude to Roman Catholicism seems to have been hostile in the extreme; Mexican priests are 'black pillars of hypocrisy and vice', he is disgusted by the reverence accorded to 'greasy beasts of friars', and all in all, 'in this country [Mexico] the perverting, debasing effects of the Catholic religion appear in naked force and would almost justify the dogma of some of our Irish Orangemen who esteem it doing God a service to get rid of a bloody Papist'.[65] However, the qualification in the last passage ('would *almost* justify') is indicative; and elsewhere Parnell attacks 'puritanical bigotry' and defends nuns as 'doing a great deal of good ... devoting themselves to God in the manner in which they feel they can alone do it effectually'.[66] In his native context he seems to have maintained this more liberal attitude; in 1850 he approached Robert Chaloner about the possibility of building a Catholic church at Rathdrum.[67] Possibly he inherited his father's combination of repulsion from Catholic doctrine allied with admiration for the social function of Irish priests.

At this stage it may be useful to attempt some definition of John Henry Parnell's character as it can be reconstructed from his journal. He was undoubtedly a man of intelligence and strength of mind, as well as a certain impatience and asperity towards what he considered affectation – whether it was the too-carefully modulated tones of a Canadian Governor's daughters,[68] the attempts of Fanny Kemble, an ex-actress, to make the grade in colonial high society,[69] or the fashion for visiting asylums and houses of correction as sights to be seen.[70] Linked with this sharpness is a power of observation beyond the ordinary; Parnell's *Journal* is far more imaginative and discursive than most Victorian travel diaries. He takes care to record long conversations with inn-keepers and chambermaids whenever he considers the opinions expressed are worth noting;[71] his views of colonial and American society are pungent, amusing and always readable. He evinces something of his famous son's dislike of social duties, as where he 'opened Mr. Forsyth's door intending to leave cards only, just heard him talking inside in time to shut the door and run away':[72] he frequently records with relief having 'escaped' a smoking-party after dinner.[73] This reclusiveness is accompanied, as so often, by a liking for rectitude in others and a strong sense of the importance of the proprieties. In New York he was shocked by the general reception accorded to an opera singer 'who made herself too famous in England by her elopement with Paganini ... I did not go, but heard that several ladies of good society in New York were present. I charitably suppose they were not acquainted with her history'.[74] Similarly, in Mexico City he thought it 'questionable taste' on the part of two English ladies to parade on the Pasao in the evening, as Mexican ladies and gallants did.[75] Such questions of correct behaviour, while not an obsession of Parnell's, were certainly a preoccupation; his great dislike of oaths, even in rough company, is also significant.

Despite his acute perception and his often humorous observations on foreign ways, he was not a natural traveller. 'I hate all foreigners', he recorded on board ship to Vera Cruz, 'especially as bedroom companions',[76] and his real interest is often reserved for those of Irish blood whom he meets abroad – like the Irishwoman in French Canada who teaches her children 'as good Irish dialect and accent as could have been taught in Connacht'.[77] In Mexico, his strongest reaction was anger at the maltreatment of horses and mules: the sight of naked Indians toiling underground in the English silver-mines merits only a passing reference. In these attitudes he emerges strongly as the young English or Anglo-Irish gentleman abroad, whose catholic interest in all he sees is nonetheless accompanied by a recurring desire to return home and an unyieldingly insular attitude. This type of young man, having made his tour for the sake of his education, rarely travels abroad at length again; and this seems to have been true of John Henry Parnell. After he returned with his new wife in 1835, his life centred round Avondale. The little that is recorded of him after this period bears out the impression created by his unconsciously revealing diary: the young man who expressed such censoriousness about indiscreet women and rowdy parties disapproved equally in later life of his rackety neighbours the Dickinsons, and of his children's amateur theatricals.[78] Later, when Emily was discovered in an illicit rendezvous with an admirer while in London, Lady Howard expressed her surprise at 'a daughter of John Parnell' thus disgracing herself;[79] an uncompromising attitude towards such peccadilloes remained one of the central features of his character until the end of his life.


## II

The one inconsistency in John Henry Parnell's life - the one impetuous act on the part of a generally sober and predictable young man – seems to have been his romantic marriage. 'This was the one notable event in the life of John Henry Parnell',[80] according to R. B. O'Brien; it was certainly the most striking.

The circumstances of the match are shadowy. Emily Dickinson wrote:

> My father was a wealthy and very handsome man, belonging to one of the best old Irish families. Soon after attaining his majority he had, while travelling with his cousin Lord Powerscourt, met, fallen violently in love with, and married the lovely and only daughter of Admiral Stewart.[81]

This is the skeleton of the story, and it is hard to enlarge upon it. Mrs Parnell herself told the story in a characteristically rambling and disconnected way to R. M. McWade in 1891. Since the words – whatever their accuracy – are her own, it is worth giving the account in full:

Mr Parnell was induced by his friend Lord Powerscourt to travel. He was his cousin. On the steamer coming they met Mr and Mrs Thomson Hankey. Mrs Hankey was related to the Biddles of Philadelphia [frequently mentioned in Parnell's journal as playing host to Powerscourt and himself]. The whole party came to Washington together. My mother called on Mrs Hankey and when the two young men heard there was a young lady in the drawing-room they also put in an appearance. This was early in 1834. Then the whole party came to see us. The two young men were sure to come too and on the occasion of that very first visit to us Mrs Hankey astonished me by beginning to quiz Mr Parnell about his admiration for me. This was something like Benedict and Beatrice and probably laid the first stone, for Mr Parnell was very shy, like many a young Englishman. His friend was not. Both were very handsome young men, but Mr Parnell was the handsomer by far. Then they went away on different visits together, but soon separated. We went to West Point as usual . . . Mr Parnell and his cousin came to West Point took immediately after our arrival there . . . I induced the proprietor of the hotel to give a ball to the cadets. I got very few dances with them because of the persistent attentions of Lord Powerscourt and Mr Parnell to me. Right in the midst of the dancing, which I was enjoying very much, Mr Parnell said to me: 'I hate this dancing; won't you come into another room?' However, I went into another room, where there were several other couples; so then he dragged me off to another room, with a similar fate. Then he got me out on to the piazza, and there were several other couples; and then he gave vent to a John Bull oath, 'Damn it', which I had not heard since my father's ship, which astonished me exceedingly. I began to think he was very bad-tempered and became a little afraid of him. So the next morning he went out to smoke with his cousin but soon left him smoking and hurried up to the hotel and asked me if I would not like to see Kosciusko's Retreat. Of course, as I had never seen it, I was glad to go and see it. There he proposed – asked me to go to Ireland with him; and going away from the Retreat we met his cousin hurrying to find out where we were. I hardly took Mr Parnell to be serious so I said to Lord Powerscourt very frankly: 'Your cousin has just asked me to go to Ireland with him but I don't like being lost in an Irish fog and I am afraid he has no house there.' That was my idea of Ireland. Lord Powerscourt laughed and said he 'thought his cousin had a mud cabin'. That was all the encouragement he gave me. Well, we had parties on horseback and different things and they left me and we went to Lebanon to see the Shaking Quakers; but the whole of this business at West Point gave me a violent headache which lasted for a week. [82]

There she ends the story of Parnell's proposal; Mrs Parnell does not detail his further advances, merely adding:

> This is but the beginning of the history of his perseverance, which ended in our marriage at Grace Church, New York, Dr Taylor officiating, the 31st of May, 1835. My mother was very much opposed to the match and she would not consent to it herself until he promised to bring me back every year to see the family. Yes, but he did not keep his promise, as he did not promise to bring the children and I was not willing to leave them. [83]

Several comments can be made about this exiguous account. First of all, though Parnell was a cousin of Powerscourt's, after Powerscourt died, the relationship between the families dropped into abeyance; when Richard Wingfield's son, the 7th viscount, wrote his *History of Powerscourt* he cannot have supposed the Parnells to be relatives or he would not have referred to them so patronisingly. [84] The 6th viscount was evidently a close friend of John Henry Parnell, but when he died (prematurely, in 1846) their families cannot have remained close. There are also several doubtful claims in Mrs Parnell's story, which cast some shadow on the accuracy of her memory. She describes her husband as a 'young Englishman', capable of a 'John Bull oath'; elsewhere she says that he belonged to 'the Church of England'. [85] These are extraordinary mistakes for the widow of an Irish squire to make. There is also the smaller point that Parnell, on the evidence of his journal, disliked smoking and abhorred swearing; and, with reference to her last sentence, it might be pointed out that scruples about leaving her children rarely bothered Mrs Parnell in later life.

Nonetheless the account is definitely authentic. The rather jumpy style, the characteristic of including completely extraneous details while glossing over important facts, the preoccupation with herself and the figure she made [86] – in all these features this chapter in McWade's scantily documented and hastily compiled book resembles (for instance) the lengthy letter about her family that Mrs Parnell wrote to T.D. Sullivan some years before. [87] Her distinctive style is of dubious advantage to the reader, but is readily identifiable.

Unsatisfactory as Mrs Parnell's long account is, it is the only first-hand account available. Her story takes place in the summer of 1834; her husband's American journal begins in the October of that year, when he had left America for a visit to Canada, and it was finished in April 1835. Thus for the period throughout which he kept the diary he was certainly in pursuit of Delia Tudor Stewart, and possibly engaged to her; when he ended it he must have known that in a month he would be returning to marry her. Yet his references to her throughout – where they can be detected – are infrequent and formal. Not too much construction need be placed on this; as has been said, the diary seems to have been written to be read, and discretion is in the forefront of Parnell's mind throughout. Nonetheless, the picture given is not of a young man in constant pursuit of a recalcitrant maiden. In fact, at every ball or party he attends, Parnell gives an inventory of the ladies present, often in a manner that suggests he was at least interested in their possibilities. In New York he 'danced with Miss Costa, who has 200,000 dollars hard cash – 60,000 pounds. She is a substantial, good-humoured little lump';[88] at Washington his attention was engaged at ball after ball by a Miss Seaton.[89] His future wife is referred to as 'Miss Stewart' or sometimes 'Miss Delia'. In New York at Christmas he and Powerscourt encountered her at many dances; Parnell's diary for this period is remarkable for the number of lines, and even complete pages, that have been scored out. His pursuit over Christmas was not unduly hot: 'I had promised to go to a party at Mrs Stewart's but feeling lazily inclined stuck to the hearth all evening'.[90] Some days later at a ball Parnell 'met Miss Stewart and danced a quadrille with her, but she was afterwards engaged to waltz with Murray and the heat was so excessive that I made an attempt to escape'.[91] At a New Year's Eve reception in Washington Powerscourt 'danced with Miss Delia in a cotillon';[92] the following day provides the only hint of anything more than a social acquaintance with the lady, when Parnell 'fulfilled my promise to Miss D. and made an expense of 6 dollars to give her The English Keepsake [an almanac] which has some beautiful engravings'.[93] If Parnell throughout this period was beseeching Delia Tudor Stewart to be his wife, he took care not to hint at it in his diary.

This is, however, not unnatural in someone of his reticence, who expected his journal to be read and was moreover not certain of having his proposal accepted; Mrs Parnell's account must still be taken as the only definitive one. John Howard Parnell believed that his parents met in Mexico,[94] which is contradicted by the evidence in his father's diary. (John Howard also gives his father's age incorrectly as 21; he was actually 23.)

The couple married in New York and returned to Avondale. The effect of what Emily Dickinson described – with characteristic dash – as 'the sudden transformation from having been the belle of New York to the solutides of Avondale'[95] will be discussed in full in the next chapter; but here it is appropriate to consider how the marriage turned out. Mrs Parnell rarely mentioned her husband, and their children do not record much of value about the relationship between their parents; but circumstantial evidence seems to show that it was not an unduly happy marriage. Country life did not agree with the bride, and she seems to have had little distraction apart from her many children. She bore eleven sons and daughters.[96] William Tudor was born in 1837 and died five years later, 'through bad vaccination'.[97] Delia was born in 1838, Hayes in 1839, Emily in 1840, John Howard in 1843, Sophia in 1845, Charles Stewart in 1846, Fanny in 1849, Henry in 1850,[98] Anna in 1852 and Theodosia in 1853. As can be seen from this list, children were born regularly to the couple – almost one a year – until 1853, but none after that year, though Mrs Parnell was only 36 years old. From about this time Mrs Parnell (usually with some of her children) seems to have resided largely in Paris.[99] It was in this year too that John Henry Parnell took Charles Stewart – aged only seven – to school at Yeovil and told the schoolmistress that he was anxious the child should spend some years in England *'with someone who would mother him* and cure his stammering'.[100] Mrs Parnell was in Paris when her husband died; she did not return until after the funeral. Nor did she inherit anything, except a small annuity, which she later renounced;[101] all his property went directly to his children. St John Ervine was told by one who knew the Parnells and Avondale that Mrs Parnell 'was considered by the people about the estate to be a "flighty" woman . . . she would go away and not see her husband for near a year again'.[102] This was, of course, what Ervine wanted to be told, believing already that Mrs Parnell was 'bad all along and mad in the end'; but circumstances seem to show that Delia Parnell began the peripatetic style which characterised her later life[103] five or six years before her husband's death.

The fact that the Parnells lived largely apart from 1853 may be at least partly explained by a tragedy that took place about that year: the accident which led to the death of their eldest son, Hayes. His death is described by Emily Dickinson as being caused by a clumsy horseman riding over him in the hunting-field.[104] John Howard recalled that Hayes 'died from consumption, which developed after a fall from his pony'[105] and Mrs Parnell recorded that his death was brought on by pleurisy.[106] But the riding accident was generally blamed as the cause of the fatality; and Mrs Dickinson significantly added:

> My mother had always dreaded these hunting-days for her children, predicting that some day one of them would be brought back dead; but her husband had invariably ridiculed her fears, maintaining that there could be no danger for his children, as they were all born riders.[107]

Not a horsewoman herself, it is likely that Mrs Parnell would have blamed her husband for allowing the tragedy to happen; this reinforces the impression that Mrs Parnell lived, to all intents and purposes, apart from her husband from 1854, and also provides a reason for the separation.

## III

Unlike the two previous squires of Avondale, John Henry Parnell never stood as M.P. for Wicklow, but it is both relevant and possible to reconstruct his political sentiments. R. B. O'Brien described him as 'a staunch Liberal',[108] and many entries in his journal bear out this judgement. In Frederickton he wrote sympathetically of an acquaintance who was 'a nephew of Dan O'Connell's and suffers accordingly from the bitter Tories of the regiment, which most of them are'. He criticised a Mr Hamilton encountered in Quebec as 'a red-hot Tory . . . nothing appeared to satisfy him but bayonetting the whole House of Assembly'; and he described at length a debate at dinner

> between Mr Ogden, the Attorney-General, a most genuine bigoted Tory of the old school and a Mr Daly, an Irish Papist, as we would call him *chez nous* . . . In heart I believe him as much of a Tory as any of the others, however on this occasion he took the Liberal side of the question [which concerned government discrimination against those in favour of Canadian legislative reform when considering applications for civil service jobs]. I was delighted to find a liberal in such company, and joined Mr Daly warmly.[109]

His own views on contemporary questions manifest a generally liberal analysis:

> The conversation turned on the North-Western Indians. Kertchikoff was expressing feelings which I believe are common to all Europeans respecting them, namely commiseration for their sufferings under the war of extermination which is carried out against them by whites wherever they come into contact. McKinna turned to me and said gravely 'It amuses me to hear so much *false* sympathy wasted on these Indians, since it is evident from certain causes producing certain effects, *Providence* has decreed that this race should become extinct and make room for the whites and civilisation. How useless and weak is it then to attempt to retard the progress of their annihilation; I for one am convinced that it would be far more humane to accelerate their destiny as much as possible' (by this he meant wholesale butchery of the poor creatures). I enquired of him what were the natural causes which he referred to: he replied 'Weakness and ignorance'. 'Cannot ignorance be remedied by education' asked I, 'and is weakness, either from inferiority of numbers or of strength, a sufficient reason for slaughtering your fellow—creatures?' 'Oh,' said he, 'it is all very well to talk thus, but the history of mankind has always shown that right must yield to might in the end and that the great body of men are only

obedient to laws because they are compelled to be so.' I was shocked at his sentiments with regard to the poor Indians, the rightful owners of the soil, but I fear that the same opinions on this topic are entertained by three-fourths of the Americans, only they do not venture to express them quite so openly. [110]

Such liberal opinions are reinforced by a sour reference elsewhere to Louis Philippe, 'who accepted monarchy and has since shown his deep respect for liberal institutions by getting rid of them upon every occasion that they interfered with his ambitious views'. [111] Given his liberality about current politics and the Indians, however, Parnell was by no means unilaterally enlightened. His first impressions of Mexican half-breeds are significant, especially considering that he wrote them down on his very first day in the country:

I could not look on these beings at first without disgust and felt for the first time in its full force the privilege of being a white man. Their character fully corresponds to their appearance – they are lazy to extremes, fond of drinking and gambling, would rather thieve than work, and totally destitute of intelligence or education, except in so far as the ipsa dicta of the priests go. [112]

On social issues he could take an even harder line, complaining after his inspection of the new prison at Philadelphia that it had been made far too comfortable. [113]

Moreover, if he considered himself a Liberal in politics, John Henry Parnell was still nothing like a Radical. A strong vein of anti-republicanism runs through his journal. 'I think that this is one of the great evils of an unlimited republic,' he wrote in New York, 'that the freedom of doing what they like with their own is denied to the rich, though fully conceded to the poor.' [114] Similar views are evident in his reaction to Jackson's Presidential levée; where to his surprise the westerners behaved themselves correctly:

Thus it is that vulgarity and rudeness will always shrink from the contact of refinement and true gentility, and this practical effort to show that all men are equal convinced me more than all the arguments in the world that all men are not equal, nor were intended to be so. [115]

Parnell's view of the British-Irish connection is not stated in his journal, but it can be deduced. He refers more than once to *'we Britishers'* [116] and *'our* transatlantic dominions' [117] (as Isaac Butt was to do); however, he was well aware of the injustice implicit in government from afar, at least as regarded judicial appointments and religious and education administration in Canada:

Who shall then wonder that in such a situation of things, with the flourishing state of Maine alongside of them, that some should begin to doubt the boasted advantage of British connexion and sigh for the change which has produced such brilliant results to their neighbours? [118]

This is not to say Parnell supported Canadian discontent; elsewhere he records incredulously that 'they demand an election council, the abolition of the land company, a civil governor instead of a military one, and several other extravagant demands'. [119] Later on he ascribes the superiority of American civilisation and commerce over that of Canada 'wholly to the disadvantage of colonial government'; but, he adds carefully, 'it is a most difficult question to determine whether if they are to remain colonies they can be governed in any other or better manner'. [120] It seems likely that, had he lived, he would have supported Butt's Home Government Association, as a thoughtful and Liberal country gentleman; how much further he would have gone is a moot question.

## IV

Emily Dickinson described her father as 'a wealthy man' at the time of his marriage. [121] That he was a man of property is undeniable; but his assets at the time of his death seem to have been limited. Before considering this circumstance, it is enlightening to review the extent of his property as it can be reconstructed from memorials in the Registry of Deeds for this period.

John Henry Parnell's direct inheritance from his father was, of course, Avondale. Under William Parnell this contained the townlands of Ballytrasna, Cassino, Crevagh, Ballylugduff, Carrignamornan, Ballinderry, Ballyteigue, Ballyeustance, Tyclash and Rockstown; [122] the Hayes estate had also included lands near Newcastle and at Ballymoreustace, which William Parnell sold [123] (probably to provide for Catherine's endowment, which he arranged about the same time), and the lands of Carrowsillagh and Balliniskea in Glenmalure, which were retained. [124] The more cursory inventory of the estate in John Henry Parnell's day omitted Ballyteigue, Crevagh and Ballinderry; but Ballyteigue probably appears under Ballyknockan (which abuts onto it), and the new names of Kingston and the Meeting of the Waters can be taken to embrace the other discrepancies; there are no memorials of sales by John Parnell of land in his area. He augmented the Avondale holding by renting 123 acres from Lord Fitzwilliam at Corballis, near Rathdrum, on a short lease. [125] He maintained this land carefully, and his family were granted £250 in lieu of this when the lease lapsed upon his death. [126] Six acres of these lands 'adjoined the approach to Avondale' [127] and as such it was in the interest of the

Parnells to retain the lease; however John Henry Parnell had only leased this holding 'by some understanding with the tenant but had no consent of the office for doing so . . . and it was contrary to rules of the property that farms should be held by persons not on the property', [128] so the lands were re-let after his death. (Robert Chaloner's correspondence includes many letters to Parnell about the farm at Corballis.) [129]

The nucleus of Parnell's property was, however, Avondale; at the time of his death St John Ervine claims it 'had a free rent-roll and was worth about £4,000 per annum'. [130] He gives no source for this information, and it seems likely that it was an approximation derived from conversations with John Howard Parnell. A Government survey of 1876 estimated the estate at 4,678 acres. [131] When John Henry Parnell inherited in 1821, the estate was committed to paying Catherine the £10,000 due to her; [132] however, he had financial resources through other family arrangements. He did not inherit anything from his uncle Arthur Parnell's sizeable estate in 1827, as the latter's will (made in 1807) left money to his brother William but not to his heirs. [133] However, by Sir John Parnell's will an estate in Armagh, Collure, was left to William Parnell 'and after his decease to furnish and suffer the first son of the said William to receive the issues and profits thereof for his own use, until he attain the age of twenty-one years' [134] – the restriction being because the lands were committed to producing £8,000 to be divided between William's younger brother and sister, Arthur and Sophia Parnell. [135] However, through Thomas Parnell, another uncle, John Henry held a mortgage on a large Dublin premises in Sackville Street; [136] and – possibly in return for re-assigning this mortgage to his uncle – in 1855 Thomas presented to John Henry 'the interest, dividends and annual proceeds of Trust monies, stocks, funds and securities' which he inherited from his sister Sophia Evans in 1855. [137]

Thus on paper at least, John Henry Parnell was a man of considerable property; and he was to add to this property on a large scale, with his purchase of the Carlow estate of Clonmore, just before he died. Before considering this purchase, however, the position regarding the Armagh estate requires clarification. This estate, referred to as Collure, [138] was held on a long lease from the Provost, Fellows and Scholars of Trinity College, Dublin. At the time of Sir John Parnell's marriage to Letitia Brooke in 1774, the estate was assigned to Lord Bangor and Lord Knapton (later Viscount de Vesci), to be held in trust by them for producing £8,000 in trust for the younger children of the marriage. A similar arrangement was outlined in Sir John's will 27 years later; Collure was bequeathed to Robert Stubber, Lord de Vesci Charles Ward and Robert Scott, 'in trust for the benefit of' William Parnell and his eldest son. John Henry Parnell paid £3,692 6s 2d (currency having been revalued in the meantime) to Sophia Parnell from the estate, as part of the earlier arrangement. The long lease from Trinity College was re-granted to John Henry Parnell in 1846, [139] in 1851 the lands were granted to him in perpetuity by the Trinity College Leasing and Perpetuity Act. [140] St John Ervine states that the head-rent due to Trinity College was £1,100 p.a., a figure he probably obtained from Mrs John Howard Parnell, whose husband inherited the property. [141] Ervine goes on to claim that when this head-rent was paid and other expenses met, there was nothing of the estate's income left over; this statement will be evaluated later, when I come to examine the estate more closely. [142] Certainly, as it was not owned outright, Collure was less of an asset than it seemed; the head-rent and running expenses may have left a very narrow margin indeed.

The most significant information about John Henry Parnell's property, however, especially with regard to the state of his affairs at the time of his unexpected death, is contained in a Memorial of a mortgage made in July 1858, exactly a year before his death. [143] This concerns the estate at Clonmore, Co. Carlow, which was left to his third son, Henry Tudor Parnell; it seems most probable that John Henry Parnell's acquisition of it was for the express purpose of providing for him. What is surprising is the extent of this estate: it comprised nearly all of the portion of County Carlow which juts into the south-west corner of Wicklow – a rough square bordered on the north, east and south by the Wicklow county boundary and on the west by the Derreen river and its tributary the Douglas. This area measured about 22 square miles, or 13,000 acres; nearly every townland named in it by the 1911 Ordnance Survey map is contained in the inventory of the Clonmore estate. [144]

Mrs Parnell wrote to T. D. Sullivan concerning these lands that 'the property of the Wicklow Howards was purchased from the Duke of Ormond, and I believe that the property which my son Henry sold was part of it; this property descended to my husband's grandfather Hugh Howard, and furnished the title – Clonmore – of the eldest son of the earls of Wicklow'. [145] She thus implies that her husband inherited these lands through his grandfather; but this was far from being the case. It is true that the lands were originally the property of the Wicklow Howards: they were initially purchased by Robert Howard, Bishop of Elphin, in 1740, and descended to his son Ralph, the first Earl. The latter's grandson, Hugh, was John Henry Parnell's maternal grandfather; Hugh inherited the Clonmore estate in 1815 when his brother, the 3rd Earl, died without issue. But when he died in 1841 it was his son Sir Ralph Howard who inherited Clonmore, not John Henry Parnell; and John Henry purchased the estate from his uncle in 1858, for the large sum of £69,469. 'It was not convenient to the said John Henry Parnell to pay the entire of the purchase money'; so he produc-

ed £13,500 'in hand, well and truly paid' and arranged with Sir Ralph
to let the remaining £55,969 'stand out on the security of the said estate thereby conveyed'. In other words, a bare year before his unexpected death John Henry Parnell undertook a mortgage for nearly
£56,000 in order to purchase a third estate.

This £56,000 was to be paid off at six per cent interest, in equal
half-yearly payments; Sir Ralph covenanted not to foreclose on the
mortgage as long as the conditions were kept up. This arrangement is
recorded in an immense Memorial, over six pages long, in the Registry
of Deeds; it was a correspondingly weighty undertaking. John Parnell
died at the very worst time, as far as this arrangement went: when the
payments of the huge principal had just begun. There were several
provisos to encourage as speedy a payment as possible; the wisest
course his widow could have taken would have been to put every
resource available to her into paying it off, but there is no evidence
that she did so.

Indeed, there are signs that even in the short period before his death
John Henry Parnell felt that it was worth lessening the acreage of
Clonmore in order to provide ready cash. In April 1859 he granted 767
acres of the estate in perpetuity to Charles Davis of Dublin at a yearly
rent of £219; in return Davis paid him £5,697. [146] In June of the same
year he made a similar arrangement with regard to 119 acres, with
another tenant. [147] He had committed himself to a good deal in taking
on the Clonmore mortgage; possibly he felt already that he had bitten
off more than could profitably be chewed.

With this in mind, it is not hard to see why Alfred MacDermott, the
Parnell's solicitor, 'found everything in a very confused state' when he
came down to Avondale after John Henry Parnell's sudden death. [148]
Parnell had not been a man of complex business interests; the only
commercial involvement which I can trace is his directorship of the
Munster and Leinster Railway Company, which lasted from 1841 to
1844. [149] In 1847 the Waterford, Wexford, Wicklow and Dublin
Railway Company was formed, with several of the same directors; but
John Henry Parnell was not one of them. (Charles Stewart Parnell
was later granted £3,000 compensation from this company when the
railway was extended through his estate.) [150] Nor was John Henry
Parnell involved in the Dublin and Wicklow Railway Company which
was formed in 1858; and – unlike his relative, Sir Ralph Howard, and
his neighbour, Colonel Acton – he was not a director of any commercial banking company. [151] He was simply a man of landed property,
who died before his one large investment could pay off. It is probably
unfair, almost definitely inaccurate, and certainly unsubstantiated to
say, as St John Ervine did, that 'Mr Parnell, living like a lord, managed to load his estate with debt'. [152] The only authority for a lordly life
at Avondale is Emily Dickinson's unreliable romancing about high life

in her far-off youth, and any debt there was had been incurred by John Henry Parnell's wish to provide an inheritance for his third son. Alfred MacDermott's first act was to pay off all the workmen not actually required; while, by order of the Court of Chancery the livestock and farming implements were sold by auction. Sufficient horses for the use of the family were kept, and the rest sold'. [153] An economy measure could also be seen in Mrs Parnell's decision to live away from the estate for the next few years; but it is more likely that this represents her personal inclination.

John Parnell's death took place on 4 July 1859. As might be expected in the case of a country gentleman of local habits, there was no announcement in the Dublin papers. The *Leinster Express* carried a brief notice twelve days later, [154] but the *Wicklow Newsletter and County Advertiser* was the only paper to have any sort of obituary:

> In the high social position which Mr Parnell occupied, he rendered himself deservedly popular by his kindly disposition, frankness, and urbanity, Steadfast in his friendships, just and impartial as a magistrate, and cordial and unreserved in his intercourse with his humbler neighbours, he will long be regretted by them and by the numerous tenantry on the large estate which he so ably managed. [155]

On 16 July, his death was followed by the demise of Henry Grattan, who lived a few miles down the Avonmore at Clara House [156] – like Parnell, the direct descendant of an eighteenth-century 'Patriot' politician who had done well out of the old House at College Green and whose sons had been content to live as liberal country gentry in one of the most pleasant parts of Wicklow. Henry Grattan had entered politics, but more in his character as local squire than in any sense of carrying on a torch; so had William Parnell, if in a more reforming spirit. It is not unlikely that John Henry Parnell might have stood at M.P. for Wicklow, had he lived longer. Like Henry Grattan's elder brother James, John Parnell's father had been a Wicklow landlord in liberal politics; the tradition was not to end with them.

# 2  'The Belle of New York in the Solitudes of Avondale': Delia Tudor Stewart Parnell

> The sudden transformation from having been the belle of New York to the solitudes of Avondale appears at first to have been a great disappointment to her.
>
> (*E. Dickinson* of her mother,
> *A patriot's mistake*, p. 5.)

My treatment of John Henry Parnell's family postulates a great divide in 1859, with his death; and before this period little is recorded of his American wife, except what she herself recalled and what she told her children. Mrs Parnell as a widow is a different proposition, and I will deal with this period of her life at a later stage. I have already discussed her marriage, and her virtual separation from her husband for the last six years of his life; in this chapter I will deal briefly with other aspects of her life and character up to her husband's death.

## I

By her own accounts in a letter to T. D. Sullivan and in reminiscences published by R. M. McWade (both scanty with regard to dates), Delia Tudor Stewart was maternally descended from a family who settled in Boston in colonial times. The first of the family in America was a Mrs Tudor, widow of a Colonel Tudor from Wales; she was a high-class baker and confectioner in Boston and her son John was Delia's great-grandfather. He was miserly and difficult; his wife maintained and educated their son William, who married Delia Jarvis, of Huguenot stock. He was a prominent man, a Judge and Advocate-General of the Revolutionary Army; he studied law with John Adams, and they remained close friends. A member for Massachusetts of the House and the Senate, he was in 1809–10 Secretary of State for the same state; there is a biography of him in the Collection of the Massachusetts Historical Society.

Of his children, Emma married Robert Hallowell Gardiner, of an old New England family; Frederic Tudor invented a freezing method for exporting ice to Cuba and thereby made his fortune;[2] William was a well-known soldier, statesman and journalist who died as Chargé d'Affaires in Rio (a scholar and essayist, he was editor and proprietor of the *North American Review*);[3] the youngest daughter, Delia Tudor, married Admiral Stewart and was the mother of Delia Tudor Stewart Parnell. Judge Tudor and his wife were influential people who entertained many French dignitaries during the 1790s, and are eulogised in the Comte de Séguier's memoirs; the *Dictionary of American Biography* describes them as 'an affluent and socially prominent Boston family'.[4]

Delia Tudor Stewart Parnell's reminiscences have a way of attributing the same qualities of beauty and intellectual accomplishment to every lady of her family whom she has cause to mention; it is thus no suprise to find that her mother was the 'Belle of Boston', spoke five languages fluently, was artistic and musical, 'studied history with an extraordinary avidity', and 'was as familiar with the abstruse sciences as the ordinary girl is with intricacies of a spring bonnet'.[5] Abroad, she created – according to her daughter – a sensation in London society. 'Her soul', Mrs Parnell summed up cryptically, 'was too great for her means and her sphere'.[6]

Dealing with her father's family Mrs Parnell displayed more reticence and considerably less coherence; the reason was probably because, owing to her parents' early separation, she heard a great deal less about them. Her father's parents were Belfast people who emigrated to Philadelphia. Mrs Parnell was assured that their family silver was emblazoned with the royal arms of Scotland, but that

> at the time of the Revolutionary war, when this diaster in this infant country was extreme, [Delia Parnell's grandfather's] widow, who besides being of Milesian origin was still further revolutionised in this land, and by his death freed from the influence of her severe Scotch husband and of the little God of Love, more potent than blood, his widow, through the urgency of her son-in-law John MacCauley of the United States Navy – melted down her plate to help suitably to rear her eight children, a matter of prime importance, and as it seems, especially as far as the youngest child Charles Stewart was concerned.[7]

I quote this lengthy and confused sentence in its entirety to illustrate the sort of obtuse and pretentious rambling that Mrs Parnell was prone to, especially in her long letter to T. D. Sullivan (although it was written as early as 1880, eighteen years before her death). The value of her recollections, even at this stage of her life, is made still more doubtful by the fact that her memories of Admiral Stewart's mother – her true singing voice and beautiful figure, even in her nineties – are almost identical to those she recalls elsewhere about her other grandmother. However, the facts of her father's remarkable career are easily enough ascertained.

After running away to sea in his youth, Charles Stewart became a naval lieutenant in 1798; by 1800 he was in command of the schooner *Experiment,* and captured the *Deux Amis* and *Diana* from the French; in 1815, commanding the *Constitution,* he captured two British warships, the *Cyane* and the *Levant* (the latter was later recaptured). For this exploit he received a gold-hilted sword from the legislature of Pennsylvania and a Gold Medal from Congress. He was later nominated for the Presidency of the United States, and was made an Admiral by Lincoln. His career was not all success, as he was court–martialled in 1826 for diplomatic breaches; however, he continued to serve in the Navy after reaching retiring age in 1857, and died aged 92 in Bordentown, New Jersey, on 6 November 1869. He married Delia Tudor in 1815, but the marriage was not a happy one; they separated in 1826. I intend to go no further into the life of Admiral Stewart here; his daughter lived chiefly with her mother, and his career has been amply recorded elsewhere.[8]

Delia Tudor Stewart was the elder child of the marriage, born in 1816; she had one brother, Charles. The two children, she recalled 'were very close; but an unfortunate occurrence which separated my father and mother resulted in our being parted for years, he going to live with father and I remaining with mother'.[9] The 'unfortunate occurrence' concerned, she says, her mother helping a refugee Spanish officer during the Spanish war against Chile and Peru, when the Admiral was quartered in the area; Stewart was court-martialled for 'violating the neutrality law' and his wife, because of 'a nervous nature', would not go personally to court to vindicate him. 'He could not forgive her at the time, and they were separated.' Delia was then ten years old; she lived with her mother until her marriage to John Parnell eight years later. Her parents' separation may have been for more mundane reasons than this story of a diplomatic breach; Emily Dickinson mentions that 'an illegitimate relation' sued for some of Admiral Stewart's money after his death in 1869,[10] and the whole tenor of Delia's references to her father suggests that her mother left him, not the other way round.[11] A reference by Emily Dickinson bears this impression out. When Emily's father died, her American grandfather suggested that she come to live with him; but

My uncle, Mr. Wigram [Catherine Parnell's husband] belonging to the sect of the Plymouth Brethren . . . determined I should not be allowed to live in such a questionable atmosphere, as he rightly considered residence under his [Admiral Stewart's] roof to be.

He therefore paid down the necessary amount required to make me a ward of court, as he knew very well the Lord Chancellor would not permit me to go to live in America. [12]

Elsewhere Mrs Dickinson states that her grandmother 'refused to live any longer with Admiral Stewart for domestic reasons'; [13] her references clearly imply a separation on the grounds of infidelity rather than because of the rather insufficient story told to R. M. McWade by Mrs Parnell.

For whatever reason Mrs Stewart left her husband, the separation was final; when Delia married John Parnell her mother followed the couple to Europe and took up residence with her son in Paris. Before this, however, she had lived with her young daughter in Washington; their life seems to have been the normal existence for those of good connections in society and ample means, with seasons in Washington and summers in Boston (with Mr and Mrs Frederic Tudor) and Maine (with Mrs Stewart's sister, Mrs Hallowell Gardiner) and Newport:

> this in the earlier days of Newport, when it was just beginning to be fashionable; there was not a cottage there; [14] everybody lived in boarding-houses; Newport people were very easily satisfied then . . . We got rye coffee and always got hot cakes; everywhere we went we got good buckwheat cakes. [15]

I quote this passage in deliberate contrast to Mrs Parnell's tendentious remarks on the Stewart family silver already quoted; [16] it is significant that such lucid writing as this last piece always occurs when she is simply recalling her youth, instead of retailing what she has been told second-hand, or what she wishes to believe.

The family was not exceptionally well-off. Delia Parnell wrote to T. D. Sullivan that her Stewart grandfather 'gave half his fortune to the Revolutionary government and so helped to impoverish his family', while her father presented the ships he captured to the government and never sued for the prize money due to him. [17] On the Tudor side her grandfather, though left a large fortune,

> generously spent a colossal fortune in benefiting individuals, the public of Boston, and its environs . . . Both sides of my family were wealthy at first, and for this land then, immensely wealthy . . . therefore had they let their means moderately take care of themselves, we would have been among the richest of the rich in this rich country. However, we have been taken care of by a wise Power and their descendants have never been seen begging their bread. [18]

Elsewhere she mentions her Tudor grandfather's 'financial troubles', [19] but does not enlarge upon them. Her uncle Frederic Tudor, 'the Ice

King', succeeded, according to Mrs Parnell, 'in building up a large fortune, restoring his family fortunes and the prestige of the Tudors for
wealth';[20] but the *Dictionary of American biography* tells a different
story, of a life spent deep in debt until his old age.[21] Elsewhere Mrs
Parnell states that her brother Charles 'was entirely the artificer of his
own fortunes':[22] she was later to inherit all his money in 1874 and the
entirety of her father's estate came to her shortly before (1869). It was
at this stage that she gave up the small annuity which was her
husband's only bequest to her.[23]

Delia's brother studied law and engineering; he became a member of
the bar, but was also involved in such engineering schemes as the
Reading railroad. He died unmarried at a comparatively young age.
Mrs Parnell gives no information about her own education; her life as
a society belle in Washington and New York seems to have been un-
disturbed by incident until the spring of 1834, when she met John
Henry Parnell and Lord Powerscourt on their Grand Tour.

## II

As the epigraph to this chapter suggests, marriage and the subsequent
introduction to Wicklow county life may have been more than Delia
Tudor Stewart expected. Of her marriage, practically all she records is
in one paragraph of the reminiscences in R. M. McWade's book:

> Our home was made in Avondale, County Wicklow, except when
> we were visiting among his [John Henry Parnell's] friends and
> when I went to Paris for the education and social advantages of
> my family. My mother and brother had a beautiful home in
> Paris. My husband was pleased to have us go there on account of
> the great advantages it afforded to me and to my children, but he
> would not let them go to school unless I was near them.[24]

*A propos* of this reflection, neither John Howard nor Charles Stewart
went to school anywhere near their mother, until John went to Paris to
study art; Charles, as described above, was sent to 'somebody who
would mother him' in Yeovil when he was only seven. Moreover, the
passage quoted above obscures the fact that she resided practically all
the time in Paris throughout the late eighteen-fifties, according to both
Emily Dickinson and John Howard Parnell; there is also evidence that
she lived for a time on the south coast of England.[25]

It would be interesting to know more of the friends the Parnells
'visited among'; Lord and Lady Wicklow are mentioned by John
Howard Parnell as frequent visitors to Avondale,[26] and the Proby
family at Glenart Castle are mentioned as close friends by Mrs Parnell
herself;[27] there were also the Brookes at Castle Howard, whose
children were playmates of the young Parnells;[28] and there must have

been many more. Nonetheless, society in rural Wicklow would have been quiet indeed after the social round of Washington and New York, especially when her husband disapproved of rowdy neighbours like the Dickinsons; his daughter Emily wrote:

> My father went in for farming on an extensive scale which, join-ed to his being an ardent lover of all kinds of sport, kept him very much in the open air, so that my mother, not caring for outdoor recreations, was in consequence left a good deal alone and naturally, in contrast to the gay life she had led in America, found it dull and lonely. However, when in due course children began to come, she no longer complained so much of loneliness or want of occupation, though she never took kindly to the coun-try or country pursuits. [29]

This is not to say that Delia Parnell was an unusually worldly nineteen-year-old; in some ways she was exactly the reverse. 'I had never seen a drunken man ... until I married and went to live in Ireland', she recalled later, 'and could not for a long time discover when a man was drunk.' [30] Her first impressions of the country were a welcome contradiction of the 'mud hut' conception with which she had teased her suitor; she wrote to T.D. Sullivan forty-five years later that the Irish were

> a race that even in the poorest looked to me, a young American nurtured among great men, when I first landed at Kingstown, as one and all gentlemen of ease as they lounged about with their hands in their pockets to keep them warm and clean while look-ing for a job: if it is true that what is bred in the bone will come out in the breeding, the Irish must have drunk in better days of congenial Parian springs and for mother milk sucked honey from Hybla, for no fashion can disguise, no hardship obliterate the keen intellect, the ready wit, the noble composure of their solid substratum, their ancient foundation; I wrote to my dear mother that the Irish made as much in a minute by their speech as others did in a week by their hands. [31]

However, it can reasonably be doubted that she ever really adapted to the Irish way of life. Her dislike of riding [32] was in itself a contravention of local custom; her references to her husband as an 'Englishman' [33] and 'a member of the Church of England' [34] suggest that she understood little of the Irish ethos.

This is not to imply that she lived outside of county society. Emily Dickinson described her mother as (in about 1849) 'a beautiful and ac-complished American, still quite a young woman ... she was par-ticularly famous for her talents as a hostess and in the good old days, when hospitality was extensively and generously practised, she had ample scope for the exercise of her talent in this respect'.[35] Here allowance must be made for Mrs Dickinson's delusions of grandeur where her early life was concerned; but her brother John Howard also recalled that 'my mother was extremely fond of entertaining'.[36] Mrs Parnell herself recalled that, in her entry into Wicklow society, her father's reputation had to some extent paved her way. A neighbour, Mrs Seaton, had a young brother who had been a midshipman aboard the *Cyane* or the *Levant* and was full of admiration for the Admiral's treatment of the crews aboard the ships he captured; Granville Leveson Proby, Lord Carysfort, who was a British admiral, had cross-ed swords with Delia Tudor Stewart Parnell's father at Gibraltar, and she 'used to fight my father's battles over again with him in a friendly way'.[37] Lord Carysfort's wife was a Howard, and an aunt of John Henry Parnell; when the latter died, the Carysforts offered his widow a home at Elton in England. 'My best and earliest friends were their sons and daughters, my husband's first cousins; to write of them my pen would tire ere it could stop.'[38]

But the impression remains of someone who cannot have been at home in Wicklow. She was to find Dublin more congenial at a later period of her life, but probably not before this; Emily Dickinson states unequivocally that when her mother took up residence at Dalkey as a widow 'she made her *first* entrance into the social atmosphere of Dublin'.[39] She lived away from Wicklow for the last years of her husband's life, and did not return until after his funeral; when she did come back, it was only to auction off his personal belongings and remove herself to Dublin.[40] The likelihood is that her husband's death liberated her completely from a way of life that was uncongenial to her, and which she had already largely rejected. When she died in 1898, none of the local gentry attended her funeral in Rathdrum or the internment in Glasnevin [41] although this may have been a reflection of her son's politics rather than of her own popularity.

## III

At this stage a brief consideration of Delia Tudor Stewart Parnell's character is of value: again, in view of how she appears in the period of her youth and marriage. John Howard Parnell repeated his sister Emily's judgement of their mother as charming, accomplished and 'a brilliant conversationalist'.[42] These are traits which are hard to ascertain from a later vantage point, but a less laudable characteristic comes through her own writings with unmistakeable clarity: a strong preoccupation with social position which at times becomes an overwhelming snobbery. Recalling her family history for R. M. McWade, she emphasises that her pastry-cook ancestress was 'a Colonel's widow', and that her aunt married 'a near relative of Sir

Benjamin Hallowell'; she refers gradiosely to 'the Tudor vault' in a Boston cemetery;[43] her tendentious reference to the royally-crested Stewart silver has been quoted above.[44] Sometimes this preoccupation produces an unintentionally hilarious effect, as where she writes of her mother's social success in London: 'The sons of George the Third crowded round her piano'.[45] She continues in this vein: 'It was said that a Duke and more than one Lord had sought her hand in vain'. At such times Mrs Parnell achieves the most outrageous heights of 'stage American' social snobbery. The history of the Stewart family gave her less room to manoeuvre, but she could still claim that 'my father was descended from Irish gentlemen, under the hollow of whose feet water could run without touching them'.[46]

Marrying John Parnell gave her ample scope to indulge her genealogical speculations. A telling passage in her recollections deals with her daughter Theodosia's marriage to Captain Claud Paget:

Lord Anglesea, the head of the family, is a cousin of the husband of Minnie Stephens of New York. There was not a family in England that would not have been proud to be allied to the Parnells . . . all the near relatives of his [Captain Paget's] family went from England [to the wedding in Paris] and thought themselves fortunate in being allied to the ancient family of Parnell. In this connection I wish to say that my son's family is one of the most ancient in Great Britain, going back to a Norman duke who was killed at the battle of Hastings, on the Norman side, and on the English side going back to the Lord High Stewarts of England, and by marriages to the Stewarts of Scotland and the Howards of England. My cousin, the Rev. Samuel Stewart, a missionary, who was connected with the Lispenard Stewarts of New York, used to say that the Stewart family were descended from Banquo's ghost. In the story, you know, Fleance, the son of Banquo, was saved. He fled to Paris and there married a princess of the house of Tudor, so that the Stewarts were descended from the Tudors.[47]

In her letter to Sullivan Mrs Parnell delved at length into the geneaology of the Wicklow Howards, coming up triumphantly with a relationship (via the Earl of Darnley) to Queen Anne though she 'did not wish to vouch for this tradition . . . without being sure of it';[48] and in later years she published in the American press a pretentious 'family tree' which showed the Parnell's descent from the 'King-maker' Earl of Warwick through Anne Ward, Sir John Parnell's mother.[49]

It is hard to know how far she carried this attitude into her own social life; it is significant, however, that she sent her sons John and Charles to Mr Wishaw's school in Chipping Norton because Lord Brabazon (the son of the Earl of Meath, who lived at Kilruddery near

Bray) and Louis Wingfield (a cousin of Lord Powerscourt) attended it
– not to an Irish school, which would have been more consistent with
the anti-British feeling later attributed to her. All in all, it is not easy
to form a complete picture of the lady at this stage of her life. What
impression can be gained is not unduly likeable, which is in large part
due to the bombastic nature of her own recollections: she had an undeniably good conceit of herself. St John Ervine referred to her as 'one
of those outspoken, strong-minded, silly women, commoner now,
perhaps, in America than anywhere else, who have been so admirably
exposed by Mr Bernard Shaw in the characters of Mrs Clandon in *You
never can tell* and Lady Britomart Undershaft in *Major Barbara*'.[50]
Fair or not, this description applies more accurately to the Mrs Parnell
of later years, when her political views received prominence. At this
stage Mrs Parnell resembles more closely another of Shaw's
characters, the posturing Raina of *Arms and the man;* she could well
have done with a chocolate-cream soldier to bring her down to earth.

The question of her sons' schooling raises the most important point
of Mrs Parnell's character, at least for the purposes of this study: the
extent of her leanings towards Irish nationalism, and how much they
affected the upbringing of her children. This is a topic to be dealt with
fully in the next section of my work;[51] but it is important to state here
that all concrete manifestations of Mrs Parnell's much-published
nationalism seem to post-date her husband's death. This is not the
traditional view of the development of Mrs Parnell's political
philosophy, which is generally formulated as Thomas Sherlock, for
one, saw it:

> Mrs Delia Parnell, the daughter of Admiral Stewart, brought to
> her Irish home of Avondale a strong American love of in-
> dependence and a hearty hate of British greed and desire for
> domination. She became in thought and feeling an Irish
> Nationalist; and from her mainly is derived the warm popular
> sympathies which glow in the breasts of four of her children.[52]

St John Ervine tells the same tale, with an opposite bias: 'She set
herself, almost from the beginning of her life at Avondale, to the mean
mischief of making bitterness and wrath between her husband's family
and their countrymen in England'.[53] Mrs Parnell herself contributed
to this picture of the young bride bearing the sacred torch of
Republicanism to the aristocratic fastnesses of Avondale. In the
reminiscences published by McWade she states: 'From the time I first
placed my foot upon Irish soil in 1835, as the bride of John Henry
Parnell, my heart and actions have been in sympathetic accord with all
movements for the liberty and prosperity of the Irish People'.[54] But
those close to her were not so emphatic. Emily Dickinson is silent on
the subject of her mother's patriotism during her marriage, and when

John Howard Parnell wrote that 'our mother was American to the core, a burning enthusiast in the cause of Irish liberty, and possessed of an inveterate hate against England',[55] he refers to a later period of her life. Even then, he goes on to say, she always instilled into her children the principle of personal loyalty to their sovereign; a letter to John Howard from his mother towards the end of her life read: 'How the Queen must despise low, mean, mischief-making extremists! They get money by arousing passions and exaggerating aims. If they succeed, rebellion and anarchy will run riot in Europe'.[56] The 'Fenianism' on Mrs Parnell's part which made such an impression on Charles' schoolmaster at Chipping Norton was articulated only from the 1860s on; the quotation above suggests that it never went very deep. Certainly, Mrs Parnell's initial political stance was harmless enough:

> My first real public action was a public speech that I made in Dublin, and I was nearly scared to death. I had started a series of musical and dramatic gatherings which were called 'Originals', because everything was to be of original Irish talent . . . The ladies who came to play brought their own quadrilles, waltzes, galops, etc . . . It was in 1861, I think . . . My part was to deliver the address of welcome which opened the series. Fully three thousand people were present, many of them being from the Viceroyal households. Lord Carlisle, though unable to attend in person, was represented by many of his aides-de-camp . . . besides my opening address I selected a portion of Emerson's poems to recite . . . In my speech I referred to the poem and to our American republic, telling the people that it was characteristic of the Americans to 'go ahead', and that I wanted the Irish also to strive to 'go ahead'. I astonished my audience, and the aides-de-camp looked nervous . . . [57]

This type of meeting could hardly have been farther removed from a political platform, though Mrs Parnell tends to represent it as such; the impression that one gains is rather of a smug self-consciousness at being an *enfant terrible* at large in Dublin Society. Her first political speech in America, she goes on to relate, was in the early 1880s, well after Charles Stewart Parnell had become an established public figure; even the modest trial run described above was not undertaken until two years after her husband's death. Mrs Parnell quotes in McWade's book a poem she wrote in 1846, struck by the famine emigration, as evidence that 'my life and my thoughts have been given to . . . the [Irish] cause'. This begins 'Dear home of my Heart, dear Erin, Farewell/My sad heart now beats to thy sorrowing knell', continues in like vein (and uninterrupted metre), and could have been written by any contemporary lady with literary pretensions and nominal powers of observation.[58] When writing to Sullivan in 1880, and even more when reminiscing in 1891, Mrs Parnell was anxious to imply that the unadulterated patriotism she imported to Avondale 'had much to do with turning the mind of my son so strongly in this direction'; [59] it is with this in mind that she emphasises not only the American Republican tradition of her mother's family, but also her maternal grandfather's impressions of Ireland in the previous century: 'He forcibly condemned from Ireland the British government there' [60] and 'his observations led him to predict the Irish Rebellion of '96 [*sic*]'. [61] The error in this last quotation is significant. It is the sort of mistake (like the belief that to be a member of the Established Church in Ireland was to be in 'the Church of England') made by someone whose involvement with Ireland cannot, at least initially, have been deep. Mrs Parnell's political analysis, and her view of the Irish cause, will be examined in depth at a later stage; in the period up to 1859, in which year she returned to Ireland and set up residence in Dublin, there seems little ground for supposing that her political beliefs were an important factor in the upbringing and conditioning of the Parnell children.

# 3   The Parnell children up to 1859

We had eleven children born, five sons and six daughters, all born at Avondale except Theodosia, who was born in Torquay, the place where the family first landed in England,[1] and Henry, who was born in Paris. All born in the same room at Avondale except Anna. Five of the eleven children are now living, three daughters and two sons. Ten of them grew up to majority. Hayes died of pleurisy and an affection of the liver at fifteen; and I lost an infant son, five years old, William Tudor, through bad vaccination.[2]

Thus wrote Mrs Parnell in 1891, reminiscing to R. M. McWade with uncharacteristic brevity and conciseness. The children were, in order of age, William (1837–42), Delia (1838–82), Hayes (1839–55), Emily (1841–1918), John (1843–1923), Sophia (1845–77), Charles (1846–91), Fanny (1849–82), Henry (1850–1915), Anna (1852–1911), and Theodosia (1853–1920).[3] There was also a boy, stillborn, who was probably the first child. In this chapter I will deal briefly with the Parnell children up to their father's death, and in particular with the early childhood of Charles Stewart. Not surprisingly, all the information on these topics comes from published reminiscences.

Before considering the general question of the Parnell children's upbringing, I will deal with each child briefly.

## I

Delia was the eldest (surviving) child, and is mentioned in both her brother's and her sister's memoirs on account of her beauty. Her education was mainly in Paris, where she met the American whom she later married. John Howard Parnell describes her visits home to Avondale during school holidays;[4] otherwise, he simply states succinctly that 'Delia was considered a great beauty, she had dark hair and complexion'.[5] (Here, as in many other cases where their accounts overlap, the style of his description is in total contrast to that of his sister Emily, who could never resist the florid cliché.[6]) As is often the case with celebrated beauties, little else about Delia is recorded. She married James Livingston Thomson, an American who lived in Paris and was 'a descendant on his mother's side of the excellent and distinguished Chancellor Livingston of the United States', according to Mrs Parnell.[7] According to Emily it was Thomson's money rather than his lineage, or even his personality, that carried weight with Delia, and she 'frankly told him so beforehand, but he was so infatuated with her that he was content to take her on any terms'.[8] The marriage thus inauspiciously entered into was solemnised in Paris about the time of John Henry Parnell's death, probably slightly before it; the marriage settlement (an annuity of £100 for Delia, chargeable upon the Avondale estate) is dated 4 June 1859.[9] Emily Dickinson credits her mother with having disapproved of the match from the outset.[10] She (Emily) refers to Thomson as a 'millionaire', a term which she tended to use with undiscriminating enthusiasm; he certainly appears to have been rich enough to keep his bride in some style in Paris, and it is significant that John Parnell did not feel required to make any further settlement on his eldest daughter than a small annuity.

Hayes was the next eldest child. Like his sister he was dark in colouring; like his younger brother Charles, he was mechanically—minded. John Parnell recalls him as 'clever ... very quiet and studious, and slightly built'.[11] Mrs Parnell's recollections of her son, who died aged fifteen, seem tainted by hindsight, referring to his 'remarkable patriotism' as well as his intellectual brilliance;[12] he even framed laws for the 'Free government' of Ireland. Whether he was unnaturally precocious or not, the manner of Hayes's death seems to have been in the long run the most influential thing about him; I have discussed this already.[13] Since consumption and pleurisy are both mentioned as causes (albeit vaguely, and in conjunction with a riding accident), it seems likely that he was tubercular.

Emily was the nearest in age to Hayes, and his 'special chum'.[14] She is the best recorded of the Parnell sisters, a fact mainly due to herself. *A patriot's mistake* is subtitled *Reminiscences of the Parnell Family*,[15] but it is really an autobiography, if a rather incoherent one. Before considering this work, John Howard Parnell's recollections of Emily as a child can be briefly considered. He remembered her as musical, vivacious, athletic and high-spirited. Although her father's favourite, he disinherited her just before his death owing to her romance with Arthur Dickinson, who lived nearby at Kingston and who, with his brothers, was forbidden to visit at Avondale; a graphic little scene in

John Howard's memoir describes amateur theatricals with the Dickinsons, and his father's disapproval. The world of *Mansfield Park* seems only a little removed from the vale of Avoca. [16]

John recalls his sister's love of horses and hunting, and her winning record in the donkey races organised by the children at Avondale; Emily's own book begins with an account of her first hunt, in the company of Hayes and her father. (Writing in 1905, she dates this as 'fifty years ago'; it must have been in fact in 1849, as she mentions that there were only six children then and that Charles was three years old.) The account of this hunt, and of the subsequent dinner-party, sets the tone of the book. It is completely self-centred, often unperceptive, extraordinarily self-opinionated, and written by someone able to blind herself to anything less than attractive in her own behaviour, as well as being basically uninterested in the actions and character of others except in so far as they affected herself. The value of *A patriot's mistake* is correspondingly limited. The book is further marred by writing which is usually bad and often obscure, and by a tendency to wild exaggeration, bordering on delusion. Mrs Parnell became 'a millionairess' upon her brother's death; [17] the hall at Avondale was 'capacious enough to drive a coach and four round'; [18] the cricket-game between the Phoenix and Leinster clubs which proved fatal to her father is transformed into 'a big international cricket match'. [19] Very few of Mrs Dickinson's statements can be taken at face-value; but her book remains, with John Howard Parnell's memoir, the only primary source available for the Parnells' family life.

To return to Emily herself, she describes herself as a weakly and delicate child, but she seems nonetheless to have been well able to hold her own. Her attachment to Arthur Monroe Dickinson began when she was twelve years old, and 'by the time we had reached the respective ages of fifteen and twenty we were very much in love and became privately engaged'. [20] Her loyalty to Dickinson, not only during their forbidden romance, but also throughout their far more trying marriage (he was to become an unbalanced dipsomaniac) is one of Emily's most likeable characteristics. Her attachment to Arthur continued throughout adolescence and she married him five years after her father's death. [21]

Up to 1859, Emily's life continued much as her sister's had done. She went to Paris about 1857, to 'finish' her education at a large and cosmopolitan boarding-school; in 1859 she went to London to be a debutante. Like Delia, she stayed with Sir Ralph and Lady Howard in Belgrave Square. In London she was expected, in her turn, to 'make a matrimonial choice'; [22] but she remained faithful to Arthur.

The London scene is described in *A patriot's mistake* with a wealth of cliché and detail, emphasising the impact which Emily made upon the cream of London society; [23] she shared the imagination of Delia

Stewart Parnell, who could visualise without any difficulty the sons of George the Third crowding round her mother's piano. [24] Emily's recitation of compliments received and social successes registered is varied by the sudden irruption of Arthur (on leave) into the house at Belgrave Square, and his tussle with the footman; St John Ervine's description of Captain Dickinson as 'a representative Lever soldier' seems well justified. [25] This contretemps was followed by a tryst with Arthur in the square, and a kiss that was observed by Lady Howard; the latter and Sir Ralph decided that their charge was not to be trusted and wrote to her father that she intended running away with Dickinson. His feelings about the family at Kingston have been described; he went straight from the cricket match in Dublin to his solicitor's, cut Emily out of his will, and died suddenly a few days later. [26]

Here Emily's account is corroborated by John Howard Parnell, and seems likely enough. By the summer of 1859, which was to change the Parnell children's lives so decisively, the pattern of Emily's life had been laid down; she did marry her 'representative Lever Soldier', and she remained headstrong and self-opinionated until she died nearly sixty years later.

In contrast to Emily's book, John Howard Parnell's *C. S. Parnell: a memoir*[27] is exactly what it purports to be. Very little of the writer, diffident and self-effacing, obtrudes into the picture; it is in no sense an autobiography. Born two years later than Emily, John Howard became after Hayes's death the eldest son. He seems to have been more shy and quiet than his high-spirited sisters and brothers; a speech defect could have been either the cause or the effect of this. His stepson, Captain Mateer, believes that he had 'a divided palate'; John Howard Parnell himself refers to being 'aflicted with stammering' as a child, but states that this was cured after a spell at school in Paris. [28] It seems to have returned, however, for Mrs Parnell wrote in 1898 that her eldest son's political career had been hampered by 'a nervous defect of speech'.[29] (His Parisian teacher is named variously as 'M. Marderon'[30] and 'M. Roderon';[31] he taught 'French, drawing, and a little painting'.) John was still at school in Paris when his father died in 1859.

As the only two boys in the family after 1854, except for Henry, who was a comparative infant, John and Charles were constant companions in escapades round the estate; *C. S. Parnell* copiously records these pastimes. Their schooldays, however, were not spent together (until they both attended Mr Wishaw's at Chipping Norton, after their father's death). This was because Charles's frequent imitations of his brother's speech hesitation both aggravated John's defect and produced a stammer in his own voice. [32] Thus John Howard, who scrupulously excludes his own reminiscences except where they involve his brother, gives us no picture of his own schooling. It seems conclusive, however, that neither he nor his brothers attended Eton, where their father, grandfather, and many of their relatives had been pupils; nor did they attend a similar school. Their education was entrusted to an odd mixture of private tuition, small private schools, Parisian tutors, and pre-university crammers.

John's character is testified to more often at a later stage of his life; but the qualities of kindness and integrity which are recalled by the son of the last steward of Avondale, Mr Hugh Gaffney, and by John Howard Parnell's stepson, Captain Mateer, seem to have been characteristic of him from his youth; but these qualities were not inconsistent with the strength of emotion which he shared with most of the family. Mrs Parnell wrote to Sullivan:

> My son John is full of pity and kindness for everyone. When a boy, having received some great provocation, but unwilling to hurt anyone weaker than himself, he seized hold of a heavy old–fashioned mahogany armchair, and saying 'I must hurt something', smashed it to pieces on the floor. [33]

This anecdote, while not exactly illustrating the 'pity and kindness' which Mrs Parnell quoted it to corroborate, is nonetheless indicative of the strength of feeling inherent in most of the Parnells.

The next oldest child was Sophia or Sophy, who seems to have been remarkable only for her beauty (of a blonde type, unlike Delia), and for her elopement with the family solicitor, which took place long after her father's death. She was only a year older than Charles, with whose childhood I will deal separately.

Fanny was two years younger than Charles, but was an especial companion of his. [34] Like Hayes, she had a literary bent; John Howard called her 'the poetess of the family and our bluestocking sister . . . she knew every book in the library at Avondale'. [35] Dark, sharp-tongued and witty, she was Charles's constant opponent in games like tin soldiers, which gave rise to the famous and too often quoted story of his gluing his army to the floor. [36] Fanny's soldiers always represented the Irish side, John Howard recalled; and, he added, 'I think that Fanny's impassioned patriotism had a great effect on Charley's convictions in later life'. [37] Fanny was one of Charles's closest companions; her early death in 1882 was to be a great shock to him. She was far closer to him, in temperament as well as age, than the equally strong-willed, but Philistine and unintellectual, Emily. (Significantly, Emily never came to share the politics of her younger brother and sisters.)

Henry Tudor Parnell, the youngest son, is a mystery figure. He is very rarely mentioned and is only referred to cursorily by John Howard Parnell. The Clonmore estate was left to him, and was probably purchased by his father with the express purpose of providing an inheritance for him; he was later to sell it off, and to marry a daughter of Dr Thomas Luby, a Fellow of Trinity College, Dublin. He studied law at Cambridge but, John Howard stated cryptically, 'was too nervous to pass his examinations'.[38] A son of his, who was mentally deficient, lived with Mr and Mrs John Howard Parnell in Glenageary during the 1920s.[39] These are the only easily ascertained facts about Henry Tudor Parnell; I will enlarge on them in a later part of my study.

Anna was next in age to Henry, but was similar in her convictions to Fanny and was often compared to her in later life. Little is recorded of her at this stage, though she was to become a more public figure than any of her sisters. She was only seven when her father died. Like Delia, Emily and Fanny, she was dark-haired and slightly built; like many of the family, she had a delicate constitution.[40] She shared with John a facility for painting, and later studied art in England.

Theodosia was the youngest child, and is described by John Howard as 'a real society belle; though of a very quiet disposition'. However, she was only six years old in 1859. Her later life was to be more conventional than that of any of her brothers or sisters, and Mrs Parnell alone records anything of it, when she describes – with obvious pleasure – her marriage to Claud Paget, a well-connected young English naval officer.[41]

Even a cursory survey of the Parnell children yields one or two rough generalisations. There seem to have been two strains of character. One was strong-minded, individualistic, and – except for Emily, who is otherwise of this group – intellectually oriented and politically minded. These are the Parnells who were often called 'mad', and they included Emily, Fanny, Anna, Charles and Hayes. The other strain was more retiring, did not enjoy the limelight, and was ready to accept a quiet and uneventful lot; they often took up residence in England. Theodosia, Delia, Sophy and Henry were of this type. John Howard alone combined the characteristics of both. In general terms, it could be said that the first group 'took after' their mother and the second after their father; simplified as it is, this is a more logical criterion of division than any other. The more retiring and un-political Parnells are not a uniformly younger or older group; nor are they only girls.

This group includes the eldest (Delia) and the youngest (Theodosia) as well as the middle child, Sophy. Thus the politically-minded children were not those who were brought up almost entirely by their mother, nor those who had known their father best; the distribution was, in terms of age and sex, completely even. The interesting thing is that, as children, the different patterns can already be seen so clearly.

The life of the Parnell family during the 1840s and 1850s is worth some comment. Nothing has been written of this except for John Parnell's careful recollections of boyhood pranks, and Emily Dickinson's patchy delusions of *la vie de chateau* lived in the grand style at Avondale. From these observations and from conversations with Mrs John Howard Parnell and Tudor MacDermott (Sophia Parnell's son), St John Ervine reconstructed a graphic picture of a totally eccentric, roistering, Leveresque country family, ignored by a bookish father and ruled by a mad matriarch who was mentally unhinged by her obsessive hate of England.

> The Parnells and their neighbours might have stepped out of the novels of Lever. Wicklow, like other Irish counties, was inhabited by a hard-living, hard-drinking set which loved hunting and gambling and loud, lavish hospitality. Mr Parnell's affection for books kept him from the rougher life of his neighbours such as the Dickinsons, but his children fell into it as if by instinct. His daughter Emily, whom he disinherited because he suspected her of having schemes to elope with a Captain Arthur Dickinson, a representative Lever soldier, gives an account of her upbringing in *A patriot's mistake* which shows that the Lever Ireland, though it no longer exists, certainly existed in the middle of the nineteenth century.[42]

Much of this, as I have shown, is unfounded. John Henry was no retiring, indecisive bookworm. His wife was not the eccentric that Ervine paints her as elsewhere, and moreover abhorred exactly the country life that he describes. The 'loud, lavish hospitality' existed more vividly in Emily Dickenson's rambling recollections than it ever had in real life. But the interesting thing about Ervine's view is that it represents – albeit largely by hypothesis – a unique attempt at a view of the Parnells as contemporaries must have seen them: he attempts to put them in some sort of contemporary context. His view is biassed and over-simplified, but it is nonetheless a worthwhile effort.

There was, moreover, some substance for his accusations that Mrs Parnell devoted less care to the bringing up of her children than she might have done. John Howard's story of Charles's infancy, when his mother, on hearing visitors while nursing him, 'hastily stowed away the future Irish Leader in the drawer of a large press, which she closed without thinking'[43] and forgot all about him, is not so amusing in its implications. Nor had she any compunction about leaving her children to go to Paris, or about sending Charles to a boarding-school when aged seven. John Howard's references to 'the succession of uneducated nurses who had charge of us elder children' [44] and to the children's appreciation of the admirable Mrs Twopenny, 'a most respectable woman' who at last succeeded these nurses, is also indicative. [45] Little enough can be reconstructed of the Parnells' early life at Avondale; but the blurred picture which emerges probably corresponds more closely to St John Ervine's over-coloured period print than to later hagiographical depictions where Delia Parnell, the angel of high-souled patriotism, instils principles of republican independence into children whose young brows are already touched with the light of dedicated nationalism. [46]

## II

After this long treatment of the context of his childhood, it is time to introduce Charles Stewart Parnell himself. He was born on 27 June 1846, and was thus a year younger than Sophia and two years older than Fanny. Despite the proximity of their ages, Sophy was not a particular playmate of his; he was closest to John and Fanny, both of whose temperaments were more similar to his own. His brother recalled him as

> a wiry little boy, very bright and playful, making fun of everybody and everything. He was fond of mechanics, like his eldest brother Hayes. He had dark brown hair, a pale complexion, very dark brown and very piercing eyes. His figure was slender and he was very small for his age. He did not grow until late, and was nicknamed 'Tom Thumb' at home. [47]

Like many children brought up by a variety of nurses, he had a tendency to be fractious; he was never, however, corporally punished, 'but only shut in a room by himself where he howled himself to sleep'. [48] (It is notable that it was his father who inflicted this punishment, in contrast to Ervine's picture of a vague and unconcerned bookworm.) His characteristics seem those of any lively and possibly over-indulged child. [49] He was, according to John Howard, 'the gayest and most vivacious of us all (as also the most domineering)'; [50] although it was Emily who always insisted on being leader in games of follow-my-leader, not (as claimed in some politicised versions of his childhood) Charles.

His relationship with his brother was what might be expected between two headstrong boys in a large family of girls:

> We had many fights, or rather tussles, for there was rarely any ill-feeling. He used to aim a blow at me and then run, catching up

anything he saw and flinging it over his shoulder at me. I followed at full speed, also catching handfuls of ornaments,
knick-knacks, sofa-cushions and even flower-pots and hurling
them at him. During one of these pell-mell chases, leaving a trail
of destruction in their wake, I remember seizing a poker from a
grate and breaking it over the back of a sofa, with no intention of
hurting him, but just in order to give him a thorough good fright
... in temper he was headstrong and self-willed, often to the
point of rudeness, while at times he showed a curious mixture of
jealousy and suspicion, which developed strongly in later years.
His love of mischief was unbounded, but underlying every action
was the rooted desire to have his own way at any cost ... Still, in
the days of his childhood as throughout life, he and I were the
best of friends.[51]

His jealousy and wilfulness are not to be marvelled at. Too much can
be, and has been, read into his boyhood characteristics. Even the
usually balanced view of his brother is too prone to hindsight, placing
great emphasis on his nurse's remark that he was 'born to rule'.[52]
Charles's childhood characteristics were not incontrovertible evidence
of his destiny to become leader of the Irish Nation. He was, as his
brother states, over-indulged. He was brought up amongst a class
never noted for its humility; his parents' union was neither a close nor
a happy one. Several of the other children developed in as headstrong
and self-willed a direction as Charles; Emily was at least as much of a
handful. A good example of the sort of exaggerated emphasis that is
laid on Charles's nursery characteristics is contained in *A patriot's
mistake:* 'Charles ... from an early age exhibited a masterful propen-
sity for dictating to and managing others, assuming the leadership and
trying to set the world and its pilgrims right'.[53] As so many later
biographers did, here Emily Dickinson is making the sketchy structure
of his nursery characteristics bear the weight of the politician that he
was to become thirty years later. John Howard Parnell, however,
makes clear that the tyrannical excesses of Charles's spoilt infancy
were greatly modified by his schooldays. After his first term at Yeovil,
'the greatest improvement was noticeable ... he seemed to have lost
his old habit of domineering'.[54] He was, in fact, a typical example of
someone exposed to the doubtful privilege of having a boarding-school
'knock some manners' into him. 'As he grew in later years', his brother
adds, 'he rapidly became more and more reserved'.[55] His sparring
relationship with John Howard continued, but there was no animosity
involved.[56] His delicacy as a child allied with his own intensely strong
will meant that he was highly-strung; John recalls that even when
Charles was aged about eleven,

at that time, during the cricket-matches, I used to notice

Charley's extreme nervousness; his fingers twitched anxiously, even while he was watching the match, and I know that in after--years he was just as nervous, though perhaps he did not show it to outsiders, in the greater game played in the House of Commons.[57]

His constitution remained delicate; besides an   attack of typhoid while at school in Yeovil, he was stricken with scarlet fever at Avondale in 1858. At this time John was separated from him, kept in quarantine in the dower-house at Casino, and the latter recalled: 'Although I had Sophy's company ... that did not make up for the loss of Charley's vivacity and ever-charming manner.'[58] Again, it is striking how the livelier Parnell children – those of the first strain mentioned above – were closest to each other, irrespective of age: there was a bond between Emily, John, Charles, Fanny and later Anna, which did not extend to Sophia, Theodosia or Henry.

In thus briefly considering the characteristics of someone who seems to have been a spoilt and headstrong child – though no more so than could reasonably be expected from his background – I must once again emphasise the fatuity of drawing any direct lines from these nursery traits to his character as a political leader. His mother was particularly fond of this kind of dissertation; writing to Sullivan she remarked:

> Charles in particular has shown that the child was father to the man, for the energy and devotion that he now manifests to his country, to those who need a mighty help, are the outgrowth of his youthful activity and consideration in favour of his family, of his feeling, just and indulgent judgement, respect and unselfishness towards all who came near him.[59]

This at least is a change from the school of thought that sees the Iron master of the Irish Party in the child who shouted at a maid for disturbing his birds' egg collection, or the politician who out-manoeuvred Gladstone in the boy who glued his soldiers to the floor; but it is no more useful or relevant. If, in fact, Charles Stewart Parnell had developed logically from the sort of child he seems to have been, he would never have made the politician of consummate patience and self-control that he became.

Charles's early life at Avondale passed in the sort of activity that might be expected. From the time when as a child he used to watch cricket on the pitch at Avondale, until he and John were old enough to organise matches among the work-boys on the estate,[60] this game was his chief pastime; other social recreations were donkey races on the lawn in front of the house,[61] visiting the Brooke children at Castle Howard,[62] and playing hockey and handball. With their father the boys went shooting, and carried home the game; he also taught them how to play cricket and took them on fishing expeditions to Aughavannagh, where he had a shooting-box. [63] A pastime more peculiar to Wicklow was driving in a donkey-cart to Aughrim and panning for gold in the river there. [64] This, at least, was a preoccupation that never deserted Charles: 'the gold found in the river he treasured, I believe, till the end of his life'.

Charles was a good cricketer; when still quite young, he was a substitute player on many of the Wicklow teams. His primary pursuit at this stage of his life was the reprehensible one of collecting birds' eggs; more enterprisingly, he was a partner with John in a potato-growing enterprise, the produce being sold in Rathdrum for pocket-money. [65]

It was just what might be expected of a county Wicklow childhood, with the usual round of cricket-matches, donkey-driving, visiting, and church on Sundays (where John made himself faint by putting his head between his knees). Since Hayes's death John Henry Parnell gave up being Master of the Hunt and sold his hounds, so riding does not play as large a part in John's early memories as in Emily's; both memoirs taken in conjunction, however, give much the same impression of childhood at Avondale up to 1859. There could have been few more attractive places to grow up in, and the Parnell children enjoyed the potentialities of the neighbourhood to the full; but it seems that they took the natural beauty of the place for granted. John Howard mentions that Mrs Twopenny (an Englishwoman) 'was very fond of the scenery round Avondale and instilled a love of the country into me which Charley, however, did not show until later'. [66]

As far as his schooling went, however, Charles Stewart Parnell's youth was not as typical as in other respects. His schooldays began at the age of seven, when his father took him to Miss Muirley's in Somerset. I have already dealt with this, quoting Miss Muirley's own account to R. B. O'Brien. (John Howard Parnell remembered it as his *mother* taking Charles to Yeovil, because he had been over-spoilt at home;[67] this would have been a drastic measure indeed, and there is no reason to doubt Miss Muirley's own memory of the incident.) Charles became a great favourite of hers, and she seems to have given him the 'mothering' that John Henry Parnell requested. She nursed him through a long spell of typhoid, and always retained an interest in his later life. The Yeovil period, however, can only have been a short-term arrangement to tide over a period of domestic awkwardness at Avondale; the school was a girls' establishment, and Charles was not enamoured of the situation. [68] At all events, his serious illness there, and the fact that he continued under medical attention after it ('his head seemed peculiarly affected' [69]) meant that he remained at home, after spending only a year or so away. [70] Here he was taught first of all by his sisters' governess, who found him too much of a handful, and then by a tutor. After this unsuccessful period he was once more sent away to school, aged eight or nine. This time he went to a Mr and Mrs Barton, who ran a school near Kirk Langley in Derbyshire. Discipline was again a problem, but he seemed to enjoy this experience; he told John that 'it was at Kirk Langley that he learned all his boyish tricks and he always referred to it as a bright spot in his memory, owing to all the fun he had there'.[71] After a year with the Bartons he left the school; St John Ervine claims that his parents were asked to remove him, but does not substantiate this. From 1856 to 1859, John Parnell recalled, Charles was educated at home once more, by one tutor after another; a Mr William Clarke, son of Dr Clarke of Rathdrum, fulfilled the office at one stage, 'and Charley as usual did not get on very well with him and was in the habit of making awful faces at him behind his back'.[72]

It is unlikely that he learnt much. His mother later wrote 'I gave great care to his education, requiring him to make accurate and fine translations from the original into the English, both in Caesar's Commentaries and Virgil';[73] but in the same vein she recalls 'religiously my son was a Protestant ... His father belonged to the Church of England and Charles was much with religious and pious people',[74] and that 'particular pains were taken to place Charles with manifestly kind and religious people'.[75] This glosses over a youthful characteristic of Charles's which John Howard explicitly emphasised: his complete impatience with religious instruction.[76] Mrs Parnell does not choose to recollect this; perhaps she never knew about it. She was rarely at Avondale in those days. Elsewhere, when she claims 'I went to Paris for the education and social advantage of my family',[77] Charles was certainly at least one exception to this rule.

The standard Charles's education reached at this stage does not seem to have been unduly high. Miss Muirley found him 'quick and interesting to teach',[78] and Mrs Parnell wrote to T. D. Sullivan that 'all my son's tutors expressed a high opinion of Charles's abilities';[79] but the impression gained from John Howard's memoir is that his brother must have been idle and hard to teach (a judgement subscribed to, after conversations with the family and others, by R. B. O'Brien). But it was not true to say, as did St John Ervine, that 'his mentality was slow';[81] there is every evidence that throughout his life he had no trouble in learning what interested him.

The normality of Charles's Wicklow childhood comes through strongly in the many anecdotes which John Howard Parnell and others tell of his early youth. Playing soldiers,[81] losing a favourite dog in a mineshaft, raiding the kitchen-garden at Avondale, constructing ponds and building rafts,[83] playing at the ruined fort on the estate,[84] instigating a firework display,[85] visiting the local 'haunted cottage'[86] – it could be the childhood of any child born into the comfortable

Plate 1 Avondale in the time
of the Parnells.
From *A Patriot's Mistake*
By courtesy of the
British Library Board

Plate 2 Charles Stewart
Parnell aged twenty.
From *A Patriot's Mistake*
By courtesy of the
British Library Board

Plate 3 Delia Tudor Stewart
Parnell.
From *Celtic Monthly* February 1881.
By courtesy of the National Library
of Ireland
By courtesy of the
British Library Board

Plate 4 Charles Stewart
Parnell aged eight.
From *A Patriot's Mistake*
By courtesy of the
British Library Board

Plate 5 Fanny Parnell.
From *Celtic Monthly*, February 1880. By
courtesy of the National Library of
Ireland

Plate 6 Theodosia Parnell.
From *Celtic Monthly*, February 1880. By
courtesy of the National Library of Ireland

Plate 7 Emily Dickinson on a favourite
horse.
From *A Patriot's Mistake*

background of the Irish landed gentry of this period.

But even at this stage, there were differences. Mrs Parnell was not a typical wife for an Irish squire; her inclinations did not lend stability to the children's background. She and her husband did not live much together; this in itself must have been unsettling, and it seems to have been the chief cause of Charles's rather premature trips to school in England. Then there was the sudden death of John Henry Parnell in 1859, at a time when Charles was the only one of his children in Ireland, and the only one to attend his funeral. The fact that he died at so disadvantageous a time where his financial affairs were concerned meant that the break in his children's way of life was to be all the greater. Avondale was let, and a new sort of life began when Charles was only thirteen. The co-existence of the country gentleman and the discontented ex-belle may have ended, to all intents and purposes, six years before the death of the former; but his way of life seems to have been the dominant influence on their children up to 1859. The influence of Delia Parnell on Charles's life and on the formation of his opinions – especially bearing in mind that he was one of the children who did *not* accompany her to Paris and attend school there – can only have been notable after 1859.

# Part III

*Parnell before politics, 1859–74*

# 1  The Parnell family

For the Parnell family, the immediate result of John Henry Parnell's death was a complete reorganisation of their lives. Avondale was to be vacated, although not at once; the family returned there after the funeral and almost immediately began to arrange the temporary disposal of the estate. This was overseen by Alfred MacDermott, described by John Howard Parnell as 'our father's solicitor'. John Parnell goes on to say that MacDermott

> found everything in a very confused state, and his first act was to pay off all the workmen not actually required; while, by order of the court [of Chancery] the livestock and farming implements were sold by auction; sufficient horses for the use of the family were kept, and the rest sold; Mr West of Mount Avon was appointed agent.[1]

Although the auction was first advertised on 30 July 1859, about three weeks after the funeral,[2] it did not take place until 11 and 12 October. There is a detailed inventory of this auction, as well as of the later sales at Casino, in an appendix to this book, but a brief glance at the list shows how thoroughly the establishment at Avondale was broken up; it would never be as extensive again. Sixty-two head of cattle were sold, twenty-two sheep and twelve horses (even though several had been reserved for family use). A great many farming implements were auctioned, and four carriages.[3] Over a year later, a further auction at Casino, the dower house (or more accurately, large cottage) nearby, disposed of more personal effects such as china, furniture, the contents of an extensive wine-cellar, and 'a good cricket-ground tent in perfect order';[4] two years later there was yet another sale of 'the property of Mrs Parnell'.[5]

The servants were, however, kept on; the house was to be let 'by order of the Court', according to Emily Dickinson,[6] and obviously required a functioning establishment. The shadowy Miss Zouche, described by John Howard Parnell as 'a devoted relative who had been acting as housekeeper',[7] remained at Avondale for a year; after this the family moved to Dublin. Emily Dickinson dates this move as the spring of 1860.[8] Neither she nor John mentioned to whom the house was let, but local newspapers of the time record Mr Thomas Edwards, chief engineer of the Dublin, Wicklow and Wexford Railway, as living there;[9] Edwards later became a friend of John Parnell's.

The family moved to Dalkey, then an upper middle-class watering-place connected by train to the city. Mrs Parnell, Emily says, 'would have liked to take her children away to London or Paris, but was prohibited by the Court from taking them out of Ireland'.[10] The location of the house 'at the seaside' was also by command of the Court of Chancery.[11] Mrs Parnell moved nearer Dublin a year later, and into the city in 1862.[12] Emily recorded this final move, to a house in Temple Street,[13] as being 'ordered by the court .. so that her elder daughters might have the advantages of a Dublin season'.[14] However, it is more likely that Mrs Parnell had simply had more than enough of seclusion. John wrote that 'our mother did not care for the country, so took a house at 14, Upper Temple Street',[15] and this seems reason enough.

Mrs Parnell was not, however, her own mistress. It is unfortunate that the Chancery Court records for this time were all destroyed in 1922; the contemporary Irish Law Reports do not record any orders made concerning the Parnell children, and for their legal position I have had to rely only on scattered references in the Registry of Deeds and the reminiscences of John Howard Parnell and Emily Dickinson. At all events, the guardians of the children were Sir Ralph Howard, their father's cousin, and Robert Johnson of Dunblane in Scotland, 'a Scotch agricultural expert and an old friend of our father's'.[16] John Howard Parnell recalled that 'Sir Ralph Howard was annoyed at being joint guardian with Mr Johnson', and Emily Dickinson states that Sir Ralph 'declining to act as "guardian of the persons", the court selected my mother for the office'.[17] Howard's refusal may have been caused by disapproval of his co-guardian, but an additional reason could have been the bad impression Emily made on him in London; he had already declined responsibility for her once before. At any rate, when the will was made known, John Howard Parnell recalled that 'our mother took steps to have us all made wards in Chancery'[18] and the Court seems to have taken the important decisions regarding the children, for the next years at least. Alfred MacDermott 'managed our affairs under the Court of Chancery'[19] and the two trustees seem to have had relatively little to do, though described in legal memorials as 'testamentary guardians'[20] as well as joint trustees of John Henry Parnell's estate.[21]

According to herself, Emily was the only child not to be made a ward of court as there was no money to be deposited on her behalf, her father having cut her out of his will;[22] she did not become a ward until G. V. Wigram, who had married her father's sister, paid out the necessary amount as a way of preventing her maternal grandfather from adopting (and, by implication, corrupting) her.[23] In any case, references to the children in legal memorials mention Emily as a ward with all the rest, and a Chancery order mentioning her is dated as early as 19 July 1859.[24]

In a consideration of the terms of John Henry Parnell's will, the destruction of the Irish Public Record Office again creates a divide that cannot be crossed. The most important provisions, however, were recalled by John Howard Parnell:

> Avondale was left to Charley, the Armagh estate (Collure) to myself; and the Carlow property to Henry. I well remember Charley standing by our mother's bed discussing our father's will and saying 'I suppose John has got Avondale', and when mother told him it was his he was greatly surprised and said he never expected it.[25]

Elsewhere he explains why the Wicklow estate did not go to himself, as the eldest son:

> Although I was the eldest son, my great-uncle and guardian, Sir Ralph Howard, had always told my father that he intended to leave me a considerable portion of his property, as under the terms of Colonel Hayes's will Avondale was always to pass to the second son. It was for that reason that under my father's will I was only left the comparatively unproductive estate in Armagh, burdened as it was, moreover, by annuities to my sisters. The relations between my father and myself were always perfectly cordial but he, naturally, did not wish to leave any of his sons unprovided for, and so left the Carlow property to Henry, as I was the prospective heir of Sir Ralph.[26]

Sir Ralph's legacy did not, in the event, work out as lucrative as the Avondale inheritance would have been, but John Henry Parnell was not to know that. There were, moreover, financial burdens on Avondale about which his son knew nothing; though not as unprofitable as Collure, it was by no means an unencumbered legacy.[27] The provision about Avondale always passing to a second son seems an unnecessary addition; there are no references to it in the many recapitulations of Samuel Hayes's will in the Memorials of the Registry of Deeds. It is likely that this was a piece of hearsay absorbed by John Howard; he elsewhere refers to Samuel Hayes as 'a close friend of our father's', which shows a very imperfect idea of the original owner of Avondale.

It is significant that John Howard Parnell never shows any rancour at the arrangement made for him by his father; and it is an equally telling reflection on his sister's character that she does. Emily Dickinson wrote sententiously that 'an unjust will never bring a blessing to the one who profits by it' [28] and elsewhere referred to John's life being ruined by his disinheritance. [29] It should be pointed out that, contrary to the impression given by her, John Parnell's 'human sympathy' was not 'crushed beneath that early act of injustice'; he seems to have struck everyone who knew him as a kind man as well as a good one. [30]

The will, then, bearing John Howard's revelation about Sir Ralph's promise in mind, was not a particularly strange one. The boys inherited the property and the girls small annuities (£100 a year), in most cases chargeable upon the Collure estate. Mrs Parnell also had a small income, which she later waived; [31] but for domestic expenses she relied upon an allowance paid to her from her sons' property by the Court of Chancery. [32] She inherited a good deal of money from her father and brother later on, but her husband was not to know this when he made his will. Indeed, she seems to have been largely ignored in John Henry Parnell's dispositions. John Howard declared that 'she had been left nothing under father's will'; [33] her husband's uncle and a friend were guardians of the children, and it was only because Sir Ralph declined to become 'guardian of the persons' that her legal connection with the children was as close as it was. Nor had she much to do with the administration of her sons' property. This no doubt had partly to do with the position of women, especially as regards property, at the time; but the scanty attention paid to John Henry's wife in his will implies a large degree of detachment, if not almost complete estrangement, between them.

There were complications in the situation in which children and guardians suddenly and unwillingly found themselves. The memorials dealing with the Parnell affairs in the Registry of Deeds have constant references to a petition heard in the Chancery Court of 'Howard and Parnell minors v. Charlotte Zouche, Delia Parnell and others'. [34] The case is not recorded in the Irish Law Reports, and the Chancery records have been destroyed; but since the case gave rise to a Chancery order of 16 May 1860, 'that C. M. West was appointed and still is receiver over the said estate and interest of the said minor Charles Parnell . . . and as such receiver is in the receipt of the yearly rents', [35] it seems to have involved an attempt on the part of one of the contestants to gain control of the administration of the Avondale estate. This order was not the end of the case, as an additional decree was made in respect of the Howard v. Zouche petition on 30 July 1867; with reference to this, Charles Stewart Parnell mortgaged Avondale and its income to Sir Ralph Howard to pay £1,500 of the debts and funeral expenses settled by Sir Ralph in favour of his late nephew. (Charles had come of age about a month before.) The case therefore seems to have been brought to determine who should administer the sizeable income of Avondale; West's receivership was called into question, but upheld by the court. What is significant is that Sir Ralph and his charges were on one side in the case, and Mrs Parnell and Miss Zouche, the housekeeper-relative mentioned by John Howard, on the other. An effort seems to have been made by Mrs Parnell to question the arrangements dictated by her husband's will; possibly her plan was for Miss Zouche, who had been managing Avondale for a year, to act as receiver of the income. At all events, West retained the post, and that is all we definitely know. It would be interesting to ascertain, for instance, on what side Alfred MacDermott, the ubiquitous family lawyer, stood; but I can find no more details of this case besides the synopsis of its outcome.

Some antipathy between Delia Parnell and her husband's relations is further indicated by the efforts of G. V. Wigram, the husband of her sister-in-law, to prevent Emily going to live in New Jersey. According to Emily, he not only made her a ward of court but also offered to adopt her. 'My mother was very much troubled by the possibility of losing me';[36] but Emily made her preferences clear and the Lord Chancellor rejected the offer. Though Emily places these recollections in the context of her life at Temple Street (1862–4), she was made an official ward in July 1859,[37] so the Wigrams must have made their feelings clear immediately after John Henry Parnell's death. The fact that they negotiated about this step through the Court instead of asking Mrs Parnell's feelings first and then abandoning the effort to adopt Emily is significant. As members of the Brethren, it is in any case unlikely that they approved of their American sister-in-law; her tastes and interests were very much of 'The World'.

The terms of their father's will, then, dictated the Parnells' life for the next years; but their mother's influence became paramount. They left Avondale, and country life; though the Court of Chancery organised their income, Mrs Parnell made most of the decisions. She could not take them out of the country to live, though it seems likely that she would have if she had been able;[38] but their life with her must still have been very different from under their father's sober rule. To realise this, a general examination of the nature of the family's life under Mrs Parnell's influence is necessary.

## II

For the years immediately following her husband's death, Mrs Parnell's life revolved of necessity round Dublin. It was not until 1865 that she 'got leave from the Court' to take the youngest members of the family with her to Paris, where she intended to set up house with her brother;[39] significantly, this was the year that John Howard came of age, and so could assume some responsibility for the rest of them. At this time the family was living at 14, Upper Temple Street. They had initially moved to Khyber Pass, a large house above the sea at Dalkey. John Howard recalled learning to swim at Kingstown Pier and off the rocks at Dalkey, boating at Bullock Harbour, fishing off the Mugglins Rocks and shooting rabbits in the grounds of the house; he and Charles also went ferreting on Dalkey Hill, 'taking with us the porter from the railway station'.[40] However pleasant for her children, this rural life cannot have suited Delia Parnell; in less than a year (the early summer of 1860) the family moved into Kingstown, renting a large house in its own park owned by the O'Conor Don.[41] This was an even shorter sojourn; in the following winter (1861–2) the elder children went to stay in Casino, the house near Avondale, while Mrs Parnell took 14, Upper Temple Street in the city, and here she stayed.[42] It was at Kingstown, in August 1860, that old Mrs Stewart, while on a visit, suddenly died; Mrs Parnell was much affected by this, and may have been ready to leave the house on this account.[43] But her whole inclination seems to have been towards city life. Furthermore, after 1862 John and Charles were at a pre-university 'crammer's', and their mother had more time to devote to social life. Once moved into the city, according to John Howard, 'Our mother [kept] open house in Temple Street, giving dinners, balls and small dances to her many Dublin friends . . . she was extremely fond of entertaining'.[44] Emily recalled of this era (1862–4): '[Sophy] and I now led a very gay life, running the giddy round of vain delights and living in a world made up of drives and rides, dinners, kettle-drums, balls, concerts and theatres, fashionable talk, and everything else what was light and sparkling'.[45] Both she and her brother attribute the extent of her mother's social involvement to her friendship with Lord Carlisle, the Lord Lieutenant at the time.

[He] was an old friend of my mother's. Now, taking advantage of such an excellent opportunity of renewing his former friendship, he 'took her under his wing' and secured to her and her daughters introductions to the best houses and families which Dublin society afforded, so that my mother's first entrance into the social atmosphere of Dublin took place under the most favourable auspices.[46]

This is the sort of reminiscence in which Mrs Dickinson took most delight, and where she usually gave her fancy free rein; but her more sober brother bears her out in this instance, remarking that the Lord Lieutenant, 'being a friend of our mother's', used to single the Parnells out at Castle functions.[47] Lord Carlisle died in December 1864;[48] Mrs

Parnell began her habit of living between Paris and Dublin shortly afterwards. The Temple Street house seems to have been used only episodically in the later 1860s, and was given up by 1870. [49] Although the children visited Avondale and occasionally Clonmore, Mrs Parnell does not seem to have left Dublin often during her residence there. She was involved in viceregal society, her own entertainments, and activities like the 'Originals' club she started in 1861, which I have described in my last section. [50] A contemporary recollection of Mrs Parnell as a Dublin hostess casts an interesting sidelight on the actuality of the sort of grand entertainments vaguely hinted at by Emily Dickinson.

> This entertainment [a haphazard house-party at the Conollys' house, Castletown] suggests another of a rather singular kind, given by an American lady, no other than the mother of the patriot, Charles Stewart Parnell, who must then have been in his frocks. It was a sort of 'go as you please' show. There was to be a late lunch, then a tea, and then a sort of dinner, to be followed by a dance. The idea was that the guest was to take up his residence in the house for this protracted period! I recall meeting there the pleasant Dion Bouccicault ... Mrs Parnell had a bevy of pretty daughters who did their best to stimulate the proceedings but the fact was, no-one knew why on earth he was there or what was to be done next, so the thing gradually languished out and, quietly folding our tents, we stole away very early. [51]

It is interesting that the anonymous author of these remembrances, while no stickler for protocol, still firmly puts Mrs Parnell's party firmly in the context of 'grotesque entertainments'. [52] His view of Lord Carlisle's circle is also significant; 'rackety' is a charitable description. Looked at in the context of these recollections, Delia Parnell's favoured position in viceregal society is a good deal less impressive than it first seems.

It is hard to know how lavishly she lived, but the allowance from the Chancery Court on which she depended until she inherited from her father and brother in 1869–72 cannot have been large. One of Charles's early schemes was to make money out of the Avondale timber 'to provide her with ample funds for her wants', as she was 'extremely fond of entertaining'. [53] By 1872 Mrs Parnell was living in Paris permanently, and from 1870 she seems to have visited America more often than Dublin. Emily and Sophy were by then married, neither of them to a man she approved of, and John and Charles had come of age. The age of her children, and their circumscribed legal position, seem to have been all that kept her in Ireland.

This is not to say that Mrs Parnell was unduly concerned with them. As early as 1861 the boys were spending months alone at Casino; and John Howard recalled, in a revealing sidelight:

> We all got into a terribly disorganised habit as to meals during our days together at Avondale, after our father had died and our mother had gone to America. The only meal during the day at which all the family and visitors were certain of meeting was dinner'.[54]

The haphazard way of life that Sir John Ervine attributed to the Parnell family is more relevant to this stage of their existence than during their father's lifetime. The family was, in a sense, dispersing. Certainly from about 1865 the life of each of them began to develop separately; from this date the Temple Street house was used infrequently and when it was given up altogether (before 1870) 'the family scattered, never again to meet all under one roof'.[55] Delia was settled in Paris, John went to America, Emily and Sophy were married, Charles had moved back to Avondale, Anna was at art school in England, Henry at school and then university; only Fanny and Theodosia were in any way consistently attached to their mother. Of the early period at Temple Street, John Parnell wrote: 'Looking back over our past lives, I can see that it was here at Temple Street that our fates were really decided. From this time forward great changes took place in the life of each of us and this may be said to have been the birth of our careers'.[56] At least part of the reason why Delia Parnell resided less continuously in Dublin after 1869 was that she could then afford to travel. Up to this she had had very little money of her own. Writing to T. D. Sullivan about the 1860s she implied that she lived in Ireland in order to be 'enabled to watch the proceedings of the agents and attornies considering my sons' estates . . . The guardians lived out of Ireland.'[57] Certainly her interest in these estates was paramount: she had no other income than what she was allowed out of them. In November 1869, however, her father died in New Jersey; in 1872 she went to live permanently in Paris with her brother, Charles Stewart, but he died in October of the following year, in Italy. She therefore not only inherited her own share of her father's money, but also – within four years – her brother's portion; and the latter also left her 'all his large fortune in Southern railroad bonds and shares'.[58] For the next month she was occupied in sorting out Stewart's Parisian affairs [59] and in late 1873 she went to New York to organise his business interests there.[60] 'She was now quite a millionairess', recalled Emily Dickinson with unconcealed satisfaction, 'and was able to make me a liberal allowance.'[61]

She was certainly comfortably off. Her distinguished father must have amassed a good deal of money (especially as he could afford to run for President some years before) and Charles Stewart was well off, appearing in several memorials in the Registry of Deeds as a sort of financial benefactor and provider of loans to the Parnell daughters, in return for holding their annuities in trust.[62] It is doubtful if Mrs Parnell's fortune was as 'immense' as Emily liked to remember; if so, her mother must have managed it remarkably badly, for she was in straitened circumstances again before long. But at the end of the period with which this chapter deals, her position looked secure. She had contacts in Paris, money in America and a family in Ireland; she divided her time between the three.

It seems doubtful that Mrs Parnell spent much, if any, time at Avondale after 1860, even when Charles had taken up residence there once more; but her children retained a close connection with Wicklow, even during the peripatetic years of 1860–4. In the late summer of 1860, for instance, John and Charles 'went down to Casino, the dower-house near Avondale, for a change; we had many friends there and were asked out repeatedly to dinners and to cricket matches, and spent many pleasant evenings with Mr Edwards [who was renting Avondale]'.[63] The next year, John recalled:

> We all went down to Casino again for the winter, Charley and I got up a shooting-party for woodcock, which were plentiful in Avondale woods. Our mother did not care for the country ... but Charley, Fanny and myself remained at Casino for some time longer, with our sister's Italian governess. We had a very happy time, for we all loved Avondale.[64]

The following Christmas (1863) John and Charles went down to Casino when they returned from school, taking Fanny with them; there they found Emily and her governess in residence. Once more they went shooting and walking and renewed their acquaintance with local people like Mrs Twopenny, Charles's old nurse.[65] John and Charles spent a fortnight of this Christmas vacation at Casino, and only had time for 'a few days' with their mother at Temple Street before returning to school.[66] When Charles was at Cambridge, Avondale was his base rather than Dublin; here, according to his brother, 'he had many social duties. The Wicklow county families constantly entertained him, and no invitation to Avondale was ever refused.' Thus the connection with Wicklow was kept up during Charles's childhood and by 1870, when he had left university, John found him living in solitary state at Avondale, except for two servants.[67] After his lengthy visit to Avondale the following year, Lord Carysfort was to urge him to 'remain here and take up your position in the county';[68] in a sense, this was simply encouraging the regularisation of a relationship which had been, if intermittent, a constant factor in Charles's and his siblings' lives since their father died.

From 1859 to 1870, then, the period during which Mrs Parnell lived in Ireland, her children kept up the Wicklow connection although she was not inclined to renew it herself.[69] How she influenced their development in other areas is not easy to chart; but one important aspect of their life is the nationalist slant to political thinking with which she is traditionally supposed to have inbued them.[70] I have referred to this before, in examining Mrs Parnell's later claim that she was an adherent of Irish Nationalism from her first days in the country;[71] a later chapter is devoted to her political involvements throughout her long life.[72] But here it is worth briefly considering the 'Fenian' nature of her sympathies during the 1860s. The idea that her opinions could be so described seems to depend on two much-told stories. The first was related to R. B. O'Brien by a classmate of John's and Charles's, almost certainly the Earl of Meath:

> 'I well remember,' says one who was at Chipping Norton with Parnell, 'the day the Parnells came. Their mother brought them. She wore a green dress and Wishaw [the headmaster] came to me and said "I say, B—, I have met one of the most extraordinary women I have ever seen – the mother of the Parnells. She is a regular rebel. I have never heard such treason in my life. Without a word of warning she opened fire on the British government and by Jove she did give it us hot. I have asked her to come for a drive, to show her the country, and you must come too for protection." So we went for a drive, but my presence did not stop Mrs Parnell from giving her views about the iniquities of the English government in Ireland'.[73]

Several observations can be made about this passage. The Parnells did not first come to Chipping Norton accompanied by their mother; John has described their arrival, alone and at night, in detail.[74] This encounter must have been another time. Further, there is nothing of the 'rebel' in Mrs Parnell's attitude as quoted; there was and is nothing treasonable about attacking 'the British government', and nothing rebellious about condemning 'the iniquities of the English government in Ireland'. Disraeli himself did as much, and more.[75] The interpretation of Mrs Parnell's views as 'Fenian' in this case was probably the Earl of Meath's; he was, in fact, exactly the kind of Wicklow aristocrat who looked on Parnell as a traitor to his class and his duty.[76] Hindsight must also be allowed for; it is unlikely that the concept of Fenianism would have sprung to the mind of an English schoolteacher in 1862. Finally, Wishaw cannot have been so very scandalised by Mrs Parnell, as he was friendly enough with the family to visit them in Ireland some years later, staying with them in Temple Street.[77] This anecdote shows that Mrs Parnell was outspoken about the British administration of Ireland, and nothing more.

The second and more weighty anecdote that is often adduced to
prove Mrs Parnell's active nationalism at this period postulates that in
the latter 1860s she was in the habit of concealing Fenian fugitives at
14, Upper Temple Street, and on one occasion had her house searched
by the police because of this. Besides turning up in most secondary
accounts of the Parnell family background, this story is told at first
hand by Emily Dickinson.[78] R. B. O'Brien was told that 'her house in
Temple Street was placed under police surveillance ... One night a
batch of detectives paid a surprise visit and insisted on searching the
premises',[79] and R. Johnston claimed that when posting a letter late
one night in Temple Street in 1866 he was told by a constable that he
was watching number 14 because 'Mrs Parnell ... hides the Fenians
on us'.[80] John Howard Parnell, however, has an interestingly different
slant to this connection:

> Owing to our mother being a prominent American woman and to
> her undisguised sympathies with the Fenian outlaws, a number
> of tramps and imposters used to call at our house in Temple
> Street for aid ... In the days of frenzied police action which
> followed the rising and Rossa's trial our mother not unnaturally
> became suspected of complicity with the Fenians owing to the
> number of visits paid by suspicious characters to our house in
> Temple Street. As a matter of fact, she had actually assisted one
> of those connected with the Manchester affair to escape to
> America in female clothing. However, one day a body of police
> suddenly appeared at our house in Temple Street with a
> search-warrant and insisted upon going through the whole
> house.[81]

But all these accounts were written with hindsight, affected by the
image of Charles Stewart Parnell as an out-and-out Nationalist and by
his mother's latter-day claims to a personal history of patriotic
fervour. It is therefore particularly interesting to find a version of the
affair written by P. J. Hanway as early as 1881, which implies a far
less extreme situation:

> [In 1867 Mrs Parnell] busied herself in lightening the burden of
> [the Fenians'] imprisonment and in pleading their claims for
> treatment less inhuman and revolting than that provided by
> English prison discipline for the most desperate classes. About
> this time an amusing incident occurred. The Parnell physician
> was suspected by the police of being an active Fenian and his
> movements were closely watched. He was in constant attendance
> on one of the family who was stricken down with cholera. But
> the police were not aware of this; the drawn blinds in the
> windows of the sick-room and the constant visits of Dr O'Reagan

left no doubt in the mind of a lynx-eyed detective that escaped
Fenians were concealed in the Parnell household. A descent on
the house was immediately ordered, but when the advance-guard
reached the darkened room and learned that it contained a
young lady suffering from Asiatic cholera, they beat a hasty and
by no means dignified retreat.[82]

This version is interesting on a number of accounts. It was written
comparatively recently after the event described; the Fenian
connection that aroused police suspicion was not Mrs Parnell, but her
doctor; there is no mention of any Fenians ever having been actually
abetted by Mrs Parnell. Furthermore, and most important, her interest
in the Fenians is described specifically in terms of their conditions of
imprisonment – in other words, Mrs Parnell was sympathetic to the
idea of amnesty, as many people were well before the foundation of the
Amnesty Association in 1869. This is, of course, a very different thing
from being 'a regular rebel'; it is also far more the sort of interest one
would expect of Mrs Parnell, with her Castle connections and her
'Originals' tea-parties. She subscribed to the *Irishman;* but so did Isaac
Butt, and other moderates like Bushe and the Rev. Gilmour of
Rathmore.[83] Moreover, a facet of her interest in Irish agitators of the
time which is recorded by both William O'Brien and John Devoy is,
significantly, that the men who received help from her were
Americans.[84] She paid the passage home of several Americans in 1866,
released on condition that they would return to the United States. And
her connection with them need not imply a great degree of political
sympathy; for a letter from one or these officers to the *Irish World*
years afterwards describes how he encountered Mrs Parnell when she
was prison-visiting in Dublin in the 1860s.[85] Again, the activity
involved is much more closely allied to the respectable Amnesty
movement than to Fenianism. Americans imprisoned in Dublin
appealed to her as a prominent compatriot, with connections in
viceregal society, and she helped them; there need have been no more
to it than that. The interests of her daughter Fanny were a different
matter, and I will come to them presently. But the 'amusing incident'
related in the *Celtic Monthly* seems a far more likely story than the
exciting tale of intrigue which found its way into Barry O'Brien's book
and which Emily Dickinson and John Parnell remembered respectively
forty and fifty years later.

In any case, if Mrs Parnell had Fenian sympathies at this stage, it is
debatable whether they noticeably affected her sons. John Howard
Parnell recalls that neither he nor Charles had much use for the
'tramps' who came to Temple Street seeking help:

> I think he [Charles] came to look upon most of the nondescript
> visitors to our house as tramps, as I did also to a certain extent.

He finally got so tired of their constant visits that he used to wait
for the so-called Fenians behind the hall-door in Temple Street
and (like Sam Weller at Ipswich), directly the door was open,
make a rush for them and kick them down the steps. [86]

He was put out by the police raid on Temple Street, but only because
the police impounded his Wicklow Rifles uniform, which he wanted to
wear to a Castle leveé. 'Charley especially disliked the idea of his
uniform being mistaken for a Fenian one . . . He distinctly resented the
idea of being stamped as a Fenian, especially as he was in the Queen's
army and was proud of the fact.'[87] His reaction to the affair was an
increased impatience with nationalist politics: 'He finally declared that
he would leave the house if anything more was said about the
Fenians.'[88] John Howard Parnell was in absolutely no doubt about his
brother's opinions at this time: 'My recollection of Charley's attitude
at the time is, as I have recounted, distinctly against his entry into
politics being in any sense due to the influence of the Fenian
movement.'[89] His sister, who differs from John Howard on so many
points, is here equally categoric:

> Charles had not as yet shown any Radical tendencies; rather the
> reverse . . . Charles evinced no sympathy with the Fenians and
> was vexed with his mother for taking the active part on their
> behalf which she did, and for mixing herself up so much with
> their affairs. [90]

Mrs O'Shea gives a similarly decisive view, and also emphasises the
slightness of Parnell's contact with his mother at this stage. [91] There
seems to be little evidence for the theory that attributes Charles
Stewart Parnell's subsequent entry into nationalist politics to the
Fenians and his mother's interest in them. Statements like Robert
McWade's about Mrs Parnell instructing her children about the
'inherited infirmities' of the British Royal Family [92] are directly
refuted by John Parnell, who wrote of her enduring admiration for
Queen Victoria and crown authority. [93] Other claims about her
influence on Charles are generally both second-hand and affected by
hind-sight. One worth examining is a saying triumphantly quoted by
St John Ervine, which he found in Frances Power Cobbe's
autobiography. Mrs Power Cobbe knew Sophia Evans, William
Parnell's sister, and wrote that she remembered Mrs Evans saying:
'There is mischief brewing! I am troubled at what is going on at
Avondale. My nephew's wife has a hatred of England and is educating
my nephew, like a little Hannibal, to hate it too'. [94] However, though
the 'little Hannibal' is intended as a reference to Charles Stewart
Parnell, the 'nephew' referred to would have been John Henry Parnell,
not one of his children, who were grand-nephews and grand-nieces of

Mrs Evans; furthermore, Mrs Cobbe, writing in 1894, dates this as 'in the 1840s', when Charles was at most three years old. Hind-sight seems again to be responsible for the flavour of this confidence, recalled half a century later by a woman who was self-confessedly the bluest of Tories; she elsewhere refers to Parnell as 'an Englishman', and 'only one example more of the supremacy of the Anglo-Saxon intellect in every land of its adoption'.[95] Her recollections of Delia Parnell's character, besides being admittedly second-hand, are likely to have been strongly influenced by the reputation that lady had gained in the meantime.

This is not to say that the whole family remained unaffected by the nationalist fervour of the 1860s. Though John records his agreement with Charles regarding the 'tramps and imposters' who visited Temple Street, he still accompanied Fanny when she walked to the *Irishman* office with her poems, whereas 'Charley made fun of her poetry and steadfastly refused to accompany her to the Fenian stronghold'.[96] John and Fanny attended O'Donovan Rossa's trial, and even bought him a bouquet which they could not summon up enough courage to throw. When the sentence was passed, 'Fanny could hardly restrain her tears and I think pictured herself as the next occupant of the dock'.[97] Fanny was, as John Howard affectionately termed her, 'an arch-rebel'; but the fervour with which she embraced the Fenian ideals did not extend to her brothers. She was a 'bluestocking' poetess (again in John Howard's terms), and was more susceptible to abstract ideas than they; whereas John and Charles both owned estates, and it was coming to grips with running them and their subsequent realisation of the possibilities of rural improvement inherent in the tenant-right movement which initially impelled them into Irish politics. This is, however, to ancitipate.

Any interest in politics which Charles Stewart Parnell evinced at this time of his life seems to have been located in the affairs of his mother's country. John Parnell states this emphatically:

> If anything can be said to have been the first impulse that direct Charley's attention towards politics, it was the American Civil War. This was a constant topic of conversation in our family circle, owing to our being American on our mother's side.[98]

At first supporting the side of the North, Charles became sympathetic to Southern claims during his visit to Alabama in 1871.[99] While the war was on, 'Charley eagerly read every item of information contained in the newspaper and discussed the details freely';[100] even after it was over , he was capable of keeping companions on a shooting-trip awake all night by talking about it, while his brother 'wondered how he could keep his interest so much alive in the politics of what was, after all, a remote country'.[101] This remarkably concentrated interest was not to be brought to bear on affairs nearer home for some years; when it was, the intellectual involvement would be even more complete, but in the 1860s Irish politics seem to have concerned Parnell little enough.

### III

Before considering Charles Stewart Parnell's life at this period in detail, it is well to deal briefly with his brothers and sisters from 1859 to 1875.

Delia had married Livingston Thomson, for his money according to all the authorities, shortly before her father died. Emily Dickinson records the intense jealousy of Delia's husband, who followed her everywhere and refused to allow her to go riding; though wealthy and living in a 'fairytale' chateau at St Germain, her life seems to have been an unrelievedly unhappy one. [102] Emily and Arthur Dickinson honeymooned at the Thomsons' Paris house, and Mrs Parnell visited there from time to time; otherwise the unfortunate Delia's life is little recorded until the death of her only child in 1882.

In contrast, Emily's life during the period under consideration is of course covered copiously in her quasi-autobiography. Her father's death, and the discrimination against her in his will that prevented her – for a time at least – from marrying Dickinson, left her deeply depressed; 'in a nature like mine, keenly felt emotions were liable to take a deep root', [103] and even the gay social life into which she and Sophy were plunged at Temple Street meant little to her. In 1862, however, she came of age and was officially betrothed to Arthur Dickinson, whose regiment was now quartered in Dublin. In April 1864 they were married. Their two-year engagement was a happy one, with Emily enjoying a social life centred round Arthur's regiment ('renowned for its entertainments, which were conducted on the most elaborate and extensive scale') and her own accomplishments as a musician:

> I had some time reached the zenith of my fame as a pianist, and was frequently asked to play at the large concerts organised for charitable purposes. My audience often consisted of a couple of thousand people . . . I excelled in the pathetic softness with which I played the passages that called for expression. These often drew tears from the eyes of my hearers. [104]

She was to need this buoyantly good conceit of herself from the early years of her marriage on. Arthur did not stay long in the army; Emily recalled that he was posted to the Cape of Good Hope, where her health would not not allow her to go, and he resigned his commission rather than leave her, saying 'I shall get a land agency and we will live in Dublin' – a telling indication of how little he expected such a job to occupy him. He then, according to Emily, became agent for the Collure estate. John Howard Parnell, however, dated this arrangement from *before* the wedding.[105] Certainly, the wedding took place shortly after John came into possession of Collure. But whether or not the Captain became agent before or after his marriage, he was to remain largely dependent upon his wife's family. Though resident at 22, Lower Pembroke Street in Dublin for some time, the Dickinsons lived more and more at Avondale. Charles settled an annuity on Emily from the estate, as well as giving her away in marriage and presenting her with a diamond necklace and bracelet as a wedding present;[106] he seems to have been friendly with his likeable but unsound brother-in-law.[107] The dependence continued; it was Mrs Parnell's legacy that enabled the Dickinsons to start hunting again, and Emily received an income from her mother after Admiral Stewart died in 1869.[108] But life at Avondale, though first described by Emily as a pleasant idyll,[109] became increasingly troubled as Arthur's lack of occupation and fondness for the United Services Club, reinforced by a naturally roistering temperament, led to a developing alcoholic problem. He was 'a very enthusiastic, genial, social character, with a strain of wildness and easily led'.[110] One of the few sincerely eloquent passages in *A patriot's mistake* (if not the only one) deals with Arthur's decline into dipsomania.[111] She genuinely loved her 'representative Lever soldier' and stuck by him, though her affection became increasingly mothering and protective. The violence of his drinking bouts increased, and he had to be bought out of numerous undefined 'scrapes'. In the early 1870s Charles (after an attempt to keep Arthur sober and in isolation at Avondale, which culminated in the Captain downing a bottle of whiskey and chasing his host out of the house) tried to persuade Emily to separate from her husband, but she refused.[112] Arthur similarly rejected an offer from the Parnell family of £500 a year on condition that he live abroad, away from Emily (who now had a baby daughter, Delia). His drinking continued, and his eccentricity increased; when drunk he was liable to burn all his clothes or throw crockery from the windows at Avondale. 'Occasionally he threw the servants down the staircase but they were so fond of him that they did not mind such rough usage'.[113] Emily showed similar ingenuousness in attributing her husband's frenzied drinking to a wish on his part that he might die before she did, because he loved her too much to outlive her,[114] whereas elsewhere she records her difficulty in dissuading him from strangling her because he 'was so fond of her';[115] but it is likely that a certain amount of self-deception was all that made her miserable existence bearable.

By the early 1870s the Dickinsons seem to have been living entirely on small incomes from the Parnell family. In 1867 Mrs Parnell had arranged for an annuity of £100 p.a. and a life-insurance of £1,000 to be made over to Arthur;[116] in 1873 Emily inherited a legacy from Sir Ralph Howard;[117] there was also her marriage settlement, which brought in £100 p.a., and the undefined allowance received from her mother. Arthur's family was not poor: his father had been a solicitor, and clerk for Co. Wicklow [118] and his uncle, Sir Drury Dickinson, was prominent in Dublin life. [119] It is possible that some annuities from this side kept the couple solvent, after Arthur's agency for Collure lapsed in 1872; but like their neighbour Lady Caroline Howard, who wrote gloomily in 1869 of residence in Shelton Abbey that 'nothing but actual poverty drives us here',[120] the Dickinsons held the unenviable position of poor relations by 1875, and were totally dependent on Charles Stewart Parnell for somewhere to live. [121]

John Howard's life for the fifteen years under review was an eventful one. He shared Charles's tutor while living in Dalkey and Kingstown, but after the sojourn at Wishaw's cramming school 'went to the School of Mining in St Stephen's Green, and there obtained two certificates for mining and geology, while I also kept up my painting'. [122] Previous to attending Chipping Norton he had 'only been to school in Paris and had not made the progress I should have done with the English language';[123] it is unlikely in any case that he would have gone to university as his interests, though intellectually oriented, were not academic.

About 1866 [124] John received a letter from his mother's brother in America suggesting that he go out there and make some money in the post-war boom. He had recently come into a legacy, and was thinking of investing it: despite the lack of encouragement from Sir Ralph Howard, he decided to go. [125] Once there, he became involved in cotton-planting and formed an affection for the American South which he was never to lose. He returned to Ireland in about a year but was back in America by 1871, experimenting with peach-farming in Alabama, where Charles visited him and prevailed upon him to return to Ireland, against his original inclination. In the spring of 1872 the two brothers were back in London, visiting Sir Ralph Howard, by now old and ailing. In a well-intentioned attempt to impart some enthusiasm about his heir's American ventures to Sir Ralph, Charles first of all biassed him against American business by describing a careless railway accident and then compounded the injury to John's interests by 'praising up my investments in land in Alabama more than they were justified'. [126] Once again, John's lack of rancour in describing such incidents – well-meant though they were – is remarkable.

Returning to Ireland, John found his affairs there needing attention. Having good-naturedly but unwisely appointed Dickinson as his agent, he found the Collure accounts badly in arrears. (Dickinson cannot have paid much attention to his sinecure; he lived at

Avondale, and Emily never mentions any visits to Armagh, let alone residence there.) John set to running his own estate, and experienced a sort of revelation:

> After two years I gave up acting as my own agent, as I saw that the tenants could not possibly pay in a bad time, as it was difficult enough to get in the rents in comparatively good times ... My collecting, although I met with considerable success in it, certainly opened my eyes to the real condition of the tenant farmers, especially as at this time Mr Butt was advocating his tenant-right principles.[127]

He and his brother were to discuss this, with far-reaching results.

In August 1873 Sir Ralph Howard died at his house in Belgrave Square.[128] The ramifications of the Howard v. Zouche and Parnell case, whatever they may have been, must by then have been forgotten; Mrs Parnell stayed with him through his last illness.[129] The will read, John Howard found that his great-uncle seemed to have been as good as his word: 'He had left me what appeared to be a very considerable fortune, derived from his English mining investments, which brought my income to an almost equal amount to what Charley received from Avondale'.[130] There was, however, drawbacks. After his conversation with Charles about John's American investments Sir Ralph had altered his will by codicil,

> leaving me in the end only half the amount of his original bequest amounting to about £4,000 a year, the other half being left to his cousin Lord Claude Hamilton [later the Duke of Abercorn], owing to the increase in value of the investments since the will was made. However, he made me liable for all the calls on the shares.[131]

Thus John, on paper destined to be at least as well provided for as his younger brother, ended up not as well off. There was, indeed, a further provision made for him which he does not mention but which recurs in memorials in the Registry of Deeds. His father's aunt, Sophia Evans, left a residual sum of £4,800 in Brazilian bonds (subject to some annuities) to her brother Henry Parnell and William George Prescott in trust for John Henry Parnell or his eldest son.[132] The money was to be invested in land, and the income descended, after a case heard in the Chancery Court in 1856[133] to John Howard Parnell. Alfred MacDermott, the family solicitor, managed the income in trust for John Howard by an arrangement made on 16 March 1868;[134] but he cannot have been well off, as the same year he took out an extra mortgage on the already heavily encumbered Armagh estate in order to borrow an undisclosed sum of money from Sir Ralph Howard, and subsequently mortgaged the income on Sophia Evans' legacy to Sir

Ralph as well.[135] This could have been an additional reason why Sir Ralph cast a cold eye on his great-nephew's subsequent American dealings; he must have lent most of the money required for them.

Nor was the inheritance of Collure a particularly enviable acquisition. Describing his attempts to collect the rents in 1872, John wrote:

> It was thought that because I had in some instances to take proceedings against the tenants I was acting harshly, but I had to provide both for my sisters' annuities and the Trinity College head-rent, which had also fallen into arrears, getting nothing for myself.[136]

This was no exaggeration. A list of Armagh townlands and landlords for 1860 in the National Library of Ireland gives the Collure estate as 1,494 acres, valued at £1,092.[137] Even if the rents were reasonably high, the profit margin after a head rent of £1,000 a year and annuities totalling £500 cannot have been much. Small wonder that he mortgaged the estate for £4,000 in 1867;[138] it could never have been a source of profit to him and as the years went by it was to weigh him down more and more.

In this commentary on John Parnell's property, extensive on paper but meaning little hard cash, he can be seen to some extent as playing as unfortunate but good-humoured Esau to Charles's unintentional Jacob − destined for preference, though through no manipulation of his own. John Henry Parnell thought he was leaving each well provided for, but Charles ended up with the choice estate in Wicklow whereas John had to mortgage Collure and his great-aunt's bequest while awaiting Sir Ralph's legacy; on top of this, Charles's well-meaning interference halved this inheritance, leaving John with little more than enough to clear his debts and keep up his commitments. Charles's own estate was not unencumbered,[139] but John had to farm in America for a living and was not conspicuously successful at it. Once again I must recur to John's extraordinary good nature in the face of undeserved adversity (or comparative adversity); the complete absence of rancour or 'side' is one of the most pleasant things about his attractive memoir.

This image of John as a person ready to oblige his decisive younger brother even at his own inconvenience enters into the last aspect of his life I intend to discuss up to 1875; his brief fling at politics in 1874. Told that he was ineligible to run in the 1874 election for Wicklow because he was High Sheriff, Charles was in no doubt what to do: John must run instead. John did not want to, but knew it was no good:

> I was therefore launched in politics, but, what proved to be more important, it was Charley who launched me and who directed

my course. For it was in the wake of my fruitless little Wicklow expedition of 1874 that he himself became drawn into the sea of politics.[140]

Entering the running late and at a disadvantage,[141] he came a very inglorious last;[142] as was to be expected. Nevertheless, he ran all the same; he was to remain steady and self-effacing in his support of his brother to the end of his life.

The next child in order of seniority was Sophy, who distinguished herself by secretly marrying Alfred MacDermott, the family solicitor, in 1862, when she was only sixteen; the marriage was not made public until she came of age in 1866. Emily Dickinson wrote with great bitterness of MacDermott as an 'ingratiating' acquaintance of Mrs Parnell's who insinuated himself into the family's affairs 'as a friend'.[143] This is not accurate; he acted as solicitor for Sir Ralph Howard, and for John Henry Parnell before the latter's death.[144] Emily further claimed that 'he first of all directed his attention towards me, which culminated in an offer of marriage' shortly after her father's death;[145] indignantly repulsed by Emily, he turned his attention to Sophy and 'persuaded her to elope with him, without the knowledge of her mother, who was ill at the time, or that of her family, even running the risk of the Lord Chancellor's anger'. After a Scots marriage the pair returned to Dublin, keeping their union a secret; MacDermott's career could have been jeopardised by such an action and Mrs Parnell, according to Emily, was bitterly disappointed by such a match for 'her peerless daughter', whose blonde beauty 'formed a bewildering picture hardly of this earth'.[146] The MacDermotts were, at all events, re-married in Dublin to satisfy public curiosity and went to live in Fitzwilliam Square. Emily wrote that the pair were known in Dublin society as 'Beauty and the Beast'; 'needless to say', she adds unnecessarily, 'which was Beauty and which was Beast'.

The impression deliberately given by Emily is that MacDermott was out to marry one of the Parnell girls for their money, and did not much care which one it turned out to be. In 1860–1, however, there was little enough coming to any of them; Mrs Parnell's American legacies had not yet come to pass, and as family solicitor MacDermott must have known of the mortgages on the family estates. Emily's dislike of MacDermott was intense and unbalanced; she blamed him for her sister's early death, and whatever passed between MacDermott and Emily before she married Dickinson left an intense and lasting antipathy. In fact, her husband in one drunken fit set off to shoot MacDermott (with an unloaded gun), but Emily dissuaded him: 'I knew', she recorded with a certain disingenuousness, 'my brother-in-law would have made a "case" out of this harmless incident if he had got the chance'.[147] John Howard Parnell is reticent about the marriage, referring to it only twice [148] and then without any of the spice provided by his sister's account.

Of Fanny, next in age (leaving out for the moment Charles Stewart), little enough is recorded at this stage. Emily described her when nineteen years old as talented, pretty, and pursued by would-be suitors in Dublin. [149] On the last count, John Parnell had something to add:

> Fanny ... was engaged to Mr Catterson Smith, the celebrated artist, who at that time, however, had not made his name, so that Charley raised strong objections to the match. I think he afterwards regretted taking this course, as Fanny never married. [150]

In any case, Fanny was despatched in 1868 to do the regulation season at her aunt's in London, but as Lady Howard died suddenly in that year her niece took up residence in Paris with her sisters Anna and Theodosia and their mother. Here she attended art school as her brother John had done, and entered society. Her mother recalled

> People said Fanny was destined to be a *grande dame*, the wife of some great character, taking an active part both in diplomatic and political life ... she thought nothing of her dress, but let me dress her as I liked. She took part in tableaux with great effect. [151]

Mrs Parnell adds with relish that 'a future Duke' wanted to marry her; but on her uncle Charles Stewart's death Fanny accompanied her mother to America and lived mostly there for the rest of her short life.

The quotation above notwithstanding, she was not as passive a character as her mother implies. Rather than being destined to become the wife of someone influential, she came to wield some political influence herself. I have already mentioned the fact that Fanny was the most active Nationalist, and possibly the *only* active Nationalist, in the Temple Street household during the 1860s. [152] Charles Stewart Parnell did not take her seriously then; [153] in some ways he was always to remain detached from Fanny's brand of nationalism. Discussing Fanny's most celebrated poem, 'Hold the Harvest', Standish O'Grady wrote:

> I saw Parnell smile when those verses were read out in court during a State trial. It was a very pleasant smile, merry and natural, as if he were highly and affectionate amused at the dithyrambics of his little sister and playfellow. He did not regard landlords as 'coronetted ghouls'. [154]

Some of his attitude towards his sister's impassioned politics probably remained since the days of Temple Street, Rossa's trial, and kicking the 'tramps' down the steps; it is unlikely that he ever really warmed to her 'heroic' poetry. But others did, and made of it a sort of anthem. Fanny was only to become 'known' in the nationalist movement after her brother's rise to pre-eminence; but by 1875 she had taken up her position.

Little is known of the younger brother, Henry Tudor Parnell, who came into the Clonmore estate in 1871. He is mentioned by Emily Dickinson as being at an Avondale cricket-party in 1867, [155] and by 1874, she claims, 'Henry Parnell had married and turned to housekeeping and superintending babies, which he varied by mountain-climbing'. [156] Debrett, on the other hand, dates his marriage as 1882, and is more reliable. In any case, he was still a law student in 1874. He was admitted to Cambridge after going to school in Ireland (at St Columba's, Rathfarnham), unlike his brothers. Entering Trinity College, Cambridge in October 1868, he matriculated in 1869; [157] according to his brother John he finished his course there but was 'too nervous to take his degree'. In January 1872 he entered Lincoln's Inn to become a barrister, and was called to the Bar in 1875; [158] but, again according to John, he never practised. His life seems to have gone largely unrecorded.

In one sphere, however, Henry's activities are detailed more extensively than any of his siblings – the disposition of his property. I have described how he had been left an enormous but largely unpaid-for estate in Carlow; [159] his solution of the debt problem was to sell off the lands bit by bit instead of retaining the whole and making the revenue pay off the mortgage. Delia Parnell claimed that her son showed 'extraordinary business capacity' when he came of age 'in the rearrangement of his property and its sale to his tenants'. [160] Whatever about the business acumen shown, the sales were by no means always to 'the tenants', and when they were, were usually to very large-scale tenants indeed; it seems likely that Mrs Parnell's terminology in reviewing these events was influenced by later land-agitation demands.

The Clonmore estate as bought by John Henry Parnell had comprised, as I have stated elsewhere, a large part of the area of Co. Carlow that juts into the south-west corner of Wicklow; [161] no measurement is given for the entire estate, but by 1859 John Henry Parnell had sold off 886 acres [162] and an advertisement for the letting of the shooting in 1868 estimated the area as 7,800 acres. [163] It could initially have been even larger than these 8,686 acres, as Sir Ralph may have repossessed some of his ward's estate between 1859 and 1868 in return for a reduction in the sum owed him; the corner of Carlow in which it was situated, and where practically every townland named on the Ordnance Survey map is included in the estate inventory, measures about 13,000 acres. The income from the estate at this time was given by St John Ervine, probably from conversations with the John Howard Parnells, as £2,000 a year; [164] this low figure is explained by the fact that most of the lands as defined in the Registry of Deeds were held by fee farm lease on very low rents.

However, if the Clonmore income was not commensurate with the estate's physical extent, Henry Parnell certainly utilised the market potential to the full. A large number of memorials in the Registry of Deeds show that from 1874 to 1876 he sold off a total of 6,760 acres for £70,425.[165] At the end of 1874 he bought a more compact estate of 617 acres in Kilkenny for £5,850.[166] In 1859 the capital sum owed on the Clonmore estate was about £50,000;[167] even if no reduction in the size of the estate took place until Henry attained his majority and began selling it off, what he made from land sales must easily have covered the debt and left a large surplus. There was, moreover, more than a thousand acres not accounted for in the land sales recorded. On the lands sold, he retained head-rents of over £500 a year.[168] The Kilkenny estate was purchased before he had sold off all of Clonmore, and he had to borrow £3,600 for further land purchases in Carlow;[169] but a memorial of the following year records a payment of £1,500 to him 'in respect of the surplus proceeds in respect of the sale after payment of encumbrances' in the matter of his estate. Nor was his position as straightforward as simply the seller of an encumbered estate; he had begun to speculate, selling the lands in Carlow bought for £3,600 in 1874, and put in Charles's name, for a profit of nearly £1,000 the following year.[170] Henry's address at this time was recorded as Chapel Street, Park Lane, London, and it seems likely that the Kilkenny estate was bought purely for an income and as an investment for some of the money realised by the Clonmore land sales; he seems to have lived in London for most of his life, and the money he made from his land deals suggests that he could have lived comfortably off investments. An article in the *Celtic Monthly* in 1881 mentions that despite owning an estate in Kilkenny he spent much of the time travelling for the sake of his health;[171] at the time of his death he was living in Lausanne.[172]

The nature of Henry's extensive land sales deserves some comment. In practically every sale, he reserved the position of head landlord, receiving a head-rent and retaining rights of hunting and mining. In the case of smaller holdings the purchaser was often the incumbent tenant, with a local address; but generally the buyers seem to have had an eye merely to income or speculation. A Dublin stockbroker, J. A. Wilson, bought 493 acres for £1,250;[173] T. F. Caldbeck of Eaton Brae, Loughlinstown, Dublin and Bartholomew Warburton Rooke of Herbert Street, Dublin, paid £12,900 for 628 acres.[174] On a smaller scale, Miss Augusta Newton of Brighton bought 97 acres at Eagle Hill which she had been leasing for years; but these transactions were not at all the same thing as selling out to the occupying tenantry, which is what Mrs Parnell implied in later years.[175] John David Vanston of

Dublin bought 943 acres for £1,510,[176] obviously as an income; and in 1875 the biggest investment deal involved, interestingly enough, a consortium of Wicklow gentry. W. J. Westby of High Park, William Kemmis of Ballinacor and William Grogan of Taney Park, with Richard Long of Wiltshire and H. L. Lopes of Kensington, bought 1,785 acres for the enormous sum of £39,000.[177] After examining such transactions, and considering the total amount realised by Henry Parnell, the purchase of Clonmore makes sense; the investment potential of the estate was obviously large, and seems to have been well exploited by Henry. He was the only Parnell brother to do well financially out of his inheritance, and seems to have led a more regulated kind of life than his brothers; his stable financial position was probably an important factor in this.

In 1875, Anna Parnell was 23; her life up to this is only scantily recorded. She accompanied her mother in Paris, studied painting, and then attended an art college in England. Details of her youth are quoted in R. M. McWade's book as given in an undated article from *Truth*. She was 'a girl of a nervous, resolute disposition – wayward, a little snappish, and absolute mistress of the house; but she was liked by humble neighbours, with whom, in their trials, she often commiserated'.[178] Her 'febrile energy, which she took from the American side of the house' made her intolerant of people whom she saw as genteel humbugs, such as the rector of Rathdrum; her only friends round Avondale were the daughters of the local miller, named Comerford, and they were considered socially beneath her – besides not being clever enough for one

> who was a regular reader, even then, of New York and Boston journals, and ... dipped into the lectures of American oratoresses who stood on the equal rights platform; the mental inferiority to which women were condemned by ecclesiastical authority was accepted as a matter of course by the miller's pleasant daughters, but it galled Miss Anna and chilled her sympathy for them; if they had revolted against St Paul she would have been their close friend in spite of the Castle prejudices that stood between her and them.[179]

According to the same source, 'Miss Anna was old enough when Mrs Beecher Stowe was being lionised in Europe' to take an interest in the slavery controversy. *Uncle Tom's cabin* was in fact first published in England in 1853, when Anna was only a year old, but it is likely that the family interests in the Civil War, described by her brother, led her to consideration of this in any case. Destined to be better known than any of her immediate family except Charles, Anna's early life was nonetheless little recorded. (Her own rigidly impersonal approach to the study of history would no doubt have approved of this.)

Research about the youngest child, Theodosia, yields even less. Only a year younger than Anna, she was antithetical in character, being mild-mannered and completely conventional. She accompanied her mother to Paris and back to London, and seems to have done little of moment until her impeccable marriage in 1880. The *Wicklow Newsletter* records her playing and singing at Rathdrum church concerts,[180] and this seems typical of the undemanding way in which she passed her life. She was the only sister to have a happy marriage, and one of the few Parnells who enjoyed a happy and undisappointed life; from the point of view of records, an almost complete obscurity seems to have been the result.

Thus, as John Howard wrote, the Temple Street period and the early 1870s seemed to fix the fates of the Parnell children. The two distinct groups defined in my last section stand out still more clearly. One type – embracing Delia, Sophy, Theodosia and Henry – had all chosen quiet lives, and except for Sophy lived outside Ireland; all were to marry fairly young. Delia showed some neurotic tendencies and Sophy had distinguished herself by her bizarre elopement, but the lives of these four remain distinctly different from those of their brothers and sisters. For this reason they are less well recorded. Of the other group, Emily, Fanny and Anna had early on made their preferences clear and had stuck by them. Emily had insisted on marrying her unsuitable husband and was living from hand to mouth at Avondale; Fanny and Anna had declared for unfashionable opinions, spinsterhood, and a bias towards the bluestocking. John, as earlier in his life, retained elements of both groups; he left Ireland for America and a self-effacing life on a Southern farm, but returned and allowed himself to be persuaded briefly into politics. In this, of course, Charles was instrumental, belonging as he did most emphatically to the strong-minded of the Parnells. He disagreed with Emily's persistence in her marriage, laughed at Fanny's patriotic fervour, and more than likely disapproved of Anna's egalitarianism; but he remained closer in spirit to these sisters and John than to the quieter ones. He also retained a closer personal connection with them; this was certainly strengthened by the fact that, Emily apart, none of this group married until very late in life, if they married at all. The close connection with John, Fanny and Emily remained, on Charles's part, throughout his life; he was equally close to Anna until their politics estranged them.[181]

# 2    The young Parnell

I remember when we arrived at Lord Carysfort's the latter said
[to Charles]: 'Now that you have come home you must take up
your position in the county.'

(In 1873) J. H. Parnell,
*C. S. Parnell*, p. 117.

Mr. Parnell is a young gentleman of no ordinary talent and
capacity, and we hope ere long to see him assume that position in
his native county which his own talents and station as well as his
ancestral antecedents so fully entitle him.

*Wicklow Newsletter*, 29 June 1867,
reporting Parnell's coming of age.

## I

For Charles Stewart Parnell, the death of his father meant as great a
break as for his brothers and sisters. He had, however, been living at
home until 1859; the change to Dalkey life was not as great as in John's
case. As before, he was educated by desultory private tuition but by the
time he was sixteen, according to John Howard Parnell, his mother
decided that this was not sufficient: she consulted Lord Meath, who
recommended a private school at Chipping Norton in England run by
the Reverend Wishaw.[1] Writing to Sullivan in 1880, Mrs Parnell
stated that it was Lady Londonderry who recommended Mr Wishaw,
'an especially kind, highly educated and accomplished tutor';[2] at all
events, the supposedly patriotic Mrs Parnell seems to have had no
hesitation in choosing for her sons an English school patronised by
people of impeccable social standing.[3] John Parnell describes their
fellow pupils as 'Lord Brabazon, Mr Pilkington (later an M.P.) and
Louis Wingfield (a cousin of Lord Powerscourt)'.[4] The school appears
to have been a small-scale crammer's, and one which did not aim at a

particularly high standard; upon Charles's expressing a wish to enter Cambridge, 'a special master' had to be engaged for him. It seems likely that the school catered mainly for those backward in their studies; though Charles was sixteen and John nearly twenty when they went there in 1863, they were, according to John, the youngest pupils there.[5] Lord Brabazon was 22 in 1863, and was probably being 'crammed' for the Civil Service examinations, which he sat in that year.[6] Pilkington was probably Sir George Augustus Pilkington (knighted in 1893), who went on to become a surgeon at Guy's Hospital and was Liberal M.P. for Southport 1884–5 and 1899–1900.[7] At Wishaw's John Parnell was taught 'writing, spelling and recitation, as having only been in school in Paris, I had not made the progress I should have done with the English language'.[8] This sort of instruction was administered by Mr Wishaw himself; Charles's requirements seem to have been more exacting than the sort of education the school usually specialised in.

He did not, however, get on well with his 'special master', and criticised his abilities to his face;[9] however, the next year he 'took a keen interest in mechanics and altogether did fairly well at his lessons'.[10] A classmate of the Parnells at Chipping Norton told Barry O'Brien the celebrated story of Charles contradicting the lexicon, and went on to give an uncomplimentary picture of his character as a schoolboy: 'We all liked John, who was a very good, genial fellow; but we did not like Charles. He was arrogant and aggressive; he tried to sit on us and we tried to sit on him. That was about the state of the case'.[11] John however recalled his brother's experience of the school as happier.[12] Since the numbers attending the school were small, the Parnells had a classroom to themselves and lodged in a cottage opposite the rectory. The small size of the school must have meant that pupils and teacher came to know one another well; Mr Wishaw and his son later visited the Parnells in Dublin, and were taken by them on a tour of the West.[13] Mrs Parnell saw 'a great improvement' in her sons after Chipping Norton; they were probably educated more consistently there than they had ever been before.

After two years at Chipping Norton John went to the College of Mining at Stephen's Green, Dublin; Charles entered Cambridge in 1865, becoming a pensioner at Magdalene, then a 'fashionable but unacademic college'. The fact that entry requirements here were less stringent than at other colleges probably influenced his choice; his secondary education cannot have been unduly thorough. I intend to deal briefly with Parnell's university career; it has been ably discussed by Mr Ged Martin in an article called 'Parnell at Cambridge: the education of an Irish nationalist',[14] and there is little to add.

Though he matriculated in Michaelmas 1865 and remained at university until 1869,[15] Parnell left Cambridge without taking a degree. This was due to his temporary suspension owing to a court case in which he was prosecuted for assault. Perhaps it was because of this that his mother, writing to McWade, was evasive about Charles's university career:

> He was sent to Cambridge on account of his father having been there; besides, he had a great talent for mathematics, and that is a great mathematical college ... I think he did not remain at college the full term for graduation, on account of a disagreement between himself and one of the professors. He left of his own accord, as his self-respect prevented his yielding and asking pardon where he thought he had been unjustly treated. [16]

John Parnell, though more accurate, was similarly brief; outlining the details of the court case and pointing out that his brother could have returned the next term but refused. [17] On the subject of his brother's life at the university, John's information is equally sparse: 'His references to undergraduate days were very brief and reserved, though he appeared to have got on badly with the other fellows and to have had many quarrels, which often resulted in blows. [18] Barry O'Brien learned slightly more from an un-named contemporary of Parnell's. [19] His rooms were in the Pepysian buildings of Magdalene, below the library. [20] His tutor was Mr Mynors Bright and one of his lecturers (in mathematics) a Mr F. Patrick, who 'used often to describe how Parnell, when he had been given the ordinary solution to a problem, would generally set about to find whether it could not be solved equally well by some other method'. [21] O'Brien also repeats a story about Parnell's chivalry in attempting to protect his tutor during a town and gown commotion, and gives an authoritative and accurate account of the circumstances of his expulsion, supplied by a Fellow of Magdalene; but O'Brien's treatment of his hero is prone to hindsight and anticipation as regards the significance of Parnell's Cambridge record. [22]

An oblique reference to Parnell by a Cambridge contemporary refers to him as a man 'keen about nothing', [23] and his record in the official history of Magdalene is certainly brief and dry:

> He entered in 1865. His college career was short, for, having been convicted of assault, he was sent down in accordance with the rule in such cases. It is understood, however, that the Master would have allowed him to return if he had wished to do so. He appears to have had few friends in the college. [24]

Even his favourite pastime of cricket did not draw him much into college life; he is recorded as playing only two matches for Magdalene. [25] He joined the Boat Club, but refused to renew his subscription, to the disapproval of the committee. [26]

The only authority to dispute the general consensus that Parnell's college career was anti-social is Emily Dickinson, who describes a reckless and happy first year at University.[27] However, this is merely to set the tone for her apocryphal tale of Parnell's seducing a country girl near Cambridge, and is probably as fantastic as the rest of the chapter, in which Mrs Dickinson allowed her considerable imagination full rein in order to demonstrate that 'whatsoever a man soweth, that shall he also reap'.[28] Conviviality was indeed present, but in a different sense. A Magdalene contemporary recalled an element there of 'sons of monied parvenus from the North of England' who were looked down upon by the 'right' sort of undergraduates and who were susceptible to rowdyism;[29] Mr Ged Martin's study points out that Parnell's companions in the escapade which led to his rustication were probably of this type. Certainly a tendency to rowdyism is amply demonstrated by the account of the court case where Parnell was convicted of assault. O'Brien gives the brunt of this in his book, and a contemporary report is quoted at length in an appendix to this study.[30] There is in it little sign of the 'conflicting evidence' charitably referred to by John Parnell; the case was an open-and-shut one. Parnell had been drunk and abusive to a stranger in the street, as well as arrogant enough to offer a policeman a bribe 'to settle the affair' (an aspect of the case which, it surprisingly, the judge did not draw attention to in his summing-up [31]). It was not the only time that Parnell was up in court on a charge of disorderliness at this stage of his life,[32] which lends further weight to the plaintiff's case – if it were needed. Long afterwards, reminiscing about the incident, Parnell told two colleagues that his opponents were 'two swell students' who attacked him; whereas actually the other party was a respectable merchant dealing in manure.[33] Either he chose to remember it differently, or his listeners supplied the gloss themselves. Either way, this shows the mythologising of a piece of run-of-the-mill loutishness.

A College meeting of the Master and three Fellows was convened five days after the court hearing (26 May), and Parnell was rusticated for the remaining two weeks of term. Though such incidents were not uncommon (the Marquis of Queensberry, a contemporary of Parnell's, was involved in several), the fact of its being brought to court was what dictated the disciplinary action.[34] The whole affair compounds the general inauspiciousness of Parnell's Cambridge career; perhaps the only important result of these four years from 1865 to 1869 was to add to the sense of his inferiority in the matter of formal education which, according to his brother, he retained throughout his life.[35] That much was inevitable. His mother had never troubled herself over-much with seeing that he had a regular and systematic education; it was not surprising that, left to himself at university, he did not make a better showing. As is usual, he only came to regret this later. But at the time, the four years spent at Cambridge seem to have been little more than a casual and inglorious interlude.

In 1867, Charles had come of age and had gone to live at Avondale; I shall deal with this part of his life in detail. Before this, it is worth considering another important interlude in his life, after his ignominious return from Cambridge: his lengthy visit to America in 1871. He went there in search of a wife, the elusive Miss Woods;[36] but unlike his father he returned disappointed. It was nevertheless an instructive visit, and John Howard Parnell, who was with his brother much of the time, has left a memorable account of it.[37]

In the spring of 1871 Parnell set off to the United States to invest some money and to follow an American girl of whom he had become enamoured in Paris. After a disappointing visit to her in Newport he travelled south to join his brother in West Point, Alabama. To his astonishment, he enjoyed some of the food; he was further surprised by the large tract of land his brother had under cultivation, and the way it was worked by negroes, whom he viewed with distrust.[38] Parnell examined the local mills, went shooting, and met neighbouring farmers; a quarrel with the local Marshal about who should give way on a footpath nearly led to a fight, shelved when Parnell's relationship to the locally-respected John Howard was discovered.[39] He met Matt Hill, an uncle of the State senator, and discussed American politics with him. He experienced a cyclone, and by mistake shot a pig which got in under the piles of the house one night, a story which 'he used often to relate with great gusto in after-days at Avondale'.[40] When John Howard could leave his farm the brothers went on a visit to the coalfields of Alabama, staying in Birmingham, which John vividly describes as a pioneer mining town. They examined the Warrior coal-mine, which belonged to an Irishman,[41] and then Charles went on to New Orleans to visit a Parisian friend named Cliphart. He was to meet John a fortnight later, at Montgomery; the cable went astray, but they met accidentally and set off for Birmingham. Both brothers were prey to superstitiousness (allegedly a traditional weakness of Irish Protestants); their presentiment of danger was borne out by a serious rail accident *en route*, in which John received serious head and neck injuries.[42] Charles nursed him for a month in Birmingham, though himself affected by internal injuries. The patient was often visited by Father Galvin, an Irish priest 'related to the Father Galvin of Rathdrum who in after-days used to assist Charley in his political fights'. After a month they returned to West Point where John, now weakening in face of his brother's injunctions to leave this barbarian country and come home, began to dispose of his cotton crop and plan his return. The brothers travelled back via the Clover Hill mines in Virginia, spent Christmas in Jersey City, and sailed home on the S.S. *City of Antwerp* on 1 January 1872. 'Charles expressed his vivid delight at being home again, as he had never really enjoyed being in America'.[43]

Nonetheless his time there had been full of incident. It would have been highly uncharacteristic for him to have kept a journal as his father did thirty-seven years before, but one cannot help wishing that he had. His tour was of a very different sort, far closer to the people and to the rougher levels of American life; Newport was his only foray into the sort of American social round which both he and his father cordially disliked, but which had marked the latter's stay so conspicuously. His mother and uncle were in Paris, so their kind of society had no claims on him; he visited the industrially exploited South when the backlash of the Civil War was still bitterly felt, and it would be fascinating to know what he made of it. John's brief account is still instructive, if only because it shows clearly the extent to which he and Charles were close friends as well as brothers. When Charles next visited America it was to be as a public figure; this early acquaintance with the country probably formed the basis of his opinions about it. It was the last free expedition of the early part of his life; he now returned to Ireland and to Avondale and was expected, as Lord Carysfort put it to him, 'to take up his position in the county'.[44]

## II

A discussion of Parnell at this stage is more coherent when carried on with reference to the several aspects of his life rather than chronologically. Thus when considering his involvement with and life in Wicklow, I will discuss first of all the estate which represented his material stake in the county, then his pastimes, social life and character at this stage.

Avondale was let out until 1867 to Thomas Edwards, chief engineer with the Dublin, Wicklow and Wexford railway company. The scale on which the farm stock had been sold off [45] suggests that Mr Edwards used only the house; the demesne lands were probably rented by neighbouring tenants. But the gardens were well utilised, and won prizes for Edwards at the Rathdrum horticultural shows during this period.[46] The Edwards family seem to have entered fully into local society, Edwards continuing to lend the cricket lawn for local matches and one of his daughters being married from Avondale in 1864 to Frederick Wright of Emma Vale, Arklow.[47] When the young Parnells visited the estate they stayed at Casino, but were friendly with Edwards. It seems the family rented the house throughout this entire period (1860–7); the railway extension in the area was a lengthy business. Avondale itself was originally to be traversed by the new line in 1861, but a report of an extraordinary meeting of the company in that year shows that the idea was dropped; owing to projected

parliamentary opposition from 'the proprietor'; though 'the persons
acting for the minor' had agreed to the scheme.[48] It seems likely that
the opposition in Parliament would have come from Sir Ralph
Howard, who was an M.P. at the time. The 'persons acting for the
minor' who had become amenable to the project could have been Delia
Parnell and Charlotte Zouche, or Charles West, the agent of the
estate; a disagreement on this question could have been involved in the
Howard v. Zouche case, but this must remain conjectural. The new
line eventually went through Parnell's land at a later stage, because
his brother tells us that Charles received £3000 compensation from the
company.[49] For the moment, however, it was diverted.

Edwards must have vacated the house by June 1867; in this month
the *Wicklow Newsletter* fulsomely reported the coming of age of
Charles Stewart Parnell as 'a worthy young squire', and his tenants'
rejoicing:

> The coming of age of Charles Stewart Parnell, Esq., of
> Avondale, in this county, was celebrated with great rejoicing and
> festivity at the family residence at Avondale on Thursday the
> 27th instant by the tenantry, retainers and work-people of the
> property.
>
> Mr Parnell, who is deservedly popular amongst all those with
> whom he is in any way connected, was unavoidably absent on
> the occasion, important business in the Court of Chancery, in
> which he was a ward during his minority, having required his
> presence before the Lord Chancellor. But a plentiful and
> sumptuous entertainment was provided by his orders for all
> those who are in any way connected with the estate, and in fact it
> might be said for all comers, and we need scarcely say that Mr
> Parnell's hospitality was largely availed of.
>
> The rejoicing was opened with large bonfires which were kept
> abalze for a considerable time and were regarded as signals for a
> regular gathering of the merry-makers of the neighbourhood.
> Many were the jokes and long was the laughter which mingled
> with the crackling of the faggots of the joy-fires, and frequent
> and hearty were the wishes expressed for the health and
> happiness of the worthy young squire.
>
> After the company had partaken of the good cheer provided
> for them, the health of Mr Parnell was proposed in a speech well
> suited for the occasion by Mr John Kavanagh of Ballyknockan,
> one of the tenants of the estate, and seconded in a short but
> appropriate manner by Mr Laurence McGrath. The toast was
> received with the greatest manifestations of goodwill, and three
> times three given for Mr Parnell with a heartiness and a
> cordiality which were infinitely creditable alike to that

gentleman and his tenantry and people. Dancing and feasting were kept up till an advanced hour in the morning, when all parties quietly returned to their homes highly delighted with their entertainment.

It is with feelings of great pleasure that we give publicity to the above narrative of festivity and rejoicing, which we fully believe were neither more nor less than the occasion required. Mr Parnell is a young gentleman of no ordinary talent and capacity and we hope were long to see him assume that position in his native county which his own talents and station as well as his ancestral antecedents so fully entitle him. [50]

The position which Parnell was now expected to fill could not have been more clearly spelled out. He had come into an estate which, according to a legal memorial of the time, totalled 3,807 acres with a rent roll of £1,789 a year, [51] plus additional quit-rents and head-rents of £290 a year. The actual financial position of the estate is something I will discuss separately; [52] but Parnell did not waste time in trying to consolidate his holding. On 13 October 1870 he wrote to W. Mills King, who held the farm at Kingston for a head-rent of £200 a year, asking what price he wanted to sell out to Parnell; [53] King replied with an estimate which Parnell felt was 'a good deal beyond the mark', and he countered with an offer of £4,500, 'a sum I consider much over the market value'. Parnell added that King's title to Kingston would be easier proved to him then to a stranger. [54] These references are from letters of Parnell's; in view of them, the sum of £3,000 which J. H. Parnell names as being the price his brother paid for the Kingston head-rent can be disregarded. [55] But he does make clear that the deal went through.

There is also evidence that from the start he threw himself into the administration of those aspects of his inheritance which most interested him. In about 1869 John Howard found him 'busily engaged with his new sawmills at Avondale, where he was trying to make money out of the timber on the estate'; [56] this mill, according to John, Charles had had built with a view to supplying funds for their mother's entertaining: it was the only one in the county besides that of Captain Bookey at Derrybawn, a 'great friend' of Parnell's. [57] This involvement, begun in the 1860s, stayed with Parnell all his life. He returned precipitately from Paris and an amorous involvement in the spring of 1871 'owing to his presence being required at the sawmills'; [58] travelling in America in the same year, he noticed the design of a bridge over the Warrior river in Alabama and decided to sketch its covering structure, 'which he wished to adapt . . . for a roof which he proposed constructing at his new sawmills in Avondale'. [59] He went to considerable danger to draw it, while John watched apprehensively for

approaching trains. By 1872 his brother recorded that Charles's chief
interest at Avondale was 'in the timber, which by means of his
sawmills he manufactured into various articles in order to provide for
the growing demand which existed in America for Irish-made
articles'.[60] When mortgaging the estate at this time,[61] Parnell made a
special reservation of 'the full right of lopping, thinning and pruning
all timbers and other trees';[62] the preoccupation with his timber and
its potential never left him.[63]

The possibilities of the estate for timber and later for mining were
what interested him most; otherwise its administration continued as
before. The Avondale gardener continued to sweep all before him at
the Rathdrum Horticultural Show;[64] the squire went shooting every
autumn at the Aughavannagh shooting-box, as his father had done
before him.[65] Here there were also valuable peat-bogs, which Parnell
examined when on shooting trips with his friend and neighbour, W. J.
Corbet of Spring Farm,[66] his brother-in-law Arthur Dickinson, or the
gamekeeper Patrick O'Toole; because of these bogs, he later 'became
interested in the production of turf'.[67] Thus far, his life resembled his
father's: Cambridge, a visit to America, and return to Avondale and
involvement with the estate which was his inheritance. But even at this
stage it was only certain aspects of estate farming which really claimed
his attention, usually those with a mechanical bent and large
money-making potential; sawmills, fuel production and mining, all of
which used up the resources of the estate without putting much back
in. It is significant that the collection of agricultural tracts and
pamphlets itemised in the Avondale Library Catalogue are dated in
John Henry Parnell's day and not that of his son and heir.[68]

In other ways too Parnell's life at this period, when he immersed
himself in Wicklow society, resembled his father's. Like the latter,
much of his socialising revolved round cricket. As a boy he had played
the game with John and the work-boys on the estate; during this stay
at Chipping Norton he played at the nearby village of Churchill and
'got a high reputation as a bat, wicket-keeper and catch'.[69] Back in
Wicklow Avondale had continued to be the local centre of cricketing
activity even after John Henry's death; in 1861 a cricket team called
'Avondale' played at the house by courtesy of Thomas Edwards,[70] and
in the following summer both John and Charles Parnell played (albeit
without great distinction) for this side.[71] In the same year Charles
appeared on the Wicklow team, though John did not.[72] By July 1863
he was captaining the Avondale team against Ballyarthur.[73] Both
brothers played for Rathdrum in the same summer. 1864 saw full
involvement, Charles being appointed to the committee of the Co.
Wicklow Cricket Club and practice days for the Club team being held
at Avondale on Mondays and Fridays.[74] It was probably this era which
the *Wicklow Newsletter* recalled in 1890 as 'those days when on the

green award of Avondale Mr Charles Stewart Parnell encouraged and developed in his usual forcible and thorough-going style the theory and practice of "The King of Games" '.[75] During this summer he was 'a principal scorer' for Rathdrum v. Arklow [76] and 'played in splendid style'[77] against Leinster; he appears as one of the Wicklow team's principal bowlers in this season. Other teams Parnell played with at this period were Lord Fitzwilliam's Twenty-Two [78] and the Twenty-Two of Wicklow, Wexford and Carlow.[79] He became, as is well known, captain of the Wicklow Eleven; the story of his so-called dictatorship of the team has often been repeated. It appeared in the *Pall Mall Budget* and was repeated by Barry O'Brien. Standish O'Grady in 1894 claimed that he was 'responsible for this story, which has had a press circulation; I had it from one of the team'.[80] This is O'Brien's version:

> 'Before Mr Parnell entered politics', says one who knew him in those days, 'he was pretty well known in the province of Leinster in the commendable character of cricketer. We considered him ill-tempered and a little hard in his conduct of that pastime. For example, when the next bat was not up to time, Mr Parnell, as captain of the fielders, used to claim a wicket. Of course, he was within his right in doing so, but his doing it was anything but relished in a country where the game is never played on the assumption that this rule will be enforced. In order to win a victory he did not hesitate to take advantage of the strict letter of the law. On one occasion a match was arranged between the Wicklow team and an eleven of the Phoenix club, to be played on the ground of the latter in the Phoenix Park. Mr Parnell's men, with great trouble and inconvenience, many of them having to take long drives in the early morning, assembled on the ground. A dispute occurred between Mr Parnell and the captain of the Phoenix team. The Wicklow men wished their own captain to give in and let the match proceed. Mr Parnell was stubborn, and rather than give up his point, marched his growling eleven back. That must have been a pleasant party so returning without their expected day's amusement, but the captain did not care. In later years Mr Parnell used to use the Irish party much as he used the Wicklow Eleven'.[81]

There is no reason to doubt the veracity of this account; nonetheless, the way of relating it should be examined. A bias is evident from the first: the use of the word 'commendable' with reference to a reputation as a cricketer implies that Parnell's political character was *not* 'commendable'. The parallel between Parnell as cricketer and as politician is heavily implicit throughout, even before the direct reference in the last sentence. Parnell's insistence on the rules is

obviously emphasised with his usage of House of Commons procedure
in mind; both, to an opponent of his, would seem similarly
'unsporting'. And finally, in the captain who 'did not care' about his
men is seen the future dictator of the Irish Party.

Indeed, the very fact that this anecdote comes from one who knew
him in cricketing circles before his entry into public life presupposes
that the story-teller would be an opponent of the politics embraced by
Parnell. Cricket was the gentry's preserve, learnt by them in school in
England, and most practised when those public-school boys were home
in Ireland during the summer vacation. The names of the Wicklow
Eleven members repeat the litany of county families who ran the
affairs of the district in the period under survey. A typical entry in
Lady Alice Howard's diary for 1874 records: 'Went to a cricket match
at Ballyarthur – Brookes, Carysforts, Sir E. and Lady Grogan and
Parnells were there'.[82] Later in the same summer she went with Lord
and Lady Wicklow 'to a cricket match at Avondale – it was very
pleasant – all the county were there – but we were nearly consumed by
midges'.[83] For the followers of cricket, 'all the county' denoted a very
narrow compass. It is unlikely that the Wicklow gentry continued to
meet each other regularly at Avondale cricket-parties for many
summers after the occasions recorded by Lady Howard, as the owner
became more and more deeply immersed in a brand of politics so
repugnant to most of his fellow-players. Mrs O'Shea recorded that 'he
never went to matches after he entered Parliament'.[84] But at the
period of Parnell's life under review, cricket and all it meant was an
important social focus for his activities; and even far later, a fortnight
before his death, he was able to recognise on a Dublin street someone
with whom he had played cricket at Avondale thirty-five years before,
and had not seen since.[85]

A less typical interest for a country gentleman of his class was his
consuming preoccupation with amateur mechanics. John Howard
wrote that at this time 'Charley was a great practical mechanic and
devoted much of his time to engineering pursuits, so that his life at
Avondale was a very busy one';[86] further evidence is found in his
fascination with the cotton-factories, grist-mills and coal and iron
mines which he found in America.[87] His interest in the Warrior River
Bridge, to which he returned again and again, is indicative of the man
who was to find his greatest relaxation from the pressures of public life
in launching 'unsinkable' model ships from Brighton Pier.

Not all his pastimes, however, were so idiosyncratic. He joined the
Wicklow Rifles in February 1865, as befitted a Wicklow landowner;[88]
according to his brother, an additional reason was that 'by doing so he
would be able to wear uniform at the Castle, as he disliked the levée
dress, declaring that it looked too much like a footman's livery'.[89] At
the same time John joined the Armagh Light Infantry, and both

brothers underwent preliminary training at the Royal Barracks before joining their regiments; they both became immersed in the accompanying social round.[90]

In the country he entered into similarly predictable pursuits. While still living at Temple Street he used to go down to Wicklow and occasionally to Clonmore on shooting-parties;[91] he went to Aughavannagh annually for the grouse, sometimes with his neighbour, Lord Carysfort.[92] His brother does not mention riding a great deal, but Mrs Dickinson recalls that in the 1860s he loved hunting.[93] She describes Parnell thoughtfully walking his mount home 'after a heavy day with the Wards', and how her brother only gave up 'his favourite recreation' when a doctor erroneously told him he had a weak heart.[94] Whatever about this, he remained fond of riding, and Mrs Dickinson told Barry O'Brien that they used to ride all over the county together.[95] He was similarly fond of walking, preferring to walk alone than in company.[96]

His amusements were, in short, not sedentary. Barry O'Brien's quotation from John Parnell is well known: ' "Did you ever see him read in those days?" I asked . . . "The only book I ever saw him read", he said, "was that" (Pointing to Youatt's *The Horse*) "and he knew that very well" '.[97] Parnell himself gave weight to the idea that he was no great reader; he told a university audience in 1877 that he knew little of Irish history and learnt that late in life,[98] and a newspaper reporter in 1880 remarked upon the dearth of modern works in the Avondale library and the fact that the owner only seemed to use parliamentary Blue Books and a few books on Ireland.[99]

This implication is borne out by an examination of the Avondale Library Catalogue of 1901.[100] The vast majority of the collection is from the eighteenth or early nineteenth century; very few of the important lots auctioned at this time are dated from Parnell's lifetime – in fact, none except for Hansard, Webb's *Irish biography* (inscribed to Anna Parnell), Froude, Joyce's *Place-names*, Lewis Carroll, issues of *Hearth and Home and Forest and Stream*, Murray on the horse, Folkard on water-fowling, Geikie on geology, and a good deal on mining and mechanics: Greenwell on mine-working, Richards on wood-working machines, Gibbs on architecture, and several architectural and building magazines. All these books comprise only about twenty of the 400 lots auctioned. The greatest part of the library dates from William Parnell's time and reflects his tastes. There are all the classics; eighteenth-century parliamentary records; Walker's *Siege of Derry;* many archaeological folios of the same period; *Pacata Hibernia;* Strafford's *Letters;* several Parliamentary Commission reports; Leland; local Irish histories; Sir John Davies; *Irish Pamphlets;* Spencer, Moryson, Molyneux, Curry, Borlase, Sir James Ware; Henri Bayle; a large collection of political pamphlets; old English histories

(Yarrington, Baker, Fuller and Ashmore). The list, in fact, reads like a bibliography of one of William Parnell's own treatises. There are also the magazines of his time – *Scribner's, The Eclectic, Pranceriana* and the *Edinburgh Review,* as well as many more. The collection of William Parnell is the nucleus of the library, and is what brings it well above the standard of the average country house. Other books seem to be random later additions, and reflect the different interests of his descendants. Anna and John would have been interested in Holbein's *Portraits* and a Hogarth folio; Mrs Delia Parnell probably supplied the American travel books and Thomas Jefferson's collected works. Many books of heraldry, peerages and baronetages testify to her preoccupation with birth and descent; most are dated from the mid-century. Emily's interests are reflected in folios on horsemanship, and Fanny's by volumes of Victorian poetry. The interests of the family are, in fact, profiled vividly and accurately by the library. As an entity, nonetheless, it is overshadowed by William Parnell's collection, coherent and showing a dominant taste; the additions are random and of unexceptional literary interest. But those first listed above as dating from Charles Stewart Parnell's lifetime show his own interests clearly – politics, riding, shooting, geology, mining, mechanics – and there is little, except for Lewis Carroll,[101] that is there purely for the pleasure of reading.

Besides being occupied by his own particular interests, Parnell seems to have led a fairly active social life at this stage. According to his brother he had 'many social duties ... The Wicklow county families constantly entertained him, and no invitation to Avondale was ever refused'.[102] About 1870, John Howard wrote:

> I found Charles still down at Avondale, busy with his sawmills, his cricket-matches and his parties. My mother was then living in Paris, as Temple Street had been given up and the family scattered, never again to meet all under the same roof. Charley often got invitations to Paris, to balls at the British Embassy, and thought nothing of making a flying trip to France to attend one; in fact, I do not think he ever missed one.[103]

But apart from such forays, his life centred round Wicklow. Here he 'spent a good deal of his time riding and hunting and dancing' with a Miss C–[104] who lived nearby,[105] but the relationship was a friendship rather than a romance. As I have mentioned, the county gathered at Avondale to play cricket, and John Parnell told Barry O'Brien that at this time 'they used to have dances in this hall [at Avondale] and the band used to be placed in the gallery'. Lady Alice Howard at Shelton entertained 'Charlie Parnell' for a shooting-party in 1874, where with Lord Listowel, Mr Brooke and Lord Wicklow, he killed 636 birds.[106] The Howards sometimes 'drove in the phaeton to Avondale' from

Shelton for a visit,[107] and Charles and Fanny Parnell came to lunch at Shelton and played tennis afterwards.[108] The Howard ladies' diaries record a life where Carysforts, Symes, Tighes, Brookes, Bayleys, Powerscourts and Howards lived in each other's pockets, constantly visiting with each other and meeting incessantly in Dublin as well as Wicklow; the Parnells were, though to a lesser extent, involved in this caucus of county society.

Politics were to sever this connection; a hint of this comes in Lady Alice's entry in her journal after the 1874 Wicklow election, which does not mention John Parnell's candidature, and laments only that Lord Fitzwilliam was beaten by Dick and O'Byrne, a Home Ruler.[109] John Parnell wrote that Lord Carysfort, who in 1873 encouraged Charles to 'remain here and take up your position in the county', later disapproved of his brother's politics to the extent that he refused to speak to him.[110] This is, however, the concern of the next section of this work.[111] Up to 1875, all the evidence is that Charles mixed fully in the kind of county society for which his birth and conditioning intended him.

In this connection, Emily Dickinson devotes a whole chapter to describing a three-day cricket match organised by Charles and Arthur Dickinson in July 1867 to celebrate the former's coming of age.[112] This description furnished St John Ervine with most of the material for his condemnation of the Avondale household as 'roistering' and 'Leveresque'. After, according to Emily, deciding on 'a real spree', Charles organised a match for the Wicklow Eleven against the Dublin officers' garrison team, to be played at Avondale. Twelve officers, a Mrs Moore and her daughters, the Dickinsons, Charles and Henry Parnell were all at Avondale for the three days. There was also a Mr Frederick C–, described casually by Mrs Dickinson as 'one of my latest admirers'.

> Numerous invitations were sent to the county gentry and also to friends and acquaintances in Dublin, from whence a military band had been bespoken, and the fame of this having got abroad enhanced considerably the importance of the event . . . tents and marquees were erected . . . the ballroom was swept and the floor polished.[113]

The first day, she continues, started with luncheon in 'the grand, medallioned dining-room' and continued after the cricket with dinner, dancing and champagne. The 'county Magnates' were all in attendance. Cricketing concentration began to lapse on the second day, and the players, to Charles's annoyance, openly preferred to dally in the woods with the ladies of the party:

> Now commenced a scene of fun and flirtation which surpassed

description and which had probably never before been equalled
as the old haunts of Avondale. In every shady nook and corner
were to be seen an isolated couple engaged in the pleasant
pastime of love-making.[114]

The hosts were not exempt from this; Arthur, in fact, had to be
dissuaded from beating up Emily's 'latest admirer'. The party on the
second night went on and on, and a young widow from Dublin who
had arrived down received the next day a letter from her solicitor
requesting her to leave as 'from rumours which had reached him with
reference to the festivities at Avondale . . . it was evident that the
house was not fit for her'.[115] Cricket was resumed the following
morning, but Charles encouraged the convivial officers to leave on a
train at midnight, as a third night would not be desirable.

The county families . . . bade hostess and host goodnight,
expressing with seeming sincerity grateful thanks for the
pleasant time they had had, but notwithstanding that they had
partaken of Charles's hospitality and enjoyed themselves
immensely, afterwards professed themselves much shocked and
abused the whole entertainment roundly.[116]

If all was exactly as described, this is not altogether surprising.
Emily's account should not, however, be taken at face-value. It has the
flavour of an often-reminisced-over story which has gained
considerably in the telling. Furthermore, as regards the large
conclusions which St John Ervine drew from the affair, the whole
tenor of the account suggests that it was not typical of Avondale life.
And it was both instigated and organised by Emily and the egregious
Arthur, whereas Charles tried to keep it strictly as a cricket-fixture,
sent the officers home early, complained about distractions, and ended
by saying: 'The next cricket match I have I won't have any ladies, or
at least only ugly ones.'[117] Finally, the occasion is not mentioned in the
*Wicklow Newsletter*, which always faithfully reported even the
smallest fixture. Bearing Mrs Dickinson's addiction to hyperbole in
mind, the whole affair was probably on a much smaller scale than she
implies.

The Dickinson's residence at Avondale at this time, however, must
have affected social life there, and Arthur's influence on Charles, then
in his early twenties, probably did lead to a certain amount of
roistering. This contention is borne out by a court case reported in the
*Wicklow Newsletter* of 24 September 1869. Headed 'A Fracas in a
Hotel', the account is of a case brought against Charles Stewart
Parnell and Arthur Dickinson at the Rathdrum Petty Sessions by
Ralph Jordan, proprietor of the Glendalough Hotel, 'for being
disorderly in the hotel on the night of the 27th July last'. Jordan stated

that Dickinson had entered the private sitting-room of a Mr and Mrs Coleman, two English guests, 'with his hat on', and on being asked to leave had retired upstairs to a room he was sharing with Parnell. When the Colemans began to play the piano downstairs Parnell and Dickinson interrupted them, demanding a dance, and were again turned away. They then took up positions in a conservatory adjacent to the Colemans' room and refused to leave, depositing their coats in the sitting-room and beginning to drink brandy and smoke cigars, while the Colemans 'received much annoyance' from them. Jordan sent for the police, but there were none in the barracks. Eventually, 'threats and blows were given and returned between the parties on both sides; a scene of the utmost confusion ensued, and it was some time before the gentlemen were separated'.

The defendants actually denied very little of this, stating that they had had every right to be where they were and that Dwyer (a friend of the Colemans) had struck the first blow. But the magistrates' judgement was completely and surprisingly in their favour:

> They thought that the fact of any person refusing to leave merely the room of a hotel was not an offence within the meaning of the Act of Parliament, and should therefore dismiss the case against Mr Parnell and Captain Dickinson; and, as they considered Mr Dwyer was to blame for commencing the disturbance, they should fine him five shillings and costs.

Understandably, Dwyer's solicitor asked for an increase in the fine so that he could appeal against the judgement; but he was refused. The magistrates' decision is, however, less extraordinary when it is seen that one of them was Captain Bookey and the other Charles Frizell; both were neighbours and social equals of Parnell, and Bookey was a particular friend of his.[118] It would have been most surprising if a hotelier from Glendalough had prosecuted the squire of Avondale at the latter's local Petty Sessions and had won his case. Parnell's tendency to aggressiveness has already been seen in several embroilments on his American tour, as well as in the celebrated assault at Cambridge; living with someone of Dickinson's temperament and drinking habits cannot have done anything to ameliorate this.

However, a tendency to make a nuisance of himself when drunk did not distinguish Parnell particularly from the rest of his class in Ireland; rather, in fact, the opposite. He was, moreover, very conscious of being one of the gentry, a fact John Howard draws attention to when describing his brother's reaction to visiting one of the more prominent citizens of Birmingham, Alabama:

> Charley, owing to his proud disposition, was greatly afraid of being mistaken for the usual Irish emigrant, the only class of our

countrymen who were to be found in these parts, and before we
went round to Colonel Powell he said to me: 'For God's sake,
John, when we see Colonel Powell don't tell him that we are
from Ireland as they have never seen a real Irish gentleman and
wouldn't know one if they did' ... However, it was already
known that we had come over from Ireland, though that did not
seem to do us much harm. Colonel Powell was an educated and
travelled man and, as we soon learned, quite recognised the
difference between the Irish emigrant and the capitalist seeking
investments. [119]

The same attitude is revealed in comments of Parnell's quoted by his
brother after they had visited a State governor: he felt that they had
been 'despised' for being Irish, and smarted under it. [120] He was always
conscious of social standing, and while in America disliked rough
company, and in particular negroes, as much as his father had. [121] But
where this attitude is most important is of course in the apparent
anomaly of his espousal of Nationalist politics. His brother noticed
this; in 1872, when John suggested that Charles enter Parliament in
support of Butt's tenant right movement, his brother answered: ' "I
would not, because I would not join that set." His pride, in other
words, prevented him moving with the Home Rulers of that time,
because they were beneath him in station'. [122] The question of the
extent to which a country gentleman was compromising his social
position by associating himself with Home Rule politics at this time is
an issue which I will deal with later. But it should be noted that one of
the members elected for Wicklow in 1874, Mr O'Byrne, was described
as a 'Home Ruler' and yet was a J.P., had been High Sheriff of the
county, had residences at Cabinteely House, Cabinteely, Glenealy in
Wicklow, and a house in Middlesex, and was a member of the
Athenaeum Club in London [123] – in other words, he was a Wicklow
country gentleman and lived as one. T. P. O'Connor, talking to R. M.
McWade in 1891, claimed that except for George Henry Moore, the
Irish cause was at this time 'abandoned by the country gentlemen, who
in other times had occasionally rushed out of their own ranks and
taken up the side of the people'; [124] but he went on to admit that the
1871 Kerry election returned Rowland Blennerhasset, who like
Parnell was 'a landlord, a Protestant and a Home Ruler. The time had
apparently come when constitutional agitation had a fair chance, and
when men of property who sympathised with the people would be
welcomed into the National ranks'. [125] There were other Home Rule
M.P.s like Esmonde and King-Harman, who were very much of
Parnell's class. This is to anticipate. But the point is nonetheless
relevant, that entry into nationalist politics was by no means a
negation of the consciousness of social standing characteristic of
Parnell in his youth, and in some ways may have reinforced it.

The social position which Parnell held, and his consciousness of it, presupposed some involvement with the affairs of the county. He was probably more than ready for this. Always proud of Wicklow – Barry O'Brien heard him say 'I am an Irishman first but a Wicklow man afterwards'[126] – the years when he lived uninterruptedly at Avondale as local squire were, according to John, 'the happiest period of my brother's life'.[127] Mrs Parnell emphasised her son's consciousness of his local position in her letter to Sullivan, ludicrously over-emphasising the seignorial position of the lord of Avondale;[128] but Parnell's position did imply a certain duty to the locality, and after taking over his inheritance he began to answer its call. From 1873 he was a J. P. and Grand Juror in the Wicklow Assizes;[129] during 1874–5 he was High Sheriff for the county.[130] At the annual Wicklow Races he held the position of Steward, along with Lord Fitzwilliam, the Earl of Wicklow, the Marquis of Downshire and other local notables.[131] After 1870 he became a member of the Synod of the Church of Ireland; he was proposed as a select vestryman in July 1870.[132] These again were more social than religious obligations. Unlike his father, however, he was not on the Board of Guardians of Rathdrum Poor Law Union.[133]

His performance as magistrate was not as remarkable as latterday stories liked to claim. The priest of his local parish wrote, when recommending him to a constituency, that 'though he is the youngest of our bench of magistrates the others defer to his opinion and when a knotty question arises postpone it till he can be present';[134] but in the period from 1873 to 1874 Parnell's presence at Rathdrum Petty Sessions is only recorded once.[135] R. M. McWade tells a story of Fanny Parnell prosecuting a man for cruelty to a donkey when Charles was sitting on the bench, and the latter fining him thirty shillings;[136] the genesis of this story must be in an account reported in the *Wicklow Newsletter* of 3 October 1874 which records that it was Parnell himself who prosecuted one Thomas Cooper for cruelty, and, when the defendant was fined two pounds ten shillings and costs, asked for the fine to be reduced, as 'his sole object in coming forward was to teach persons like the defendant that they cannot ill-treat poor dumb animals'. Parnell's own attendance as magistrate was perfunctory, at least at this stage. But the mere fact of his being one, and of being High Sheriff as young as twenty-eight shows that he was entering into the round of local duties and 'taking up his position in the county'.

There was so far very little in his life and development which was at odds with his background and position; this is also true of his love-life, which involved a certain amount of romance, though no more than was to be expected. At school in Chipping Norton, his brother records that Charles had a sweetheart in the neighbourhood;[137] always an exceptionally good-looking man, he early became accustomed to admiration. An Italian governess of Emily's 'took a great fancy to

Charles',[138] and in Wicklow society he 'was invited out a good deal and
was a thorough favourite with the girls'.[139] At viceregal balls, he
'danced with all the pretty girls',[140] but his first 'really serious
entanglement', according to John, was with an American girl whom he
encountered in Paris, probably about 1870, at a time when he was
frequently visiting his family there and 'was strongly urged by his
uncle to marry one of the heiresses whom he was constantly
meeting'.[141] The lady in question happened to be rich, but from
Charles's point of view it was a genuine love affair. 'Their engagement
was everywhere recognised'; Charles visited her family in Rome in
autumn 1870 and, returning to Avondale, 'prepared the house for the
reception of his expected bride'.[142] In 1871, however, she precipitately
returned to America and when he followed her there he was told that
'she did not intend to marry him, as he was only an Irish gentleman,
without any particular name in public'.[143] John implies that the girl's
parents influenced her against the match. He records that Charles was
depressed and melancholy for weeks after the blow, and when he
recovered 'his attitude towards women for many years afterwards was
a cold and even a suspicious one'.[144] In 1880 John and Theodosia
called on Miss Woods, the faithless fiancée, in Newport, She was now
married, and they had the satisfaction of hearing her express her
regret at not having married their brother – 'How happy we would
have been!'

John Parnell placed great emphasis on the importance of this early
involvement:

> Had it turned out as he expected, it would have meant his living
> a contented and comfortable life at Avondale, on the Continent,
> or in America. His jilting undoubtedly helped to drive his
> energies into politics, for he was deeply hurt at the idea of being
> considered a country gentleman without any special abilities.[145]

Emily Dickinson also said that 'his entrance into a parliamentary
political career had its origin in a woman',[146] and told a similar story
but in a garbled version.[147] Much of this seems fantasy, with
conversations freely recounted verbatim, and all the other trappings of
Emily's unreliable romancings. But Parnell himself bore out his
brother's tale by telling T. P. O'Connor that it was a jilting that
brought him into politics.[148]

Totally unreliable, however, is a story to which Emily gave
currency, about a local farmer's daughter who was seduced and
abandoned by her brother while he was at Cambridge.[149] Henry
Harrison and Dr Ged Martin criticised this account pertinently, and it
is not even worth examining in detail. Indeed, Emily practically admits
she made it up: 'Remembering chance words and allusions and the
sudden termination of his college career ... I discovered with a flash of
insight the whole cause of his altered and careworn looks.'[150] The

'flash of insight' obligingly supplied a wealth of circumstantial detail as well as the novelettish outline; neither deserves serious consideration. Before Harrison's refutation, Henry Tudor Parnell went to some trouble to discredit his sister's story; when her book appeared in 1906 he corresponded with the Master of Magdalene, receiving corroboration that no such incident had ever been heard of, and wrote to the newspapers denying that there was any veracity in the tale.[151] Emily told Henry that she had the story from their mother and Sir Ralph Howard (both conveniently dead), thus contradicting her own assertion that she and Arthur 'discovered' the secret from Charles himself. Henry, who believed both this assertion and the subsequent contention of Emily's that the incident was the reason why Charles was left nothing by Sir Ralph's will, went on to deduce that 'some interested person' who would benefit from their uncle's estate put the tale about to discredit Charles. However, Howard's will had been made long before 1869, and Charles was never intended to be beneficiary of it. The genesis of the story was in Mrs Dickinson's sensation-hungry and slightly unbalanced imagination; there is no need to look further.

It was by no means unnatural that Parnell remained unmarried, especially with an abortive love-affair behind him. Besides being personally attractive, he was well-off and independent; the Miss C— and Miss P—[152] of neighbouring county families, whom he squired and whose fathers would have liked to see marry him, were kept at a distance; so was another American beauty, to escape from whom he fled to Paris in 1873.[153] He was, in fact, 'a catch' and probably knew it. There is no reason to be surprised at his marital caution, much less to credit the apocryphal stories invented to 'explain' it.

'I have so little to go upon as regards things spoken', wrote John Parnell of his brother's character, 'and as regards things written, nothing at all'.[154] Any student of Parnell encounters the same difficulty. When those who knew him recalled his character, they were always influenced by his 'image', the reputation of a proud, impassive man of iron, which was generated by his parliamentary eminence. One of the most valuable aspects of John Parnell's book is that it recalls his brother as he was before the image took over. Though he often refers forward to Parnell's aloofness, 'the robe that attracted the loyalty and even the wild enthusiasm of his own countrymen, while at the same time repelling their intimacy',[155] John also unequivocally admits that he found 'just a trace of affectation in this sphinx-like attitude towards the world in general';[156] he had, after all, known him before.

John was doubly entitled to make such an observation, because he knew his brother better than anyone else – except Mrs O'Shea. John's treatment of Charles's character in the period under review is endlessly instructive, because it isolates two ostensibly contradictory traits. One was the legendary 'closeness' – 'My idea is to mind my own affairs and leave other people's alone' [157] and the other was a marked tendency to be aggressively disputative: 'Charley was very fond of arguing; we all said he would have made a splendid lawyer, for, try as we would, we could never get the better of him in argument'. [158] Without adopting an unduly psychological approach, it is still possible to see a certain conflict in Parnell's character between introvert and extrovert characteristics; the latter seem to have been more natural to him, but, in much the same way as his early schooling suppressed his rowdiness, his later experience seems to have subdued his aggressiveness.

This conflict went with a certain tension always noticeable in Parnell's make-up. At Chipping Norton, according to his brother, 'his highly-strung, nervous temperament was even then noticeable'; [159] at this time too his 'closeness' became characteristic. [160] In Alabama, following his rejection by Miss Woods, he lapsed completely into melancholia. [161] Sleep-walking was characteristic of him, and is mentioned in connection with his American visit and with his sojourn at Cambridge; [162] this tendency is often discussed in conjunction with something called, by both Barry O'Brien and John Parnell, 'nervous attacks'. [163] He seems, in fact, to have been of an exceptionally nervous temperament; after the railway accident in America, he insisted on travelling outside, on the steps of the last carriage, in case he had to jump off. [164] This sort of nervousness is usually mentioned in conjunction with Parnell's over-emphasised susceptibility to superstition, but his brother categorically relates this tendency to his later life. [165] Moreover, 'spiritualism and palmistry ... he always regarded with great contempt, and laughed at Fanny and myself for going round to have our fortunes told'.

What comes through most strikingly at this stage of his life is Charles Stewart Parnell's strong-mindedness. He had grown up used to getting his own way, and according to his brother 'was used to having his slightest whim obeyed'. [166] Thus when he turned to the unwilling John before the 1874 Wicklow election 'and said "John, we must run you," I knew that his mind was made up and that I must either follow the course he had set for me or break with him once for all'. [167] Others were not favourably impressed by this characteristic; one remembers the Earl of Meath's description of him as 'arrogant and assertive'. The thread of aggressiveness that appears in several of Parnell's American encounters [168] is repeated in the court cases where he appeared as defendant, in Cambridge and Rathdrum. But this was not an uncommon characteristic of the young country gentlemen of his era and his background. There is no real evidence that it ever made him unpopular – much, indeed, to the contrary. [169] His active social life alone is an indication of this. But he had strong opinions on what to do and what not to do. It is significant that he abandoned his pursuit of Miss Woods as 'undignified' [170] and that in a mining town during his American visit he was 'thoroughly disgusted with this mode of living, as he had always been accustomed to the best of everything and did not relish sitting down to dinner with a very ruffianly-looking crowd'. [171] I have already mentioned his well-developed sense of social standing.

But with these unexceptional traits, there remained unpredictable depths – such as for instance the great mental application he could bring to bear on a subject in which he had a special interest. John Parnell sums up the background to the 'enigmatic' nature of his brother's character with reference to this:

> Charles kept his own counsel even as a boy. As a man this trait was developed to such an extent that it was only on very rare occasions that one caught a glimpse of the real man beneath the courteous but frigid exterior ... It must be remembered that then as ever he was always a questioner rather than an informant. He wanted to get every scrap of information and every shade of opinion on any subject in which he took a real interest but at the same time he did not like disclosing his own views, especially when they were, so to speak, in the melting-pot. Once he arrived at a definite opinion he used to express it (and then only when he considered such an expression of opinion to be absolutely unavoidable) in as few words as possible, giving no reasons, however, for his having arrived at that opinion.
>
> As he gradually grew out of childhood this reserve of Charley's became more and more accentuated. The greater portion of it was undoubtedly due to a mixture of nervousness and pride resulting in a sort of shy repulsion towards allowing his inner thoughts and real nature to appear on the surface, to be at the mercy of the multitude. [172]

But, he adds carefully, there was also a trace of affectation in this attitude. This is the sort of salt, added in painstakingly measured quantities, which makes John Parnell's diffident reflections doubly valuable – most of all at this patchily recorded period of his brother's life.

## III

Dealing with this stage of Parnell's life, his brother refers to him as 'a pretty well-to-do country gentleman'; [173] on the face of it, there seems no reason to doubt that contention. Avondale was a lucrative and extensive estate; there were also farms in Kildare and a share in the Dublin property which had been included in Hayes's bequest. [174] According to John, Charles had enough money to be able to invest in American mines, even though 'he had ... to keep the whole of the family, who had no money except the small annuities coming to them out of my property in Armagh'. [175] As early as 1869 Parnell was considering investing in American interests; in 1871, when he set off in pursuit of Miss Woods, he did so 'after discussing American investments with his uncle [Charles Stewart] ... [and] armed with several business letters of introduction'. [176] He already had invested in the Clover Hill coal-mine in Virginia, along with his mother and his uncle; [177] a visit to coal and iron fields in Birmingham, Alabama, interested him greatly and he decided to put £3,000 into them. [178] A partnership agreement was drawn up with the owners, whereby Parnell was to put up £3000 capital; he was also interested in buying up pine-lands nearby, where John believed the coal seam continued, at only a dollar an acre. [179] But his stubbornness and his insistence on complete control led to an impasse in the negotiations, and he neither invested the £3,000 nor bought up the pine-lands. [180] He retained his interest in American investments, however, and John describes him on the train back to New York, sitting up all night discussing finance with his broker. [181] Charles's departure from America was, in fact, complicated by his being hounded by 'a Wall Street sharper who had heard that he had only just come over from Ireland and had persuaded him before going South to contract for some shares in a bogus company'. [182] The 'sharper' entered a lawsuit against Parnell, who felt it prudent to remain in New Jersey until he left. John gives no details about this, and does not say whether his brother actually parted with any money; the incident is interesting for showing the extent to which Parnell's American trip was involved with finance.

His interest remained. In 1872, on a visit to Paris, he discussed American finance endlessly with his uncle, who was expected to leave him something on his death. [183] This expectation was not fulfilled. But looking at Charles Stewart Parnell's fortunes as indicated in his brother's book, one feels that the legacy was not especially needed. With a valuable property behind him and money to invest abroad, Parnell appears as a more than ordinarily well-off country gentleman.

This is, however, only half the story. Evidence in the Registry of deeds shows that not only was the Avondale estate encumbered by far more than the family expenses mentioned by John Parnell, but Parnell himself must have been in debt by the early 1870s; and to some extent the claims on his estate which initially occasioned the celebrated Parnell Tribute of 1883 originated long before his entry into politics.

When he came of age in 1867, he provided his guardians, Sir Ralph Howard and Robert Johnson, with a mortgage on Avondale in return for an extension of loan for a sum of £1,500, which he owed them on behalf of his father's debts; [184] two years later C. M. West, his ex-agent, obtained judgement against him in the Court of the Queen's Bench for £7,000. [185] No details of the case are recorded in the Irish Law Reports, nor is there any account of it elsewhere, and I cannot ascertain what occasioned the lawsuit; but only £3,500 was paid over after the judgement, security for the rest being Parnell's Kildare farms, some of the Wicklow estate, and his share of the houses in Stephen's Green. [186] This outstanding £3,500, at a rate of six per cent interest per annum, remained unpaid until September 1883; [187] the National Tribute had reached £15,000 by this month, [188] though it was not paid over until December, and it seems probable that the expectation of it provided the wherewithal to pay the debt.

Nor was this the only liability incurred by Parnell in 1869 – or by any means the largest. In this year he mortgaged the estate to George Woulfe of Bishop's Lane, Kildare, and Paul Askin, of 40 Lower Sackville Street, Dublin, for £12,000. [189] The reasons for his need of this large sum go back over half a century, to William Parnell's bequest to his daughter Catherine (Charles Stewart Parnell's aunt) of £10,000, drawable on Avondale. Catherine, while retaining her claim to this, had not demanded it from her brother John Henry. When she died (12 September 1867) she left to her husband, George Vicesimus Wigram, 'absolutely all that she had power to give, including the sum of ten thousand pounds wherein described, as then lent to her brother'. [190] By 1870, when Wigram received the administration of the estate, Charles Stewart Parnell had come into full possession of 'the hereditaments charged with the said two several sums of five thousand pounds'. Wigram, though a member of the Brethren, does not appear to have shared the attractive lack of interest in money so characteristic of Lord Congleton; he required the ten thousand pounds from Parnell so peremptorily that the latter had to instruct Woulfe and Askin to pay it out at once, even before all investigations necessary for closing the loan had been completed. What happened was, in effect, that the mortgage which Catherine Wigram could have claimed on Avondale was transferred to Woulfe and Askin, for £12,000, £10,000 of which had to be paid over at once to Catherine's heir. The estate was, as mentioned above, already liable to a loan of £1,500 from Parnell's guardians; by an agreement of 1871, they undertook to allow priority to the repayment of the far larger debt to Woulfe and Askin. [191] A mortgage dated 1872 shows that the latter loan was not to be one of short duration; Woulfe was by now dead, and Parnell applied to Askin and William Hobson of the Bank of Ireland in Listowel for a further loan of £1,000 on the mortgage. This was 'assented to, and paid in hand'. [192] In the same year, the Avondale estate, already three times mortgaged, was made liable to an annuity to Emily of £100 p.a. 'for her own sake and separate use, free from the debts, engagements and control of her husband';[193] a debt of £350 to the Rev. John Ebbs was also due to these assets. These arrangements on Emily's behalf coincide with the attempts she describes her family making to free her from dependence on Dickinson.[194]

The interesting thing is that these mortgages are dated so early in Parnell's life. By 1872 the estate was liable for nearly eighteen and a half thousand pounds, from the mortgages to Askin, Howard and West, plus family annuities. By the time Parnell's affairs reached a crisis point in 1882–3 the debts must have totalled far more, but the course was set from 1867 when Parnell's majority coincided with Catherine Wigram's death and her husband's claiming the portion due to her from Avondale. He probably had no compunction about this; he had already taken John Henry Parnell to court over some interest outstanding on the £10,000 [195] and, as I have mentioned, he seems to have been no friend to Mrs Parnell.

For all his enthusiasm about American investments in 1871, then, Charles Parnell was not really the 'well-to-do country gentleman' he appeared to be. Moreover, the investment he had made in the Clover Hill coal-mine in Virginia was to fail when the mine ran out soon afterwards, as John Parnell's geological knowledge had foretold it would.[196] Even before politics began to make demands on his time and resources, Parnell was not rich. The Avondale rent-roll brought in £1,789;[197] the income from the Kildare farms and the Stephen's Green houses probably brought this to over £2,000. But he owed £18,500 at an annual interest rate of six per cent, which was £1,100 a year; there was an extra £100 p.a. to Emily, and a similar annuity to Delia (the other sisters drew their incomes from Collure); and he paid out at least £4,500 in 1870 for the Kingston head-rent.[198] It was also, as his brother pointed out, up to him to support the family, or those of them that happened to be living in Ireland at any time. There cannot have been a large margin in his annual balance-sheet; little wonder that sawmills and mining, with their prospects of quick capital returns, attracted him to the point of obsession. In later life Parnell was heard to remark that politics were 'the only thing which ever made him any money';[199] this is usually taken as ironic, but there may be more truth in it than in the common contention that political involvement led to financial ruin. His affairs, as this brief survey shows, were running towards an increasing debt as early as 1871, when he was twenty five years old, and fully four years before he entered parliament.

# 3 *The entry into politics*

The Irish heart is untainted with the socialistic venom. Irishmen pay position and ancient lineage a deference which is equally free from envy and servility. They welcome heartily into their ranks scions of 'the good old stock' . . . The success of Charles Stewart Parnell is hoped for by every Irish fireside.

*Freeman's Journal*, 10 March
1874; leader on the Dublin election.

Colonel Taylor: 'He had not the honour of knowing Mr Parnell' – A voice: 'Who does?' – Laughter and 'hear, hear'.

*Irish Times*, 14 March 1874,
reporting a Conservative
meeting at Kingstown.

## I

The reasons for Parnell's precipitate entry into politics in 1874 form a thread which recurs again and again in this study; it is a question which stands at the centre of my work. The quotation from Henry Harrison at the beginning of this book shows that my lengthy study of his family antecedents can have a direct relevance to this question: Parnell *can* be seen as 'the logical outcome' of all that had gone before him, of his family background and his own conditioning. How conscious he himself was of this is disputable. Devoy, after meeting him in 1879 was quite categoric that he knew nothing about his relatives' history, or indeed about history itself.[1] Henry Parnell's book about the Irish Catholics is listed in the Avondale library catalogue, and William Parnell's works were also there in Charles's lifetime; but the impression that he was not a reader is reinforced by this reflection of Devoy's. About Parnell's knowledge of Sir Henry, Devoy is, however, contradicted by Parnell's 1874 election address, which mentions his campaigning for Catholics. There is, moreover, a clue to Parnell's development towards politics in Devoy's last observation, that 'about the then conditions of Ireland he was thoroughly and minutely informed'. He may have known little about the course of Irish history, even as written about by his forebears; but as an intelligent and argumentative boy and young man, he was always interested in current affairs. His brother, whose record is invaluable in this as in other respects, points out that Charles was passionately interested in the American Civil War, to the extent of arguing incessantly about it long after it was over.[2] John Parnell then makes a direct connection to his later personal involvement: 'If anything can be said to have been the first impulse that directed Charley's attention towards politics, it was the American Civil War'.[3] The depth of his interest in this certainly presupposes an involvement in current affairs which has rarely been attributed to him, but which seems completely to be expected in view of what can be seen of his character at the time.

The next factor which John Parnell isolates as influencing his brother's drift towards a political stance is more questionable. This concerns the effect on Parnell of the Fenian movement: 'if the American Civil War may be said to have first aroused Charley's interest in politics, it was certainly the Fenian outbreak that concentrated that interest on Irish affairs'.[4] Barry O'Brien in 1898 was even more definite about this,[5] though he was questioned on the issue by Henry Harrison.[6] O'Brien was influenced by Parnell's celebrated interruption on behalf of the Manchester Martyrs in the House of Commons, and his sister recalled his indignation at their execution;[7] but this did not necessarily imply Fenian sympathies, any more than an involvement with the Amnesty movement at that time did. The effect on Butt of the Fenian inspiration is undeniable; Parnell's response to it is not testified to as unequivocally. His own references to this influence which appear long afterwards in isolated speeches do not deserve the weight Barry O'Brien gives them,[8] at least in the pre-1874 context. Before the Special Commission, Parnell's responses to Asquith's questions about the background to this political involvement make no reference to any interest in the Fenians, though this could have been calculated on his part: 'I cannot say I was very much interested in political questions at that time. I had been observing matters; but I was chiefly interested in local matters; attending my own business.'[9]

Moreover, even while attributing his brother's political development to Fenian influence, John Howard Parnell continually emphasises that 'with the Fenian doctrine itself, and with the Fenian methods, he was never really in sympathy'.[10] His impatience with Fanny's emotional nationalism and his annoyance at being taken for a Fenian sympathiser by the police raiding-party in 1867 bear this out.

Furthermore, there is a considerable time-lapse between the high point of Fenian fever in 1867 and Parnell's sudden stand in the 1874 election. This gap is doubly suggestive when it is realised that at its close come two phenomena of the early 1870s which shortly antedate Parnell's entry into politics: the Ballot Act and the tenant right movement. These two factors had far more to do with Parnell's precipitation into politics than the chimera of the Fenian ideal. Giving evidence before the Special Commission in 1889, Parnell himself left no doubt about this:

> The passing of the Ballot Act in 1872 was the first public event which more intimately directed my attention to politics. I thought that arising out of the passage of that Act the political situation in Ireland was capable of a very great change. I had some knowledge, not a very deep knowledge, of Irish history and had read about the independent opposition movement of Sir Charles Gavan Duffy and the late Sir Frederick Lucas in 1852; and whenever I thought about politics I always thought that that would be an ideal movement for the benefit of Ireland. [11]

His brother states categorically that what Parnell wanted to see amended at this time was primarily the position of the tenants, the abuses of whose position 'he saw more and more in their naked hideousness as he went about among his tenants on the Avondale estate'. [12] John had come to similar conclusions after his experiences on the encumbered Armagh lands; [13] when the brothers returned to Ireland from America in 1872, Charles 'found Butt's tenant-right campaign in full swing and studied it closely in the newspapers of all shades of opinions, though his comments were few and far between'. [14] In the years following Parnell's entry into parliament, Andrew Kettle noticed his particular interest in Tenant Right, recalling that 'he attended all our meetings;' [13] Before 1874, John Parnell recalled, he suggested that Charles take up politics and this cause, and enter parliament, and was told briefly 'I could not, because I would not join that set'. Barry O'Brien emphasised the importance of the Ballot Act and tenant right as formative influences on Parnell; probably from a conversation with John Howard Parnell, he describes Charles' reaction to his brother's encouragement to enter politics as saying: 'I did not see my way. I am in favour of the tenants and Home Rule, but I do not know any of the men who are working the movement.' [16] The less diplomatic rejoinder recorded in John's book seems more likely; nor does O'Brien's further interpolation of Parnell as saying 'the whole question is English dominion. That is what is to be dealt with', ring true for 1872. It reads like an effort to link Parnell's decision back to the Fenian example; and the man who in the 1868 election had worked for Lord Milton's Liberal candidature [17] was not someone who had been fired with enthusiasm for nationalism by the Fenian rising of the previous year.

Nor is there any reason to look for such inspiration. Given that Parnell came from a family with a tradition of public service, that he was interested in tenant right, that he understood the implications of the Ballot Act, that he found himself master of a sizeable estate and at a loose end in his personal life – a bachelor, not ready to embark upon another engagement – there is nothing incongruous about his sudden entry into politics. (The Ballot Act, it might be added, had a further result, noted by Dr Thornley and applicable to Parnell's circumscribed financial position: it 'greatly decreased the cost of political campaigning which faced a prospective candidate and at once reduced the disadvantage . . . of a candidate of slender means'.) [18] The step was, as Harrison saw, 'a logical outcome'. The sort of politics he entered were not as untoward as they may seem. The trend of Parnell's later politics was unpredictable; at this later stage also, the Fenian influence on him became something to reckon with. But the development towards his entry into politics in 1874, if – as his brother termed it – 'a shrouded growth', was in no way an unnatural one.

## II

Even Parnell's actual decision to contest an election, sudden as it was, does not seem to have stupefied those who knew him well. The circumstances of his decision, as described by John Parnell, are well known:

> His actual decision was a sudden and even a dramatic one. It took place one night early in 1874, when Charley and I were dining with our sister Emily and her husband Captain Dickinson at their house at 22, Lower Pembroke Street, Dublin . . . The conversation at dinner itself was of a light nature . . . Afterwards, however, it drifted into an argument as to tenant right and Butt's movement in general. Charley took little active part in the arguments advanced for either side. Suddenly, when we had discussed the situation from all points of view, Charley cried: 'By jove, John, it would be a grand opening for me to enter politics!' This frank avowal by one who had always been so reticent as to his real views took our breath away for a moment. Then we all cried, carried away by the idea and the firm conviction of his words, 'Yes, it would. It is a splendid opportunity.' Once his mind was made up, Charley never wasted time in words . . . Accordingly, we had hardly time to express our approval when, without any other words of explanation, he went on to say, betraying no excitement: 'John, will you and Dickinson come down with me to the *Freeman's* office?' [19]

As John told the story, he stayed behind while Parnell and Dickinson went off to see the editor; in two hours they returned crestfallen, having been told that, as Parnell was High Sheriff of Wicklow, he was ineligible to stand. Next morning, the Lord Lieutenant refused to accept his resignation there and then, so Charles was too late to run in the election for his native county; his brother recalls his anger at 'what he conceived to be a slight on the part of the Lord Lieutenant', and his ensuing resentment.

Eighteen years earlier Barry O'Brien told substantially the same story, probably gleaned from conversation with John Parnell and Dwyer Gray, whose father had been proprietor of the *Freeman* at the time. According to O'Brien, Dickinson suggested to Parnell that he run for Wicklow, and it was John who accompanied him to the newspaper office; but such discrepancies do not affect the substance of the story.[20] Emily did not mention the incident in her book, though she was probably a witness of the scene; it is doubtful if much of value has been lost by her omission.

John, as I have mentioned elsewhere, ran in the Wicklow election instead of Charles, and did ingloriously.[21] A letter in the *Freeman's Journal* following the election tells why: O'Byrne and O'Mahony came into the field while John Parnell was 'consulting Sir John Gray as to the propriety of coming forward', both running on the Home Rule ticket. John backed down; however, on 31 January O'Mahony changed his mind (the writs had been issued on 27 January) and John Parnell published his address at short notice on 2 February. The point made by the writer (Richard Johnson of Arklow) was that Parnell came forward as soon as he could in the circumstances; but the confusion engendered accounted for his defeat.[22] O'Byrne headed the poll with 1,511 votes; Dick, the conservative, followed with 1,146. The unsuccessful candidates were Lord Fitzwilliam with 927 and John Parnell with 553.[23] O'Byrne, the successful Home Ruler, was, as I have said, a country gentleman of extensive connections;[24] he was also strongly in favour of tenant-farmers' Defence Associations.[25] Had Charles Stewart Parnell run against him, they would have presented very much the same political image.

Failure at the Wicklow election, however, did not exhaust the gamut of possibilities. Though Parnell told the Special Commission in 1889 that: 'I did not stand for any constituency in Ireland in 1874, for I was High Sheriff of my own county',[26] he was not telling the truth. His ineligibility as candidate for Wicklow did not extend to other constituencies; it only affected him in that county because he would have been in charge of counting his own votes. A month after the Wicklow election, he *did* stand for another constituency – the county of Dublin. Despite his resounding defeat, it is a campaign worth examining; many of the important issues concerning Parnell's entry into politics appear during its course.

The Dublin county seat had been held by the Rt hon. T. C. Taylor for the Conservatives for 23 years in 1874, a record that was looked at askance even by 'a Conservative registered freeholder of the county' who wrote to the *Freemen's Journal* on 3 March asking why 'Colonel Taylor should be allowed to walk over the course without a question in the coming election for the county'. Others evidently felt the same. The County Dublin Tenants' Association looked hard for someone to oppose Taylor, even consulting Cardinal Cullen about it, and eventually lined up Parnell at three days' notice. [27] Parnell undertook to pay the costs of the election, returning the £300 which the Home Rule League offered him; it was to cost him, according to several sources, £2,000. [28] The *Freeman* carried a leader on 9 March which introduced Parnell as a candidate for the election, and set the tone of his campaign; an almost complete reliance on the Parnell family record and on the desirability of someone of Parnell's social position and religion, as broadening the base of the Home Rule party. [29] Sir John Parnell was eulogised as a genius of extraordinary debating power and cultural gifts; [30] his genius was equalled only by his integrity, and he refused all bribes to countenance the Union. Here the editor, overtaken by confusion, wrote that 'beneath the heart of the Rt hon. *Henry* Parnell there throbbed a heart as patriotic and as incorruptible as that of the Martyr of Utica', and that 'he struggled to save from death that Irish Parliament in which he had so often and so fearlessly asserted the rights of his Catholic fellow-countrymen', but the message came through clearly:

> Today Charles Stewart Parnell, a grandson of Sir Henry Parnell's, comes forward to solicit on the ancestral platform the suffrages of the electors of the county of Dublin. Mr Parnell is a gentleman of fortune and position, and High Sheriff of the county of Wicklow. In his address he pledges himself to the full popular programme – Home Rule, security of tenure, denominational education, and Amnesty. He also promises to support the last demands of the Irish Civil Servants. He has received the unanimous support of the Home Rule League, and the County Dublin Tenants' Defence Association, and it only needs organisation and zeal to secure the return for the county of so eligible a candidate.

This important editorial thus emphasises two of what may be called the 'passive advantages' of the candidate, as they had little to do with his personal qualities: the myth of his family and the significance of his social position. The editorial goes on to animadvert upon a third passive advantage – the iniquity of Parnell's opponent. Taylor was seen as hand in glove with Disraeli, who had just made him Chancellor of the Duchy of Lancaster,[31] and the Government's veiled threats about the 'confiscatory' Disestablishment Act and the undesirability of denominational education were the bane of the *Freeman*. Quoting a speech of the Chief Secretary, Hicks-Beach, the leader drew the conclusion that the Conservatives intended a coercive and hostile policy towards Ireland. Political meetings of the campaign show the same tendency to concentrate on Taylor's disadvantages rather than Parnell's advantages.[32] The similarly passive virtue of the advantage of Parnell's social position – the emphasis on what he represented rather than what he was – is also recurrent throughout the campaign. When summing up the election, the *Irish Times* admitted that

> the Home Rule Party could scarcely have found a more eligible candidate than Mr Parnell: a gentleman of property and influence in his native county and the holder of an office of high dignity, he was open neither to the suspicion of being a political adventurer nor of being actuated by revolutionary motives.[33]

The second epigraph to this chapter shows that the *Freeman* was equally conscious of this; it was an advantage to be able to claim that 'Irishmen pay position and ancient lineage a deference which is equally free from deference and servility',[34] and to adduce Parnell's candidature as evidence. Even if he was a landlord, it was pointed out, he was a good one; A. M. Sullivan remarked at a Home Rule meeting that Parnell 'received today from the tenants of his extensive estates the identical amount of rent that the tenants paid his grandfather ninety years ago'.[35] The Conservatives did their best to discredit this image by circulating a broadsheet headed: *'Parnell of Avondale and Tombay as a Landlord'* which claimed – allegedly by order of the editor of the *Freeman's Journal* – that 'a gentleman by the name of Parnell' had been involved in many disputes with his tenants, and showed 'some sharpness' in his dealings with them.[36] The basis for this story was true, but it involved Parnell's brother, Henry.[37] Both the *Freeman's Journal* and Parnell himself angrily repudiated the charge, and attacked the unethical method of making it.[38] Many other references show that the opposition were highly conscious of the advantage to the Home Rulers of a candidate of Parnell's standing. The *Evening Mail* significantly saw Parnell's candidature as *'unseemly'*, as well as 'unchivalrous and factious'.[39] and Colonel Taylor made the same accusation of a lack of gentlemanly solidarity on Parnell's part when he told a political meeting at Rathmines: 'referring to his rival . . . that he had been at school at Eton with his father, and he was sure, if he now lived, his son would not be in the field against him'.[40] Another speaker said that he would only look on Parnell 'in the light of an adventurer'.[41]

Closely connected with this was the similar emphasis laid on the

Home Rule candidate's religion. Canon Lynch of Blanchardstown, an influential tenant right priest, spoke on Parnell's platforms, saying 'he was delighted that it was a Protestant gentleman that was coming forward with a promise to get justice for Ireland';[42] T. D. Sullivan welcomed political meetings where he saw 'Catholics with their worthy clergy on the platform . . . meeting under the shadow of the Catholic steeple to aid the candidature of a liberal Protestant',[43] and was roundly cheered. And, along with the advantage of his Ascendancy background, the aura of the candidate's family mystique was incessantly invoked. When the *Freeman* ran out of eulogies about Sir John Parnell, it filled a leader with details about Sir Henry's support of the Catholics.[44] At political meetings, Jonah Barrington's comments on Sir John Parnell were read – one presumes selectively – to an appreciative crowd.[45] In a flight of fancy and anachronism the *Freeman* stated that the Home Rule candidate 'carries in this contest that good green flag under which his ancestors did yeoman service'.[46] Throughout, Parnell's family record was treated as one of his prime recommendations – not least in his own election address.[47]

Apart from his election address, indeed, the candidate seems to have had little enough to say for himself; this reinforces the impression that what he represented merely by sitting on a Home Rule platform was considered enough. The address was a predictable one; I have given it in full in an Appendix.[48] At election meetings, Parnell seems to have taken little part; again, his presence was the main thing. Reports of these meetings often do not bother to quote his speech, merely noting that he 'reiterated the sentiments contained in his public address'.[49] The one modest speech of Parnell's quoted in the *Freeman* is, however, interesting:

> He [Parnell] now believed they should poll a very considerable majority. As regarded his principles he put Home Rule first: because it embodied everything else. He thought it comprised everything that Irishmen wished for; because when they had Home Rule they would be able to make those laws for which the country had been yearning for years . . . He believed that when they got Home Rule – and he was certain that they would get some part of it before long – they should have their manufactures encouraged; they should have their fisheries developed; they should have their gentry living at home and spending their money amongst them and coming forward on the public platform to represent the liberties of the country.[50]

The moderation of this speech speaks for itself; nothing could be further from the fire-breathing nationalism attributed to their opponent by Taylor's supporters. Moreover, this view of Parnell's corresponds very closely to his grandfather's sixty years earlier.[51]

Where his grandfather passionately called upon the Irish country gentlemen to enter parliament and work responsibly for their tenants, and where he eulogised the betterment of living-conditions that followed independence, he used much the same language as Charles Stewart Parnell in 1874. It seems likely that at this stage the latter's opinions were not in essence noticeably more 'advanced' than those of his grandfather. On the large questions of nationalism and land ownership he did not commit himself very far; writing to Lord Howth to ask for his support in the election, he contented himself with saying that 'I think there is an important principle at stake',[52] and did not enlarge upon it. Significantly, his opponents saw him as a man out of his depth. Colonel Taylor told a meeting at Kingstown that

> he hoped they would support him against a stranger, and one who had been put forward by very violent and he might say very dangerous men. He had not the honour of knowing Mr Parnell – A voice: 'Who does?' – Laughter and 'hear, hear' – but he could not help thinking that Mr Parnell was sorry for himself, or if he was not sorry for himself yet, then that he would be bye and bye, that those experienced and artful dodgers had seized hold of him and taken him in.[53]

In part this attitude was a reaction to Parnell's youthfulness and social background, but not entirely; there were other scions of 'the gentry' standing on Home Rule platforms in 1874. The League was certainly anxious to have him; Butt admitted having 'pressed' Parnell into accepting the Dublin nomination,[54] and the *Evening Mail* reported that it was only 'after a good deal of searching' that a candidate had been found to oppose Taylor.[55] But at least in part, the idea that Parnell was being made use of by the Home Rule League without realising it must have come from his own reticence on public platforms. He was presented as a figurehead; and to a large extent he acted like one.

Figurehead or not, the League spared no effort on his campaign. The Conservative *Irish Times* sourly admitted that his publicity machine was far more active than Taylor's.[56] Far more Home Rule League meetings were reported than Tory gatherings, even in the Conservative papers; the energy of the Parnellite canvassers was admitted by all.[57] Gray and the *Freeman* kept up a constant barrage of pro-Parnell leaders and anti-Taylor invective and shortly before polling day claimed enthusiastically that

> there's not a farmer's hearth in the Donegal hills, not a village gathering in the wave-washed valleys of Kerry, where the Dublin election is not the main topic of conversation and where the most ardent wishes are not breathed for the success of Parnell and Home Rule.[58]

But when it came to the point it was the voters of Dublin county and not Donegal mountain-men or Kerry farmers who were to decide the outcome, and their answer was unequivocal. Parnell received 1,235 votes and Taylor 2,183. It should be pointed out, however, that such a decisive result was not expected. The morning after polling day the *Freeman* felt qualified to state that Parnell would win; he had a majority in Drumcondra and Coolock, and had done 'particularly well' in Kingstown, Dalkey and Blackrock. [59] On the same day even the *Irish Times* granted that it would be a close-run thing. [60] But after the results the Conservative tone changed from cautiousness to jubilation. The Ballot Act, according to the *Irish Times*, had made no difference; Colonel Taylor's last opponent, in 1865, had received over three hundred more votes than Parnell managed to secure. [61] Despite the vigour of the Home Rulers' organisation, the same paper continued, they had failed because they frightened off Liberals and moderates; Parnell's advantages, enumerated in detail, [62] made no difference. The Freeman was as gloomy as the *Times* was jubilant after the polling. Admitting an emphatic defeat – 'it would be worse than puerile to try to disguise the real character of the result' [63] – it blamed the apathy of the Liberal voters, abuse of the ballot, Taylor's personal popularity, the traditional Toryism of Dublin, and, most of all, 'a disastrous want of organisation in the Liberal ranks'. Nonetheless, the conclusion looked on the bright side; Parnell's 1,235 votes meant that 'the ballot . . . has shown the way to brighter things . . . and has given the present occupant notice to quit'.

This was a more optimistic view than circumstances should have permitted. Parnell had lost, and lost badly. But the Dublin election showed the strength of organisation that could be put at his disposal; between the *Freeman's Journal* and his energetic election agents, he had been given all the publicity and exposure he could desire. In a safer seat, he could do well; and a year later one was found for him.

## III

On 29 March 1875 John Martin died from a chill caught at John Mitchel's graveside a few weeks before. Born in 1812, Martin had been a radical Young Irelander and had edited the *Irish Felon;* as 'Honest John Martin', he had been a greatly respected M.P. for Meath. Two days after his death the *Freeman's Journal* was speculating about probable contestants for the vacant seat: on 2 April Parnell's election address was published. [64] He had been, since the Dublin failure, waiting in the wings: a well-phrased letter from him to the *Freeman* in March 1875 had warmly pressed Mitchel's case as regarded the celebrated Tipperary election, and forwarded £25 for Mitchel's expenses. [65] Moreover, after Mitchel's death, Parnell himself had been interested in standing for the vacant seat. A letter from Father Richard Galvin, the parish priest of Rathdrum, to a Tipperary priest on 23 March 1875 declared that Parnell 'would contest Tipperary against any conservative'. Galvin praised Parnell as an excellent landlord, and described his family tradition as a liberal one – referring to Sir Ralph Howard as well as John Henry Parnell, and maintaining that Charles Stewart Parnell, whom he had known for years, would 'prove true to the traditions of his family'.[66] William Dillon wrote two days later to John Madden (a Tipperary Home Ruler who twice stood for Monaghan without success) that he had had several long talks with Parnell, and though he had been at first 'inclined to distrust him rather, as I thought his publishing that letter sending £25 towards the expenses of Mr Mitchel's election looked very like an election dodge', he had now decided Parnell was 'a very thorough and sincere Home Ruler'. Dillon, however, doubted that the National party in Tipperary would support him 'even supposing he is all I believe him to be', and had in any case heard from John Dillon that they were not considering taking an active part in the election anyway. Dillon was, however, keen that Madden meet Parnell and advise him 'as to what priests he ought to call on'. Parnell wanted to visit Tipperary; and though Dillon had his own reasons for not going with him, he asked Madden to assist Parnell in Clonmel on the following Wednesday, and to introduce him to Charles Doran of Queenstown – to whom this letter could be forwarded,[67] and who had helped canvass for Mitchel in Tipperary.

Madden wrote to Doran, enclosing Dillon's letter, after replying to the latter that he would meet Parnell but promised no support. The National interest in Tipperary did intend a contest, but had not yet decided upon a candidate.[68] The next day, however, John Martin died. Writing to Doran again, Madden decided to postpone a decision until after Martin's funeral; but he enclosed a letter from Kickham to the parish priest of Mullinahone, which 'spoke well' of Parnell while 'not advocating' him: presumably because of Kickham's more radical political views. However, as Madden prophetically observed, 'Parnell's will now probably turn his attention to Meath', where a contest was more certain.[69] But the Tipperary negotiations show that influential channels of communication were being utilised on Parnell's behalf, and that he was anxious to emphasise his 'honesty' and his difference from 'Whig Home Rulers'.[70]

Parnell's election address was followed three days later by a declaration on the part of J. T. Hinds, who had seconded Parnell's nomination for the Dublin seat a year before,[71] that he also was offering himself as a Home Rule candidate. There was a Conservative candidate as well, Mr James L. Napper of Loughcrew.

In the week that intervened between the announcement of the

second Home Rule candidate on 5 April and the nomination meeting
scheduled for 12 April, the *Freeman* made no secret of its preferences.
Though Hinds evidently felt he had a right to the nomination and was
not prepared to stand down, his canvassing went largely unrecorded;
whereas Parnell's visits to Drogheda,[72] Navan,[73] Athboy[74] and
Kells[75] were fully reported and his every utterance approvingly
quoted. At the nomination meeting in Navan on 12 April Parnell was
adopted as candidate and the *Freeman* had a stern admonishment to
make against any possibility of internecine strife; Hinds might be a fit
enough candidate, but the county had chosen Parnell, and the paper
endorsed the choice with a paragraph of fulsome praise.[76] Napper was
dismissed as 'in the list of the Liberal-Conservatives – a combination
of ambition and half-heartedness',[77] and in spite of the fact that he
was both resident in Meath and locally popular, his cautious approval
of 'a paper Irish Parliament' was heartily ridiculed by the *Freeman*.[78]

The county meeting which nominated Parnell had, in fact, taken a
stronger line against Hinds than the *Freeman* did. He had opposed
Disestablishment, and was vilified by the influential Catholic clergy
because of it. Despite the marshalling of forces against him, however,
Hinds refused to back down. His nomination was entered on 15 April,
despite a Home Rule League deputation who asked him to stand
aside,[79] and his addresses continued to appear until polling day.

If the clergy opposed Hinds, they were overwhelmingly and
vociferously behind his rival. As has been seen, Father Galvin had
written to the Tipperary priests about Parnell's projected stand there;
Galvin now circulated a similar letter to the Meath priests.[80] As early
as 5 April Parnell was visiting local priests and the Bishop of Kells, Dr
Nulty,[81] and the support he received was unquestioning. Reporting the
county meeting which nominated Parnell, the *Freeman* remarked that
'the occasion was of particular interest from the fact that it was
expected the clergy would express their views on the subject in
question';[82] in the general election for Louth two months earlier, the
contest had seen a conflict between priests and bishop over the
former's work on behalf of the Home Rule candidate.[83] But on 12
April 1875 in the neighbouring county, there was no doubt about the
direction in which clerical support lay. Wherever the subject concerned
Mr Hind's unsuitablenss, the pastors waxed wrathful to the point of
vindictiveness:

> Rev. Fr. Tormey said . . . that Mr Hinds had before this set at
> nought the feelings of the people of the county and opposed the
> wishes of the priests, and they all knew what had been the result
> . . . When the established church was toppling to its final fall, the
> name of Mr Hinds figured amongst the defenders of that church,
> and he showed himself an enemy to the people.[84]

The same priest spoke glowingly of Parnell.[85] Father Tormey proposed Parnell; another cleric, Father Lynch, also spoke for him, as did Father Behan, the local parish priest. There were several more of the local clergy in attendance.[86] T. D. Sullivan, speaking at this meeting, 'was delighted to see on the platform so many of the revered and faithful guides of the Irish people, for he knew, as they all knew, that Ireland must ever be safe so long as her people and her priests act together'.[87] Clerical support for Parnell was kept up throughout the campaign, as the *Freeman* approvingly noted,[88] and on the day before voting 'in almost every parish and district an active canvass was made by the ever-faithful and watchful priests of the county;[89] the paper went on to refer to 'our glorious Protestant patriots', including in the roll Sir John and Sir Henry Parnell.[90]

Parnell himself was then, as later in his career, more than careful about alienating the religious guardians of local opinion. In his speeches he spoke strongly for denominational education,[91] although, he told Davitt long afterwards, there was clerical disapproval of some of his references and he was informed: 'the priests of Meath know nothing about John Stuart Mill'.[92] Even before the Meath election, a letter in the *Wicklow Newsletter* from Rev. James Redmond, a Catholic archdeacon, shows that Parnell was cultivating the clerical element: Father Redmond approvingly quoted a letter he had received from Parnell, 'our patriotic High Sheriff', about the death of a prominent Catholic businessman in Arklow.[93] Hinds' chances were non-existent after his denunciation by the priests of Meath; Parnell's were immeasurably strengthened by their support, and their organisational importance – far greater in the Meath election than it had been in the Dublin campaign – was one of his strongest weapons.

Besides his religious incongruity, the other obvious anomaly of Parnell's position was that he was a landlord standing for tenant right. His supporters were conscious of this and Kirk, the Home Rule M.P. for Louth who seconded Parnell's nomination, drew attention to it openly:

> He reminded them that they were advocating the cause of a landlord, but a landlord who had never himself, nor his father before him, evicted a tenant or changed the rent-roll of his estate. This was more than could be said of the great majority of landed proprietors in Ireland. At the Land Conference in Dublin he defended the principle of fixity of tenure; and he (Mr Kirk) was a tenant-farmer himself and he had scarcely say he would not speak in favour of a landlord whom he did not believe to be a good man and true.[94]

At the same meeting, the candidate himself felt it the first priority to clarify this question, and opened his speech by saying:

It might be thought because he was a landlord he had no interest in the tenant, or might try to prevent the tenant having his interest in the land recognised by the state. If it were the wish of any landlord to come forward and say that his tenant had not as just and as good an interest in his farm as the landlord, such a possibility was rendered impracticable and had been in fact removed by Mr Gladstone's Act of 1870. He was not going to praise Mr Gladstone's Act, for it had been proved to be miserably inadequate and had in some respects done harm to the tenants, having coverted some good landlords into bad ones, and because it had not given the slightest protection to the tenantry over three-quarters of Ireland. He however, as a landlord, maintained that the tenant has property in the land as well as the landlord and they should hold fast to that principle and endeavour to pass a bill which would define what the interest of the tenant is and which would protect that interest. Without fixity of tenure and fair rents the tenants would never be happy, nor would the country be prosperous.[95]

It is interesting that this lengthy definition of his land policy was put first in Parnell's nomination-meeting speech, and that by contrast his profession of adherence to the Home Rule principle, which followed, seems almost perfunctory.[96] He did, however, warn that 'if she [England] refuse to Ireland what her people demand as a right, the day would come when Ireland would have her opportunity in England's weakness', and was cheered for it. His supporters continued to describe him as a 'patriot', and to prove this, his ancestral record was adduced time and time again. In front of his progression from the station to the town centre of Navan for the nomination meeting were carried, according to the *Freeman*, 'two time-worn banners of the Irish Volunteers, the property of Mr Parnell, under which his ancestor had fought'.[97] Leaders in the same newspaper referred to 'his two ancestors who in old times upheld the national cause'.[98] This patriotic emphasis, as well as Parnell's own references to nationalism (more outspoken than in the Dublin campaign), were obviously dictated by the fact that both Hinds and Napper subscribed to the principle of some kind of native self-determination; it was to Parnell's advantage to be further left, and adopt the full orthodoxy. The *Freeman's Journal* described him as

> finally and above all ... an Irishman – Irish bred, Irish born, 'racy of the soil', knowing its history, devoted to its interests; no English interloper fishing for a seat in this island and too ready to swallow, with a wry face, of course, any pledge which might help him to it.[99]

But it should be pointed out that even his opponents never saw him as representing a 'dangerous' kind of nationalism. Even the *Irish Times* found some scant comfort, after he was elected, in the fact that

> the principles of which Mr Parnell is the exponent are thoroughly constitutional ... and it ought to be a source of satisfaction to those who are interested in the future of this country that a gentleman who is far removed from the suspicion of association with the disloyal has been chosen to advocate them in the House of Commons. [100]

The combination of family record, clerical backing, honourable experience in the field of battle, and the constant admonishments of the *Freeman* in his favour was invincible. Parnell received 1,771 votes, Napper 902, and the stubbornly importunate Hinds, 133. The reaction of the *Freeman's Journal* was unashamedly crowing: 'The "patriotic" attorney is nowhere; the good landlord but bad politician is hopelessly outvoted; the young Irish patriot is at the head of the poll. The election is in many ways full of important lessons'. [101] One of these lessons, significantly, was that

> with grateful Ireland ancestral services now, as at all previous periods, weigh most deeply; it is no offence to the hon. member for Meath to say that nothing so strongly recommended him to the electors of the great county for which he sits as the fact that those whose blood he inherits and whose name he bears in the old times loved and lived and laboured for Ireland. [102]

According to the *Freeman*, the importance of Parnell's record in the Dublin election was only secondary. The *Irish Times* laid the same emphasis on the candidate's ancestral record: 'his name alone suggests the principles on which he appealed to the county'. [103] As far as simple facts are concerned, the family record – as I have previously concluded – had little to do with Irish patriotism: but the myth was what mattered. Nor was Parnell himself particularly knowledgeable about the ancestors so frequently referred to; if his ideas approximated to those of any of his forebears it was to William Parnell's – like his grandson, a landlord in politics who believed in a better land system and home government, for the most pragmatic of reasons. But the myth, along with Parnell's adherence to the line approved by the clerics who were so influential in his election, was of primary importance. So was the strong backing afforded him by the *Freeman*. In all this, the candidate himself does not come through very strongly. He had entered politics from a position in life which presupposed public involvement of one kind or another, and had chosen the party whose platform and principles agreed most closely with his own. That he must have been at least ambivalent about several other facets of the

Home Rule orthodoxy is implied by the previous chapter in this section of my study. But the nature of the politics into which he entered – possibly from boredom as much as anything else, and from a sense of hiatus in his personal life – was to change dramatically in the next five years; and he himself was at first to assist, and then control this change. That he entered politics with any inkling of what was to happen is doubtful; there is no evidence for it in his previous conditioning. His commitment to nationalism – the extent of which always remained arguable – followed on his entry into politics; it did not antedate this. In April 1875, the squire of Avondale became the hon. member for Meath; the process was to a large extent aided by emphasising his family history, from great-grandfather on, and by playing down the Wicklow gentry background which had been equally important in his conditioning, but from which his peculiar upbringing had kept him slightly apart. A wheel had turned full circle; and the early elements of this study here come together.

In time, Parnell's character as politician eclipsed and took over from the life of a country gentleman; but this was to come later. The final sections of my study will examine the connections he retained with Wicklow, with Avondale, and with his family, until his death.

# Part IV

*Parnell and Wicklow, 1875–91*

# 1    *Parnell and Avondale*

## I

A consideration of Parnell's connections with his Irish home during his parliamentary career must begin with some reference to the frequency of his visits there. It is a well-known truism that these remained regular up to 1882, but from 1883 become more and more infrequent – a phenomenon usually attributed to the influence of Mrs O'Shea. Barry O'Brien wrote regretfully:

> The rest and solace which he had once found in the old home in the Wicklow vale, he now sought in the new retreat of a London suburb ... There were weeks, months, which he could have spent in Ireland, to the immense advantage of the National movement, but for this unfortunate attachment to that unhappy lady.[1]

Others were less restrained in voicing the same opinion.[2] William O'Brien subscribed to this theory, but maintained that Parnell 'never broke off that we would now call wireless communication with the front in Ireland'.[3] With regard to sojourns in Avondale, Mrs O'Shea herself had an explanation:

> He often went over to Ireland expressly to see how things were going there, but after 1880 he could never stay even a few days there in peace. The after-effects of the awful famine, in such terrible cases of poverty and woe as were brought to his notice the moment he arrived in his old home, made it impossible for him to remain there at all. No one man could deal charitably with all the poor people and live, and as time went on Mr Parnell's visits became necessarily shorter, for the demands were so many and the poverty so great that he could not carry the burden and continue the political life necessary to their alleviation.[4]

It should, nonetheless, be pointed out that such scruples did not prevent Parnell pouring thousands of pounds into mines and quarries on the estate, for very little return, until the end of his life.[5] A simpler explanation for his absences lies in the nature of the politics of the time. Up to 1882 the matrix of Irish politics was, so to speak, in the field; decision-making and policy originated in the land agitation in Ireland, and here Parnell concentrated his attention and energies. After his release from Kilmainham his politics revolved round the House of Commons; despite assertions by Frank Hugh O'Donnell and others,[6] his attendance there was not as erratic as has been claimed.[7] His tendency to remain in London from this time was accentuated by the fact that he made his home at Eltham from exactly this period. Barry O'Brien, always judicious, placed 'health and public policy' second on his list of reasons for Parnell's absences from Ireland, though deciding Mrs O'Shea was the prime cause; but it is possible, and even plausible, to reverse his order of priority.

Moreover, Parnell did continue to return home. The chronicler of his movements is frustrated at this, as at all other, junctures of his life by the paucity of personal records available; but from data such as contemporary newspapers and the dates on autograph letters I have compiled an incomplete calendar of Parnell's movements from 1875 to 1891. This shows that before 1880 he was more or less continuously at Avondale during parliamentary recesses from August until November;[8] and after Kilmainham he spent some weeks at Avondale in the summer and autumn of 1882, coming back to Ireland again before Christmas. 1883 was one of the few years when he was not in Aughavannagh for the opening of the grouse season; but he visited Ireland at least twice in June and July, and was there for much of December. In 1884 he was in Ireland in February and April, and visited Ireland in May, August and September; 1885 saw him there for most of January and almost continuously from August to November. In 1886 there were visits, mostly on political business, in the early part of the year, and the usual protracted stay at Aughavannagh in August. In 1887, a year when Parnell was 'dangerously ill', his movements are little recorded; but he was in Avondale on 30 August for an indefinite period. In 1888 there were visits in January and, as usual, August. In 1889 the parliamentary session carried well into August, with Parnell in regular attendance, but he visited Wicklow as soon as possible, being in Aughavannagh on 25 August. His movements are only scantily recorded for 1890, but he was in Wicklow during August, when some labour troubles at his quarries broke out; and, as is well known, from December of this year until his death ten months later he crossed to Ireland at least once a week. Few of these last visits brought him to Avondale, however, or anywhere near it.

It is undeniable that his visits became less and less frequent; but to state, as he himself did in 1880, that 'since I forsook agriculture for politics I have not slept six nights in Avondale House',[9] is a gross misrepresentation; he had been there for several consecutive weeks in the autumn of 1878 and 1879. Emily Dickinson recalled that the Irish Party used to meet at Avondale during the Land War,[10] and Davitt describes such an occasion in September 1882.[11] Only in the late eighties, according to Mrs Dickinson, did her brother's visits become 'few and far between';[12] and though a reporter from the *World* in 1880 found Avondale so 'barren and neglected' that 'one could fancy that the coverings had just been drawn off the furniture at the expiration of a Chancery suit',[13] this was at a particular juncture when his Irish visits rarely brought him near Wicklow. In 1882 a *Nation* reporter found that 'the mansion is being painted inside and outside, and arrrangements are being made to restore the demesne and pleasure grounds to the order and beauty for which they were so distinguished before Mr Parnell devoted all his time and energies to public affairs'.[14]

By the end of the 1880s, however, the forlorn aspect of the place was being attested to on all sides. T. P. O'Connor found it with peeling paint and barely furnished interior,[15] while yet another roving reporter (this time from the *Spectator*) decided in 1890 that it was 'a depressing house, with the master a long time away, the hall grate fireless, and the library the only room bearing any signs of use'.[16] But even though Parnell's visits decreased in frequency, the connection remained a close one. In Eltham, Brighton, or even the House of Commons, he was continually preoccupied with findings from his mines and quarries at home; the estate's finances and the large mortgage on it came to have a political importance in 1883;[17] and throughout his career the supposed anomaly of his position as a landlord at the head of a land reform movement was brought up again and again.

To understand the nature of Parnell's connection with Avondale, his particular attitude towards the estate must be emphasised. John Parnell told the following anecdote to illustrate his brother's dislike of bluster:

> We were walking down the road to the sawmills [at Avondale] when I noticed that some of his men working on a field near-by were taking things very easily, even for Irish labourers. I said to him: 'Why don't you call out to those fellows, Charley, and get them to hurry up? They look like being all day over that field if they go on like that.' He replied, with a shurg of his shoulders: 'I know that, but if I wanted to make them hear I should have to shout, and I dislike shouting.' We walked on in silence.[18]

It is, however, even more illustrative of his attitude to Avondale. Later, John goes on to say, Charles had a word with the workmen, but at the time it wasn't worth it. This, one feels, is closely connected with the fact that they were working 'on a field'. Had they been idling over the sawmills or the quarrying Parnell would have shouted, and shouted loudly.

Though knowledgeable about farming, Parnell's primary preoccupation remained with the industrial resources of his estate. He was, in this respect, a model nineteenth-century man.'He often told me that Ireland had hundreds of industries lying idle for want of working, and he was particularly anxious to have them opened up. He also believed that Ireland was full of mineral wealth hidden beneath her soil.'[19] The celebrated cattle-shed at Avondale which he designed, inspired by the new railway station at Brighton, was the only facet of dairying which is recorded as having preoccupied him. Even this remained roofless while the new sawmill and the house for its manager were completed; the shed probably cost a fraction of the £3,000 laid out on the latter buildings.[20] There is no evidence that he actually neglected the farming of his land in favour of his industrial preoccupations; at the same time, he applied for a Public Works loan of £1,200 and built a number of cottages.[21] The fact that the estate supported so many people meant that he could not afford to let farming go by the board. In 1884 a newspaper reporter spoke of 'upwards of 150 employed on the place'[22] and even when the new sawmill was in its infancy it required 25 full-time workers. Little wonder that he took up book-keeping in an attempt to check estate accounts, 'and many weeks sat immersed in double entry, estate account-keeping, commercial book-keeping, etc.'[23] In an appendix to his memoir John Howard Parnell gives a valuable account of his brother visiting Avondale in 1885 and checking up on the work in progress; but, then, as ever, his chief interest was in the welfare of his industries.

The agriculture of his estate, however, could not be ignored; and until the end of his life he kept in touch with his agent, William Kerr, about comparatively minor points. Kerr, Parnell told Mrs O'Shea, was 'a duffer about anything except book-keeping'[24] and needed 'advising and admonishing all day';[25] an example of this advice is a letter of Parnell's in May 1890 which tells Kerr to 'take necessary legal steps to obtain compensation from Saunders anent the heifers' and instructs him in detail about a new brand of cabbage:

> I find that 'Thousand-headed' is the name of the cabbage, and that the seed need not be sown until the end of June; it will then be fit to transplant after the oats have been reaped and will be first-rate food for ewes to yean [sic] upon early in February – it would be well to prepare the upper half of the garden to transplant some of the plants into in September or August.[26]

If an industrial engineer by inclination, circumstances had, after all made him a farmer. On a visit home in 1883 his brother recollected him entering into 'a long consultation' with his herd, Henry Gaffney, about cattle,[27] and T. P. O'Connor gives a lively picture of the Irish leader instructing Tim Healy in the mysteries of general agriculture:

> Mr Parnell had been a practical farmer during a portion of his life and would talk learnedly about the rearing of pigs, the calving of cows, and the top-dressing of land. Tim, reared in town and offices, was like most of the other leaders of the agrarian movement, unable to tell the difference between a horse and a cow, or between a field of potatoes and oats. Parnell quite gravely answered all the questions that Tim put to him, explaining all these mysteries in very simple and intelligible language.[28]

This question of Parnell's agricultural knowledge comes up when considering an interesting article in the *North American Review* of April 1880, under Parnell's name.[29] Nothing was less typical of Parnell than to write a magazine article, and in fact the article was written by Fanny and signed by her brother.[30] But much of the article concerns itself with purely agricultural matters, and gives a pithy and logical explanation of the decrease of grazing-land in Ireland; where the author writes of the effects of dampness and non-fertilisation, he knows exactly what he is talking about. It seems likely that Parnell provided his sister with the facts, and they are well substantiated. Andrew Kettle, himself an experienced farmer, often talked of agriculture to Parnell and was impressed by his knowledge of cattle: 'he had done a good deal in the stock line, but not much in tillage; one of his comments was that anyone could sell cattle but that it takes a good judge to buy them'.[31]

The traditional aspects of the estate and its economy, however, were treated cursorily by him. No individual trees or plantations at Avondale are ascribed to him, although he depleted the surrounding woods for his sawmills; and though he encouraged his mother to improve the terracing and views around the house, he himself 'had no time' to do so.[32] His agent stated that Parnell believed in 'the great value of timber in adding to [scenery] . . . I have known a tree to be felled here, in rather a prominent position, and his grief was so great that he told me he would prefer to lose one hundred pounds'.[33] Generally speaking, however, the finanical consideration seems to have carried the day. The turf bog he owned on Blackrock mountain at Aughavannagh held great attraction for him, and he sometimes walked there with John (once at two in the morning) to inspect it; he also rented a 'peat-litter industry' in Kildare.[34] His whole interest in his peat was, as John said, 'to get a market for it', and the revenue would probably have been diverted to his quarries, or, later, his mines. Avondale had, according to John, a fine orchard; but he regretfully recorded that his brother had all the trees cut down 'because he did not like apples'. [35] He was not a sentimental farmer; it is more than likely that he wanted some wood to try on his sawmill.

This sawmill remained a preoccupation all his life. From his early days as squire at Avondale he had operated a small one, as did his friends Captain Bookey at Derrybawn and Charles Barton at Annamoe. In 1876, visiting the Philadelphia Independence Centenary Exhibition, he studied the Machinery Hall, and the new suspension bridge in the same town; he was still, as when he had sketched the Warrior River Bridge, in 1871, planning a new sawmill. This was completed by 1885. It was situated by the river, 'under Kingston', near the main entrance to Avondale, and was built of wood and iron. Parnell also designed the water-way, race-lock and dam in the river, which ran the mill; the turbine-wheel was brought in America and in supervising its fitting Parnell nearly lost a finger. [36] John noticed in 1885 that his brother worked in the mill himself along with the men 'and, I was told, planed harder than anyone there'. [37] When Andrew Kettle visited Avondale a year later Parnell demonstrated the sawmill turbine in action, starting up the machinery himself – 'and this', Kettle added, 'on a Sunday'. [38] The old, smaller sawmill remained in operation, helping to produce beech paving-setts for Dublin Corporation; later stone setts became more popular, and these were produced in the Parnell quarries. A reporter from the *Nation* visited the Avondale sawmill in its early days:

> The sawmill, from its foundation to the erection of its machinery, I was informed, was constructed from the plans and under the direct supervision of Mr Parnell himself. When I entered there were some half-dozen saws at work, and as many lathes, the motive power being a turbine-wheel turned by a water-race from the Avonmore and equal to fifty horse-power. The wood being sawn and turned was oak, thinned from the woods of several miles' extent surrounding Avondale House. The men and youths at work were, a few years ago, ordinary farm labourers. They all seemed exceedingly active and skilful; their industry is stimulated by a rate of wages increasing by a certain amount each year, with piece-work rates in very busy times. Several of the lads whom I was were engaged in turning and painting brush-heads, while their elders were sawing up the trees sent in by the wood-ranger and cutting them into appropriate lengths. [39]

Ten years later, at the beginning of 1891, the Avondale sawmills were producing heavier articles, such as pavement blocks and railway sleepers. 'Beech blocks from these mills', recorded the *Freeman,* 'have been used in the laying down of Grafton Street and Suffolk street in wood pavement, and have been considered of great service and utility'; but William Kerr would have preferred to have 'first subjected them to the hardening process called "creosoting" '. [40]

As Parnell knew, however, wooden paving blocks were rapidly becoming outdated by stone setts, which he himself produced at Arklow. [41] The sawmills, like everything else at Avondale, had declined when John Parnell took over the estate in 1891; arriving there, 'Charley's workmen all gathered round me in a body, imploring me with tears and outstretched hands, to do something for them'. [42] The only hope was in the sawmills; and, instead of oak brush handles or beech paving setts, John Parnell found there was a market for elm coffin-timbers, out of which 'grew quite a thriving business'. The coffin-timbers seem to have had a gloomy appositeness; the estate continued to sink further into debt, and was sold off at the end of the decade. Had the superstitious Chief been alive, he would have expected no more. His delight at seeing his beloved sawmill revived would certainly have been negated by the ill-omened use to which it was put.

## II

By the mid-eighties, at any rate, a new industrial resource had taken over Parnell's imagination. This was his celebrated stone-quarrying venture. He had been interested in using the stone on his estate since the 1870s; on his visit to the Philadelphia exhibition 'he took special interest in the stone-cutting machinery'; by 1882 he was working a quarry rented from a neighbour without much return, but in this year wrote excitedly to Katherine O'Shea that he had 'discovered several quarries *on my own land,* much nearer to the railway station than the one we are working on, and for which we have to pay a very heavy royalty'. [43] Production increased after this, and in June 1883 it was decided at a Dublin Corporation meeting that 'a small order on trial' should be given to Parnell for stone paving setts. [44] One hundred tons at twenty-four shillings a ton were ordered. The Lord Mayor announced his pleasure at this sign of the exploitation of the natural resources of the country; Mr McEvoy sharply remarked that he was 'glad to find Mr Parnell turning his attention to matters of practical interest to the welfare of the country instead of those to which he had hitherto devoted himself'; Mr Shackleton countered by hoping 'it would not divert his attention from his more important work'. By the beginning of the next year the city engineer, Parke Neville, had inspected the granite setts produced by Parnell's men at Ballinaclash, and pronounced the stone good:

But the dressing of the stone was most defective, and such as that it would be impossible to make close joints or even courses in pavements executed with them. This defect could be remedied by the employment of skilled and experience sett dressers, and I gave every information in my power to Mr Kerr (Mr Parnell's agent) how to overcome this difficulty. [45]

When the *Nation* published this report by Neville, Kerr wrote in to say that the engineer had visited the quarries in September, 1883, at their inception; they now, in January 1884, employed several top-quality dressers and could turn out from 70 to 200 tons weekly. He also stated that Neville had subsequently ordered 800 tons of setts for O'Connell Bridge, 700 tons of which had already been delivered. Production at Ballinaclash was up to and above the standard of the Welsh quarries hitherto patronised by Dublin Corporation, and they gave a great deal of local employment.

John Parnell states that the stone at Ballinaclash was too brittle to be really suitable; but if this was an important drawback, the Corporation would hardly have favoured the quarry with such a large order. John goes on to say that his brother employed at least twenty men at one quarry alone (near the Avonmore River); [46] he also had another in Mount Avon wood. The stone he needed was whinstone, a volcanic or basaltic product, which was used by his Welsh rivals. John believed that, despite the unsuitability of his brother's quarries, 'those whom he consulted advised him to continue quarrying it, with the result that he lost many thousands of pounds'. [47] A flag quarry also lost money, and had to be abandoned. Kerr's report, however, suggests that the stone was more usable than John Howard remembers.

In 1884, in any case, an engineer named Patrick MacDonald told Parnell of an entire hill of whinstone near Arklow – Big Rock, on Lord Carysfort's land. Parnell, hearing who the owner was, said 'he won't let me have it, because he disapproves of my politics', though MacDonald felt that Carysfort would care only whether he got his royalties or not. As it turned out, Carysfort later said that he would have rented the quarries directly to Parnell, 'if only to provide work for the people'. [48] Be this as it may, Parnell inspected the location secretly, and approved of it; Joseph Hetherington of Manchester, a granite merchant, leased the hill from Carysfort for 31 years in December 1884, and then assigned the lease to Parnell. [49]

Production began at Big Rock in 1885, and the whinstone proved suitable; but the initial outlay was over £10,000 and – probably because he had to keep prices down to competitive Welsh levels – Parnell found that 'sett-making by itself did not pay' and had to spend a further £5,000 on machinery to convert the refuse into by-products like macadam and cement dust. This, according to John, 'began to pay almost immediately it was adopted.' Even more ambitious was the inclined railway line Parnell built from Big Rock to Arklow harbour; it was a mile and five-eighths long and cost £1,200, [50] and was intended for exporting the finished stone. He imported advisors from Wales, and also skilled stone-cutters, who were 'housed on the mountain-side, in a number of little huts'. [51] According to his wife, Parnell experimented with profit-sharing among the workers to increase production, and found it successful; [52] we have already seen that he tried out a piece-work incentive among his sawmill workers.

Finally, on 20 August 1885, Parnell had the satisfaction of showing a sub-committee of the Paving and Lighting Committee of Dublin Corporation round the quarry at Big Rock. The party included the Lord Mayor, the professor of natural experimental philosophy at Cambridge, Dr James Dewar, and the previously dissatisfied City Engineer, Parke Neville. Parnell met them at Rathdrum and brought them to Arklow, where a celebratory bazarr had been organised by the local priest, Father Dunphy. The quarries were inspected and all agreed that the setts produced there were equal to anything English. At the bazaar in the evening Parnell spoke on the promotion of native industry; his own 'little industry', he said, would never have got this far without the encouragement of Dublin Corporation, and he related this to the function of a native parliament in patronising home industries. He told how he had given a lower quotation than the Welsh quarries to the Corporation, and how the Welsh had then combined to undercut his price again; but the Corporation had spurned their offer, knowing that once Parnell's quarries were eliminated the Welsh would raise their prices again. He thanked the Corporation for this, and the evening wound up with mutual expressions of appreciation and good-will. [53]

There was, however, an opportunity for criticism here; and one of the few parliamentary appearances made by Parnell in early 1886 was on 18 March, when, 'still looking very ill', he came down to the House to hear a question from a Welsh member who accused the Dublin Corporation of jobbery with respect to their preference for Parnell's stone. [54] The questioner felt that in the circumstances the Corporation had forfeited their right to the £100,000 they had received from the Local Government Board. John Morley replied on behalf of the Government that this loan was not subject to any condition about the way the work was carried out; and in any case, he stated that when tenders for paving setts had been invited the previous autumn the best tenders were from Ballintoy (22 shillings a ton) and Arklow (24 shillings), which, taking into account the greater specific gravity of the former stone, were about equal. The Welsh tenders had uniformly been 27 shillings. The Parnellites cheered, and Morley affirmed that setts were now being ordered from both Ballintoy and Arklow.

Not all local opinion was favourable to the Big Rock quarries. In 1889 Owen Fogarty, an anti-Parnellite member of the Arklow Harbour Commission, accused the quarries of owing shipping dues to the harbour, with a good deal of publicity; this drew an angry letter from William Kerr to the local paper. [55] Kerr claimed that Fogarty's real intention was to 'scandalise' and bring in religious-political issues which he – Kerr – had hitherto avoided; in a further letter he stated that there had been a deliberate policy hatched at 'a sort of cabinet council' and anti-nationalist elements on the Commission to blacken Parnell's name. [56] Certainly, religious-political issues were to arise before long in the question of quarry administration, with a great deal of attendant publicity; I deal with this elsewhere.

By 1891, the *Freeman* recorded angrily, the Corporation had switched their entire order to the Antrim quarry, due to 'jobbery' and Tory influence. [57] By this time, however, Parnell's men were capable of producing polished granite ornaments of exhibition standard, [58] and he was exporting macadam to Birkenhead, Swansea, Cardiff, Newport, and as far abroad as Gibraltar and North Germany. [59] A newspaper report said that the supply of stone at Big Rock was 'inexhaustible, and the further in the excavations of the rock go, the better the quality becomes; the largest orders in paving setts can be executed, and Mr Parnell means to leave nothing undone to develop the industry to the fullest extent'. [60] The quarries became celebrated as a local 'sight'; staying at Glenart Castle in 1890, Lady Alice Howard was driven 'to Arklow Rock after luncheon, and saw Parnell's quarries', [61] and as late as 1916 Joseph McCarroll of Wicklow wrote of them to John Parnell as 'a standing proof of his fostering of industrial development'. [62]

But by 1891 it was the need of employment that kept the quarries going rather than the commercial demand. Writing to the *Freeman a propos* a labour dispute in this year, [63] William Kerr stated that, though the quarries paid out £5,000 to £10,000 a year in wages and had relieved distress greatly, 'at the present moment we have about fifteen thousand tons of setts and macadam on hands and the greater part of this was made so as to keep employment going and people from starving'. Kerr estimated this stock as worth £6,000. Both he and Parnell[64] made it clear that if wages were raised from 13 and 14 shillings a week to 15 shillings, the quarry would be unable to keep operating. At its height, it had employed over 200 men; [65] but in 1891 only eighty were working there. [66] In August 1891 a letter from Kerr to the *Wicklow People* mentioned that production had temporarily stopped because of over-stocking and export difficulties. 10,000 tons of macadam and 6,000 tons of setts were lying at Big Rock. His attempts to arrange a steamer for the quarries' own use had almost been successful, but were temporarily abandoned because the harbour was not safe enough. [67] Further difficulties arose over a landing-stage

Parnell proposed building for his own use at the termination of his railway-track in Arklow harbour. The anti-Parnellite element on the Harbour Board insisted upon several 'hedging' clauses before allowing this; they wished the stage to be their property, and insisted on several important rights over it. Kerr angrily threatened to take away, not only the quarry custom from the harbour, but also Parnell's offer of free stone for harbour improvement works.[68] The disagreement became bitter, with broadsides delivered from Kerr at Avondale, and a special meeting of the Board on 3 October where tempers ran high.[69] A compromise was arranged, with both sides backing down; but by then, Parnell was dead.[70]

Despite such disputes, and the labour troubles mentioned below,[71] he had nonetheless remained sanguine about the quarries to the end of his life. A month before his death he wrote optimistically to his wife that Kerr was 'getting up a small company to buy a steamer, and I think he may succeed'.[72] The quarries, however, were not lucrative enough to pay Parnell's debts after he died; in 1895 John Parnell purchased the lease and equipment from his sister-in-law, together with 'the goodwill of the business there', but he was forced to sell Avondale four years later.[73] The Parnell quarries, as McCarroll wrote, remained; and John Parnell emphasised that few of his brother's acquaintances realised just how deeply the quarries had preoccupied him during his career.[74] This is no more than the truth. Parnell was preoccupied with his stone-works to the point of obsession. It is significant that he used his political 'drawing-power' to encourage publicity for the Arklow quarry when the Dublin sub-committee visited it, although he usually kept private and public life rigorously separate; and it is even more telling that, though ill and politically inactive at the time, he exerted himself to attend parliament to hear the reception of a question about his stoneworking contract. The quarries preoccupied him even more than the sawmills; the only facet of his 'estate industries' which held more fascination for him was the more glamorous, but less productive mining operations which he carried on all through his political career.

## III

Mining in Wicklow throughout this period was not a preoccupation of Parnell's alone. In January 1882 a talk on the 'Industrial Resources of Ireland' given by G.P. Bevan to the Society of Arts in London emphasised the potential of copper and iron mines in Wicklow and the decrease in their exploitation over the past few decades;[75] a select commiteee meeting on Irish industries a few years later discussed pyrites and gold in Wicklow, and a member said 'there were grounds for encouraging further work for the discovery of gold in the Wicklow district'.[76] It is not clear when Parnell's obsession with mine-working began; but an article in the *Nation* of 20 November 1880 recorded that 'for years past he has been making borings for lead and in his latest attempt he has succeeded in striking the lode.' By then, a mine-shaft sunk near the Avonmore was connected by a steel rope to the sawmill machinery which thus supplied power for a water-pump as the boring was in an extremely wet location. Parnell, according to the newspaper report, was 'sanguine that the recently discovered lode will become a commercial success; he has expended a large sum of money on these mining investigations, but hitherto he has met with no pecuniary reward.'

This mineshaft by the river near Kingston had been sunk by Parnell himself, and had another purpose: to rediscover the copper seam worked by the Connoree Copper Company years before, and reopened by accident when the railway bridge was built across the Avonmore. There were also, however, disused lead mines already bored on the estate, and it was in connection with these that Parnell wrote to Mrs O'Shea in 1881:

> I have satisfied myself by two separate tests today that there is a good deal of silver in the dark stone of which there is so much in the old mine. In fact, nearly the whole lode consists of this (the miners are working on it in the North level). I cannot say how many ounces there will be to the ton until I get it assayed, but if there should be six or eight ounces to the ton it ought to pay to work.[77]

In 1883, however, John Parnell found his brother still indefinite about the actual location of the supposed copper seam near Kingston;[78] four years later, his examinations of the old lead mines had still not yielded any information as to whether the seam might run across his own land, though 'one of his tenants told him that his father, whilst driving his cattle across the mountain, found that one of them, while cropping the short grass, had scraped bare a vein of lead; the man, however, had forgotten the exact place where this was believed to have occurred'.[79] Such impreciseness did not daunt Parnell; on the contrary, it encouraged him. At this time, John tells us, Charles explained his pet scheme to him – an idea to which he recurred again and again:

> 'When I am able, I will get the Dublin, Wicklow and Wexford Railway, in conjunction with the Great Southern Railway, to build a line from the Meeting of the Waters right through Glenmalure to the Kilkenny coalfield, tapping the lead and iron mines on their way.' His great idea was to connect the iron at Avoca and Rathdrum with the coal at Kilkenny.[80]

By this time – 1887 – Parnell had sunk the first shaft in his search for gold, having found gold traces in a quartz vein located in a field rented from him by one Nicholas Devereux. In 1888 he told Davitt that he had been looking for gold 'for fourteen years', but his searches seem to have been desultory until this 'breakthrough'. [81] The same field contained yellow ochre, and he expected to find an accompanying vein of copper; this never materialised, but the search for gold was in any case his predominant interest.

Questioned by Barry O'Brien about shooting trips with Parnell to Aughavannagh, John Redmond recalled: 'He [Parnell] was always looking for gold in Wicklow, Gold, sport, and the applied sciences were his subjects out of parliament'. [82] From the mid-eighties began his passion for assaying, when samples of ore were constantly arriving from Kerr at Avondale for analysis by Parnell in his workshops at Eltham and Brighton; in 1885 he diverted a troublesome South African encountered on the Irish Mail by showing him some iron pyrites specimens which he was carrying 'in his trouser pocket'. [83] The lack of definite results never worried him; his operations were carried on beyond all reasonable proportion to what they yielded. In August 1887 he wrote to Mrs O'Shea that 'the new mine is improving, so I have been tempted to continue it for a short while longer'; [82] by the time of the Special Commission hearings Parnell was convinced that at last he had struck gold, and this preoccupation possessed him to the exclusion of all else.

He was not the only person to believe in an imminent gold rush in the Wicklow hills this year; a letter in the *Wicklow Newsletter* in January 1889 enthusiastically described the incalculable amount of gold around Croghan Mountain, [85] and in June a *Freeman* correspondent excitedly reported 'considerable quantities of floating gold' in the river near Aughrim. [86] The *Wicklow Newsletter* jeered at this claim, pointing out that ' "the difficulty of pitching upon the particular spot where it lies" has been recognised, unfortunately, in the county since the days of King O'Toole;' [87] but in October 'Mr Doyle, an expert gold-finder' was investigating likely localities at Ballymanus and by January 1890 had decided that working them would pay. [88] However, Parnell, equally convinced, had more opportunity to carry through his plan, and all through the Special Commission hearings he thought of it. Davitt watched him unwrapping a parcel and taking out a tiny nugget as they sat in court one day, and noticed how Parnell's attention was totally claimed by this 'find' – the result of fourteen years' search. [89] Davitt thought this obsession of Parnell's eclipsed his interest in all that was happening; indeed, at the far more dramatic moment of the publication of Pigott's forgeries, he had insisted on completing some assaying before going up to London from Eltham. [90] Henniker Heaton met Parnell when he appeared in the House that evening. The Irish leader on whom all eyes were naturally turned, in-

stantly engaged him in urgent conversation; which, to Heaton's surprise was entirely about a gold strike in Australia, of which Heaton
had specimens – he gave Parnell some of the lode, which Parnell
analysed enthusiastically (and accurately) at Eltham. [91]

By February 1888 Parnell was sufficiently encouraged by his findings to apply to the Commissioner of Woods, Forests and Land
Preserves for a licence 'to search for, raise, mine, and wash gold or
gold ores or gravel in the county of Wicklow'. [92] He had found gold, he
wrote,

> in two of the tracts coloured blue [on an accompanying map]
> both in the gravel and in quartz lodes, not much in the latter,
> but sufficient to give good hopes from further explorations; I
> have found gold in the gravel in such quantities in several places
> as to make me believe that it could be washed for under the
> hydraulic system as profitably as in any place in California, and
> in this my opinion is supported by a mining engineer of large
> Californian experience. [93]

Six months later he acknowledged the grant of a twenty-one year lease
empowering him to raise gold, and asked for the right of following
mineral lodes discovered on his property 'across the river Avonmore in
an easterly, and across the river Avonbeg in a westerly, direction'. [94]
This too was granted, and in December 1888 Parnell asked for the
lease to be extended to lands west of the Avonmore, as he had
'discovered several gold-bearing lodes in this additional area'.
Moreover,

> I have spent a good sum in assaying and prospecting them, and if
> you regarded the matter as an alternative, I should prefer it to
> the original area coloured blue in your map, which I have not yet
> examined; I have drawn the boundaries so as to exclude
> cultivated land, the area being entirely composed of wild moun-
> tains and valleys. [95]

This latter consideration did not mean that no-one was inconvenienced
by Parnell's mining operations. Writing, probably to Kerr, in May
1890, he gave instructions to 'divide your force of miners and start on
Ballycapple at once – Boyle will know the most likely spot, *and it is
probable the tenant may be induced to dispense with the month's
notice*'. [96] The extension of mining operations in this year bore fruit,
though not in relation to the gold he searched for. In March 1890 the
*Wicklow Newsletter* reported that Parnell's Ballycapple investigations
'have been eminently successful and there is every likelihood of a
profitable return upon the investment', [97] and in December, the month
of the Irish party split over Parnell's leadership, he told a reporter
from another paper that he

heard today of the successful issue of some mining operations; the letter I received relates to the search for the continuation in depth of the great lode of magnetic iron ore which was worked last about two hundred years ago for the supply of the iron furnaces at Clash, near my native home. [98]

He had started searching for this a year before, and had now located a thirty-foot wide seam a hundred feet down; its composition was sixty per cent metallic iron and ten per cent manganese, 'thus proving it to be in the very first rank of the iron ores of the world'. He was unable for the moment to smelt it locally, but should like to do so; already his quarries and mines were employing over 250 men. Parnell then enlarged in expansive terms upon his plan to connect the Kilkenny coalfield by rail with the iron ore of east Wicklow, via the iron ore deposits centred round Shillelagh; he also prophesied the utilisation of the river Barrow and the sea-port of Waterford. Using existing services, only thirty miles of new railroad would be needed to complete the linkage. With 'public money and private capital', the coalfields of Tyrone could similarly be connected with the Antrim iron mines. Parnell spoke of these plans at length and with passion; the *Freeman* reporter who wrote that he was 'almost as ardent a miner as an Irish politician' understated the case.

This reporter travelled round Parnell's mines with him a week later and recorded his minute knowledge of the geography and geology of the terrain. 'His mind appeared to have banished all thoughts of the thrilling scenes through which he had passed'; in fact, he probably looked upon the political embroilments of the time as an unwelcome interruption, although his eye was still bandaged from the quicklime thrown at Kilkenny a few days before.

> Indeed, it was strange to watch the individual as he climbed fences and made his way through rough and hilly fields and to reflect occasionally that he, apparently with undisturbed mind, was the man about whom the whole world was talking. At one point he conversed with men who were above the ground, at another he explained some technicality in the art to your representative, and throughout showed how completely he had mastered the subject, and how completely he was absorbed in its various workings and speculations. [99]

Parnell had come down on the 8 a.m. train from Dublin and was met by Kerr at Glenealy station, whence they drove to Ballycapple and Ballard. After two hours' consultation with the miners and an inspection of the newly-discovered lode, he drove on to Arklow. Here he was recognised, and arrived at Father Dunphy's house surrounded by a friendly crowd. Here he lunched, before inspecting his quarries, where construction on the inclined railroad was about to begin. In the evening he dined with his sister Emily at Bray; by seven o'clock he was on board the mailboat for England.

Thus at the busiest time of his life, and the most desperate stage of his career, he still returned to his mines as often as possible. At the Leinster Hall convention in 1891, Katharine Tynan noticed him absorbed in conversation with a mining expert while enthusiastic adherents attempted in vain to attract his attention;[100] and, once in Wicklow, he lost himself completely in their administration. He was back at Ballard and Ballycapple on 3 January 1891; but neither at this time, nor at any period after the euphoria of 1889, did Parnell mention his gold 'finds' to reporters or anyone else; his widow took the balanced view that 'the working was far too laborious and expensive to be profitable otherwise than as a hobby'[101] and possibly Parnell came to share this opinion. His iron mines continued to obsess him all through the frantic last year of his life. In a passage which is as striking as William O'Brien's celebrated description of the Chief materialising in the fog at Greenwich Observatory in 1886,[102] Standish O'Grady wrote:

> I saw him twice during the last year of his life. Once, while driving in the county of Wicklow on the coldest day which I had ever experienced, the day of a tremendous blizzard in England, on a lonely hillside, I came full-tilt on him. He too was driving. He sat on one side of an outside car drawn by a white horse. The agent of his Wicklow estates was on the other. The driver was on the box. Parnell was muffled in the most copious manner, quite a hill of rugs, cloaks and shawls. The agent, Kerr, now dead, stopped to talk with me. I knew him slightly. Then he suddenly introduced me to his companion; I had not previously recognised him. There, on the hillside, I had some ten minutes' conversation with Parnell who, however, did nearly all the talking. He talked almost altogether about his mines and quarries; on that subject he was almost cracked. He had men in his employment for many years, probing and boring over all those mountains. A good deal of his fortune must have been spent on that hobby. On the day I met him he was on his way to inspect some such borings. He believed that at last he had struck iron, and was going to do great things in the bowels of the earth. His boyish enthusiasm about these holes had something in it half diverting, half pathetic. At that time he was in the full career of his campaign against his revolted followers.[103]

There is much in this evocative anecdote which recalls O'Brien's view of Parnell in 1886. The muffled-up dress, almost amounting to a disguise; evidence of eccentricity, to the extent that one questioned his sanity; and the mystique of a leader who was already almost a fable, symbolised by his appearance in a mounting storm, drawn by a white horse. But equally significant are details like Parnell doing 'almost all the talking', which was not characteristic behaviour of the man – except where mineralogy was concerned. It is also interesting that, although Parnell repeated the news of an iron strike, he made no mention of gold; this chimera must have been regretfully abandoned by 1891. O'Grady implies that the iron strike was also more in Parnell's mind than anywhere else; how far this is true is impossible to ascertain (Katharine Tynan heard that 'whenever he showed signs of closing down the mines they were "salted" by someone interested in keeping them going';[104]) but others believed in it as well as he. More than twenty years later, when John Parnell was writing his memoir of his brother, Joseph McCarroll of the Wicklow Town Commissioners wrote to him that 'there was no question of the ore not being there, and in abundance'.[105] Such optimism would have been after Parnell's own heart. His insouciant attitude towards the unproductive mines recalls Maria Edgeworth's Sir Ulick O'Shane.[106] In Parnell's time Avondale became neglected, and the demesne, once an arboreal showpiece, was denuded of much of its timber; it was left to a British ministry in 1904 to plant seeds and seedlings from all over the world and to restore the plantings in the tradition of Samuel Hayes. Parnell, on the other hand, would have been happy to see Wicklow, Carlow and Kilkenny become a model Black Country, and to run railways through the loveliest mountain valleys in the area. Nowadays the visitor to Wicklow thinks of Parnell as he drives from Laragh down the beautiful vale of Clara to Rathdrum; it would be far more apposite to remember him as one continues from Rathdrum through Avoca to Arklow. The road goes by Castle Howard, Ballyarthur, Shelton Abbey and Glenart Castle, the strongholds of county magnates in Parnell's time; but the river is dead and the air foul, due to an intensive chemicals industry in the region. Parnell would have felt the price was worth paying; had he lived, and been successful in his mining operations, there would be little enough left of County Wicklow, as we know it, today.

# 2   *Parnell and his tenants*

Does he [Parnell] wish to extricate himself from an anomalous position, so that, being disembarrassed by any connection with landlordism, he may be free to take any line of action he pleases in a new and more revolutionary agitation? Time will tell.

Editorial in *The Times* headed
'Mr Parnell selling his estate', quoted
in *Wicklow Newsletter*, 16 December 1882.

## I

The anomaly of Parnell's position as a landlord at the head of a land reform movement, though most marked in the 1879–81 period, remained obvious all his life. Political opponents rarely let slip an opportunity of drawing attention to it; efforts to prove that the Land League leader did not practise what he preached were frequent throughout Parnell's career. Such accusations had the effect, useful for my purpose, of provoking a spate of letters to newspapers and general resolutions; they also inspired more than one newspaper editor to send a roving reporter to Rathdrum to see what he could glean. Thus there is more evidence available regarding Parnell's relations with his tenants than any other sphere of his activities as a landlord.

The political importance of this relationship was seen from the beginning of Parnell's career; I have mentioned the emphasis laid upon his status as landlord in his first election campaigns, [1] and the circular about Parnell sent by the parish priest of Rathdrum to the Meath clergy in 1875 declared that 'all his tenants here are comfortable and independent, with good long leases . . . I have never heard of a case of oppression or extermination attributed to him'. [2] Many secondary records of Parnell's life claim that his tenants were not insensible of the delicacy of his political position as regards his private affairs, and acted accordingly. His brother recalled that tenants on the estate 'very often took advantage of his good nature and not only did not pay their rents, but almost denuded his Aughavannagh shooting of game'; [3] elsewhere, when explaining Parnell's penury at the time of the National Tribute, John wrote: 'During the famine years very few of the tenants of the Avondale estate paid their rents, and even after the famine was over they kept up this custom largely, finding that he was an easy-going landlord and could not bear the idea of eviction'. [4] Whatever Parnell's personal attitude towards eviction, his political position after 1879 could not have borne it. There is no evidence that he would have evicted in any case; but the anecdote which John goes on to recount implies that his brother felt some resentment at the leniency he was compelled to practise. This tells of a faithful supporter running after Parnell's carriage after a political meeting, and Parnell ignoring the demonstration: "let him run a little longer," said Charley, "seeing that I have let his rent run for seven years". [5] Sir William Butler, shooting with Parnell in 1889, remarked on the people coming out of cottages and saluting 'the Chief'; but, he added, 'it seemed as though they were not there, and when one of our party said that one of the most effusive cap-wavers had not paid any rent for five years, Parnell paid no more heed to the remark than to the waving'. [6]

He was not always as impassive; and he usually recollected where arrears were owed. At Aughavannagh in 1882 John Redmond heard him call a tenant to task for failing to keep the game preserves clear in August: ' "Whitty," said Parnell, "you have been on the land for many years, you never pay me any rent, and all I ask you is to keep the sheep off the mountains when I am out shooting, and, you old villain you, you don't even do that" '. [7] But, if he was well aware when his tenants 'took advantage', he was always on good terms with them. Everyone attests to this. [8] Part of the reason may have been that Parnell was always absolutely at ease with working-men; never an egalitarian, he would not have seen any reason why he should not be. This lack of constraint followed naturally from his aristocratic attitude – not, as might initially be supposed, from the reverse. Rather ingenuously he told Barry O'Brien: 'I like looking at working-men. A working-man has a pleasant life, when he has plenty to do and is fairly treated'; [9] whatever capital his opponents might make out of his seignorial position at Avondale, he felt totally at ease there. When St John Ervine was writing his biography of Parnell, a correspondent informed him: 'I know . . . a rabid Unionist who to this day *loves* Parnell. He says that Mr Parnell was not a talkative man, but that he would chat freely and laugh heartily with the people about Avondale, and the quarrymen and the miners; but that with upstarts he would have nothing to do.' [10] Political colleagues like T. P. O'Connor and William O'Brien noticed the unforced familiarity with which he treated his tenantry. [11] Justin

McCarthy also recorded this, and told an attractive story in illustration, about an English visitor to Avondale seeing over a new cottage built by Parnell; the chimney smoked abominably but the inhabitant refused to tell Parnell for fear of disappointing him. [12] The esteem in which Parnell's tenants held him was further attested to by the celebrated Avondale ploughing matches, which I deal with elsewhere. [13]

## II

In Wicklow as everywhere else, however, the landlord–tenant balance was upset by the Land War; I intend briefly to consider the history of this period in Wicklow before considering in detail Parnell's position *vis-à-vis* his tenants.

Wicklow had a tradition of good, if conservative, landlords and a prosperous tenantry; [14] even in the distressed year of 1879, feeling in the county did not run as high as elsewhere, as a letter in the Wicklow *Newsletter* of 21 June 1879 complained. 'In this year of depression . . . why is this county particularly, I had almost said shamefully, silent?' The anonymous correspondent went on to denounce landowners, 'many of them M.P.s professing "Home Rule" and advocating tenant-right', for hanging back from rent reductions on behalf of their 'highly rack-rented and impoverished peasantry'. Another letter in the next issue agreed completely, while pointing out that there were some good landlords in Wicklow nevertheless; again, landowning M.P.s were particularly singled out for attack. This began a correspondence in the newspaper which shows on the one hand a feeling that Wicklow was particularly fortunate in its landlords, and, on the other, a sense that the county was hanging back from its duty. [15] By September the controversy had reached the deliberations of the Rathdrum Board of Guardians, to whom a resolution was presented calling for rent reduction petitions to be generally adopted; the chairman, Colonel Tighe, a landlord, deprecated the introduction of class conflict into the proceedings, and nervously eulogised the traditionally good landlord–tenant relations in the county. He was, however, opposed by the radical element and eventually left the meeting with other 'ex officio' guardians like Colonel Tottenham and William Kemmis. The rump of the Board (who did not number any scions of the landowning Wicklow gentry) triumphantly passed the resolution, and looked forward to some militant local action. [16]

By December, few landlords had taken the heavy hints about abatement dropped in newspaper correspondence and committee meetings all over the county, or been encouraged by the *Wicklow Newsletter's* practice of printing the names of abating landlords whenever possible. [17] January saw the first 'large and enthusiastic' tenant-right meeting in Rathdrum, addressed by W. J. Corbet, M.P. for the county, as well as Sexton and Davitt.[18] Andrew O'Byrne, the other Member, and a 'nominal Home Ruler,' implicitly denounced for not reducing his rents, did not attend; but the name of Parnell, 'whom Wicklow claimed for her own', was cheered, and Davitt called for the formation of a Land League branch in the town to 'meet Mr Parnell at the railway station and conduct him back to Avondale' when he returned from America.

O'Byrne was by now a marked man, and despite anxious letters denying that he had purposely avoided attending the land meeting [19] and a hasty abatement of all his rents,[20] he stood down at the 1880 election; the connection between landlord and politician had been spelled out too clearly for his comfort. In the election W. J. Corbet and J. C. McCoan, Home Rulers, beat the Conservative candidates W. W. Fitzwilliam Hume-Dick and Robert Gun-Cunningham, Wicklow landlords of the old school;[21] on the night of the election a crowd in Rathdrum stoned the residence of the Conservative agent there.[22] The way seemed clear for widespread land agitation.

This was not, however, what happened. Corbet, himself a Wicklow landowner, was at the head of most demonstrations, and was always moderate; when a zealous supporter mentioned that the landlords 'wanted lead' he threatened to step down unless such language ceased.[23] Moreover, despite Davitt's invitation, no Land League branch was formed in Rathdrum, or anywhere in the county, until November 1880.[24] Another was founded, at Tinahely, in December.[25] But even landlords as important as Lord Brabazon soon became prepared to reduce rents up to fifty per cent;[26] the only *cause célèbre* at this time took place, predictably enough, on the Fitzwilliam estate, where an old man died following his eviction.[27] Land meetings increased in number throughout January 1881;[28] but Corbet's speeches extenuated many landlords, while execrating Fitzwilliam. In February 1881 even W. F. Littledale of Whaley Abbey, who had provoked wild scenes at an earlier eviction, abated his rents.[29] Organisation continued; the Ladies' Land League had formed three branches in the county by March 1881.[30] A county meeting of the Land League at Wicklow on 25 March drew a crowd that even the hostile *Wicklow Newsletter* (which approved of abating landlords but could not abide the League) admitted numbered 4,000.[31] But at such meetings the tone remained unfailingly moderate.[32] A later meeting at Rathdrum emphasised proudly the absence of violent crime in the county.[33] Moreover, the second Home Rule member for the county, J. C McCoan, was no extremist; he voted against the Parnellites on the second reading of the Land Bill and was shortly afterwards censured by the organisation.[34]

A prime cause of the moderate attitude taken by Wicklow opinion was that the landlords seem to have come some of the way to meet land agitation demands. Father Dunphy, the parish priest of Arklow, was a well-known nationalist and Land Leaguer; but even he wrote, while specifically describing the case-histories of ill-treated tenants in other counties:

> The local landed proprietors ... have come forward at this critical time and given their tenants substantial reductions in rent, some even less than Griffith's Valuation ... Such landlords have never forfeited the traditions of their families, always kind and considerate to those who held under them. Surely the present peaceable state of the country is due in great part to their kind and indulgent treatment of the tillers of the soil. [35]

This seignorial sense of duty did not mean sympathy for land reform; on the Rathdrum Board of Guardians the landlord element continued to oppose such motions, and sometimes to win hard-fought victories. [36] But the peaceable state of the county was generally remarked upon. [37] Though Baron Dowse noted at the summer assizes of 1881 that six out of the ten cases before him 'had reference to the present condition of the county', none of them involved personal violence. [38] The *Wicklow Newsletter* continued to give most prominence to events like the Wicklow and Bray regattas, the Delgany cottage-garden show, and cricket fixtures at the great houses of the county – with no sense of fiddling while Rome burned. At a Wicklow Land League meeting a visitor from the central branch made a point of asking whether it was true that 'in this neighbourhood they had not much reason to complain of bad landlords?' The rather defensive answer was that 'to an extent', this was true. [39] The visitor, Mr Heffernan, went on to give a slightly admonishing address upon the necessity of condemning *all* landlords; he seems to have felt his audience needed reminding. Nonetheless, complaints like that of one of the Mount Kennedy tenants, who remarked imaginatively that Colonel Gun-Cunningham was 'a modern Pharaoh', remained infrequent; [40] and speaking at Rathdrum in December 1881, John Redmond remarked that 'within the last month he had heard a statement that in the county of Wicklow the spirit of the people was not as high or as determined as it ought to be'. [41] Not all his audience can have agreed with his subsequent contention that the Avondale ploughing match gave the lie to this statement. [42]

It is necessary, however, to distinguish between the east of the county and the west, where land was poorer, model estates fewer, and landlords harsher. The Land League meetings at Carnew and Baltinglass were correspondingly more extreme. Fitzwilliam was vilified by the parish priest of Clonegal as the worst of landlords; [43] the first arrests when County Wicklow was proclaimed in October 1881 were those of the president and secretary of Baltinglass Land League.[44] It was in the same area that Wicklow landlords first felt it necessary to band together; on 31 October 1881 the Shillelagh Mutual Defence Association was formed under the aegis of the Hon. John Fitzwilliam.[45] The following February, when Corbet asked the Chief Secretary why the county continued to be proclaimed despite the peaceable conditions there, Forster's reason was the intimidation in West Wicklow, especially round Baltinglass.[46] In September of the same year a magistrates' meeting made the same distinction between the state of the county east and west;[47] the Grand Jury in November 1882 still referred to Baltinglass as a centre of intimidation.[48] By 1883 the *Wicklow Newsletter* triumphantly pointed to the peaceful nature of the county as evidence that the Land League never really appealed to Wicklowmen except in 'the extreme west'. By 1885, however, even Fitzwilliam was giving up to fifty per cent abatement on a half-year's rent,[49] and the land question had been shelved long before this.

Even at the height of the agitation, West Wicklow never had a particularly active record. Although a thousand people massed in Wicklow on the night of Parnell's arrest, and the shops of Rathdrum were closed in mourning,[50] the height of seditious activity was the illicit posting of No Rent Manifesto notices;[51] landlord organisations were not formed at Rathdrum and Newtownmountkennedy until two months after the Shillelagh meeting, and no landlord in the east of the county equalled Fitzwilliam's donation to the Mutual Defence Fund of £1,000.[52] Henry Monk mentioned at a Rathdrum branch meeting that several landlords had refused to join on the grounds that boycotting did not happen in the area;[53] large rent reductions continued to be granted. In the troubled month of December 1881 Corbet announced: 'The people of Wicklow have been remarkable all through these trying times for the quiet way in which they have conducted themselves; and I am informed that the constabulary authorities have thought it unnecessary to bring an additional force of police into Rathdrum on this occasion.'[54] A year later, the *Wicklow Newsletter* satirically described Corbet's political image: 'bland and deliberate, as is his habit [and] much less violent than his compatriots . . . The gentleman and the man of culture could not wholly lose himself in the agitator and the party-politician'.[55] But Corbet had reason for moderation. East Wicklow landlords reduced their rents drastically; in February 1881 Lord Powerscourt and his tenants arranged to decide rents by each side appointing a rent valuer, and a disinterested third party umpiring the findings; good relations were thus preserved, and none of his tenants appeared in the Land Courts.[56] Expediency was an important motive; the landlords continued to fight their corner, and when a Home Rule Candidate named John Gaskin attempted to get on to the Rathdrum Board of Guardians (whose meetings had taken on an increasingly political complexion), the aristocratic Truell–Dick–Cunningham faction used all their proxy and property votes to keep him out – so energetically that when Gaskin demanded a re-count it was discovered that their influence had been exaggerated and Gaskin won the ensuing re-election. [57] But the land-agitation, never revolutionary, was nearly over. In the summer assizes of 1882 Baron Dowse admitted the small incidence of crime in Wicklow except for threatening letters; [58] rents were being paid promptly to Lord Fitzwilliam's agent at Coolattin in September, [59] and by the end of 1884, according to the *Newsletter*, Wicklow had seen 'the last of the Land Act', the sub-commissioners having held only one sitting which heard very few cases: 'the rent question in Wicklow may be considered as settled'. [60] Rent reductions continued to be made, even by the most conservative of landlords; [61] but the demand for abatement was not as urgent as it had been, and the Plan of Campaign fell noticeably flat on the one local estate where it was tried upon any scale. [62]

### III

Even in the context of this moderation, however, the landlord of Avondale was still head of the Land League, and it was inevitable that some capital should be made out of his position. His name was among those of the first Wicklow landlords to give a universal abatement in November 1879, when he gave a reduction of twenty per cent and bog leave to all tenants; [63] in December 1880 he lowered the rents of his Glenmalure lands to Griffith's valuation. [64] But on 5 October 1880 a letter appeared in the *Irish Times* from 'A Constant Reader' which drew attention to what quickly became known as 'the Parnell lease'. The letter stated simply:

> The following extract, taken from a memorial in the office of the Registry of Deeds, may be interesting to your readers and to the Land League: 1880, B.44, no. 199, memorial of lease dated 18th August, Charles Stuart [*sic*] Parnell of the one part and of the other part –, in consideration of the surrender of a former lease and in lieu and bar of all claim for improvements, past or future, disturbance or otherwise, by the said –, the said Charles Stewart Parnell demise, etc.

The implication was clear: Parnell, champion of radical land reform, had denied one of his own tenants a fair lease. This letter was followed by another communication two days later, signed 'A Tenant': 'What has Mr Parnell done for his tenants, or what does he intend to do for them? Will he make them a present of their farms, or will he lower their rents? . . . Talk is cheap, but acts are of some weight. Perhaps Mr Parnell will condescend to give us tenants this information.' [65] Few of

Parnell's tenants could have been in the habit of sending letters to the *Irish Times;* it seems likely that this letter came from the same source as the first, and that both had to do with the other party to the 'Parnell lease' – Charles Mathew West of Mount Avon, who had written rather prematurely to the *Wicklow Newsletter* on 5 October that he would *not*, as rumoured, be 'the first applicant to come before the Land Commission with reference to a lease made to me by Mr C. S. Parnell, M.P.'.[66] Nor would this have been the first disagreement between the two; in 1869 West had taken Parnell to court over money owing to him, half of which was still outstanding in 1880.[67]

In any case, the 'exposure' had its desired effect. A week later the *Irish Times* recorded with satisfaction that at a meeting of the Westport Town Commissioners, a member remarked that 'he [Parnell] certainly sets a very bad example to the Irish landlords; I saw a copy of the lease in a Dublin paper and its clauses are the most stringent I have ever seen . . . they are worse than those of the Duke of Leinster's lease'.[68] The paper did what it could to encourage such widespread discussion, devoting an editorial to the subject which asked: 'Who has not now heard of the Parnell lease?' and emphasised the universal nature of the controversy. This leader went on to quote a letter from Alfred MacDermott, Parnell's solicitor, who raised the points that the lease was to a 'gentleman', not a tenant farmer; that the improvements clause had not been objected to at the time; and that the holding (twenty three acres and a house) was not a farm. But, the *Irish Times* pointed out, West's solicitor contradicted this: the holding *was* a farm, and the only reason his client did not object to the improvements clause was because it would affect, not himself, but a purchaser of the lease from him.

This refutation of MacDermott was heavily underlined by the *Irish Times,* which went on to remark disingenuously that 'we shall not allow ourselves to assume that there is no way out of the maze; if there be, we shall be delighted to be the means of letting the public see it'. But if Parnell could not explain the anomaly, then the Land League must require him to repudiate the lease, and not let such an arrangement occur again.[69]

Thus the political conclusion was drawn speedily and categorically: if Parnell himself was open to question as a landlord, then his authority over the League was flawed. Nor did the pressure cease here. Another letter in the same paper during this month claimed maltreatment of tenants at Carrignamuck and Corrignameel in Glenmalure, part of the Avondale estate. Parnell had supposedly induced these tenants, Shiel and Kavanagh, to grant him possession of the mountain pastures for shooting in return for being allowed to run sheep on it; but in 1872, when the tenants sowed out crops there as usual, he charged them with wilful trespass and summoned them before

Hacketstown Petty Sessions to try and dispossess them. The case was, however, dismissed. The writer of this letter also claimed that Parnell let out Blackrock mountain at £60 per annum, while its poor law valuation was £20 10s; and, finally, that Parnell had, as his brother's agent, speculated in property in Carlow. Clonmore had been bought by his father on mortgage for £56,000; Parnell had raised rents, evicted those who did not pay, and then sold off the estate at enough profit to buy an estate in Kilkenny. The letter was, like the rest, anonymous, being signed simply 'Inquirer'; [70] it shows evidence of research in the Registry of Deeds, and thus is likely to have come from the same pen as the letter 'exposing' the Parnell lease.

The *Irish Times*, strangely, did not draw attention in its editorial to 'Inquirer's' letter, or publicly investigate any of the assertions therein. Possibly, having tested the ground, the paper found it would not bear much weight. The Carlow transactions were, of course, Henry Tudor Parnell's; his brother's only connection with these dealings was to act as trustees for one day during a conveyancing. [71] The rent of Blackrock is not recorded individually upon the Avondale rent schedule, [72] but had Parnell really trebled the poor law valuation the *Irish Times* would not have left the matter there; and in a letter to the *Nation* a month later the Blackrock tenants indignantly affirmed that they were only required to pay Griffith's valuation. [73] And the anecdote about Shiel and Kavanagh contains its own contradiction; Parnell may have allowed them graze sheep on the shooting, but no arrangement was made about sowing crops there. The dispossession attempted would have referred to the mountain territory only; the tenants obviously had other farms for their livelihood. Moreover, for Parnell to claim mountain for shooting in 1872, a comparatively easy time, was not unreasonable; especially if he conceded grazing rights to the tenants.

Thus the hostile press did not seize on this evidence to bolster up their case; and at the end of October, vindication for Parnell in respect of the Parnell lease had come from the unlikely quarter of a Protestant clergyman in Dingle. On 30 October the *Nation* published a letter sent by Rev. C. McCarthy, C. R. A. M., ex-siz. TCD., to the *Kerry Sentinel* on the 15th. McCarthy, a warm supporter of Parnell, had been 'greatly startled by the lease at first'; but he had lived in Rathdrum, and 'knew a little of the Mr West to whom Mr Parnell has given the lease so long talked of '. McCarthy went on to point out a vital fact, unmentioned by MacDermott: a year before, West had attempted to sell his interest in Mount Avon, but since the lease was nearly expired, no-one would buy it. [74] The place was beautifully kept up, wooded, landscaped, and in a fine position above the Meeting of the Waters; it was not in Parnell's own interest to renew West's lease to enable him to sell it off; but all the same, when West requested a renewal, after his unsuccessful attempt to sell, Parnell granted it to him. It was not in

Parnell's power to grant a longer lease than thirty-one years, as Mount Avon was legally in settlement, and could not be let in perpetuity, by the law of entail. Moreover, the rent West paid for the land, all meadow, was only £1 an acre. Therefore,

> Mr Parnell had done what no other landlord in Ireland would do in the interest of the tenant. He has cancelled in his interest an unexpired lease in order that the tenant may be in a position to realise a handsome sum from the sale which otherwise he could not realise; and as to his giving the tenant only 31 years, this the present existing law compels him to do. . . . I add that the place is not, strictly speaking, an agricultural farm at all. It is in every idea and essential a gentleman's place. Mr West has, however, another farm in the county by many times larger, and the sum he would be able to realise by the sale of Mr Parnell's place would fully stock and crop it, and leave him a good sum in addition in his pocket. The whole matter I have written on ought to be placed before the public by the Land League, and I feel surprised that they allow the fair and unsullied reputation of their chief to be severely criticised by an inimical press without an attempt at its vindication.

McCarthy more or less waived the question of the restrictive improvements clause in the lease, except to point out that Parnell and his father had been responsible for the plantings and landscaping of Mount Avon. But his letter nonetheless illuminates the case, since it seems conclusive that Parnell was, as McCarthy reiterated, granting the lease as a favour to West to help him sell Mount Avon. It seems at first paradoxical that Parnell should thus have facilitated a man who had taken him to court eleven years before;[75] but on that occasion West had obtained judgement against Parnell for £7,000, and in 1880 £3,500 was still outstanding.[76] West held a mortgage on some of Parnell's property for this sum, and was thus in a position to demand such a concession as a lease renewal in his favour. He had been appointed agent of the estate and receiver of the rents in 1859, and had had to have his receivership verified by a court of law;[77] he cannot have been on good terms with Parnell, and if he did not actually instigate the campaign about 'the Parnell lease', and he did nothing to clarify the position.

At any rate, McCarthy's letter stopped the controversy.[78] By now, however, Parnell's seignorial position had begun to attract general attention. On 1 November another anonymous correspondent of the *Irish Times* attacked Parnell, this time from the Left. Why did Mr Parnell not hand over his land to his tenants, asked the writer, 'and come forward with clean hands? His lease tells his integrity'. 'X' then went on to call upon all landlords to renounce their right to ownership.

Nor was this the only interest inspired by the Lease controversy. The London *Standard* sent a reporter to Avondale, and the result was a long and absorbing article on 'Mr Parnell as landlord'.[79]

The article began with a reference to West's notorious lease, quoting a statement of Parnell's that West's health had been bad and the renewal was to enable him to sell; Parnell knew nothing of the legal details.[80] McDermott, in other words, had inserted the improvements clause; he was, according to T. P. O'Connor, 'of different political opinions' to Parnell.[81] The lease thus disposed of, the reporter went on to describe his eight visits to tenants on different parts of Parnell's estate. He found that two owed over three years' rent, and two over one year's. Rents were near the government valuation, and one tenant had bought out his lease for £170, building three cottages on his four acres of land. This last tenant had complaints to make, but the reporter did not set much store by them:

> He [the tenant, George Warren] said that he had never seen him [Parnell] or at least not for a long time. He had made a hundred complaints to the woodranger about a rotten tree that he feared would fall on a little outhouse he had built, and no attention had been vouchsafed him. He thought the land was high-rented – £12 10s for about four acres – but it is below the Government valuation, which is £14, and besides contains the two cottages mentioned which let for £9 2s yearly, and the larger of the two is divided into separate tenements. Mr Warren is anxious to sell his interest for £500, and I was told Mr Parnell thinks of purchasing the plot for the purpose of erecting a hotel on it, to accommodate visitors to Wicklow's scenery.[82]

Warren was, in other words, by no means a subsistence-level tenant. However, visiting two neighbouring farms, the reporter found 'an air of misery and discomfort', and three years of rent unpaid. One farm, of twenty five acres, was held by a widow who 'saw no prospect of paying any rent for a long time'. The neighbouring farm, of thirty five acres, was in as bad a state; outhouses were crumbling, living-conditions filthy, 'and', concluded the reporter, 'not a penny of rent paid for three years from a combined farm of 60 acres of the best land in Ireland, let at 30s an acre, with a reduction of 20 per cent'. By implication, Parnell was, if anything, too lenient a landlord.

On the other hand, Peter Byrne, who held fifty acres on a 200-year lease, 'seemed very prosperous' and was 'an intelligent and active farmer'; he had undertaken to pay Parnell the government valuation, although his lease only stipulated half of this amount. Laurence McGrath held a farm under a similar arrangement, and the positions of both men indicated more than ordinarily good landlord–tenant relations. John Kavanagh, who rented eighty acres, also held land from another landlord, W. F. Littledale of Whaley Abbey. Kavanagh had no complaints about Parnell, and was 'very much dissatisfied' with Littledale; but, significantly, while he had paid Littledale in full, he owed Parnell a year's rent.[83] Good landlord relations did not seem to be conducive to prompt payments; John Parnell's claim that Charles's tenants took advantage of his leniency as well as of his principles seems here substantiated.

The *Standard* also inspected one of the Avondale labourer's cottages and found it 'exceedingly damp'; but all in all, the survey was what the *Nation* jubilantly pronounced it to be: 'A Remarkable Vindication'. As regards West's lease, 'Mr Parnell would – to consider the matter from the lowest point of view – hardly have been fool enough to do privately what, when done by others, he had publicly denounced'; and the *Standard* had shown that in this case he had in fact 'behaved with a generosity that has been badly repaid'.[84]

This seems to have held true for his general rent policy. In October 1890 a case was brought against Parnell by William Smith of Leeson Park, Dublin, who had a claim on one-fifth of two-thirds of the rent yielded by Tyclash, on the Avondale estate – probably the outcome of one of the provisions in Samuel Hayes's will.[85] Kerr's defence was that by 1890 so few of the Tyclash rents were being paid that Smith's portion of the income was only £7, which he had refused to accept.[86] The Land League landlord had by then, as the *Wicklow Newsletter* implied, been thoroughly hoist by his own petard. His rent policy at Avondale was consistent with his views from 1880 on. This contention is borne out by a letter sent to the *Freeman* in that year by twenty two of Parnell's tenants. Its message was unequivocal.

> We hereby declare that Mr Parnell is treating us, his tenants, exactly according to his public declarations made at public meetings attended by him.
> We are only asked to pay Griffith's valuation and are not asked for arrears. If the reductions in rent given us of late years have not reduced our rent to Griffith's valuation, we will be allowed the difference at next payment of rent.[87]

Two of the signatories were Shiel and Kavanagh of Corrignameel, the tenants whom Parnell had been accused of ill-treating over the shooting-rights; another was James Whitty, the old man whom Redmond heard Parnell admonishing about not paying rent and not clearing the coverts.[88] Such altercations do not seem to have affected the esteem in which Parnell was generally held by his tenantry. Moreover, in the affairs of an estate the size of Avondale, tenants' business could easily be misrepresented to outsiders. Thus when the *Irish Times* gave prominence in 1882 to 'an ejectment process against three tenants named Ebbs, Kavanagh and Brennan, for non-payment

of rent of a farm . . . on Mr Parnell's estate',[89] the *Nation* was able to
point out that there were two middlemen involved in the arrangement,
and that Parnell had nothing to do with it.[90] Parnell let eighty acres to
Mrs Courtney at ten shillings an acre; she sublet to Daniel Kavanagh
at £1 15s an acre; he in turn let the land to Peter Brennan at £2 6s an
acre. The ejectment suit was in Kavanagh's name against Brennan.
The *Wicklow Newsletter* covered the case in detail to furnish an attack
against Kavanagh, who had been a prominent Land Leaguer; but
incidental to this point was a complete vindication of Parnell, who was
in fact owed large arrears by Mrs Courtenay and head-rents by both
Kavanagh and Brennan.[91]

In 1884 an American visitor found Parnell's standing immensely
high in the Rathdrum area: 'the only fault found apparently amongst
the people in this neighbourhood is that "Master Charles" does not
marry and settle down on the place, instead of flying about the country
as if he had no intention of perpetuating the honoured name of
Parnell'.[92] The same year saw a large demonstration at Avondale
when fifty acres were ploughed up by local farmers as a gesture of
esteem. But although the Land War was over, and Parnell's attention
increasingly diverted from land to political issues, any tenant of his
claiming unfair treatment was usually sure of a publicised hearing.[93]
When the *Irish Times* and *Daily Express* published in 1887 Thomas
Kennedy's complaints of rack-renting and eviction at Avondale, the
*Freeman* remarked:

> If our Tory contemporaries exhibited a tithe of the interest
> which they have shown in this fictitious case of Mr Kennedy in
> the real and terrible hardships of the poor people under Lord
> Clanricarde in Galway, Lord Lansdowne in Queen's County, the
> Ponsonby tenants in the south or the Shirley tenants in the
> north, the Land Question would be hastened instead of impeded,
> as it now is by them, on its way to the inevitable settlement.[94]

In the same issue a long letter from William Kerr appeared, refuting
Kennedy's allegations and giving an account which is notable both for
evidence of Parnell as a thoughtful farmer and for Kerr's
long-suffering tone with regard to the Avondale tenants. Kennedy had
been temporarily let twenty acres of the demesne, for grazing only, at
£75 – 'probably the very best piece of land in Mr Parnell's hands'.
Parnell had manured and limed it, at considerable cost. In 1882 a new
arrangement was made whereby Kennedy paid £55 and delivered a
hundred pounds of manure annually as top-dressing on the land. After
two years, Kennedy ignored the manure duty. Significantly, Kerr went
on to generalise: 'we put up with this for a couple of years, when we
found it judicious to take into our own hands all lands let in this
fashion; because *the people took advantage of Mr Parnell's political*

*position* and gave us, as in Kennedy's case, considerable trouble'. By 1886, Kerr continued, Kennedy had received a twenty five per cent rent reduction, so was only paying £40 for the lands at Casino. Kerr decided to ask him to vacate the farm and offered him land at Garrymore for a year's grazing. He did not, as Kennedy claimed, drive cattle off Casino. Kennedy had damaged and impoverished the land; and Garrymore was not a second-best farm, but had been manured and limed by Parnell. Kennedy moved there, but tried to back out of the arrangement after six months, only paying half the rent; 'he also used most unnecessary observations'. Kerr offered to settle for £40; Kennedy refused and deserted Garrymore, leaving it neglected and 'a perfect common'. In conclusion, Kerr added that Kennedy had received particular aid from Parnell over the years: 'this is gratitude with a vengeance'. There seems no reason to doubt his lengthy account, which went uncontradicted. Casino was part of the demesne, standing inside the gates and including the 'dower house'; it would only have been let as a temporary measure. Moreover, Kennedy was not a poor tenant, nor even, strictly speaking, a farmer; the *Wicklow Newsletter* mentioned that he owned a shop in Rathdrum. [95] What is interesting is the general way Kerr's letter refers to such treatment of Parnell by his tenants; he states categorically that Kennedy was not the only one to behave thus, and his own patience seems to have been strained to the utmost.

Another publicised case in the same year involved, once more, the vexed question of the Glenmalure shooting. [96] Parnell summoned Matthew Kavanagh, for trespass of cattle. Parnell's case was that Kavanagh surrendered his holding in 1869 and was re-let it at the same rent but without a free grazing right; Kavanagh denied having made such an arrangement. The case, heard at the Hacketstown Petty Sessions, was left to the parties concerned to come to an agreement; and the hostile *Wicklow Newsletter* made what little it could from the evidence. [97]

Thus throughout Parnell's career, political capital was made of tenants' complaints. But during the Split, when there was a greater opportunity than ever for an attack of this sort, none of his tenants seem to have used it, or let themselves be used. Possibly an older loyalty than that conducive to immediate advantage came through; and exploitation of a landlord whom circumstances as well as principles forced to be easy-going became less fair game. In any case, there was better capital to be made by the anti Parnellites elsewhere: Parnell was by 1891 a large-scale employer of industrial labour.

In June 1891 at Carlow, during the by-election campaign there, two of Parnell's workmen from the Arklow quarries appeared on the platform at a meeting. They attacked their wages and working-conditions and alleged religious discrimination in the quarry administration. The two men, Larkin and Hughes, were leaders of a strike at the quarries; they were introduced to the meeting by Mr Condon, M.P. They claimed they were given 1s 8d a day when the quarries opened, and when they demanded more, they were threatened with closure. Parnell, it was alleged, sacked an English Catholic foreman in favour of a Belfast Orangeman, who raised the wages for workers from Belfast to 1s 10d a day and operated a shop which the employees were forced to patronise. The working-day was ten hours long, and conditions extremely hard.[98]

Once again the Avondale agent had to take up the cudgels in the national press. The *Weekly Freeman* of 4 July 1891 published a long letter from Kerr. After pointing out that 'the object of importing into the election contest a stray labourer from Mr Parnell's quarries is obvious', he went on to give details of the organisation at Arklow. The amount of wages paid out over the last ten years had been from £5,000 to £10,000 a year; the benefits to the locality were well attested to, and the works had relieved a good deal of distress. Kerr himself organised the wages; and until 15 June 1891, no one demanded any raise. On this date Parnell visited Arklow and a few workers, 'by some notorious enemies of his put in motion', demanded 15s a week. They were already getting 12s and 13s; such a rise would, Kerr said, compel the closure of the quarries. Larkin had already struck before, with his brother, but had asked to be reinstated. He had left the quarry a couple of weeks before he appeared on the Carlow platform. As for Hughes, he had been discharged frequently 'owing to his own behaviour'. There had been others from the quarry at the Carlow meeting, but these had 'a few days afterwards applied to be re-engaged and admitted their folly in being led away';

With regard to working conditions, Kerr stated that the malcontents had been engaged in loading wagons with twelve hundredweight each of stones and transporting them fifty yards to a stonebreaker. Wages for this were 13s and 14s a week. Kerr said that he had 'personal knowledge of several quarries and of other classes of employment throughout Ireland, and in no place were wages paid in a country place so high as ours'. By now, Kerr continued, the quarries were producing a surplus; but Parnell was keeping production going to provide maximum employment and was himself losing by it, as well as having paid out a great deal of money on equipment. The hours worked, which Larkin objected to, were from 7:00 a.m. to 6:00 p.m., Monday to Friday with an hour off for dinner; Saturday was a half-day. He concluded by pointing out how Parnell had lavished money on the Arklow harbour works and helped the unemployment situation there – not to mention his mining operations, where 'thousands of pounds have been spent upon the workers'. Parnell was, his agent stressed, if anything too indulgent an employer.

Kerr was here claiming too much. The strike of 1891 was not the first of the labour troubles at Big Rock. Before the Split, in August 1890, a strike began when the Northern foreman (Samuel McAllister) was accused of being involved in planning an Orange march in Arklow for the twelfth of July (Arklow being at this time rocked by religious riots sparked off by open-air Protestant evangelical meetings). The main instigator of the strike was, according to the *Wicklow Newsletter*, 'a quarry labourer, a man possessed of much more than the ordinary intelligence of his class'.[99] He induced his fellows to go out on strike on 11 August; the strike lasted a week. Parnell promised a full investigation, during which McAllister was to be suspended, and the men resumed work. The *Wicklow Newsletter* believed that McAllister, who was not re-employed, was sacrificed to 'priestly favour and mob popularity'; but Kerr denied this, alleging that McAllister had 'many faults'.[100] These faults can be guessed, for Kerr also wrote to the *Newry Telegraph*, which had attacked Parnell's quarry administration, and in his letter he castigated the Protestant bigots whose proselytising had wrecked the hitherto peaceful relations between the two religions in Arklow.

But the labour difficulties at Big Rock went deeper than religion. The un-named 'quarry labourer' may have been connected with union activity in the area, which was pronounced at the time. Unionisation difficulties led to strikes among Arklow dockers in November 1890,[101] and by the end of the following January a Labour Union had been formed in Wicklow.[102] Nor were all the strikers in the following summer merely political tools of the anti-Parnellite party. During the 1891 difficulties a meeting was convened at Arklow 'of the men at present on strike at Mr Parnell's quarries at Arklow and the carters employed at the works' in the rooms of the local branch of the Labourers' Union.[103] This meeting protested against 'the statements made by Larkin and others' at the Carlow meeting, 'with a view to prejudicing the minds of the labourers of that county against Mr Parnell', and passed a resolution of support to be sent to the head of the local Parnell Leadership Committee. These men were, therefore, politically sympathetic to Parnell; but they were nonetheless out on strike. There must have been cause for dissatisfaction beyond that stirred up by anti-Parnellite *agents provocateurs*. There had been agitation for wage increases before this, contrary to Kerr's assertion. Parnell admitted this during the Carlow campaign.[104] He went on to state that those now demanding more 'had been incited to act in that matter for political purposes, in order to damage him, by some of the seceders in the town of Arklow'; this is contradicted by the strikers' meeting which repudiated the political use of their cause. Parnell concluded that he would not give the extra rise 'under these circumstances'; but he also held that 'in any case' the work could not afford it. He was already employing only a third of the 250 labourers who had worked the quarries at their peak, and Kerr stated that a large surplus of produce was accruing. The stone-workers would have had reason for discontent without outside instigation.

It is likely that Parnell viewed his relationship with the quarry-workers differently from that with his tenants. Many of the former were imported from Wales or the north of Ireland; there was not the same tradition at work. He disliked the land system, worked against it publicly, and seems to have treated his tenants accordingly; rents were let run, and their interests looked after. But with this view of the estate went a correspondingly modern attitude to its resources, whether timber, stone or iron. Here Parnell looked for efficiency and profit, and was prepared to stand his ground. He had, after all, told Davitt in 1890 that he 'would not tolerate' trades unions if he was at the head of a government: 'they are opposed to individual liberty and should be kept down as Bismarck keeps them under in Germany'.[105] But for a tenant family like the Gaffneys, who were closely connected with him from 1880 until his death, he had nothing but consideration. Mrs O'Shea recorded how he invariably brought Fortnum and Mason's tea for Norah Gaffney when he returned to Avondale. Her son, Hugh Gaffney, had been an unofficial messenger for the Ladies Land League, and was arrested as a suspect; Katherine Tynan remembered Parnell worrying about the effect of this on Mrs Gaffney's health.[106] Hugh became steward and head gardener and managed Avondale after Kerr's death; as an officer of the Rathdrum branch of the Land League, he identified with Parnell's politics to the end of his life. One of the best-educated men in the parish, he became local secretary of the National League and then the United Ireland League down to 1918; he worked on the Avondale demesne until two years before his death in 1937.[107] Hugh Gaffney's aunt by marriage, Mary Gaffney, had been Parnell's nurse and was later the cook at Avondale; her husband, Peter Gaffney, had been valet to John Henry Parnell. Connections like this went far back into Parnell's life, and into his parents' lives; it would have been strange if his attitude to Avondale had not been close and warm.

Before leaving the subject of tenant relations on the estate, we may look finally at Parnell's specific rent policy. Parnell told Andrew Kettle in 1879 that his tenants were 'paying him badly';[108] the questions from the *Standard* report in 1880 show that rents on the holdings visited were not excessive, and had been let run for several years. Patrick Moore paid £28 5s for sixteen acres, valued at £20; John Warren paid £12 10s for four acres, valued at £14; John and May Carroll paid 30s an acre, and Peter Byrne paid the government valuation of 20s an acre for his fifty acres. The rents had been reduced by twenty per cent that year[109] and the letter from Parnell's tenants to the *Freeman* stated that only Griffith's valuation was required of them. [110] This is verified by a circular Parnell issued to his tenants about this time, stating: 'In order to obviate any error on the part of anyone representing him, henceforth until the Irish Land Question is settled on the basis of the Land League principles, no farm tenant shall be asked to pay higher rent than the poor-law or Griffith's valuation'. [111] In 1882, asked how the No Rent Manifesto was working, Parnell replied grimly: 'All I know about it is that my own tenants are acting strictly up to it'; [112] as I have mentioned, this trend continued. By 1888, as has been seen, stories about lengthy and unclaimed arrears on the estate were beginning to proliferate. [113] In 1887 William Blunt heard from Davitt that 'nobody suffered more from the land agitation' than Parnell, and that many of his tenants 'pay him no rent to the present day' [114] and by 1890 some areas were yielding hardly any rent at all. [115]

Only one case, in fact, is recorded where Parnell took a tenant to law for arrears – and this tenant was the widow and executrix of his old adversary, Charles Mathew West, who had created such difficulties over the Mount Avon lease. By 1884 West was dead, and £168 of rent were outstanding on Mount Avon. Parnell had brought an action for recovery of the sum during West's lifetime, but had not proceeded with it. By 1884, however, he had paid West the £3,500 he owed him; and in April of that year he entered an action against Mrs West for three years' rent. [116]

No political capital was made out of the case. Part of the reason may have been that Parnell was no longer at the head of radical land agitation; but it was by now well-known that West's position was not that of a simple tenant farmer, and this must have been equally influential. The incident suggests that Parnell was not averse to prosecution for rent when the tenant could afford it – and had made things as difficult for Parnell as West had done. Parnell never at any time saw landlords as the diabolical creations visualised in his sister Fanny's poetry. The article upon which they collaborated in the *North American Review* in 1880 referred only to *absentees* as 'bloodsuckers'; and he refuted accusations that the Land League was 'communistic' by saying that 'it was no more communistic than to compel the owner of a private hoard of provisions on board a wreck to share it with his starving companions'. [117] This analogy was consistent with the position of his poorer tenants in the early eighties, but it did not exclude the determined pursuance of Charles West for the rent which he owed Parnell, and which Parnell knew he was able to pay. His feelings on land nationalisation are well known. Even as regards land purchase, when someone asked him why, since he was in favour of the principle, none of his tenants had been granted purchase, his answer was characteristic: 'They have not asked me.' [118] In fact, one of Parnell's tenants was engaged in purchasing part of the estate when he died. [119]

But in practical terms, a tenant at Avondale would have gained little by purchase, given their strong position with regard to letting rents run. To sum up, even a detailed examination of Parnell's relations with his general tenantry (if not those with his industrial work-force) does nothing to contradict T. P. O'Connor's assertion: 'For some years Mr Parnell attended to his estate with great assiduity ... whatever may have been the record of his brother [Henry] his own, I believe, was perfect. He never evicted anybody; he attended to his estates; he was very popular.'[120]

# 3  *Avondale and Parnell's life-style*

'When the character of Mr Parnell is assailed, I would be wanting in my duty if I did not state to the country at large what I know. I will give you my opinion, or rather the opinion of his house-keeper at Avondale, who told it to Father Galvin, who told it to me. She told exactly his mode of living, and here it is. When Mr Parnell goes to Avondale for a little rest he gets up at seven o'clock and after a light breakfast he takes his hatchet or his saw and goes out, and comes in the evening at six o'clock to his dinner, and then, if the housekeeper forgot to put a glass of wine on the table, he would not think it worth his while to say a word about it. Now, sir, she said for a fact that Mr Parnell never put his foot inside Dublin except on very special business. Do you mean to tell me, if he is the man he's reported to be now, that that's the career he would carry on?'

> Alderman Ryan, at a Cork Corporation meeting
> called to consider the O'Shea divorce petition;
> quoted in *Wicklow Newsletter*, 18 January 1890.

## I

Parnell's visits to Avondale became, as has been seen, more and more infrequent;[1] there is, therefore, little evidence of his life-style when he was there during the 1880s. During the latter part of his life, his visits seem to have been primarily concerned with overseeing the mines and the quarries; if Avondale had ever been a centre of hospitality and socialising, as Emily Dickinson and her mother liked to recall, these days were long gone by 1880. In this year a newspaper interview with Parnell at Avondale recorded:

Mr Parnell is very abstemious, drinking little but water and tea. He smokes a great deal, and is never in want of a good 'weed',

which he proffers very liberally to his friends. At the same time
he keeps a neat little wine-cellar and can, when the occasion
arises, regale his friends with a choice vintage. In other respects
his style of living is very homely. His only retainers are the
venerable matron we have already seen, and a man who looks
after his horse, the garden, and the general affairs of the house.
In the intervals of agitation he is a great rider, a moderately keen
sportsman, something of a farmer, and often speaks of himself as
a Cinncinnatus who has been regretfully compelled to relinquish
his cabbages. Mr Parnell has always been a more or less solitary
man, seeing little company and leading a rather introspective
life.[2]

Parnell must have cut down on his heavy smoking when he came
under the strict regimen of Mrs O'Shea in the early 1880s; otherwise,
these details are borne out elsewhere. The 'venerable matron' would
have been Mary Gaffney, Parnell's old nurse, who was still
housekeeper at this time; elsewhere in the same article she is described
as 'floating out of a side apartment' into the hall, expressing surprise
at the master's return, and vaguely offering something to eat. John
Parnell gives a similarly haphazard picture of life at Avondale. Parnell
rose late (the attribution to him in the epigraph of early-morning
rising is certainly inaccurate), and had a large lunch-breakfast at noon
– porridge, a chop, oatmeal toast – and for his next meal had dinner,
at any convenient hour, preferring mutton or trout. As for routine,
there were no fixed mealtimes: the dining-room saw one long
succession of meals, like the Mad Hatter's tea-party in *Alice in
Wonderland*.[3] Those who were entertained at Avondale recall it as the
essence of simplicity. T. P. O'Connor would not have agreed with John
Parnell that 'you could have what you liked when you liked'. When
Parnell suggested a picnic at Glendalough, 'T.P.' naively expected
hampers of cold chicken and champagne, but the Chief went into the
kitchen at Avondale, made two sandwiches of oatmeal bread and
butter, wrapped them up, and so they set off.[4] While Parnell stayed at
Avondale, O'Connor recorded, 'all the necessities in the way of food
and drink were supplied from the hotel in Rathdrum' – and Parnell
owed them a bill of several hundred pounds by 1883.[5]

This is not to say that he was a careless or a casual host. In London
he sometimes entertained colleagues at dinner-parties, and Justin
McCarthy recalled more than once Parnell's charm as a host, despite
his own lack of interest in fine culinary points.[6] But such occasions
were not his *métier*, Mrs O'Shea tell of his 'grim determination' as he
set off to the few social occasions which she persuaded him to attend.[7]

There was one sphere of entertaining, however, which Parnell loved
and at which he shone: shooting-parties at Aughavannagh in August.
Here he could dispense both with formality and with unnecessary

conversation; and here he himself was happiest and most at ease. In 1879 a letter to his wine merchant shows him ordering five dozen claret and a gallon of whiskey to be sent to Avondale in August;[8] a party generally convened at Aughavannagh for the latter part of the month, and Parnell himself spent as much of the autumn there as circumstances allowed. (He was shooting at Aughavannagh with J. J. O'Kelly on 8 October 1881, the day before the Wexford speech for which he was jailed,[9] and when William Corbet, his friend, colleague and neighbour, visited Parnell in Kilmainham he found that the prisoner's chief concern was that a projected shooting expedition together 'had been rather rudely interrupted'. He insisted that Corbet go by himself, and furnished him with a letter to the Aughavannagh gamekeeper.[10])

Parnell's companions on these shoots were generally close political colleagues. In 1882 John Redmond was with him [11] and in 1884 his brother William;[12] in 1886 the party included Henry Campbell and Corbet,[13] and in 1889 Sir Thomas Esmonde, Timothy Harrington, J. J. O'Kelly, Corbet, and Sir William Butler, who then lived at Delgany.[14] It was a habit of Parnell's to send back birds to some of his colleagues in London; McCarthy recalls this 'graceful little courtesy'[15] and Barry O'Brien quotes a letter of Parnell's which bears him out.[16]

Life at Aughavannagh was simple. According to T. P. O'Connor, 'the household arrangements were extremely primitive and everybody had more or less to cook for himself after the manner of soldiers on a campaign'.[17] William Redmond described the house as having 'only a very few habitable rooms' and being 'in very bad repair'.[18] Mrs O'Shea insisted on 'getting together hampers of provisions for him to take over with him [to Aughavannagh] as the arrangements he had been used to before I met him were decidedly primitive and very trying to his health'.[19] A particularly interesting description of an expedition to Aughavannagh is given by Sir William Butler in his autobiography, and is worth quoting at some length. Butler dates the anecdote as 1888, but the *Freeman* records his shooting with Parnell at Aughavannagh in 1889, and he does not seem to have visited there twice.[20]

> Parnell was at this time at the summit of his power. His mountain home at Aughavannagh lay some twenty miles distant from us at Delgany. When the grouse-shooting began in August I got a letter from the Irish Leader in London asking me to join him at Aughavannagh. I accepted with delight ... [The *Times* Commission] had kept Mr Parnell in London for a few days after the 12th August, and it was on the 16th that he arrived at Aughavannagh ... When he arrived at Aughavannagh no outward manifestation was visible that the master and owner of

the place and shooting had come. Things went on as usual among the five or six guests – all political members of his own party except myself. No part of the large mountain area which was his property had been reserved for him. We had shot over it in detached parties on the previous days. The weather was glorious.

The building in which we lived was an old three-company barracks built in 1798 at a cross-roads in the lower part of the valley, which was then a rallying-point for the insurgents, Holt and Dwyer, and their daring bands. It was a gaunt, bare, stone structure, half-ruined, its central portion, the quarters for the officers, being still habitable. It stood about nine hundred feet above sea-level; and although not much of a view was obtainable from the old square limestone windows of the house, the moment one quitted the door great sweeps of heathery hill could be seen curving upward to Lugnaquilla to the west or mixing themselves with lower mountains to the north and east.

From the shoulders of Lugnaquilla the eye was able to reach into great distances to the south-west. The air was of indescribable freshness. The day following his arrival, Parnell asked me to shoot with him on a mountain to the south of the old barrack. We rode to the ground; the walking was exceedingly rough, the ground being full of tussocks in which grouse lay well but men fell easily. Parnell, who at this time was on a special regimen of food and liquid and looked far from strong, nevertheless crossed these hummocky uplands with a light and easy step, shot surely and quickly, and seemed thoroughly to enjoy the sport. At halts he talked freely, sometimes of a parish priest in the neighbouring county who seemed to imagine that political support in the constituency carried some collateral right of poaching his (Parnell's) bog. 'As I knew that he would be out on the 12th I sent – (one of my friends) down to join him a year ago, so that I might get a few of my own birds; but the result of that attempt was that the reverend sportsman lodged a good deal of the shot of one of his barrels in my friend's knee, laying him up for six months.'

In the evening we had pleasant conversation. He spoke little of politics; said no ill of anybody ... The quality in Parnell that impressed me most was the entire absence of sense or thought of superiority. Even in the most trifling details of life this was apparent. When he opened his gun-case the gun was found rusty; but he would take no help in the cleaning of it; he did it himself. He did not seem to be self-conscious in anything ... If anything occurred to call for the exercise of his courtesy as host and master, it was given instantly. I was obliged to leave the party in the afternoon, and the car which as to take me home was on the road some distance away from the ground we were shooting over. When I had to say good-bye, he stopped shooting, took three or four brace of grouse from the bag, and, carrying them himself to the car, put the birds in the 'well' of the vehicle with a courteous message to my wife. [21]

This account of Butler's presents a picture of Parnell 'off duty' which is available nowhere else except in his brother's memoir, chapters of his wife's biography, the recorded reminiscences of Henry Harrison, and occasional chapters in the recollections of William O'Brien. Butler illuminates Parnell's kindness, ease of manner, lack of presumption, and the attractive sense of humour (seen in the story about the priest) which more superficial observers denied him. These are qualities which John and Katharine Parnell, William O'Brien, and Henry Harrison, who knew him best, are alone in recording. Aughavannagh was not a particularly good preserve; during the Land War, according to John Parnell, the tenants almost denuded it of game [22] and Parnell told Mrs O'Shea that 'three or four days broke the back of that little shoot, anyhow'. [23] But the pleasure it gave him was completely disproportionate to the value of the game. Aughavannagh and the grouse season there represented the one part of the country gentleman tradition with which Parnell never lost touch.

In other areas of Avondale life, a combination of lengthening absences and the exigencies of his political career separated Parnell from the pastimes associated with his position. One of these was hunting. He was always a keen horseman; Mrs Dickinson recalled long rides together through the mountains [24] and Mrs O'Shea said he was a 'fine horseman', though 'not a man who had very much knowledge of horses'. [25] This may have been so by her standards – she had helped run a stud farm in the early days of her marriage to O'Shea – but others vouched for Parnell's expertise in this field. [26] He knew Youatt's *The Horse* 'very well', [27] and Sir William Butler remembered Parnell telling him how to correlate the movement of a horse's ear to incipient lameness. [28] Parnell once surprised William O'Brien by remarking to him, on a visit to Mallow, that 'the only good things the Irish landlords have to show for themselves are their hounds and perhaps, in the Roscommon country, their horses'. [29] It was an observation which may have been prompted by the fact that the Land League chose to carry the war into the landlords' camp by picketing their meets and obstructing their hunting, and in this respect Parnell's own position had a degree of ambivalence. The president of the League being one of the gentry and fond of riding could be used by opponents much as his position as landlord was; and a letter from the parish priest of Durrow in the *Leinster Leader* of 24 September 1881 shows that this was so.

The letter violently attached the 'frivolity' of hunting and contradicted statements in the Tory press that Parnell supported it. On the contrary, he agreed with its suppression as 'a step in the emancipation of the people from a dominant, worthless, insulting class'. [30]

Parnell's attitude to hunting was, however, less inflexible than that attributed to him by the zealous Father Rowan. In the *Freeman* of 12 November 1881 there appeared a Central News Agency telegram which stated that Parnell had 'written from Kilmainham to the leading members of the County Wicklow Hunt, enclosing a cheque for his subscription towards the hounds, and stating that he is strongly in favour of maintaining hunting and hopes it will not be stopped'. This was not altogether accurate, and Parnell himself clarified his position by writing to the newspaper two days later:

> I notice a paragraph in the *Freeman* of yesterday that I have written from Kilmainham to the leading members of the County Wicklow Hunt ... I wish to say that my letter was not written from Kilmainham, but from Avondale the day before my arrest, and that it had sole reference to the County Wicklow Harriers, to which I had been in the habit of subscribing, and which have not been rendered unpopular by the acts of the Master, or, so far as I know, of anyone who hunts with them. [31]

He carefully avoided condemning the practice; and the fact that he himself subscribed to the local hunt showed a different attitude to Father Rowan's. Eight years later he could raise a laugh at the Special Commission hearings by courteously explaining a suspicious cheque-stub as his subscription to the Harriers; but in the fiercer days of the Land War and afterwards, the *Nation* carried weekly reports of hunts 'stopped', and a great many agitators shared the feelings of the parish priest of Durrow. This was, moreover, no less true of Wicklow than of anywhere else; in 1884 the Rathdrum National League passed a resolution unanimously to 'stop the hunting of the local pack of harriers', [32] and in the western part of the county the Shillelagh branch took similar action. [33] Parnell did not feel this way; but the whole issue, small though it seems, serves as an illustration of the impossibility of becoming leader of the Land League while remaining the squire of Avondale in any traditional sense.

## II

I have already emphasised Parnell's shaky financial position in 1875. He owed a loan of £13,000 which he had had to borrow to pay off a family debt to his uncle by marriage, and two mortgages of £1,500 and £3,500 on his property. [34] None of these encumbrances were paid off before 1883, when the National Tribute brought him temporary relief;

but by his death in 1891 he was once more steeped in debt. According
to his brother, Charles had been left 'Avondale and £4,000 a year'.[35]
This may be an exaggeration. The *Nation* believed in 1879 that 'his
property does not bring him in more than £1,500 a year';[36] the rent
roll was in fact £1,789 a year, and there were additional properties in
Kildare and probably some investments.[37] In any case, the interest
alone on Parnell's debts was £1,100 a year and he also paid Emily and
Delia £100 a year each. He would have had to live carefully and
manage his affairs astutely to pay back what he owed.

This, of course, is exactly what he did not do. In 1878 he must have
been attempting to manage carefully, for he was asking for extensions
on debts as small as one of £20 to his wine-merchant.[38] But political
life proved expensive,[39] and Parnell's rent policy decreased his income
from Avondale. Finally, according to his brother, by 1881 he had so
little money that in order to be able to send something to his mother
after her stock-market losses he had to ask John to mortgage some
shares on his behalf.[40] This is not altogether surprising. Since his
majority, besides contracting the large debt already mentioned, he had
paid out at least £4,500 to purchase the head rent of the Kingston
lands on his property;[42] his election expenses for Meath had been
£2,000, paid for by himself;[42] he had spent, according to John, 'at
least £3,000' on his celebrated sawmills and cattle-shed. Even by this
stage he had spent on mining what the *Nation* cautiously described as
'a large sum of money . . . with no pecuniary reward';[43] John Parnell
put it at several hundred pounds. It was little wonder that his capital
debts remained undiminished.

There were, moreover, the expenses of his new political career. As
early as January 1880 the London correspondent of the *Irish Times*
wrote that he had paid out £3,000 of his own money for political
purposes.[44] Nor is this uncorroborated. T. M. Healy wrote to his
father in 1879 that Parnell had personally guaranteed to stand his
election costs for contesting Ennis,[45] and John Parnell claimed that
financial support from his brother did not stop at such expenses: he
actually paid some M.P.s an allowance.[46] In 1889 the *Nation* declared
that investigation of Parnell's bank account by the Special
Commission 'disclosed the fact that after the collapse of the Land
League agitation and when the subscriptions from America had almost
altogether ceased, Mr Parnell's own private purse supplied the sinews
of war'.[47] About the time referred to, Justin McCarthy wrote to Mrs
Praed of 'a subscription made up at [Parnell's] suggestion for a very
deserving Irishman who has ruined his business and his prospects for
the sake of trying to advance the Irish Cause . . . most of the
contribution came from Parnell'.[48] The picture of Parnell using his
own resources for the salaries of his followers is one that recurs; F. H.
O'Donnell referred to him paying 'his *diadoichi* . . . 8 to 10 pounds a

week',[49] and John Parnell told an uncharacteristically bitter story in this respect: it concerned Parnell driving past two members of his party on their way to Avondale from Rathdrum, remarking curtly 'they are only coming up to put their hands in my pockets and get some more money'.[50] By the time he wrote his book, John had an axe to grind against the Irish party.[51] But others bear him out; and it seems likely that the money Parnell spent on politics escalated greatly during the last years of his life. Though Henry Harrison, who entered politics in 1890, recalled that candidates 'rich as well as politically robust' were preferred wherever possible,[52] this was not a common combination; and Barry O'Brien quotes a letter written to him by Parnell in 1891 asking him to stand for Parliament – and offering to pay his expenses, although he had 'wanted a man with money'.[53]

How much of the money Parnell spent on politics was actually his own is debatable. Dr Cruise O'Brien confirmed John Howard Parnell's belief in an article in 1946,[54] but in his book *Parnell and his Party* he rescinded this judgement; from a sworn affidavit by T. M. Healy, it is evident that Parnell personally drew the income of the no. 1 fund in Paris and used this money to finance individual members as well as the National League.[55] Thus John Parnell, examining his brother's financial records after the latter's death, would have assumed such debits on his personal account to represent his own money.

Healy, however, dates Parnell's use of the fund income 'from 1882 to 1890'; before the setting up of the Paris funds and after the Split, there is no reason to doubt that his own money was used for political expenses. But the implication added by John Parnell, that this was the reason for his brother's constant financial trouble and eventual colossal debts, is unsubstantiated and unnecessary; bad management and personal expenses account more than adequately for that.

In December 1882, the newspapers first carried the announcement that Parnell had filed a petition for the sale of Avondale to clear its incumbrances.[56] An editorial in the *Nation*, while admitting that there was a mortgage of £13,000 on the estate, stated that this was 'not regarded as constituting any great burden on the estate, and the reasons for the intended sale, it is said, must be sought elsewhere'; the writer suggested 'pressures from without', but did not define them.[57] The leader went on to call on the Irish people to 'take practical steps in the matter'. In the next issue, however, a hasty qualification was added:

No action of this kind is deemed to be necessary by friends of Mr Parnell, who have taken all the circumstances into consideration, and who mean to give them still further attention. The repugnance felt by the hon. gentleman himself to any such movement accounts for much in their view of the case.[58]

The petition for sale had been filed on 29 November 1882; the order was made absolute in the following February. [59] In the next month the *Nation* was once more emboldened to return to the question of a public subscription fund. While admitting Parnell's initial reluctance, the newspaper claimed that 'circumstances ... have altered materially within the last few weeks'; [60] the reference was to the efforts of English politicians, especially Forster, to heap opprobrium upon Parnell in the House of Commons. A demonstration of trust was called for. From this time, the newspapers carried a weekly record of the subscription fund to date; the Papal attitude was declared in May, and subscriptions flooded in; in December, as is well known, the immense cheque for £37,011 17s was handed to a taciturn Parnell by the Lord Mayor of Dublin. [61] His financial troubles must have seemed over.

This was, however, not so. According to John Parnell, in an appendix to his book which bears the rather defensive title of 'Where the Tribute went to', [62] the £10,000 which Parnell owed because of the debt to Wigram remained outstanding 'and I had finally to pay it off'; [63] the Tribute money went into mining operations, instead of clearing liabilities, and even the bills which Charles persuaded John to back in 1881 for their mother went unpaid; for this John had 'to sell what little capital I had'. [64]

On this topic, however, John's word is not entirely reliable. A memorial in the Registry of Deeds shows that by an arrangement of December 1882 John admitted responsibility for half the money owed to Wigram under their grandfather's will; and, this £10,000 having been 'paid out of his own proper money borrowed for that purpose' by Charles, a 'compromise had been entered into' in respect of Charles' ensuing claim of £5,000 from John. John was to pay Charles £2,500 down, with four per cent of this sum computed from 1870 (the date when Charles had paid off Wigram). Furthermore, John Parnell was also indebted to his brother for £1,515, which as the balance of a sum of £4,000 borrowed from the Hibernian Bank by Charles for John's use. John Parnell owed Charles £5,065; £2,500 capital, £1,050 interest on this, and £1,515 outstanding on a previous debt; and Charles waived the other half of the £5,000 due from John to him for the Wigram debt. John made over to Charles a mortgage on Collure, and covenanted with him to pay £1,500 on 1 July 1883 and the remainder in equal half-yearly payments. [65]

This may have been the reason why Charles never cleared the £3,000 backed by John's mortgaging his shares in 1881. Possibly he was simply cancelling out the amount of John's debt to him – a debt which John never mentioned in his book. John is, moreover, not strictly accurate in stating that the debt to Wigram was never paid. It was paid in 1870, by a loan raised for the purpose; and the loan thus raised, owing to Paul Askin and W. C. Hobson, was paid off in

September 1883, as was Parnell's debt of £3,500 to C. M. West. [66] But the mortgage was not cancelled: Askin and Hobson transferred it to the trusteeship of Henry Tudor Parnell. [67] This means that the money with which Parnell paid them must have been borrowed from his younger brother, in whose interest the unpaid mortgage subsequently stood. As was evident to anyone who cared to read the relevant column in the *Nation,* the Tribute had reached £15,000 by September 1883; Henry Parnell knew his loan was safe. But he may have been too sanguine. There is no reference in the Registry of Deeds to the mortgage being cleared; and we have John's word, usually reliable, that he had to clear the debt incurred by the £10,000 left by William Parnell to his daughter Catherine so many years before. By 1883, however, the debt was no longer payable to Catherine's heirs, but to her nephew Henry – the only son of John Henry Parnell who made a financial success of his life.

Charles's debt to Henry may not have been for the full £13,000 he owed Askin and Hobson; John mentions that Avondale was 're-mortgaged' for £6,000 after 1883, [68] and the arrangement with Henry is the only one legally recorded – although Parnell was planning to raise another mortgage on the estate when he died. [69] He may have paid off the remaining £7,000 with the tribute money, and left £6,000 outstanding on the mortgage. In any case, the evidence is that the estate remained in debt even after the Tribute; one is compelled to wonder what Parnell's expenses were from 1883 to 1891.

John stated unequivocally that his brother spent £10,000 upon establishing the Big Rock quarries at Arklow, and a further £5,000 on machinery before they began to pay. [70] Kerr recorded that wages at the quarries varied from £5,000 to £10,000 a year; [71] in 1888 Parnell estimated the average amount he spent yearly upon wages in the quarries and mines as £8,000. [72] There were also the wages of the workers at Avondale which, according to John Parnell, cost £50 a week. Thus Parnell's outgoings in the 1880s were enormous; he had good reason to claim in 1890 that the Tribute had been 'spent by me in Ireland, amongst the working-men of Wicklow'. [73] Considering that the Dublin Corporation sett contract had lapsed [74] and a large production surplus was collecting at Big Rock, and that the mining venture never really passed beyond the exploration stage, the returns for this huge outlay were infinitesimal. By 1888, Parnell stated privately that he 'could show by my books that I have spent upwards of seven thousand pounds prospecting for minerals in Wicklow'; [75] with the increase of such operations in 1890, costs must have advanced far beyond this. Nor did his industrial expenses stop at his own operations; he donated £2,000 to the Arklow Harbour works as well as supplying them with free stone [76] and declared in 1891 that he had spent £5,000 altogether on public works in Wicklow. [77] In January 1891 he spent a further

£1,200 on the railway connection from Big Rock to Arklow. [78] When the Tribute had been used to pay off £3,500 to West, £7,000 of Askin and Hobson's debt, and £1,500 owing from Parnell to his guardians' heirs, the remaining £25,000 had yet to cover further personal debts, the £15,000 used in setting up Big Rock, and £7,000 spent on mining by 1888, with a large additional outlay on the Ballycapple mines in 1890. Avondale was by now producing a good deal less than its original £1,789 p.a., and Parnell's small share in some Dublin property added little to his annual income. [79] He had an improvident mother and impoverished sister to support, as well as an expensive political career and a London establishment to keep going. It would have been extraordinary if he had not got as swiftly into debt as he was extricated from it.

Nor did he make much effort to do otherwise. Though he was careful about some expenses, when his own foibles were concerned his extravagance was unbounded. T. P. O'Connor described his 'absolute indifference to money'; he ran up bills 'unconsciously', and on one occasion gave a lunch at the Café Royal where he tipped the waiter a half sovereign but left the bill unpaid. [86] Despite the Tribute he applied for a loan of £1,200 in 1885 to improve his estate, [81] and his brother recalled him as being 'in financial trouble' in 1887. [82] He got £5,000 damages from *The Times* in 1889, and it was claimed that he kept £5,000 of the £10,000 subscribed by Cecil Rhodes to the Home Rule Party. [83] His enemies further claimed that he kept the balance of the money raised to pay the costs of the Speical Commission legal defence, amounting to £10,000. [84] Parnell denied these charges in a speech at Wicklow on 31 May 1891. [85] He said the balance from the Commission fund was a small one, nothing like £10,000, and he was 'keeping it in hand'; £5,000 of Rhodes's money had gone to William O'Brien for the evicted tenants and most of the remainder of party expenses; he was again keeping only a small balance 'in hand'. Whatever about the accuracy of these studiously vague assertions, Parnell's financial position in 1891 was worse than it had ever been. In August he was ordered to pay O'Shea's divorce case costs, amounting to £700. [86] In September he arranged a loan from the Hibernian Bank, promising his wife 'the first thousand' of it for immediate demands; [87] in October, just before his death, he wrote to MacDermott, his solicitor, about raising a speedy mortgage. [88] Moreover, earlier in the year he began preparations to sell part of Avondale – the lands of Ballyknockan, 131 acres adjoining the demesne. A memorial in the Registry of Deeds shows Emily Dickinson releasing these lands from liability for her annuity as the remainder of the estate was 'of ample security' and Parnell was 'desirous to sell' the land in question. [89] Other records show that the arrangement was to sell the Ballyknockan farm to the occupying tenant, Peter Brennan, for £900; in March 1888 before the arrangement was made with the Land Commission, Brennan and Parnell had reached a private agreement regarding the price an¹ terms of sale. The arrangement was completed by Mrs Katharine Parnell as administrator in 1892. Perhaps this transaction was intended merely as the first in a policy of selling out Avondale to those tenants who wished to purchase; but Parnell died before it could go further, and he realised no money in this way. John Parnell in 1916 stated that the debts accumulated by his brother by 1891 amounted to £50,000, 'a figure which I have just verified'; Sir Henry Lucy was told by 'an intimate friend of Parnell's' that 'his premature death was contributed to by actual poverty'.[90] Between 1881 and 1891, his brother added, Parnell had spent £90,000.[91]

There is, as I have noted, no need to attribute this to politics, Standish O'Grady thought that 'a good deal of this fortune' must have gone on his 'holes in the ground',[92] and these indeed seem to have swallowed up all that was put into them without yielding much in the way of profit. Parnell himself gave the lie to the idea that politics dissipated his fortune, in fact, he claimed the reverse was true:

> I remember him in 1887 [John Parnell wrote], complaining of the financial difficulties in which he again found himself involved, and saying to me: 'Well, John, politics is the only thing I ever got any money from, and I am looking for another subscription now.' I think he was quite serious when he said it, but, of course, a fresh tribute was not forthcoming.[93]

The cynicism of this remark, coupled with his previous casual acceptance of the £37,000 in 1883, seems breathtaking. But it was in essence no more than the truth. As has been shown in the last section of my study, he entered politics heavily in debt. Whatever money came Parnell's way in the years after 1875 did not come from his rent-roll, which is to his credit; but neither did it come from his mining or his quarrying, which never testified to his common-sense.

# 4    *Parnell and Wicklow*

We are all willing to believe that Mr Parnell is not guilty. Although he seldom comes home he is a Wicklow man, and one has what is known as a *gra* for one's old neighbour, no matter what political banner he fights under.

> Editorial in *Wicklow Newsletter*, 4 January 1890, about the O'Shea divorce petition.

## I

Such associations [with the 1798 Rising] perhaps explain partly why Mr Parnell revolted uneasily against the lot of a country gentleman. In some ways, he was admirably fitted for that quiet lot. He loves animals and outdoor pursuits, and with his taste for the exact sciences he would have been a revolutionary farmer of a fine type. When he came home from his English training he seemed to fall well into that life, becoming a magistrate and High Sheriff of his county, and captain of the Wicklow Eleven at cricket. Well would he have administered his estate, with his keen sympathy for his own folk, for whom his coldness changes to a simple kindliness. [1]

Thus an English newspaper in 1890 analysed the social context from which Parnell chose to abdicate: giving, as many others did, the relevant but rather inadequate reason of the county's eighteenth century rebel tradition. As the epigraph to this chapter shows, even Unionist opinion in Wicklow recognised that Parnell had some sort of stake in the county. It is true that his position in local affairs did not become what his background would have led an observer to expect, but his connection with Wicklow remained a strong one, and it had its own character.

As early as January 1880 Thomas Sexton prophesied that 'a day

would come when people would come to Rathdrum like pilgrims'
because of its association with Parnell;[2] indeed, the flow had already
started, since excursions to Avondale became from an early date a
popular outing for nationalist and semi-nationalist organisations.[3] It
was also in 1880 that Rathdrum mounted a triumphal reception for
Parnell on his return from America, complete with a band, bonfires
and a triumphal arch erected over the entrance to Avondale.[4] He was,
by then, the local celebrity.

The local duties of the squire of Avondale, however, preoccupied
him less and less. He attended some meetings of the Rathdrum Board
of Guardians, although not officially on the board,[5] but only up to
1878. This was also the last year to see him as a steward of the
Wicklow steeplechases.[6] In 1878 as well his name appeared on the
donation list for the Wicklow Regatta[7] and he chaired a Relief Fund
Committee composed of 'the principal inhabitants of Rathdrum
parish'.[8] But these are the last records of Parnell as active in the
context of the county establishment.

One official link, however, remained with the heritage to which he
had been born; though 1876 was the last year to see him sworn on to
the Grand Jury,[9] he remained a J.P. This is not to say he was active;
he sat at Rathdrum Petty Sessions only once after his entry into
politics.[10] But the involvement led to some raised eyebrows
comparatively early in his career. After he told the celebrated anecdote
from his American tour about the donation of '$5 for bread and $20
for lead' at the meeting in the Rotunjo on 30 April 1880[11] a
correspondent wrote to the *Nation*, demanding; 'Is this gentleman a
justice of the peace for Co. Wicklow?'[12] The same question occurred to
Earl Fortescue in August of the following year, when he asked in the
House of Lords whether Parnell was still a magistrate. When the
answer was 'yes', another member pointed out that Parnell's record
was hardly synonymous with law and order.[13] 1881 was the last year
of Parnell's magistracy; the dichotomy of his position became absolute
with his arrest in October.

His connection with Protestant parish affairs is less easily traced. In
1875 his name headed the list of donors to the Rathdrum Parochial
Fund,[14] and in 1879 he was recorded as one of the two synodsmen of
Rathdrum Parish.[15] But no Parnells are ever recorded at the many
Rathdrum parochial functions described in detail by the *Wicklow
Newsletter*. In 1890 a hostile M.P. asked: 'What has Mr C. S. Parnell,
M.P., done for Protestantism, that would entitle him to claim to
belong to that religious denomination?'[16] This seems a not
unreasonable question, especially in view of Mrs Katharine Parnell's
later statements about her husband's religious beliefs;[17] but it drew an
angry letter from Bernard Manning, the secretary of Rathdrum Parish
Vestry, emphasising Parnell's generous contribution to parish funds

and constant interest in Church affairs.[18] The *Wicklow Newsletter* added sourly that in the last statement of Rathdrum Parish accounts Parnell had given £10 to the sustenation fund and £2 to the school fund, out of a total collection of £170; this seemed to the editor little enough, considering that 'his residence and most of his property is situate . . . in the centre of the parish'. Manning's letter probably owed more to loyalty than a desire to clear the name of an unappreciated philanthropist.

Without officiating directly, however, Parnell continued to be interested in the affairs of the county, especially where they touched upon his own preoccupations. It was largely through his influence in the county and in London that the Wicklow Town and Harbour commission obtained a loan from the Treasury to build a breakwater and steamboat pier.[19] In 1880 a government loan of £50,000 was secured;[20] the improvements were completed in 1883. Corbet (who came to be known as 'the local question member')[21] had pressed strongly for the harbour scheme in parliament, backed by Parnell; the scheme took on a larger importance and a political complexion because of comparisons with the Arklow harbour works which Lord Carysfort instigated at the same time. The issue was more than a not-so-friendly rivalry between the two neighbouring ports. Parnell consistently emphasised the fact that the Wicklow scheme had been the result of local initiative and enterprise, whereas the Arklow plan was the preserve of Lord Carysfort and the Board of Works, and correspondingly was dogged by failure and inefficiency.[22] From the anti-nationalist side, the *Wicklow Newsletter* jeered at Parnell's uncharacteristically flowery assertion that 'as long as the foundations of the earth last these piers will stand,[28] with regard to the Wicklow harbour. The *Newsletter* claimed that the Arklow works were uncompleted, and anyway not a parallel case; the issue rapidly became a party one. At the convention to nominate M.P.s for the county in October 1885, Parnell's speech was almost entirely taken up with the question of the respective harbour improvements, and Corbet faithfully returned to the same point again and again.[24]

The two schemes did not, however, continue to remain political rivals. The history of the Arklow plan had initially been completely Lord Carysfort's preserve: in 1876 he secured a government grant for £13,000 towards it and was accordingly eulogised by the *Wicklow Newsletter*, always suitably unctuous where the gentry were concerned.[25] But the land surrounding the harbour was owned by the Wicklow Mining Company, who refused to surrender their lease,[26] and though the storms of the following winter finished off the old harbour,[27] the scheme had by June 1877 'definitely fallen through'.[28]

When Corbet and Parnell began to press for the Wicklow harbour scheme in 1880 Carysfort objected, stating the priority of Arklow's claim.[29] While Corbet professed sympathy for Arklow's case it was the Wicklow scheme which was ratified, and Carysfort recorded his regret in a strongly-worded letter to the *Wicklow Newsletter;*[30] for his opposition he was assaulted by a group of ill-wishers in the streets of Wicklow.[31]

Corbet now, however, took up the cudgels on behalf of Arklow[32] and secured a government loan of £20,000 in 1881 to buy out the mining company's lease and start harbour works.[33] He also obtained a free grant of £15,000. Work began under the aegis of Carysfort, and led to an increase in the rivalry between the two schemes, described above. In 1885, however, Carysfort was voted out of the chairmanship of the Arklow Town Commissioners, and replaced by the president of the local National League branch;[34] and from this point, Parnell began to adopt the cause of the Arklow harbour. In 1887, the *Wicklow Newsletter* was delighted to announce the co-operation of Parnell and Lord Carysfort over the issue: a phenomenon which marks the beginning of a completely new attitude on the part of that paper towards the Irish Leader, now seen as a local benefactor – and thus, it might be said, acting once more like one of the gentry.

The harbour works in 1877 were unfinished and unsatisfactory; by the beginning of 1890, Parnell and Carysfort had each offered £2,000 towards them and Parnell was pressing for a government loan of £5,000; Kerr told an Arklow ratepayers' meeting that his employer 'had had frequent interviews with Mr Jackson at the Treasury about this'.[345] The new alliance, however, was not an easy one. Parnell did not refrain from referring to the work hitherto done on the harbour scheme as useless, and the money spent thereon simply wasted; the political nature of the question was only just submerged. In March 1890 the *Wicklow Newsletter* printed a long correspondence between William McPhail, editor and proprietor of the paper, and Parnell's agent, William Kerr. Kerr had accused the *Newsletter* of discriminating against the Parnell interest by printing letters from Edward Kearon, a Unionist member of the Arklow Harbour Commission, who had taken issue with Parnell over the latter's denigration of the previous harbour works. Kerr felt keenly the degeneration of the harbour issue into party politics, especially since his own political ideas were very different from his employer's, whose interests he nonetheless defended with passionate loyalty. 'You know', he wrote plaintively to McPhail, 'that I am quite as good a Conservative as yourself, or Kearon.' But Parnell, he went on, was large-minded enough to put the town's good above politics, and they should do the same.[36]

This was not strictly true; Parnell's remarks about the chequered history of Arklow harbour invariably made the most of the comparative failure of the scheme under Carysfort's control.

Moreover, his efforts were not without a tincture of self-interest; the successful growth of his quarrying venture near Arklow depended upon an efficient outlet. Nonetheless, his efforts were greatly appreciated. When, after Parnell's and Corbet's activity throughout the summer session of 1890, £3,500 was made available to the Harbour Commission as a free grant and another £3,500 as a loan, the *Nation* pointed out: 'Arklow's prosperity and the promise of its future progress are to a considerable extent the creation of Mr Parnell. He has nursed and managed its industrial resources in a way that gives a rare earnest of his success in the management of a wider field.'[37] Parnell's speech to the Arklow Town Commissioners on 23 August 1890, in which he made the offer known, brought him great kudos; and neither Carysfort's name nor his exertions were so much as mentioned, even by the faithful *Wicklow Newsletter*, which so far forgot its allegiances as to remark that 'this is real Home Rule'.[38]

Parnell's involvement with the harbour did not stop there; he now interested himself in the mechanics of the task, writing to the Arklow Town Commissioners with advice about the location and material of the piers and offering 'dry rubble and material at 3d a ton, the royalty payable by me', for his quarries – the value of this being calculated at over £2,000.[39] A local Harbour Board took over from the Board of Works, and work was scheduled to begin early in 1891. Also at this time began the construction of Parnell's railway from his quarries to the sea; the same engineer was to oversee both,[40] and he followed Parnell's ideas and plans closely.

The relationship between the patron and the Harbour Board was not to be the happy one that events seemed to presage. The close connection between Parnell's private industry and his interest in the Arklow harbour was resented; attempts were made to prevent him having a landing-stage for his own use, and Kerr was goaded to the point of threatening to withdraw the offer of free stone.[41] Most important of all was the re-surfacing of the political issue – no longer the simple alignment of Parnell's sympathisers versus those of Carysfort, but the muddier and more backstabbing ethics of the Split. At first an effort was made to preserve a superficial amity; when Parnell visited Arklow on 27 January 1891 accompanied by a *Freeman* reporter, the latter found:

> There is something very touching in the regard entertained for Mr Parnell by his neighbours. He has lived amongst them and worked for them and, knowing him, they esteem him. The practical interest which he takes in the development of the country's resources has been abundantly evidenced in Arklow and the vicinity.[42]

The reporter went on to eulogise Parnell's 'delicacy of feeling' in avoiding political allusions while replying to the addresses of welcome presented by trades bodies and other local organisations; but the Harbour Board, less delicate, had noticeably absented themselves from all receptions held for Parnell since the party Split. [43] The chairman of this body, Daniel Condren, was particularly anti-Parnellite and at a subsequent meeting the plans of Parnell and Strype, the engineer, regarding which pier to start work on first, were disagreed with acrimoniously for the first time. [44] At the end of Parnell's life, as I have mentioned, his agent was embroiled in a bitter quarrel with the Commissioners about their obstruction of his plans for a landing-stage; his exertions on behalf of the scheme were but little mentioned.

It is unlikely, however, that politics were much in his own mind where the subject was concerned. In Arklow and its harbour Parnell could see some material result of his industrial plans for Wicklow; and these were closer to his heart than anything else. His personal fortunes were involved in these plans, but his vision was essentially a broader one than that. Wicklow, its minerals, stone-quarries and sea-ports, was to him a microcosm of the sort of industrial potential he visualised in all of Ireland; this is evident throughout his career, from the time when in Kilmainham in 1881 his first enquiries of a visitor were about the progress of Wicklow Harbour, [45] to the time and attention he devoted to the Arklow works in the last frantic year of his life.

Nor was the appreciation of Arklow businessmen the only tribute paid by Wicklow opinion to Parnell. The affectionate relationship between him − as land leader and local celebrity rather than squire − and the farmers round Rathdrum is well attested to by the celebrated Avondale ploughing matches. This tradition began when Parnell was in Kilmainham, and unable to administer his estate. In December 1881 the following notice was posted up in Rathdrum: 'The crops of our leader, the illustrious Charles Stewart Parnell, are to be put in on the 15th December. Assemble in your thousands with carts, ploughs, and horses, and show by your presence that you are not unmindful of the benefit conferred by him upon the Irish people.' [46] One of the signatories, Patrick Byrne, was a tenant of Parnell's; [47] but the other names (Nicholas O'Brien and Thomas Flinter) do not appear on the Avondale rent-roll, and general newspaper opinion held that the affair was organised by the Land League.

The ploughing and manuring on 15 December of Parnell's fields at Garrymore (near Rathdrum) and Avondale was on a scale far larger than the announcement − despite its casual reference to 'thousands' − implied. Volunteers came from Wicklow, Wexford, Carlow and even as far as Tipperary; [48] 600 carts were available for carting manure, with 183 ploughs decorated by green ribbons and laurels and a 'multitude' of labourers; local industries like Comerford's mills and Cronybyrne tanneries gave their workers the day off to attend, [49] and special trains were laid on from Dublin.[50] The work, which according to the *Wicklow Newsletter* involved only a dozen acres, was completed in two hours, and though it 'was of the most unromantic kind it bore the appearance more of a festivity than a labour',[51] the celebrations were out of all proportion to a mere agricultural task. Tents were erected and provisions marketed; the Gorey Brass Band and 'Parnell's Own Band' from Rathdrum provided music. A dung-cart bearing an effigy of 'the last landlord' caused considerable amusement; it made a circuit of the fields, and then a four-pronged fork was driven through the 'landlord's heart. On a more sedate note, a select group was shown around the house and behaved, remarked the *Wicklow Newsletter* irreverently, 'as if the corpse of the master were lying in state in one of the rooms above'.[52]

William Kerr supervised the affair, but the agricultural nature of the meeting was quickly taken over by politics. The attendance list was headed by W. J. Corbet M.P., J. E. Redmond M.P., Andrew Kettle M.P., and 'Professor' Henry George;[53] the speedy ploughing and manuring were followed by speeches and resolutions. The Land League had been proclaimed since 1880; the affair gave it a golden chance for a 'legal meeting'. Redmond's speech emphasised the political nature of the gathering: 'It had another and greater significance besides that of an expression of the affection and constancy of a people towards an individual man. It was a demonstration in favour of the principles for which this man and his friends are suffering.'

Other speeches on the same occasion mentioned the Parnell family myth, still potent and by now well established in the orthodox Home Rule canon of belief:

> He [the speaker, Joseph McCarroll] had seen that day in Parnell's home the banners of the glorious Volunteers of 1882. Looking at them and knowing the blood which flowed in the veins of their leader, and that his days of childhood had been spent among the relics and associations of so glorious a history, he felt that it was impossible for Parnell to be anything but a patriot and a leader.[54]

Though the crowd numbered thousands it remained orderly, and only three constables were in attendance.[55] Nor was this to be the only such occasion; Corbet announced in concluding the meeting that another 'Avondale ploughing match' would be held in the spring.

Two months later, on 16 February 1882, 500 ploughs broke up 50 acres of pasture for tillage, before – according to the *Nation* – fifteen to twenty thousand spectators, and taking only four hours.[56] Many encamped at Avondale overnight, but there was no confusion; and, although there were musical bands in attendance, there was no drinking. A few were shown over the house; no speeches were made; and 'much effort had been made to prevent the demonstration in any way assuming a political character'.[57] (The *Wicklow Newsletter* stated that this was 'in compliance with strict injunctions from Kilamainham'.)[58] The *Irish Times* was not convinced by the meeting's ostensibly innocent nature: 'Although going by the name of a "ploughing match" on a large scale, it was to all intents and purposes a monster Land League display, in which the strength of the organisation and completeness of its discipline were as much sought to be shown as gratitude to its leader.'[59]

The next demonstration was on 30 March 1882, when 70 teams saw to the ploughing and harrowing of the demesne farm; Kerr and Andrew Kettle supervised them.[60] There were no speeches and the *Wicklow Newsletter* put the attendance at 'a few dozens only', since 'the affair was not intended to bear the character of a demonstration'. Moreover, and significantly, 'several of the farmers of the neighbourhood who are not identified with the Home Rule Party sent their teams to assist in the preparation of the land for the sowing'.[61] Parnell's local position had by now become the prime cause of the ploughing matches, rather than the opportunity for political expression which they afforded.

A similar undertaking was planned for the turnip-sowing in May, but if it came off it was not recorded in the newspapers; the next occasion mentioned was a reaping-party of 'some hundreds' who harvested fifty acres of oats on 5 September, helped on by the Rathdrum Brass Band.[62] Andrew Kettle lent two machines and attended the work; otherwise the attendance was mainly of local people, and no speeches were made.[63]

January 1883, however, saw a return to large-scale agricultural demonstrations at Avondale. On 17 January, once more organised by Andrew Kettle, 150 ploughs worked 30 acres at Avondale and 60 ploughs were operated on 20 acres at Garrymore.[64] Speeches were made by Joseph McCarroll of the Wicklow Town Commissioners, and others; Kerr entertained a large group to lunch at Avondale. On this occasion a field of Parnell's neighbour, Mrs Lambert, was also ploughed; she was the sister of a local clergyman associated with political movements. But the attendance did not exceed 700, and there were no special trains laid on or prominent politicians involved, as in the headier days of 1881.

The local newspaper summed up: 'As an agricultural demonstration and a proof of the "comfortable case" of the Wicklow tenant farmer, and the excellence of their cattle, the affair was very successful, but as a political demonstration, or even as a "show", it was a failure.'[65]

This trend continued. The following March, 30 acres of oats were sown and harrowed by 40 teams,[66] but there was no further demonstration until January 1884, when 50 acres were ploughed and 6 acres of potatoes gathered.[67] 160 ploughs and 100 carts performed the work; Andrew Kettle and James F. Grehan of Cabinteely were the principal organisers. The *Freeman* recorded: 'In its extent and the warmth of the zeal shown by the farmers to participate in the work it recalled the memorable occasion when many farmers and labourers took part in a similar work when Mr Parnell was in Kilmainham as a suspect.'[68] But it was, in practice, a different kind of affair. Most of the names recorded in attendance were local people, and the majority were from the Parnell lands like Carrignameel, Ballyknockan and Ballinderry; Andrew Kettle was the only M.P. there, and there were no speeches. The land agitation had become subdued, and this is the last 'ploughing match' recorded at Avondale.

The Rathdrum area had, nonetheless, been active during the era of advanced agitation – at least in the context of Wicklow's peaceful history in the period.[69] Evictions had occurred on the Littledale estate nearby which had resulted in respectable farmers' wives assaulting policemen and being jailed for nine months.[70] When the Mooney family at Newbawn were to be evicted, eight or ten Land Leaguers helped them barricade the house and 200 police had to be called in. All concerned received prison sentences.[71] Hugh Gaffney, an employee of Parnell's, was an officer of the Land League and was responsible for plastering Rathdrum Police Station with copies of the No Rent Manifesto one memorable night; before the Land League was proclaimed he helped to organise meetings where Dillon, Redmond and others spoke; he was also influential in the ploughing matches.[72] He and other Parnellites canvassed strenuously for Parnell's candidates in 1891. The 1892 election in Wicklow saw the defeat of the Parnellites, W. J. Corbet in East Wicklow and John Parnell in West Wicklow; both seats were won by the official Irish Party candidates, John Sweetman and James O'Connor. But Rathdrum, it is held, remained Parnellite to the end; the tradition of supporting the local squire probably helped to reinforce adulation of the fabled chief who recalled the epic days of the Land War. The ploughing matches, at all events, bear witness to a local support that partook of both elements.

## II

Parnell, remarked Captain O'Shea to Sir E. T. Cook, 'was a pariah, and none of his own class would have a word to say to him'.[73] But the attitude of Parnell's own class towards him in Wicklow life is not as easily charted as that of his tenants, or the Arklow townspeople; there is no specific record of opinion to draw upon. A good gauge is provided by the redoubtably Tory *Wicklow Newsletter;* but while always adopting a reverent tone towards the gentry, this journal catered for a lower level of local interest, and so cannot be taken as a measure of 'county' opinion. The opinion of the county is, however, easily reckoned: Parnell was *de facto* a class traitor, and should be treated as such.

The importance of Parnell's upper-class background was never underestimated by his own supporters. An address presented to him in 1883 declared that 'in a time of national prostration you stepped out of the ranks of selfish aristocracy and flung youth and fortune into the service of the Irish cause';[74] and when times were more malicious, in May 1891, the *Nation* claimed that 'it was the peculiar surroundings of the Protestant Squireen' which constituted Parnell's attraction for the Home Rulers in the first place.[75] The same accusation had been made by Parnell's opponents in the very first election he fought.[76] A similar point was raised by an English opponent of his, who wrote to the *Cumberland Press* in June 1891 that Parnell, basically English, became leader 'by the help of able men of Celtic blood'.[77] Frank Hugh O'Donnell amplified this idea: 'I doubt very much if Mr Parnell saw for a considerable time the attractions which his personality offered to a huge class of agitators in Ireland. They wanted a "country gintleman". They got him.'[78]

Though the idea of Parnell as figurehead will not stand up to examination, the frequency of such accusations shows that his background was an issue very much in people's minds. Gladstone listed 'advantage of birth' as a reason for Parnell's ascendancy[79] and Sir William Butler, an ardent admirer of his, believed that the Irish recognised 'the factor of birth' as an element in Parnell's supremacy.[80]

Certainly, an upper-class conditioning had formed a great deal of his character. But the people amongst whom he grew up rejected him when his politics diverged from theirs. I have referred to his belief that Lord Carysfort would refuse to rent him his quarry 'because he disapproves of my politics';[81] yet Carysfort was Parnell's father's first cousin, and had been a companion of John and Charles on shooting parties in Wicklow before the latter's entry into politics.[82] The Carysforts were one of the few families actually named by Mrs Delia Parnell as close friends of hers in Wicklow society.[83] Parnell's alienation from Carysfort cannot have been total, for they co-operated over the Arklow harbour scheme in the late eighties,[84] though not closely.

But with other neighbours, the estrangement was complete. Charles Barton of Annamoe was a close contemporary of Parnell's, only two years younger than he. Like Parnell, he built an ambitious sawmill on his demesne, and he shared Parnell's enthusiasm for cricket. As a young man Parnell often came to play cricket on the lawn in front of Glendalough House, a fine neo-Gothic pile built at Annamoe in 1838 by Barton's father; here, local tradition has it, a boy emptied a claret-cup into Parnell's boots before a match and was soundly thrashed for his ill-conceived jape. Barton was an enlightened man, a good landlord and employer, and a close contemporary of Parnell's in every way, as well as a neighbour; but he was also a Unionist, and when Parnell entered Home Rule politics, Barton simply never spoke to him again. [85]

This was, it appears, just one instance of what became a general practice. An obituary notice of W. F. Hume-Dick, at one time Conservative M.P. for Wicklow, described him significantly as 'a near neighbour and *one-time friend*' of Parnell's. [86] John Parnell mentions that the Parnells became estranged from the Brookes of Castle Howard, friends since childhood, because of politics; [87] and Emily Dickinson, who described high life among Wicklow society in her youth with the regret of one mourning Saturn's Golden Age, wrote that after her brother's name became identified with Home Rule, 'social life wore a very different aspect; cold looks and distant bows took the place in many cases of the hearty and friendly cordiality of happier times; therefore invitations were not at all so plentiful as of yore'. [88] Even after Parnell's death, she expected to be ' "shelved" on account of politics' in Dublin society. [89] This was not, in the event, the case; and it appears unlikely that the Wicklow gentry visited the sins of the brother upon his non-political sisters. Lady Alice Howard was the strongest of Tories, and never mentioned the name of 'Charlie Parnell', who had once attended shooting-parties with her at Shelton Abbey, after 1875; but when she visited Paris in 1882, one of her first actions was to pay a call on his sister, Delia, who had never deserted the social fold. [90]

Moreover, even with regard to Parnell himself, a certain class solidarity remained. He was, as I have said, no believer in social equality; [91] and a perceptive reporter from *Tinsley's Magazine*, who heard an extremist speech of Parnell's in 1881, noted:

> A strange feeling took hold of me after he had concluded. It was that it would be a grave error to suppose him to be a great lover of the farming class. I could not even think that he disliked his own class, the landlords, though his words about them were strong and the reverse of complimentary. [92]

Enough fellow-feeling remained for Standish O'Grady, who knew Wicklow well, to be able to remark that 'even the gentry of Leinster, his neighbours, liked him and watched his strange career as their enemy with a certain amused and affectionate interest'. [93] St John Ervine said the same thing. [94] And when a fund was opened in 1888 for Parnell's legal expenses arising out of the *Times* Special Commission, the Earl of Bessborough was one of the first subscribers: 'He knew

Parnell well when living in the county Wicklow, and always found him in business and other matters to be a truthful man; and he forwarded £10 "as a proof of my reliance on his word".'[95]

But the mainstream of county opinion was heavily against the renegade in their midst. When an employee from Avondale looked for employment at Guinness's after Parnell's death he was refused on account of his connection with 'that rebel';[96] the Guinness family owned much land in county Wicklow, and represented county conservatism at its strongest. And it was not only in the House of Commons that Parnell had to learn to put up the impassive mask to hostility, so tellingly described by Henry Harrison;[97] Davitt tells of how Parnell had to sit in the Irish Mail train from Holyhead to London listening to someone in the same carriage declaring that 'Parnell was *a renegade to his own class* and ought to be shot for stirring up the country against the landlords'.[98] Though a neighbour like Sir William Butler at Delgany could admire Parnell fervently, Butler was not in a position analogous to those who 'ran' the county and owned estates there; he could, in a sense, 'afford' to admire Parnell, and he also had a good deal more intelligence and breadth of view than the average county magnate. As he mentions, he was the only member of the shooting-party at Aughavannagh, which he recorded, who was not a member of the Home Rule Party.[99] The rift between Parnell and his neighbours among the county gentry was unbridgeable by 1888.

The strength of their feeling is testified to by the language used by those who attended a meeting in Molesworth Hall, Dublin, on 23 October 1885 to form an 'East Wicklow Loyalists' Union' as a branch of the I.L.P.U.[100] The meeting was chaired by the Earl of Meath, Lord Lieutenant of Wicklow; the attendance reads like the roll of magistrates for the county. Lords Wicklow, Carysfort and Powerscourt were prominent, along with two Fitzwilliams; names like Howard-Brooke, Casement, Tottenham, Saunders, Latouche, Acton and Erck follow. Out of the sixty-seven named in attendance, twenty-one were J.P.s.[101] Some were Liberals and some Conservatives, and they made it clear from the first that their political allegiances differed widely;[102] but Liberals and Conservatives united when 'dismemberment of Empire, with certain already proclaimed socialistic violences included in the deed' was at issue.[103] The committee formed included members of both parties. Significantly, the most remarkable feature of the meeting, and the one upon which newspapers of all political hues concentrated, was the opening speech by Lord Meath – a blistering personal attack on Parnell as a 'dictator' and an 'anarchistic communistic revolutionary'. Meath spoke with the voice of the Wicklow gentry against the apostate they had spawned, and his fellows cheered his every word.

Such was the beginning of the gentry's counter-organisation. A much smaller meeting at Baltinglass on 25 October 1885 established a West Wicklow branch of the I.L.P.U., presided over by W. W. Fitzwilliam Hume-Dick, Tory candidate for the division;[104] but support was less forthcoming. West Wicklow had far fewer landlords and its record in the Land War was far more active.[105] The gentry in the west of the county may have felt more beleagured, and been correspondingly more extreme in their Unionism; a Loyalist meeting in Baltinglass on 17 July 1885 was held under the auspices of a Belfast Orange Lodge.[106] But there were far fewer of the gentry to support the movement, and they had less money at their disposal.

The Wicklow I.L.P.U. met in force several times before the 1886 Home Rule Bill was introduced;[107] on 6 May 1885 Lady Alice Howard recorded in her diary a visit to Kilruddery 'to begin a Ladies' branch of the Loyal and Patriotic Union in Bray',[108] and in the previous month a branch of the Union had been formed on Parnell's own doorstep in Rathdrum.[109] But the Unionist candidates went down badly before Corbet and Garret Byrne, the Home Rule candidates, in the elections of 1885 and 1886,[110] and their meetings became more and more rare.

This does not mean that the county attitude to Parnell softened with time; feelings went too deep for that. A telling letter in the *Nation* of 27 November 1880 from Parnell's tenants in West Wicklow protested 'in the strongest possible terms against the false statements and cowardly slanders constantly uttered from the bench in Hacketstown court and from the chair in Baltinglass Board-room by a J.P., Colonel Dennis' about their landlord; and the *Freeman* recorded five years later that the ' "Loyalists" of East Wicklow' were by far the most virulent of the anti-Parnell element in Ireland.[111] He was, as the man in the railway carriage remarked, 'a renegade to his own class' – or, more accurately, to what appeared to be the interests of his own class – and he was treated accordingly. When he died, the unionism of, for instance, William McPhail, proprietor of the *Wicklow Newsletter*, could allow that Parnell was a benefactor to Wicklow and state that 'how much his heart was centred here, and how deep an interest he displayed in the home of his childhood, was little thought of;'[112] but Lady Alice Howard, who had once known him well, merely noted in her diary that 'C. Parnell died . . . They gave him a tremendous public funeral and buried him at Glasnevin'.[113] It is unlikely that Parnell returned the implacable enmity he received from the people he had grown up among; as the *Tinsley Magazine* reporter noted, he did not seem to dislike his own class, and he was no egalitarian. But he had to face this attitude, and it must have shaped his impassive public persona at least as much as did the vituperation he received from the opposing parliamentary benches.

## III

This survey of Parnell and Wicklow during the years of his political ascendancy has not held to any chronological scheme; I have preferred to consider facets of his involvement with the county as they arose. But it is appropriate to conclude with a brief look at opinion in the county following the party split, and the echoes that Parnell's last battles raised in Wicklow.

By 1891 the county had two newspapers, McPhail's Conservative *Wicklow Newsletter* and the *Wicklow People*, which had begun life as a National League broadsheet in 1883 and was put on a commercial basis by Joseph Smyth in 1886. [114] The *Newsletter* was invariably hostile to Parnell, the *People* fulsome in his praises. By 1890, however, the *Newsletter* had swung to grudging praise of Parnell's efforts on behalf of the county's ports, and his largesse as an employer; as the epigraph to the last chapter shows, he was seen as an 'old neighbour', albeit an apostate one, [115] and McPhail's reaction to the divorce case was non-commital – except that he stated unequivocally as early as February 1890 that Parnell would let the case 'go by default' so that he could marry Katherine O'Shea. [116] When this happened, the *Newsletter* remained uncharacteristically silent; but the *People* rounded both fast and furiously upon the erstwhile local saint. Partly because it was a chance to take a different line from his rival, but also as a continuation of his support for Parnell as a local benefactor, it fell to McPhail to take on the incongruous task of defending the disgraced national leader. He attacked the Arklow Town Commissioners for snubbing the man who 'from his sickbed dragged himself to the House of Commons and kept his weary vigils to vote and assist at the passing through the different stages of the Arklow Harbour Bill'; [117] he appended critical editorial notes to anti-Parnellite letters in the paper; [118] he gave full coverage to the activities of the Parnell Leadership Committee in the county, [119] and he attributed large attendances to Parnell's political meetings. [120]

There was, in any case, only one anti-Parnellite organisation in Wicklow, predictably enough located in Arklow. Joseph McCarroll, chairman of the Wicklow Town Commissioners, headed the Parnell Leadership Committee in the town of Wicklow; perhaps the rivalry between the two harbours carried over into Split politics. Both Wicklow M.P.s were Parnellites, Corbet passionately so; though himself a Catholic, he was not afraid to attack local priests publicly on the issue. [121] At a large meeting in Wicklow in June 1891, Parnell spoke warmly of his native county, 'where I lived for fifteen years amongst you', [122] but he tailored his speeches to traditional Wicklow opinion, and while attacking Gladstone and calling for 'legitimate freedom', he hastily added: 'I don't mean separation from England, or anything of the kind.' He knew of old that his support in Wicklow did not come from hillside men.

It came, in fact, from older loyalties, to the potency of which even the *Newsletter* was not immune – though McPhail had to remind his readers (and, one feels, himself) in July 1891 that 'to all true Unionists the cause of Mr McCarthy and Mr Parnell is the same'. [123] The *Wicklow People,* on the other hand, published any and every calumny about Parnell and his new wife, often relating the statements to Wicklow – he was bringing 'Mrs O'Shea' to Aughavannagh, he had taken a house at Bray for her to entertain her London friends, and so on [124] – which brought the faithful Kerr, in a fever-pitch of rage, to threaten the editor with 'a good thrashing'; [125] but the *Newsletter* never entered these grubby lists.

Support for Parnell at Wicklow political meetings often recurred to the Parnell family's 'patriotic' record [126] and Parnell's own munificence to the county: [127] two uncontroversial local issues, one mythological and one referring purely to Parnell's personal life, but both potent. The issue of English dictation was rarely mentioned; when Wicklow supported Parnell, it was on the basis of the themes of family history and local position, which I have tried to illustrate throughout this study.

The *Wicklow Newsletter* gave him its non-political support until the end. A grief-stricken editorial of 10 October 1891 mourned the death of a benefactor who was too little appreciated in his lifetime:

> What he has done for the people of the county, and what he intended to do, will never be adequately realised . . . How painful it is to reflect that the implacable animosity that pursued him to his death grew luxuriantly and was fostered industriously where he should have been most looked up to. We are not now speaking in a political sense, but in a purely local and personal vein.

McPhail went on to attack those employees of Parnell's from Arklow who had 'denounced a generous and affectionate employer at the Carlow election'. Both these men and the politicians who instigated such backstabbing deserved every execration. 'Mr Parnell's life was sacrificed for Ireland. No matter how we may condemn his policy, he lived to aid her progress.' It was with every truth that he had told the Archbishop of Cashel that the inhabitants of Arklow could explain what he had done with the Tribute; and, the editor added accurately, 'it was known to be a fact in Wicklow that the profits of his labours were but little commensurate with his outlay'. In conclusion, 'We hope his memory will be long revered, and that those who thwarted his progress in local enterprise will be among the first to render him the homage that his memory deserves.' The editorial was followed by a biographical note which made full mention of the Parnell family's long

connection with Wicklow, and their relation to the Howard and
Carysfort families. The whole obituary could be that of a Wicklow
gentleman and local benefactor who had never stepped out of his
prescribed sphere. Family tradition and local position had much to do
with Parnell's entry into politics; and it was these elements in his
career that local opinion recurred to at his death.

# Part V

*Parnell and his family, 1875–91*

# 1   *The non-political Parnells*

'That's the fascination': soliloquised Leopold Bloom when struck by
the sight of John Howard Parnell walking up College Street, 'the
name; all a bit touched.'[1] 'Touched' or not – and to this day one is told
in Wicklow that 'the Parnells were all mad' – the fascination of the
name held good before Bloom's day as well as after it. As Parnell's
fame grew, the character and doings of his family became almost as
much of a public preoccupation as did his own; and when he died and
his reputation became mythologised, the Parnells took on the status of
family figures in a Greek tragedy.

But the reputation of, and interest in, the Parnell family was not
solely and simply as a function of the great man; they made their own
reputation. This was not, of course, true for all of them; and the
discrepancy has dictated my treatment of Parnell and his family in this
chapter. Attached as he may have been to Theodosia, or even Henry,
the public knew little of these 'non-political' Parnells; they kept,
probably by design, well clear of the limelight. Thus I have dealt
sparingly with the members of the family who had no part in public
life, both because the records of their quiet careers are scanty, and
because their own reputation has little part in forming or fortifying
their brother's myth. But the lives of Mrs Delia Parnell and of Fanny,
Anna and John have a different kind of significance in relation to
Charles Stewart Parnell, as well as having an interest of their own;
therefore, in this section it is upon these members of the Parnell family
that I will concentrate, first of all dealing with the non-political
Parnells in this chapter.

Discussing the Parnell children in their childhood, I drew a
distinction between the 'two strains' amongst them. The
strong-minded, individualist group were Charles, Emily, Fanny, Anna
and Hayes; these, except for Emily and Hayes (who died aged fifteen)
were politically-minded, close-knit, and stayed single or married late in
life. The other stream included Delia, Sophia, Theodosia and Henry.

All married young, were more self-effacing and conventional, and all except Sophia chose to live outside Ireland. John Howard alone combined some attributes of both groups; his temperament belongs to the second, but his career places him among the first.

Of the non-political Parnells, Delia, Sophia and Theodosia may be first – and briefly – considered. Sophia did not live to see her brother achieve prominence. She had, as I have told, married Alfred MacDermott secretly in 1862 and publicly on 22 May 1866. [2] She lived at 43, Fitzwilliam Square, and according to Emily 'her early marriage to a rather ordinary man made her very conventional'. [3] She lectured Emily upon indiscreet friendships with men other than her husband, gave up social life to devote herself to her three children, and 'never confessed to' repenting of her headlong marriage. [4] Throughout her account of Sophia's life, Emily's strong bias against MacDermott manifests itself; [5] it is unfortunate that we have only her word to rely upon, especially where Sophia's early death in February 1877 is concerned. This was brought on by nursing her children through scarlatina while herself pregnant; Emily states contradictorily both that Sophia 'insisted' upon doing this and that she was forced to because MacDermott refused to hire a nurse which she requested. [6] Sophia was only thirty-two when she died; MacDermott's 'remorse' was such, Emily tells us, that he was pitied even by 'his worst enemies' – by whom she probably meant herself. Nonetheless, she vowed never to forgive him.

Other members of the family were less intractable. The memorials in the Dublin Registry of Deeds show that MacDermott continued as solicitor for John and Henry Parnell as well as for Charles – despite the conservative politics attributed to him. [7] A family connection remained as well as this professional link; when John Howard Parnell and his mother came to Ireland the winter after Parnell's death, it was to MacDermott's house in Fitzwilliam Square that they first made their way. [8] The family friendship with MacDermott had begun before his precipitate marriage to Sophia; it continued after her death. He had, after all, been solicitor to John Henry Parnell as well as to his sons. [9] Emily may have blamed her brother-in-law for Sophia's early death, but it seems unlikely that any other member of the family did. There were, in any case, Sophia's four children to consider; [10] they were half Parnell. And the connection was strong enough for one of them, Tudor MacDermott, to earn himself a niche in Irish history by administering a horsewhipping to T. M. Healy after one of the latter's more foul-mouthed references to Parnell's widow in 1891.

Of Delia, who died not long afterwards, there is little to record – and most of the information available comes from the unsteady memory of Emily Dickinson. Delia's hardheaded marriage to Livingston Thomson continued to turn out badly; his jealousy reached the point where he forbade her to go out riding, whereupon she attempted suicide,[11] and was only rescued by the intervention of her sister Anna, staying in Paris at the time. She was, Emily admits, 'of a very undemonstrative and of an apparently cold temperament', but her husband's jealousy remained undimmed; and we have more than Emily's word for it that she was beautiful, for she was accorded the doubtful privilege of being considered 'the most strikingly beautiful woman he had ever met' by no less worldly a judge than Willie O'Shea.[12]

Unhappy as she was, Delia concentrated her affection upon her only son Henry, who was born in 1861. She does not seem to have left Paris often, although her husband had relaxed in his attitude since her attempt to do away with herself. John Howard mentions that she was in America in the late 1870s,[13] but he may have meant Theodosia, who was living there at the time; he confuses the two sisters elsewhere.[14] In April 1882 Henry Thomson, by then a music student living alone in Paris, died of Typhus fever, undiagnosed till it was too late; this provided the occasion for Parnell's celebrated parole from Kilmainham, when he travelled to Paris to console his sister. From here he wrote to Emily that Delia was 'much cut up by her dreadful loss, but is somewhat better now; my being here has done her a great deal of good';[15] he wrote in similar terms to Mrs O'Shea.[16] Delia, was, however, inconsolable; she became a recluse after her son's death and died, according to John Howard, in 1882. It seems likely that whatever neurotic tendencies she already had were accentuated by her loss. The exact date and place of her death are unrecorded, as are the other details of her unhappy life; in the recollections both of Emily and her mother she figures more as the provider of a suitably glamorous background than as a person of any intrinsic interest. The newspapers did not report her death, and neither Katharine Parnell nor John Howard Parnell mention the event as being the sort of upheaval that, for instance, Fanny's was; it is likely that her influence upon her great brother did not carry far beyond childhood.

Between Parnell and his youngest sister, however, a closer connection seems to have existed. John Howard, who spent summer holidays with Theodosia in the fashionable fastness of Newport, R.I., described her as 'a real society belle, though of a very quiet disposition';[17] a contemporary portrait of her in the *Celtic Magazine* shows a strikingly attractive blonde girl, smartly dressed, with more delicate features than the other Parnell women.[18] In the late 1870s she lived at Bordentown, New Jersey, with her mother and sisters Fanny and Anna. She was active enough in her support of her sisters' work for the Irish cause to earn praise from the *Celtic Monthly*,[19] and accompanied her mother and brother upon the latter's American speaking tour in 1879–80; but it was said that 'though an ardent Land

Leaguer too, she lacked the practical, untiring methods of her sisters
Fanny and Anna'.[20] It seems likely that her aid was dictated more by
good nature than anything else; her name was not linked with Irish
politics after her marriage in July 1880.

Theodosia returned to Europe with her mother, sister, and brother
Charles in March 1880. T. M. Healy, who was on the same ship, was
interested to notice that, although Parnell had told him Fanny was his
favourite sister, 'he often paced the decks with Theodosia'.[21] Healy
also wrote, more outspokenly, to his brother Maurice: '[Parnell] is
sublimely indifferent [to his mother and Anna] . . . I was surprised,
therefore, to see that he showed a great deal of attention to his
youngest sister while on board'.[22] This, to Healy, was all the more
remarkable because of the cavalier attitude the family had towards one
another's doings:

> She [Theodosia] announced her intention of going to Paris the
> night we got to New York, and neither of the others, nor the
> mother, seemed in the least surprised, or to care a damn, and
> Parnell himself said 'Ah!' although none of them had ever heard
> of the project before.[23]

But the casual relationship between them, especially where travel
plans were concerned, was only to be expected after the haphazard and
geographically scattered way that Mrs Parnell had brought her
children up.[24] Parnell certainly seems to have felt a real warmth for
his youngest sister; he travelled to Paris for her wedding at a busy time
in 1880,[25] and writing to Emily from Paris in 1882 he mentioned: 'I
shall be sure to call to see Theodosia and Claude before I return to
Ireland', adding a worried postscript – 'I am sorry to hear Theodosia is
not looking at all strong.'[26]

Theodosia married Claude Paget, a naval officer two years older
than she was, on 21 July 1880. Born in 1851, he had the sort of
impeccable family connections which delighted his mother-in-law; his
father, Colonel Leopold Grimston Paget (1824–92) was grandson of
the first Earl of Uxbridge and nephew of the first Marquis of Anglesea.
Claude entered the Navy in 1864 and became a lieutenant in 1875; he
was to retire as Commander in 1896.[27] Writing in 1891, Mrs Parnell
emphasised both the Paget family tree and the fact that Claude's
relatives 'thought themselves fortunate in being allied to the ancient
family of Parnell'.[28] Besides the pleasure of being allied to the
Parnells, the lieutenant had the more concrete good fortune to marry
someone who was, according to a memorial in the Registry of Deeds,
'entitled in her own right' to ten thousand dollars in American railway
stock and twelve thousand dollars invested in a coal company;[29] she
also had an annuity of £100 from the Collure estate, by her father's
will.[30] There was one son born of the marriage in 1891, named Cyril

Nevil. The couple bought a house on the Thames at Weybridge, where – after Paget's early retirement – their time was taken up, according to Emily Dickinson, 'with horses and cycling, cultivating roses and peacocks';[31] a picture of an English upper middle-class idyll far removed from the more stormy and star-crossed fortunes of the rest of the Parnell family.

## II

Emily, though equally non-political, is a case in point. By 1875 her husband was a committed alcoholic, and they were largely dependent upon Charles for support.[32] In February 1882 her mother described her as 'living at Avondale';[33] Emily tells us that she went there about this time with her daughter Delia at Charles's invitation 'for a few months', when proceedings were brought against Arthur for assault and he had to leave the country.[34] He was gone for six months. Theodosia and Claude Paget came for a summer at Avondale, with an entourage of dogs and horses;[35] Emily stayed on into the winter. At this juncture, she received an unexpected legacy from 'my uncle, Mr Bligh' – or so she tells us.[36]

In any case, Emily could now afford to pay off the plaintiff in Arthur's assault case; and, better still, Arthur had managed to stop drinking during his sojourn abroad. At this point, her quiet life at Avondale, enlivened only by the Leveresque escapades of a permanently drunken groom[37] and 'occasional visits from neighbouring county families',[38] was suddenly brought to an end: not, however, by the expected return of the prodigal, but by a telegram announcing his sudden death in Brussels. Emily believed this to have been caused by the shock to his system induced by unaccustomed abstinence. The event, undated by his widow, is reported in the *Wicklow Newsletter* as having taken place on 12 December 1883.[39]

Emily had still retained a house in Dublin – or, more probably, the lease on one. She now gave it up and relapsed into melancholy at Avondale. She was horrified that among the messages of condolence she received after Arthur's death were some which tended to thoughtless but understandable congratulation; and she refused to entertain the advances of old beaux.[40] 'The next winter' – probably 1884 – she moved back to Dublin for a few months, then to London, then Richmond, then Jersey, and finally spent an unhappy winter in Guernsey, where her relationship to Parnell meant that the unfriendly natives 'visited their disapproval and wrath on the head of his unoffending sister'.[41] In the early spring (probably of 1886) she returned to Ireland. Her daughter Delia had left boarding-school and needed taking care of; Mrs Parnell was in financial trouble, and Arthur's debts had swallowed all of Emily's money (she does not mention what part of her travels of the past two years played in this process). Permanent residence at Avondale 'was no longer a mere question of choice, but absolutely indispensable'. Here she lived regularly with her headstrong and discontented daughter until the end of Parnell's life.

Thus, despite the grandiose and inaccurate style of Emily's memoir, her account is one of particular interest: because she was the only member of Parnell's family who occupied a fixed position in his life. The others, to whom he was in many ways more closely connected, only crossed his path at intervals; they lived abroad or did not move in his circle at home. Emily, however, was at Avondale more or less throughout her brother's political career; she had the sort of consistent view of him which was shared by no one else except Mrs O'Shea. It is, therefore, still more of a pity that her account places so little value upon consistency, or accuracy.

Moreover, their relationship, at least according to Emily, was close: they disagreed about politics, but tacitly preferred not to discuss them.[42] He came straight to Avondale upon hearing of Arthur's death; at this point, Emily says, 'my brother's affection shone out in full lustre'.[43] He organised the removal of Arthur's body from Brussels, settled his affairs there, and attended the funeral of the unfortunate Captain at Ballinatone.[44] Parnell stayed on with his sister, consoling her and attempting to distract her.[45] After she took up residence in Avondale, whenever he returned there on his brief visits they used to take long rides together and explore far into the mountains; on these 'we talked of every subject under the sun except politics'. Andrew Kettle, visiting Avondale in 1890, watched them returning from such an expedition, and remarked 'they both looked to advantage on horseback'.[46]

Even before Arthur's death, they had been closely connected. Parnell spent the day before his arrest in 1881 with Emily and her daughter at Avondale;[47] she was one of the first visitors allowed him in Kilmainham, and 'constantly' called on him there.[48] She was, she states, never searched and 'had quite the run of the prison'; but when she offered to carry letters for her brother he 'chivalrously refused'. Here Emily's account is probably inaccurate; Parnell wrote to Mrs O'Shea that it was not until March 1882 that he was allowed to see Emily in private.[49] And it is hard not to suppose that chivalry had less to do with his refusal of her services than apprehensiveness about Emily's tendency to garrulity and self-glorification. She also claims that she often stayed in the room when Parnell was discussing political tactis with his political colleagues at Avondale, and that when Davitt once complained about her presence he was told by Parnell: 'She is quite safe'. If 'safe' with political matters, however, which were probably largely above her head, Emily would have been decidedly risky with letters to Katharine O'Shea; and this is most likely to have been what was in Parnell's mind when he refused to use her as courier.

As far as appearances went, the relationship between the two was not as warm as might be supposed from Emily's memoir. Barry O'Brien was told of their reunion after Kilmainham by a companion of Parnell's on his return to Avondale: Parnell remained 'absolutely unmoved' throughout the passionate demonstrations of the household, and Emily remained as cool as he. [50] It is tempting to infer from this that Emily wildly exaggerated her brother's closeness to her; but I believe such an inference is unwarranted. For one thing, O'Brien does not mention that Parnell had seen his sister often in Kilmainham; they were not meeting after an unbroken absence, as he implies. Furthermore, much of the 'lack of feeling' implicit in the passage may be attributed to Parnell's social manner. As I have previously shown, it is incontestable that the feelings between Parnell and his estate workers were the warmest possible; [51] and their reaction at his homecoming shows this. Yet he treated their welcome, if O'Brien's anecdote be taken at face-value, as casually as he did Emily's cool greeting. But they knew him too well to expect anything else; and so did Emily. [52]

Her closeness to him does not presuppose a great understanding of his personality, his life, or his politics – significantly, her account of the O'Shea liaison is fanciful garble. [53] She evidently knew next to nothing about it. And she was, as she states, opposed to his politics; at one point, indeed, she claims that after Kilmainham he set to 'working towards the broader tenets of socialism'! [54] Where it suits her dramatic purpose she is capable of referring to 'the promised land of Home Rule' and 'the great structure of his [Parnell's] life-work'; [55] but there seems little doubt that her general attitude to his politics was disapproval, further coloured by the unpleasant difference she found that his reputation made to her own social life in Dublin. [56]

She was, however, furious about the secession in Committee Room Fifteen and determined to see him through his last campaign; they spent more time together in this last year than at any time since childhood. [57] When he went to meetings near Wicklow, she attended them; when he spent a night at home, she kept him company. She describes his outward cheerfulness and his desire for companionship – and the one time she found him alone 'with a look on his face . . . of a despondency which saw no ray of light far off'. [58] Barry O'Brien has written of the same thing; [59] and Patrick O'Brien told him of Parnell asking if he could come to the theatre with himself and Emily in 1891, [60] when he was almost pathetically anxious for company. Most of what she writes of this period has the ring of truth; as has the account of the last time she saw him. Emily and Delia took rooms at Bray to attend the Cabinteely meeting; Parnell drove to the meeting with them, and the carriage went past Khyber Pass, Dalkey, where they had lived as children immediately after their father's death.[61] They reminisced enthusiastically about this; but the easy tone of the evening was spoiled by the shattering of the carriage windows by the over-eager crowd at the meeting – to both the superstitious Parnells, an act of great ill-omen. After the meeting they dined at the Royal Marine Hotel at Kingstown; Parnell walked with his sister and niece to the Bray train and said goodbye. The Creggs meeting was two weeks later; and he did not come to Avondale again.

It is significant that about the Creggs meeting, which she did not attend, Emily supplies irrelevant and totally imaginary details, such as Parnell swaying and falling senseless at the end of his address. It is equally typical that of her dash to Brighton after his death (also mentioned by her mother)[62] she says nothing except that she was not allowed to view Parnell's remains by 'his small band of followers';[63] one longs to hear more. But in her account of Parnell following her from room to room in Avondale during 1891, uncharacteristically 'making conversation', in her memory of him deliberately forgetting politics on their long rides together in the Wicklow hills, in the kindness and sympathy he showed to her when Arthur's unexpected death left her stranded at Avondale in 1883, Emily's book bears witness to a closeness between brother and sister which lasted from childhood, through deep-rooted differences of conviction, attitudes and character. Emily lived too long; in old age she was to become that saddest of sights, a 'character' round the streets of Dublin, and to write a book which in many ways travestied her dead brother's reputation. But what is worthwhile in her memoir is easily discernible from the mass of chaff which surrounds it; and even the inaccurate or simply fanciful aspects of the book themselves tell us something of the unfortunate woman who wrote it. For all her differences from her brother, she was still a Parnell – and one who was closer to him than many others of the family.

## III

Henry, the youngest Parnell son, remains a shadowy figure throughout this period. He had, as I have discussed, made money out of his inheritance[64] selling off most of the Clonmore lands by 1875; in this year he was admitted to the Bar at Lincoln's Inn.[65] He never, however, practised as a barrister, though giving this as his profession on legal documents; John Howard tells us that Henry never took his degree examination at Cambridge because he was 'too nervous',[66] and possibly this inertia was due to the same reason. Other records state that he spent much of his time travelling because of his delicate health.[67]

He married Penelope Jane Luby on 21 October 1882; the wedding was not mentioned in the Dublin papers, although the bride's father had been a well-known Fellow of Trinity College. It probably took place in London; Penelope's address, as well as her mother's, was given as the Grosvenor Hotel of Buckingham Palace Road,[68] and her father had died in 1870.[69] Penelope was a cousin of the celebrated Fenian, T. C. Luby, but this interesting link does not seem to have meant that Henry Parnell had leanings towards Irish nationalism; Thomas Clarke Luby was if anything an even more anomalous product of his background than Charles Stewart Parnell.[70] There were three children born of the marriage: Henry Maurice Stewart (in 1884), Maud Yolan Howard (in 1886) and Harold de Mowbray (in 1889). The last-named was slightly simple-minded; in later years he lived with John Howard Parnell at Glenageary. But up to 1891, little enough is known of Henry Parnell's family. They lived, ironically, at the sort of watering-places on the south coast of England so favoured by Henry's brother and Mrs O'Shea at the same time. In 1884 Henry was living at Folkestone,[71] in 1891 at Ramsgate,[72] and T. P. O'Connor records him as being resident at Brighton;[73] while Parnell, looking for a discreet retreat in the early 1880s, rented a house at Eastbourne with a view to purchasing it only to discover to his surprise and chagrin that Henry was living in the same town.[74]

This reaction, as well as the ignorance it shows on Parnell's part about his brother's whereabouts, implies that there was not a close link between him and Henry. T. P. O'Connor states (though without corroboration) that Henry had a persecution mania and suffered from the delusion that he was constantly being followed[75] and this may provide an explanation for his shadowy life-style as well as clarifying what John Parnell meant by his casual reference to Henry's nervousness.

The only record we have of Henry is, appropriately enough, contained in his land dealings. With the profits of his Clonmore sales he had bought a six-hundred acre estate in Co. Kilkenny;[76] he also retained about three hundred acres of the Clonmore estate.[77] He used these assets as the most absentee of landlords; we find him raising money on the security of the Carlow lands in 1884 and 1891,[78] and putting part of the Kilkenny estate in the trusteeship of his mother-in-law and Alfred MacDermott as security for £6,000 which was advanced to him when he married Penelope Luby.[79] He seems to have managed these Irish lands through a middleman; and it has already been seen how his harsh reputation affected his brother's career, both in the Dublin election of 1875, when the Conservatives circulated a broadsheet proclaiming 'Mr Parnell's many disputes with his tenants at Tombay',[80] and in an anonymous letter to the *Irish Times* in 1880 which accused Parnell of being party to the Clonmore land speculations.[81] Whether or not the accusers were completely ingenuous in mistaking the identity of the landlord, the effect was strong enough. A correspondent of Michael Davitt's in 1885, complaining that Parnell was not condemned as roundly as other landlords, added: 'I have heard it said that his brother is as bad a landlord as any other';[82] Davitt himself remarked on the same thing to W. S. Blunt in 1887.[83] Both T. P. O'Connor and St John Ervine describe Henry Parnell as a strong conservative, without stating their authority.[84] It seems that his attitude as landlord did not suggest any sympathy with his brother's political activity; and although he made some effort to defend his brother's reputation when Emily wrote her fanciful account of Parnell's Cambridge love-life in 1906,[85] this is the only record we have of his attitude towards Parnell's public image.

Withal he remains, as I have said, elusive. The one record of a personal appearance in the period under review is at a strangely appropriate time. Katharine Tynan, standing in the crowd at the City Hall during the lying in state of Parnell's body on 11 October 1891, was suddenly shocked 'to come face to face with Mr Henry Parnell, who bore a striking resemblance to his brother'.[86] During Parnell's lifetime his younger brother never appeared as one of the family, even taking into account the extreme looseness of their relation to each other; at his brother's death, Henry simply makes a shadowy appearance as one of the public filing past the bier. It is fully consonant with his unrecorded and slightly enigmatic life.

# 2 Delia Tudor Stewart Parnell

Woman's mission is chiefly to pity and aid the feeble, the suffering, and in her sons, how wide it may become! History shows that, for good or evil, often as is the mother, so is the son, and private life shows too often that as is the mother for nullity, frivolity and selfishness, so is the son. Many a man who could respond on some angelic mission to Béranger's lines

> plaignez le peuple, il souffre, et tout grand homme
> auprès du peuple est l'envoyé de Dieu

has surely felt and acknowledged a mother's sacred influence.

Delia T. S. Parnell to T. D. Sullivan, 21 January 1880.

Except in that he derived from her, I doubt that she influenced him very much. In old age she was a flamboyant person, very American, obviously 'a handful' who must have been a trial to her grave and dignified son.

Katharine Tynan, *Memories* (London, 1924), p. 5.

## I

In the early 1870s, Mrs Parnell returned to America, where she lived for most of the rest of her son's life. In her long letter to T. D. Sullivan she gives the date of leaving Ireland as 1874.[1] She lived at Ironsides, Bordentown, New Jersey, the Stewarts' family home. This was a large, gabled house – three stories including an enlarged basement – near the road at Bordentown, but surrounded by trees; the back of the house looked out over the river Delaware. There was a farm attached. Furnace-heated within, Ironsides was judged by Davitt 'the best-appointed house he ever visited';[2] Delia Parnell left it only for sojourns in the New York Hotel and brief trips to Europe. Early in 1878 she visited England;[3] in 1880 she accompanied Parnell on his return to Europe, probably to attend Theodosia's wedding in Paris; [4] the newspapers of February 1882 record her leaving New York for a visit to Ireland; [5] she visited Avondale after Arthur Dickinson's death, in 1884; and in September 1886 she came to Avondale again and stayed there until late in 1887. [6] She was back in America in 1889, [7] and did not return to Ireland until some months after Parnell's death.

Thus for most of the period under consideration her background was American. But she remained nonetheless in the news, as far as Irish opinion was concerned. Her political dabblings, which I will deal with separately, [8] were only one of the reasons for this; her own eccentricity and the instability of her personal fortunes were at least as influential. Reports of her ill-health were given prominence in the early 1880s; [9] when her health was not newsworthy, there were still such episodes as her narrow escape from death when walking on the railroad track near Bordentown in October 1883; a signalman had to lift her aside as a train rushed by, Mrs Parnell being inexplicably 'unaware' of its approach. [10] In early 1884 she was in the news owing to a number of acts of vandalism and persecution carried out against her at Bordentown – her farm animals had been poisoned and outbuildings destroyed. [11] Always ready to speak her piece, Mrs Parnell gave an interview to the *Boston Pilot* in which she spoke of the many depredations carried out by people hostile to 'the inmates of this house'; but she cut short the surprised interviewer's questions by remarking obscurely 'I do not care to talk about these things, though; they do not trouble me much; perhaps my cat and the dogs gave offence and merited their death – who knows?' and preferring to show him round the house instead. [12]

In this and in other interviews, Mrs Parnell shows herself as always more than ready to receive the gentlemen of the press, but less prepared to be pinned down to coherent facts; this is especially true of her political pronouncements. [13] But increasingly throughout the 1880s she became reported less for her political attitudes and more for the vicissitudes in her personal fortunes. Money always seems to have been a problem with her; and in her position, financial embarrassment could become a distressingly public predicament. She does not seem to have found such publicity disturbing; but there is little doubt that her famous son did not accept it so easily.

Though undergoing financial crises in 1873 and 1881, [14] the first major publicity Mrs Parnell's precarious finances received was in July 1885, when 'a number of New York ladies resolved to initiate a movement for a testimonial to Mrs Delia T. S. Parnell, in recognition of her services to the Irish cause and on account of her present financial embarrassments'. [15] Ellen Ford was the moving spirit behind this, and the evidence of Mrs Parnell's penury which inspired her was the announcement that the house at Bordentown was going to be put up for sale.[16] Thus not only the idea of a testimonial, but the actual reason for such a subscription, were closely analogous to the way the 'Irish people' had shown their appreciation of Parnell two years before.[17] No more was heard of the New York ladies' testimonial; but I do not think it fanciful to believe that Mrs Parnell herself was conscious of the parallel with the Parnell Tribute and hoped by the announcement of the sale of Ironsides to reap a similar reward. She told a reporter about this time that she 'felt rather bitterly towards the Parnell Fund people and the Irish "patriots" generally, who, she thought, had treated her shabbily'.[18] Moreover, even when the subscription-fund idea was not pursued, there was no further mention at this time of the proposed sale of Ironsides.

There was, however, further mention of Mrs Parnell's pecuniary embarrassments, as publicly as possible. On 20 February 1886 a *Washington Post* journalist reported:

> In a common tenement fourth floor, over a liquor store, in a crowded portion of the city, lives an old lady of seventy, whose condition is a reproach to her American countrymen and Irish partisans. She is Mrs Parnell, mother of the popular Home Rule Leader of Ireland . . . Your correspondent called on her today. At first the people in the vicinity declared that no such woman lived thereabout, but the liquor dealer handed him a key and said 'unlock the door and go up to the top of the house'. The directions were followed, after pulling the bell-handle in vain, and at the top of the fourth flight of narrow stairs the invalid lady was found. The halls smell like Constantinople, and evidently plumbers are much needed. The tenement in which Mrs Parnell is confined consists of four small rooms, and the family, whose guest she is, numbers a man and his wife and son and two men boarders. Mrs Parnell has been confined to her room for four months with neuralgia and gout, only climbing to the roof three or four times in that period for a breath of air. She was so low a month ago that she was believed to be dying, rheumatism having attacked the heart, but she rallied.[19]

The same reporter had met Mrs Parnell in palmier days during the early 1880s, when she lived at the New York Hotel and moved in 'society'; but 'at this time the old lady does not seem to have one dollar she can call her own'. She informed him that she could no longer afford to live at Ironsides, which may have been true; but she also said that she had bequeathed it to Charles, which patently was not. Other pathetic details followed; neighbours testified that they sent up soup to the old lady and believed it was shameful that some sort of public fund should not be raised for her.[20] The inevitable conclusion followed, worded to carry an implication of hypocrisy on Parnell's part similar to the many reports of supposed maltreatment of his tenants during the Land War:[21] 'Mr Charles Parnell ought to know that were it not for charity, there would be some danger of his mother being evicted and made the victim of rent-rack'.[22]

This lengthy report was publicised, in one form or another, in Irish and English newspapers;[23] though he made no public statement about it at this stage, Parnell must have been worried enough about his mother to insist that she come to Ireland, for she arrived in Dublin the following September and stayed at Avondale for well over a year.[24] 'Notwithstanding her recent illness', a reporter noted, 'Mrs Parnell looked well and sprightly'; she stated that she had not been in Ireland for a dozen years (despite the visit which, according to Emily, she made after Arthur's death in 1884) and that her stay was to be 'purely a domestic one'.[25] A spectator at her leavetaking at New York found her 'almost entirely recovered . . . [with] much of the old energy that has always marked her life'.[26] On her way through Dublin she visited the Lord Mayor and spoke to reporters; but a witness of her arrival at Rathdrum saw her as a less impressive figure:

> After staying a few minutes at the Fitzwilliam Hotel she hired a jaunting-car and drove off to Avondale, the residence of her son, whither she was accompanied by Mr. P. O'Brien, M.P. Mrs Parnell, who seemed to be in feeble health, wore a dark straw bonnet, profusely trimmed in blue ribbon, a mantle of broche velvet, and a dress of the same sombre hue, while her entire luggage consisted of two very small boxes. After the long journey there was no-one to meet her at the station, not even the 'Uncrowned King', and as the car left the precincts of the railway, not a solitary cheer was raised. The bystanders, some dozen in number, seemed to gaze upon the lady as if she were a curiosity.[27]

It is hard not to feel that this picture – unfriendly as it may be – is more consistent with the lady who gave erratic newspaper interviews with reporters and made inconsequential speeches in public whenever the occasion demanded.[28] 'Curiosity' or not, she settled in at Avondale, deciding to re-plan the terracing round the house,[29] receiving a complimentary address from the Wicklow National League in July 1887,[30] distributing prizes at a bazaar at Avondale the same summer,[31] and the following Christmas presiding over the sort of grandiose but haphazard entertainment in which she had delighted during her Temple Street days.[32] But she must have returned to America at some point in 1888–9; for in November 1889 statements about Mrs Parnell's finances, personal debility, and the threatened loss of the Stewart family home appeared once again in the New York *Herald* and *Standard*.[33] The *Freeman's Journal* received anxious enquiries about her;[34] and John Boyle O'Reilly editor of the *Boston Pilot* quoted a typical letter to the paper: 'I am surprised to see that the *Pilot* has not opened a public subscription for the relief of the venerable mother of Mr Parnell. I am one who wish to subscribe. It is scandalous that she should be left in want.'[35] The *Pilot*, however held that there was no need for such a subscription, 'at least for the present', and warned about the unfair political capital that was being made out of the issue.[36] Boyle O'Reilly lived in America, and does not seem to have taken Mrs Parnell's crises as seriously as others did; he may have known her better. But political capital had already been made of the matter in England. Justin McCarthy wrote to Mrs Campbell Praed in the same month:

> Some of the tory Unionists took up the report and wrote as if Parnell, wallowing in wealth, had deliberately consigned his aged parent to starvation. The *St. James Gazette* was particularly brutal about 'son Charles' ... Luckily, Parnell reads hardly any newspapers and so will not see most of the attacks against him and his family.[37]

Parnell, was, however, affected enough to give a long and uncharacteristically forthcoming interview on the subject of his mother's much-publicised penury; it deserves a lengthy quotation.

> The hon. gentleman stated that he had been very much surprised by the intelligence, and had at once cabled to his agents in New York to supply Mrs Parnell with funds. He had had no reason to suppose that his mother was pressed for funds, as on previous occasions she had always applied to him and he had always promptly remitted the sum she required. Since his last remittance, however, although she had frequently written him, her letters did not complain of any want of funds, or contain any application for money, but, on the contrary, indicated that she was in good spirits and spoke of her intention to realise the crops of the Bordentown estate, which had been stored during the last three or four years for a rise in prices, and which she anticipated would realise six or seven hundred pounds.
>
> Mr Parnell thinks that his mother's income and crops may have been attached to await the issue of some legal proceedings, and that the present alleged pressure may have arisen from this circumstance. With regard to the threatened sale by foreclosure of her Bordentown estate, Mr Parnell does not think there is any risk of such a contingency, as some years ago he had given instructions to his American bankers to guard against this by making the necessary advances if they were at any time required. He has always found it very difficult to obtain exact information

as to the condition of his mother's affairs and health ... Mrs
Parnell has always declined to reside anywhere but in America,
although her son has frequently tried to induce her to live at
Avondale, where he would have more chance of taking care of
her.[38]

There is a strong implication in this statement that Mrs Parnell's
money troubles were largely of her own making. She had been left a
good deal of property by her father and brother in 1869 and 1873,[39]
but much of this was lost, according to John Howard Parnell, in the
Black Friday stockmarket panic of 1873.[40] There must, however, have
been something left, for in the succeeding years Mrs Parnell continued
to play the stockmarket. An article about her by P. J. Hanway in 1881,
for which much of the information seems to have come from the lady
herself, states: 'Mrs Parnell, having inherited various descriptions
of property, was forced to study finance. Her knowledge of the subject,
in all its ramifications, coupled with a keen natural perception,
enabled her to save a share of her fortune from the wreck and ruin
wrought by the panic of 1873'.[41] This was one way of looking at it.
Staying in New York in the same year, T. P. O'Connor heard that 'she
was an incessant gambler on the stock exchange';[42] he was astounded
at the change in her appearance during his visit there, from having
been 'very well-dressed' to wearing 'shabby clothes' and claiming she
had 'become almost a pauper'. He heard that this decline was due to
losses in stockmarket speculation. There is also the evidence of a court
case heard in March 1892, during which it was disclosed that Mrs
Parnell had been entrusted in 1876 with a sum of $4,538 by a Miss
Smith, 'to be used at her discretion in speculating in stocks for the
benefit and at the risk of the owner'.[43] Mrs Parnell lost the money,
and 'did not communicate the fact to Miss Smith, but attempted to
retrieve the losses by using her own money. After further losses Mrs
Parnell remitted over £3,000 to Miss Smith, allowing her to believe
that the sum was the proceeds of her investment.' The court case was
brought by the administrators of Miss Smith's estate after the latter's
death; they sought the return of the sum of money originally entrusted
to Mrs Parnell, but they lost their case.

This seems a strange way to conduct the tricky business of
investment; but whatever about the wisdom of her stockmarket
dealings, Mrs Parnell evidently imagined herself an adept at it. She
had, moreover some money to invest, besides what was left over of her
family fortune; the House of Representatives voted her a pension of
$1,200 a year on 9 May 1880.[44] This was reduced by an amendment to
$600; but small as it was, this pension should have been enough, with
her other resources, to keep her out of the squalor of the liquor-store
tenement. Yet it was only a year afterwards that she told T. P.

O'Connor that she had become a pauper; and at the same time Parnell asked his brother John to back bills for £3,000 for their mother, who was 'practically destitute'.[45] It seems likely that this was to provide the £3,000 paid over to the unsuspecting Miss Smith. A weakness for the stock market would explain the recurring crises in Delia Parnell's financial life, as well as her refusal either to return to Avondale or to stay permanently at Bordentown. Emily Dickinson refers to the 'total failure' of her mother's affairs in 1886 through unfortunate speculations;[46] her losses were not simply a result of the 1873 panic. It seems likely that a similarly unlucky flutter caused her sudden and unexpected destitution in 1889. Her weakness for this pastime, unfortunate enough in any case considering her circumstances, was doubly unpleasant for Parnell; besides placing his mother in unsavoury circumstances, the results of her financial peccadilloes, as I have shown, more than once provided ammunition for hostile public opinion in his political career.

Thus the life-style for which Mrs Parnell was notable before her son's entry into public life – which I have described before as 'rackety'[47] did not change substantially when he became a world figure. Nor is this altogether surprising. Much of the reason must lie in Mrs Parnell's own character, which could be kindly described as 'erratic'. Henry Harrison took furious exception to St John Ervine's description of her as 'deranged' or even as 'outspoken, strong-minded and silly'.[48] But even if Ervine was working from secondary sources, so to a great extent was Harrison; he only met Mrs Parnell 'on two or three occasions'[49] and he was, moreover, a fiercely chivalrous judge.[51] Those who met her as early as 1880 had strong doubts about her mental stability. In this year Tim Healy wrote to his brother from America:

> They are the most extraordinary family I ever came across. The mother, I think, is a little 'off her nut' in some ways, and, for that matter, so are all the rest of them! . . . The mother supposes that Parnell is constantly dogged by spies, and that her own correspondence is opened by the Government. She used to wire Parnell that she had a detective of her own, detecting the Government detective! She gave me a huge code which she advised should be used in writing or telegraphing to her, arranged somewhat in this fashion: 'The main street must depend for support on the Irish vote, which holds the balance of power – Rugose'. She remarked, smilingly but in the greatest confidence, that if that happened the main street *would* look rather rugose. About which I said there was little doubt – seeing that it might be looking that way all the days of its life before I should know any difference, or what was the matter with it! Did

you ever hear such a word? She is a very amiable old lady, but why she imagines such a vain thing as that her son or I were going to write or telegraph to her is more than I can understand, as she had no previous warranty for such a supposition. [51]

Another Irish Party member who knew Mrs Parnell was T. P. O'Connor. In his hasty and over-sentimentalised *C. S. Parnell: a memory,* written in 1891, he wrote that 'underneath her impassivity there was the keenest appreciation of all that was going on'. [52] But later, writing his own memoirs long after Parnell had died, he was far less circumspect:

> I settled down in a hotel in New York in 1881 largely because Mrs Parnell, the mother of my chief, resided there . . . I found her a very strange being. She talked slowly and deliberately, but almost perpetually . . . It was hard to say whether she could be described as wholly sane. She had unlimited powers of speech. As a rule she spoke for an hour at a time; I never knew at the end of her speech what she had said, except that once she told a story of two men testing each other's power of holding their legs in a bucket of hot water, and how when one man conquered it was discovered that he had a wooden leg. [53]

O'Connor, like everyone else who met her, emphasised the extreme physical likeness between Parnell and his mother; Swift MacNeill, meeting her at a dinner some years later, was struck by the same thing but did not, it is only fair to add, notice any particular eccentricity. [54] But the combination of her erratic life-style, the accounts of Healy and O'Connor, and the extraordinarily florid, grandiose and rambling style in which she expressed herself (seen in her letter to T. D. Sullivan and the reminiscences she wrote for McWade's book) [55] suggests a mind that can fairly be judged not quite in balance. Her self-absorption, which led easily to self-delusion where her importance in political matters was concerned, [56] enabled her to confide the most trivial and pathetic facts about herself to both Sullivan and McWade; perhaps reaching some sort of apotheosis in a lengthy and embarrassingly bad poem which she quotes proudly in McWade's book as having been written by her when ill in 1889. [57] The other marked characteristic in her writing is an overwhelming preoccupation with social standing and an obsession with the rather fuzzy by-ways of 'noble' genealogy; [58] St John Ervine was exercising unaccustomed restraint when he wrote that 'she loved the assemblies of the rich and influential'. [59] The impression left is inescapable: that anyone so full of confused self-importance and so prone to rambling dissertation in her writing (both in 1880 and 1891) could only have been yet more so when encountered in person.

## II

Up to this my conclusions about Mrs Parnell have been based upon evidence regarding her personal life; but they are, I believe, reinforced by a consideration of her political involvement throughout the 1880s. I have shown that the reputation of a Fenian firebrand of the 1860s, which Parnell's biographers have attributed to her, seems to be based upon the most nebulous evidence;[60] her political activity in the later part of her life only seems to have post-dated her son's rise to eminence, and to have mainly consisted of lending her presence on party platforms. In 1878 she approached Davitt in New York and gave him messages for Parnell, but these seem to have been of a purely domestic character;[61] during her son's American tour in 1880 she figured upon platforms at receptions.[62] Her first public speech, however, was not until the foundation of the American Land League;[63] and her first real activity came in October 1880 with the foundation of the Ladies' Land League in America by Fanny.[64] Though John Howard describes his mother as simply 'an enthusiastic supporter' of this organisation,[65] she was in fact the titular president of it; but this does not seem to have connoted a position which required either policy-making powers or organisational aptitude, both of which were supplied by Fanny and by Ellen Ford.[66] Mrs Parnell's attendance at Irish-American meetings in 1881 was, according to T. P. O'Connor, dedicated in the extreme: and she generally spoke 'for an hour or more, patiently and indefatigably'.[67] When she first spoke at a Ladies' Land League meeting in New York, Mrs Parnell herself recalled, she was 'greatly frightened'; she states that it was her first public appearance since the 'Originals' tea-party in Dublin many years before,[68] although John Howard believed that her first speech was at an American Land League meeting. She practised assiduously for the Ladies' meeting, trying out her speech on Fanny in their room at the New York Hotel.[69] She also travelled with Ellen Ford on organising tours for the Ladies' League; but recalling her political involvements for McWade, she mentioned only one speech, reprinted in the *Irish Nation* of New York in the middle 1880s, and an article she wrote for the New York *Daily News* in 1883. 'Most of my public life and my public speeches and writing I deem it unnecessary to refer to', she added; 'I deem it unnecessary to say more of myself.'[70] This was not strictly true; she went on to reminisce a great deal about herself, but in the familiar vein of her childhood literary triumphs and distinguished family connections – not in the context of political activity, which probably stretched very little further than the references she had already given, and in which she was never really at home.[71]

Her political reputation, in fact, seems to have coincided with the rise to eminence of her daughters, and to have ended with the decline of the Ladies' Land League in 1882. In the hectic days of 1880 and 1881 she achieved the status of a celebrity; the *Nation* on New Year's Day 1881 carried a front-page portrait of her, and many branches of the Ladies' Land League in Ireland and America were named after her. By 1883, such public appearances as her speech at an Irish meeting in Jersey in December [72] were rare, and her political assertions becoming increasingly vague. [73] In the same year she summoned Patrick Egan, recently arrived in America, to visit her in order to bring 'good tidings and elucidation of the actual crisis in Irish affairs'; [74] there is a strong impression that she had retired to the wings and was playing Cordelia as sympathiser and inspiration rather than leader of the fray. A similar impression is gained from her Delphic utterances at Liverpool *en route* to Ireland in 1886 [75] and by the letter she wrote to William O'Brien in the same year, congratulating him and his colleagues on their work for the evicted tenants and asking him to pay 'a weak and suffering old woman a visit at Avondale'. [76]

In August and September of 1884 she made some announcements about a project of Parnell's to encourage the duty-free importation of Irish goods, [77] and she declared that the Irish vote in the coming Presidential election could be used to support whichever candidate would embrace the idea; [78] but although she met the leaders of the Irish National League in America to discuss the project, it seems unlikely that there was much in it. Significantly, Alexander Sullivan consistently refused the presidency of the Irish National League in America at this time because he was going to canvass for Blaine and felt that the Irish-American vote should not be promised to either party; it is probable that this was a generally-held attitude. [79] Mrs Parnell's last entry on the political stage was after the Parnell Split. She spoke about 'my son and Mr Gladstone' at Irish National League meetings in America, where her 'strong personal epithets with regard to Mr Gladstone ... were received with applause'. [80] But her interest here was primarily personal; her speeches limited themselves to the personal rather than the political issues involved, as did her letters on the subject to John Howard Parnell. [81] And in her episodic political appearances throughout the period, it was the personal connection with Charles Stewart, and to a lesser extent with Fanny and Anna, which both motivated her and provided her with a ready-made political reputation.

This thesis is supported by an examination of her political pronouncements over the period under review. Where her speeches are reported verbatim, they are at best vague and disconnected and at worst, almost incomprehensible. She generally spoke, she told McWade, 'from very few notes, which nobody could understand by myself'; [82] the same, unfortunately was often true of her actual speeches. Speaking, for instance, upon ladies and the Irish land question in New York in March 1881, she continually recurred to 'the land question in America'; she seems to have been under the impression that this was her subject. Then she digressed cryptically into unrelated matters, of which she evidently felt she could speak with more authority: 'A great change has come over the financial world; and if you heard it as I do, you would be surprised.' The English Government, she added obscurely, 'has transferred its allegiance from the land to the landlord'. In an aside of elephantine coyness, she told the ladies in the audience: 'I trust you not only have a good many strings to your beaux, but a good many beaux to your strings; that was my habit when I was a girl, and it was an agreeable one.' And her conclusion was equally incongruous:

> We are all born here on earth; the air, sunlight and water were created for the use of every one of us on this globe. I trust that the women here will do their utmost to make the land as free as the other two [sic] . . . This question appeals to everybody − to the hope and aspirations which a mother entertains for her son. Go to lectures on religion, education and industrial matters. There is nothing more interesting in the world than the industrial matters of this enormous country, and they will form the great centre of everything in this world when they will throw the industries of Great Britain out of the field altogether. [83]

What any of this had to do with the Irish land question is uncertain. She was nonetheless applauded throughout; as T. P. O'Connor wrote of her at this time, 'her speeches, without any disrespect, appeared to be somewhat rigmarole ... but the immense respect felt for her personally, and for her son, always secured her an attentive, though a puzzled, audience'. [84] She saw herself, moreover, as a person of political significance. I have quoted Healy's mystification at her belief that he and Parnell would be constantly telegraphing and writing to her in code; [85] and at a land meeting in April 1881 she told her audience that that if her son was arrested 'she would go to Ireland herself and see if a daughter of "Old Ironsides" and a grand-daughter of Washington's aide-de-camp would be arrested' [86] − considerations which would hardly have weighed too heavily with Dublin Castle. In the same month she told a Brooklyn land meeting, in all seriousness, that 'Mr Gladstone had made overtures to her son *and also her* and had said "only let your son pull with us and he will be the saviour of Ireland" ' [87] − an assertion which can reasonably be accounted a delusion. Later in 1881 the Washington *National Republican* went to interview Mrs Parnell and Ellen Ford about the Ladies' Land League; Mrs Parnell talked incessantly, while Miss Ford, the reporter added ironically, 'believed in work − not mere talk'. Where large issues were concerned, Mrs Parnell became eloquent. When asked, however, about the forthcoming Land Bill and its prospects Mrs Parnell's answers became briefer and more evasive; she eventually said 'but come, let us talk about the – about livelier topics, in short'. [88] The recorded interview ended here; but it is a fair guess that the 'livelier topics' included herself and her family history.

As I have said, her political appearances became infrequent after 1881, though on her way to Ireland she spoke at a meeting of Father Sheehy's in Liverpool; here Mrs Parnell declared hyperbolically that 'Ireland was the keystone of the universe and on it depended the future of the world'. The principles of Home Rule should be introduced into England, Scotland and Wales, as 'they would ensure their prosperity and peace; for if those principles were placed there they should eventually have no wars, and they would bring about a state which might justly be described as a millenium' [89] – a truth which her listeners were expected to accept as self-evident, for Mrs Parnell enlarged upon it no further.

Just before leaving America at this time, she had attended an Irish-American convention in Chicago and magnanimously 'expressed great satisfacton at the manner in which [it] was conducted'; [90] as she departed from New York, an old friend told a reporter from the New York *Herald*: 'There is no better-informed woman on either side of the Atlantic today than Charles Stewart Parnell's mother; she reads without glasses and translates four languages.' [91] But, however admirable, these qualities are not necessarily indicative of political acumen; and appearances on public platforms with her daughters, pronouncements to newspaper correspondents, or even her title as president of the Ladies' Land League are no stronger arguments. Mrs Parnell's position in Irish-American politics cannot, as Healy's and O'Connor's reminiscences show, have been of practical importance. The *Celtic Magazine* told of how, when Gordon Bennett was awaiting a decision from Parnell whether he would accept Bennett's offer of a place on the Distribution Committee of the New York *Herald* Famine Fund and stop his American campaign, Mrs Parnell mounted a seven-hour vigil outside the *Herald* office to find out her son's answer. Besides showing a lack of political perception on Mrs Parnell's part – no one else who knew Parnell could have expected him to accept Bennetts ludicrous offer – this incident suggests that she had little part in her son's political confidence. [92] As O'Connor stated, it was respect for her position and connections that guaranteed her position in nationalist politics, rather than any ability or acumen of her own.

What ideas she had appear to have been alarmingly contradictory. She warned a National Republican reporter about revolutionary forces 'actively at work', [93] and Wilfred Scawen Blunt was told by Dr Duggan, the Bishop of Chicago, about a 'curious conversation' he had with Mrs Parnell in 1886, during which he was told 'there were half a dozen men in America ready to produce half a million each, but not for a land campaign or a campaign in parliament' [94] – which seems to imply a sympathetic connection with extreme nationalism. But she also ingenuously presented as a point in Mrs O'Shea's favour in 1891 that 'her immediate family were on terms of the closest intimacy with Queen Victoria, and the members of the Royal Family were proud to recognise her as their friend'; [95] and she wrote to John Howard Parnell in the 1890s of the wisdom and goodness of Queen Victoria, [96] as well as the iniquity of extremists. These exhortations, remarks John Howard, 'she must often have addressed to Charley as well during his lifetime'. [97] If she did, they went strangely with the more extreme political stance which she sometimes adopted. But, like many strong-minded old women, consistency probably seemed of little account to her.

There is also a suggestion that as the 1880s progressed her political interest failed to keep up with events. It is significant that, when listing her son's achievements in 1891, she fixed on a strange collection of facts, some vague, some inaccurate, and all related to the early part of his career: 'He compelled the English Government to make a grant of £170,000; he caused the passage of the Seed and Potato Bill and the Irish Relief Bill; he called into existence the Mansion House Committee, the Marlborough Committee, and the Land League Committee.' [98] She adds that he alleviated the lot of the evicted tenants and presented the Irish cause poignantly to the American people. But, in what purports to be a summing-up of her son's entire career, she relies entirely upon 'these facts, published in 1880' [99] to define his achievement. There is no mention of land purchase, or the creation of an unparalleled kind of political party, or even of the changing of the English political balance and the adoption of a Home Rule platform by the Liberals. It is tempting to wonder how much of Parnell's later career was actually grasped by his mother.

The dark days of 1891 brought her on to public platforms once more, where she attacked Gladstone and those who had 'betrayed Parnell with a kiss'. [100] Her alignment with her son meant some contradiction of her previous attitudes. In 1882 she had written to the New York *Herald* that the Irish Catholic priests 'exemplify on earth the sublimest relations between God and man . . . It is just that the Irish Catholic priests should feel that whatever in the least touches the welfare of their people touches the apple of their eye'. [101] In 1891, however, she confided to John Howard; 'the Roman Catholic organisation has become an abomination to man and to God . . . God will render them full measure for their murderous, fiendish thoughts and actions'. [102] Even allowing for natural partisanship, the *volte-face* is remarkable. Her letters to John Howard at this time are extremely strongly expressed, [103] and it was, naturally enough, the personal aspect of the Split which absorbed her – the future of Parnell rather than of Home Rule or the Irish Party. When Parnell died, her invective knew no bounds. Although, she wrote to John Howard Parnell, 'the cruel blow prostrated me almost irrevocably – left me all but dead', she still, characteristically, was 'kept up enough to see two or three reporters to tell what I thought'. She continued:

> I would have died rather than not denounce poor, poor Charley's murderers and called [sic] down vengeance on them. Gladstone will suffer for his knavish, brutal wickedness to his dying day . . . The widow, the mother, is heard in heaven. Your brother's blood cries aloud for vengeance. [104]

The role of Cordelia had given way to that of Hecuba. As in a happier period of her life, Mrs Parnell's opinion became newsworthy because of her relationship to her son; and, as she had always done, she was prepared to utilise the opportunity for publicised self-expression to the full.

## III

In conclusion then, what influence did Mrs Parnell have over her son during his political career? I have quoted a comment of Katharine Tynan's as an epigraph to this chapter, because I believe it to be nearer the truth than the vague assertions usually made about her effect on Parnell's political development and the inspiration she provided during his short, meteoric career. She was certainly, as Katherine Tynan supposed, 'something of a "handful" '; it also seems likely that she was indeed a trial to her son. [105] He was, naturally, fond of her; even Healy, while amazed at the nonchalant attitude of the family towards each other's movements, felt that Parnell was 'certainly very fond of his mother' – to the extent of sending her a telegram, carefully worded in French, simply to tell her of his safe arrival at Toronto in 1880. [106] It seems probable that Mrs Parnell was someone who had to be humoured; she could certainly be exasperating. Mrs O'Shea was amused to hear that Parnell's mother, on her visit to Avondale during 1887, had taken over the celebrated new cattle-shed for 'an entertainment', evicting the occupants and laying down a temporary floor; Parnell was less amused, and tried to insist on the restoration of the shed to its occupants. [107] The entertainment went on; it was duly advertised in the *Wicklow Newsletter* in December: 'Miss Bessie Byrne, the distinguished American actress, assisted by the Gasparro brothers and some local friends, will give a dramatic and musical entertainment at Avondale on Tuesday, the 16th inst. Mrs Delia T. S. Parnell will also give an address.' [109] It would be intriguing to know more. But the only account is in a slightly jaundiced letter from Parnell to Mrs O'Shea, after his arrival in Avondale a few weeks later: 'Miss B. B. was very old, very ugly, and very vulgar; in fact, E. [Emily] says, the worst sponge that ever got hold of my mother. She drank nothing but whisky, and took it to bed with her. There was dancing after the theatricals till six in the morning.'[109] Even had this gaiety not affected his cattle-shed (where a reporter visiting Avondale three years after Parnell's death saw the decorations and garlands still *in situ,* withered and decayed),[110] it would not have been to Parnell's liking. The language he uses is revealing: his mother was evidently prone to being 'got hold of' by 'sponges'. Perhaps he was thinking back to the Fenian 'tramps' he used to kick down the steps at Temple Street.

There is every evidence that he had great patience with his mother; his wife reiterates that 'to all his brothers and sisters, and most of all to his mother, Parnell was most generous and affectionate',[111] and John Howard Parnell corroborates this judgement.[112] But it is difficult to believe that he wrote the letter to her attributed to him, shortly before his death:

> I am weary, dear mother, of these troubles, weary unto death; but it is all in a good cause ... The statements my enemies have so often made regarding my relations with you are on a par with the endless calumnies they shoot upon me from behind every bush. Let them pass. They will die of their own venom. It would indeed be dignifying them to notice their existence![113]

This letter is quoted by Barry O'Brien, and the originals of most of the other letters he uses are to be found in the National Library of Ireland: but not this one. There is no facsimile of it in his book, nor in Mrs Katharine Parnell's memoir, which also quotes it. Of the letters which Parnell *did* write, not one is couched in this awkward and formal phraseology, nor embodies anything approaching such nauseating pomposity. He wrote as he spoke, whether in a letter of businesslike farming advice to William Kerr,[114] a friendly note to Justin McCarthy,[115] or his love-letters to Katharine O'Shea from Kilmainham.[116] Indeed, a fault universally found with these latter letters, when the recipient published them to a scandalised world in 1914, was that they were *not* highflown or carefully phrased.[117] The letter Mrs Parnell claimed to have received from her son just before his death is in a style diametrically opposed to his own – which is to say that it exactly resembles the way she wrote herself. She must have been O'Brien's authority for this unlikely and atypical letter; I believe that, given the odd balance of her mind, it is on the same level of authenticity as her claim in 1881 that Gladstone had told her that her son could be the saviour of Ireland. Where reality did not come up to the mark Mrs Parnell expected of it, she was capable of making the necessary adjustment herself.

The image she presented to the general public was not that of an erratic, slightly unbalanced, rambling old woman with a weakness for making pointless speeches to captive audiences and gambling on the stock exchange. When it was announced in 1886 that Parnell was ill with 'a gastric attack and complications' and under his mother's care, Frank Hugh O'Donnell wrote a spluttering satire called 'The Leader's Mamma' which pictured a weakling Parnell attached to his mother's apron-strings.[118] However, in the real state of affairs, it was not his mother who was nursing Parnell, but the woman who lived with him as a wife; and in 1886 Mrs Parnell was in no condition to nurse anybody, even herself. She had, moreover, a rather unreal view of her son – as when, in the same year, having written a poem about the evicted tenants, she asked him if it should be published under his name or hers.[119] To entertain the idea of Parnell's name appearing under some of his mother's execrable verse in a monthly magazine shows a very vague grasp of his personality as well as of his carefully preserved public persona. Only slightly less unrealistic is her assertion elsewhere that in 1886 he planned to set up house with herself and Emily 'near London, where we might have spent together our remaining days and assisted him in his labour'.[120] Mrs Parnell may have cherished this idea; her son, living only for his suburban haven at Eltham, never could have done. This lack of realism was something she had in common with her son Charles, who could delude himself that the money poured down mines in Wicklow year after year was well spent; a consistent lack of realism, it can be argued, motivated him through the last wrecking year of his life. But it was not the sort of common characteristic which made for a close bond between mother and son. Fond of his mother Parnell certainly was; but during his political career her effect upon his life was either to provoke attacks from the hostile press upon his hard-heartedness whenever her most recent financial scrape came into the news, or to visit upon him, either at Avondale or in London, her latest erratic scheme or self-delusion. What she was in the 1880s is the logical development of the discontented and self-glorifying Boston belle who accepted John Henry Parnell and Avondale in 1835 and found it more than she could cope with.[121] She took the pleasure that most women would in having a famous son; and her own life reflected a larger share of his fame than that of most mothers. But so many of her characteristics were antithetical to his that the way she lived her life under this refracted limelight cannot have pleased him greatly.

# 3 The muse of Bordentown: Fanny Parnell, 1875–82

Such perfect beings die young. Their path is one of undiminished lustre which can end only in heaven, and that soon.

Mrs Delia Parnell, of her daughter Fanny,
in R. M. McWade's *Life of Stewart Parnell*, p. 80.

## I

Fanny Parnell held a unique place in the pantheon of Irish nationalism during the nineteenth century; in a way she holds it still. She was often compared to 'Speranza', the muse of nationalism in the 1840s; but her life was more ardently committed, and her political involvement far more profound, than her predecessor's, and unlike Speranza, she died at the height of her mystique. I shall deal primarily with Fanny's politics and poetry during the late 1870s and early 1880s in this chapter; but before this a brief consideration of her life and character is necessary.

In 1874 she had accompanied her mother to America.[1] Her health first began to fail at this stage; but it was Fanny rather than her mother who organised the house and farm at Bordentown, and she helped Mrs Parnell through the financial reversals attendant upon the Black Friday panic of the previous year.[2] From 1879 Fanny added to this the labour of organising relief funds and the Ladies' Land League in America; she also managed to produce countless poems, and a pamphlet called *Hovels of Ireland* which went through several editions in a few months of 1880.[3] Breakdowns in her health became increasingly frequent; in October 1880 she was to ill even to attend the inaugural meeting of her Ladies' Land League,[4] and from October of the following year until her death in July 1882 her literary output almost stopped – which could only have been an indication of debility. The actual cause of her death is uncertain. Emily Dickinson believed that Fanny died of rheumatic fever after a bout of malaria;[5] her mother repeated this.[6] Barry O'Brien was told by Willie Redmond, who was staying at Bordentown when she died, that Fanny died very suddenly in her sleep.[7] T. P. O'Connor implied that there was a possibility of suicide;[8] Tim Healy declared unequivocally but without any substantiated authority that 'she died of an overdose of a sleeping draught'.[9] This seems pure conjecture – possibly based on the fact that, according to her mother, 'Fanny's nerves gave way' while in America.[10] Certainly her last poems show a gloomy preoccupation with mortality and bear titles like 'After Death' and 'The End of All'; but this could simply have been a reflection of the lengthy illness which all the newspaper accounts of the time attribute to her. When she died, at all events, she had become a national figure both in Ireland and America.

On the surface, she was an unlikely celebrity. 'You could not help thinking', wrote a friend, 'that she felt as if it were amusing that she should be expected to possess any influence'.[11] She found, in fact, a great deal in life amusing, and seems to have had a sense of humour which goes strangely with the bathos of her worse poems. John and Emily describe her as a lively, spirited girl; those who met her when she had a reputation for writing intense poetry were surprised by her gaiety.[12] She was capable of smart repartee, as when a deputation came to tell her that the Ladies' Land League were to be toasted at James Redpath's farewell dinner in the words 'the hand that rocks the cradle rules the world'; Fanny refused to attend, replying tartly that 'the Ladies' Land League could not properly respond to that toast, since it was so recently organised by two single ladies who had given up all hope of ever rocking a cradle'.[13] But with her lightness went a deep intellectual commitment to nationalism, and more than a dash of the Parnell eccentricity, as Tim Healy noted in 1879:

> When I first met her she was gay and feminine, without a trace of the poetess or bluestocking. She chaffed about Dillon because, she said, he left his slippers in one hotel and his night-shirt in another . . . Then she complained that John Devoy had failed to obey her mandate to steal a black cat from the New York *Herald* office, which, she maintained, brought Gordon Bennett all his luck. I gasped, but she was serious.[14]

She could, of course, have simply been succumbing to the temptation to pull the sober Devoy's leg. John Parnell, however, recalled that she was addicted to spiritualism;[15] and all who knew here were struck by her nervous tension. A spectator at her first public appearance recalled that the effort of speaking almost exhausted her.[16] William O'Brien thought of her as 'one with all the Promethean passion and the Promethean unhappiness of the poet';[17] a friend who wrote a posthumous appreciation of her felt that she was more withdrawn than she seemed. Leaving the domestic circle was 'an extreme wrench' and 'her appearing in public was so much out of her line that every emergence gave her a fresh shock'; she could only be induced to give very brief speeches. [18]

This nervous tension was probably what enabled her to produce a prodigous amount of intellectual work, as well as leading to her physical breakdown. She was also gifted with a strong intelligence, as evinced in her articles and pamphlet [19] – and, above all, with a charm and attractiveness which must have greatly smoothed her way long the thorny path of political organisation. [20] In 1879 someone who had read her work but never met her

> expected to find her a lady of mature years and serious manner, but was agreeably disappointed ... to behold in her a beautiful lady in all the enjoyment of youth, with large, speaking eyes, above the medium height, of willowy form, joyous in spirits, lively in expression. [21]

A picture of her in the *Celtic Monthly* of February 1880 shows a determined-looking, handsome girl with the strong Parnell chin and an attractive half-smile; a contemporary attributed to her 'several of the elements of beauty'. [22] Added to personal attractiveness was a thoughtfulness of manner; arriving in America, the young Tim Healy found her 'womanly in providing "creature comforts" after my voyage, and loud in the praise of oyster soup, which she ordered for me', [23] and an anecdote dating from shortly before her death shows her in a particularly likeable light. The United Land League of Philadelphia sent a deputation to reap the harvest at Bordentown, as had recently been done as a tribute to her brother at Avondale. Fanny thanked them gracefully but declined: 'There are', she said 'a number of poor people around me that I employ every year. I have always employed them, and your doing the work would deprive them of their means of living.' [24] Her mother, one feels, would have accepted the tribute and gloried in it; but Fanny was a lady of very different qualities.

## II

Fanny's politics were of a no less different order. The enthusiasm whith which she had attended the Fenian trials in youth stayed with her in later years; she witnessed the beginnings of parliamentary obstruction on a visit to England, and during the twenty-six hour sitting of 31 July 1877 she stayed in the Ladies' Gallery all night. [25] The element in Irish politics of the time with which she was most connected was the Ladies' Land League. The operations of this extraordinary and endlessly absorbing movement in Ireland are quite correctly associated with the name of Anna Parnell; I deal with these below.[26] But the movement had its inception in America, from an idea of Fanny's in the summer of 1880.

Previously to this, she had thrown herself into the welter of organisation connected with her brother's American tour and the Famine Fund begun in 1879. Fanny was an indefatigable correspondent and organiser as well as writer of verse; Davitt called her 'a practical as well as a poetic reformer' [27] and from 1879 on, references to her in John Devoy's correspondence become regular.[28] Her importance to Parnell at this time was not, as with her mother, largely imagined; in February 1880 William Dillon wrote to Devoy: that Fanny had 'full instructions' from Parnell about all that had to be done politically.[29] Probably as a result of this Fanny wrote to Devoy shortly afterwards, giving him details of her brother's itinerary and plans, and adding forcible and exacting instructions about 'heading off the *Herald*' in organising Irish relief collections.[30] Devoy blamed Fanny for the rumours in 1879 that the Land League was receiving assistance from the Skirmishing Fund,[31] and his correspondence contains many uncomplimentary references to her which his answers seem to have let go uncontradicted. Possibly the affair of Bennett's cat still rankled; but there were more profound differences than that between them.[32] Fanny nevertheless continued to organise. A constant preoccupation of hers was the failure of the Land League in Ireland to acknowledge American subscriptions, thus ensuring a good deal of unnecessary pique and alienation. She wrote angrily to T. D. Sullivan in 1881 about this, giving examples and castigating Parnell and Dillon for their dilatoriness.[33] Many letters in the Land League papers bear out her accusations.[34] Fanny keenly felt this cavalier acceptance of American donations; she had organised such expedients as the collecting boxes in post officers all over the United States [35] to which she refers in her letter to Devoy, and she resented the deflection of funds to the Marlborough Committee or, more pernicious still, to Gordon Bennett and the New York *Herald*.

At this time, she and Anna lived entirely in the New York Hotel, working for the famine relief organisation 'at least ten hours a day', according to an observer.

> We often marvelled at the strength and assiduity of those frail girls at that time. They appeared to be always at work, and yet they were ever anxious for more. They never grew tired. Their great minds over-matched their bodies for the time, and carried them along in one continuous effort. They worked, too, in such a way that the actions of one nearly always fitted into and supplemented those of the other. Occasionally, though, some of

Anna's plans would run foul of those of Fanny, or some of Fanny's machinery would stand in the way of one of Anna's pet projects. Then there would be a momentary pause and a little debate. It was delightful to hear them, in the parlours of the New York Hotel, set those things straight and again branch off on their respective lines with fresh impulse and new resolve. [36]

At this stage, the sisters were working on the Famine Relief Committee; but shortly afterwards, in the summer of 1880, a particular brain-child of Fanny's was brought into being. The Ladies' Land league reached its apotheosis under Anna in Sackville Street the following year; but in the beginning the idea was completely Fanny's. She wrote to Mrs M. F. Sullivan when the latter was writing *Ireland of today* in 1882:

> As nobody could possibly give you as correct an account of the Ladies' Land League in America and Ireland as myself, and as I have seen many garbled and untrue accounts published, I hasten to supply you with as brief a sketch as possible . . . The idea first occurred to me in July 1880. The funds of the Land League, which had increased so rapidly when Mr Dillon and my brother were here in this country, had fallen off to almost nothing, a few hundred dollars a week; and it occurred to me that by setting the women at work much needed stimulus would be given to the men. I mentioned the idea to Mr Davitt a few days afterwards and he was delighted with it. [37]

Fanny thought about the idea 'for several weeks' and then launched an appeal to Irishwomen in America. On 12 August 1880 she wrote a letter to the *Irish World* and other newspapers, emphasising the extreme nature of the situation developing, calling for added support for the Land League, and exhorting women to found a sister organisation. [38] Weeks passed without a response; finally an answer came from Miss Jane Byrne of New York, and a trickle of others followed. A New York Ladies' Land League was set up by Fanny and Jane Byrne. The first meeting was held at the New York Hotel on 15 October 1880: 'The constitution I had drawn up was accepted. We selected an executive, nominated my mother for president, and took up a collection for $100, which was sent to Patrick Egan the next day'. [39] The Ladies' Land League was under way. All over America branches sprang up; 'I was overwhelmed', wrote Fanny, 'with applications for copies of our constitution, for letters to be read out at meetings, for advice how to organise, etc. For two months I wrote letters incessantly, day and night.' [40] It was not long before the idea of organisation in Ireland, 'where the real work would soon lie', began to preoccupy her. The *Nation* in December 1880 quoted a letter written by Fanny the previous month to three sisters who wished to organise a similar movement in Ireland.[41] Fanny told them the ladies might take over if the men were imprisoned. A month later she wrote a public letter in similar terms.[42] Requests for advice came back across the Atlantic: 'I gave them as minute instructions as I could, but not having any leader they remained feeble and obscure, till it became evident that the Coercion Act would be passed and that all the members of the Irish National Land League would be in danger of being arrested'.[43] At this point, the end of 1880, Anna was asked to take over the organisation in Ireland; the continuation of the tale is part of her story, and I will deal with it accordingly.[44]

The extension of the new organisation to Ireland added to Fanny's fund-raising work; public speaking was now added to her exhausting paperwork, and in the summer of 1881 she made a tour of the north-eastern states and Canada to raise money for the League. She was by now a political celebrity. Of her speech at Montreal on 5 July a reporter wrote: 'It is simply impossible to adequately describe the scene . . . the entire audience arose to its feet and appeared to be positively carried away by enthusiasm.'[45] In Ireland, lockets containing her portrait were hawked for a shilling each; her poetry was given prominence in every nationalist journal. Her relationship to her brother may have helped to bring her to prominence; but her political activity by 1882 earned her a position as a political force in her own right.

What, then, were her own views? It is difficult to define the attitudes of those connected with Irish land agitation at this time; whether they leaned to Fenianism or parliamentarianism, the urgency of the land question and the runaway success of the League often seems to have relegated these issues to the background at the time, and it is only in retrospect that any kind of considered stance can be attributed. Thus it was with Fanny Parnell. She had been a sympathiser with Fenianism in the 1860s; her poetry for the *Irish People* and her attendance at Rossa's trial show this conclusively. But her later attitude is less clear-cut. An obituary remarked that she was uninterested in parliamentary tactics because she was 'a pronounced rebel to the British rule in Ireland';[46] but American Fenians like William Carroll were caustic about the extent of her nationalism as early as 1879, when Carroll wrote to Devoy:

I suppose you got and noted the *Evening News* I sent you with Miss Parnell's opinions about the Fund and the Fenians, which indeed are not given as mere opinions, but as facts patent enough to her. It will be news to all the Fenians that I ever met to learn that they would be satisfied with a Home Rule government and a British Queen. However, it is not Irish to contradict a lady, and so we leave Miss Parnell to see what she will see of Fenians' love for British Queens before she adds another twenty-two years to her present record of summers. [47]

Carroll put Fanny's age as eight years younger than it was, but his chivalry stopped there; Fanny and the Land League became the bane of his political life, and he finally resigned from the chairmanship of the executive board of Clan na Gael over the question of supporting them. Plans like the mooted 'Irish-American Land League' which Parnell and Dillon were organising when suddenly recalled to Ireland in March 1880 were anathema to such hard-line Fenians; in connection with this scheme, Carroll fulminated against 'the party of "respectables" Miss Fanny invited to the family gathering'. [48] Nor could his mind have been eased by speeches of Fanny's like one in Montreal where she emphasised that 'the English government is not by any means the worst enemy the Irish people have . . . it is the feudal government in Ireland that has created so deplorable a state of affairs in the country'; [49] thus, she implied, the government had to be improved rather than destroyed. She emphasised the Land League's non-violent nature in the same speech; and in August 1880 she wrote to the *Irish World:*

> My own individual opinion is that the Land League is right to confine itself to 'the inch beyond the saw' and to employ nothing but moral force means as long as they are of use. When things arrive at such a pitch that moral force measures will be no longer of any use, then let the Land League disband. [50]

She went on to call upon the Irish 'of every shade of nationalist opinion' to support the League; this seems to have become by now her priority, the issue of parliamentarian tactics versus physical force having become a secondary issue. One of her contemporaries supports this contention:

> She was perfectly at ease in all Irish organisations. It mattered little to her whether they were of the physical or moral force doctrine . . . She had a use for every man and every idea, and with all the ease in the world assigned every organisation its place and gave it full credit for its work. In this way she exercised great influence in uniting the various contending elements which went to make up the Land League. [51]

She did not always find this an easy path to follow. John Parnell, after paying a tribute to her ability to resolve friction, went on to describe her anger and annoyance at overhearing 'some very nasty remarks made both about our brother and herself' when she was visiting a house in Providence, Rhode Island; the offending people were

members of 'the extreme section of Mr Ford's party'.[52] A good sample
of the way hard-line Irish-American nationalists looked upon Fanny's
work is to be found in the letters of William Carroll to John Devoy,
some of which I have already quoted. An interesting characteristic of
Carroll's letters is that he seems to have resented the Parnell family
connection at least as much as the constitutional politics that the
League stood for: 'Mr Parnell and family' were running Irish affairs
'in the family interest . . . as pro-English as if prepared in Downing
Street'.[53] Like Devoy, Carroll thought Fanny indiscreet in her public
statements about the aid given by the Skirmishing Fund to the Land
League;[54] he also thought that she and her friends were 'building up a
concern to crush V.C. and I.R.B.' and that the end result would be
that Ireland would once more 'find herself deceived by spouters' – a
scarcely veiled reference to Fanny's fervid poetry.[55] Carroll was
further infuriated by the personal adulation received by Fanny and
her brother; he felt that Clan na Gael should be 'placed again on its
feet in the dignified position it is entitled to assume, instead of cringing
at the feet of Miss Fanny and "her brother" '.[56] Parnell, he felt, would
set up 'a new C.O.I.R. – ship with all the family and family servants as
assistant C.O.I.R.s'.[57] Such attacks cannot have been restricted
entirely to private correspondence; and Fanny seems to have been
especially sensitive to criticism of the family. Mrs Parnell told R. M.
McWade that the day before Fanny died, after a talk with Davitt, she
said to her mother 'with extreme distress and terror: "Oh, Mamma,
Davitt hates Charlie!" '[58] 'Oh no, my dear', Mrs Parnell replied, 'you
mistake'. This cannot have been great comfort to Fanny, who had
listened to backbiting Fenian resentment in the house at Providence,
and by now had had three years of constant political organisation and
manoeuvring to contend with. Others must have thought much as
Carroll did, and not kept their opinions to themselves.

What her own political opinions were remains a question hard to
answer. Had she outlived the Land War, it would be easier to define
her political stance. The trend of her social thought was certainly more
radical than her brother's; though he put his name to the introduction
of her pamphlet *Hovels of Ireland*, it is unlikely that he subscribed to
many of the opinions therein:

> All through history it is the mob (so-called) that really ends by
> winning. In the warfare of plebeian against patrician it is the
> plebeian that scores the final victory. The blind instinct of the
> multitude, often wrong but much oftener right, is one of the
> most powerful of God's instruments of civilisation. It reminds
> the minority, the upper classes, of what it would be only too glad
> to forget: that with the accidental privilege of greater education,
> intelligence, wealth, go stern duties; that if it neglects to perform

its duties, if it begins to fancy that its gifts are to be used for its own good alone, the great threatening majority everywhere around it will inflict terrible punishment on it. [59]

Fanny continues this passage from *Hovels of Ireland* with an interesting analysis of the enormous crimes of British government in Ireland – among which she emphasises the distortion of the Irish image through what would nowadays be called the media. The doctrine of Irish inferiority, she felt, was broadcast so publicly that it had become an article of faith, believed in by the Irish people themselves; Irish literary figures, for instance, went to England, and earned credit for England, too often ending up by maligning their real country. [60] Her case is sharply and cleverly put (sagaciously relying for evidence upon the reports of English officials and agricultural commissions in Ireland); it would be interesting to know more about Fanny's social thought. A qualification should be added, however, about the question of her progressivism; she wrote to T. D. Sullivan in 1881 and left no doubt about her opinions regarding both the *Irish World* school of thought and radical social theory:

It is being said that the Dublin Land League is being turned into an advertising bureau for the *Irish World!* For my own part, I consider it a great misfortune that the Land League ever had any connection with the *Irish World*. The *I.W.* has sent to the Land League some $50,000. It would have paid the Land League to have given the *I.W.* $50,000 to say nothing about them. It is the recognised organ of the Communists in America and has been excommunicated by all the Catholic clergy. I have read this paper regularly for the last four years, as I like to see everybody's views of a question, and my deliberate conclusion is that, while the paper is safe enough for educated people and contains some very excellent ideas, it is a paper calculated to do much mischief in the hands of an only partially-educated and simple-minded peasantry. [61]

There speaks Parnell's sister; and this impression is borne out by references to her letters to Sullivan, where she states roundly after Philip Callan's election in 1881 that 'Louth should be disenfranchised as far as representation by honest men goes' [62] and refers to 'the pernicious influence of Mr Dwyer Gray'. [63] But enough of the Parnell enigma remains around Fanny's political stance to preclude a pat judgement. She was for the Land League in the most unequivocal manner possible; where she stood on larger political issues is not so clearly seen. She was certainly, where the league was concerned, politically detached; as she wrote to Sullivan, she 'liked to see everybody's views of a question'. This was never the approach of the

Clan na Gael stalwarts, and cannot have brought her any closer to them. She was, in any case, something of an anomaly in Irish-American politics; not only because, like her brother, her background and vested interest in the Irish *status quo* argued against it, but also because of her social and literary gifts. Her mother wrote, with barely-concealed regret:

> [There was] certainly a great difference between her happy, peaceful time in Dublin, her brilliant time in Paris and London, and her time of devotion in aiding her brother's movement, often doing the work of friends in addition to her own. She threw herself out of her social sphere, like her brother, just at the time when she might have made a great home, had loving ones about her, and chosen enjoyments, interests and occupations wherein her great talents, which amounted to genius, would have shone pre-eminent and gained celebrity for her. [64]

The 'social sphere' meant more to her mother than it did to Fanny; and the 'celebrity' she gained in Ireland reached a pitch it never would have achieved in the more refined air of international salons. Her political activity brought Fanny prominence; her poetry ensured it. And an examination of some of her celebrated verse clarifies both the reasons for the extent of her fame and the uncertainty surrounding her political prejudices.

## III

Time has not dealt kindly with Fanny Parnell's poetry. Only one poem of hers was included by Lennox Robinson when compiling his *Golden treasury of Irish verse,* and this was not one of her typical products, but the introspective and gloomy 'After Death'. [65] But her martial and violent verses ring out in issue after issue of the *Boston Pilot* and the *Nation* from 1879 to 1882 had a life all their own, and an effect that was unparalleled – even if their mediocrity is more apparent to us than to a readership which identified closely with Fanny's subjects and revelled in her gothic imagery. To discuss the poems even briefly it would be desirable to be able to refer to a fair sample of them in their entirety; but since a twenty-syllable line and a sixteen-verse poem were nothing unusual for this poet, I have only reproduced one of her poems in full, 'Hold the Harvest', which is to be found in an appendix. (Only one collection of her poems was published, in an American pamphlet edition after her death; [66] and I have not been able to find a copy of this.)

Before examining Fanny's poetry, it should be pointed out that even in her lifetime the more literary of Irish nationalists never over-rated her poetry. Charles J. Kickham wrote waspishly to Dr T. J. Crean in 1881:

> Miss Fanny Parnell wrote some nice pieces for the *Irish People* –
> for which she insisted upon being paid. Now she writes like this:
> > Gladstone is sunk supine
> > To quivering slush'. [67]

This was in fact a misquotation; the complete extract, from 'To England; or, the Land Bill of 1881' is even more distasteful and runs thus:

> You, Gladstone, sunk supine to quivering slush –
> > You, Forster, with the seal of Cain in breast and dye –
> > You, Bright, whose slopping tongue can gloss and gush –. [68]

Even when writing her obituary in the *Nation*, T. D. Sullivan, who himself wrote poetry, could not bring himself to praise Fanny's verses unequivocally: 'she seems either not to have cared about or not to have studied the minor but still indispensable requirements of metrical composition'. [69] John O'Leary, a careful and courteous critic, wrote: 'All [the verses] I have seen from that lady's hand are, I think, rather rhetoric than poetry, though very vigorous and sonorous rhetoric indeed'; he went on to quote some lines from Fanny's first poem for the *Irish People* and added:

> [The story] was one of men who, at the call of their leader, first
> slew their wives and children and then themselves rather than
> yield themselves prisoners and consequently slaves. The moral
> was, of course, everything we could desire, though the example is
> one that can scarcely be followed in later times, when conquest
> involves moral rather than material enslavement. [70]

Fanny would not have argued with this; it was a habit of hers to over-state her case when presenting it poetically. Although she believed the Land League should be non-violent, [71] her verses addressed its members in the most violent martial language. This, of course, was at the heart of her effectiveness. To illustrate the point, it is necessary only to look at her most celebrated poem, 'Hold the Harvest'. It is also probably her best work – and certainly the quintessence of what made her reputation. It appeared in the *Nation* during the summer of 1880, and seized the national imagination at once. It was attacked in the *Daily Telegraph*, praised by George Augustus Sala, and finally ensured immortal fame by being read aloud by Attorney-General Law in court during the State Trials of 1880. Davitt described this scene memorably; with the court being carried away despite itself by this 'Marseillaise of the Irish peasant', and bursting out into impromptu applause. [72] It still deserves to be read;

Davitt's judgement is not exaggeration. There is passion in it, as well
as the more obvious qualities of rhythm and eloquence. If some of the
imagery is overdone, such as the corpses of murdered peasants
providing 'ghastly compost' for their descendants' crops, it is still hard
to fault the lines on the poor man's God, whose 'angels stand with
flaming sword on every mount and moor', there are flashes of feeling
in the poem which can evoke for us the transfigured, epic quality of
the Land League struggle like no other literary record of the time.

'Hold the Harvest' made Fanny's name famous. She was rebuked
for her 'outburst of poetical licence', for her 'strong vocabulary of
abuse', and for 'turning viciously' upon emigrants (whom she had
categorised as 'lucre-loving wretches' and 'sordid churls').[73] A weighty
article in the *Edinburgh Review* on 'Irish discontent' itemised her
poetry as a prime cause of nationalist unrest.[74] G. A. Sala, while
professing himself 'thousands of leagues apart' from Fanny's politics,
admired 'Hold the Harvest' as 'peculiarly eloquent, nervous, and, after
a manner, "cogent" ; he compared it to Julia Ward Howe's 'John
Brown's Body'.[75] Fanny herself seems to have enjoyed the mixture of
bouquets and condemnation suddenly showered upon her. She wrote
to T. D. Sullivan in February 1881:

> You really are too kind to say so many flattering things about my
> 'varses'. But I have been more flattered still by receiving the
> distinction of some half-dozen anonymous and chastening letters
> from various parts of England and Ireland, elicited by the
> 'unspeakable indignation', as one writer phrased it, 'of every
> woman in Great Britain at my villainous, vulgar and unfeminine
> lines'. So you see, honours have come thick upon me.[76]

She never wrote anything quite as effective as 'Hold the Harvest'
again; but her position was assured.

Her poetry remains of compelling interest. It is over-written and
hovers disconcertingly on the edge of banality; she shared some of
Kipling's qualities, but lacked the incisiveness which saved much of his
similarly rhythmic, racy, didactic verse from becoming doggerel. She
could also produce a splendid 'howler', as where she refers to St
Patrick driving out of Ireland 'the crawling snake and skulking
wolf',[77] and she was capable of making a stanza in an otherwise
regularly-constructed poem one line shorter than all the rest.[78] The
body of her poetry, however, repays examination; there are several
issues which surface again and again in it, and help to illuminate the
political position of the author. Was it, for instance, Fenian poetry? To
decide this, it is necessary to go back to the poems Fanny wrote for the
*Irish People* in the 1860s:

O Brethren, prove the mettle of your swords by noble deeds:

> Far better he who in the patriot's strike untimely bleeds
> Than he who spends a long, inglorious life in heaping gold
> With heart that unto Erin's sacred cause is false and cold . . . [79]

Lines like these, whatever about their poetic quality, bear an unequivocal message. There is, moreover, a continuation of the same spirit in Fanny's Land War poetry. In April 1881 she wrote:

> The blood of martyrs is the choicest seed God sows.
> A thousandfold, at last, the wondrous harvest springs;
> From every fertile crop a Truth triumphant grows,
> And to the living from the slain Hope's mission brings. [80]

This epitomises a preoccupation of Fanny's: the heritage of dead patriots, phrased in the unfortunate metaphor which she may have borrowed from the 'Marseillaise', of a bloody fertiliser spread over Irish fields. The same idea recurs again and again in 'Hold the Harvest', with the subsequent message only thinly veiled:

> The yellow corn starts blithely up; beneath it lies a grave,
> Your father died in 'forty-eight; his life for yours he gave;
> He died that you, his son, might learn there is no helper nigh,
> Except for him who, save in fight, has sworn *he will not die.*

Elsewhere she refers to John Mitchel 'teaching the one old way where lies the serf's salvation', [81] which seems to leave no doubt. Some of the imagery in these later poems seems consciously to use the phoenix symbol that came to be connected with Fenianism, as where she writes of those who have died for Ireland:

> Lo! Yonder, like white-hot beacons, they light up the path we
>   should tread,
> Pure flames on the heavenly watch towers; shall we weep for
>   those happy dead? [82]

This seems to subscribe to that traditional dogma of Irish Republicanism: the personal good fortune of those vouchsafed a death in the Irish cause. In the same poem Fanny promises that England ('the Scarlet Woman that's drunken, with the blood and tears of her slaves') shall reap the whirlwind; there seems little doubt that this visitation will be a bloody one.

One of the most interesting things about Fanny's poetry, however, is how accurately it reflects her mood of the time; and in a long panegyric to John Dillon, whom she saw as an amalgam of 'Galahad the chaste' and El Cid, she shows that her particular pantheon of Irish heroes was not restricted to advocates of physical force. The eighteen verses of this poem constitute a breathless celebration of Wolfe Tone, Emmet, Mitchel, Smith, O'Brien, and the rest; but O'Connell receives more than honourable mention, and so does Grattan.[83] Moreover, in several of her Land War poems there is a strong injunction to use moral rather than physical force. This is most evident in 'Coercion: Hold the Rent', which alone comes anywhere near the inspiring effect of 'Hold the Harvest';

> Hold your peace and hold your hands – not a finger on them
>      lay, boys;
> Let the pike and rifle stand; we have found a better way, boys.[84]

With this theme, and equally inconsistent with the Fenian spirit, there is a growing preoccupation with social issues – the sort of approach which I have remarked upon in her *Hovels of Ireland*.[85]

> From every wayside hovel, from every pauper's cell,
> From every reeking garret, from every liquor-hell,
> From every jail and brothel, from every death-bed ditch,
> The cry is swelling – surging – *'Now cursed be the rich!'*
>
> The world is changing – changing – and down the long
>      years
> I see slow revolutions wrought out with pangs and fears;
> In vain to creed and custom we cling with shaking hands,
> Upon the shifting quick-sands our social palace stands.[86]

The same element is found in another poem:

> ... Hear again the people's first and final cry:
> 'No more for you, O Lords! we'll dig and grind;
> No more for you the castle, and for us the stye.
> No more your gyves our equal limbs shall bind . . .'[87]

I have stated that Fanny's poetry tended to reflect her political preoccupation of the time; thus, when between August and November 1880 she was preoccupied with planning the Ladies' Land League she wrote:

> Vain, ah vain, is a woman's prayer!
> Vain is a woman's hot despair!
> Naught can she do, naught can she dare –
> I am a woman, I can do naught for thee, Ireland, mother![88]

By the same token, when she was worried in 1881 about rural support for the Land League and writing letters about this to the papers, she also expressed her feelings on the subject in verse. The *Nation* in February 1881 published a letter from her about faint-heartedness among the Irish farmers: 'Should this be true, then the Irish farmers are not worth fighting for. At all costs, the tenants must stand firm. Otherwise I shall call on America to leave them to their fate.'[89] At the same time the *Boston Pilot* published eleven verses of Fanny's addressed 'To the Farmers of Ireland' and bearing the same emphatic message.[90] Much of Fanny's poetry of this time contains a fierce attack on the apathy and subservience which she felt might sap the strength of the land movement. It is a recurring message in 'Hold the Harvest':

> The serpent's curse upon you lies – ye writhe within the dust,
> Ye fill your mouths with beggar's swill, ye grovel for a crust.

The same preoccupation obsessed her sister Anna,[91] and possibly their brother as well.[92] In this way, the violent phraseology of her poetry has an explanation other than that of being a literal call to arms: she was attempting to galvanise the more sluggish of the League's supporters into action.

There is undeniably a consistent strain of anti-British feeling throughout Fanny's work. Lines like those addressed 'To England', which refer to her as a 'red-fanged and clawed' monster provide ample illustration.[93] Nor was her dislike restricted to aspects of British rule in Ireland. In 'What shall we weep for' she attacks the hypocrisy of English imperialism abroad;[94] and this verse from 'To the Land Leaguers' shows a general disgust with the English way of life:

> From grim Britannia's bowels, where souls are slain for coal,
> Where all her iron Juggernauts o'er endless victims roll;
> From London's slums of horror, where vice with hunger meets,
> Breeding men to fill her prisons, and girls to fill her streets . . .[95]

Davitt, who knew Fanny well, wrote that she hated England intensely and was 'a rebel to her heart's core'.[96] This is largely true; but it would be dangerous to draw too simple a conclusion from it as to Fanny's political stance. It will be by now becoming clear that the political feeling manifest in Fanny's poems is difficult to characterise – except that the land issue is seen as of more paramount importance than political independence, despite the violent tone and anti-British sentiment for which her lines were so celebrated.

One final characteristic is important: the intense religious feeling which runs through nearly all of her work. T. D. Sullivan wrote that Fanny 'occasionally selected sacred subjects, and was rather fond of dwelling on the mystery of life'.[97] This is an understatement. Not only was she addicted to writing hagiographical poems addressed to churchmen like Father Sheehy, Archbishop Croke, and Pope Leo XIII;[98] religious references turn up in almost every poem she wrote. Biblical allusions and Christological parallels appear in her poems to John Dillon[99] and the Land Leaguers;[100] her reaction to the Clogher Massacres was to wonder for an instant 'Is there no God?' but to find an answer in religion.[101] The poems on the Pope and Dr Croke strike a pitch of breathless adulation which the most ardent Catholic would be hard-pressed to equal. Whatever about the casual attitude to formal religion among the Parnells of which Tim Healy complained to his brother,[102] there is no question but that Fanny subscribed to some sort of fervid ultramontanism. The general nature of her references shows that she reverenced all Catholic clergy, and not only those who distinguished themselves in the land agitation. She certainly saw the land cause as a holy war; she said so categorically in several poems. To the imperatives of holding one's own, overcoming political apathy and driving out social injustice, her poetry added the injunction of a religious crusade; given her eloquence and manipulation of violent imagery, the powerful and heady effect of Fanny's poetry was assured. I have avoided discussing her verses in a literary context. Influences like Thomas Davis can easily be discerned – as can, less obviously, those of Lord Byron and Edgar Allan Poe. But it was not for its literary quality that her poetry was admired in Fanny's lifetime – just as, because of the lack of this, it has not been anthologised since her death. It is the immediacy of her rhetoric which captures the imagination now – most memorably in 'Hold the Harvest', less so in other poems. And this immediacy leads to the reflection in her verses of all the diverse strands which made up her own emotional, peculiar nationalism – no less forceful for its peculiarity, as her hard work in political organisation shows. Seen this way, her poetry is doubly illuminating: as a memorial to the strength of the feelings aroused by the Land War and the inspiration behind the works as well as the words of Fanny herself.

## IV

Of Parnell's strong attachment to Fanny there is little doubt. He told both Tim Healy and Mrs O'Shea that she was his favourite sister;[103] he entrusted details of the organisation of his American tour to her;[104] and several anecdotes suggest that there was a deep and warm bond between them. Standish O'Grady noted how affectionately Parnell smiled when the Attorney-General read 'Hold the Harvest' during the State Trials.[105] An anonymous writer in the *Irish-American* witnessed a touching scene when Parnell departed from America in 1876, when he found Fanny hiding in a doorway at a crowded reception, waiting for a chance to say goodbye to her brother.[106] And though Fanny complained in a letter to T. D. Sullivan that 'it is no use writing to my brother, for he never reads the letters of any of the members of his own family',[107] this does not mean that a warm bond did not exist between them. Parnell and his sister were close enough for him to be almost prostrated with grief when she died. He avoided the House of Commons for weeks, and appeared to those who saw him to be greatly stricken.[108] Mrs O'Shea broke the news to him, after seeing it in the morning papers at Eltham while Parnell was still asleep; 'for a time he utterly broke down'.[109] The suddenness of Fanny's death made it an added shock. That day she had driven to the post-office, exercised the dogs, and gone for a walk with William Redmond and Michael Davitt, guests at Bordentown at the time.[110] Redmond told Barry O'Brien:

> I was at Parnell's house, Ironsides, Bordentown, when Fanny Parnell died. She died very suddenly. One day she went out for a walk. She returned in a great state of excitement with a copy of the New York *Herald* in her hand. It was the time of the Egyptian War, and there was a rumour of an English defeat. I remember well seeing Fanny burst into the drawing-room, waving the paper over her head, and saying 'Oh, mother, there is an Egyptian victory. Arabi has whipped the Britishers. It is grand'. That was the last time I saw Fanny Parnell alive. Next day she died quite suddenly.[111]

Contemporary accounts state that she died that evening (20 July 1881), when lying down after dinner.[112] Her mother saw her walk with Redmond and Davitt (whom Mrs Parnell disliked) as a contributory cause of her collapse, telling McWade: 'She died of exhaustion and a weak heart after walking through the hot sun to provide entertainment for Mr Michael Davitt and Mr W. Redmond, whom she had invited to Ironsides.'[113] This seems an over-simple view of the case. It has been stated that she died of tuberculosis,[114] and a weak chest would account for her recurring illnesses over the preceding years and her swift decline following a change of climate. But the immediate cause of her death – discounting Healy's and O'Connor's vague assertions about suicide[115] – was some sort of sudden heart failure.

The effect on Parnell of Fanny's death was not limited simply to the loss of someone he loved; the obsequies which followed affected him where he was most sensitive. When he was still in a state of shock, Mrs O'Shea recalled,

> a cable arrived for him – sent on from London – saying that his sister's body was to be embalmed and brought to Ireland, and his horror and indignation were extreme; he immediately wrote out a message for me to cable from London on his behalf, absolutely forbidding the embalment of his sister's body and saying that she was to be buried in America.[116]

'The idea of death', she adds, 'was at all times very painful to him, but that anyone should be embalmed and taken from one place to another after death was to him unspeakably awful'. This decision of Parnell's however, was not generally popular. Irish America had decided that Fanny, rapidly becoming the object of a death-cult, should have the funeral of a martyred heroine. John Boyle O'Reilly, the influential editor of the *Boston Pilot,* had rather prematurely written an obituary poem called 'The Dead Singer' which depicted Fanny lying 'in the sacred clay of her country' after sailing the Atlantic 'in state on the mourning-ship, like the lily-maid Elaine'; possibly feeling he had a vested interest, he headed what can only be called a campaign to have Fanny's body brought to Ireland. On 25 July there was an immense funeral, with the remains viewed at Bordentown, and John Parnell and his mother (the latter prostrated until just before the service) as chief mourners. The coffin was then removed to Riverview Cemetery, Trenton, to await the expected shipment to Ireland, an Irish shipping firm having offered to take the casket over free of charge. Despite Parnell's feelings, Fanny had been fully and grotesquely embalmed, and one can understand his repugnance; the papers of the time show her body lying bedecked and flower-strewn on an embroidered pillow, wreathed with shamrocks. A death-mask was taken by a prominent Philadelphia sculptor, and the body lay in state at Trenton until a decision was come to about its eventual fate.

On 8 August 1882 a meeting was held in New York of prominent Land Leaguers to discuss the question. Boyle O'Reilly, unable to attend, sent a telegram reading: 'Let her be buried in Ireland, her dead lips will speak more powerfully than ours living.' It was claimed that 'Mrs Parnell and all her friends in this country desire that the body be taken to Ireland'; Dillon had been asked if the body would be received there, twenty-five delegates had already been chosen to accompany it, and reception preparations were in progress.

There was, however, the large though unarticulated obstacle of Parnell's wishes. Plans were kept at a standstill; Fanny's remains continued to lie at Trenton. Eventually a telegram from New York on 19 October 1882 announced that the body was brought to the Tudor vault at Boston that day. A poem to Fanny's memory in the *Nation* remarked pointedly that the Irish people would be

> . . happier still could our fond wish restore thee
> To rest in thy own native isle of the sea. [117]

Several similar comments were made; but in this respect at least, Parnell had had his way.

The transference of the coffin to Boston was nonetheless an occasion for demonstration. John Parnell came over from Ireland, where he had been in the meantime; Mrs Parnell was once again 'prostrated' and unable to accompany the funeral train, though she was seen waving from Ironsides as it went past the house on its way from Philadelphia. When the train stopped at Camden, New Jersey, *en route,* the remains were viewed once again, by seven thousand spectators. 'The face looked perfectly natural and lifelike', remarked an observer, 'and it seemed difficult to realise that Miss Parnell had been dead for nearly three months.'[118] There were further demonstrations in New York, and an immense procession in Boston, where the body was at last interred in the cemetery at Mount Auburn, Cambridge.

John Boyle O'Reilly remained intransigent. An editorial in the *Boston Pilot* remarked:

> We shall not say that the funeral of Miss Fanny Parnell took place last week in Boston; that word we reserve for the last transfer of her remains, when the Irish people of Boston shall bear her body down to the sea and send it to its natural home in the bosom of the land she lived and died for . . . We persist in the belief that the spirit of the poetess will not rest till her body be buried in Ireland; it was her living dream; she never thought of lying in a vault in a Boston churchyard.[119]

All round, Fanny's death aroused strong emotions. An article in the *Celtic Magazine* remarked on the extraordinarily profound effect of her demise upon the Irish-American consciousness: far deeper than that of John Martin, John O'Mahoney, or even John Mitchel. Moreover, the same writer added, hers was not reflected glory: her fame was completely independent of that of her brother.[120] The poems written in her memory at the time[121] proclaim a cult that was almost religious. Beautiful, poetic, young, generous, prophetic and noble, Fanny was all but canonised by Irish-American opinion; more than one poem about her said that she was not dead, but would arise again to sing Ireland's final liberty – as she had herself poetically prophesied.[122] It became a habit in Boston to make a pilgrimage to Fanny's grave on Memorial Day (30 May), with speeches, floral tributes, and a general demonstration of grief;[123] such visits were still being paid eight years after her death. Her influence and inspiration were of a unique type during her lifetime; she remained a cult figure after her death.

# 4 'The pain and strain of years':
## the political activity and disillusionment of Anna Parnell

When I first began my journey
My step was firm and light
And I hoped to reach a shelter
Before the fall of night.

But a band of thieves beset me
Quite early in the day;
They robbed me and then they cast me
All bleeding by the way.

And since that hour I have crawled,
A cripple blind with tears,
While each step I've made has cost me
The pain and strain of years.

Anna Parnell, 'The Journey' in *Old tales and new*
(Dublin, late 1890s).

One thinks of her fading further and further away from the actual world. She glided through life as one who had very little to do with the hard facts of it; and yet she was exquisitely human. Her life ought to have been written, for she was a great woman, and yet I think that she herself would have preferred that her name be writ in water.

Katherine Tynan (of Anna Parnell), *Twenty-five years*
(London, 1913), p. 98.

# I

Anna Parnell's reputation is linked indissolubly with Fanny's; they are generally remembered together, and the Ladies' Land League as their joint creation. They were, however, very different types of woman. They both believed in the Irish land struggle and worked passionately for it; they both wrote poetry; they were both – though in very different ways – heroines of their time. But there were not many more resemblances between them; and while Fanny's permanent ill-health and sudden death earned her a martyr's reputation, it is arguable that Anna, who lived on for nearly thirty years after Fanny's death and the end of the land agitation, is the more truly tragic figure.

She struck most people who met her as an extraordinary person; there is no doubt that she was, as Katherine Tynan said, 'a great woman'.[1] There is however, a curious nebulousness about the personal impression she made – again remarked upon by Katharine Tynan in the second epigraph to this chapter. Anna's sister Emily described her as 'generous to a fault', of angelic qualities and great sympathy;[2] but she says next to nothing else about her, and there was evidently little contact between them. T. P. O'Connor, who claimed to 'know her very well', did not find Anna a particularly pleasing personality; angular in appearance, with a cold manner masking intense feeling.[3] But by far the most complete picture has been left by Katharine Tynan, who worked with her and loved her. She recorded that, as well as sharing Parnell's mystery and aloofness, Anna had 'his extraordinary charm in great measure'[4] and an amazing 'presence', always felt as soon as she arrived at the Ladies' Land League office in Sackville Street:

> You might not lift your eyes from your letter-writing for members of Parliament, country priests, released suspects, American journalists, revolutionary leaders; but you would certainly lift them and turn about when the little lady, whose very atmosphere was gentleness, glided gently into place.[5]

She was of the stuff of heroines; 'and what soft, gentle stuff it was!' Katharine Tynan remembered Anna's constant small gifts to the girls who worked with her, her shyness, charm and sensitivity; unlike O'Connor, she found Anna's 'small, pale face strangely attractive'.[6] Despite a strong sense of humour and a lovely laugh, she objected to any form of coarseness. 'I cannot say', wrote Katharine Tynan, 'if religion influenced her at all, or if she was anything but a gentle stoic.' She visited Katharine at her father's farmhouse at Clondalkin and talked about writing poetry. Her friend's characterisation of Anna is as the most gentle, sensitive and other-worldly of sprites.

And yet this was the woman who crossed a river on a supporter's back so that she could be present to hector police constables at an eviction,[7] who burst through a bodyguard and stopped Lord Spencer's horse in Westmoreland Street,[8] who answered the enquiry 'You surely don't think they would shoot [an agent]?' with the terrible reply 'I'm afraid not; in these parts anger evaporates in threats.'[9] She worked all day and night in the Land League offices, made speeches of remarkable pungency, and wrote a memoir of the Land War which is sharp, forceful, cogent and brutally honest. Even Katharine Tynan, while describing Anna 'with her curiously gentle, gliding pace, in her neat dress, the very embodiment ... of a delicate, austere lady, just verging on spinsterhood',[10] still noted that Anna alone of Dublin ladies could walk down Grafton Street by herself after the shops shut — which would have ruined any other woman's reputation. Michael Davitt gives some inkling of the contradiction between her appearance and her character, describing her peculiar blend of a fragile appearance and a resolutely revolutionary spirit.[11] She had a special quality of steely strength, allied to the Parnell nervousness of temperament; in many ways, she was the most formidable character of the family.

She had, moreover, a certain intellectual arrogance which helps to explain some of the ostensible contradictions in her character. This comes out again and again in her unpublished memoir of the Land League (characteristically entitled 'The tale of a great sham'); she constantly refers to the stupidity, slow-wittedness, and lack of intelligence of the English, the landlords, recalcitrant tenants, and anyone else who opposed her. She also took an almost brutal attitude about the victims of the Phoenix Park murders, feeling no compunction either to speak well of the dead or to admit that it was tragic mischance that killed Lord Frederick Cavendish; she implied instead that the murderers were unjustly accused, tried and sentenced.[12] There is no question but that she possessed an extreme independence of mind which enabled her to pursue the most unfasionable or unpopular opinions with single-minded determination. She obviously liked Katharine Tynan, who saw the kindest side to her; Miss Tynan was an intelligent woman, worth spending time with. But all the evidence shows that not only did Anna avoid suffering fools gladly: she refused to entertain them at all.

## II

In the early 1870s, Anna was at the Metropolitan School of Art, where 'she was a diligent student, apparently the gentlest of the gentle, and nothing surprised her teachers and classfellows more than her [later] appearance in the political world'.[13] But a political consciousness was never far below the surface, ever since the days when her unconventional opinions outraged the vicar's wife in Rathdrum and her feminism shocked Mr Comerford's placid daughters. [14] Certainly by 1877 she was following her brother's political career assiduously; in this year she attended parliamentary sessions regularly and later wrote a three-part article for the *Celtic Monthly* about the Irish party's obstructionist tactics in the House of Commons. [15] This article repays examination; there is much in it that prefigures Anna's later political activity and position.

These 'notes from the ladies' cage' begin with a recapitulation of the Irish Party's recent history at Westminster – seen from the ladies' gallery, the underprivileged position of which is described with characteristic sharpness. Anna describes the Irish Party with an ingenuousness she was later to revoke; she believed at this time that they 'enjoyed the remarkable distinction of being the only [party] which has never had any internal dissensions or rivalries'. [16] She is, however, perceptive about the effects and implications of obstruction, as regards the attitude of the English to the Irish cause. Unexpectedly, after describing Butt's opposition to the new policy, she praises him for courageously standing out against it instead of tacitly opposing it but claiming the credit for the successes it brought – which he could easily have done. Dealing with the actual debates which were obstructed – on the Mutiny Acts, political prisoners, army estimates, and so on – she is straightforward, sharp and rather abrupt in style, but the effect is lightened by touches of asperity where members are personally mentioned: Mr Raikes 'looked as if he had been taken out of a ditch drowned', Mr Lowther's features resembled 'a horse of uncertain lineage'. [17] The effect of obstruction upon the maddened wives of English M.P.s is described with frank and satiric pleasure.

As Parnell moves to the centre of the parliamentary stage, is suspended, and joins her in the ladies' cage, the pace of Anna's narrative mounts; [18] her conclusion to her article was characteristically extreme, and typically élitist: she *regretted* the general adherence of the party to the new policy after Butt's deposition, on the grounds that the ensuing infusion of moderate opinion meant that the process was not pushed as far as it might have been. [19] These articles, as well as giving a good history of the obstructionist debates, show clearly where Anne's own sympathies lie; and they portray somebody with a keen interest in political agitation, and the tendency to élitism which so often characterises a dedicated revolutionary.

By the time her articles were published, Anna was in America and was herself absorbed in the organisation of the Famine Relief Fund. A spirited letter of hers to the New York *Herald* in December 1879 attacked the 'murderous programme' of the English government in Ireland, and spoke of the 'enormous power of passive resistance' to be brought against it; she added that American support would be in the interests of the United States itself, as otherwise the American labour

market would be flooded with Irish immigrants. [20] Nor was her support
of the land movement restricted to articles and letters; I have quoted a
description of her working with Fanny in the New York Hotel at this
time. [21] She seems to have shared the organisational work evenly with
Fanny; Tim Healy, arriving in February 1880 at New York, found
Anna involved as much as her sister, and wrote unkindly to Maurice
that they were 'mutually jealous of each other's efforts'. [22] He found
Anna as formidable as Fanny:

> The Parnell girls are their brother's sisters! They have a central
> relief office here, and Anna Parnell goes down every day, though
> the committee employs two clerks, to work for hours over the
> Land League and relief business . . . The demands on Parnell to
> visit places keep pouring in continually, but John Dillon's
> capacity is referred to by Miss Parnell with acerbity, and I find
> to my dismay that I am regarded as a 'Heaven-sent genius' to set
> everything right. I would not like to repeat Miss Parnell's
> comments on Dillon, and you need not mention this to anyone
> . . . Miss Parnell says a lot of people are offended because they
> cannot get replies to their letters and invitations . . . In spite of
> their present graciousness and compliments, I shall be the next
> victim if anything goes wrong. [23]

The American correspondence of the Land League in the National
Library of Ireland shows that Anna was deeply involved in League
business by 1880; [24] there are several businesslike and rather
peremptory letters from her for this period. As with Fanny, the
question of acknowledgement of American donations was a
preoccupation of hers; finally in desperation she suggested a sort of
'form letter' that could be printed up, with suitably comprehensive
wording, and sent off to donors. [25] The confusion of finance for 'relief'
and for 'organisation' is also a frequent topic. Her hard work was
eulogised by J. J. W. O'Donoghue, editor of the New York
*Chronicle*, [26] Davitt also mentions her diligence at this time. [27] Her
work for the American relief organisation, however, was simply
Anna's apprenticeship to political activity; she was about to embark
upon the movement which altered the face of Irish agitation and
brought her first of all great fame and then a bitter disillusionment
which lasted for the rest of her long life. The movement was the
Ladies' Land League.

As has been seen, [28] this organisation was started by Fanny in
America in the autumn of 1880. By December of that year, Fanny was
clear in her mind that the L.L.L. (as I shall henceforward refer to the
movement) would have to be extended to Ireland; she suggested that
Anna should see to this. But Anna was not unduly enthusiastic – her
reasons being, according to Fanny, 'first, because she doubted her own

executive ability, and secondly, because she thought the Irish women would be afraid to join'.[29] In the event, Anna was given little choice; 'the executive of the Irish National Land League', wrote Fanny with satisfaction, 'passed by a unanimous vote a motion requesting my sister Anna to come forward and organise a Ladies' Land League similar to the one that had already been in existence, with such excellent results, in America'.[30] This was largely due to Davitt, and Anna made no bones about the fact in a speech of April 1881 when she stated that the L.L.L. was 'wholly his work' and that if she had been consulted, she would have hesitated.[31] Davitt, writing in 1904, said that this statement of Anna's was 'too modest';[32] but since Fanny corroborates the story of Anna's reluctance, it seems likely that she was being accurate. Certainly, it was Davitt's enthusiasm which made the Land League Executive adopt the idea; numerous accounts tell of the opposition that was at first offered.[33] Andrew Kettle was one member who became rapidly converted. He was extremely dubious at first, but when he met Anna his enthusiasm became unlimited. She had a better knowledge, he wrote, of both the nature of Irish rural society and the measures necessary to change it than anyone he ever met, and would have brought the Land War to a better conclusion than her brother.[34] This was an impressive tribute from Kettle, who was not usually so eloquent. His account is also significant for showing that the elements which came to the surface in 1882, when the L.L.L. was destroyed, were there from the beginning: antipathy to the idea among the Land League executive, and a very different analysis of the land situation on Anna's part from that of her brother. Parnell, Dillon and Brennan were strongly against the idea, which later earned them a scornful gibe from Francis Sheey-Skeffington, a keen feminist: 'They were imbued with the old "protective" idea of man's relation to woman.'[35] But it is equally likely that Anna had made her political stance known to them, and it was not entirely to their liking.

The first rumours of a Ladies' organisation in Ireland began in November 1880;[36] Anna arrived in Dublin in December; and concrete plans for the new organisation began in early January. It was to share the premises at no. 39, Upper Sackville Street, with the Land League; existing Land League branches were to organise sister movements; the support of the evicted tenants and the encouragement of resistance to land-grabbing were to be the ladies' special provinces. They were to see to the erection of wooden huts for the evicted, and the support of prisoners' families; as coercion increased, the ladies were to decide what would 'by the expenditure of money' provide most opposition to the government.[37] Thus it was *from the beginning* an expensive programme – a point to bear in mind when considering the later disbanding of the movement on the grounds of undue extravagance.

From the beginning, there were differences of opinion about its organisation. Dillon wanted the L.L.L. to be like the St Vincent De Paul Society: a charity movement. Anna, we are told, 'strongly objected' – as can easily be imagined.[38] She claimed full organisational powers, working in co-operation with 'the men's organisation' – a telling phrase. (In her 'Tale' she tells of an inexplicable parcel of ragged clothing arriving at Sackville Street; the Ladies' anger at being considered simply as do-gooders evaporated in laughter when it was discovered that the clothes were intended for the Distressed Ladies' Organisation nearby, to enable them to attend Castle functions.)

Many of the women who worked with Anna would have shared her attitude. The names beside hers on the early manifestoes are those of Anne Stritch, Nan Lynch and Harriet Byrne;[39] they were the secretaries of the Executive. The treasurers were Mrs Maloney and Miss O'Leary.[40] Organisers included Mrs Moore, Hannah Reynolds and Mary O'Connor (both later arrested). Dillon's cousin, Mrs Deane, was president, and Mrs A. M. Sullivan a prominent committee member.[41] The spirit that guided the most influential women, according to Katharine Tynan, was the tradition of well-educated, idealistic nationalism. Girls like the Lynch sisters had gone to convent schools abroad and travelled widely as governesses; the Walshe and Nally girls had been connected with the Land League since its inception in County Mayo. While many of the membership were there simply to write letters at dictation, Anna had still attracted a central group of remarkable women. Katharine Tynan herself was 'only one of the rank and file, and a frivolous one';[42] her fondest memories of the L.L.L. were of making tea and eating cakes, and to her 'the memory of the League rooms in those days had something of the effect of an agreeable picnic'.[43] But the central organisation of the League was more businesslike – and required greater sacrifices. Elsewhere Katharine Tynan describes a visit to the Walshe sisters, and one girl bursting into the other's room late at night with orders from Miss Parnell to go to Paris 'now, tonight, this minute';[44] the occasion was the illicit printing of *United Ireland*, which was carried out by the Ladies in an atmosphere far from that of an 'agreeable picnic'.

This was an example of the sort of work which devolved upon the L.L.L. after the Land League was proclaimed in October 1881. Even before these frantic days, however, their work was of a character, and of a standard, which would then have been considered most unladylike. The organisation was elaborate; there was, besides the Executive already named, a 'reserve executive' of twenty-one ladies ready to take over in case of arrests.[45] The local organisations were closely linked to Sackville Street, an important part of their work being to send up data for what was called 'the book of Kells' – an immense dossier on every estate in Ireland, including details of tenants, rents, valuations, attitudes, evictions, and the character and record of landlords and agents. Weekly reports from local branches were fed into this Domesday book; this constituted the chief bureaucratic work [46] and shows the level to which organisation was carried – as well as the realism with which Anna combated the inefficiency of the Land League, of which she so often complained. [47] Besides this massive record, the central office also had to co-ordinate the local activities such as attending evictions and building wooden huts for the evicted – these last being intended both to provide shelter and to enable the evicted tenants to ward off land-grabbers. Though they furnished 210 cabins for evicted tenants in one year, they were often prevented by police from erecting them; [48] writing in 1907, Anna admitted that this system did not work, those huts that eventually got built proving unfit to live in. Nonetheless, the psychological effect of such an effort must have been considerable – as must have been the pecuniary help offered prisoners' families. To this last, however, Anna had an objection which she states again and again in her 'Tale': there was no way of knowing whether this money would not, in fact, go towards paying the rent instead of feeding the family. And here was the crux of one of the great differences between the L.L.L. and the men: 'The Land League', Anna wrote acidly in after years, 'had by no means the same objection to rent being paid as we had'. [49]

There was, as I have said, a difference in approach from the beginning. In her memoir Anna consistently makes the point that, in spite of the fact that the Land League talked in grandiose terms, the Ladies found an almost complete dearth of organisation when they began to operate in country areas; and this was accompanied by what can only be called the lack of a consistent ideology on the part of the men. A monster meeting, Anna believed, was not as productive as a few people monitoring an eviction proceeding, [50] and the Ladies put this belief into practice. The circular reissued by the L.L.L. in 1881 detailing the procedure to be followed where evictions were concerned shows an approach that was business-like, efficient and practical. [51] Anna came to look upon the Land League as a mixture of hypocrisy, bombast and narrow-sightedness; they let the time for a rent strike go by, and then issued the useless No Rent Manifesto, and this to her summed up the 'sham' which was at the heart of the movement. The two organisations seem to have had at best an uneasy alliance; Anna wrote of the early days of the L.L.L.: 'It did not surprise me to hear complaints from the travelling members of the Ladies' Land League that it was very difficult to do anything where 'A MAN' had been shortly before, because they were so extravagantly liberal with promises.' [52] I should state here that this view of Anna's from the vantage point of 1907 was not hindsight; it is borne out by her speeches and policies of 1881–2. [53] How far her opinions were shared by her colleagues is another matter; but of her primacy in the L.L.L.

there is no doubt whatsoever, so the importance of this point is negligible.

When the time came for the Ladies to take over from the proclaimed Land League in October 1881 they were not, according to Anna, prepared enough – despite the fact that their address of February had outlined this as one of their tasks. The housing scheme was the only areas of administration in which they had had any considerable experience. There was also, she bitterly remarked later, the certainty of strong animosity against them at the time:

> Besides our experience in housing, we were in possession of another distinct advantage in the knowledge we had that whatever we might do, we were equally certain to be blamed for it – an assurance which is a great help to clear and impartial judgement.[54]

Knowing that they would be criticised in any case, and annoyed at the small budget vouchsafed them, the Ladies deliberately embarked upon an active and money-spending programme from October 1881 until the following spring. 'The men' – as other witnesses besides Anna have recounted – were not at all behind them in the implications of this; and neither, admitted Anna, were the tenants. Her memoir contains many references to their tendency to backslide, and their plaguing the Ladies with demands to honour the Land League's promise of paying legal costs – which Anna saw merely as granting them the money which would enable them to pay their rents. Again, one notices her élitist attitude towards the people in whose name she was working. 'I only wished' she added ruefully, 'the tenants would be as determined with the landlords as they were with us'.[55]

What the Ladies' activity provoked is well known. Organisers like Hannah Reynolds and Mary O'Connor were arrested; thousands of angry women joined in their place. The whole organisation was to be arrested, it was rumoured, until measles broke out in the women's prison and, as Anna remarked with her sardonic humour, 'the government probably thought it would be rough on the Governor to have both the measles and the Ladies' Land League on his hands at once'. Even before they had taken over from the men, Archbishop McHale had denounced the L.L.L. as 'forgetting the modesty of their sex and the high dignity of their womanhood' and 'so far disavowing their birthright of modesty as to parade in the public gaze in a character unworthy a child of Mary'.[56] This had only served to call forth angry attacks on McHale himself and fervent eulogies of the Ladies.[57] When Forster attempted to have them arrested under antique statutes intended to curb prostitution, the members of the L.L.L. were elevated yet further to martyrdom. They lived in constant anticipation of arrest; their papers had to be duplicated and hidden in unsuspecting repositories ranging from a city wine-merchant's premises to the house of 'a respectable Protestant landlady in Rathmines'. [58] When the L.L.L. was itself proclaimed, Anna arranged for simultaneous convocations all over Ireland, and the government did not follow the idea through. The Ladies saw to the continued printing of *United Ireland* from as far afield as Liverpool and Paris, and distributed it in Ireland – 'the pleasantest part of all the work of the Ladies' Land League', Anna recalled, '[as] it was something that could, at any rate, be done, and did not seem to be so painfully like trying to make ropes of sea-sand as so much of our other tasks did'. [59] When Forster resigned and the Kilmainham leaders were released, the L.L.L. was given much of the credit – an attitude which infuriated Anna, who believed there should be no assumption of an 'end' to the Land War. She had never had any patience with the Land Bill of 1881, and even when confronted with the fact that the mass of tenants chose to abide by it, she wanted to continue the fight on their behalf: showing yet again a marked disdain for what was – however regrettably – the popular opinion. This, however, belongs to a later section of this chapter. [60]

During their struggle, moreover, the actions of the Ladies had laid them open to accusations from the released moderates. One charge was extravagance; the other, condoning of agrarian violence. Davitt wrote that the ladies deliberately did not enquire into the methods used by outlawed League militants. [61] Elsewhere, he states categorically that the L.L.L. organised 'intimidation' [62] and that 'no district in which some form of opposition had not been offered to an evicting landlord or obnoxious agent would receive grants from Dublin until the weapon of the boycott was applied; districts were known as "courageous" or "timid" as they merited this distinction by their record'. [63] Certainly Anna's memoir is loud in its denunciations of the weak spirit of the tenants; but she seems to restrict this concept to their approach to paying rents. However, the line between violent and passive resistance, always hard to draw, is illegibly smudged in the case of the Land War; numerous studies of the subject have failed to elucidate the exact extent to which the League condoned violence. Anna's position in this respect is as ambivalent as any other Land Leader's – and she often expressed herself in this respect with consumate political artistry. This is shown in a speech she made at Drumcolliher on 26 June 1881, where she referred to a tenant's threat to shoot a landlord and a voice from the crowd remarked 'Right he was.' Anna answered: 'Well, I will not go into the question of whether he was right or not – I certainly don't think he was, because he had not anything to shoot him with [laughter] and you ought never to threaten that which you know you have not power to carry out.' [64] The question was thus skilfully left open. Anna had, by then, found her element. The reluctant organiser of December 1880 was well on her way to becoming the heroine of Captain Moonlight's reign in the following winter. To further elucidate both her own career in the L.L.L. and the political rationale behind the organisation itself, a consideration of Anna's own activity throughout the period is necessary.

## III

By the beginning of February 1881, the L.L.L. was organised; they issued their first manifesto on 4 February [65] and on 13 February Anna made her début as a public speaker. [66] Characteristically, she requested that there be no 'demonstration' upon her arrival at the platform, and she refused to ride in a carriage pulled by her admirers; her distaste for the sort of emotionalism called for by 'the men' is clearly evident. Even more significant were the words of her speech – the first of countless talks she was to give up and down the country. She emphasised, shortly and sharply, that the L.L.L. was not a charity movement: its object was relief and organisation. [67] The objects of relief outlined by Anna were the evicted tenants, the families of prisoners, and the prisoners themselves; but a more active policy than simple relief was indicated in her concluding injunction to boycott the R.I.C. men in their town, to refuse to entertain them in their houses, and to refuse to talk to them in the street; this echoed the call to female solidarity and independence articulated elsewhere in her speech.

She found receptive audiences all over Ireland; by the end of February branches had proliferated in the country and a London organisation under Mrs A. M. Sullivan had its headquarters at the Westminster Palace Hotel. [68] During the month Anna appeared to rural gatherings in Naas, Cliffoney and Ballyhaunis, where she attracted bands on station platforms and laudatory addresses – not only as 'a lady of highly cultured intelligence, independent mind, and undoubted courage', but also as 'the sister of the heroic leader of the Irish people' – the repetition of which connection must have made Anna doubly impatient with all the paraphernalia attendant upon being a celebrity. The limelight could not, however, be avoided – especially when her opinions were as extreme as they were. On 28 February, at Naas, she tentatively suggested a rent strike in coerced areas; [69] on 6 March she became involved in a controversy about a speech of hers in which she was supposed to have doubted the existence of the next world, [70] which may have influenced Archbishop McHale in his ill-considered attack upon her organisation at this time. [71] Later in March Anna travelled to England to visit the many branches of the L.L.L. springing up there. She made a powerful speech at Liverpool in reply to an attack on the L.L.L. in the *Standard*, and was widely reported for it. [72] On 20 March she was back in Ireland and into the middle of the controversy aroused by McHale's denunciation; she only referred to him indirectly, as such able vindicators as A. M. Sullivan and Archbishop Croke had already taken up the cudgels in defence of the Ladies' reputations.[73]

All this time Anna's speeches show a conception of the L.L.L. which she was later to articulate in her 'Tale of a great sham'. Organisation and research were emphasised; it was the business of the Ladies to study landlordism and 'be able to pass a competitive examination in it'.[74] The business of the tenants was to stand fast; the fact that Tipperary, for instance, was not proclaimed 'appeared to her [Anna] the greatest slur that had been cast on Tipperary for a long time' and she called upon the tenants to refute it.[75] At Charleville a few days later she castigated 'the men' for having paid rent on the Saunders estate; she would 'do a thing she had never done before' and 'go outside the sphere of relief business' by advising the wives to pay for groceries and the like in hard cash only – and thus prevent their husbands from saving up money to pay rent while they ran into debt. The fact that none of the ladies' husbands were imprisoned was 'no credit to them'; and those who accused her of unfeminine extremism were 'old men and old women'.[76]

As Anna's political counsels grew more extreme, the pace of her activity quickened. 'The energy of Miss Anna Parnell is something extraordinary', remarked the *Nation* admiringly in April 1881; 'her desire to serve the cause of the Irish tenant is so great that she hardly gives herself a moment's rest.'[77] On 17 March she was in Navan, on 24 March at Charleville, the following day in Kilmallock, and on 27 March at Kanturk; she made speeches at each place, and at the same time was supervising the rapidly increasing and diversifying office-work in Sackville Street. At most of the meetings which she attended, Anna made remarks about 'the men' of a more or less acid nature; the only member of the Land League Executive whom she refers to in a complimentary way is Davitt who was now in prison once again.[78] Addresses which referred to her femininity were sure to draw a sharp riposte; when a complimentary resolution mentioned that she was 'prepared to work as well as weep', she answered that she would leave the weeping to the men.[79] In several speeches she attacked the idea of emigration;[80] she also called for an increase in American subscriptions;[81] and she did not shirk criticising the country branches of the L.L.L. for failing to report the atrocities of local landlords and police.[82] And she skirted the issue of violence by an increasingly narrow margin. The only reason to practise restraint, she told one of the largest L.L.L. meetings to date, on 5 June 1881 at Tulla, was to keep out of jail; but 'she did not mean to preach the immoral and cowardly doctrine that it was wrong never to resist the law; all she wanted to say was that she never allowed the other side to choose the time and the place for the people to resist the law'. [83]

She herself set an example by appearing in the field at evictions – bidding against Emergencymen at a stock auction on the Gormanston estate in May, [84] and playing a conspicuous part in the evictions at Mitchelstown in August. [85] Here she instructed tenants not to pay rents, hectored the superintending R.M. until she was allowed to accompany the sheriff on his rounds, and then headed off his party at cottages while she exhorted the tenants to hold firm. [86] Many of the rents *were* paid, which must have infuriated her; but it was literally 'at the point of a bayonet' and, as the *Cork Herald* remarked, 'her presence was anything but welcome to those whose business it was to get the rents paid'. Nonetheless, she had demanded that nothing be handed over; [87] though the eviction campaign, according to the *Nation*, 'had kept the entire district for nearly a fortnight on the edge of civil war', [88] and she was welcomed into Fermoy as a heroine, Anna saw it as a failure.

A month earlier she had disagreed violently with someone who mentioned the Irish people were poor and helpless, retorting: 'The Irish people are poor because they choose to be poor; the country is rich, and its wealth is in the hands of the tenant farmers; if they choose, they can keep up the Land League'. [89] Whether they chose or not was the crux or the matter; and the new Land Bill gave the tenants an incentive to decide upon the alternative. Anna never believed, as her brother did, that 'the starving man is not a good Nationalist'; [90] she viewed the Land Act of 1881 as a miserable half-measure, designed to deflect the Land War from its rightful conclusion, and her speeches of the summer of 1881 all carry this implication. The Bill received the Royal Assent on 22 August; Anna's speeches from this date show an increase in radicalism and more and more passionate appeals to the Irish tenants to choose open war instead of appeasement. At this stage, of course, her brother's public utterances took a similar path – but with a weight of sophisticated political calculation behind the decision which does not apply to Anna's case. In a month's time he was to write privately that the 'movement was breaking fast' and that it was politically fortunate that he should be arrested; [91] this attitude, together with the expedient of 'testing the Bill', was the sort of approach which was anathema to his sister, and which did nothing to elevate her opinion of 'the men'. In the mounting anger of her public utterances from September 1881 on can be traced the beginnings of her open break with Parnell the following summer.

It was at this juncture that she chose to carry the war into the enemy's country. She had made a tour of the L.L.L. branches in Britain the previous March; but her visit to Scotland and the North of England in the autumn was attended by a completely new kind of publicity. In late August she and John Redmond spoke at a meeting of the Glasgow Irish; much money was raised for the Land League, and Anna's speech referred to Gladstone in terms which make her brother's celebrated utterances at Wexford seem the essence of moderation. The Prime Minister, she told the Glasgow audience, 'is a wretched, hypocritical, bloodthirsty miscreant . . . who is having your own countrymen and countruwomen slaughtered now at home to suit his own vanity'; she enjoined the Irish in Glasgow never again to vote for him.[92] Nor was this a statement made in the flush of rhetoric, as the newspapers pointed out: her steady, quiet delivery made it all the more telling.[93]

Anna went on to speak at Edinburgh, Greenock and Dundee, and her approach did not become any more moderate. At Edinburgh she told her audience that 'she could see no advantage in shooting Mr Forster or Mr Gladstone, as these gentlemen living were doing a service to Ireland which if they were dead they could not do; they were teaching the Irish people the utter folly and weakness of trusting any English statesman, or any Englishman, to work reform for Ireland'.[94] Scottish opinion was outraged by her; the fact that a Land League in the Orkneys was mooted and founded during the northern tour cannot have set many minds at rest. At Greenock the provost refused to chair a meeting to which she was invited because of her 'indulgence in very violent and unbecoming language'; Anna lambasted him at a subsequent meeting in Dundee, to 'a perfect hurricane of applause'.[95]

On 6 September she returned to Glasgow for the inaugural meeting of a L.L.L. branch. She then returned to Ireland; but a month later she visited the North of England, speaking scornfully of Gladstone's threat to employ the resources of civilisation.[96] The following month she visited England again, speaking at Blackburn, Liverpool and Bradford[97] and publicising the Political Prisoners' Aid Society recently founded by the L.L.L. She also attacked the Irish police, judges, juries and any tenants who were disposed to accept the Land Act – though these, she claimed, were a tiny minority. Whether or not she believed this, it is impossible to say; but it is certain that, unlike her brother, she wanted it to be true.

By now, of course, 'the men' were in jail and the Land League proclaimed; the fact that Anna was in Liverpool and attacking the judicial system in her speeches must have been connected with her action at this time in producing a pamphlet exposing jury-packing which named jury panels all over Ireland; she had 20,000 of these printed at her own expense in Liverpool and delivered them illicitly from her Dublin home at number 7, Hume Street, aided in the venture by Mrs Jennie Wyse-Power and Patrick O'Brien.[98] The attempts of Dublin Castle to suppress this pamphlet led to O'Brien's arrest, and to the hiding of caches of copies all over Dublin. Perhaps it was some of these pamphlets which Anna entrusted under false pretences to the cautious and prudent Alfred Webb, who had helped her in some underground printing ventures for the L.L.L.; Webb recalled in his unpublished autobiography that Parnell later expressed his regret and disapproval at his sister's Machiavellian manoeuvre.[99] After October 1881 the L.L.L. had little time to afford scruples about such matters; as Anna told a meeting at Liverpool, they 'now had to work very much underground and in the dark'.[100] In parts of Mayo, she added, 'the tenant farmers were actually afraid to be seen speaking to a strange lady for fear she might be a representative of the Land League'. They were not all Furies, as Katharine Tynan was careful to point out;[101] this is borne out by Alfred Webb's delightful account of how he visited Sackville Street at the time 'when the leading Lady Land Leaguers were looked upon as Joans of Arc', and found the ladies sitting in silence, one behind the other in the large central office, each combing the hair of the girl in front of her.[102] But, as he pointed out, the principals of the movement were not present at the time. Anna, for one, was rapidly becoming completely involved in organisation; after her English tour in November she appeared at fewer and fewer public meetings, and it was at this time that Katharine Tynan remembers her working until after midnight every night and then walking alone across the city to Hume Street. The accounts of weekly L.L.L. meetings given in the *Nation* during the winter of 1881–2 show the vast increase in business handled.[103] Organisation involved the delineation of policy and the elucidation of what the Land League meant; in November 1881, when confusion was caused by an open letter from Kilmainham about what tenants' cases deserved assistance, Anna wrote to the *Freeman* that all deserving cases would be aided and only those who had saved up relief money to pay rent would be abandoned.[104]

It was about this time that Anna became a sort of folk heroine; when a meeting of the Children's Land League (an offshoot of the L.L.L.) was broken up in Kerry the same month, there was a procession of children through the village 'cheering for *Miss* Parnell and the Land League',[105] which implies that she held a position in the popular imagination almost equal to her brother's. Fame in Ireland was accompanied by notoriety in England; Mrs O'Shea told of Anna being burnt in effigy with the Pope outside her gate one Guy Fawkes Day in Eltham.[106] Her status was enhanced by the official proclamation of the L.L.L. by the R.I.C. on 16 December, when it was announced that the suppression of the Land League on 20 October had also included that of the Ladies.[107] Anna had to organise an alternative headquarters in London, in the care of Helen Taylor at Kensington; speaking in the North of England at the end of the year, she mentioned that she had heard of the imminence of her own arrest and had been making preparations.[108] At a meeting in Liverpool she

referred to Herbert Gladstone as a 'sneaking spalpeen' and ridiculed
Forster for his measures against the Ladies, to consummate effect. [109]
In the New Year she was back in Dublin, chairing the fourth meeting
of the L.L.L. since its official suppression, and attacking the
*Freeman's Journal* for supposing that the political prisoners' Fund
would close at £10,000; this, she said, was not nearly enough,
considering that even before the recent wave of arrests they had been
spending £400 a week upon the prisoners. By the end of January,
several of the Ladies were themselves in jail; [110] but there was no
retrenchment in activity as far as Anna was concerned. In one area
there was a new departure; the support of English tenants. The
colliery owners at Ushaw Moor in Durham had evicted some miners
from their cottages; the L.L.L. sent them a donation of £50 and a
resolution of sympathy which was, according to local opinion, more
than the Trades Union offered. An address of thanks from the miners
'expressed a strong hope that the English working classes would see
their way towards reciprocating the kindness of the Irish people'. [111]
This would have been exactly to Anna's way of thinking; but it is a fair
supposition that 'the men' would have seen it as a dangerous precedent
and rank extravagance.

The Ladies were, in fact, getting through a great deal of money; it
was to be one of the accusations levelled against them after the release
of the Kilmainham prisoners, that they spent £70,000 sent from Paris
without accounting for it. It should be pointed out, however, that two
separate sources – Davitt's 'Secret History of the Land League' in
Cashman's biography and Mrs. M. F. Sullivan's account of the
movement for *Redpath's Weekly* in 1882 – give a list of accounts
submitted by Anna which add up to very nearly this amount. By June
1882, as much as £865 a week was being spent upon evicted tenants by
the L.L.L.; [112] the Ladies' special work, that of building houses for the
evicted tenants, was still an important preoccupation. Throughout the
spring of 1882 Anna had been less in the public eye than usual, due to
the death of public meetings. But on 14 June 1882, walking down
Westmoreland Street, she jumped out before Lord Spencer's horse,
caught it by the bridle, and hectored the Lord Lieutenant about the
forced stopping of building huts for tenants evicted near Limerick.
According to the newspapers Spencer was 'puzzled', and told an
aide-de-camp to escort her back to the pavement. [113] In a letter
complaining about the treatment of the tenants which she sent to the
press, Anna gave a characteristically different account:

> I met Lord Spencer on his way to the Castle subsequently, and
> asked him, whether the statement [that the building of the huts
> had been suppressed] was true? He answered that he could not
> hear what I was saying; but he could hear perfectly well, and I

told him so, to which he replied steadfastly, 'I cannot', and
refused to say anything else; from this I came to the conclusion
that Lord Spencer is really ashamed of himself, and would be
glad to escape from the odious position he has put himself in. [114]

But already the money for aiding evicted tenants was being choked off
by 'the men', released a month before. In July Anna was to be
prostrated by the news of Fanny's death; in August the L.L.L. would
breathe its last, and Anna would enter a political wilderness of
bitterness and disillusionment.

## IV

The outline of how the L.L.L. came to be disbanded is well known,
attested to by many authorities. Parnell, infuriated by the Ladies'
extremism and financial extravagance, cut off their funds and the
movement collapsed, leaving an implacable estrangement between him
and his sister. [115] The sequence of events was, however, rather more
complex than that, and Anna's own account is enlightening about this.
After Forster's resignation and the release of 'the men', there was a
reaction which infuriated her: it was assumed that the Ladies had
'beaten Forster' and that the fight was over. 'This fictitious triumph',
she wrote, 'was even worse than the cold atmosphere of censure that
we had so long been used to'; [116] Anna saw the rapprochement with
Gladstone as a terrible betrayal. There was, for the exhausted Ladies,
only one advantage: 'our long nightmare was over . . . they could have
no excuse for leaving the work they had made on our shoulders for
much longer'. [117] But at a meeting with the released M.P.s the L.L.L.
was amazed to be met with polite surprise from the men when it
announced that it wanted to quit. The reasons it gave were first,
simple exhaustion (Anna wrote time and time again of how she would
have welcomed prison 'for a rest'), and, second, that 'it was morally
impossible for us to go on working with the men' – which to her
'hardly sounded emphatic enough'. [118] She admits in her memoir,
however, that such antipathy may not have been universal. The
executive of the L.L.L. numbered twenty-five, not all of them closely
connected with its organisation; the anomosity between the two
leagues may not have been realised by all the ladies involved.

In any case, the Ladies consented to continue for the present. The
Kilmainham Treaty had left everyone exhausted by the Land League,
Anna remarked, except the Government; 'for the Land Leaguers
worked just as hard for a sham as anybody could have done for a
reality'. [119] Demands for legal costs continued to flood in from evicted
tenants, for there was no pause in the landlords' machinery. Anna, as
usual, far preferred to concentrate upon housing the evicted tenants;

her distrust of money payments was unabated. But the Land League refused to allocate money for housing, and remained evasive about what their position was as regarded a full-scale resistance to paying rents, which the Ladies still advocated. Relations between the Leagues deteriorated. May, June and July of 1882 passed without any explanation while the ladies were 'kept to the grindstone' – and the Land League, to Anna's extreme annoyance, used the L.L.L.'s account to make grants for legal costs and then refused to reimburse the Ladies from Paris. The L.L.L.'s bank began to worry; Anna told them to stop the cheques if they liked, hoping that this would force the men to resolve the situation. The Ladies did not wish to dissolve, and precipitate a public quarrel; and they were not emphatic enough with the men in private. They were still, moreover, expected to do all the hard work.

The men's policy came out into the open when the L.L.L. overdraft reached £5,000. They refused to discharge it unless the Ladies dissolved – while still undertaking to take over the job of considering all applications for legal aid and making recommendations upon them to the men. In other words, they were to lose autonomy and continue as workhorses – working on a scheme with which Anna, at any rate, fundamentally disagreed. When the men presented this ultimatum, in the form of a document to be signed by the Ladies, the remaining scales dropped from their eyes. [120] They did not fear legal distraint, since the leading Ladies had followed Anna's example and located their personal savings far away from Ireland. So they told the men that they would hand over their records and do any outstanding secretarial work, but would cooperate no further.

There seemed only two ways out of the deadlock: dissolution and failure to honour their debts, or compliance with the men's request. Finally, the Ladies overcame the difficulty by sleight of hand. They copied out the Land League ultimatum, leaving out the clause which bound them to consider applications incurred by the men. This meant in effect no work at all, since the Ladies had regularly avoided making any such recommendations. They signed the altered document 'lavishly' and returned it. The men welcomed it. Either they never noticed the alteration until the Ladies' debts had been paid, or they just decided to take the easy way out. 'Perhaps', noted Anna with acerbity, 'they thought there was no end to our folly; if they did, perhaps the thought was not unnatural'. [121]

In August 1881 the L.L.L. was dissolved. There had been one last scare that the small emergency fund would be inadequate to cover some final obligations to evicted tenants; but it proved sufficient. 'So at length the ghost of the Ladies' Land League rested in peace.' [122]

This was the substance of Anna's account, written twenty-two years afterwards; but it seems definite that hindsight was no part of her attitude, and that her reaction in 1882 was much as she recalled it in 1907. On 19 July 1882 she wrote a long lettter to a priest named Father Cantwell which was printed in the *Nation;* her point was that at this stage evictions and landlord oppression must be expected to *increase*. Landlordism had not been given the death-blow; instead the beast had been enraged by superficial wounding. Moreover, the Land Courts would work to the advantage of the landlord in facilitating the raising of rents 'if once they can break down the pressure on the Land Court from the other side'. Therefore, she continued, the supreme effort was needed *now;* it was no longer sufficient to rely upon Irish America; the tenants must plan ahead and organise by subscribing a shilling in the pound on the valuation of the estates where they lived; and this must be collected before the landlord could claim it for rent. [123]

Given the condition of rural Ireland in the late summer of 1882, this was not a realistic assessment. Landlordism may not have been killed outright, but the principle of the 1881 act was far nearer to a death-blow than to the glancing injury which was Anna's estimate of it. However, accurate or not, the point is that Anna's analysis of the situation was the same in 1882 as she outlined it to be in 1907; her approach to the Land Act, to the question of advancing money for legal costs, and her whole attitude to the course the Land War should take was as different from that of her brother as it could possibly be. Given this, it was impossible that there should not be friction between the two organisations as soon as the Land League leaders were released.

Nonetheless, the extent of this difference is never mentioned by the memoirs of those prominent during the era; the L.L.L. is generally treated in an indulgent and slightly dismissive way, with its members portrayed as eccentric hoydens. Anna wrote furiously to Dr Sigerson in 1907 that all the memoirs of the 1880s 'have libelled and ridiculed us in the most outrageous way'. [124] Andrew Kettle gives the most sympathetic view of them; his ideas about land were closer to Anna's than to her brother's. But his memoir was not published until long after Anna's death. Davitt alone implies that the Ladies were implacably opposed to Parnell's approach, when he described Parnell grimly telling him that 'they told me in Dublin, after my release, that I ought to have remained in Kilmainham'; [125] Davitt defended the organisation to Parnell (though this did not prevent Anna from dismissing his *Fall of feudalism* as 'a mass of lies'). [126] Most accounts, however, accept the view that the L.L.L. was disapproved of simply because of its 'extremism' and overspending; the antipathies that had existed since its foundation are never mentioned.

Here again, however, the invaluable Katharine Tynan adds some vivid details from the Ladies' side: she describes Parnell's dislike of the L.L.L. from the beginning, and his 'grim smile' at being treated irreverently by the organisation's treasurer. [127] There was also, according to Katharine Tynan, gossip about the O'Shea affair in the Ladies' office; someone jestingly referred to it in front of Anna and was silenced by 'Miss Parnell's pale, sibylline smile'. [128] She stated that Parnell knew of this gossip, but she admitted that she was unable to remember whether it was during the heyday of the L.L.L. or later that a lady who had spoken of the affair received from Parnell a letter that was 'a masterpiece of dignified and terrible rebuke'. [129] These sidelights conform the likelihood that Parnell never felt warmly towards the organisation from the beginning.

There was certainly open war from the moment Parnell stepped outside Kilmainham. William O'Brien recognised that the Ladies would naturally be critical of the Treaty, but added contradictorily that the only argument Parnell had with them was financial. [130] This is unnecessarily ingenuous. Davitt described to Barry O'Brien Parnell's fury on meeting him after his release from Dartmoor, when they journeyed down to London together: he emphasised Parnell's fury at the 'anarchy' let loose by the Ladies, and the disagreement he had with Davitt some weeks later when he first tried to stop their funds. [131] Davitt told the same story in his own memoir six years later. [132] Parnell's own view of his disagreement with Davitt over the matter is given in a letter he wrote on 20 August to Mrs O'Shea:

> The two D's [Dillon and Davitt] have quarrelled with me because I won't allow any further expenditure by the Ladies and because I have made arrangements to make the payments myself for the future. They were in hopes of creating a party against me in the country by distributing the funds amongst their own creatures, and are proportionately disappointed. [133]

At several points throughout her memoir, Parnell's wife makes references to the folly of the L.L.L., with their 'incitements to crime and wild expenditure'. [134] Mrs O'Shea believed that 'Parnell wrote to her [Anna] again and again from prison, pointing out the crass folly of the criminality for which the Ladies' Land League now solely existed'; [135] this is unlikely, for Parnell wrote to Sir Charles Russell in 1889: 'I know nothing about the distribution of the *Irish World* by the Ladies' Land League; I was then in Kilmainham and was not allowed to communicate with them.' [136] and he had by then little reason to prevaricate about the subject. But while contradicting the assertion that he often wrote to Anna in disapproving terms, this reference suggests that the Ladies were more directly involved with radical nationalism than was the Land League – a contention which is borne out by references to them in W. M. Lomasney's correspondence with John Devoy in February 1881, which mentions telegraphing to Anna 'in such a way that she alone could understand it'. [137] Given Parnell's initial dislike of the movement, his disapproval of the tendencies of their policy while he was in prison, and his own change of approach when he came out of Kilmainham, it was inevitable that he should have suppressed the L.L.L. as soon as he could. The factor of expense provided him with both an excuse and a strategy for this, but was not in itself a primary cause.

The account of the suppression given by Anna in her 'Tale', therefore, is a valid one; but it has one serious discrepancy. Why, one asks, did Anna herself – by now a national celebrity and a woman of influence as well as inspiration – simply accept the inevitability of dissolution without even an attempt at public justification, much less an effort to keep the Ladies' Land League afloat? She had stormed into Tim Healy's lodgings and attacked him because of articles he wrote (at Parnell's instigation) criticising the L.L.L.; [138] and her defiant letter to Father Cantwell on 19 May shows that she was prepared to continue organising the tenants. Yet after this opening volley she fired no more shots, and the L.L.L. was dissolved in August. There is an important omission here; and it arises, not from any desire on Anna's part to mislead, but from her peculiar approach to writing history. She believes that persons were unimportant as their actions, unlike those of groups or classes, 'are not met with again' in history. [139] And her 'de-personalising' approach meant that she left out what must be considered a vital factor in the suppression of the L.L.L. – the fact that on 20 July 1882, the very day after Anna wrote to Father Cantwell stressing that the fight must go on, Fanny Parnell died in her bed at Bordentown; and Anna was instantly precipitated into a nervous and physical breakdown from which she did not emerge until the end of the summer.

A fortnight after Fanny's death she was still dangerously ill and unable to work; [140] meetings of the L.L.L. were at first cancelled, and then began to convene without her. [141] She did not attend any of the meetings which organised the dissolution of the L.L.L. and appointed a working committee to wind up business. Early in August her condition had been critical, and Parnell and other members of the family had been summoned to Dublin; even after a partial recovery, her doctors said she could not work again 'for a long time'. [142] Contemporary opinion attributed her breakdown as much to overwork as to grief, stating that 'strong men have broken down under labours less severe', much less someone of her frail constitution and self-denying habits. [143] Katharine Tynan remembered Anna's extremely distressed state long after Fanny's death; she could not be left alone in Hume Street, where she paced up and down her room all night. All the evidence shows that she was completely shattered, mentally and physically, at the very juncture when she needed reserves of strength most; and the comparative ease with which the Ladies' organisation gave way is explained.

There is, moreover, some indication that when she recovered, Anna refused to consider herself as party to the submission. When the National Executive of the L.L.L. announced its dissolution in August, it stated that local branches could decide for themselves whether or not to continue;[144] and as late as December English branches were still meeting, one of which sent a small sum 'to Miss Anna Parnell in aid of the evicted tenants'. Anna replied with a letter which acknowledged receipt of the donation and asked the ladies to continue in their efforts to secure money in aid of the evicted tenants.[145] When her illness was over, she may have attempted to struggle on.

She was, however, by now out of the political picture; and so she was to remain. Her attitude continued unbending. Early in the following year a branch of the L.L.L. still active in St Louis sent her $200 'for the poor of Ireland', and she wrote back refusing to 'act as almoner', and blaming the Irish tenantry's insistence on paying rent for their present misfortunes.[146]

This letter was written from 7, Hume Street, as was a note she sent Katharine Tynan in August 1885, acknowledging her gift of a book of poetry;[147] but in 1886 William O'Brien heard that she had taken up residence in a painters' colony on the Cornish coast.[148] Up to her departure she still followed Irish politics; in February 1886 she wrote to the *Freeman* defending T. D. Sullivan, who had been criticised for his opposition to O'Shea's candidature in Galway. Anna praised the *Nation* for having sided with the obstructionists in the 1870s instead of 'doing as others did, holding back and waiting for events before taking sides' – probably a blow aimed at the *Freeman* itself.[149] She went on to give her own views on O'Shea's return, eventually taking a surprisingly conciliatory position: while she agreed with Sullivan's view of a 'Gladstone Whig' being chosen for an Irish constituency, the matter should be let drop. If the Irish party wanted O'Shea, they might as well have him, and make the best they could of the bargain. The *Freeman* did not print Anna's letter; she sent a draft of it to Sullivan himself, who incorporated it in his memoirs.[150]

She was still living in Cornwall in 1889. Katharine Tynan, entering the New Gallery in Regent Street with her old friend W. B. Yeats in the summer of that year, was startled to find Anna there 'in rapt contemplation of a picture'.[151] Anna had been painting in Cornwall, and had come up to London for the day. To Katharine Tynan's surprise, her companion was mistaken by Miss Parnell for John Dillon : 'a most unlikely thing'. On finding out who it was, 'she was very much interested'. What the poet thought of being taken for Dillon is not recorded. It must have been an encounter worth witnessing.

It is not surprising to find her living in Cornwall. She certainly disliked England; but she felt for Ireland a lasting bitterness. Her experiences in land agitation and politics had left her in 1882 with an attitude which she gives vent to in one of the few passages of her 'Tale' to reflect her own feelings:

> However long I might live, I knew it would never again be possible for me to believe that any body of Irishmen meant a word of anything they said. It is true that I had been inside the Land League. Allowing, however, for the utmost difference between the views of insiders and outsiders, a feeling must have been created amongst the latter that something had been very wrong in the Land League, for so much cry to have ended in so little wool. [152]

She therefore decided that the Irish Party lost credibility generally, and the right sort of person stopped identifying with it after 1882; self-seekers and humbugs came to the fore. She felt this analysis borne out by the Home Rule Bill, which she saw as a hypocritical 'absurdity'; [153] even the Plan of Campaign came too late and was not based on a sound principle; [154] and the later Land Acts she considered pro-landlord, if anything. The collapse of the disciplined Irish Party in 1891–2 seemed to bear out her gloomiest prognostications. When she wrote bitterly about the decline of Irish politics, the élitism of her own approach is finally and categorically stated:

> The only difference between the Irish ship of state as she has now become and what she had been before is that the colours under which she had previously sailed in secret are now nailed to the mast. Anybody who does not like the flag need no longer have anything to do with it. Those to whom it was invisible once can see it now, and no victims need waste their strength, money and time under a misapprehension as to its real nature. This gain is surely a set-off to the infinitesimally small chance, which is all that has been lost, of *a minority being able to seize some unexpectedly magnificent opportunity and by its aid turn the national rudder against the dead weight of the majority.* [155]

The Irish tendency to neutralise action by too much talk beforehand is something she attacks mercilessly in the closing pages of her account; and she perceptively expected 'armed rebellion to be the next thing either tried or played at here', for if the Fenian tradition had once been ridiculed, the Land League and the Irish Party had by 1907 made themselves every bit as open to ridicule. Anna did not live to see Easter Week 1916; but it would not have surprised her, and there were many elements in its making which would have appealed to her greatly.

Anna never spoke to her brother again after 1882. His wife wrote that he regretted this, and several times made overtures to his sister, 'of whom he was really fond, and for whose strength of mind and will he had much respect'; but she never acknowledged his letters, and when they met by accident once or twice she resolutely cut him dead.[156] Parnell told William O'Brien the same story; he asked O'Brien for news of her in 1886, and added: 'She has never spoken a word to me since I stopped that account of the Ladies' Land League'.[157] Anna, he told O'Brien, 'might have been great in anything'. He had spoken of her to Andrew Kettle in similarly glowing terms some years before, as someone 'never at a loss, and never mistaken in her judgement'.[158] This was long before the rift between brother and sister. But some sort of admiration for Anna's great qualities must have remained in Parnell's mind, as well as a residual affection. The same was probably true from Anna's side; Katharine Tynan wrote that 'they were devoted to each other'.[159] It is likely that Anna's arrogance and pride had a good deal to do with the maintenance of the break between them; judging from her writing, it was her chief fault. But she had more to be arrogant about than most people. Her loyalties were shown in 1891 to be with her brother; perhaps her attitude was reinforced by her contempt for 'the dead weight of the majority'. A typical flash of Anna's spirit comes out in a letter she wrote to the *Irish Times* after Parnell's death, objecting to the choice of Glasnevin as a burial place: she said that the statement that her brother's body 'belonged to the Irish people' was only true if their having killed him gave them a title to it.[160] A few years before, she had written a poem in which she stated that she would welcome death as a release from 'this world's Hell'; the alienation and bitterness testified to on every page of her 'Tale of a great sham' had entered her soul after the collapse of the Ladies' Land League, and settled there henceforth. Alfred Webb wrote of her brother that 'he broke his life; it was not rounded off and perfected';[161] the same was true of Anna, though instead of dying dramatically amid the destruction of her life's work, she lived on in disillusionment – one of the most likeable, and possibly the most admirable, of the Parnells. The publication of memoirs about the period of her political activity which ridiculed the L.L.L. or dismissed it indulgently was galling to her; she felt cheated by her contemporaries and undervalued by posterity. As well as painting, she found refuge in writing poetry, most of it satirical parody in an anti-British vein. Some of her more personal verses, however, have a sparseness and a memorable simplicity reminiscent of her sister's American namesake, Emily Dickinson. The title of my study of Anna comes from one such poem, 'The Journey', an allegorical view of her career and life; its bleak stanzas provide a fitting conclusion.

> When I first began my journey
> My step was firm and light,
> And I hoped to reach a shelter

Before the fall of night.

But a band of thieves beset me
Quite early in the day;
They robbed me and then they cast me
All bleeding by the way.

And since that hour I have crawled,
A cripple, blind with tears;
While each step I've made has cost me
The pain and strain of years.

I've had no shelter from the storm,
No screen against the heat;
The sun has beat against my head,
The shards have cut my feet.

My fellow-travellers on the road
Bound for the selfsame goal
With purse and staff and scrip equipped
And limbs and raiment whole,

All point at me with scorn, and say:
'Why does he choose to roam?
For travelling he is not fit;
Cripples should stay at home'.

Alas! they do not know that I
Was once as fit as they
And that there is no turning back
For those who go this way.

The long dark shadows of the night
Are closing on me now,
And its clammy dews are lying
Heavily on my brow.

I see the light of the City
Where I may never win
And I know there's warmth and comfort
For those who are within;

And alone in the cold and darkness
I know that I must die,
And unburied in the desert
My bones will always lie.

# 5 Charles Stewart and John Howard

From 1875 until his brother's death in 1891, John Howard had little to do with Ireland; the most valuable passages in his memoir have to do with the period before Parnell entered politics. Nonetheless, the brothers remained closely connected; there was a bond between them which absence did not erode. However, because the relationship between the two brothers is something which I have referred to regularly throughout this study,[1] my treatment of John Howard at this point will be brief. His life after Parnell's death is better chronicled than that of any other member of the family; but during his brother's political ascendancy, John Howard remains a figure in the wings.

In view of the fact that he wrote a memoir, this seems an unexpected contention; but the most remarkable thing about John Parnell's book is the extent to which he rigorously excludes himself from it except where his life intersects with that of his brother. Possibly he was too conscious of the travesty published by his sister Emily some years before, in every chapter of which the author plays a starring and obtrusive role. In John's case, the omission of his own experiences is to be regretted. He tells us that he continued his experimental farming in the South, and travelled widely through the United States.[2] He had left for America just after his failure in the 1874 Wicklow election,[3] but returned in time for his brother's unsuccessful candidacy for Co. Dublin in the same year.[4] He then went back to Georgia, and next met his brother in New York during October 1876, when they visited the Independence Centenary exhibition at Philadelphia together.[5] They met again during Parnell's frantic American tour in 1880;[6] but they did not see each other again until John visited Avondale with his mother. He dates this as autumn 1885,[7] but she does not seem to have left America in that year, and John did not accompany her on her return to Avondale in 1886,[8] so this joint visit was probably in 1884, when Mrs Parnell came to Ireland after Arthur Dickinson's death.[9]

John returned to America, but was back in Wicklow in time to go shooting at Aughavannagh in 1886, and again in 1887; he was in England during the Special Commission hearings of 1889.[10] This seems to have been his last contact with Parnell. He heard of his brother's unexpected death in Atlanta,[11] and did not arrive back in Ireland until December 1891.[12]

John admits himself that he saw little of his brother in the 1880s, but states that he was 'in constant communication with [him] and followed his career in the newspapers'.[13] Communicating with Parnell was never easy; elsewhere John admits: 'even I, when I wished to arrange to meet him, had to do so by telegram, as if I sent on a letter in advance he rarely took much notice and I had to go and rout him out wherever he was stopping'.[14] When they did spend time together it was usually in Ireland, where the old associations of Avondale and their common interests in farming and mechanics kept up the strong bond between them. And John had an added interest in keeping in touch with his brother; for, as his candidature in the Wicklow election implied, he was politically sympathetic to Parnell's career.

This is not to say he can fairly be classed as a 'political Parnell'; I have said before that he alone partook of the elements of the two divisions of John Henry's Parnell's children.[15] He was primarily interested in experimental agriculture, and politics came only second to this – an attitude which he was capable of attributing rather ingenuously to others as well:

> I attributed a good deal of the antagonism shown towards me [in the Wicklow election] to the fact that I was the first to import frozen fruit from America to Ireland, which was followed by the importation of frozen meat, which local farmers thought would greatly injure their trade.[16]

In fact, John's transportation of frozen goods never became anything like a regular trade; and there were plenty of other reasons for his lack of support in the Wicklow election. He had stood unexpectedly, as the last moment, with no political record, and without wanting to in the first place; his brother, in fact, made his speeches for him. And as one of the local gentry suddenly running on a Home Rule ticket, he not unnaturally would have appeared in the guise of an opportunist. There was also the matter of there being initially two Home Rulers in the field already, and of John's indecisive temporary withdrawal.[17] Yet it was typical of the man that he found a simple and rather naïve answer to his failure in his agricultural pursuits; and even more typical that he returned to his farming with no regret whatsoever.

His interest, however, remained. He knew Patrick Ford in New York, and was in the habit of visiting him;[18] he met Davitt in American in 1878 and talked to him about the land question. In 1880 he helped Patrick Moran, the editor of the *Atlanta Constitution*, to found a Land League branch in that city; he also worked on the organisation of one in Savannah,[19] and he mentions in his memoir that he 'attended many meetings in New York'. John was a prominent enough figure in Irish-American politics at this time to be invited to the elaborate farewell dinner given by the Land League of New York to James Redpath in June 1881;[20] in the spring of that year he addressed a meeting of the New York Land League where he spoke of the universality of interest among the Irish in the land question and called for money: 'The agitation is not yet over; I am afraid it is only the beginning, because I do not think Gladstone will bring in a bill which will suit. I think Gladstone is willing, but those old fogey Englishmen will not let him do any good.'[21] Again, this analysis is what one would expect; a direct, rather over-simplified view, expressed with a moderation foreign to his sisters and – at this stage – to his brother. The same approach is to be seen in an interview which the *Chicago Citizen* conducted with him in February 1882; John volunteered the opinion that Parnell would continue his present tactics, the current ministry would be overthrown, and Home Rule quickly attained.[22] If Anna was infuriated by Charles in 1882, she must long since have become disillusioned with John's diffidently optimistic moderation.

Nonetheless, he was 'political' enough for his private life to have a certain publicity-value – reinforced, as time went by and the myth grew, by the fact that he was Parnell's brother. And, like the great man, he was vulnerable to publicity through his position as a landlord. There was evidently talk about this from an early stage; in her letter to T. D. Sullivan in 1880 Mrs Parnell said, ungrammatically but emphatically:

> He [John] has not evicted any tenants, though his are well able to pay their rents to him, at least in many cases having money in bank [sic] and have so far, I believe, paid him nothing, though offered a good reduction, while he, not being the head landlord, is obliged to use a legacy to pay Trinity College, the head landlord, the old rent demanded by them, and for fear of eviction himself.[23]

He may not always have been so indulgent. The *Irish Times* of 25 August 1882 carried a paragraph announcing that the previous Saturday 'a number of bailiffs proceeded to Mr John H. Parnell's estate in this county [of Armagh] and seized four farms for non-payment of rent – one in the townland of Lisoosley, and theree in the townland of Keenaghan'. These farms were to be put up for sale; the tenants evicted put up no opposition. This contention went uncontradicted; Lisoosley and Keenaghan were indeed part of the

Collure estate, and John was in financial trouble in 1882. [24] Nor was
this the only opportunity given the Tory press to point out what was,
they claimed, a serious anomaly. In November 1885 the *Irish Times*
reported that some of John's tenants at Moy, Co. Armagh, were served
writs for rents 'not a month overdue; in every one of these cases the
tenants, for sums of a few pounds, will be put to 30/– costs'. [25] The
paper went on to claim, incorrectly, that Charles Stewart had an
interest in the estate and fixed these rents, 'known as the greatest rack
rents in the county . . . but that was before Mr Parnell was known as a
politician'. The Collure rents had been reduced in the Land Courts
over the past few years – one from £63 15s 0d to £42. Such jibes may
have seemed insignificant at the time; but they had an undoubted
political importance, and memories about such things were long. In
1891 a rumour was abroad that John Parnell intended to contest a seat
at the next election for his brother's party, and the *Nation* snidely
remarked: 'We suppose that the choice has fallen upon him because of
his services to and sufferings for his country; the tenants of Mr Parnell
in county Armagh will more than ever appreciate the meaning of Mr
Parnell's pretensions'. [26] At the time of the evictions, however, there
were slightly extenuating circumstances – which the *Nation* in those
days would have been only too ready to point out. An eviction for
non-payment of rent in late 1882 was different from evicting in 1880
or 1881 – or so a moderate like John Parnell would certainly have felt.
Moreover, Collure was held from Trinity College under their
Perpetuity Leasing Act – and such estates were notoriously badly
managed by their head landlord. In 1882 Trinity sent a deputation to
Forster to lodge an objection to accusations that they 'crushed' leasees,
who were 'poor cultivators of the soil'; their case was that the college
estates were let to wealthy middlemen, and if anyone was responsible
for ill-treatment of tenants, it was the latter. [27] This drew a long, angry
and carefully substantiated letter from Lord Leitrim about the college
estates; he pointed out that Trinity raised head-rents to the middlemen
arbitrarily and unreasonably, and without considering any
improvements. In many cases (as with Collure) [28] there was already
very little profit margin between rents received and rent due. Others
wrote in similar terms. The last rent rise had been in 1882; John
Parnell's pressure on his tenants may have been forced upon him.

He was, as I have mentioned, in financial difficulties in 1882. [29] He
was still liable for a quarter of the £10,000 owed by Charles on
Avondale for the Wigram mortgage – an arrangement which pursues
the Parnell's muddled financial lives throughout the period like a
family spectre. John also owed his brother £1,515 outstanding on a
private loan. The interest alone on what he owed of Wigram's money
came to £1,050 in 1882. [30] For the £5,065 thus owed by him to
Charles in this year, the latter got a mortgage on Collure. I have

already referred to John's silence on this subject when he recalled that Charles asked him to back bills for £3,000 in 1881 to help their mother.[31] On these debts falling due, according to John, 'I had to sell what little capital I had, while my promising fruit business was crippled for want of money'. It is unlikely, however, that he was ever in the position of making much wealth out of his American business. He had to work extremely hard at it, and was mentioned in agricultural journals for his experimental ventures;[32] he was celebrated for growing peaches of unrivalled size, as well as for his innovations in frozen shipment. But time and time again in reading his memoir one is struck by the number of might-have-beens which marked his attitude and his life – his missed chance to inherit Avondale, his fling at politics, the alteration of his great-uncle's will,[33] the near misses where financial success was concerned: such as his advice to Charles to buy up one-lands in the American south when he had a chance to do so for a dollar an acre.[34] The same holds good for the many agricultural and industrial ventures which he planned at Avondale in the 1890s.[35] T. P. O'Connor said of him that 'he had the Parnell inclination to go in for enterprises that promised fortune and left only debt, and poor Parnell had to make up the losses'.[36] Whatever about his brother making up his losses, it is hard to avoid the conclusion that John was not cut out for success.

Perhaps partly because of this, he worshipped his brilliant brother; this comes clearly through every page of his memoir. His personal diffidence and his devotion to Charles have led to some unnecessarily dismissive judgements of him. T. P. O'Connor wrote: '[John] had some likeness to his brother, but it was a likeness that was rather like a caricature; he was a very amiable, very harmless, and rather a stupid man'.[37] Joyce's Simon Dedalus said that when they put John in Parliament, Parnell would come back from the grave and lead him out of the House of Commons by the arm.[38] This was not altogether likely, since Parnell had wanted his brother to run for parliament in 1884;[39] but such an interpretation of Charles' attitude towards his kindly, stammering elder brother is not inaccurate. John himself testifies to something like it in several revealing incidents:

> He and I were travelling together by train, when a number of enthusiasts followed us into the carriage. He straightened himself from his usual half-reclining position in the corner of the carriage, which he adopted when travelling, and said to me pettishly: 'Can't you get those people out of the carriage, John? They're annoying me.' I had to set about the very uncomfortable task of going up to each person and asking him whether he would mind leaving the carriage, as my brother wished to be alone.[40]

Nor was this peremptory tone an unusual one; at Avondale, John recalled, 'he used often to say: "Now, John, you might take a basket and go and pick some barberries for me" '.[41] There was also the incident of the two brothers meeting in Kildare Street and Charles – then at the height of his fame – not saluting John except by the most inconspicuous of winks: an action which John quite properly puts down to 'affectation'.[42] The untouched aura which Parnell cultivated did not allow a casual encounter on a Dublin street. When the acquaintance thus cavalierly treated was the celebrity's own brother, there was good excuse for resentment. The fact that John was not blind to the 'trace of affectation ... in this sphinx-like attitude towards the world in general' shows that he retained a degree of detachment; he had, after all, known his brother when there was nothing to single him out for greatness. But there was no element of bitterness in his attitude – though it might have been forgiven in one who was so often the loser by his brother's good fortune. From his side, Parnell does not seem to have made a habit of subjecting John to his 'sphinx-like attitude'. 'He was always specially fond', recalled John, 'of quizzing me with a kind of dry but always good-natured humour';[43] and at Avondale in 1884 he enthusiastically brought John over his sawmills and mining works, and listened to what he had to say.[44] The fact that Parnell inherited Avondale over his brother's head never seems to have come between them. John says that his brother often 'expressed regret' at this fact to him,[45] but this can have been scant comfort as he watched his brother pouring money into mines and quarries as mortgages accrued on the family estate – although, it is only fair to add, he himself would probably have done no differently.

Throughout Parnell's career, then, though seeing comparatively little of each other, the brothers' relationship was a close one. As was the Parnells' habit, their arrangements to meet were haphazard; a typical instance was when John and his mother came to Ireland in 1884 and 'found to our surprise that all our family had left Dublin';[46] they had to go to the reliable Alfred MacDermott to discover that Charles happened to be at Morrison's Hotel, and Emily was still down at Avondale. 'We are a peculiar family', Parnell once told William O'Brien, 'we are all very fond of each other, but somehow we do not seem to get on so well when we are too much together'.[47] This was, in general terms, no more than the truth. But, as in their childhood, between the two brothers there was a close bond which was only emphasised by their great dissimiliarity of character, and by the habit of the younger to expect the elder to do things for him as a matter of course. John accepted his role no less naturally; he was not made of the stuff of greatness, and he recognised it was equally as he realised his brother's genius. But there was a good deal more to him than O'Connor's description allows. He is a vital figure against which to define his brother; and his memoir is, I believe (despite several terminological inaccuracies) an under-rated source of material about Parnell. The balance of the brothers' relationship was set up before Charles became famous, and altered little during his career; this is why a chapter about their interaction upon each other between 1875 and 1891 need be no longer than this one. The life of John Howard Parnell took a more active turn after his brother's death, and his fortunes during this period will form the framework for a conclusion to this study. For, in a sense, John's life was as moulded and defined by that of his brother after the latter's death as much as it ever was while he was alive. It is typical of John that he ends his book with Charles' death; and although he was to experience bitter disillusionment both over Irish politics and the fortunes of Avondale in the 1890s, he rarely if ever allows a mention of this to enter his book. Their relationship tells as much about Parnell as it does about his brother. They were at the same time as unlike and as closely united as two brothers could be: yet another facet of the Parnell paradox. Parnell was fond of Theodosia and Emily, suffered his mother's excesses with equanimity, admired Fanny, and fought with Anna; but the retiring, diffident John Howard – politically sympathetic but rarely with him during his career, and whom Charles treated with a certain thoughtlessness and authority which both brothers accepted as completely natural – seems to have known him better than any of them.

*Epilogue: The Parnells and
Avondale after 1891*

# Epilogue: The Parnells and Avondale after 1891

No story of Greek history by a Greek dramatist tells of a family tragedy more striking and more complete.

T. P. O'Connor, *Memories of an old parliamentarian*, ii, 331.

## I

John Howard Parnell first arrived back in Avondale in December 1891, two months after his brother's sudden death amid the wreckage of his career. Almost at once he began his efforts both to retain Avondale and to take his brother's place: both destined to fail through a combination of unpropitious circumstances, lack of sympathy, and his own indecision and failure to appreciate and to cope with the realities of his position. He took up a position in Rathdrum life, became involved in nationlistic politics, and made brief return trips to America to bring back fruit-tree seedlings and other expedients to make Avondale pay.[1] His plans, which he publicised indefatigably, were to refurbish the orchards, establish cottage-industries (making baskets, walking-sticks and other articles), and keep the quarries going.[2] He bought the quarries from his sister-in-law, received orders for his new industries, and by 1896 described these involvements as 'getting nearly beyond my power'.[3]

But such optimism cannot have been carried unduly far. The quarries were soon sold again, and John's brave and imaginative little industries were not enough to make Avondale viable. It was primarily a landed estate, and he made no more money out of it on this level than his brother had done. The difference was that John attempted to; but without success. Case after case came to the Rathdrum Land Commission court, where Avondale tenants claimed a reduction, and generally got one.[4] Though hostile opinion attacked John for over-renting, it was the *valuation* which was, in most cases, reassessed;

the tenants were being asked no more than this. The reason for their objections at this time was simple; they were, for the first time in a long while, being pursued for their rents. John was prepared to bring ejectment suits for repeated non-payment, though he was otherwise a liberal enough landlord.[5] No tenant started proceedings to purchase; John would have seen no reason why they should not go on paying rent. But, as with his brother, his own peculiar position ensured maximum publicity for this.

Again like his brother, he ignored traditional farming in favour of schemes which never worked out. The fruit-trees were weakened by early frost; the wooden articles were discriminated against on the English market, and lack of capital forced him to sell out to an English company. 'We allow foreigners to grab everything', he lamented, 'to the destruction of our race.'[6]

His own experience certainly bore this out; and it was as true for the quarries as the other industries. John had bought them for £1,200 to prevent a Welsh company getting them, but was forced to sell out to a Scot a year later.[7] The quarries, already ailing at the time of Parnell's death, had ground to a halt afterwards; difficulties with the Arklow Harbour Board continued,[8] and the hiatus was prolonged by Kerr's sudden death only a month after his employer. John's plan was to form limited company to work them; for this, a foreign interest was necessary. By 1895 a hundred men were at work again with new machinery, a widened tramway, and a new railway;[9] but this was not possible with John's resources alone, and by 1898 he had sold his share in what were still called 'the Parnell Quarries'.[10]

From 1891, the destitution of the Parnell family had been more or less openly discussed, with rumours of mortgages and relief funds; it was generally felt that no matter what happened, the estate would have to be sold.[11] John raised several small mortgages,[12] but pinned all hopes upon his industries; and in May 1895 he wrote sadly to John Redmond: 'we will have to vacate Avondale any moment ... there is nothing to keep things going here'.[13] His incorrigible lack of realism continued, however; even while writing desperately to an American creditor for extension of an overdue loan, he was capable of adding a postscript about 'finding out if English primroses, wild ones, would bring a good price if they could be brought over by refrigerator'.[14] He also asked John Redmond if the Irish Party would back a bill for £100; Redmond's confidence cannot have been increased by John's additional note that he 'did not know what is to be done about the bills at Avondale for the last three months'.[15]

In 1898 he was receiving a small income of £150 a year as City Marshal of Dublin – a ceremonial post which, according to T. P. O'Connor, was arranged for him by the Parnellite Dublin Corporation.[16] It carried with it the duties of Registrar of

Pawnbrokers, which brought in an added £500 or so. He soon became involved in acrimonious disputes with the Pawnbrokers' Association, who could influence his salary,[17] and with the Irish Party over his taking part in the ceremonies attendant upon Queen Victoria's visit to Dublin.[18] Nor did he like the situation. 'It is my daily bread', he wrote gloomily to a friend, 'but it is a position not suited to my tastes at all, as I have been engaged all my life in natural enterprises'.[19]

In 1901 he could write proudly that he was practically out of debt;[20] but by then he had been deeply disappointed in other spheres. One of these was politics. In 1892 he had sounded out the ground with the Irish Party,[21] and put his name up for the West Wicklow election, without campaigning. In 1895 he was narrowly elected for Meath – the first Independent victory there for three elections.[22] The *Independent* was jubilant, foretelling that he would be 'a tower of strength to his party';[23] but this was to rate poor John too highly. He rarely spoke at Westminster, where his stammer must have been a terrible handicap. Despite dutiful platform appearances and equivocal public statements, his real appeal was based solely on his relationship to his brother – whose mantle, as the *Wicklow Newsletter* unkindly put it, he had been persuaded to believe had fallen on himself.[24] He was painfully conscious of being held of little account; he told a reporter that he 'saw the situation plainly enough, though perhaps people think I don't',[25] and later told Redmond of the 'contempt and dislike' with which he had always been treated by other Irish members.[26] Though John himself said 'a man must have a very mean mind to quarrel with me',[27] his very inoffensiveness must have made him a marked man at this most squalid and back-biting era of Irish politics. Moreover, his attitude during the storm over the Queen's visit in 1900 made things no easier; he wrote to Redmond that he was 'in a social position different from other nationalists' and would not jeopardise it by boycotting the ceremonies. 'We have no quarrel with the Queen's doings ... my brother would have taken the same view'.[28] But Redmond's own welcoming of the Royal visit had been violently attacked by other Irish members;[29] John's separation from the Irish party was now inevitable.

He was put out by what he accurately termed a 'trick'. No other candidate contested his constituency in 1900, so John did not need to place a deposit; but minutes before nominations closed J. L. Carew suddenly entered his name and the necessary deposit for an opposed candidate. John had no time to complete similar formalities, and was disqualified, Carew being returned unopposed.[30]

It was little wonder that after this shabbiness John ran as an independent in the next election; but he was beaten by the official candidate.[31] Even before he was expelled from politics, a deep disillusionment had set in; a long letter to an American friend described bitterly the apathy, obstruction and hypocrisy he had encountered in his industrial and political efforts, and his dislike of what Ireland had become.[32] Ironically, his sister Anna had made many of the same points after a very different process which led to a similarly bitter disillusionment. John's efforts to 'keep up my brother's memory'[33] met with further disappointment in the episode which set the seal upon his long canon of disappointments in the 1890s: the way Avondale was finally disposed of.

**II**

As early as March 1893, Alfred Macdermott had filed a petition for the sale of Avondale; the one thing, as Emily Dickinson observed, upon which all the solicitors could agree.[34] Court cases were being brought for recovery of debts, and much of the stock was already auctioned off. The actual sale was held off for five years; John wanted most of the tenants to purchase their holdings, and he himself planned to buy back the demesne.[35] The tenants themselves wanted some of the estate to be disposed of under the Land Act,[36] but nothing came of this. In any case, by 1899 a scheme was afoot for 'saving Avondale', backed by the Irish Party. The plan was for the estate to be bought as a 'Parnell monument'. This concept led to dissension. The Parnells felt 'political debts' had brought things to this pass, notably the £5,000 raised by Parnell on a bank mortgage and now imprisoned in the Paris Funds.[37] They therefore assumed that the plan was to buy back the estate for the family. The Irish Party, however, wanted it for 'the nation'; and the ultimate object of the appeal remained very vague. A fund-raising tour of America produced $50,000, including $10,000 from Tammany Hall 'to secure the retention of the Parnell homestead in the family'.[38] John, however, was soon involved in acrimonious arguments with Redmond, who earmarked only a certain proportion of the fund for redeeming Avondale and wanted the house as 'a public monument' in any case; John felt the Party's plans would make 'gate-keepers' of the family and cause local unemployment.[39] He finally went ahead with a plan of his own, selling the estate in 1900 to a Dublin businessman called Boylan for £8,000 on condition that he could repurchase in two years.[40] For the next two years John mounted countless schemes to buy back the estate, backed by some body or other; but Boylan's price went up, the Irish Party refused to co-operate, and even when the effects were auctioned off John had to let the library go to an English buyer.[41] In an endless correspondence with Redmond John mooted plan after plan; Boylan even extended the option; but nothing came of it. In 1904 Boylan died and Sir Horace Plunkett persuaded the Board of Agriculture to buy the estate for £10,000 and start a forestry school there. By then Avondale had in reality been long lost to the Parnells, but John never got over it. He hated 'the English government' owning it and objected to trees being cut down and employees laid off; one of the few bitter passages in his memoir (which avoids all mention of his own political efforts and personal disappointments after 1891) deals with it. [42] It is surprising that Avondale's future as a forestry school did not please him; it was a more worthwhile fate than many of the alternatives suggested. But he was not easy to please where the estate was concerned; and the Irish Party was, from his point of view, unnecessarily flinty about the Monument Fund. He must have been an irritating man to do business with, with his sudden bursts of optimism and his flashes of stiff-necked pride. But it is hard not to think that he was treated meanly.

The same is true for the epilogue to the disposition of the estate: Redmond's takeover of Aughavannagh. In the 1890s Redmond and others rented the shooting there; John suggested that he and Redmond combine to take the lease for the barracks when it came up for renewal, and renovate the building. [43] The arrangement was never satisfactory, punctuated by squabbles over sharing expenses and embittered by disagreements in other areas. John eventually sold Redmond the lease, but only after lengthy and acrimonious haggling; Redmond refused to meet John for discussions. One of John's final stipulations when the sale at last went through was that the place be kept in memory of his brother; perhaps he saw it as a sort of monument. [44]

In any case, he no longer went there much. He used a cottage at Avondale for fishing trips to Rathdrum from his new residence at Upper Mount Street in Dublin; [45] later he rented fishing at Laragh Castle in County Wicklow and is remembered round Annamoe as a lonely figure walking the roads in the area. He remained City Marshal, though Joyce's Leopold Bloom heard he never wore his uniform; Haines and Buck Mulligan watched him, a grey ghost of a man, playing chess in the D.B.C. cafe. [46] His last years were not lonely; in 1907 he married Olivia Mateer, the widow of Archibald Mateer of Carlingford, Co. Louth. They lived first at Clarinda Park, Dun Laioghaire, near where John and the rest of the family had rented the O'Conor Don's house fifty years before. Later they moved to Sion House, Glenageary, which cannot have been far from the first house, Khyber Pass, in which Delia Parnell installed her family after her husband's death. His stepson, Captain Mateer, remembers visits to Wicklow, but the connection with Avondale was gone. John published *C. S. Parnell: a memoir* in 1916, and lived on until 1923, the last of the Parnell children to die. The obituaries were kind but dismissive; [47] one mentioned that he had became a subscriber to the Unionist Party; and a photograph showed him proudly displaying one of his prize peaches from Georgia. [48] This recalled what was probably the happiest period of his life; what followed his brother's death was a protracted, saddening anti-climax. He could have said, as his sister Emily did, that 'this was the only reward that patriotism had brought us';[49] but he did not, for that was never his style.

### III

After 1891, the remainder of Parnell's family lived as they always had done. Mrs Parnell continued to reside in America, after a brief visit to Ireland in December 1891.[50] She issued some political dicta upon the presidential election of 1892,[51] and she was in Ireland again in 1894.[52] However, in April 1895 most newspapers carried reports describing how she had been attacked and robbed near Bordentown;[52] she received severe head injuries. A delegation from the Independent Party which visited her a month later found her 'at the point of death':[54] by March 1896 she had rented out Ironsides and was living at Trenton. She was described as possessing all her faculties, but not yet fully recovered; she intended going abroad to join Anna.[55]

She was still, as ever, capable of giving interviews. American papers in the summer of 1896 carried reports of her opinions regarding Parnell's death:

> Mrs Parnell believes her son was either assassinated by English agents or is still alive. She leans to the latter conviction. She says the night he died he retired to bed complaining of rheumatism in his left arm, and his death was pronounced by physicians to have been caused by rheumatism of the heart. 'Whoever heard', she asked, 'of rheumatism passing from a man's left arm to his heart and killing him in a single night?' Mrs Parnell has a number of theories to account for her son's alleged disappearance.[56]

In the same interview, she declared her intention of selling up Ironsides and returning to Avondale, and she arrived there for the last time in September 1896. Having fallen badly on her voyage over, she was 'very infirm'; Emily Dickinson, meeting her at Kingsbridge, found her 'a changed and broken figure'.[57] While at Avondale, financial worries surrounded her. Emily Dickinson describes her 'going without certain luxuries to which her age and her position entitled her',[58] and in March 1897 some movement was made among nationalist groups to begin a 'Parnell family fund'; it was reported that 'Mrs Delia Stewart Parnell and some members of her family are in deep distress'.[59] There were many subscriptions, but this fund rapidly became absorbed into the Parnell monument collection.

Delia Parnell lived on at Avondale until her death in March 1898. Emily describes her as passing a sedentary life, as 'she did not like driving';[60] well into her eighties, she liked country life as little as ever.

Her death followed a bizarre and terrible incident. A dinner-party was organised by Emily (and later described by her to great dramatic effect)[61] where her mother shone conversationally as in the days of her youth; Mrs Parnell retired late, and arose early to breakfast in her room. Sitting by the fire, she either fell into the flames or her clothes caught a spark from it; she was found ablaze, with the room 'afire at several points'. After her rescue, she rallied a little, but died the following day, 27 March 1898.

There was an enormous funeral at Glasnevin on 1 April 1898; the intention had been for a private ceremony at Rathdrum [62] but the Independent party made it a great occasion. Delegates came from all over Ireland, and there was a procession through Dublin, which numbered celebrities like Maud Gonne.[63] But in the many long lists of notables at Mrs Parnell's funeral, there is no mention of any of her neighbours among the Wicklow gentry. In her death as in life, what defined her was her son's reputation: not the Irish county circle she had married into over fifty years before and to which she had never been able to adapt.

The end of the remaining Parnells can be told briefly. Anna died in 1911. She remained reclusive after 1891. T. P. O'Connor and others heard she was penniless and attempting to get a book of poems published: 'We got the poems published and sent her a sum which was supposed to be the profits – entirely imaginary – of the sale of the book.'[64] She contributed an introduction to Jennie Wyse-Power's *Words of the dead chief* in 1894, which repeated the judgements of her political days, and foreshadowed what she was to say in her 'Tale of a great sham': 'the smallest minority owes no allegiance to the proudest majority on the smallest matter of principle'.[65] She was not, however, forgotten: in 1899 the *Independent* held a competition for an essay on 'the most remarkable woman in Irish history' and Anna was high on the list of the most popular subjects (in the catholic company of St Brigid, Devoragilla, Ann Devlin, Maire, Sarah Curran and Deirdre.)[66] She appeared in Dublin in 1907–8, when she gave a lecture on the Ladies' Land League,[67] and campaigned for C. J. Dolan, who was standing as Sinn Fein candidate for Leitrim.[68] It did not prefigure a return to politics; it was said later that she was pelted with eggs on the hustings and refused to speak in Ireland again.[69]

She had not remained closely in touch with her family, though she sailed to America after the attack on her mother in 1895. She also corresponded with her sister Theodosia, who was in touch with her at the time of her death and who wrote to Helena Molony, a friend of Anna's, about the 'Tale of a great sham' and Anna's anxiety to have it published.[70] But when a middle-aged woman calling herself 'Cerisa Palmer' was drowned in the sea-baths at Ilfracombe on 20 September 1911, it was some days before it could be ascertained that this was

Anna. She swam out to sea, ignoring the attendant's advice, was
pulled under in the heavy swell, and drowned very quickly. Giving
evidence at the inquest, her landlady remarked that 'she had said it
was not much of a day to go bathing and deceased said "Rubbish" . . .
Miss Palmer preferred to do as she pleased'.[71] Anna's indomitable,
astringent spirit comes strongly through the report of the inquest
proceedings – as strongly as through the absorbing memoir which she
left behind her.

Henry died four years later, in November 1915, at Lausanne.[72] He
remained out of the picture in the years after his brother's death,
except for writing to the newspapers contradicting Emily's assertions
about Parnell's life at Cambridge.[73] He continued to raise an income
from his Irish estate.[74] By 1897 he was living abroad, in Heidelburg.[75]
A son of his, Harold de Mowbray, lived with John Parnell and his wife
after 1915. Henry's residence on the Continent, together with his
self-effacing life-style, makes his movements no easier to chart at the
end of his life than at its beginning.

Emily, on the contrary, died in a blaze of publicity. The last years of
her life seem to have been confused and unhappy. John had found her
'almost starving' at Avondale in 1891.[76] She moved to Bray in 1892,
and spent the summers there for the next few years. Her daughter
married a man named O'Clery, of whom Emily disapproved; he died
after three years, and Delia became a nurse; she was living at
Avondale when Mrs Parnell died in 1898. When Avondale was sold,
Emily moved to Dublin, and Delia emigrated to Australia, meeting an
Englishman named Wright on board ship and marrying him on
arrival. As for Emily, she re-entered Dublin life and bought two
horses.

> No longer young, I yet looked younger than I was, and my seat
> on horseback, for which I had ever been remarkable, was as good
> as of yore . . . sometimes I drove the pair of superb animals,
> conscious of their pedigree, together in a phaeton, on which
> occasions their high-stepping action was the admiration of
> Dublin.[77]

But this was not how others saw her; it was at exactly this period that
Joyce's invaluable observer mentions 'his [Parnell's] other sister, Mrs
Dickinson, driving round with scarlet harness, bolt upright like
Surgeon MacArdle'.[78] T. P. O'Connor described her eccentricity as
'wildly and publicly developed', and was told of her 'driving about
Dublin in the weirdest garments – flaring yellow or some such
outrageous colour'.[79] In these days, as 'a prominent and somewhat
grotesque figure in Dublin life', there is a strange echo of her mother
about Emily; she even gave an 'American tea', which recalled the
far-off days of Lord Carlisle.[80] As she tells the story, she was

impoverished at the height of her social success by the cessation of her annuity from her brother's estate, so she 'decided to leave Dublin and abandon my meteoric reappearance in social circles'; [81] when she wrote these words, at the end of her haphazard memoir, she was living in a remote fishing-village, where she was sustained by visits from Irish friends and her one good friend, 'Lady –' (another echo of Delia Tudor Stewart Parnell). A grandiloquent farewell to her readers from this unaccustomed tranquillity ends the book.

But this was not the end of the story. [82] *A patriot's mistake* was published in 1905, and made her some money. She characteristically spent this by moving into a Dublin hotel and living lavishly for a while. At this point, when she was living as though she had money, she meet a guardsman named Captain Cuthbert Ricketts, younger than she; they were hastily married and went to Monte Carlo. Within days, the arrangement foundered; John Howard Parnell, who knew little of all this, was summoned out to Monte Carlo, where he found an hysterical Emily abandoned by Ricketts. The stability of her mind was, not surprisingly, further affected by this experience; she was more or less unaccountable from this period on.

She lived on and off with John Howard; but she was resident in Wales in May 1918. She was under a doctor's care, but left and came to Dublin. She stayed in a hotel for some days, and then on 13 May made her way to the South Dublin Union Poorhouse, where she demanded entry as a pauper and gave her name as 'Miss Roberts'. [83] She died there six days later, and was only then identified. In a statement to the papers, John Parnell said that she had £1,000 from Captain Dickinson, £1,000 from Sir Ralph Howard, and a life annuity for £100 which she had sold for £650 'a few years ago' (thus giving the lie to Emily's statement that this had lapsed after she re-entered public life). [84] She had also inherited £850 from her mother, and her book had brought her £600. She had therefore enough capital to live off. It is unlikely that Emily would have used her capital wisely; she had already commuted one annuity, and splashed out on her book's earnings. But she could have gone to John's house to stay; it seems unquestionable, as Mrs John Parnell surmised, that 'her mind was somewhat deranged'; [85] it had been so for many years, and she died as unreasonably as she had lived.

Only John and Theodosia were left, and she died on 17 March 1920. In April 1893 her husband had been in charge of a District Coastguard Station on the Clare coast, [86] but by 1911 the Pagets were living at Weybridge again. [87] Claud Paget died in 1917; when Theodosia died three years later she was living at 38 Denbigh Street, Pimlico. [88] With John's death three years later, the Avondale Parnells were all gone. With them snapped the last threads leading back to the background and the family which had, far more than has been recognised, defined and influenced the life of the greatest of them all.

*Conclusion*

# Conclusion

This study of Parnell, as its subtitle implies, is an exercise in contextual history. The man has often been seen as a phenomenon, a Hero after Carlyle's mould, and Heroes, like Patrick Kavanagh's Gods, make their own importance: environmental influences are dismissed into insignificance. By seeing Parnell against his background – in the continuing Wicklow tradition, as well as surrounded by his extraordinary family – I have attempted to redress the balance. He may well remain a hero: his political career is no part of my study here. But along the way enough of the often-adduced myths surrounding his *persona* have been re-examined to show aspects of the man in a different light.

The family myth which played such an important part in launching him politically was totally distorted: Sir John Parnell was at best an ambiguous 'Patriot'. Charles Stewart Parnell was not a well-off young gentleman who aspired to do his duty for the national ideal, and lost his fortune in the process: he was an aggressive young county buck, with an estate that was heavily encumbered by debts long before he entered politics. His mother, influential as she was, can no longer be seen as a fervent nationalist who educated her children in political principles from the cradle: she seems instead to have been intellectually lightweight, socially snobbish, mentally erratic, and far out of her depth as regards her son's politics. What influence she had on him and on his sisters was more to do with a sense of alienation from county opinion than with any positive political analysis. Moreover, Parnell's sisters Fanny and Anna have never been given their due: Fanny was more formidable than she has been painted, and Anna had a far more original importance than most publications have credited her with.

There are many other misconceptions which I have attempted to elucidate. But there are also, more importantly, some important positive aspects of Parnell's background which have never been properly emphasised. Sir John Parnell's importance in dictating the family tradition may have been a latter-day myth: but in the under-estimated figure of William Parnell is a potent influence. Equally important on the larger canvas is the whole fabric of Wicklow landed gentry – always conservative but including both a better type of landlord than elsewhere and odd examples of an enlightened social approach in James Grattan and William Parnell himself. Parnell's position in Wicklow society and his continuing relationships with the county provide a new definition of what has previously been seen simply as his eccentricity. His industries, for instance, took up more of his time (and his money) than has been recognised, especially in the later years of his life. Wicklow was not something he left behind him. It can be suddenly enlightening to consider his career in this light: to see him as a reforming Wicklow gentleman, with the inherent conservatism and arrogance of his class, but a 'modern' outlook where industry was concerned, and a readiness to accept the ending of the old land system (which had never proved profitable in his own case). His extraordinary qualities, of course, remain; and even before his death, too much of what he represented had been elevated to myth for it to be possible, or even valid, to demythologise him now. But he was not a myth to his brothers and sisters, nor to the Gaffney family at Avondale, nor to the long-suffering William Kerr. And he was not a myth to his 'county' contemporaries like Lord Meath, who had been to school with him, or the Bartons who had played cricket with him, or Lord Carysfort, who had urged him to take up his position in the county: nor to those who sniped at him on the Arklow Harbour Board. He was part of what all these people represented: he came from this background, and he remained far more integrated into it than has generally been realised.

Each section of this study has its own conclusions: some of these are repeated and amplified throughout. My study has been, in a sense, empirical, working from the broadest definitions (the Wicklow gentry and the Parnell family history) down to the particular product of this environment. Such a process was initially dictated by the dearth of specific Parnell papers; but I think it has its own validity. It has, however, necessitated an approach lengthier, more 'literary', and of a more narrative nature, than most analyses. Along with this, the same ground has sometimes been retraced. The intention is for an overall pattern to emerge: to see, in the broadest sense, a phenomenal politician defined against the non-phenomenal aspects of his background and his life. My approach, and the sharply compartmentalised structure of this study, precludes a pat conclusion. There is no 'therefore' at the end of this process: but I hope there are several overwhelming inferences, which I have attempted to draw out throughout and to indicate here. I have limited myself to certain areas of study as regards Parnell – those which have so often been ignored before.

The facts of Parnell's public life (though not their interpretation) have become almost a cliché: I have thus been left freer to examine his background as separate from his career. But the continuing influence of what surrounded him is what matters. When Sir Lewis Namier decided to examine the meaning of eighteenth-century politics along the same lines that Aeschylus used to determine the flight of crook-taloned birds, he was accused of not seeing the wood for the trees. This book in no way sets itself up to be Namierist. But as regards what made Parnell, it is an attempt to get into the wood: to examine what grows at the back of it, from the immense and atrophied trunks of past generations down to side-shoots, latter-day saplings and the surrounding undergrowth; with the eventual object of retreating to a new vantage and seeing trees and wood together.

# Appendices

Appendices

# Appendix 1:
# Avondale auction inventories

*Wicklow Newsletter,* 30 July 1859: Preliminary notice of Avondale auction by Daniel Johnson, Auctioneer, Rathdrum.

*Ibid.* 1 October 1859: Inventory of auction to be held 11–12 October:

Cattle (62 head):
6 dairy cows
3 forward and one backward springers
13 $3\frac{1}{2}$ year old bullocks
14 Kerry heifers
25 high-bred heifers
1 bull

Sheep (22 head):
15 wethers
7 ewes

Horses (12):
5 year old bay mare
7 year old brown mare in foal
5 year old grey harness-horse
4 year old promising filly
3 farm-horses
5 colts and fillies

Agricultural produce:
1 stack old oats
5 acres prime potatoes
10 acres swede and Aberdeen turnips, mangolds and carrots

Farming implements:
3 drays and creels
2 farm cars
1 new timber carriage

Winnowing machine
Donkey cart and harness
Water cart
4 wheelbarrows
Stone dray
Field and garden rollers
Beam, scales, weights
Long and short garden ladders
Crate of window glass
Fencing wire
2 ploughs and swings
1 double harrow
5 sets cart-harness
3 pairs backbands and traces
Farm and garden tools
Crowbars
40 sacks
Oat-bins
Stable appointments

Carriages:
1 travelling-chariot
1 phaeton
1 covered car
1 outside jaunting-car

Harness:
1 set brass-mounted double harness
1 set brass-mounted single harness
Tandem harness
Ladies' and gentlemen's saddles and bridles

Guns:
2 double-barrelled
1 rifle
1 revolver

*Wicklow Newsletter,* 20 October 1860: Announcement of the late Mr John Henry Parnell's oat crop – 60 stacks.

*Wicklow Newsletter,* 1 December 1860: Announcement of a further auction, to be held at Casino on 7 December inst.

'Rare old port wines, sherry, madeira, claret, champagne, liqueurs, casked whiskey.'
3 cows
A good deal of furniture and china.
2 jaunting-cars.

1 covered car.
Saddle and harness.
'A good cricket-ground tent, in perfect order.'

*Wicklow Newsletter,* 19 December 1863: A further auction at Casino advertised, of 'the property of Mrs Parnell'.
Much of the furniture listed is the same as in the auction of 7 December, but there are far fewer outside effects.

# Appendix 2:
# Charles Stewart Parnell's election addresses

*Freeman's Journal*, 9 March 1874:

*To the electors of the County of Dublin*

Gentlemen − In compliance with influential requests, I offer myself as candidate for your county at the approaching election.

Upon the great question of Home Rule I will by all means seek the restoration to Ireland of our domestic Parliament, upon the basis of the resolutions passed at the National Conference and the principles of the Home Rule League, of whose Council I am an active member.

If elected to Parliament I will give my cordial adherence to the resolutions adopted at the Conference of Irish Members, and will act independently alike of all English parties. The wishes and feelings of the Irish people are in favour of Religious Education. In these feelings I concur, and I will earnestly endeavour to obtain for Ireland a system of education in all its branches Primary, Intermediate and University − which will deal impartially with all Religious Denominations by affording to every parent the opportunity of obtaining for his child an education combined with that religious teaching of which his conscience approves.

I believe security for his tenure and the fruits of his industry to be equally necessary to do justice to the tenant and to promote the prosperity of the whole community. I will, therefore, support such an extension of the ancient and historic Tenant Right of Ulster, in all its integrity, to the other parts of Ireland, as will secure to the tenants continuous occupation, at fair rents, and upon this subject I adopt the declarations of the Tenant Right Conferences held in Dublin and Belfast.

I think the time has long since come when a complete and unconditional Amnesty ought to be extended to all the prisoners, without distinction, who are suffering for taking part in transactions arising out of political movements in Ireland.

I am in favour of the Revision and Amendment of the Grand Jury Laws.

I will earnestly advocate a removal of the grievances of which the Civil Servants of Ireland so justly complain. I have seen with indignation of the rejection of their demand to be placed on an equality with those who are employed in England. I will use my best endeavours to obtain for them the advantages which they have asked for in vain, but to which they are so clearly entitled.

If I appear before you as an untried man, my name and my family are not unknown in Irish politics. My ancestor, Sir John Parnell, in the old Irish Parliament was the active and energetic advocate of the removal of the disabilities which affected his Catholic fellow-countrymen. In the evil days of corruption he lost a great office and refused a peerage to oppose the fatal measure of Union. His successor, Sir Henry Parnell, rendered in the British Parliament services to the cause of Catholic Emancipation and of Ireland which the Irish people have not forgotten.

If you adopt me I will endeavour, and I think I can promise, that no act of mine will ever discredit the name which has been associated with these recollections.

I am, Gentlemen, your faithful servant,

Charles Stewart Parnell

Parnell's address to the Meath electors was almost identical. It was published in the *Freeman's Journal*, 2 April 1875.
The first paragraph read:

> Gentlemen – the untimely death of the single-minded and noble Irishman who so well and faithfully served you in Parliment has caused a vacancy in the representation for your County. I offer myself for your adoption as a candidate.

The main body of the address was as above, from 'Upon the great question of Home Rule . . . 'to' . . . Revision and Amendment of the Grand Jury Laws.' However, the paragraph about the Civil Servants' grievances was replaced by the following:

> I do not appear before you as an untried man. In March 1874 I contested the county of Dublin against Colonel Taylor, the Government candidate, at the request of the Irish Home Rule League.

This was followed by a paragraph beginning 'Neither are my name or family unknown in Irish politics . . . ', which read as the second last paragraph of the previous address; and the concluding paragraph was also identical.

# Appendix 3:
# Hugh Gaffney's recollections of the Parnell family

The Parnells' life at Avondale was vividly put before me in conversations with Mr Hugh Gaffney of Roundwood, Co. Wicklow, whose mother, Maria Gaffney, was housekeeper to John Howard Parnell and Emily Dickinson, and whose great-aunt, Mary Gaffney, was Charles Stewart Parnell's nursemaid. Mr Gaffney's father, Peter Gaffney, worked on the estate as a boy, was valet to John Henry Parnell for the last years of the latter's life, and then became a steward of the estate for Mrs Parnell. The family was descended from a Hugh Gaffney who came from the Parnells' estate in Armagh, and they lived in Avondale House, not in an estate cottage; the bond was a close one. Mr Gaffney's memories of what his parents and great-aunt told him are sharp, decisive and endlessly interesting; however, as they are not first-hand recollections, I have decided to put them in an appendix rather than drawing on them as sources throughout my narrative.

The general view thus given of the Parnell *ménage* in its early days is in direct contrast to Emily Dickinson's memories of seignorial splendour. The Parnells, Mr Gaffney states, 'never lived it up', except for organising cricket matches. The house was 'plain and neglected'; Mrs Parnell was 'proud', and 'didn't mix with the county'. The family did not entertain; nor were they particularly good 'church people' (they did not, for instance, read the lesson in Rathdrum Church). They had, Mr Gaffney recollects, no carriages, unlike the Byrnes of Crony Byrne; Peter Gaffney drove them in a sidecar wherever they wanted, and as a boy he remembered walking into Wicklow town to collect their letters, as there was no carriage to be sent. Nonetheless, the family was noted for its charity, though not for its wealth.

Many of Mr Gaffney's recollections deal with Avondale after the death of John Henry Parnell; but Mary Gaffney, who travelled from Ballyshannon to Avondale in 1848 to be a nursemaid to Charles Stewart Parnell, lived until 1916 and retained a clear mind until the end; a perspicacious and intelligent woman, she was – with Peter

Gaffney, Mr Gaffney's father – one of the best educated people in the parish. Their recollections of the Parnells are still remembered by Mr Gaffney; and the details I have adduced here are illuminating, though essentially secondary, data.

# Appendix 4:
# Account of C. S. Parnell's court case in Cambridge Independent Press of 22 May 1869

Assault by an Undergraduate – Hamilton v. Parnell
A Jury Case
Poland Adcock for Parnell, Cockerall for Hamilton

The action was brought to recover £26-5-0 for an assault and £6-15-0 for damage done to plaintiff's coat and trousers in consequence of such an assault. The plantiff is a merchant at Harston, and the defendant an undergraduate at Magdalene College. On Saturday the 1st of May the plaintiff was on his way towards the station when he found the defendant lying upon the ground and a friend standing near him. He roused them and for his attention the defendant rushed at him and committed the assault complained of. Several attempts [were made] at an amicable arrangement by giving something to the hospital and paying the costs, which proved unsuccessful.

Mr Edward Charles Hamilton, examined by Mr Adcock, said he was a merchant at Harston and on the evening of the 1st of May, between 10 and halfpast, was on the station road in company with his servant. When opposite Newman's public-house saw a man lying full-length in the gutter and a gentleman standing over him. Plaintiff went up to them and said, 'What is the matter?' and the gentleman said, 'Oh, my friend is only very drunk and we have sent for a cab to take him home.' Plaintiff then offered his assistance and the gentleman said 'No, we do not want any of you or your d–d help; go about your own business.' Plaintiff replied – 'When one offers assistance they are not usually insulted', and was about to walk on when all of a sudden the gentleman lying in the gutter jumped up and hit plaintiff with a violent blow in the mouth, cutting his lip and nose. Defendant then struck plaintiff another blow on the collarbone, which disabled his arm for three days, and after that kicked him severely on the right knee, which caused great pain. The clothes, which were stained with blood, and also the trousers (a new pair) were torn in the struggle. The value of the coat was £5-5-0 and the trousers £1-10-0. After the assault a policeman was met and he was requested to take the defendant's address, which he did. Plaintiff then went to the police-station.

Cross-examined: Dealt in manure. Was going to the station upon business. When walking down the road to the police-station the defendant's manner was that of a drunken man. Did not strike defendant before he hit me, or at any time. Mr Bentley, defendant's friend, did not strike anyone and my man Allen did not hit the defendant until I was on the ground.

Mr Charles Stewart Parnell, the defendant, was called by Mr Adcock and said he resided in Co. Wicklow, Ireland, and between 9 and 10 in the evening went in company with Messrs Hoole, Forster and Bentley, all undergraduates of Magdalene, in a fly to the station and at the refreshment rooms had some champagne, sherry and biscuits, left in about half an hour, and then went out of the station and sat on the side of the road while his friends went for a fly. While he was sitting on the side of the road he heard someone say 'Hullo, what is the matter with this 'ere cove?' and Bentley replied that they did not want any of their interference; plaintiff then said he did not expect to meet with such b—y impertinence and came opposite him, and witness asked what he meant by insulting his friend, and plantiff then said 'Your friend has been impertinent and I will not have any from you', witness then struck at plaintiff and missed him, the plaintiff then struck witness a severe blow on the eye, and witness then retaliated by knocking plaintiff down.

By the Judge: I did not kick him.

Witness resumed. The plaintiff's man then knocked me down and struck me twice in the right eye. As soon as I got him down I picked him up again (laughter). After that a policeman met us and I gave him my name; received a letter on the 5th, and went the next day to Ireland.

Chief Inspector Robinson was called and proved that the plaintiff made a complaint at the police station relative to an assault committed upon him by an undergraduate. He described the nature of the injuries the plaintiff had sustained.

P. C. Carter proved taking the defendant's name, and stated he was offered money to settle the affair. The defendant was the worse for liquor. In cross-examination he said the defendant was not in such a state as would have justified him (witness) taking him into custody.

Mr Benson, a surgeon, proved examining the plaintiff on the afternoon of the 6th and described the injuries; he was of the opinion that the injury to the knee was most probably the result of a kick. He first saw the plaintiff on the 6th of May.

Mr Cockerall, for the defendant, dwelt strongly upon the fact that the plaintiff did not see the surgeon until after the letter, describing the assault as provoked [sic] cruel, cowardly and disgraceful had been sent by Mr Adcock, and suggested that the interview with the surgeon was concocted at that gentlemen's office. He must admit that an assault was committed, and duty must guess of the nature from the conflicting statements. As to the damage done to the clothes, that must be left out of the question.

Mr Robert Bentley was called by Mr Cockerell and stated in answer to the learned counsel that he could not swear whether the defendant was sitting or lying or in a reclining sort of position. Saw the plaintiff and his man come and thought one of them said 'What is the matter with this man?' Witness told them to mind their own business, and might have said their own d–d business. Parnell then said what do you mean by insulting my friend, and he and plaintiff then had a little shake-up and the defendant got the best of it. I think the other man did his best (laughter).Did not see the plaintiff strike the defendant, but saw him knocked down, but not kicked.

His Honour, in summing up the case to the jury, said that there was no doubt an assault had been committed, and the only question for their consideration was the amount of damages. It was a most unfortunate thing that these young gentlemen should hire a fly to go to the station for the sole purpose of taking wine; he did not say there was any moral turpitude in the act, but had they not committed this indiscretion then they would have escaped this unfortunate occurrence. If they believed the plaintiff *in toto*, then a most violent and disgraceful act was committed. The question for them was, did the evidence of the defendant modify the plaintiff's statement, and he was bound to tell them that the weight of evidence was in the plaintiff's favour, in fact it would be no excuse had the plaintiff used the language attributed to him. He thought that it was a great pity the case had not been settled out of court. They must dismiss from their minds, however, all allusions which had been made as to giving the damages to the Hospital.

The Jury, after a short consultation, returned a verdict for the plaintiff, with twenty guineas damages.

# Appendix 5:
## 'Hold the harvest'

(This was first published in the early autumn of 1880; the fullest version I could find was in R. M. McWade's *Life of Stewart Parnell*, pp. 57–8.)

Now, are you men are you kine, ye tillers of the soil?
Would you be free, or evermore the rich man's cattle toil?
The shadow on the dial hangs that points the fatal hour –
Now hold your own! Or, branded slaves, forever cringe and
   cower.

The serpent's curse upon you lies – ye writhe within the dust,
Ye fill your mouths with beggar's swill, ye grovel for a crust,
Your lords have set their bloodstained heels upon your
   shameful heads,
Yet they are kind – they leave you still their ditches for your
   beds!

Oh, by the God who made us all – the seigneur and the serf –
Rise up! and swear to hold this day your own green Irish turf;
Rise up! and plant your feet like men where now you crawl as
   slaves,
And make your harvest-fields your camps, or make of them your
   graves.

The birds of prey are hovering round, the vultures wheel and
   swoop –
They come, the coronetted ghouls! with drumbeat and with
   troop –
They come to fatten on your flesh, your children's and your
   wives'–
Ye die but once – hold fast your lands and, if you can, your lives.

Let go the trembling emigrant – not such as he you need,

Let go the lucre-loving wretch that flies his land for need,
Let not one coward stay to clog your manhood's waking power,
Let not one sordid churl pollute the Nation's natal hour.

Yes, let them go! The catiff rout that shirk the struggle now,
The light that crowns your victory shall scorch each recreant
    brown.
And in the annals of your race black parallels in shame
Shall stand by traitor's and by spy's the base deserter's name.

Three hundred years your crops have sprung, by murdered
    corpses fed;
Your butchered sires, your famished sires, for ghastly compost
    spread;
Their bones have fertilised your fields, their blood has fall'n like
    rain,
They died that you might eat and live — God! have they died in
    vain?

The yellow corn starts blithely up — beneath it lies a grave,
Your father died in 'forty-eight; his life for yours he gave;
He died that you, his son, might learn there is no helper nigh
Except for him who, save in fight, has sworn *he will not die.*

The hour has struck, Fate holds the dice, we stand with bated
    breath;
Now who shall have our harvests fair — 'tis Life that plays with
    Death;
Now who shall have our Motherland? 'Tis Right that plays with
    Might;
The peasants' arms were weak indeed in that unequal fight!

But God is on the peasants' side, the God that loves the poor;
His angels stand with flaming sword on every mount and moor.
They guard the poor man's flocks and herds, they guard his
    ripening grain;
The robber sinks beneath their curse beside his ill-got gain.

O pallid serfs! whose groans and prayers have wearied Heav'n
    full long,
Look up! there is a law above, beyond all legal wrong;
Rise up! the answer to your prayers shall come, tornado-borne,
And ye shall hold your homesteads dear, and ye shall reap the
    corn!

But your own hands upraised to guard shall draw the answer
    down,

And bold and stern the deeds must be that oath and prayer shall
   crown;
God only fights for those who fight – now hush the useless moan,
And set your faces as a flint, and swear to Hold Your Own.

# Bibliography

One or two of these classifications may seem unnecessarily catholic: but the alternative was for a proliferation of sub-headings, with very few entries under each. The entries under each heading below are numbered, and in alphabetical order: where a note is needed about classification under particular headings, I have put it in the apposite place.

A disadvantage arising from following a plan as simple as the one above is that it does not allow for emphasis of particular works whose importance, in a sense, transcends their classification. J. H. Parnell's

*C. S. Parnell: a memoir* (A VII, no. 37) for instance, was one of the most important source-works for this book, and I should like to emphasise that here. A secondary work which has been under-estimated is St John Ervine's *Parnell* (B I, no. 2): though popularised and racy, it contains important insights into Parnell's Wicklow background. However, the really important sources for my work have classifications to themselves: the memorials in the Registry of Deeds, the assorted MSS in the National Library, and the contemporary newspapers (A I, A II, and A VI). The Registry of Deeds, if gone into in depth, provides an invaluable repository for family history – or at least for that vital aspect of it which deals with the transference of property through the generations. It also goes a long way towards making good the deficiency caused by the lack of estate maps for Avondale: enough details are given about the various areas of the estate to build up a comprehensive idea of it. Of the MSS in the National Library, John Henry Parnell's 'Journal' (A II, no. 1) was especially illuminating, and has not, I think, been much looked at before. Delia Tudor Stewart Parnell's long letter to T. D. Sullivan (A II, no. 6) was as instructive for the manner in which it is written as for its actual contents. The body of estate memoranda for Wicklow was again useful in my empirical process: the Fitzwilliam papers (A II, no. 10) were invaluable, as were the copious diaries of Lady Alice Howard and Lady Caroline Howard in the Wicklow Papers (A II, no. 8), and James Grattan's notebooks (A II, no. 9). Among other MSS, the letters of Parnell's at Avondale House (A III, no. 1) are especially useful for providing facts about his mining venture.

Newspapers were important for building up a picture of Parnell's relations with Wicklow throughout his career, and no journal was more useful for this than William McPhail's quirky, expansive, 'rural Tory' *Wicklow Newsletter* (A VI, no. 21) which I used exhaustively. Among contemporary reference works, I used *Thom's Directory* (A VII, no. 19) extensively, especially for the introduction to my work.

Contemporary memoirs were most important, for reflections of contemporary opinion as well as hard facts. The anonymous recollection of Fanny Parnell in the Celtic Magazine (A VIII, no. 10) provided some valuable insights: books by men like Henry Harrison (A VIII, no. 20), Sir William Butler (A VIII, no. 3), and Andrew Kettle (A VIII, no. 20), who saw Parnell outside his political context, were particularly useful. Emily Dickinson's maddening memoir (A VIII, no. 9) was a staple, but had to be handled gingerly; the same was true for the recollections by Katharine Parnell (A VIII, no. 36) and by Delia T. S. Parnell in McWade's book (A VIII, no. 26).

As is obvious from my text, the works of William Parnell (A IX, nos. 13–16) were basic source-material for an important section of my work; the many contemporary guides to Co. Wicklow, also under the

heading of 'other contemporary writing' (A IX, nos. 5, 7, 18, 2, 23),
were important in the first section on the county.

Of later works, I have already mentioned Ervine's book; Barry
O'Brien's biography at the time of writing still towers above all the
rest (B I, no. 8), a state of affairs which will soon be altered by the
publication of Dr F. S. L. Lyons' Life of Parnell. The special-subject
classification included books which I consulted throughout as well as
some writing on very specific topics. Dr Ged Martin's article covered
comprehensively a whole area of Parnell's youth which would
otherwise have been an important section of my study, and Professor
Moody's unpublished work on Anna Parnell both provided references
and suggested a line of approach.

# A: PRIMARY SOURCES

### I: Memorials in the Registry of Deeds, Dublin

Up to 1831, these are catalogued by a volume number, the first in the series: the next number denotes page, and the third, the actual number of the memorial. Thus 255 . 324 . 165063 means volume 255, page 324, Memorial number 165063. From 1831, Deeds are catalogued differently: the year is given, then the volume number for that particular year, then the memorial number. They are listed in order of volume number.

For the property of Sir John Parnell and his father:

| | | |
|---|---|---|
| 255 . | 324 . | 165063 |
| 257 . | 20 . | 165130 |
| 261 . | 558 . | 198645 |
| 263 . | 237 . | 167471 |
| 265 . | 236 . | 174973 |
| 265 . | 629 . | 180088 |
| 268 . | 493 . | 171255 |
| 294 . | 500 . | 195546 |
| 295 . | 291 . | 196191 |
| 297 . | 572 . | 196187 |
| 297 . | 573 . | 196188 |
| 297 . | 574 . | 196189 |
| 297 . | 575 . | 196190 |
| 297 . | 605 . | 196321 |
| 298 . | 558 . | 198645 |
| 299 . | 324 . | 165063 |
| 302 . | 104 . | 199336 |
| 305 . | 91 . | 200603 |
| 306 . | 430 . | 204032 |
| 307 . | 337 . | 207370 |
| 310 . | 478 . | 207393 |
| 311 . | 349 . | 210628 |
| 320 . | 60 . | 210729 |
| 320 . | 195 . | 215257 |
| 325 . | 411 . | 221496 |
| 325 . | 413 . | 221497 |
| 326 . | 492 . | 216733 |
| 328 . | 434 . | 221573 |
| 331 . | 234 . | 221494 |
| 331 . | 236 . | 221495 |
| 337 . | 52 . | 225275 |
| 337 . | 161 . | 226446 |
| 340 . | 363 . | 229788 |
| 341 . | 122 . | 227795 |
| 342 . | 181 . | 229242 |
| 344 . | 342 . | 231887 |
| 344 . | 343 . | 231888 |
| 349 . | 343 . | 234564 |
| 352 . | 99 . | 236805 |
| 353 . | 128 . | 236804 |

| | | | | | |
|---|---|---|---|---|---|
| 354 | . | 345 | . | 237896 |
| 354 | . | 501 | . | 240151 |
| 354 | . | 503 | . | 240152 |
| 355 | . | 31 | . | 236879 |
| 358 | . | 559 | . | 243093 |
| 362 | . | 137 | . | 242921 |
| 363 | . | 564 | . | 246215 |
| 365 | . | 476 | . | 246476 |
| 367 | . | 137 | . | 246326 |
| 369 | . | 54 | . | 246350 |
| 374 | . | 33 | . | 247754 |
| 377 | . | 413 | . | 255133 |
| 383 | . | 252 | . | 253775 |
| 389 | . | 77 | . | 255741 |
| 389 | . | 495 | . | 257043 |
| 395 | . | 421 | . | 262305 |
| 399 | . | 429 | . | 264379 |
| 406 | . | 411 | . | 267091 |
| 422 | . | 349 | . | 276490 |
| 428 | . | 253 | . | 280110 |
| 444 | . | 532 | . | 289565 |
| 451 | . | 310 | . | 289929 |
| 460 | . | 505 | . | 295172 |
| 464 | . | 540 | . | 297562 |
| 464 | . | 541 | . | 297563 |
| 493 | . | 446 | . | 323719 |
| 493 | . | 447 | . | 323726 |
| 503 | . | 229 | . | 323770 |
| 509 | . | 489 | . | 335814 |
| 515 | . | 518 | . | 335813 |
| 516 | . | 99 | . | 336348 |
| 527 | . | 581 | . | 252571 |
| 528 | . | 286 | . | 346613 |
| 531 | . | 334 | . | 351104 |
| 537 | . | 523 | . | 354070 |
| 542 | . | 14 | . | 255716 |
| 560 | . | 449 | . | 375622 |
| 569 | . | 557 | . | 383941 |
| 596 | . | 290 | . | 406658 |

For the property of Samuel Hayes:

| | | | | | |
|---|---|---|---|---|---|
| 255 | . | 222 | . | 164473 |
| 286 | . | 511 | . | 190098 |
| 303 | . | 707 | . | 204104 |
| 313 | . | 538 | . | 210289 |
| 316 | . | 293 | . | 212062 |
| 331 | . | 479 | . | 222929 |
| 332 | . | 203 | . | 224121 |
| 348 | . | 288 | . | 234231 |
| 356 | . | 293 | . | 240259 |
| 472 | . | 424 | . | 303548 |
| 478 | . | 160 | . | 308062 |
| 760 | . | 103 | . | 516038 |
| 786 | . | 555 | . | 532090 |

For the property of William Parnell:

```
544  .  137  .  361412
549  .  443  .  364504
553  .  340  .  368788
560  .  431  .  375487
573  .   12  .  383112
601  .   33  .  407707
614  .  560  .  426386
690  .  195  .  474148
749  .   53  .  509388
761  .  252  .  516787
```

For the property of John Henry Parnell:

```
774  .  263  .  524598
786  .  255  .  532090
857  .   64  .  572064
```

(Henceforward catalogued under year)

```
1834:  1  .  83
1835:  14  .  173
1836:  2  .  145
1842:  15  .  181
1844:  17  .  127
1845:  13  .  299
1847:  12  .  212
1848:  5  .  122
1852:  26  .  282
1853:  26  .  110
1854:  24  .  128,  25  .  105,  29  .  288
1855:  23  .  9,  32  .  132
1857:  6  .  172
1858:  5  .  227,  25  .  123
1859:  12  .  26,  19  .  138,  29  .  251
```

For the property of the Parnell family after 1859:

```
1862:  12  .  72,    12  .  73,    16.21,    16  .  22,    18  .  112,
33  .  97
1863:  17  .  141,  17  .  142
1864:  31  .  161
1865:  3  .  160,  26  .  95
1866:  21  .  202,  26  .  282
1867:  2  .  16,  28  .  193,  32  .  68
1868:  14  .  134,  14  .  135,  18  .  214,  33  .  136
1869:  7  .  96,  24  .  134,  27  .  67
1870:  32  .  192
1871:  9  .  61
1872:  6  .  140,  11  .  47,  23  .  238
1873:  19  .  249,  24  .  178,  25  .  77,  26  .  97,  26  .  101
1874:  26  .  180,  29  .  11,  30  .  132,  30  .  177,  32  .  45,
34  .  85,    34  .  86,    42  .  8,    44  .  259,    47  .  287,
47  .  289
```

1875: 2 . 246,   3 . 263,   3 . 224,   15 . 212,   30 . 262,
37 . 38
1876: 1 . 77,   4 . 28
1879: 17 . 9
1880: 44 . 199,   46 . 209
1882: 12 . 284,   36 . 27
1883: 37 . 27,   39 . 1
1884: 5 . 234,   39 . 1
1885: 4 . 95,   15 . 230
1889: 28 . 182
1891: 22 . 53,   50,   145
1893: 23 . 191,   51 . 106,   59 . 81
1894: 30 . 178,   34 . 8
1895: 5 . 203,   5 . 204
1896: 20 . 141
1899: 94 . 220,   94 . 221


II: **MSS in the National Library of Ireland**

1. Parnell material
   'Journal of a tour in the U.S. and Canada, 1834–5' by John Henry Parnell: MS 2036
2. Letters of C. S. Parnell: MSS 5934, 15, 735, 10, 416
   Avondale rent-roll, 1899–1900: MSS 12, 144
   Anna Parnell material (including 'The tale of a great sham'): MSS 12, 144
2. Land League Papers
   Including letters of Anna Parnell's among the American material: MS 8291
3. Redmond Papers
   Including letters from J. H. Parnell: MSS 15, 220
4. Sigerson correspondence
   Including letters from Anna Parnell: MS 8100
5. List of Armagh townlands and landlords, c. 1860
   Helpful in defining the Collure estate: MS 2716
6. Sullivan Papers
   Including letters from Delia T. S. Parnell, Fanny Parnell and Anna Parnell: MS 8237
7. Estate Maps
   Maps of the estates of Sir John Parnell in Leix and Cheshire by Samuel Byron, 1789, with additional maps by William Delaney, 1803–5: MSS 21 F 18 (1–17)
8. Wicklow papers
   Family commonplace-books, letters and diaries of the Howard family, c. 1820–70: MSS 3575, 3577–8, 3594–3625, 4799–4803, 4810
9. James Grattan material
   Estate accounts: MSS 5515, 5382–3
   James Grattan's diaries and notebooks, 1820–53: MSS 5776–9, 3847–53, and his library catalogue in 1825: MS 4704
10. Fitzwilliam papers
    Estate accounts and memoranda, tenants' ledgers, rentals, eviction and emigration books, agent's correspondence, 1820–70: MSS 3983–4, 3986–7, 3991, 3993, 3996–9, 4954–6, 4959, 4962–3, 4965–7, 4969–72, 4976, 4987–92, 4995–6, 6073, 6077–81, 6083–7, 6119–20, 8816, 12, 163, n.19–20 pp. 211–12
11. Powerscourt Papers
    Principally estate records and accounts, 1820–70; MSS 1763, 2740, 3163–4, 3167–77, 4882–6, 4888–93

12. Some miscellaneous MSS to do with Wicklow, 1820–70
    Crofton estate accounts: MSS 2065, 7233
    Brabazon estate valuation, 1823: MS 8742
    Loftus servant roll, 1825: MS 4329
    Miscellaneous diaries of Loftus family: MS n. 3318 p. 2936
    Proby rental, 1826: MS 1149
    Massy estate accounts: MS 3928
    Truell family letters: MS n.4581 p.4547
    'Tour of Wicklow' by Dorothea Barker, 1827: MS 2194

### III: **Other MSS**

1. Letters relating to Parnell's estate management, 1875–91, preserved at Avondale House
2. Autograph letter of C. S. Parnell in T. C. D. MS 2241
3. Autobiography of Alfred Webb in Library of Society of Friends, Dublin
4. Some letters from the Doran and Davitt papers shown to me by Professor T. W. Moody
5. Diary of George M. Drought, R. M., Baltinglass, Co. Wicklow, 1839–43, in S.P.O., Dublin: VII, Centre T/48
6. Family papers in the possession of the present (eighth) Lord Congleton

### IV: **Printed contemporary correspondence**

1. Historical Manuscripts Commission
   Report on Manuscripts in various collections, vi (London, 1909). Report on Manuscripts of J. B. Fortescue, preserved at Dropmore, vols. iii (1899), iv (1905), vi (1908), viii (1912)
2. *Journal and Correspondence of William, Lord Auckland,* with a preface by the Bishop of Bath and Wells, G. Hogge, (4 vols., London, 1860–2)
3. *Memoir and correspondence of Viscount Castlereagh, 2nd. Marquess of Londonderry, edited by his brother.* C. W. Vane, Marquess of Londonderry (12 vols., London, 1848–53)
4. *Correspondence of Charles, first Marquis Cornwallis,* ed. C. Ross (3 vols., London, 1859)
5. *Devoy's Post bag,* ed. Wm. O'Brien and Desmond Ryan (2 vols., Dublin, 1928)
6. *Memoir of the life and correspondence of the rt. hon. Henry Flood* (Dublin, 1838)
7. *Lord Melbourne's papers,* ed. L. L. Sanders, with a preface by Earl Cowper (London, 1890)
8. *Memoirs, journal and correspondence of Thomas Moore,* ed. Lord John Russell (8 vols., London, 1853–6.)
9. F. W. Newman, *A personal narrative in letters, principally from Turkey* (2 vols., London 1856)

### V: **Parliamentary records**

1. *The parliamentary Register: or history of the proceedings and debates of the house of Commons of Ireland,* 1782–1800
2. *A report of the debate in the house of Commons of Ireland on 15 and 16 January 1800 on the subject of a Union* (Dublin, 1800)
3. *Parliamentary Debates,* ed. T. C. Hansard, first, second and third series
4. *Summary of the returns of owners of land in Ireland,* H. C. 1876 (422) vol. lxxx.

### VI: **Contemporary periodicals**

As my footnotes indicate, reference to periodicals formed an important part of my source-work throughout. I have therefore only given the dates for those newspapers and magazines which I merely consulted for limited periods or specific topics; the rest were used generally at almost every stage of my work.

1. *Cambridge Independent Press*, 1869
2. *Celtic Magazine* (New York), 1882
3. *Celtic Monthly* (New York), 1880–2
4. *Daily Express* (Dublin)
5. *Daily Nation* (Dublin)
6. *Edinburgh Review*, 1805, 1821
7. *Evening Herald* (Dublin)
8. *Evening Mail* (Dublin)
9. *Evening Telegraph* (Dublin)
10. *Freeman's Journal* (Dublin)
11. *Irish Independent* (Dublin)
12. *Irish Sale Catalogues*, 1901
13. *Irish Times* (Dublin)
14. *Leinster Express* (Laois), 1859–75
15. *Nation* (Dublin)
16. *Quarterly Review* (London 1815–21)
17. *Scots Magazine* (Edinburgh), 1821
18. *The Times* (London)
19. *United Ireland* (Dublin)
20. *Walker's Hibernian Magazine* (Dublin)
21. *Wicklow Newsletter and General Advertiser*
22. *Wicklow People*

VII: **Contemporary works of reference**

1. S.A. Allibone, A Dictionary of English Literature (London, 1870)
2. *Annual Register*
3. M. Archdale, *The peerage of Ireland* (Dublin, 1789)
4. J. Bateman, *The great Landowners of Great Britain and Ireland* (1883; ed. D. Spring, Leicester University Press, 1971)
5. *Burke's landed gentry of Great Britain and Ireland* (6th ed., 1879, and 9th ed., 1889)
7. *Burke's peerage and baronetage* (42nd ed., 1880, and 44th ed., 1892)
8. *Debrett's illustrated Peerage and baronetage* (London, 1864)
9. *Dictionary of living authors* (anon., Dublin, 1816)
10. F. M. Farrar, *Irish marriages, being an index to the marriages in Walker's Hibernian Magazine, 1771 to 1812* (2 vols., London, 1897)
11. J. Foster, *Alumni Oxonienses, 1715–1886* (Oxford, 1886)
12. J. Foster, *Men at the Bar* (London, 1885)
13. *Foster's Peerage* (London, 1883)
14. Vicary Gibbs, *The complete peerage of England, Scotland and Ireland* (London, 1910)
15. R. J. Griffith, *General Valuation of Ireland* (3 vols., London, 1836–48)
16. J. H. Hayden, *A book of Dignities* (London, 1890)
17. *Irish Law Reports, 1859–75*
18. J. Lodge, *The peerage of Ireland* (Dublin, 1789)
19. *Thom's Irish almanac and official directory* (Dublin, 1844)
20. *Thom's Irish Who's Who* (Dublin, 1923)
21. *Walford's county families of the United Kingdom* (London, 1920)
22. Alfred Webb, *A compendium of Irish biography* (Dublin, 1878)
23. *Who's Who* (1913)

VIII: **Memoirs by contemporaries**

Under this heading I have included biographies, autobiographies, contemporary biographical articles, and historical works (e.g. nos 8, 17, and 33) which have an important content of contemporary biography.

1. 'Fanny Parnell' (anonymous) in *Celtic Magazine,* vol. I no. 2 (Sept. 1881), pp. 28–92
2. *Recollections of Dublin Castle and Dublin society by a citizen* (anonymous) (London, 1902)
3. Sir Jonah Barrington, *Personal sketches of his own times* (3 vols., London, 1817–32)
4. W. S. Blunt, *The land war in Ireland, being a personal narrative of events* (London, 1912)
5. Sir William Butler, *An autobiography* (London, 1911)
6. Frances Power Cobbe, *The Life of Frances Power Cobbe, by herself* (2 vols., London, 1894)
7. W. J. Corbet, 'Parnell as a prisoner in Kilmainham' in *Irish Weekly Independent,* 7 Oct, 1893
8. M. Davitt, *The fall of feudalism in Ireland* (London and New York, 1904)
9. J. Devoy, 'How Parnell accepted the leadership' in *Gaelic American,* 26, Sept. 1906
10. J. Devoy, *Recollections of an Irish rebel* (London, 1929)
11. E. Dickinson, *A patriot's mistake: reminiscences of the Parnell family, by a daughter of the house* (London, 1905)
12. R. B. Cunninghame Graham, 'An Tighearna: a memory of Parnell' in *Dana* (Nov. 1904), pp. 183–99
13. J. Grant, *Random recollections of the house of Commons* (London, 1836)
14. H. Grattan, *Memoir of the life and times of Henry Grattan, by his son* (5 vols., London, 1839–46)
15. H. Groves, *A memoir of the second Lord Congleton* (London, 1884)
16. P. J. Hanway, 'Mrs Delia Tudor Stewart Parnell' in *Celtic Monthly* vol v, no. 4 (April 1881), pp. 326–9
17. H. Harrison, *Parnell vindicated: the lifting of the veil* (London, 1931)
18. T. M. Healy, 'A great man's fancies: some reminiscences of Charles Stewart Parnell' in *Westminster Budget,* vol. ii no. 41 (10 Nov. 1893), pp. 9–11; and no. 43 (24 Nov. 1893), pp. 23–5.
19. T. M. Healy, *Letters and leaders of my day* (2 vols., London, 1929)
20. J. J. Horgan, *Parnell to Pearse: some recollections and reflections* (Dublin, 1948)
21. A. Kettle, *The material for victory,* ed. L. J. Kettle (Dublin, 1958)
22. J. McCarthy, *Reminiscences* (Dublin, 1899)
23. J. McCarthy and Mrs Campbell Praed, *Our book of memories* (London, 1912)
24. S. MacNeill, *What I have seen and heard* (London, 1925)
25. R. M. McWade, 'Anna Parnell', in *Celtic Magazine,* vol. i., no. 2 (Sept. 1882), pp. 251–2
26. R. M. McWade, *The uncrowned king: the life and public services of the Hon.*
27. Wm. O'Brien, *An olive branch in Ireland, and its history* (London, 1910)
28. Wm. O'Brien, *Evening memories* (Dublin, 1920)
29. Wm. O'Brien, *Recollections* (London, 1905)
30. Wm. O'Brien, *The Parnell of real life* (London, 1926)
31. T. P. O'Connor, *C. S. Parnell, a memory* (London, 1891)
32. T. P. O'Connor, *Memories of an old parliamentarian* (2 vols., London, 1929)
33. F. H. O'Donnell, *A history of the Irish parliamentary party* (2 vols., London, 1910)
34. Standish O'Grady, 'Parnell: some personal reminiscences' in *The story of Ireland* (London, 1904), pp. 202–13
35. J. O'Leary, *Recollections of Fenians and Fenianism* (2 vols., London, 1896)
36. E. I. O'Reilly, 'Charles Stewart Parnell' in *Celtic Monthly* vol. iii, no. 1. (Jan. 1880), pp. 80–2
37. K. O'Shea, *Charles Stewart Parnell: his love story and political life* (2 vols.,

London, 1914)
38. J. H. Parnell, *C. S. Parnell: a memoir* (London, 1916)
39. W. Stewart Trench, *Realities of Irish life* (London, 1868; reprinted 1956, with an
    introduction by Patrick Kavanagh)
40. K. Tynan, *Memories* (London, 1924)
41. K. Tynan, 'Mr. Parnell's home, sketched by a lady' in *Weekly Freeman*, 6 Sept.
    1884
42. K. Tynan, *Twenty-five years* (London, 1913)
43. J. Wyse-Power, 'Recollections of Anna Parnell' in *Dublin Metropolitan Magazine*
    (Spring 1935), pp. 15–17, 28

IX: **Other Contemporary writing**

(This classification includes pamphlets, contemporary histories, and works of the
Parnell family specifically referred to: a full bibliography of Sir Henry Brooke
Parnell's works will be found in the text.)
1. Sir Jonah Barrington, *Historic memories of Ireland* (2 vols., London, 1835)
2. Sir Jonah Barrington, *The rise and fall of the Irish nation* (Dublin, 1833)
3. Sir John Carr, *The stranger in Ireland* (London, 1806)
4. W. P. Coyne, *Ireland, industrial and agricultural* (Dublin, 1902)
5. T. Cromwell, *Excursions through Ireland: a complete guide for the traveller and
    tourist* (London, 1820)
6. M. Davitt, *The 'Times' Parnell Commission: speech delivered by Michael Davitt
    in defence of the Land League* (London, 1890)
7. R. Frazer, *A general view of the agriculture and mineralogy, present state and
    circumstances, of the county of Wicklow, with observations on the means of their
    improvement, drawn up for the Dublin society* (Dublin, 1801)
8. Samuel Hayes, *A practical treatise on planting in Ireland* (Dublin, 1794)
9. F. M. Jennings, *An enquiry into the causes of poverty and discontent in Ireland
    with suggestions for their removal* (Dublin, 1866)
10. Anna Parnell, *Old tales and new* [poems] (Dublin, c. 1905)
11. C. S. Parnell, 'The Irish land question' in *North American Review*, vol. cxxx
    (April 1880), pp. 388–406
12. Sir Henry Brooke Parnell, *A history of the Penal Laws against Irish catholics
    from the Treaty of Limerick to the Union* (London, 1808)
13. William Parnell, *An enquiry into the causes of popular discontent in Ireland by
    an Irish country gentleman* (Dublin, 1805)
14. William Parnell, *An historical apology for the Irish Catholics* (Dublin, 1807)
15. William Parnell, *A letter to the editor of the Quarterly Review* (Dublin, 1820)
16. William Parnell, *Maurice and Berghetta, or, the priest of Rahery: a tale* (London,
    1819)
17. F. Plowden, *Historical review of the state of Ireland* (London, 1803)
18. *The Post-chaise companion through Ireland* (Dublin, 1803)
19. *Proceedings at a farewell dinner given to James Redpath by the New York Land
    League, 1 June 1881* (anonymously compiled, New York, 1881)
20. E. K. Purnell, *Magdalene College* (Cambridge College Histories, London, 1904)
21. T. Radcliffe, *Report on the agriculture of Wicklow* (Dublin, 1812)
22. M. Wingfield, 8th Viscount Powerscourt, *A history and description of
    Powerscourt* (Dublin, 1903)
23. G. N. Wright, *Guide to the County Wicklow* (London, 1822)

## B: LATER WORKS

I: **Biography**

1. D. Cashman, *Life of Michael Davitt and the secret history of the Land League by*

*Michael Davitt* (London, 1883 or 1884)
2. St John Ervine, *Parnell* (London, 1925)
3. Marie Hughes, 'The Parnell family: Dublin associations' in *Dublin Historical Record*, xvi, no. 3 (March 1961), pp. 86–97
4. Marie Hughes, 'The Parnell Sisters' in *Dublin Historical Record*, xxi, no. 1 (March, 1966), pp. 14–27
5. R. Johnston, *Parnell and the Parnells* (London, 1888)
6. F. S. I. Lyons, *John Dillon* (Dublin, 1968)
7. E. McCracken, 'Samuel Hayes of Avondale' in *Irish Forestry*, vol. 25, no. 1 (Spring, 1968)
8. A. Malcomson, *Isaac Corry, 1755–1813: 'an adventurer in the field of politics'* (P.R.O.N.I., 1974)
9. A. Malcomson, 'John Foster and the Speakership of the Irish House of Commons', *R. I. A. Proc* vol. 72, section c. no. 11; (Dublin, 1972)
10. R. B. O'Brien, *Life of Charles Stewart Parnell* (2 vols., London, 1898)
11. M. M. O'Hara, *Chief and tribune: Parnell and Davitt* (London, 1919)
12. F. Sheehy-Skeffington, *Michael Davitt* (2nd ed., London, 1967)
13. T. Sherlock, *Charles Stewart Parnell* (London, 1882)
14. 'William Parnell's death' with bibliography, in *Irish Book Lover*, viii, (December, 1921)

II: **Works of reference**

1. *Admissions register of Lincoln's Inns*, vol. ii (London, 1896)
2. *Burke's Peerage, baronetage and knightage* (London, 1970)
3. J. S. Crone, *A concise dictionary of Irish biography* (Dublin, 1928)
4. *Dod's electoral facts* (London, 1889)
5. S. Lee (ed.), *Dictionary of National Biography* (London, 1915–)
6. J. A. Venn (ed.), *Alumni cantabrigiensis*, part ii. vol. v, (Cambridge, 1953)
7. J. Vincent and M. Stenton (eds.), *McCalmont's parliamentary poll-book* (8th ed., Brighton, 1972)

III: **Special subjects**

1. D. J. Beattie, *Brethren: the story of a great recovery* (Kilmarnock, 1940)
2. Sydney Buxton, *Finance and politics: an historical study* (London, 1888)
3. R. D. Edwards and T. D. Williams (eds.), *The great famine: studies in Irish history, 1845–52* (Dublin, 1956)
4. J. A. Froude, *The English in Ireland in the eighteenth century* (3 vols., London, 1881)
5. E. M. Johnston, *Great Britain and Ireland, 1760–1800: a study in political administration* (St Andrews, 1963)
6. W. E. M. Lecky, *History of Ireland in the eighteenth century* (5 vols., London, 1892)
7. F. S. L. Lyons, 'The economic ideas of Parnell' in *Historical Studies*, ii (1959), pp. 60–78.
8. L. J. McCaffrey, 'Home Rule and the general election of 1874' in *I.H.S.*, ix, no. 34 (September 1954) pp. 190–212
9. J. R. McCullough, *The literature of political economy* (2nd ed., London, 1938)
10. R. B. McDowell, *The Irish administration, 1801–1914*, (London, 1964)
11. R. B. McDowell, *Public opinion and government policy in Ireland, 1801–46* (London, 1952)
12. R. B. McDowell (ed.), *Social life in Ireland, 1800–45* (Dublin, 1857)
13. Ged Martin, 'Parnell at Cambridge: the education of an Irish nationalist in *I.H.S.*, xix, no. 73 (March 1974) pp. 72–82
14. T. W. Moody, 'Anna Parnell and the Land League', a paper delivered to the Conference on Irish Studies in New York, 20 March 1965, and published in *Her-*

*mathena* no. cxvii, 1974, pp 15–16; kindly shown to me by Professor Moody while still unpublished.

15. C. C. O'Brien, *Parnell and his party* (3rd ed., Oxford, 1968)
16. P. Rogers, *The Irish volunteers and Catholic emancipation* (London, 1934)
17. 'The Rosanna press' in *Irish Book Lover,* vol. iv (October 1912), p. 54
18. D. Thornley, *Isaac Butt and Home Rule* (London, 1964)

# Notes to the text

## Introduction: Nineteenth-century Wicklow

1. J. Bateman, *The great landowners of Great Britain and Ireland* (1883), ed. D. Spring, (Leicester University Press, 1971). Also see the parliamentary White Paper, 'A summary of the returns of owners of land in Ireland', H. C. 1876 (422) vol. lxxx.

2. See above. The average Wicklow holding recorded was 478.05 acres. By 1866, only Carlow had fewer holdings listed at under £4 R. V. By 1876, though Wicklow was the 16th largest county in Ireland, only 7 counties had a smaller total number of landowners, and five of these counties were far smaller in area than Wicklow. 507 Wicklow owners were listed in 1876; only 95 lived outside the county, and most of these in Dublin.

3. For the Fitzwilliam estate in this period see N.L.I., Fitzwilliam Papers, MSS 3983-4, 3986-7, 3991, 3993, 3996-9, 4954-6, 4959, 4962, 4965-7, 4969-72, 4976, 4987-92, 4995-6, 6073, 6077-81, 6083-7, 6119-20, 8816, 12, 163, pp. 211-2. n. 19-20.

4. See *Thom's Directory*, 1848–52.

5. N.L.I., Tottenham estate accounts, MSS 3836–44.

6. See N.L.I., Fitzwilliam estate papers, MSS 4973, p.211, n. 19, p.201 n.6.

7. The density decrease for 1841–51 was 34 for Wicklow, compared to a national average of 49, and 17 for the next decade, when the national figure was 25.

8. R. D. Edwards and T. D. Williams (eds.), *The great famine: studies in Irish history 1845–52* (Dublin, 1956).

9. See N.L.I., Fitzwilliam tenants' ledger, MS 6082.

10. *Thom's Directory*, 1962.

11. Edwards and Williams, *The great famine*, p.430.

12. N.L.I., Fitzwilliam papers, MS 3982, pp. 85–6.

13. *Ibid*. p. 192.

14. On the Powerscourt estate only 4 tenants went permanently into arrears between 1844 and 1854 (N.L.I., Powerscourt accounts, MS 3164).

15. For Grattan's varied policies see N.L.I., James Grattan's notebook for 1846–7, MS 5382.

16. Edwards and Williams, *The great famine*, p. 430.

17. N.L.I., MS 5382. 'Two Haze girls called, handsome, fat, and well-dressed; they asked for money to go to America, this after robbing me of £62 and who knows how much more. M. Brophy could not make up £15, though I saw plenty in his haggard. H. Harrison is playing the same trick, and B. Nolan wants until January. Such men if they do not pay must give bills ... it looks like a combined move.' I should add that Gratton's evidence is of a different order, as regards both reliability and impartiality, from that of the average landlord.

18. N.L.I., Wicklow Papers, MS 4792.

19. N.L.I., Tottenham Papers, MS p.4937 n.4905.

20. Diary of G. M. Drought, R.M., 1839–43 (S.P.O. Dublin, VII, Centre T/48). I am indebted to Kevin Mellyn for knowledge of this absorbing and enlightening record.

21. See N.L.I., Crofton Papers, MS 2065, and Loftus Servant Roll, 1840, MS 4399.

22. An interesting example is to compare the work-diaries of two woodrangers on the Fitzwilliam estate (N.L.I., MS 12,163). From 1865 to 1868, Patrick Murphy patrolled a large area of the Fitzwilliam lands; his diary reports tenants for sharing accommodation, subletting, selling hay, not manuring, and drawing away soil, many offenders recurring again and again. In 1868 Moses Mulally succeeded to the same post, and had a similar diary to keep; but he only records a fraction of such offences, usually confining himself to reporting poaching and extracting 'promises' against further disobedience.

23. See N.L.I., Fitzwilliam Papers, Poor Shop accounts, MS 4962.

24. N.L.I., James Grattan's notebook for 1822, MS 5776.

25. From £62 (1850–1) to £156 (155–6) in 6 years. N.L.I., Powerscourt accounts, MS 1763.

26. N.L.I., Wicklow Papers, Lady Caroline Howard's diary, MS 4792.

27. The lengthy correspondence about the whole affair is in N.L.I., Fitzwilliam Papers, MS 8816.

28. N.L.I., James Grattan's notebook for 1823, MS 5977.

29. M. Wingfield, *A history and description of Powerscourt* (Dublin, 1903), p. 117.

30. Preserved in the Wicklow Papers, N.L.I., MSS 4810, 4814. For the Wicklow printing-presses see *Irish Book Lover*, iv, 16, 54.

31. For Grattan's library see N.L.I., MS 4704; William Parnell's is discussed above, p. 117.

32. N.L.I., Wicklow Papers, MS 3579.

33. N.L.I., Grattan's notebook for 1830, MS 3853.

34. For Grattan's account of this election campaign see N.L.I., MS 3853.

35. The Tighes were descended from the Ponsonbys; James Grattan was the second son of the great Henry Grattan.

## Part I: The Avondale inheritance

### 1. Sir John Parnell and his family

1. See R. B. O'Brien, *Parnell*, i, 1–12; T. S. Sherlock, *Life of C. S. Parnell* (Dublin, 1882), pp. 4–12; R. Johnston, *Parnell and the Parnells* (London, 1888), pp. 1–12; M. M. O'Hara, *Chief and Tribune* (Dublin, 1919), pp. 1–4; T. P. O'Connor, *Memories of an old parliamentarian* (2 vols., London, 1929), i, 96–7.

2. For instance M. M. O'Hara, who in *Chief and tribune* refers to him as 'one of Grattan's Parliament's ornaments; one of that immortal band whose integrity and patriotism almost redeemed it from its sordid treachery' (p.3).

3. Henry Grattan's son wrote: 'He was honest, straightforward and independent . . . as Chancellor of the Exchequer he was not deficient' (*Life and times of Henry Grattan*, v, 144). Jonah Barrington, master of faint praise, remarked: 'As a financier, he was not perfect; as a statesman, he was not deep; as a courtier, he was not polished; but as an officer he was not corrupt' (*Rise and fall of the Irish nation* (Dublin, 1833), p.84). Elsewhere Barrington refers to Parnell's 'singular combination of indolence and vigour . . . a sloven and a gentleman' (*Historic memoirs of Ireland* (2 vols., London, 1835), 1, 121).

4. Sir Jonah Barrington, *Rise and fall of the Irish nation*, p. 83.

5. 'Parnell . . . revealed the true sentiments of the government when he lamented the necessity for introducing the measure but also expressed his belief that "the liberality of the public mind would of itself have totally obliterated all distinctions in

twenty years." ' (*History of Ireland in the eighteenth century* (5 vols., London, 1892), iii, 142. Also see *Parl. reg. Ire.*, xiii, 330).

6. *The English in Ireland in the eighteenth century*, iii, 47.

7. 18 February 1782; *Parl. reg. Ire.*, xii, 180. Also see his defence of the Protestant establishment on 26 February 1790, *ibid.* x, 330.

8. See speech of 25 February 1793 (*ibid.* xiii, 320).

9. Dundas to Grenville, 17 October 1791: Fortescue MSS, vol. ii, H.M.C. (1905), p. 462. Also see same to same, 4 September 1791, *ibid.*

10. Buckingham to Grenville, 1 February 1799; Fortescue MSS, vol. ii, H.M.C. (1905), p. 462.

11. See Lecky, *Ireland in the eighteenth century*, iii, 76.

12. Undated and unsigned state paper in Fortescue MSS, vol. iii, H.M.C. (1899), p. 549.

13. He accused them of attempting 'to overturn the constitution of the country'; see *Parl. reg. Ire.*, ii, 268.

14. See a speech of 20 March 1791 in *ibid.* xi, 378.

15. See for instance speeches of 6 March 1786 in *ibid.* vi, 279, and 29 February 1788, *ibid.* viii, 365.

16. 1 February 1790; *ibid.* vi, 239.

17. 'Why destroy the whole of the ancient system? Why wrest the power and patronage from the hands of the crown? Why alter the established form of the state? Does any man envy the *rage for experiment* which has involved so great a part of Europe in misery? And if not, why should this country, going rapidly forward to prosperity, enjoying her rights and liberties, prospering in commerce and increasing in wealth, risk the possession of peace, wealth and happiness to indulge the crude schemes of speculative innovators?' 26 March 1791; *ibid.* xi, 375.

18. 2 February 1787; *ibid.* vii, 80, 82.

19. See Lecky, *Ireland in the eighteenth century*, vi, 437.

20. Castlereagh to Pitt, 29 March. 1799; C. W. Vane, *Memoirs and Correspondence of Viscount Castlereagh* (12 vols., London, 1848–53), ii, 243.

21. For Corry's attacks see *Parl. reg. Ire.*, vi, 30, 40, 47, 73, 82, 83, 156; vii, 44, 83, 98, 117, 294, 252, 286, 380; viii, 14, 22, 77, 95, 237.

22. *Ibid.* xii, 73.

23. *Ibid.* xii, 13, 84.

24. Westmoreland to Grenville, 8 February 1791; Fortescue MSS, ii, H.M.C. (1894), p. 30.

25. Parnell to William Knox of Georgia (undated), Knox MSS, Rep. on MSS in various coll., vi. H.M.C. (1909), pp. 243–4.

26. See Anthony Malcomson, *Isaac Corry, 1755–1813; 'an adventurer in the field of politics'* (1974). This is a monograph published by the P.R.O. of N. Ireland, and is most informative both about Corry himself and about politics within the Administration in the Union period.

27. Letter in Congleton papers, Bundle C.I am indebted to Dr Anthony Malcomson, who has compiled a report on these papers, for this and any other references to them.

28. *Ireland in the eighteenth century*, iii, 247.

29. See H. Grattan, *Memoir of life and times of Henry Grattan*, iv, 23. Grattan felt the post was 'not the best suited to his habit or his disposition', and he was in addition 'not as sanguine in his hopes as some of the party and doubted the realisation of their wishes'.

30. *Ibid.*

31. In 1790 he said of Grattan: 'The gentleman who has bespattered us with so much foul language puts me in mind of a bird that I once saw hanging in Covent Garden; on everyone who passed by it cast the most bitter reproaches and the most opprobrious names, but nobody felt the abuse; they knew it was the bird's custom' (*Parl. reg. Ire.*, x, 277); Their exchanges were, however, usually less polished: Grattan

incensed Parnell the same year by accusing him of fraudulent calculations.

32. J. A. Froude, *The English in Ireland in the eighteenth century*, iii, 102.

33. *Parl. reg. Ire.*, xv, 205, and xvi, 70.

34. See *ibid.* vii, 88. 'We are connected with England by blood, by affection, and by interest ... the safety of our constitution in church and state depends upon that connection ... England certainly is our best friend and the connection we have with her will support the constitution of this country against every clamorous incendiary that would attempt to shake it ... England is not only our best friend politically, but she is our best friend commercially.'

35. Elliot to Castlereagh, 28 November 1798; *Castlereagh Correspondence*, ii, 29. Elliot, however, felt that Pitt should have begun to treat with Parnell sooner.

36. Portland to Cornwallis, 24 December 1798; *ibid.* ii, 53.

37. Thus Cooke to Auckland, 15 January 1799: '[Parnell] says he could not take a forward part if he did not suffer himself to be considered as an advisor of the measure, and that his judgement is against it as being very dangerous and not necessary and that a measure of the greatest danger can only be justified by necessity'. *Auckland Correspondence*, iv, 77.

38. In this month Parnell drew up a memorandum of the transactions leading to his dismissal, preserved in the Congleton papers.

39. E. Cook to Wm. Wickham, 12 April 1799; *Cornwallis Correspondence*, iii, 86.

40. 18 January 1799; *Auckland Correspondence*, iv, 77.

41. Parnell to Lord Hobart, 28 January 1799, in Congleton Papers, Bundle A.

42. See several letters from Lord Hobart and Theophilus Jones, *ibid.*

43. See *Parl. reg. Ire.*, xx, 80–2.

44. 16 January 1799; Fortescue MSS, iv, H.M.C. (1905), p. 423.

45. Carysfort to Grenville, 23 January 1799; *ibid.* 449.

46. Buckingham to Grenville, 14 February 1799. 'Under the impression which is now prevalent on both sides that this measure will be carried, it is plain that many of these honest patriots are looking for a bridge on which to get back. Parnell said yesterday that Mr Pitt and Foster were at issue who should be minister of Ireland; from which wise observation it is clear that this mock-monarch has promised him "th'earldom of Hereford" in the shape of his old office, for which he is languishing.' *Ibid.* 472.

47. Cooke to Grenville, 10 February 1800; Fortescue MSS, vi. H.M.C. (1908), p. 122. Cooke compared Parnell's position to that of Foster, who was implacably opposed, and Downshire, whose conduct was dictated by 'pique'.

48. 'He had for some time been somewhat ailing but was going about as usual when he became suddenly faint while conversing with some of his family and died almost instantaneously.' *Gentleman's Magazine*, December 1801, part ii, p. 1153.

49. Cornwallis to Portland, 9 March 1800; *Cornwallis Correspondence*, iv, 207. A contemporary rumour attributed Parnell's death to a stroke brought on by 'over-indulgence in the pleasures of the table'. See A. Malcomson, *Isaac Corry: 'an adventurer in the field of politics'*, p. 11.

50. See Sir John Carr, *The stranger in Ireland* (London, 1806), p. 160. This erroneous iconography associated with Parnell was to become more and more potent with the passing of years and the growth of nationalism; and Dr Anthony Malcomson has pointed out that exactly the same sort of process occurred with Foster's posthumous reputation. ('John Foster and the speakership of the Irish House of Commons', *R. I. A. Proc.*, vol. 72, section C, no. 11; Dublin, 1972). About 1845, for instance, the Newry Repeal Club proposed calling itself the Foster club; whereas the fact of the matter was that Foster, and most of those who like Parnell and himself opposed the Union because it weakened the Ascendancy, became staunchly unionist once the act came into operation.

51. Sir Jonah Barrington, *Rise and fall of the Irish nation*, p. 83, and Addington's tribute after Parnell's death in the House of Commons, quoted in *Gentleman's*

*Magazine,* December 1801, part ii, p. 1155.

52. Parnell to Lord Hobart, 28 January 1799; in Congleton Papers, Bundle A.

53. N.L.I., MS 21 F 18: Maps of the estate of Sir John Parnell, from surveys compiled by various hands, by Samuel Byron, 1789.

54. 635 acres at Fethard, Co. Tipperary, 24 acres at Listowsky, Co. Armagh, and 112 acres at Loughnaun, King's County. See Reg. of Deeds, Mem. 261.583, 173152, 302.104.19936, 305.91.200603.

55. This was assigned in trust to Lord Bangor and Lord Knapton by the first Sir John Parnell as part of the settlement on his son's marriage to Letitia Brooke. See *ibid.* 344.343.231888.

56. 'Statement of my father's property' in Congleton Papers, Bundle A.

57. Reg. of Deeds, Mem. 363.564.246215.

58. For details of these houses see *ibid.* 255.324.165063, 257.20.165130, 265.629.180088, 294.500,19546, 298.558.198645, 391.349.210628, 320.195.215257, 337.52.225275, 337.161.276446.

59. *Ibid.* 428.253.280110.

60. *Ibid.* 344.343.231886.

61. A rare exception was in 1784, when he sold lands at Carrignapark and Donamase for £2,424; see *ibid.* 389.77.255741.

62. On 21 August 1805. The step required some encouragement from her brother William, who told her Evans would have £4,000 a year on his father's death and would probably then buy a seat in Parliament, enabling her to live part of the year in London. See a letter of 31 May 1805 in Congleton Papers, Bundle G. Sophia died in 1853, Evans in 1842.

63. See Mervyn Wingfield, *History of Powerscourt,* p. 97, and Henry Groves, *Life of the second Lord Congleton* (London, 1884), p. 11.

64. He wrote many treatises on finance, anticipating later measures of Peel and Gladstone, and perhaps inevitably this earned him an indictment by Grenville as 'a rash, economical innovator'; he was anti-protectionist and advocated income taxation at a rate of $1\frac{1}{2}$ to 2 per cent as well as military retrenchment. He also proselytised for 'advanced' causes like the secret ballot and the abolition of flogging, as well as campaigning for Catholic relief. As Secretary at War he quarrelled with his superiors more than once and was eventually dismissed for voting against the government on the Russian-Dutch war question. He also pressed various Irish reform causes.

65. His family had to 'collect everything in the house with which [their] father could commit suicide . . . he suffered from want of sleep at nights and when asked about his feelings his constant answer was that he felt "very low" . . . he had lost his interest in things; he tried to read but used to give it up . . . [His valet] said that he never spoke to a servant except to give orders'. Inquest report quoted in *Annual Register* for 1842, Chronicle, pp. 103–4.

66. See family tree for details.

67. The present (8th) Lord Congleton agrees that he knows of no connection maintained at this time; this is, however, still in the nature of proving a negative, and must be counted a hypothesis.

68. H. Groves, *A memoir of the second Lord Congleton.* Also see F. W. Newman, *Personal narrative, principally in letters from Turkey* (London, 1856), and D. J. Beattie, *Brethren: the story of a great recovery* (Kilmarnock, 1940).

69. Edmund Gosse, *Father and son* (ed. Allen Lane, 1949), p. 44.

70. I am indebted to the present Lord Congleton for these references from family papers in his possession.

71. Personal reminiscence of Captain A. J. P. Mateer, John Howard Parnell's stepson, in 1972.

## 2. The Avondale tradition

1. The 1876 government survey recorded it as 4,678 acres, but a legal memorial about the same time shows it to have been 3,807 acres (Reg. of Deeds, Mem. for 1869, 27.67). The larger figure probably includes farms originally part of the Hayes estate but sold off by William Parnell in 1803–5 (*ibid.* 549.443.364504 and 553.340.368788).

2. A Samuel Hayes, son of John Hayes of Dublin, matriculated at Oxford in 1762, aged 19. J. Foster (ed.), *Alumni Oxoniensis 1715–1866*, p. 633.

3. He sat on committees concerning the site of a Botanic garden and the exhibition of agricultural implements from abroad in Dublin. For details of his involvements see *Walker's Hibernian Magazine*, 1795, p. 568, and Eileen McCracken, 'Samuel Hayes and Avondale' in *Irish Forestry*, xxv, no. 1 (Spring 1968).

4. 10 March 1788; *Parl. reg. Ire.*, ii, 384.

5. 21 January 1788; *ibid.* viii, 17.

6. Quoted by himself in parliament, 14 February 1790; *ibid.* vi, 221, 230.

7. 16 February 1788; *ibid.* vii, 262.

8. See E. Johnston, 'Members of the Irish parliament, 1784–7' in *R.I.A. Proc.*, vol. 71, section C, no. 5, p. 184. He had been brought in by his neighbour Mr Tighe, whose wife (a niece of Ponsonby) owned the borough of Wicklow.

9. *Parl. reg. Ire.*, vii, 227.

10. See Reg. of Deeds, Mem. 472.424.303548, 303.707. 204647, 332.203.224121, 313.538.210289, 356.293.240258.

11. Pamphlet of 1794 quoted by McCracken, 'Samuel Hayes and Avondale'.

12. See *A general view of the agriculture, mineralogy, present state and circumstances of Co. Wicklow, with observations on the means of their improvement*, drawn up for the Dublin Society by R. Frazer (Dublin, 1801).

13. Reg. of Deeds, Mem. 553.340.368785 refers to it.

14. She was born in 1750, daughter of Thomas Le Hunte, M.P. for Wexford. For her pedigree see J. Lodge, *Peerage of Ireland* (Dublin, 1789).

15. Reg. of Deeds, Mem. 255.222.164473.

16. *Ibid.* 311.349.210628.

17. Authorities have always been uncertain about the relationship; R. Johnston called them 'cousins' (*Parnell and the Parnells*, p.9) but J. H. Parnell believed Hayes was 'no relation'.

18. He 'excelled in the cultivation of the liberal sciences' and was 'unequalled in chaste literature', according to the *Freeman's Journal*, 15 February 1821. (A letter in the Congleton papers, Bundle C, shows him explaining to his father that the extra expense in sending him to university as a fellow commoner is justified.)

19. *Sermons partly translated, partly imitated from Massillon and Bourdaloue, designed for the use of country schools in Ireland* (London 1816).

20. Dublin, 1820. The review which he answered was in the *Quarterly Review*, xxi, 471–86. *The priest of Rahery* was revised and reprinted in London under Parnell's own name in 1825.

21. *Freeman's Journal*, 15 February 1821.

22. See Reg. of Deeds, Mem. 553.340.308788 and 373.12.383112.

23. *Ibid.* 601.35.407709.

24. Thomas Cromwell, *Excursion through Ireland* (London, 1820), iii, 145–6.

25. See Sir John Carr, *The stranger in Ireland*, p. 150, which refers to the house being let to Lady Wicklow. William spent summers in a cottage in the grounds.

26. *Freeman's Journal*, 15 February 1821; also see *D.N.B.*

27. He describes this process in his *Letter to the editor of the Quarterly Review* (cited below as *Letter*), p. 27.

28. *Enquiry*, pp. 38–9.

29. See R. Frazer, *A general view of Co. Wicklow*.

30. See *Enquiry*, p. 36.

31. *Maurice and Berghetta*, Introduction, xiv.

32. *Ibid.* xii.

33. 15 April 1818; Hansard 1, xxxviii, 93.

34. 2 June 1818; *ibid.*, xxxviii, 1170.

35. W. Parnell to Henry Brooke Parnell, 29 April 1802; Congleton Papers, Bundle H. There is some slight doubt about the authorship of this letter, but William seems the most likely author.

36. 2 June 1820; Hansard 2, i, 803.

37. See for instance debates on the Irish window tax, on his brother's motion to investigate the office of chief constable in Ireland, on fining whiskey stills, on Irish coercion, etc.; Hansard 1, xxxviii, 55, 262, 1014; xxix, 1432; xli, 877; xlii, 102.

38. See *ibid.* l, xxxix, 1479; xi, 1051–2.

39. In 1818; see Grattan's notebook for 1821, N.L.I., MS 5776.

40. *Ibid.* Though catalogued as 1822, this section of the diary is evidently from an earlier date.

41. Part i, p. 86: 'Works which have been greatly esteemed by the highest authorities for their elegance of style, the statesmanlike principles which they enforce, and the pure Patriotism of the author.'

42. See Moore's *Memoirs*, ed. Lord John Russell (London, 1856), vii. 109; journal entry for 25 August 1835. Parnell had asked Moore to verify the tradition that he wrote the poem at Avondale by composing some lines to that effect, which Parnell wanted to inscribe on the seat in the Abbey churchyard where the poet was supposed to have sat. Moore, however, preferred to leave the matter in doubt.

43. *Enquiry*, p. 12.

44. *Ibid.* This passage abounds in felicitous metaphors; answering a hypothetical protest that the Catholic position is greatly 'improved', he retorts: 'It is very little comfort to the man who has his eyes put out at Tunis, that he might have had his nose cut off if he had lived at Acre.'

45. As where he claims that 'they never violated a woman', and gives his hostile editor an opportunity to correct him by quoting a proclamation of the Commander-in-Chief at Wexford which shows that they indubitably did.

46. Here, as elsewhere, he was well ahead of his time. Though the Municipal Reform Act of 1840 provided elective bodies, the franchise was high and many local offices remained in the appointment of the Lord Lieutenant. Really representative local bodies of the kind Parnell advocated did not make their appearance until the local government Act of 1898.

47. Parnell's basically conservative respect for property is also indicated by a letter of 29 April 1802 to his brother advising him to 'Talk of liberty, etc., but let property and tranquillity be ever the aim. . . . of your political life.' Congleton Papers, Bundle G.

48. *Enquiry*, pp. 59 *et seq.*

49. 26 May 1818; Hansard 1, xxxviii, 969.

50. *Enquiry*, p. 64.

51. A thesis which may have been inspired by Sir John Davies's *Discovery*.

52. *Apology*, p. 143.

53. *Ibid.* p. 145.

54. *Ibid.* p. 142.

55. *Allibone's dictionary of literature*, iii, 1510.

56. Again, purely from first-hand accounts. Much of his criticism accurately foretells the disasters of the 1840s.

57. No. xlii, pp. 47–86.

58. *A letter to the editor of the Quarterly Review* (Dublin, 1820).

59. *Ibid.* p. 13.

60. *Ibid.* p. 16.

61. *Quarterly Review*, xxiii, no. xlv, pp. 360–73.
62. *Ibid.* p. 373.
63. K. O'Shea, *Parnell*, ii, 161; J. McCarthy, *Reminiscences*, ii, 99.

## Part II: The family of John Henry Parnell

### 1. The country gentleman

1. See, for instance, a comprehensive and otherwise accurate account by Marie Hughes, 'The Parnell Family' in *Dublin Hist. Rec.*, xvi, no. 3 (March 1961), pp. 86–95.
2. See Reg. of Deeds, Mem. 761.252.516787.
3. See *ibid.* 786.555.532090; also *ibid.* for 1835, 14.173.
4. See *ibid.* 786.555.532090. Thomas Hall, a solicitor, was the guardian appointed by the court for John Henry Parnell.
5. See Catherine's marriage settlement, *ibid.* for 1835, 14.173.
6. See J. H. Parnell's 'Journal of a Tour in the United States', 1834–5 (hereafter cited as 'Journal'), p. 109, where he recalls Christmases of 'pockets full of money' and 'old family servants' wishing one a happy Christmas.
7. *Alumni Cantabrigiensis*, ed. J. A. Venn (1953), part II, v, 33.
8. Purchased from Mrs Parnell (widow of John Howard Parnell) in 1926; now in N.L.I. (MS 2036).
9. As in p. 47, where he copies passages from the newspapers that 'explain the defects of the present state of government in the United States'.
10. 'Journal', p. 76.
11. See p. 86 for a description of upper-class American youth simultaneously devouring ice-cream, oysters and champagne as if famished.
12. 'Journal', p. 154.
13. *Ibid.* p. 28.
14. See *ibid.* 29, 77.
15. At Philadelphia; *ibid.* p. 114.
16. See below, p.
17. The italics are mine.
18. 'Journal', p. 129.
19. *Ibid.* p. 51.
20. *Ibid.* p. 55.
21. *Ibid.* p. 57.
22. *Ibid.* p. 63.
23. *Ibid.* p. 64.
24. *Ibid.* p. 34.
25. See Reg. of Deeds, Mem. for 1836, 2.145. She was a daughter of Lord Roden. Her marriage portion was £2,000, with other payments making up £4,000; Catherine Parnell was a considerable heiress by comparison.
26. J. H. Parnell, *C. S. Parnell: A memoir* (London 1916), p. 9.
27. Emily Monroe Dickinson, *A patriot's mistake* (London 1905), pp. 1–7.
28. R. B. O'Brien, *The life of Charles Stewart Parnell, 1846–91* (2 vols., London, 1898), i, 20.
29. *Sp. Comm. Proc.*, ii, 695.
30. *Wicklow Newsletter*, 7 April 1860.
31. See 'Fanny Parnell' (anonymous) in *Celtic Magazine*, vol. i, no. 2 (September 1882) p. 281. The less specific reference comes from a letter from Joseph McCarroll to J. H. Parnell, Appendix E in the latter's *C. S. Parnell*.
32. 'Journal', 21 October 1834.
33. *Ibid.* p. 242.
34. *Ibid.* p. 103.

35. *Ibid.* p. 257.

36. *Ibid.*

37. *Ibid.*

38. See *Thom's Directory* for the period.

39. 8 November 1848, see Robert Chaloner's Letter Book 1842–52, (N.L.I., Fitzwilliam Papers MS 3987), p. 234.

40. 3 July 1852. *Ibid.* p. 410.

41. See *Thom's Directory*, 1849, p. 559.

42. *Ibid.* 1850, p. 445.

43. *Ibid.* 1851, p. 620.

44. See *ibid.* 1852–9.

45. *Ibid.* 1853.

46. 21 April 1849, Robert Chaloner's Letter Book, p. 252.

47. See introduction.

48. Reg. of Deeds Mem. for 1848, 5.122.

49. Fitzwilliam Tenants' Memoranda, 1843–65 (N.L.I., Fitzwilliam Papers, MS 4967), pp. 149–50.

50. Fitzwilliam Tenants' Memoranda, 1862 (N.L.I., Fitzwilliam Papers, MS 4967), p. 18.

51. See Fitzwilliam papers (N.L.I., MS 10,696) for proceedings brought against John Howard Parnell in 1899 for the rent; also letters to John Redmond from Frank Brooke and J. H. Parnell clarifying the position.

52. See *Thom's Directory*.

53. 'Journal', p. 106.

54. *Thom's Directory*, 1841, p. 194.

55. *Ibid.* 1847.

56. Quoted in R. M. McWade, *The Uncrowned king: an account of the life and public services of the hon. Stewart Parnell* (Philadelphia, 1891), p. 73.

57. 'Journal', p. 263.

58. *Ibid.* p. 167.

59. *Ibid.* p. 233.

60. See J. H. Parnell, p. 38.

61. G. V. Wigram: b. 1805, 20th child of Sir George Wigram, a London shipowner and merchant; had been an army subaltern, but was 'brought to the Lord' and entered Queen's College, Oxford to take holy orders. He wrote *The Englishman's Hebrew and Chaldee concordance to the Old Testament*, and a cognate version for the Greek New Testament, upon which venture he spent most of his money. He also wrote *Hymns for the poor of the flock*, for the use of the Darbyite wing of the Movement – which body he warmly supported in the split of 1845.

62. 'Journal', p. 258.

63. *Ibid.* p. 93.

64. *Ibid.* p. 115.

65. *Ibid.* pp. 217, 284, 176.

66. *Ibid.* p. 61. Nonetheless, his impressions of the Abbess of the convent tend towards cynicism: 'a large, fat, fresh-looking woman who had been evidently no stranger to the world and even now does not seem to mortify herself much'.

67. And was not encouraged. Letter of 25 Feb. 1850, Chaloner's Letter Book (N.L.I., Fitzwilliam papers, MS 3987), p. 299.

68. 'So that it was a considerable tax on one's hearing to pay proper attention to their remarks.' Their father was Sir Archibald Campbell. 'Journal', p. 4.

69. 'Mrs Pierce Butler (Fanny Kemble) was there, trying to look like a Heroine'. *Ibid.* p. 89.

70. 'One sees enough of the mad and vicious in every day's occurrences without going out of one's way to look for them.'

71. See 'Journal', pp. 18–19.

72. *Ibid.* p. 38.

73. For instance *ibid.* p. 43. Also see p. 83: 'Nothing to do but make morning calls on ladies, which I detest.'

74. *Ibid.* p. 76.

75. *Ibid.* p. 262. He had found ladies of this country 'in their immorality, worse even than Spanish or Italian ladies' and that their faces 'always appear to be clouded with a hidden consciousness of guilt, so different from the fresh, innocent countenance of an English or American girl'. *Ibid.* p. 262.

76. See *ibid.* p. 282.

77. *Ibid.* p. 11.

78. J. H. Parnell, p. 37; see below, p.

79. E. Dickinson, p. 27; see below, p.

80. O'Brien, *Parnell,* i, 20.

81. E. Dickinson, p. 5.

82. R. M. McWade, *Life of Stewart Parnell,* p. 44.

83. *Ibid.*

84. See Mervyn Wingfield, *A history and description of Powerscourt* (Dublin 1903), p. 97. 'Old Tom Parnell', the engineer who laid out the drives, 'was a very poor man . . . very rough in exterior but most kindly in heart'. He was in fact an uncle of John Henry Parnell – one of William Parnell's two younger brothers. Later in the chapter, C. S. Parnell is referred to as 'his nephew the agitator'.

85. McWade, *Life of Stewart Parnell,* p. 50.

86. I have not included a passage about the great estimation she was held in by the West Point cadets, which she introduces into the middle of her account of the unfortunate Parnell's pursuit of her.

87. Now in the Sullivan MSS (N.L.I., Sullivan Papers, MS 8237/6), and dated 21 January 1880. Used by Thomas Sherlock for his early biography of Parnell, published from the *Nation* office in 1881; I have cited it below simply as 'Letter to Sullivan'.

88. 'Journal', p. 69.

89. *Ibid.* pp. 136 *et seq.*

90. *Ibid.* p. 118.

91. *Ibid.* p. 124.

92. *Ibid.* p. 128.

93. *Ibid.* p. 131.

94. J. H. Parnell, p. 9.

95. E. Dickinson, p. 5.

96. One other child – a boy – was still-born, and was probably her first.

97. R. M. McWade, *Life of Stewart Parnell,* p. 46.

98. Accounting to Debrett. J. H. Parnell, not always accurate about dates, states Henry was born in 1850, but this was the date of Theodosia's birth.

99. See E. Dickinson, p. 10.

100. O'Brien, *Parnell,* i, 37; the significant phrasing could possibly be J. H. Parnell's, though O'Brien had the advantage of corresponding with the schoolmistress herself in 1898.

101. Letter to Sullivan, p. 3. (For a full reference, see n. 87 above.)

102. St John Ervine, *Parnell,* p. 26.

103. She lived between Paris, Bordentown (New Jersey) and Avondale.

104. E. Dickinson, p. 9. She states the accident as happening when she was 13, and Mrs Parnell states that Hayes was 15 at the time; both statements mean that the year was 1854.

105. J. H. Parnell, p. 11.

106. Letter to Sullivan.

107. E. Dickinson, p. 9.

108. O'Brien, *Parnell,* i. 20.

109. 'Journal', p. 34.

110. *Ibid.* p. 105.
111. *Ibid.* p. 103.
112. *Ibid.* p. 170.
113. *Ibid.* p. 80.
114. *A propos* the opera-house controversy mentioned above, p. 37.
115. 'Journal', pp. 130–1.
116. See *ibid.* p. 66.
117. *Ibid.* p. 15.
118. *Ibid.* entry for 15 Oct. 1834.
119. *Ibid.* p. 27.
120. *Ibid.* p. 58.
121. E. Dickinson, p. 5.
122. See Reg. of Deeds, Mem. 760.103.516033.
123. See *ibid.* 4553.340.368788 and 573.12.383112.
124. John Parnell also inherited a third share in a Stephen's Green house which had been part of Alice Hayes's property and brought him £36 18s per annum – *ibid.* for 1834, 1.83.
125. 123 ac., 3 rd., 54½ p., at £154 1s 6d. p.a. See Fitzwilliam tenants' memoranda, 1843–65 (N.L.I., Fitzwilliam papers, MS 4967, pp. 149–50); see above, p.
126. See *ibid.* Also 'Tenants' Memoranda for 1862' (N.L.I., Fitzwilliam Papers, MS 4995, p. 40) and account entry of 4 June 1863 in Fitzwilliam Tenants' Accounts (N.L.I., Fitzwilliam papers, MS 6119, p. 24).
127. Fitzwilliam Tenants' Memoranda 1843–65 (N.L.I., Fitzwilliam Papers, MS 4967, p. 150).
128. N.L.I., MS 4967, p. 150.
129. See Chaloner's Letter book (N.L.I., Fitzwilliam Papers, MS 3987), pp. 123, 153, 243, 275, 281, 299, 341.
130. St John Ervine, *Parnell*, p. 51.
131. *Summary of the returns of owners of land in Ireland*, HC 1876 (422), vol. lxxx.
132. See Reg. of Deeds, Mem. for 1835, 14.173.
133. John Parnell, son of Sir Henry Brooke Parnell (later Lord Congleton), eventually inherited most of Arthur's property. See *ibid.* 857.64.572064.
134. *Ibid.* for 1844, 17.127.
135. *Ibid.* for 1844, 17.127.
136. John Henry lent Thomas £784 in return for being assigned the mortgage, which was for £1,153. See *ibid.* for 1853, 26.110.
137. The amount is not specified, but Mrs Evans died childless and a widow, so it must have been the bulk of her estate; this impression is reinforced by the fact that there were several annuities due on the sum inherited. See *ibid.* for 1855, 23.9.
138. In various memorials the lands are listed as Aghinlig, Keenaghan, Kinnagoe, Lisasley, Mullaghring and Timacronnor. See *Ibid.* for 1847, 12.212.
139. *Ibid.* for 1857, 6.172.
140. *Ibid.*
141. St John Ervine, *Parnell*, p. 51. The total rental in 1780 was £1,157 according to a statement in the Congleton Papers (Bundle 4).
142. The only rents mentioned for the period are certainly low: £47 2s 4d for 52 acres (Reg. of deeds, Mem. for 1857, 6.172) and £16 17s 0d for 21 acres (*ibid.* for 1858, 5.227).
143. *Ibid.* for 1858, 25.123.
144. See *ibid.* for 1858, 25.123. 'The manor and lordship of Clonmore and all those the castles, town and lands of Killelongford, Kingsholding, Little Scotland, Ballyshane, Ballyduff, Ballynakill, Ballynagilkey, Ballysallagh, Knockballystile, Creerin, Raheen, Raheendrohogue, Rahinshinogue, Cullenagh, Tombreagh, Drumguin, Ballycullane, Constable Hill, Brownbogg, Ballaghclay, Killneany,

Cronoskeagh, Eagle Hill, Hacketstown, Rathnegrew, Raheeneels, Ballykilduff, Minamaul, Monsteel; and Carrowree'.

145. Letter to Sullivan (see note 101 above).

146. Reg. of Deeds, Mem. for 1859, 12.26.

147. *Ibid.* 29.251. The rent was £25 11s 9d; the purchase price was unmentioned.

148. J. H. Parnell, p. 40.

149. *Thom's Directory*, 1841, p. 194. It had a capital of £800,000 and shares were £100 each.

150. J. H. Parnell, p. 44.

151. See *Thom's Directory* for the period. (Sir Ralph was a director of the Bank of Ireland, as well as having subsidiary commercial interests.)

152. St John Ervine, *Parnell*, p.53.

153. J. H. Parnell, p. 40.

154. *Leinster Express*, 16 July 1859.

155. *Wicklow Newsletter*, 9 July 1859.

156. *Ibid.* 23 July 1859. He was the youngest son of the great Henry Grattan.


## 2. 'The Belle of New York'

1. In vol. xviii. He is mentioned at length in the *Dictionary of American biography*, which gives his dates as 1750–1819.

2. For further details of Frederic Tudor see Daniel J. Boorstin, *The Americans: the National experience* (N.Y., 1965), Part 1, Chapter 2.

3. He lived from 1779 to 1830.

4. *Dictionary of American biography*, xix, 47–8.

5. Quoted in R. M. McWade, *Life of Stewart Parnell*, p. 34.

6. D. T. S. Parnell to T. D. Sullivan, 21 Jan. 1880, p. 18 (N.L.I., Sullivan Papers, MS 8237/6; hereafter cited as 'Letter to Sullivan').

7. *Ibid.* p. 7.

8. See *A biographical sketch and the services of Commodore Charles Stewart*, (1838); *The Stewart clan magazine*, October 1830; E. S. Ellis, 'Old Ironsides', in *Chatauquan*, July 1898; J. Frost, *American naval biographies* (New York, 1844); C. Morris, *Heroes of the navy in America* (1907); C. J. Peterson, *The American navy and biographical sketches of American naval heroes* (1858); Fenimore Cooper, *History of the American navy; Public ledger* (Philadelphia), 8 November 1869.

9. Quoted in R. M. McWade, *Life of Stewart Parnell*, p. 38.

10. E. Dickinson, p. 210.

11. Letter to Sullivan, p. 18.

12. E. Dickinson, p. 38. Wigram later offered to adopt Emily outright.

13. *Ibid.* p. 7.

14. Mrs Parnell refers, of course, to the baronial piles erected by great industrial families in the late nineteenth century and ironically called 'the Newport cottages'.

15. Quoted in R. M. McWade, *Life of Stewart Parnell*, p. 43.

16. Above, p.55.

17. Letter to Sullivan, pp. 8–9.

18. *Ibid.* That both sides of the family were originally 'immensely wealthy' seems unsubstantiated, and contradicted by her own evidence.

19. R. M. McWade, *Life of Stewart Parnell*, p. 35.

20. Letter to Sullivan, p. 13.

21. *Dictionary of American biography*, xix, 48.

22. Quoted in R. M. McWade, *Life of Stewart Parnell*, p. 38.

23. Letter to Sullivan, p. 3.

24. Quoted in R. M. McWade, *Life of Stewart Parnell*, p. 46.

25. Theodosia was born at Torquay (*ibid.*); and Charles Stewart Parnell told Sir

Robert Edgecumbe that he had lived there as a child, though when driven there he was unable to remember in which house (O'Brien, *Parnell*, ii, 157). He also had an idea that he had been born at Brighton (T. P. O'Connor, *Memories of an old parliamentarian* (London, 1929) i, 98), although he was baptised at Rathdrum.

26. J. H. Parnell, p. 3.
27. Letter to Sullivan, p. 11.
28. J. H. Parnell, p. 3.
29. E. Dickinson, p. 5.
30. Quoted in R. M. McWade, *Life of Stewart Parnell*, p. 26.
31. Letter to Sullivan, p. 10.
32. E. Dickinson, p. 9.
33. R. M. McWade, *Life of Stewart Parnell*, p. 44.
34. *Ibid.* p. 50.
35. E. Dickinson, p. 4.
36. J. H. Parnell, p. 61.
37. Letter to Sullivan, p. 11.
38. *Ibid.*
39. E. Dickinson, p. 36. My italics.
40. *Ibid.* p. 80.
41. See full attendance list in *Daily Nation*, 2 April 1898; none of the familiar names of the Wicklow county families are mentioned.
42. J. H. Parnell, p. 10.
43. R. M. McWade, *Life of Stewart Parnell*, p. 33.
44. See p.
45. R. M. McWade, *Life of Stewart Parnell*, p. 34.
46. This is presumably a reference to the belief that a high instep indicates good breeding. Letter to Sullivan, p. 10.
47. R. M. McWade, *Life of Stewart Parnell*, p. 49.
48. Letter to Sullivan, p. 12.
49. See Davitt, *Fall of feudalism*, pp. 658–9. For Anne Ward see above, part I, p.4.
50. St John Ervine, *Parnell*, p. 24.
51. See above, p.90.
52. The patriotic children were John Charles, Fanny and Anna; T. Sherlock, *Parnell*, p. 30. See also R. Johnston, *Parnell and the Parnells* (London and Dublin 1888), p. 18, and R. M. McWade, *Life of Stewart Parnell*, p. 103.
53. St John Ervine, *Parnell*, p. 24.
54. R. M. McWade, *Life of Stewart Parnell*, p. 61.
55. J. H. Parnell, p. 128.
56. *Ibid.*
57. R. M. McWade, *Life of Stewart Parnell*, p. 61.
58. *Ibid.* p. 64.
59. *Ibid.*
60. Letter to Sullivan, p. 21.
61. McWade, *Life of Stewart Parnell*, p. 30.

### 3. The Parnell children

1. The reference is to the Norman Duke, a companion of William the Conqueror, who is mentioned by Mrs Parnell as ancestor of the Parnells.
2. R. M. McWade, *Life of Stewart Parnell*, p. 46.
3. I have compiled these dates from J. H. Parnell's memoir, Burke's *Landed gentry of Ireland*, and Debrett's *Peerage*.
4. J. H. Parnell, p. 12.
5. *Ibid.*

6. E. Dickinson, pp. 10–11.

7. Letter to Sullivan, last page (un-numbered).

8. E. Dickinson, p. 45.

9. Reg of Deeds, Mem. for 1859, 19.138.

10. E. Dickinson, p. 46.

11. J. H. Parnell, pp. 10–11.

12. Letter to Sullivan, p. 13.

13. Above, pp. 46, 66.

14. E. Dickinson, p. 8.

15. Published London, 1905.

16. J. H. Parnell, pp. 7–8. The play was *She stoops to conquer;* Charles Stewart played a page.

17. E. Dickinson, p. 79.

18. *Ibid.* p. 8. The hall is imposing enough, but by no means as grand as that.

19. *Ibid.* p. 30.

20. *Ibid.* p. 10.

21. The whole story is strikingly reminiscent of a contemporary whose patience in love was also rewarded by a disastrous union; three years after Emily Dickinson's wedding, after an equally long engagement, Katharine Wood married another dashing young subaltern, called Willie O'Shea. See Katharine O'Shea, *Charles Stewart Parnell: His love story and political life* (2 vols., London, 1914), i, chs. 2–6.

22. E. Dickinson, p. 12.

23. *Ibid.* pp. 21–3. Of her presentation at court she remarks: 'Like all the family, I had that keen enjoyment of life and artistic appreciation of form and colour which goes with the Celtic blood, though some of my charm came from my American mother. My freshness and youth, set off with the Paris gown and the *joie de vie* which I have always possessed, attracted a good deal of attention and won more than a passing smile from the royal personages present.'

24. See above, p. 61.

25. St John Ervine, *Parnell*, p. 40.

26. E. Dickinson, pp. 27–31.

27. Published London, 1916.

28. J. H. Parnell, p. 29.

29. Quoted in R. M. McWade, *Life of Stewart Parnell*, p. 46.

30. J. H. Parnell, p. 29.

31. *Ibid.* p. 38.

32. *Ibid.* p. 27.

33. Letter to Sullivan, last page.

34. J. H. Parnell, pp. 13, 20.

35. *Ibid.* p. 13.

36. Originally told in T. Sherlock, *Parnell;* given in full in J. M. Parnell's *C. S. Parnell*, p. 20; used to damning effect in St John Ervine's *Parnell* in 1925.

37. J. H. Parnell, p. 21.

38. *Ibid.* p. 11.

39. He was known locally as 'young Parnell', and was a familiar figure round the locality until his death in the 1930s.

40. J. H. Parnell, p. 13.

41. R.M. McWade, *Life of Stewart Parnell*, p.48. See above, p. 61.

42. St John Ervine, *Parnell*, p. 40.

43. J. H. Parnell, p. 19.

44. *Ibid.*

45. Mrs Twopenny is mentioned in J. H. Parnell's memoir; but long before the publication of this, an article by T. M. Healy in the *Westminster Budget*, 10 November 1893 (vol. ii, no. 41, pp. 9–11), recalled how Parnell used to compare Rowland Winn, the Tory whip at Westminster, to 'an old nurse I had – she had a very

queer name – Mrs Twopenny'. As Healy told it, Parnell would go on to recall Mrs Twopenny in fits and snatches between Parliamentary speeches, emphasising his fear of her and her fund of frightening stories. Healy gained the impression that 'it was from this antique serving-woman the Irish leader drew whatever tendency towards the "Abberglaubisch" his childhood received'.

46. An illuminated address which accompanied the Parnell Tribute, now in T. C. D. MSS collection, contains many scenes of this kind.

47. J. H. Parnell, p. 11.
48. *Ibid.* p. 20.
49. *Ibid.* p. 24.
50. *Ibid.*
51. *Ibid.*
52. *Ibid.* p. 26.
53. E. Dickinson, p. 9.
54. J. H. Parnell, p. 27.
55. *Ibid.*
56. *Ibid.* p. 30.
57. *Ibid.* p. 31.
58. *Ibid.* p. 34.
59. Letter to Sullivan, p. 54.
60. J. H. Parnell, pp. 13, 22.
61. *Ibid.* p. 30.
62. *Ibid.* p. 24.
63. *Ibid.* pp. 31-2.
64. *Ibid.*
65. *Ibid.* p. 33.
66. *Ibid.* p. 19.
67. *Ibid.* p. 26.
68. *Ibid.* 'He complained to me afterwards that they all made love to him and bothered him out of his life. In any case, he resented being sent to a girls' school, on the grounds that it was not manly.'
69. *Ibid.*
70. He returned home in 1855; his illness took place late in 1854. O'Brien, *Parnell,* i, 37.
71. J. H. Parnell, p. 32.
72. *Ibid.* p. 35.
73. R. M. McWade, *Life of Stewart Parnell,* p. 51. Also see her rather smug anecdote to Sullivan describing how travellers on the Rathdrum stage exclaimed that 'that little fellow has been wonderfully well taught'.
74. R. M. McWade, *Life of Stewart Parnell,* p. 50.
75. Letter to Sullivan, p. 5.
76. J. H. Parnell, p. 28. He consistently ridiculed attempts to provide religious education.
77. R. M. McWade, *Life of Stewart Parnell,* p. 46.
78. O'Brien, *Parnell,* i, 37.
79. Letter to Sullivan, p. 5.
80. St John Ervine, *Parnell,* p. 30.
81. J. H. Parnell, p. 20.
82. *Ibid.* p. 30.
83. *Ibid.* p. 33.
84. *Ibid.* p. 34.
85. *Ibid.* p. 36.
86. *Ibid.*

## Part III: Parnell before politics

### 1. The Parnell family

1. J. H. Parnell, p. 39.
2. *Wicklow Newsletter and General Advertiser*, 30 July 1859.
3. See inventory published in *Wicklow Newsletter*, 1 October 1859.
4. See *ibid.* 1 December 1860.
5. *Ibid* 19 December 1863.
6. E. Dickinson, *A patriot's mistake* (London, 1905), p. 33.
7. J. H. Parnell, p. 41.
8. E. Dickinson, p. 33.
9. The railway was being extended to the area at this time. Edwards appears as resident at Avondale in records like the Rathdrum Horticultural Show prizes, *Wicklow newsletter*, 20 August 1864.
10. E. Dickinson, p. 34.
11. J. H. Parnell, p. 34. The house was called Khyber Pass; it is now the Killiney Heights Hotel. John Howard Parnell returned to this area towards the end of his life, and was living at Glenageary when he died.
12. The intermediate house was in Kingstown and belonged to the O'Connor Don – 'Granite Lodge', near Clarinda Park.
13. No. 14, now part of the Children's Hospital.
14. E. Dickinson, p. 35.
15. J. H. Parnell, p. 45.
16. *Ibid.* p. 39.
17. E. Dickinson, p. 33.
18. J. H. Parnell, p. 39.
19. *Ibid.*
20. Reg. of Deeds. Mem. for 1862, 18.112. They were appointed so on 4 April 1860.
21. *Ibid.* for 1863, 17.141.
22. E. Dickinson, p. 37.
23. *Ibid.* See part II of this work, chap. 2, p. 56.
24. Reg. of Deeds, Mem. for 1862, 18.112.
25. J. H. Parnell, p. 39.
26. *Ibid.* p. 114.
27. See above, part III, chap. 2. pp.129–30.
28. E. Dickinson, p. 34.
29. Ibid. p. 192.
30. See, for instance, recollections of Captain Mateer and Hugh Gaffney, both of whom knew him well.
31. See her letter to T. D. Sullivan, 21 January 1880 (N.L.I., Sullivan Papers, MS 8237/6), p. 3: 'So far from inheriting my husband's property I gave up the dower I might have had, hoping that my dear brother's bequest to me would be enough'.
32. E. Dickinson, p. 33.
33. J. H. Parnell, p. 61.
34. See Reg. of Deeds, Mem. for 1862, 18.112.
35. *Ibid.*
36. E. Dickinson, pp. 37–8.
37. See Reg. of Deeds, Mem. for 1862, 18.112.
38. Emily Dickinson states this quite categorically. See *A patriot's mistake*, p. 34.
39. E. Dickinson, p. 65.
40. J. H. Parnell, p. 41.
41. *Ibid.* p. 43. The house was 'Granite Lodge', Clarinda Park.
42. *Ibid.* p. 45.
43. *Ibid.* p. 44.

44. *Ibid.* pp. 54 and 61.

45. E. Dickinson, p. 37.

46. *Ibid.*

47. J. H. Parnell, p. 55.

48. He was George William Frederick Howard, the seventh earl, b. 1802. As Lord Morpeth, he was Chief Secretary of Ireland 1835–41. A Liberal, he was in favour of Roman Catholic claims and The Law Reform. He was Lord Lieutenant from 1855 to 1858, and resumed the office when Palmerston returned to power in 1859. He retired in October 1864. See *Annual Register,* 1864, p. 183, for his great personal popularity in Dublin. For an irreverent and entertaining account of the social side of his viceroyalty see *Recollections of Dublin Castle and of Dublin society by a citizen,* (London 1902), pp. 60–81.

49. J. H. Parnell, p. 62.

50. See R. M. McWade, *Life of Stewart Parnell,* p. 61; also above, part III, chap. 2, p.63.

51. *Recollections of Dublin Castle and of Dublin society by a citizen* (London 1902), pp. 130–1.

52. *Ibid.* p. 128.

53. J. H. Parnell, p. 61.

54. *Ibid.* p. 178.

55. *Ibid.* p. 62.

56. *Ibid.* p. 46.

57. Letter to Sullivan, p. 4.

58. J. H. Parnell, p. 115.

59. *Ibid.* p. 116.

60. *Ibid.* p. 117.

61. E. Dickinson, p. 79.

62. See Reg. of Deeds, Mem. for 1866, 21.202. where Stewart undertook to pay the debts chargeable on Sophy regarding her father's affairs and the Howard v. Zouche case: also Mem. for 1867, 32.68, where the trusteeship of Sophy's annuity and an insurance policy for £1,000 was made over by Stewart to Emily and Arthur Dickinson.

63. J. H. Parnell, p. 44.

64. *Ibid.*

65. *Ibid.* p. 50.

66. *Ibid.* p. 51.

67. *Ibid.* p. 59.

68. *Ibid.* p. 117.

69. Her name, for instance, never appears in the lists of donations to local charities published in the *Wicklow Newsletter* for this period.

70. See T. Sherlock, *Life of C.S. Parnell* (Dublin 1882), p. 30; R. Johnston, *Parnell and the Parnells* (London and Dublin, 1888); p. 18; R. M. McWade, *Life of Stewart Parnell,* p. 103.

71. See above, part II, chap. 2, pp. 62–4.

72. Below, part V, chap. 2.

73. O'Brien, *Parnell,* i, 39. The Earl was then Lord Brabazon, elsewhere named as a classmate by John Howard Parnell.

74. J. H. Parnell, p. 48.

75. For instance in the House of Commons, 16 February 1844.

76. And often said as much. See below, part IV, chap. 4, ii, for his activities in the East Wicklow Loyal & Patriotic Union.

77. J. H. Parnell, p. 58.

78. E. Dickinson, p. 60. Justin McCarthy, for instance, retails the story in his *Reminiscences,* ii, 109 (wrongly placing it as at Avondale) and attributes Parnell's political orientation from the incident.

79. O'Brien, *Parnell,* i, p. 47.

80. R. Johnston, *Parnell and the Parnells, p.19*

81. J. H. Parnell, pp. 69–71.

82. See *Celtic Monthly,* May 1881, pp. 328–9.

83. See John Devoy, *Recollections of an Irish Rebel* (London, 1929), p. 43.

84. See *ibid;* also William O'Brien, *Evening memories,* pp. 58–9.

85. See 'Fanny Parnell' (anonymous) in *Celtic magazine,* vol. i, no. 2 (September 1882), p. 284.

86. J. H. Parnell, p. 69.

87. *Ibid.,* p. 71

88. *Ibid.*

89. *Ibid.* p. 72.

90. E. Dickinson, p. 60.

91. K. O'Shea, i, 127.

92. R. M. McWade, *Life of Stewart Parnell,* p. 75.

93. J. H. Parnell, p. 128. See above, part II, chap. 2, pp. 62–3.

94. F. Power Cobbe, *The Life of Frances Power Cobbe, by herself* (2 vols., London, 1894), i, p. 186.

95. *Ibid.* i, p. 187.

96. J. H. Parnell, p. 69.

97. *Ibid.*

98. *Ibid.* p. 125.

99. *Ibid.* p. 87.

100. *Ibid.* p. 55.

101. *Ibid.* p. 125.

102. See E. Dickinson, pp. 45–7.

103. *Ibid.* p. 31.

104. *Ibid.* p. 40.

105. J. H. Parnell, p. 59.

106. E. Dickinson, p. 45.

107. See above. p. 120.

108. E. Dickinson, p. 79.

109. *Ibid.* pp. 71–3.

110. *Ibid.*

111. *Ibid.* p. 86. 'What words can describe the torture of witnessing the slow but sure descent of one you love, of seeing him go from bad to worse, and feeling your utter impotency to save him? of watching his frantic struggles to resist the temptation, only to fall again in the end, and saddest of all, the sight of his remorse and repentance, his fears and promises of reformation – in fact, the piteous spectacle of a strong man drinking himself slowly but surely to death?'

112. *Ibid.* p. 90. Charles's request caused 'the only estrangement that ever existed between him and me'.

113. *Ibid.* p. 97.

114. *Ibid.* p. 85.

115. *Ibid.* p. 97.

116. Reg. of Deeds, Mem. for 1867, 32.68.

117. E. Dickinson, p. 120.

118. See *Wicklow Newsletter,* 11 August 1860. The Clerkship alone was worth £800 p.a. The auction of his effects (*ibid.* 22 October 1864) shows him to have been a man of substance.

119. See *Celtic Monthly,* April 1881, p. 329.

120. See Lady Caroline Howard's journal for 1869 (N.L.I., Wicklow Papers, MS 4792).

121. References in the *Wicklow Newsletter* of this period refer to them as 'The Dickinsons of Avondale'.

122. J. H. Parnell, p. 45.

123. *Ibid.* p. 49.

124. According to his book, this was 1869; but a memorial in the Registry of Deeds records him as resident in America in December 1866 (Mem. for 1867 2.16).

125. J. H. Parnell, p. 58.

126. *Ibid.* p. 111.

127. *Ibid.* p. 113.

128. See *The Times,* 9 August 1873, p. 16.

129. She must have adopted the casual Irish attitude towards litigation; in no other country could families, then as now, bring lawsuits against each other as readily or forget them so easily.

130. J. H. Parnell, p. 114.

131. *Ibid.* p. 115.

132. Reg. of Deeds, Mem. for 1868, 14.134.

133. John Henry Parnell and John Howard Parnell v. the rt. hon. Henry Parnell and William George Prescott.

134. Reg. of Deeds, Mem. for 1870, 32.192.

135. *Ibid.* for 1868, 14.135.

136. J. H. Parnell, p. 112.

137. N.L.I., MS 2716. The Ordnance Survey put the estate at 1,747 acres in its entirety (Reg. of Deeds, Mem. for 1867, 2.16). For details of estate leases see *ibid.* for 1865, 26.95, and for 1867, 2.16.

138. Reserving many rights, ranging from advowsons to minerals, for T.C.D. Mortgage to W. Smith and M. Fenton, Reg. of Deeds, Mem. for 1867, 2.16.

139. See above, pp. 127–30.

140. J. H. Parnell, pp. 123–4.

141. A. letter from R. T. C. Johnson in the *Freeman's Journal,* 5 March 1874, p. 7, explains this. See below, pp.

142. The results were: Andrew O'Byrne (H.R.) – 1,511; Fitzwilliam Dick (C.) – 1,146; Lord Fitzwilliam, (L.) – 927; and J. H. Parnell (H.R.) – 553. J. Vincent and M. Stenton (eds.,) *McCalmont's parliamentary pollbook* (8th ed., Brighton, 1971).

143. E. Dickinson, p. 34.

144. See J. H. Parnell, and *Wicklow Newsletter,* 1 June 1867.

145. E. Dickinson, p. 34.

146. *Ibid.* pp. 34, 61.

147. *Ibid.* p. 89.

148. J. H. Parnell, pp. 41, 45.

149. E. Dickinson, p. 65.

150. J. H. Parnell, p. 46. He places this incident in the context of the year 1862; it must have been a good deal later, as Fanny and Charles were only thirteen and sixteen years old respectively at this time.

151. R. M. McWade, *Life of Stewart Parnell,* p. 71.

152. See above, pp. 69, 94.

153. *Ibid.*

154. Standish O'Grady, *The story of Ireland,* p. 325.

155. E. Dickinson, p. 66.

156. *Ibid.* p. 123.

157. J. A. Venn (ed.), *Alumni Cantabrigiensis* (Cambridge, 1953), part ii, vol. vi, p. 33.

158. *Ibid.*

159. See above, part ii, chap. 1, pp. 51–2.

160. D. T. S. Parnell to T. D. Sullivan, 21 January 1880, (N.L.I., Sullivan Papers, MS 8237/6).

161. See above, part ii, chap. 1, p. 51.

162. Reg. of Deeds, Mem. for 1859, 12.26 and 29.251.

163. *Wicklow Newsletter,* 5 September 1868.

164. St John Ervine, *Parnell,* p. 52.

165. See Reg. of Deeds, Mem. for 1974, 24.178, 25.77, 26.97, 26.101, 26.180, 29.11, 30.132, 30.177, 32.45, 42.8, 44.259; for 1875, 8.224, 37.38; for 1876, 1.77, 4.28.

166. The lands of Garnagale (244 ac.), Ballynascarne (216 ac.), and Glenreagh (157 ac.), The rent roll was £451 p.a. See *ibid.* for 1874, 47.287, for a detailed schedule of the estate.

167. Originally £56,000, but less £5,697 for 767 acres sold off in 1859 (*ibid.* for 1859, 12.26) and an undisclosed sum made by the sale of 119 acres (*ibid.* 29.251).

168. See references in n. 165, above. The head-rents reserved totalled £509 p.a.

169. Reg. of Deeds, Mem. for 1874, 47.289.

170. The lands were Blindeanis and Ballinagilkey in Rathvilly, comprising 422 acres. After putting the title in his brother's name, Henry sold them to Major Glascott of Wicklow for £4,500. See *ibid.* 1875, 2.246, and for 1876, 1.77.

171. *Celtic Monthly,* April 1881, vol. v, no. 4, pp. 326–9. Mr Hugh Gaffney of Roundwood, Co. Wicklow, recalled that a great-uncle of his accompanied Henry Parnell on a trip to Madeira for the sake of his health when he was still quite young.

172. See Debrett's *Peerage.*

173. See Reg. of Deeds, Mem. for 1874, 26.101.

174. *Ibid.* 30.132.

175. For the Eagle Hill sale, see *ibid.* 32.345.

176. See *ibid.* for 1874, 42.8.

177. *Ibid.* for 1875, 37.38. The rent roll was £1,050 p.a. Kemmis and Lopes were acting as trustees for Quentin Dick, another Wicklow landowner (and M.P. for the county).

178. R. M. McWade, *Life of Stewart Parnell,* p. 73.

179. *Ibid.* p. 74.

180. *Wicklow Newsletter,* 19 September 1874.

181. See above, part V, chap. 4, p. 282.


## 2. The young Parnell

1. J. H. Parnell, p. 47.

2. D. T. S. Parnell to T. D. Sullivan, 21 January 1880. Letter in Sullivan Papers, N.L.I., MS 8237/6, p. 5; hereafter cited as 'Letter to Sullivan'.

3. As regards radical opinion and social practice she seems to have resembled Samuel Johnson's friend Mrs Macaulay, who was 'a great republican'; but when Johnson begged that in that case her footman be allowed to dine with them, 'she never liked him since'. See F. A. Pottle (ed.), *Boswell's London Journal, 1762–63* (The Reprint Society, London, 1950), p. 308.

4. J. H. Parnell, p. 48.

5. Earlier John states that they were respectively fifteen and nineteen years old, but this is not consistent with the dating as 'four years after our father's death'. I am assuming the Parnells began at Chipping Norton in autumn 1863. Charles entered Cambridge two years later, in 1865.

6. *Who's who* (London 1913), p. 1372.

7. *Ibid.* p. 1603. He was, in fact, two years younger than Charles, so the Parnells were not the most junior pupils.

8. J. H. Parnell, p. 48.

9. *Ibid.*

10. *Ibid.* p. 50.

11. O'Brien, *Parnell,* i, p. 38. The informant ('B—') was probably the Earl of

Meath, who had been Lord Brabazon at the time.

12. J. H. Parnell, p. 49.

13. *Ibid.* p. 58.

14. Ged Martin, 'Parnell at Cambridge: the education of an Irish nationalist', in *I.H.S.*, xix, no. 73 (March 1974), pp. 72–82.

15. *Alumni Cantabrigiensis*, part 2, vol. vi, p. 32.

16. R. M. McWade, *Life of Stewart Parnell*, p. 51.

17. J. H. Parnell, p. 52.

18. *Ibid.*

19. *Parnell*, i, p. 80.

20. A. C. Benson made an attempt to have a commemorative plaque erected in 1910, but gave up in the face of several objections. In 1920 the issue of the rooms' location was again raised and the incumbent, an Ulster undergraduate, insisted on moving out of them. A plaque was eventually put up in 1967. (Ged Martin, 'Parnell at Cambridge'.)

21. R. B. O'Brien, *Parnell*, i, p. 80.

22. *Ibid.* p. 64.

23. 'During the whole of my residence at Magdalene I do not think there were in the college more than, at the outside, three or four genuine loafers, men, that is, who were keen about nothing. And one of these, strange to say, afterwards attained considerable eminence in a career which in a special degree demanded energy and activity.' Samuel Sproston, *Magdalene in the Sixties*, quoted in Ged Martin, 'Parnell at Cambridge'.

24. E. K. Purnell, *Magdalene College* (London 1904), Cambridge College Histories series, p. 195.

25. 7 June 1867 and 3 May 1869; see *Cambridge Chronicle*.

26. S. Sproston, *Magdalene in the Sixties*.

27. E. Dickinson, p. 49.

28. *Ibid.* This story is effectively demolished by Henry Harrison and Ged Martin; see below.

29. Samuel Sproston, *Magdalene in the sixties*. See Ged Martin, 'Parnell at Cambridge'.

30. *Cambridge Independent Press*, 22 May 1869, p. 6; see above p. 320.

31. Parnell told Davitt years later that he gave the policeman a coin which he thought was a sovereign, but turned out to be a shilling, and that this was what offended the constable. M. Davitt, *The fall of feudalism in Ireland* (London and New York, 1904), p. 107.

32. See above, p. 120.

33. A. Kettle, *The material for victory* (ed. L. J. Kettle, Dublin, 1958), p. 68.

34. See Ged Martin, 'Parnell at Cambridge'.

35. J. H. Parnell, p. 54. 'There is no doubt that the fact of his never having been at a real school, and having a continued change of tutors, coupled with the perfunctory nature of his studies at college, considerably hampered him in after-life. He often expressed to me his regret that he had not received a better education, and even that he had not devoted himself with more application to such opportunities as he had for study. One result was that he was always afraid of lapsing into an error of grammar or spelling, and for a considerable time wrote out his speeches word for word, and carefully corrected them before delivery. His letters also ... show frequent signs of erasure and alteration.'

36. See below.

37. See J. H. Parnell, part III, chapters 3 and 4.

38. *Ibid.* p. 82.

39. *Ibid.* p. 84.

40. *Ibid.* p. 86.

41. A Mr Dunne, *Ibid.* pp. 91–4.

42. *Ibid.* p. 98.

43. *Ibid.* p. 111.
44. *Ibid.* p. 117.
45. See Appendix.
46. See for instance *Wicklow Newsletter*, 20 August 1864.
47. October 19 1864. See *ibid.* 22 October 1864.
48. 13 April 1861. The meeting took place on 5 April.
49. J. H. Parnell, p. 44.
50. Wicklow Newsletter, 29 June 1867.
51. See Reg. of Deeds, Mem. for 1869, 26.67. The schedule was as follows:

| Lands | Quit-, Chief, Head-Rents | | | Grand Denomination | Gross Yearly Rents | | |
|---|---|---|---|---|---|---|---|
| | £ | s | d | | £ | s | d |
| Ballytrasna | | | | | | | |
| (Ballyknockan) | 4 | 0 | 3¾ | Ballytrasna | 237 | 15 | 10 |
| Kingston | 200 | 0 | 0 | ibid | 225 | 5 | 11 |
| Ibid., | 3 | 1 | 1¾ | ibid | 301 | 13 | 0 |
| The Meetings | 2 | 11 | 9½ | ibid | 124 | 13 | 10 |
| Tyclash | 9 | 3 | 1 | ibid | 36 | 11 | 9 |
| Ballyteague | 2 | 2 | 0½ | ibid | 16 | 10 | 0 |
| Ballyeustace | | 2 | 1½ | ibid | 65 | 0 | 0 |
| Garrymore | 48 | 18 | 0 | Glenmalure | 42 | 18 | 4 |
| Clonkeen | 4 | 1 | 2½ | ibid | | | |
| Caravellagh | | | | | | | |
| (Corasillagh) | none | | | ibid | 63 | 15 | 0 |
| Bomaskea | none | | | ibid | 57 | 18 | 0 |
| Carrignamuck | none | | | Aughavannagh | 74 | 4 | 0 |
| Carrignaweel | none | | | ibid | 75 | 15 | 0 |
| Avondale | 1 | 13 | 0 | Ballytrasna | 260 | 0 | 0 |
| Casino | none | | | ibid | 94 | 10 | 0 |
| Aughavanagh | 15 | 0 | 0 | Aughavannagh | 80 | 0 | 0 |
| Corraskillaand | | | | | | | |
| Branskey mines | none | | | ibid | 40 | 0 | 0 |
| | | | | | | | |
| 3807 ac lr 38p | 280 | 19 | 9 | | 1789 | 10 | 11 |

52. See above, pp. 127–30.
53. C. S. Parnell to J. Mills King, 13 October 1870 (N.L.I., Parnell Letters, MS 15,735).
54. Same to same, 23 November 1870 (T.C.D., letters of C. S. Parnell, MS 2241).
55. J. H. Parnell, p. 287.
56. *Ibid.* p. 59.
57. *Ibid.* p. 62. Bookey was later found drowned after yachting in the Mediterranean. These sawmills were not in fact the only ones in the country; Peter Boland of Arklow owned one worth £2,000 in 1874. (See *Wicklow Newsletter,* 4 December 1874); and John Barton of Annamoe had a larger mill than Bookey's in the 1870s.
58. J.H. Parnell, p. 76.
59. *Ibid.* pp. 92–3.
60. *Ibid.* p. 113.
61. See below. Reg. of Deeds, Mem. for 1871, 23.178.
62. *Ibid.*
63. As late as 1972 an Annamoe neighbour remembered seeing Parnell ride over to ask for a beech tree to try his sawmill on.
64. See *Wicklow Newsletter,* 5 September 1869. Thomas Gaffney took 'first prize for winter onions, potato, onions, parsnips, lettuce, flat Dutch and Bangor potatoes,

white gooseberries and apples; second prize for celery, carrots, York cabbage, drumhead cabbage, red gooseberries, white currants, dahlias, asters, verbenas, stocks, hollyhocks and marigolds'. Also see *ibid.* 14 August 1869, for similar successes in the following year.

65. J. H. Parnell, p. 63.

66. Later one of Parnell's earliest political supporters.

67. J. H. Parnell, p. 111.

68. See *Irish Sale Catalogues*, 1901, in N.L.I.

69. J. H. Parnell, p. 51.

70. See *Wicklow Newsletter*, 7 September 1861.

71. *Ibid.* 7 June 1862. Playing against Mr Hodgson's eleven, Charles made four not out.

72. *Ibid.* 12 July 1862 and 16 August 1862, when Charles made 26 for South Wicklow against North Wicklow and received a special mention.

73. And bowled out four of the opposition. *Ibid.* 25 July 1863.

74. *Ibid.* 18 June 1864.

75. *Ibid.* editorial, 10 May 1890.

76. *Ibid.* 25 June 1864.

77. *Ibid.* 9 July 1864.

78. See *ibid.* and *Irish Times*, 29 August, 1868.

79. *Wicklow Newsletter*, 18 September 1869.

80. Standish O'Grady, *Story of Ireland*, pp. 207–8.

81. O'Brien, *Parnell*, i, p. 52.

82. Lady Alice Howard's Diary for 1874, entry for 4 August (N.L.I., Wicklow Papers, MS 3600).

83. *Ibid.* entry for 6 September. (N.L.I., Wicklow papers, MS 3600).

84. K. O'Shea, ii, 49.

85. See *Wicklow Newsletter*, 26 September 1891.

86. J. H. Parnell, p. 58.

87. See *ibid.* part III, ch. 4. In the Birmingham coal-mines 'he went into every detail of the methods of production with the keenest attention', and examining a grist-mill near West Point he was disappointed when the owner would not dismantle it to show him a certain component' (p. 84).

88. See *Wicklow Newsletter*, 4 March 1865, for his appointment as a lieutenant on 25 February 1865.

89. J. H. Parnell, p. 54.

90. *Ibid.* p. 55.

91. *Ibid.* p. 56.

92. *Ibid.* pp. 63, 117.

93. E. Dickinson, p. 59.

94. *Ibid.* p. 60.

95. O'Brien, *Parnell*, i, p. 53.

96. J. H. Parnell, p. 52.

97. O'Brien, *Parnell*, i, p. 53.

98. At a speech in University College, Dublin, on 13 December 1877. See *Nation*, 22 December 1877.

99. See an article quoted from *Irish World* in *Nation*, 4 December 1880.

100. See *Irish Sale Catalogues* (1901) in N.L.I.

101. He often used to read this without a smile, remarking that it was 'a curious book' – thus anticipating much later interpretations of it as a masterpiece of surrealism. See K. O'Shea, i, 166.

102. J. H. Parnell, p. 58.

103. *Ibid.* p. 62.

104. Possibly Comerford or Chaloner.

105. J. H. Parnell, p. 73.

106. Lady Alice Howard's diary for 1874, entry for 11 November (N.L.I., Wicklow Papers, NS 3600).

107. *Ibid.* 18 November.

108. *Ibid.* 26 September.

109. *Ibid.* 10 February.

110. J. H. Parnell, pp. 117, 282. In the 1880s Parnell wanted to buy whinstone from the Carysfort quarries, but felt it was not even worth his while asking for it; he only heard indirectly that Carysfort was willing to sell it to him. See above, part IV, p. 156.

111. See below, part IV.

112. See E. Dickinson, chapter 5.

113. Mrs Dickinson's recollections of how she organised the event are reminiscent of Dr Fagan planning the Llanabba School Sports in Evelyn Waugh's *Decline and Fall*, even down to the incongruous band. The overtones of grandiose pretension and self-delusion are also similar.

114. E. Dickinson, p. 71.

115. *Ibid.* p. 76. Her bedroom had been invaded by the officers, in an accidental manner, the night before.

116. *Ibid.* p. 77.

117. *Ibid.* p. 79.

118. J. H. Parnell, p. 101.

119. *Ibid.* p. 90.

120. O'Brien, *Parnell*, i, p. 55.

121. J. H. Parnell, p. 82.

122. *Ibid.* p. 131.

123. See *Thom's Directory*, 1872, p. 1282.

124. R. M. McWade, *Life of Stewart Parnell*, p. 108.

125. *Ibid.*

126. O'Brien, *Parnell*, i, p. 54.

127. J. H. Parnell, p. 64.

128. Letter to Sullivan. R. B. Cunninghame Graham in an article on Parnell in *Dana* in 1904 claimed he was not popular 'even on his own estate', but Graham was self-confessedly a 'desultory' friend of Parnell's and the statement is unsubstantiated.

129. See *Wicklow Newsletter*, 22 March 1873; also *Thom's Directory*.

130. *Wicklow Newsletter*, 25 July 1874 and *Thom's Directory*.

131. See *Wicklow Newsletter*, 7 May 1870, 18 March 1871 and 15 March 1873, 20 April 1872.

132. *Ibid.* 16 July 1870; also O'Brien, *Parnell*, i, p. 57.

133. Although he attended meetings of the Board from time to time.

134. Standish O'Grady, *Story of Ireland*, p. 208.

135. *Wicklow Newsletter*, 2 October 1875.

136. R. M. McWade, *Life of Stewart Parnell*, p. 106. According to McWade, Fanny then paid the fine herself.

137. J. H. Parnell, p. 49.

138. *Ibid.* p. 50.

139. *Ibid.* p. 52.

140. *Ibid.* p. 53.

141. *Ibid.* p. 74.

142. *Ibid.* p. 76.

143. *Ibid.* p. 78.

144. *Ibid.* p. 80.

145. *Ibid.* p. 130.

146. E. Dickinson, p. 111.

147. *Ibid.* pp. 111–19.

148. T. P. O'Connor, *Memories of an old parliamentarian*, i, 234. Though Parnell

told Mrs O'Shea a different version of his American love-affair (see K. O'Shea, i, 138), wherein he was the pursued rather than the pursuer, this was at their first *rendez-vous* and may have been prompted by the politics of flirtation.

149. E. Dickinson, pp. 50–9.

150. *Ibid.* p. 59.

151. Ged Martin has dealt with these efforts fully, using the Magdalene College archives, bundle 'C. S. Parnell, 1906'. see 'Parnell at Cambridge', pp. 76:8.

152. See E. Dickinson, p. 71 and J. H. Parnell, p. 74.

153. J. H. Parnell, p. 116.

154. *Ibid.* p. 125.

155. *Ibid.* p. 127.

156. *Ibid.* p. 126.

157. *Ibid.* p. 48.

158. *Ibid.* p. 52.

159. *Ibid.* p. 47.

160. *Ibid.* p. 52.

161. *Ibid.* p. 78–9.

162. See *ibid.* p. 83 and O'Brien, *Parnell*, i, p. 39.

163. See above. Henry Parnell used the phrase as well, writing to the Master of Magdalene about his brother.

164. J. H. Parnell, p. 98. Also see his worrying when the ship's engines suddenly stopped on the journey home, p. 110.

165. *Ibid.* p. 263. 'I did not notice any particular instances of superstition in Charley during his childhood and boyhood. But in later life a tendency to ascribe an omen for good or ill to the most trivial occurrence and to see the finger of fate in the most commonplace objects became very noticeable. I think it was after the railway accident in America that Charley first began to develop this curious trait in his character'.

166. *Ibid.* p. 84.

167. *Ibid.* p. 124.

168. See *ibid.* p. 105, where Parnell nearly thrashed a Mr Field, whom John 'had always found a most respectable man and got on very well with'.

169. See for instance Standish O'Grady, *The story of Ireland*, p. 211; 'Those who were nearest to him liked him best. His brothers and sisters seem to have loved him much. Even the gentry of Leinster, his neighbours, liked him and watched his strange career as their enemy with a certain amused and affectionate interest.'

170. J. H. Parnell, p. 79.

171. *Ibid.* p. 90.

172. *Ibid.* p. 125.

173. *Ibid.* p. 61.

174. Deerpark, Co. Kildare, and Moorelawn, near Kilcullen, plus 5/9 of numbers 74, 75, 76 and 77, St Stephen's Green. See Reg. of Deeds, Mem. for 1869, 24.134.

175. J. H. Parnell, p. 61.

176. *Ibid.* p. 77.

177. *Ibid.* pp. 79, 88, 106: amount unspecified.

178. *Ibid.* p. 94.

179. *Ibid.* p. 103.

180. *Ibid.*

181. *Ibid.* p. 108.

182. *Ibid.*

183. *Ibid.* p. 111.

184. Reg. of Deeds, Mem. for 1867, 28.193.

185. 23 June 1869. See *ibid.* for 1869, 24.134.

186. *Ibid.*

187. According to a later marginal note in the memorial.

188. According to the *Nation*, which kept a weekly tally.

189. Reg. of Deeds, Mem. for 1869, 27.67.

190. *Ibid.* for 1871, 23.173. The reference to this debt as a 'loan' suggests that this is the basis for the idea that she made over Avondale to her brother to help him gain Delia Stewart's hand in marriage. See above, part II, p. 34.

191. *Ibid.* 21.178.

192. *Ibid.* for 1872, 11.47. Hobson presumably inherited this loan from Woulfe.

193. *Ibid.* for 1872, 23.238.

194. E. Dickinson, p. 90. See above, chap. 1, pp. 96–7.

195. See Reg. of Deeds, Mem. for 1871, 23.123. £769 4s 8d in interest was owing in 1835, and John Henry Parnell was ordered by judgement of the court of Exchequer to pay £1,538 9s 4d as a 'penal' sum – exactly double the amount owed. This could be the debt of John Henry's paid by the trustees of his will, for whose repayment Charles mortgaged the estate for £1,500 – see above, note 184, for reference.

196. J. H. Parnell, p. 100.

197. See Reg. of Deeds, Mem. for 1869, 27.67; for details, 51, above.

198. See above, p. 113.

199. J. H. Parnell, p. 288. See above, Part IV, chap. 3, p. 196.


## 3. The entry into politics

1. *Gaelic American*, 29 September 1906, Devoy's description of his meeting with Parnell in Morrison's Hotel in April 1879. Also see O'Brien, *Parnell*, i, p. 43. In 1869, 'he knew nothing of the career of his great-grandfather Sir John Parnell, or his grand-uncle, Sir Henry, or his grandfather'. He certainly, however knew enough about them by the time he wrote his election address in 1874 (see Appendix). For a discussion of Parnell's historical knowledge and the political implications of the question see F.S.L. Lyons, 'The political ideas of Parnell, in *Historical Journal*, xvi (1973), 749–76.

2. J. H. Parnell, pp. 55, 57, 87, 125.

3. *Ibid.* p. 125.

4. *Ibid.* p. 127.

5. O'Brien, *Parnell*, i, 44.

6. H. Harrison, *Parnell vindicated*, p. 46.

7. See O'Brien, *Parnell*, i, 53. Emily Dickinson told him: 'The only political incident which seemed to affect him [Parnell] was the execution of the Manchester Martyrs. He was very indignant about that'. See also J. H. Parnell, p. 129.

8. O'Brien, *Parnell*, i, 44. 'How came Parnell, then, to turn his attention to Irish affairs? . . . He has told us that it was the Fenian movement that first awakened his interest in Ireland'.

9. *Special Comm. 1888 proc.*, ii, 694.

10. J. H. Parnell, p. 127.

11. *Special comm. 1888 proc.*, ii, 694.

12. J. H. Parnell, p. 129.

13. *Ibid.* p. 131.

14. *Ibid.*

15. A. Kettle, *The material for victory*, p. 19.

16. O'Brien, *Parnell*, i, 57. The discrepancy between this answer and the pithy remark repeated by John Parnell in his own book could have been due to free interpretation on O'Brien's part, or characteristic tactfulness on John Parnell's, when being questioned by O'Brien. O'Brien also quotes an acquaintance of Parnell's from the 1870s as saying that Parnell then 'knew nothing about Home Rule' (i, 73).

17. See *Special Comm. 1888 proc.*, ii, 694 and H. Harrison, *Parnell vindicated*, p. 438.

18. D. Thornley, *Isaac Butt and Home Rule* (London, 1964), p. 210.

19. J. H. Parnell, p. 121.

20. O'Brien, *Parnell*, i, 70–1.

21. See above, chap. 1, p. 99.

22. *F. J.*, 5 March 1874, p. 7; letter from Richard T. C. Johnson, Arklow.

23. See *McCalmont's parliamentary poll book*, 8th ed., by J. Vincent and M. Stenton (Brighton, 1971).

24. See above, chap. 2, p. 122.

25. See his letter on the subject in *Wicklow Newsletter*, 1 March 1873. Tenants' agitation was lively in Wicklow at this time; see reports, *ibid.* 1 January 1870, and 25 December 1969.

26. *Special Comm. 1888 proc.*, ii, 694.

27. A. Kettle, *The material for victory*, pp. 17–18. See above, p. 139 for further references to the difficulty of finding someone.

28. See O'Brien, *Parnell*, i, 75, and A. Kettle, *The material for victory*, p. 18. A letter from Joseph McCarroll to J. H. Parnell (*C. S. Parnell*, p. 291) also says Parnell met the expenses, but puts them at a fanciful £15,000. Also see Swift MacNeill, *What I have seen and heard*, p. 145.

29. See *Freeman's Journal*, 9 March 1874, first leader.

30. 'In that age of intellectual giants, Parnell was a distinguished man. To great debating power, great culture and great abilities he added an exact knowledge of finance'. *Ibid.*

31. This was why he was standing for re-election.

32. See especially the Kingstown meeting reported in the *Freeman's Journal*, 12 March 1874; Galbraith's speech at Rathmines, 16 March 1874, reported in *Freeman*, 17 March; also leader, *ibid.* 12 March.

33. *Irish Times*, 20 March 1874.

34. *Freeman's Journal*, 11 March 1874.

35. *Ibid.* 13 April 1874, reporting a meeting at Fairview on 12 April.

36. See *ibid.* 17 March 1874, for details of this broadsheet.

37. See also letter in *Irish Times*, 16 October 1880, which makes a similar accusation. See also above, part V, chap. 1, p.223.

38. A letter from Parnell, *ibid.*, said 'It is unnecessary to characterise the motives and taste which suggested and sanctioned the publication of such a document, and I have no doubt the honourable and intelligent electors of the county of Dublin will treat it with the contempt it so eminently merits'.

39. 9 March 1974. My italics.

40. *Freeman's Journal*, 13 March 1874.

41. *Ibid.*

42. *Ibid.*

43. *Ibid.* 16 March 1874, *a propos* a Blanchardstown meeting.

44. This time more accurately; see 14 March 1874.

45. Meetings at Blanchardstown and Clondalkin reported in *Freeman's Journal* 16 March 1874.

46. *Ibid.* leader.

47. See Appendix.

48. See below.

49. *Freeman's Journal*, 17 March 1874, *a propos* a meeting in Rathmines.

50. *Ibid.* 12 March 1874. The occasion was a meeting at Kingstown.

51. See William Parnell, *Enquiry into the causes of popular discontent in Ireland*, p. 59. Under Grattan's parliament, 'every gentleman built a palace and surrounded it with a paradise; the before-forgotten peasantry became objects of benevolence; their houses were made more convenient, their wages raised; agriculture was created and new enterprise given to commerce. No expression can give an idea of the improvements which took place in Ireland immediately on the development of its national dignity'. Also see *ibid.* p. 61, on the advantages of the gentry living at home.

52. C. S. Parnell to Lord Howth, 14 March 1874 (N.L.I., Parnell Letters, MS 5934).

53. *Irish Times,* 14 March 1874. Long afterwards Parnell was attacked in the House of Commons by someone who said that until the Dublin election, 'people had never heard of him'. This elicited the characteristic answer: 'Never mind: – people have heard of me since'. (Justin McCarthy, *Reminiscences,* ii, 101.)

54. *Freeman's Journal,* 12 March 1874; report of Home Rule meeting at Kingstown. Parnell's election address stated that he was standing 'in compliance with influential requests'.

55. 9 March 1874.

56. 19 March 1874.

57. See summing-up of election, *ibid.* 20 March 1874.

58. Leader of 16 March 1874.

59. 19 March 1874.

60. *Irish Times,* 19 March 1874.

61. White received 1,644 votes in the 1865 election.

62. See quotation given above, p. 137.

63. *Freeman's Journal,* 20 March 1874, leader.

64. Substantially the same as his Dublin address. See Appendix.

65. See *F.J.,* 6 March 1875. Parnell carefully stated that he 'did not address you on the subject of Mr John Mitchel's political opinions', but thought 'it must become everyone to protest against the decision of an obscure legal question by a party vote, in hot blood, in the House of Commons'.

66. Fr. Richard Galvin to Fr. Hickey, 23 March 1875 (Doran papers, shown to me by courtesy of Dr Leon O Broin).

67. William Dillon to J. F. Madden, 27 March 1875 *ibid.*

68. J. F. Madden to C. J. Doran, 28 March 1875 (*ibid*).

69. Same to same, 30 March 1875 (*ibid*).

70. Both phrases used by Dillon and Madden.

71. See *Freeman's Journal,* 16 March 1874.

72. *Ibid.* 5 April 1875.

73. *Ibid.* 6 April 1875.

74. *Ibid.*

75. *Ibid.* 10 April 1875.

76. *Ibid.* leader, 13 April 1875.

77. *Ibid.* 12 April 1875.

78. *Ibid.* 13 April 1875.

79. *Ibid* 15 April 1875.

80. Reprinted in *Nation,* 23 August 1879.

81. See *Freeman's Journal,* 5 April 1875.

82. *Ibid.* 13 April 1875.

83. See D. Thornley, *Isaac Butt and Home Rule,* p. 180.

84. *Freeman's Journal,* 13 April 1875.

85. *Ibid.* See N.L.I., Parnell letters MS 15,735, for a warm letter from Parnell to Tormey in 1879.

86. This although, as Dr Thornley has shown, 'nowhere in 1874 was the participation of the clergy as striking a feature of political activity as it had been in 1868'. (*Isaac Butt and Home Rule,* p. 180.) The Parnell v. Hinds contest brought the Disestablishment issue back into local politics in this instance.

87. *Freeman's Journal,* 13 April 1875.

88. 'The priests are now addressing the people in favour of Mr Parnell'. 15 April 1875.

89. A letter of Parnell's to one Fr. George Taafe thanked him afterwards for his 'kind exertions on my behalf during the Meath election' (N.L.I., Parnell letters, MS 5934; letter dated 26 January 1876).

90. *Freeman's Journal*, 17 April 1875. In the Home Rule Party of 1874 Catholics outnumbered Protestants by 46 to 13 (Thornley, *Isaac Butt and Home Rule*, p. 210). But see L. J. McCaffrey, 'Home Rule and the General Election of 1874' in *I.H.S.*, vol. ix, no. 34 (September 1954), p. 191, for the strong Protestant tradition in the movement.

91. See a speech of his reported in *Freeman's Journal*, 13 April 1875 'For their sake and for the sake of their children and their children's children, the education of the country ought to be under the proper control of the clergy,'

92. Davitt, *Fall of feudalism*, p. 175.

93. Parnell wrote: 'It must be said that the example and deeds of such men are of national importance; and we feel more acutely their removal by the hand of providence from amongst us, since so many of kindred nature, the best of Ireland's sons, are compelled for want of a career at home to devote their talents to the service of other countries'. *Wicklow Newsletter*, 5 December 1874. Again, the sentiment could be William Parnell's.

94. *Freeman's Journal*, 13 April 1875. Kirk also referred to Parnell's good record as a landlord at an election meeting in Navan on 8 April. See *ibid.* 9 April 1874.

95. *Ibid.* 13 April 1875. At this stage there was, of course, still a large landowning element among the Home Rulers – Dr Thornley finds 18 who were landowners, 4 who were younger sons of landowners, and 1 who was an elder son (*Isaac Butt and Home Rule*, p. 207). But in 1874 only 29 per cent of the new Home Rulers came from the landed class, compared with in influx of 46 per cent in the previous election. The proportion was to drop further.

96. 'Ever since he first could think of he had the principles of that movement fixed in his heart, for he always believed that the day would come when the voice of the people in this country would rule her affairs and make her laws, and that was what he understood by Home Rule.' Regarding the primary emphasis on the land question, see L. J. McCaffrey, 'Home Rule and the General Election of 1874', *I.H.S.*, ix, no. 34 (September 1954), pp. 196–7; he finds that tenant right was 'the main issue in the contest' during the 1874 election.

97. A total flight of the imagination. *Freeman's Journal*, 13 April 1875.

98. *Ibid.* 16 April 1875.

99. *Ibid.* 19 April 1875, leader.

100. *Irish Times*, 20 April 1875.

101. *Freeman's Journal*, 19 April 1875.

102. *Ibid.*

103. *Irish Times*, 20 April 1875.

# Part IV: Parnell and Wicklow

## 1. Parnell and Avondale

1. *Parnell*, ii, 164.

2. See for instance T. P. O'Connor, *Memories of an old parliamentarian* (London, 1929).

3. W. O'Brien, *Evening memories* (Dublin, 1920), p. 79.

4. K. O'Shea, ii, pp. 49–50.

5. See below, chap. 1, section II.

6. F. H. O'Donnell, *History of the Irish parliamentary party* (London, 1910), i, 289.

7. See a letter in the *Weekly Freeman*, 28 March 1891, from W. A. McDonald. Headed 'Has Mr Parnell neglected his duty?', it comprises a detailed study of Parnell's parliamentary attendance from 1886 to 1890, and shows it to have been both regular and active.

8. See also T. P. O'Connor, *C. S. Parnell: a memory* (London, 1891), p. 18: 'He

always returned there with delight during the Parliamentary recesses in the first days of his political life'.

9. Interview in the New York *Daily World,* quoted in *Nation,* 4 December 1880.

10. E. Dickinson, p. 110.

11. Davitt, *Fall of feudalism,* p. 372.

12. E. Dickinson, p. 159.

13. *Nation,* 4 December 1890.

14. *Ibid.* 8 April 1882.

15. *C. S. Parnell: a memory,* pp. 18–19.

16. Quoted in *Nation,* 25 October 1890. The article was probably by Katharine Tynan, who later recalled being taken to Avondale and writing about it in 1890. Her impression was one of 'unrelieved gloom . . . not helped by the fact that the man who was showing us over the house had an epileptic fit in the dining room'. (K. Tynan, *Twenty-five years* (London, 1913), p. 330.)

17. See above, pp. 192–5

18. J. H. Parnell, p. 176.

19. *Ibid.* p. 280.

20. *Ibid.* p. 288. His mother later infuriated him by evicting the cattle and converting the shed for a dance (K. O'Shea, i, 183). See above, part V, chap 2, p. 238

21. Reg. of Deeds, Mem. for 1885, 4.95; also *Weekley Freeman,* 6 September 1884. The cottages still stand, on the left before the entrance to Avondale, and are remembered locally as 'built by Parnell'.

22. *Weekly Freeman,* 6 September 1884.

23. K. O'Shea, i, 183.

24. *Ibid.* ii, 53.

25. *Ibid.* ii, 134.

26. Parnell to W. Kerr, 19 May 1890 (N.L.I., Parnell letters, MS 15,735).

27. J. H. Parnell, p. 278.

28. T. P. O'Connor, *C. S. Parnell: a memory,* p. 22.

29. Titled 'The Irish land question'; vol. cxxx, pp. 381–406.

30. See T. M. Healy, *Letters and leaders of my day,* i, 87: T. M. Healy to Maurice Healy, 20 March 1880. Healy had just been in America with the Parnells. Also see M. M. O'Hara, *Chief and tribune,* p. 150, for an anecdote where Parnell tells Fanny: 'They'll all know it isn't mine, it's much too good!'

31. A. Kettle, *The material for victory,* p. 26. See also *ibid.* p. 84. Kettle thought that the reason why he and Parnell got on well was because both had 'a strong streak of mysticism', but it seems more likely to have been based on their mutual agricultural interests.

32. J. H. Parnell, p. 281.

33. W. Kerr to *Wicklow Newsletter,* 1 February 1890.

34. C. S. Parnell to P. J. McGough, 24 June 1891, regarding evidence in Campbell v. *Cork Herald* libel case. *Nation,* 4 July 1891.

35. J. H. Parnell, p. 180.

36. See *Nation,* 4 December 1880.

37. J. H. Parnell, p. 279.

38. A. Kettle, *The material for victory,* p. 69.

39. 'Mr Parnell as landlord' in *Nation* November 1880.

40. *Weekly Freeman,* 10 January 1891.

41. See above p. 156.

42. J. H. Parnell, p. 256.

43. K. O'Shea, ii, 53.

44. *Nation,* 9 June 1883, See *Irish Times,* 3 August 1882, for a letter from one Henry Kinahan urging Irish enterprise in quarrying whinstone setts and mentioning locations in Wicklow where the ideal material occurs.

45. *Nation,* 26 January 1884.

46. J. H. Parnell, p. 279.
47. *Ibid.* p. 282.
48. *Ibid.*
49. See Reg. of Deeds, Mem. for 1895, 5.203, which records Mrs Katharine Parnell's assignation of the lands to John Parnell for £2,230. John's book states that Patrick MacDonald took a twelve-year lease from Carysfort, but the Registry of Deeds records Hetherington as the middle-man.
50. Built January–February 1891. See *Weekly Freeman*, 10 January 1891.
51. J. H. Parnell, p. 282.
52. K. O'Shea, ii, 53.
53. *Nation*, 29 August 1885. The *Weekly Freeman* of 10 January 1891 said that the Welsh price had been 26 shillings a ton, and Parnell's 24 shillings a ton.
54. See report in *Nation*, 27 March 1886.
55. See *Wicklow Newsletter*, 2 September 1889. Fogarty had claimed Parnell's quarries owed £50; Kerr said it was £16, and had been awaiting collection at the quarry office for weeks.
56. Letter in *Wicklow Newsletter*, 12 October 1889. See also a letter from James Doyle, harbourmaster, in *ibid.* 5 October 1889.
57. *Weekly Freeman*, 20 January 1891.
58. K. O'Shea, ii, 53. A vase and a Celtic cross from the quarry workshops were exhibited in London and Cork.
59. *Weekly Freeman*, 20 January 1891.
60. *Ibid.*
61. Diary of Lady Alice Howard for 1890, entry for 9 September (N.L.I., Wicklow Papers, MS 3608).
62. J. H. Parnell, p. 292.
63. 4 July 1891. For details of the dispute, see above pp. 179–81.
64. See Parnell's speech at Carlow on 28 June 1891, reported in *Nation*, 4 July 1891. Katharine Tynan was told long afterwards that the strike was because of two big new contracts, which it was felt could push up wages; but what the men claimed 'represented the profits' (*Twenty-five years*, p. 320).
65. Letter from Kerr in *Weekly Freeman*, 4 July 1891.
66. Parnell's speech at Carlow; see n.59 above.
67. See *Wicklow Newsletter*, 29 August 1891.
68. Letter in *ibid.* 19 September 1891.
69. Held on 28 September 1891; see *ibid.* 3 October 1891.
70. See *ibid.* 17 October 1891, for the belated reconciliation.
71. See below, p.
72. Parnell to Katharine Parnell from Avondale, 1 September 1891; see K.O'Shea, ii, 262.
73. See Reg. of Deeds, Mem. for 1895, 5.203.
74. J. H. Parnell, p. 285.
75. The meeting took place on 11 January. See *Wicklow Newsletter*, 14 January 1882.
76. House of Commons, 2 July 1885. See *ibid.* 4 July 1885.
77. C. S. Parnell to Katharine O'Shea, 4 October 1881; K. O'Shea, i, 201.
78. J. H. Parnell, p. 278.
79. *Ibid.*
80. *Ibid.* p. 286. John supposed that his brother formed the idea on his tour of the Alabama coal and iron mines in 1871.
81. Davitt, *Fall of feudalism*, p. 597.
82. O'Brien, *Parnell*, i, 367.
83. *Ibid.* ii, 112.
84. K. O'Shea, ii, 133.
85. From James Hall of Arklow; *Wicklow Newsletter*, 19 January 1889.

86. *Freeman's Journal,* 19 January 1889. Near Croghan is the optimistically named Goldmine River.

87. *Wicklow Newsletter,* 22 June 1889.

88. *Ibid.* 5 October 1889 and 11 January 1890.

89. Davitt, *Fall of feudalism,* p. 597.

90. K. O'Shea, ii, 130.

91. From an article by Sir John Henniker Heaton in *Leisure Hour,* quoted by St John Ervine in *Parnell,* p. 231. Heaton, who owned land and newspapers in Australia, was M.P. for Canterbury, 1885–1910.

92. C. S. Parnell to Commissioner for Woods, etc., 8 February 1888 (MS at Avondale; part of a collection of Parnell Letters and memorabilia kept in storage there: cited below as 'MSS at Avondale'. I am indebted to the Minister of Lands for permission to quote from these).

93. *Ibid.*

94. C. S. Parnell to George Gully, Department of Woods and Forests, 20 August 1888 (MSS at Avondale).

95. C. S. Parnell to George Gully, 3 December 1888 (N.L.I., Parnell letters, MS 15, 735).

96. Letter of 19 May 1890 (N.L.I. Parnell letters, MS 15, 735). My italics.

97. *Wicklow Newsletter,* 29 March 1890.

98. *Weekly Freeman,* 20 December, 1890. The *Wicklow Newsletter* of the same date approvingly noted the intelligence as well.

99. *Weekly Freeman,* 27 December 1890, additional details in *Wicklow Newsletter,* 27 December 1890.

100. K. Tynan, *Twenty-five years,* p. 320.

101. K. O'Shea, i, 184.

102. W. O'Brien, *The Parnell of real life,* p. 125: 'The apparition of a poet plunged in some divine anguish, or a mad scientist mourning over the fate of some forlorn invention'. See C. Cruise O'Brien. *Parnell and his party,* pp. 246–7.

103. S. O'Grady, *The story of Ireland,* p. 203.

104. K. Tynan, *Memories* (London, 1924), p. 5.

105. J. H. Parnell, p. 293.

106. Maria Edgeworth, *Ormond* (2nd ed. London, 1857); *Tales and novels* (10 vols.) ix, 274. 'How do your silver mines go on, Sir Ulick? I hear all the silver mines in Ireland turn out to be lead.' 'I wish they did,' said Sir Ulick, 'for then we could turn all our lead to gold.'

## 2. Parnell and his tenants

1. See part III above, chap. 3, p. 137.

2. See *Nation,* 23 August 1879. This 1874 circular letter was quoted after the 'papist rats' controversy, as evidence of Parnell's good relations with Catholics.

3. J. H. Parnell, p. 154.

4. *Ibid.* p. 287.

5. *Ibid.*

6. Sir William Butler, *An autobiography* (London, 1911), p. 354.

7. O'Brien, *Parnell,* i, 366.

8. Except R. B. Cunninghame Graham in 'An Tighearna: a memory of Parnell', *Dana* (November 1904), pp. 183–99 – and he never visited Parnell in Ireland.

9. O'Brien, *Parnell,* ii, 180. See also K. O'Shea, ii, 243.

10. St John Ervine, *Parnell,* p. 217.

11. W. O'Brien, *The Parnell of real life,* p. 57; T. P. O'Connor, *Memoirs of an old Parliamentarian,* i, 98, and *C. S. Parnell: a memory,* p. 28.

12. J. McCarthy, *Reminiscences* (London, 1899), ii, 94. This house may well have been one of the six labourers' cottages which, according to Wicklow tradition, the

Grand Jury ordered to be built on Parnell's land to spite him; Parnell, so the story goes, took over the building of the cottages at his own expense and situated each on its own half acre (see *Irish Press,* 19 July 1957).

13. See above, pp. 202–5.

14. See Introduction.

15. See letters in *Wicklow Newsletter,* 19 July and 27 September 1879.

16. *Ibid.* 27 September 1879.

17. See, for instance, *ibid.* 15 November and 20 December.

18. The meeting took place on 1 January 1880. See *ibid.* 3 January 1880.

19. *Ibid.* 10 January 1880.

20. See letters in *ibid.* 28 February, 6 March, 13 March.

21. See *ibid.* 10 April 1880.

22. *Ibid.*

23. At a demonstration in Rathdrum. See *ibid.* 13 November 1880.

24. *Ibid.* 4 December 1880. Mr Lawlor, Moncha, was appointed president and Mr Byrne, Ballinderry, vice-president, of the Rathdrum branch.

25. 6 December 1880. See *ibid.* 11 December 1880.

26. *Ibid.* 18 December 1880.

27. See a letter from Corbet, *ibid.* 25 December 1880.

28. There were meetings at Barndarraig, Rathdrum, Roundwood, Arklow and Tinahely in this month.

29. See *Wicklow Newsletter,* 19 February 1881.

30. In Rathdrum, Barndarraig and Kilbride – *ibid.* 19 February and 19 March.

31. *Ibid.* 26 March 1881.

32. At Wicklow, Corbet spoke of the 'respect' that both he and Parnell entertained for the constabulary.

33. Meeting on 20 April 1881. See *Wicklow Newsletter,* 23 April 1881.

34. See *ibid.* 28 May 1881 and 4 June 1881, and McCoan's unrepentant letter in *ibid.* 18 June 1881; also a speech he made in Tinahely on 16 May 1883, reported in *ibid.* 19 May 1883, and finally, for his letter of resignation from the party, *ibid.* 2 June 1883.

35. Letter in *ibid.* 9 July 1881.

36. See meeting reported in *ibid.* 16 July 1881.

37. See report of Land League meeting at Wicklow, *ibid.*

38. See *ibid.* 30 July 1881. The 6 cases were of incitement, intimidation, forcible possession (2), prevention of duty, and obstruction.

39. *Ibid.* 13 August 1881.

40. Letter in *ibid.* 27 August 1881.

41. *Ibid.* 7 December 1881.

42. See above, pp. 202–5.

43. See *Wicklow Newsletter,* 8 October 1881.

44. On 24 October 1881 – *ibid.* 29 October.

45. *Ibid.* 12 November 1881.

46. *Ibid.* 10 February 1882, also see *ibid.* 22 July 1882.

47. *Ibid.* 2 September 1882.

48. *Ibid.* 4 November 1882.

49. *Ibid.* 19 December 1885 and 14 May 1887.

50. *Ibid.* 15 October 1881.

51. *Ibid.* 3 December 1881.

52. *Ibid.* 12 December 1881.

53. *Ibid.*

54. The occasion was the Avondale ploughing match: *ibid.* 17 December 1881. Also see a speech of J. McCarroll's at a Wicklow land meeting *ibid.* 6 May 1882.

55. *A propos* a nationalist meeting at Bray. *Ibid.* 6 January 1883.

56. See *ibid.* 15 April 1882.

57. See *ibid.* 17 June, 5 August, 19 August, and 12 September 1882.

58. *Ibid.* 29 July 1882.

59. *Ibid.* 23 September 1882.

60. *Ibid.* 27 December 1884.

61. See *ibid.* 19 December 1885, 16 October 1886, 26 February 1887, and 7 December 1889.

62. The Brooke estate at Coolgreany. See *ibid.* 1886 and 1887, for many reports on the experiment.

63. *Ibid.* 15 November 1879.

64. *Ibid.* 18 December 1879.

65. *Irish Times*, 7 October 1880.

66. *Wicklow Newsletter*, 8 October 1880.

67. See above, part III, Chap 2, p. 00.

68. *Irish Times*, 12 October 1880.

69. Editorial, *ibid.* 16 October, 1880.

70. *Ibid.* 26 October 1880.

71. See part III above, chap. 2, p. 103, also T. H. Healy, *Letters and Leaders*, i, 261–2. Healy attributed these accusations to Walter Long.

72. See Reg. of Deeds, Mem. for 1869, 27.67.

73. *Nation*, 27 November 1880. See above, p. 177, for full quotation.

74. Mount Avon was advertised for sale in the *Wicklow Newsletter* of 13 and 20 September 1879; the renewal lease was dated August 1880.

75. See Reg. of Deeds, Mem. for 1869, 24.134, and above, part III, chap. 2, p. 129.

76. It was not paid until September 1883; see marginal note, *ibid.*

77. See part III above, p. 84.

78. Although the *Irish Times* of 4 November reported another *contretemps* at the Westport Town Commissioners' meeting; after an acrimonious debate on the subject of the lease Mr Egan, an anti-Parnellite, was left in possession of the field when his opponent, Mr Muffeney, 'rushed out of the room in a rage'.

79. Reprinted *Nation*, 20 November 1880. I am indebted to Dr F. S. L. Lyons for first drawing my attention to this article.

80. The rent was £61 p.a. for about 50 acres; the valuation was £58.

81. T. P. O'Connor, *C. S. Parnell: a memory*, p. 27.

82. Warren was well aware of the tourist potential of his plot, having, the reporter said, disfigured 'Thomas Moore's tree' by nailing up a board on it which read:

Tourist Read

Moore's name in letters of gold

Who made Avoca's sweet vale

To be a name of praise around the world.

His tree he wrote under is here.

Ne plus ultra;

Vice versa.

Cead Mile Falthe.

Mr Warren, the reporter added, had 'some local reputation as a poet'.

83. A reference to W. F. Littledale in the unpublished diary of Alfred Webb (now in the Soc. of Friends' Library, Eustace St, Dublin) describes him as 'a crusty conservative concerning Ireland ... a type of excellent men, landlords, blind to the necessities of the situation in Ireland' (vol. ii, 316–17).

84. Editorial in *Nation*, 20 November 1880.

85. See *Wicklow Newsletter*, 4 October 1890.

86. *Irish Times*, 4 October 1890, and *Wicklow Newsletter*, 11 October 1890.

87. Reprinted in *Nation*, 27 November 1880.

88. See above, p. 167.

89. *Irish Times*, 31 October 1882.

90. *Nation*, 4 November 1882.

91. *Wicklow Newsletter*, 15 July 1882.

92. *Weekly Freeman*, 6 September 1884. The visitor was Miss Jennie Byrne.

93. J. A. McClintock of Kingstown wrote to Michael Davitt on 7 July 1885 complaining that he had read of an eviction suit of Parnell's brought against tenants of Ballysax, Co. Kildare in April, and pointing out the anomaly: however, I can find no newspaper reference to this. I am indebted to Prof. T. W. Moody for this reference from the Davitt papers.

94. *Weekly Freeman*, 4 June 1887. The allegations had appeared in the *Irish Times* and *Daily Express* of 26 May 1887 – the latter newspaper noting the contradiction between Parnell's political image as 'the tenants' intrepid champion and devoted friend' and his private character of 'a landlord . . . as unyielding and exacting as any of them'.

95. *Wicklow Newsletter*, 28 May 1887.

96. See above, pp. 173–4.

97. *Wicklow Newsletter*, 5 November 1887.

98. *Ibid.* 27 June 1891.

99. *Ibid.* 13 September 1890. There are numerous references to the religious animosity in Arklow in issues of the *Newsletter* from May to September.

100. Letter in *ibid.* 1 November 1890.

101. *Ibid.* 29 November 1890.

102. *Ibid.* 31 January 1891.

103. *Weekly Freeman*, 4 July 1891.

104. He also said their wages had been increased a month previously, 'through the representation of the local Labourers' Union'. See *Nation*, 4 July 1891.

105. Davitt, *Fall of feudalism*, p. 636. Davitt, however, felt that Parnell might have been overstating his case so as to deflect the conversation away from the divorce case.

106. K. Tynan, *Twenty-five years*, p. 88.

107. See his obituary, *Wicklow people*, 20 August 1937. He was born in 1864. His wife died in July 1946; see *ibid.* 6 July 1946. Some recollections of Avondale by his son Hugh form an Appendix to this study.

108. A Kettle, *The material for victory*, p. 21.

109. See E. I. O'Reilly, 'Charles Stewart Parnell' in *Celtic Monthly*, vol. iii, no. 1 (January 1880), pp. 80–2; also *Nation*, 20 November 1880.

110. *Nation*, 27 November 1880; see above, p. 177.

111. *Ibid.*

112. O'Brien, *Parnell*, i, 335.

113. See above, p. 178.

114. W. S. Blunt, *The land war in Ireland*, p. 276.

115. Above, p. 177.

116. *Nation*, 26 April 1884, and *Weekly Freeman*, 22 March and 26 April 1884. Mrs West claimed that her husband had sold the lease to a man called Dalton when Parnell was in Kilmainham; but she produced no legal evidence, and lost the case. Her solicitor attempted to make Parnell attend the hearing, but this was over-ruled.

117. C. S. Parnell, 'The Irish Land', in *North American Review*, April 1880.

118. M. M. O'Hara. *Chief and tribune*, p. 119. The questioner was John Sweetman.

119. See above p. 195.

120. T. P. O'Connor, *C. S. Parnell: a memory*, p. 28.

## 3. Avondale and Parnell's life-style

1. See Introduction above.

2. From *Irish world*, quoted in *Nation*, 4 December 1880.

3. J. H. Parnell, p. 178.

4. T. P. O'Connor, *Memories of an old parliamentarian*, i, 99.

5. *Ibid.* i, 373.

6. Justin McCarthy, *Reminiscences*, ii, 93, and *Our book of memories* (with Mrs Campbell Praed, London, 1912), p. 15.

7. K. O'Shea, ii, 245.

8. C. S. Parnell to Messrs Twigg and Brett, 17 August 1879 (N.L.I., Parnell letters, MS 10, 416).

9. T. M. Healy, *Letters and leaders*, i, 136.

10. W. Corbet, 'Parnell as a prisoner in Kilmainham' in *Irish Weekly Independent*, 7 October 1893.

11. O'Brien, *Parnell*, i, 366.

12. See an article by William Redmond in *Irish Weekly Independent*, 6 October 1894.

13. J. H. Parnell, p. 281.

14. *Weekly Freeman*, 25 August 1889.

15. J. McCarthy, *Reminiscences*, ii, 94.

16. O'Brien, *Parnell*, ii, 97, C. S. Parnell to J. McCarthy, 15 August 1886: 'We have been having some nice weather here the last two or three days, and some sport; I am sending you a brace of birds by parcel post this morning.'

17. T. P. O'Connor, *C. S. Parnell: a memory*, p. 13.

18. *Irish Weekly Independent*, 6 October 1894.

19. K. O'Shea, ii, 150.

20. See *Weekly Freeman*, 29 August 1889.

21. Sir William Butler, *Autobiography*, p. 351.

22. J. H. Parnell, p. 155.

23. K. O'Shea, ii, 151. Nevertheless, in a week's shooting in 1889 the party bagged 'over 200 grouse and a number of hares' – *Weekly Freeman*, 25 August 1889.

24. E. Dickinson, p. 159.

25. K. O'Shea, ii, 76.

26. Except R. B. Cunninghame Graham, who talked to Parnell of horses and thought he 'knew little' about them ('An Tighearna' in *Dana*, November 1904, p. 195). But Graham never saw him at Avondale; and was moreover himself a renowned judge of horseflesh.

27. O'Brien, *Parnell*, i, 53.

28. Sir William Butler, *Autobiography*, p. 353.

29. W. O'Brien, *The Parnell of real life*, p. 14.

30. Letter from Rev. Fr Rowan, Durrow, in *Leinster Leader*, 24 September 1881.

31. *Freeman's Journal*, 14 November 1881.

32. *Wicklow Newsletter*, 22 March 1884.

33. *Ibid.* 8 November 1884.

34. See part III, above, pp. 127–30.

35. J. H. Parnell, p. 303.

36. *Nation*, 8 November 1879.

37. He became, for instance, by 1891 the third largest shareholder in the *Freeman's Journal*, after Caroline Agnes Grey (11,260 shares) and Dr Croke (510 shares), being in possession of 300 shares. See *Weekly Freeman*, 26 September 1891, account of shareholder's meeting.

38. C. S. Parnell to Messrs Twigg and Brett, dated 'August 1879' (N.L.I., Parnell letters, MS 10, 416). The letter asks for an extension on a debt of £19 17s, which was eventually paid in November.

39. See above, pp. 191–2.

40. J. H. Parnell, p. 286. The sum thus raised was £3,000.

41. C. S. Parnell to W. Mills King, 13 October 1870 (N.L.I., Parnell letters, MS 15, 735). John Parnell thought his brother paid only £3,000, but he attributed another £1,500 spent at this time to 'doing up Mount Avon House' – p. 287. See above, part III, p. 113.

42. See above, part III, p. 136.

43. *Nation*, 20 November 1880.

44. Quoted in *ibid*. 31 January 1880.

45. T. M. Healy to his father, 17 July 1879; quoted in the former's *Letters and leaders*, i, 68.

46. J. H. Parnell, p. 209.

47. *Nation*, 11 May 1889.

48. Letter (undated) quoted in *Our book of memories*, p. 22.

49. F. H. O'Donnell, *History of the Irish parliamentary party* (London, 1910), i, 134.

50. J. H. Parnell, p. 289.

51. See below, Epilogue.

52. See C. C. O'Brien, *Parnell and his party* (2nd ed., Oxford, 1968), p. 139, note. Also see *ibid*. pp. 136–40, for the whole question of party finance.

53. O'Brien, *Parnell*, ii, 290.

54. C. C. O'Brien, 'The machinery of the Irish Parliamentary Party', in *I.H.S.*, March 1946, p. 73, n.2.

55. Quoted in C. C. O'Brien, *Parnell and his party*, p. 139, n.3. Healy's affidavit was dated 26 April 1892.

56. A notice to claimants on the estate was placed in the *Wicklow Newsletter* of 10 March 1883 by Alfred MacDermott.

57. *Nation*, 16 December 1882.

58. *Ibid*. 23 December 1882. This 'repugnance' may provide a reason for Parnell's cavalier reception of the cheque, referred to below.

59. *Ibid*. 10 March, 1883.

60. *Ibid*. 17 March 1883.

61. O'Brien, *Parnell*, ii, 27–8.

62. J. H. Parnell, p. 286.

63. *Ibid*. p. 289.

64. *Ibid*. p. 209.

65. Reg. of Deeds, Mem. for 1882, 12.284.

66. *Ibid*. for 1883, 37.27 and 39.1.

67. *Ibid*. for 1883, 39.1.

68. J. H. Parnell, p. 209.

69. K. O'Shea, ii, 269.

70. J. H. Parnell, p. 287.

71. Letter from W. Kerr in *Weekly Freeman*, 4 July 1891.

72. C. S. Parnell to Commissioner of Woods, Forests and Land Revenue, 8 February 1888 (MSS at Avondale).

73. *Weekly Freeman*, 20 December 1890.

74. See above p. 158.

75. C. S. Parnell's letter quoted in n.72 above.

76. Letter from W. Kerr in *Weekly Freeman*, 4 July 1891.

77. Speech at Wicklow on 31 May 1891; see *Nation*, 6 June 1891.

78. *Weekly Freeman*, 10 January 1891.

79. See Reg. of Deeds, Mem. for 1879, 17.9; 1884, 5.234; and 1884, 41.232.

80. T. P. O'Connor, *Memories of an old parliamentarian*, ii, 60–1. T. M. Healy (*Letters and Leaders*, i, 307) tells the same story of the unpaid Café Royal bill, but states it was a dinner given by Parnell in honour of General Collins, the American Consul. William O'Brien said the dinner was for Senator Jones of Florida and when O'Brien reminded of the expense, Parnell asked him to 'settle it with your own cheque ... I hate to give my signature to people I don't know' (*Evening memories*, p. 120). Mrs O'Shea denied that he was 'near', but said he was 'careful' about *small* expenses (O'Shea, ii, 248).

81. Reg. of Deeds, Mem. for 1885, 4.95.

82. J. H. Parnell, p. 288.

83. See Swift MacNeill, *What I have seen and heard* (London, 1925), pp. 264–6, J. McCarthy and Mrs Praed, *Our book of memories*, p. 216, and T. M. Healy, *Letters and leaders*, ii, pp. 195, 343–4.

84. T. M. Healy, *Letters and leaders*, i, 343. A letter from Healy to his brother Maurice dated 15 December 1890 reads: 'Lewis's bill, including all expenses, was £31,000. Parnell put the balance in his pocket, amounting to £10,000'.

85. Speech reported in *Nation*, 6 June 1891.

86. *Wicklow Newsletter*, 1 August 1891.

87. K. O'Shea, ii, 262.

88. *Ibid.* ii, 269.

89. Reg. of Deeds, Mem. for 1891. 22.53. The land was 131 acres, 3 roods, and 33 perches, let at a fee farm rent of £42.

90. J. H. Parnell, p. 288; Henry Lucy, *Diary of a journalist* (London, 1920–1), ii, 56.

91. J. H. Parnell, p. 288.

92. Standish O'Grady, *Story of Ireland*, p. 203; see above, p. 164.

93. J. H. Parnell, p. 288.

## 4. Parnell and Wicklow

1. From an article about Parnell in *The Speaker*, quoted in *Nation*, 25 October 1890.

2. At a Land League meeting in Rathdrum. See *Nation*, 10 January 1880.

3. See *Nation*, 29 May 1880, for a Whit Monday excursion by the St Nicholas of Myra Catholic Total Abstinence League, Dublin, to Avondale (where they cannot have been welcomed by Arthur Dickinson); *Weekly Freeman*, 11 August 1883, for the plans of the C. S. Parnell branch of the National League to visit Avondale on 12 August – later abandoned because the railway could not accommodate the large number of people who wanted to make the journey; the *Wicklow Newsletter*, 8 April 1882, for a request from the Aid Society for the Commercial Young Men of Dublin, to visit Avondale; *ibid.* 3 June 1889 for 'a picnic visit from the Commercial United Prisoners' Aid Society'. On the largest scale of all were the 'Avondale Athletic Sports and Pony Races' held on August 14 and 16 1887 in connection with the Sisters of Mercy Bazaar.

4. *Nation*, 3 April 1880.

5. See *Wicklow Newsletter*, 19 August 1876, 16 December 1876, 30 November 1878.

6. *Ibid.* 6 April 1878.

7. *Ibid.* 31 August 1878.

8. *Ibid.* 28 December 1878.

9. *Ibid.* 25 March 1876.

10. On 17 August 1876; his fellow-magistrate was the ubiquitous C. M. West. See *ibid.* 26 August 1876.

11. See O'Brien, *Parnell*, i, 224.

12. *Nation*, 8 May 1880.

13. *Ibid.* 27 August 1881.

14. With £17 – Lord Fitzwilliam being next, with £10. *Wicklow Newsletter* 17 June 1876.

15. *Ibid.* 19 April 1879.

16. Mr Russell, M.P. His statement was quoted in the *Irish Times*, where Manning saw it (see below).

17. K. O'Shea, ii, 246–7.

18. See *Wicklow Newsletter*, 1 February 1890.

19. See letter from J. McCarroll to J. H. Parnell, quoted in J. H. Parnell, p. 292.

20. See *Wicklow Newsletter*, 29 May, 4 September, and 25 December, 1880.

21. *Ibid.* 13 June 1885.

22. See especially a speech of Parnell's at a St Patrick's Day banquet in 1885, reported in *ibid.* 21 March 1885.

23. *Ibid.*

24. See for instance a speech of his quoted in *ibid.* 1 May 1886.

25. 'Let Arklow cherish the name and memory of him who risked his life for her poor in time of sickness and distress, and who incessantly labours for her advancement'. *Ibid.* 8 January 1876.

26. See letter from Carysfort in *ibid.* 22 July 1876.

27. See *ibid.* 6 January 1877, and *Nation*, 18 January 1877.

28. See letter from M. Shea in *Wicklow Newsletter*, 30 June 1877. Also statement of Parnell's in H. of C., 18 July 1878 – see *ibid.* 20 July 1848.

29. See his letter to the Wicklow cesspayers in *ibid.* 16 October 1880.

30. *Ibid.* 25 December 1880.

31. *Ibid.* 26 November 1881.

32. *Ibid.* 21 May 1881.

33. See *ibid.* 26 November 1881.

34. See *Weekly Freeman*, 7 November 1885. The fact that Carysfort took so much part in local affairs in the first place is a further indication of the peculiar ethos of Wicklow.

35. See *Wicklow Newsletter*, 1 February 1890; also 18 January 1890.

36. *Ibid.* 1 March 1890. Kerr and Kearon had first crossed swords in the *Irish Times;* McPhail only printed Kearon's missives, but in reply to Kerr's lengthy attack, he blandly denied all question of bias.

37. *Nation*, 23 August 1890.

38. *Wicklow Newsletter*, 6 September 1890.

39. See *Weekly Freeman*, 13 September 1890 and 10 January 1891; also *Wicklow Newsletter* 13 September and 27 December 1890.

40. Mr Strype, C. E. *Weekly Freeman*, 10 January 1891.

41. See above, p. 201.

42. *Weekly Freeman*, 31 January 1891.

43. See *Wicklow Newsletter*, 31 January 1891; also editorial, *ibid.* 3 January 1891.

44. *Ibid.* 31 January 1891.

45. 'Parnell as a prisoner in Kilmainham' in *Irish Weekly Independent*, 7 October 1883.

46. *Nation*, 7 December 1881.

47. See letter signed by him in *ibid.* 27 November 1880.

48. *Wicklow Newsletter*, 17 December 1881.

49. *Ibid.*

50. *Ibid.*

51. *Ibid.*

52. *Ibid.*

53. *Nation*, 24 December 1881.

54. Quoted in *Wicklow Newsletter*, 17 December 1881.

55. *Nation*, 24 December 1881.

56. *Ibid.* 18 February 1882, and T. Sherlock, *Charles Stewart Parnell* (Dublin, 1882), p. 97.

57. *Nation*, 18 February 1882.

58. *Wicklow Newsletter*, 18 February 1882.

59. *Irish Times*, 18 February 1882. The *Wicklow Newsletter* of the same date gloomily concurred.

60. *Nation*, 8 April 1882.

61. *Wicklow Newsletter*, 1 April 188.

62. See *Nation*, 9 September 1882.

63. See also *Wicklow Newsletter*, 9 September 1882, which also played down the

importance of the gathering.

64. *Nation,* 20 January 1883.

65. *Wicklow Newsletter,* 20 January 1883.

66. On 27 March 1883. See *Nation,* 31 March 1883.

67. *Ibid.* 26 January 1884.

68. *Weekly Freeman,* 26 January 1884.

69. See above, pp. 168–72.

70. See *Wicklow People,* 27 June 1927.

71. *Ibid.*

72. *Ibid.;* for him also see above, chap. 2, p. 182.

73. J. S. Mill, *Life of Sir E. T. Cook* (London, 1921), p. 107.

74. National Tribute Address from the people of Dublin (T. C. D., MS no. 2576).

75. *Nation,* 30 May 1891. This 'caused him to be selected by Mr A. M. Sullivan as a man who would have some attraction for the mild Tories and who might lead many waverers into the National Movement if he were received himself'.

76. See above, part III, chap. 3, p. 139.

77. Quoted in *Nation,* 20 June 1891.

78. F. H. O'Donnell, *History of the Irish parliamentary party,* i, 256.

79. Writing to Barry O'Brien on 11 December 1895. See O'Brien, *Parnell,* ii, 354.

80. *Autobiography,* p. 354.

81. J. H. Parnell, p. 282; see above, p. 156.

82. J. H. Parnell, p. 117.

83. Delia T. S. Parnell, to T. D. Sullivan, 21 January 1880 (N.L.I., Sullivan Papers, MS 8237/6).

84. See above.

85. Reminiscence of Mr R. C. Barton of Glendalough House in 1973.

86. *Wicklow Newsletter,* 24 September 1892. The italics are mine.

87. J. H. Parnell, p. 24.

88. E. Dickinson, p. 173.

89. *Ibid.* p. 231.

90. Lady Alice Howard's diary for 1882, entry for 23 February (N.L.I., Wicklow papers, MS 3604).

91. See above, p. 167.

92. Quoted in *Nation,* 8 April 1882.

93. Standish O'Grady, *The story of Ireland,* p. 211.

94. St John Ervine, *Parnell,* p. 61.

95. *Nation,* 1 September 1888.

96. Reminiscence of Mr Hugh Gaffney of Roundwood in 1973.

97. H. Harrison, *Parnell vindicated,* pp. 63–4.

98. Davitt, *Fall of feudalism,* p. 189. My italics.

99. See above, p. 188.

100. *Irish Times,* 24 October 1885 and 7 November 1885; *Weekly Freeman* and *Wicklow Newsletter,* 31 October 1885.

101. *Thom's Directory,* 1885.

102. For instance, when Lord Powerscourt said that 'a measure of local legislative power' was possible for Ireland, Colonel Tottenham felt bound to disagree. In the year to come, Powerscourt was to describe himself as a 'Home Ruler' – see *Nation,* 19 June 1886.

103. *Irish Times,* 24 October 1885.

104. See *ibid.* 26 October 1885.

105. See above, p. 170.

106. *Wicklow Newsletter,* 25 July 1885.

107. See *ibid.* 27 March 1886, 3 April 1886, 24 April 1886.

108. Lady Alice Howard's diary, entry for 6 May 1885 (N.L.I., Wicklow Papers, MS 3604).

109. *Wicklow Newsletter,* 3 April 1886.
110. 1885 East Wicklow: Corbet – 3,385 and Tottenham – (C.) 1,000
West Wicklow: Byrne – 3,721 and Hume-Dick – (C.) 871
1886 East Wicklow: Corbet – 3,101 and Tottenham – 984
West Wicklow: Byrne – 3,531 and Hume-Dick – 856
*Wicklow Newsletter,* 5 and 12 December 1885; and *ibid.* 10 and 17, July 1886.
111. *Weekly Freeman,* 31 October 1885.
112. *Wicklow Newsletter,* 10 October 1891 (editorial).
113. Diary of Lady Alice Edward, entries for 6 and 10 October 1891 (N.L.I., Wicklow Papers, MS 3609).
114. See *Wicklow Newsletter,* 19 June 1886.
115. See above, p. 197.
116. *Wicklow Newsletter,* 22 February 1890.
117. *Ibid.* 3 January 1891.
118. *Ibid.* 17 January 1891.
119. *Ibid.* 28 March 1891.
120. *Ibid.* 31 May 1891.
121. See *ibid.* 6 June 1891, for his speech traducing Fr Francis McEnery for switching his allegiance after Gladstone's dictation after having supported Parnell in the aftermath of the divorce.
122. *Ibid.*
123. *Ibid.* 11 July 1891.
124. See Kerr's indignant letters in *ibid.* 29 August, 5 September and 12 September 1891.
125. *Ibid.*
126. See addresses at Wicklow meeting of 31 March – *ibid.* 6 June 1891.
127. See Joseph McCarroll's speech at a Parnellite meeting in Wicklow on 11 August 1891 – *ibid.* 15 August 1891.

## Part V: Parnell and his family

### 1. The non-political Parnells

1. James Joyce, *Ulysses* (Random House edition, New York, 1961), p. 165.
2. See above, part II, chap. 1, pp. 100–101. Also Burke's *Baronetage and Peerage* (1970) under Congleton.
3. E. Dickinson, p. 94.
4. *Ibid.* pp. 91–2.
5. See above, part III, chap. 1, p. 100. for discussion of this antipathy.
6. E. Dickinson, pp. 99–101.
7. See T. P. O'Connor, *C. S. Parnell: a memory* (London, 1891), p. 27, for a reference to MacDermott's politics.
8. J. H. Parnell, p. 256.
9. He mentioned this in several legal affirmations.
10. The child that Sophia died giving birth to, a girl, survived. See E. Dickinson, p. 101.
11. *Ibid.* p. 102.
12. K. O'Shea, ii, 45.
13. J. H. Parnell, p. 148.
14. *Ibid.* p. 195.
15. C. S. Parnell to E. Dickinson, 17 April 1882 (N.L.I., Parnell letters, MS 15,735).
16. K. O'Shea, i, 245–6.
17. J. H. Parnell, p. 80.

18. See *Celtic Monthly,* vol. iii, no. 2 (February 1880), p. 104.

19. *Ibid.* p. 197.

20. 'Fanny Parnell' (anonymous) in *Celtic Monthly* Magazine, vol. i, no. 2 (September 1882), p. 286.

21. T. M. Healy, *Letters and leaders,* i, 85.

22. *Ibid.* i, 87.

23. *Ibid.*

24. See above, part III, chap. 1, pp. 87–8.

25. K. O'Shea, i, 136; C. S. Parnell to K. O'Shea, 17 July 1880.

26. C. S. Parnell to E. Dickinson, 17 April 1882 (N.L.I., Parnell letters, MS 15,735).

27. Debrett's *Peerage* (1900).

28. R. M. McWade, *Life of Stewart Parnell* (incorporating reminiscences of Delia T. S. Parnell), p. 48.

29. Reg. of Deeds, Mem. for 1880, 49.209.

30. *Ibid.*

31. E. Dickinson, p. 191.

32. See above, part III, chap. 1, pp. 96–7.

33. In an interview quoted in *Nation,* 4 February 1882.

34. E. Dickinson, p. 141.

35. *Ibid.* p. 142.

36. *Ibid.* p. 146. She had no 'uncle' named Bligh, though two of her father's cousins had married into the Bligh family, Earls of Darnley (see family tree). This legacy is unmentioned in a public statement of Emily's finances published after her death (*Irish Times,* 27 May 1918).

37. E. Dickinson, pp. 143–6.

38. *Ibid.* p. 149.

39. *Wicklow Newsletter,* 15 December 1883.

40. E. Dickinson, chapter xii.

41. *Ibid.* pp. 168–9.

42. *Ibid.* p. 158.

43. *Ibid.* p. 154.

44. Promising the ever-anxious Mrs O'Shea not to catch cold by standing about in the churchyard. See K. O'Shea, ii, 53–4; C. S. Parnell to K. O'Shea, undated.

45. E. Dickinson, p. 155.

46. A. Kettle, *The material for victory,* p. 84.

47. E. Dickinson, p. 104.

48. See *ibid.* chap. viii.

49. K. O'Shea, i, 238; C. S. Parnell to K. O'Shea, 16 March 1882.

50. O'Brien, *Parnell,* i, 349.

51. See above, part IV, chap. 2, pp. 167, 184.

52. On this point, see K. O'Shea, ii, 244: 'He had much pride of family and family affection, but he was utterly undemonstrative and shy . . . I do not think his family ever realised how strong his affection for them was'.

53. E. Dickinson, pp. 137–41.

54. *Ibid.* p. 136.

55. *Ibid.* p. 177.

56. *Ibid.* pp. 173–4.

57. *Ibid,* p. 178.

58. *Ibid.* p. 179.

59. O'Brien, *Parnell,* ii, 341–4.

60. *Ibid.* ii, 342.

61. See above, part III, chap. 1, p. 86.

62. R. M. McWade, *Life of Stewart Parnell,* p. 49.

63. E. Dickinson, p. 186.

64. See above, part III, chap. 1, pp. 102–4.

65. *Register of Admissions to Lincoln's Inn* (London 1896), ii, 352.

66. J. H. Parnell, p. 11.

67. P. J. Hanway, 'Mrs Parnell', in *Celtic Monthly*, vol. v, no. 4 (April 1881), pp. 326–9.

68. See Reg. of Deeds, Mem. for 1882, 36.27.

69. His library was auctioned in this year. See a *Catalogue of books for auction by J. Fleming Jones in Dublin* (Dublin 1870).

70. See F. S. L. Lyons, *Ireland since the famine* (London 1971), p. 115; also J. O'Leary, *Recollections of Fenians and Fenianism* (London, 1890) for numerous references.

71. Reg. of Deeds, Mem. for 1884, 239.86.

72. *Ibid.* for 1891, 50.145.

73. T. P. O'Connor, *C. S. Parnell: a memory*, p. 25.

74. K. O'Shea, ii, 72–3.

75. T. P. O'Connor, *Memories of an old parliamentarian*, ii, 330.

76. Reg. of Deeds, Mem. for 1874, 47.27. See above, part III, chap. 1, p. 103.

77. *Ibid.* for 1891, 50.145.

78. *Ibid.* for 1882, 36.27.

79. *Ibid.*

80. See above, part III, chap. 3, p. 000.

81. *Irish Times*, 26 October 1880. See above, part IV, chap, 2, p. 137.

82. J. A. McClintock to M. Davitt, 7 July 1885; Davitt papers. I am indebted to Professor T. W. Moody for this reference.

83. W. S. Blunt, *The land war in Ireland* (London, 1912), p. 270.

84. T. P. O'Connor, *C. S. Parnell: a memory*, p. 25; St John Ervine, *Parnell*, p. 98.

85. See above, part III, chap. 2, p. 125.

86. Katharine Tynan, *Twenty-five years*, p. 348. T. P. O'Connor also remarked the resemblance, noticing Henry in a café in Germany (*Memories of an old parliamentarian*, ii, 330).

## 2. Delia Tudor Stewart Parnell

1. Delia T. S. Parnell to T. D. Sullivan, 21 January 1880, (N.L.I., Sullivan Papers, MS 8237 (6) ), p. 3. For the rest of this chapter quoted as 'Letter to Sullivan'.

2. Interview with Mrs Parnell in *Boston Pilot*, reprinted in *Nation*, 10 May 1884.

3. T. M. Healy, *Letters and leaders*, i, 62.

4. *Ibid.* i, 85.

5. *Nation*, 4 February 1882.

6. *Ibid.* 2 October 1886; *Wicklow Newsletter*, 3 December 1887.

7. *Wicklow Newsletter*, 23 November 1889.

8. See above, pp. 233–8.

9. See *Nation*, 5 November 1881; also a letter to Patrick Egan quoted in *ibid.* 7 April 1883, where she refers to 'my long illness, delicacy and debility'; also *ibid*, 7 July 1883.

10. *Ibid.* 13 October 1883.

11. *Ibid.* 22 March 1884, 3 May 1884, 10 May 1884.

12. *Ibid.* 10 May 1884.

13. See above, pp. 234–7.

14. J. H. Parnell, p. 138; T. P. O'Connor, *Memories of an old parliamentarian*, i, 217.

15. New York *Herald*, 15 July 1885; *Nation*, 1 August 1885.

16. New York *Herald*, 22 July 1885; *Weekly Freeman*, 8 August 1885.

17. See above, part IV, chap. 3, pp. 192–3.

18. *Washington Post*, 20 February 1886. Quoted in *Wicklow Newsletter*, 20 March 1886.

19. *Ibid.*

20. *Wicklow Newsletter*, 20 March 1886, quoting from *Washington Post*.

21. See above, part IV, chap. 2.

22. *Wicklow Newsletter*, 20 March 1886, from *Washington Post*.

23. See London *Daily News*, 15 March 1886, and *Nation* 20 March 1886.

24. See *Nation*, 2 October 1886, for a report of her arrival.

25. *Ibid.*

26. *Weekly Freeman*, 2 October 1886.

27. *Ibid.*

28. See above, p. 234.

29. J. H. Parnell, p. 281.

30. *Wicklow Newsletter*, 2 July 1887.

31. *Ibid.* 16 August 1887.

32. See above, p. 238, also above, part III, chap. 1, pp. 86–7.

33. See *Wicklow Newsletter*, 23 November 1889.

34. *Weekly Freeman*, 14 December 1889.

35. *Ibid.*

36. *Ibid.*

37. J. McCarthy to Mrs Campbell Praed, November 1889, in *Our book of memories* (London, 1912), p. 209.

38. *Wicklow Newsletter*, 30 November 1889.

39. See above, part III, chap. 1, p. 88.

40. J. H. Parnell, p. 138.

41. P. J. Hanway, 'Mrs Delia T. S. Parnell', in *Celtic Monthly*, vol. v, no. 4 (April 1881), pp. 326–9.

42. T. P. O'Connor, *Memories of an old parliamentarian*, i, 217.

43. See *Wicklow Newsletter*, 26 March 1892.

44. *Nation*, 21 June 1880.

45. J. H. Parnell, p. 286.

46. E. Dickinson, p. 171.

47. Above, part III, chap. 1, p. 87.

48. St John Ervine, *Parnell*, pp. 24, 38, 37, 40. Harrison attacks these contentions in *Parnell vindicated*, pp. 47–50, 427.

49. *Parnell vindicated*, p. 50.

50. She herself would not have relished Harrison's judgement that she had considerable '*untrained*' intellectual powers. She told P. J. Hanway that she was versed in history, mathematics, music, drawing, chemistry, astronomy, and had 'attained the rare accomplishment of speaking and writing in all the modern languages of Europe, besides Latin and Greek'.

51. T. M. Healy to Maurice Healy, 20 March 1880; *Letters and leaders*, i, 87.

52. T. P. O'Connor, *C. S. Parnell: a memory*, p. 17.

53. T. P. O'Connor, *Memories of an old parliamentarian*, i, 217 and ii, 330.

54 *What I have seen and heard*, p. 147.

55 See above, part II, chap. 2, p. 55.

56 See T. M. Healy's letter quoted on previous page; also above, p. 236.

57 R. M. McWade, *Life of Stewart Parnell*, pp. 65–6.

58 See above, part II, chap. 2, pp. 60–61.

59 St John Ervine, *Parnell*, p. 40.

60 See above, part III, chap. 1, pp. 90–94.

61 J. H. Parnell, p. 153.

62 *Ibid.* p. 158.

63 *Ibid.* p. 269.

64 See above, p. 245.

65 J. H. Parnell, p. 154.

66 See above, p. 245.

67 T. P. O'Connor, *Memories of an old parliamentarian*, i, 217.

68 See above, part II, chap. 2, p. 63.

69. R. M. McWade, *Life of Stewart Parnell*, pp. 63–4.

70. *Ibid.*

71. See above, p. 237.

72. See *Nation*, 29 December 1883.

73. See above, p. 237.

74. *Nation*, 7 April 1883.

75. See above, p. 236.

76. William O'Brien, *Evening memories*, p. 96. He dates this as 'about 1885', but Mrs Parnell does not seem to have been in Ireland that year.

77. See *Weekly Freeman*, 23 August 1884.

78. *Ibid.* 6 September 1884.

79. *Ibid.* In 1888, Mrs Parnell was an unequivocal supporter of Cleveland's, and they appeared together on a New York platform. See E. P. Oberholzer, *A history of the U.S. since the Civil War* (5 vols., New York, 1917–37), 5, 68.

80. At a meeting in Cinncinnati. See *Weekly Freeman*, 18 April 1891.

81. J. H. Parnell, pp. 132, 252–3; also above, p. 238.

82. R. M. McWade, *Life of Stewart Parnell*, p. 65.

83. *Nation*, 19 March 1881.

84. T. P. O'Connor, *Memories of an old parliamentarian*, i, 217.

85. See above, p. 232.

86. *Nation*, 2 April 1881.

87. *Ibid.* 16 April 1881. My italics.

88. Washington *National Republican*, 4 August 1881; quoted in *Nation*, 27 August 1881.

89. *Nation*, 2 October 1886. The meeting was held on 27 September.

90. *Weekly Freeman*, 22 October 1886.

91. *Ibid.*

92. See 'Fanny Parnell' (anonymous), in *Celtic Magazine*, vol. i, no. 2 (September 1882), pp. 280–92.

93. See above, p. 235.

94. W. S. Blunt, *The land war in Ireland*, p. 341.

95. R. M. McWade, *Life of Stewart Parnell*, p. 403.

96. J. H. Parnell, p. 129.

97. *Ibid.*

98. McWade, *Life of Stewart Parnell*, p. 55.

99. *Ibid.*

100. She said this at a meeting at Cinncinnati, reported in *Weekly Freeman*, 18 April 1891.

101. See *Nation*, 8 July 1882.

102. J. H. Parnell, p. 253.

103. See *ibid.* p. 132.

104. *Ibid.* pp. 252–3.

105. Besides the fact that Katharine Tynan knew the family in Dublin, it is significant that both of her parents were Wicklow people and she had heard much of the Parnells from them.

106. O'Brien, *Parnell*, i, 205. Healy did not mention, however, that this was a reasonable step to take considering that a Canadian Orange Lodge had threatened him before his visit. See J. H. Parnell, pp. 160–1.

107. K. O'Shea, i, 184.

108. *Wicklow Newsletter*, 3 December 1887.

109. C. S. Parnell to K. O'Shea, 4 January 1888, quoted in K. O'Shea, ii, 134.

110. *Irish Weekly Independent,* 6 October 1894.

111. K. O'Shea, ii, 176.

112. J. H. Parnell, pp. 255, 281.

113. O'Brien, *Parnell,* ii, 348.

114. See above, part IV, chap. 1, p. 152.

115. As in the one quoted in O'Brien, *Parnell,* ii, 97.

116. See K. O'Shea, i, chapters 23–4.

117. See for instance the *Standard,* 19 May 1914, where a review of *Charles Stewart Parnell* referred scathingly to the banality of the Kilmainham letters, saying they resembled 'letters from a love-sick clerk of twenty-two'.

118. This appeared on 21 December 1886. See T. M. Healy, *Letters and leaders,* i, 266–7.

119. R. M. McWade, *Life of Stewart Parnell,* p. 53.

120. *Ibid.* p. 55.

121. See above, part II, chap. 2.

### 3. Fanny Parnell

1. 'Fanny Parnell' (anonymous) in *Celtic Magazine,* vol. i, no. 2 (September 1882), pp. 280–92; in this chapter cited as 'Fanny Parnell'.

2. *Ibid.*

3. T. M. Healy to Maurice Healy, 20 March 1880, in *Letters and leaders,* i, 87.

4. 'Fanny Parnell', p. 289.

5. E. Dickinson, p. 121.

6. R. M. McWade, *Life of Stewart Parnell,* p. 72: 'Here she got malaria . . . Here she died of exhaustion and a weak heart.'

7. O'Brien, *Parnell,* i, 373, n.1.

8. T. P. O'Connor, *Memories of an old parliamentarian,* i, 219.

9. T. M. Healy, *Letters and leaders,* i, 81.

10. R. M. McWade, *Life of Stewart Parnell,* p. 72.

11. 'An appreciation of Fanny Parnell' by 'J. M.' in *Nation,* 5 August 1882.

12. See T. M. Healy, *Letters and leaders,* i, 81, and 'Fanny Parnell', p. 286.

13. *Proceedings of a farewell dinner for James Redpath,* 1 June 1881 (pamphlet, New York, 1881: Bradstreet Press). The 'two ladies' were herself and Ellen Ford. In the same spirit, Fanny (a spinster) once remarked to T. P. O'Connor that 'man proposes and God disposes' was in her experience inaccurate; she found that man never proposed at all.

14. T. M. Healy, *Letters and leaders,* ii, 81.

15. J. H. Parnell, p. 116.

16. *Nation,* 12 August 1882. She made an unforgettable impression, 'with intense, austere face, quivering, slight figure, and thrilling voice, full of all-consuming earnestness'.

17. W. O'Brien, *Recollections* (London, 1905), p. 332.

18. *Nation,* 5 August, 1882.

19. See above, p. 248–9.

20. See J. H. Parnell, p. 163, where he says as much.

21. 'Fanny Parnell', p. 286.

22. Appreciation by 'J. M.' in *Nation,* 5 August 1882.

23. T. M. Healy, *Letters and leaders,* i, 81.

24. 'Fanny Parnell', p. 290.

25. O'Brien, *Parnell,* i, 136.

26. See chap. 4, below.

27. Davitt, *Fall of feudalism,* p. 256.

28. See above, p. 246.

29. *Devoy's Post bag*, i, 481; W. Dillon to Devoy, 1 February 1880.

30. *Ibid.* i, 487; Fanny Parnell to Devoy, 10 February 1880. Her original contribution was the system of collection through nationally-dispersed 'ballot-boxes'.

31. See *ibid.* i, 468.

32. See above, p. 248.

33. Fanny Parnell to T. D. Sullivan, 5 May 1881 (N.L.I., Sullivan Papers, MS 8237 (4) ).

34. See Land League material in N.L.I., MS 8291 (1).

35. See 'Fanny Parnell', p. 285.

36. *Ibid.* p. 286.

37. M. F. Sullivan, an article in *Redpath's Weekly*, quoted at length in 'Fanny Parnell', p. 288.

38. Reprinted in *Nation*, 28 August, 1880.

39. 'Fanny Parnell', p. 289.

40. *Ibid.*

41. *Nation*, 25 December 1880.

42. *Ibid.* 1 January 1881. Fanny's letter was dated 14 December 1880.

43. 'Fanny Parnell', p. 290.

44. See below, chap. 4.

45. *Nation*, 25 July, 1881.

46. 'Fanny Parnell', p. 285.

47. W. Carroll to Devoy, 5 December 1879; *Devoy's Post bag*, i, 466.

48. *Ibid.* i, 522.

49. See *Nation*, 25 July 1881.

50. Letter of 12 August 1880, quoted in *Nation*, 28 August 1880.

51. 'Fanny Parnell', p. 287.

52. J. H. Parnell, p. 164.

53. W. Carroll to Devoy, *Devoy's Post bag*, i, 521; 29 April 1880.

54. Same to same, 11 May 1880; *ibid*, i, 530.

55. W. Carroll to Devoy, 29 April 1880; *Devoy's Post bag*, i, 520.

56. *Ibid.*

57. Same to same, 29 April 1880; *ibid.* i, 522.

58. R. M. McWade, *Life of Stewart Parnell*, p. 73.

59. From *Hovels of Ireland;* quoted in 'Fanny Parnell', p. 287.

60. *Ibid.*

61. Fanny Parnell to T. D. Sullivan, 4 February 1881 (N.L.I., Sullivan papers, MS 8237 (4) ).

62. Same to same, 5 May 1881; *ibid.*

63. *Ibid.*

64. R. M. McWade, *Life of Stewart Parnell*, p. 80.

65. See *Nation*, 12 August 1882.

66. According to the *D.N.B.*, vol. xv, p. 342.

67. C. J. Kickham to Dr. T. J. Crean, 23 Nov. 1881 (MS in possession of Mr James Cusack of Clonmel), quoted in J. Maher, *The valley near Slievenamon* (Mullinahone, 1942). I am indebted to R. V. Comerford for this reference.

68. See *Nation*, 1 October 1881.

69. *Nation*, 29 July 1882.

70. J. O'Leary, *Recollections of Fenians and Fenianism*, ii, 29–31.

71. See her letter to the *Irish World* in August 1880, quoted above, p. 247.

72. Davitt, *Fall of feudalism*, pp. 291–2.

73. *Daily Telegraph* review; quoted in the *Irish Times*, 23 September 1880.

74. 'Irish Discontent' in *Edinburgh Review*, vol. 155, no. 1 (January 1882), pp. 155–85.

75. See *Celtic Monthly*, vol. iv, no. 6 (December 1880), p. 614.

76. Fanny Parnell to T. D. Sullivan, 4 February 1881 (N.L.I., Sullivan Papers, MS 8237 (4).

77. Verse 18 of 'The Great Archbishop'. See *Nation*, 16 July 1881.

78. Verse 3 of 'Coercion – Hold the Rent'. See Davitt, *Fall of feudalism*, pp. 266–7.

79. 'The Poor Man to his Country'; see *Irish People*, 1 October 1864.

80. 'The Clogher Massacre'; see *Celtic Monthly*, vol. v, no. 4, (April 1881), p. 367.

81. 'John Dillon'; printed in the *Boston Pilot* at the time of his American tour in 1880.

82. 'To the Land Leaguers'; see *Celtic Monthly*, vol. v, no. 3 (September 1880), p. 241.

83. See n. 81.

84. See Davitt, *Fall of feudalism*, pp. 266–7.

85. See above, p. 248.

86. 'To the Land Leaguers'; see n. 82.

87. 'To England; or, the Land Bill of 1881', see *Nation*, 1 October, 1881.

88. 'Ireland, Mother' (published in November 1880).

89. *Nation*, 26 February 1881.

90. Reprinted *Nation*, 5 March 1881.

91. See above, p. 271.

92. See his celebrated letter to Mrs O'Shea from Kilmainham where he refers to the movement as 'hollow and wanting in solidity' – C. S. Parnell to K. O'Shea, 14 February 1882; K. O'Shea, i, 235.

93. See *Nation*, 1 October 1881.

94. See *Nation*, 17 July 1880.

95. See *Celtic Monthly*, vol. v, no. 3 (September 1880), p. 241.

96. Davitt, *Fall of feudalism*, p. 370.

97. *Nation*, 29 July 1882.

98. See *Nation*, 19 March, 16 July, 20 August 1881.

99. See n.81.

100. See *Celtic Monthly*, vol. v, no. 3 (September 1880), p. 241.

101. See *Ibid.* no. 4 (April 1881), p. 367.

102. T. M. Healy, *Letters and leaders*, i, 87: 'The only religion Parnell himself has is to believe that Friday is an unlucky day ... The mother and sisters share his religious condition'.

103. T. M. Healy, *Letters and leaders*, i, 85; K. O'Shea, ii, 44.

104. See above, p. 244.

105. Standish O'Grady, *The story of Ireland*, p. 207.

106. Quoted in *Nation*, 12 August, 1882: the anecdote is wrongly dated 1879.

107. Fanny Parnell to T. D. Sullivan, 4 February 1881, (N.L.I., Sullivan Papers, MS 8237 (4) ).

108. *Nation*, 2 September 1882: 'Mr Parnell has not been in the House since the death of his sister ... I am told by a gentleman who did have an interview with him on private business that he appeared to have suffered greatly'.

109. K. O'Shea, ii, 44.

110. *Nation*, 5 August 1882.

111. O'Brien, *Parnell*, i, 373, n.1.

112. See *Nation*, 5 August 1881.

113. R. M. McWade, *Life of Stewart Parnell*, p. 72.

114. In Anna's obituary; the *Irish Times*, 25 September, 1911.

115. See above, p. 242.

116. K. O'Shea, ii, 45.

117. *Nation*, 21 October 1882.

118. *Ibid.* 11 October, 1882.

119. *Ibid.*

120. 'Fanny Parnell', p. 280.

121. See *ibid.* for a selection.
122. In 'After Death'; see *Nation*, 12 August 1882.
123. See *ibid.* 23 June 1883, 18 June 1887, 14 June 1890.

## 4. Anna Parnell

1. See the second epigraph to this chapter.
2. E. Dickinson, pp. 206–7.
3. T. P. O'Connor, *Memories of an old parliamentarian*, i, 219.
4. K. Tynan, *Twenty-five years*, p. 73.
5. *Ibid.*
6. *Ibid.* p. 82.
7. 'Miss Anna Parnell' by R. M. McWade in *Celtic Magazine*, vol. i, no. 2 (September 1882), pp. 251–2.
8. See above, p. 275.
9. McWade, 'Miss Anna Parnell', p. 252.
10. K. Tynan, *Twenty-five years*, p. 83.
11. Davitt, *Fall of feudalism*, p. 300.
12. Anna Parnell, 'Tale of a great sham', Anna Parnell papers (N.L.I., MS 12, 144, pp. 214–15); hereafter cited simply as 'Tale'. This important manuscript was first brought to light and drawn attention to by Professor T. W. Moody, in a paper read to the Conference on Irish Studies in New York on 20 March 1965. I am indebted to him for allowing me to use his paper as an important source for this chapter.
13. *Nation*, 23 April 1881.
14. See above, part III, chap. 1, p. 104.
15. Anna Parnell, 'How they do in the House of Commons: Notes from the ladies' cage'; *Celtic Monthly*, vol. iii, no. 5 (May, 1880) pp. 469–72; no. 6 (June 1880), pp. 537–41; vol. iv, no. 1 (July 1880), pp. 17–21. Hereafter cited as 'How they do', part 1, 2 or 3, with page number.
16. 'How they do', part 1, p. 470.
17. These men were respectively Chairman of Committees and Secretary of the Colonies.
18. 'How they do', part 3, p. 18.
19. *Ibid.* p. 21.
20. See *Nation*, 27 December 1879. The letter was written from Trenton on 3 December.
21. See above, p. 244.
22. T. M. Healy, *Letters and leaders*, i, 87; letter of 20 March 1880.
23. T. M. Healy to Maurice Healy, 25 February 1880; *ibid.* i, 80.
24. Land League papers (N.L.I., MS 8291 (11) ).
25. Letter of 15 July 1880 (unaddressed) in Land League papers (N.L.I., MS 8291 (1) ).
26. J. J. W. O'Donogue to C. S. Parnell, 10 August 1880, Land League Papers (N.L.I., MS 8291) (1) ).
27. Davitt, *Fall of feudalism*, p. 251.
28. See above, pp. 245–6.
29. Fanny Parnell to M. F. Sullivan, quoted in 'Fanny Parnell', p. 288.
30. *Ibid.*
31. Speech at Kilmallock, 25 March 1881 – reported in *Nation*, 26 March 1881, and quoted by Davitt in *Fall of feudalism*, p. 230.
32. Davitt, *Fall of feudalism*, p. 300.
33. See for instance, A. Kettle, *The material for victory*, p. 48; Davitt, *Fall of feudalism*, p. 298.
34. A. Kettle, *The material for victory*, p. 48.
35. F. Sheehy-Skeffington, *Michael Davitt* (2nd ed., London, 1967), p. 90.

36. M. M. O'Hara, *Chief and tribune*, p. 151.

37. Davitt, *Fall of feudalism*, p. 300.

38. See 'Anna Parnell' by Mrs Jennie Wyse-Power, in *Dublin Metropolitan Magazine* (Spring 1935), pp. 15–17, 28.

39. See L.L.L. addresses of 4 February 1881, reported in *Nation*, 12 February 1881.

40. 'Secret History of the Land League by Michael Davitt' in D. Cashman, *Life of Michael Davitt* (London, 1883 or 1884), p. 230.

41. W. O'Brien, *Recollections*, p. 376.

42. K. Tynan, *Twenty-five years*, p. 79.

43. *Ibid.* p. 84.

44. *Ibid.* p. 99.

45. D. Cashman, *Michael Davitt*, p. 230.

46. *Ibid.* p. 231.

47. 'Tale', pp. 163 *et seq.*

48. D. Cashman, *Michael Davitt*, p. 232.

49. 'Tale', p. 188.

50. *Ibid.* p. 72.

51. Quoted in Davitt's speech before the Special Commission, pp. 268–9.

52. 'Tale', p. 160.

53. See above, p. 271.

54. 'Tale', p. 171.

55. *Ibid.* p. 179.

56. See *Nation*, 19 March 1881, for the full text of this pastoral.

57. From Archbishop Croke among others. See Davitt, *Fall of feudalism*, pp. 314–15.

58. Jennie Wyse-Power, 'Anna Parnell', in *Dublin Metropolitan Magazine* (Spring 1935).

59. 'Tale,' p. 185.

60. See above, p. 278.

61. Davitt, *Fall of feudalism*, p. 340.

62. *Ibid.*

63. *Ibid.* p. 341.

64. *Nation*, 2 July 1881.

65. See *ibid.* 12 February 1881.

66. *Ibid.* 19 February 1881.

67. See *ibid.*

68. *Ibid.* 26 February 1881.

69. *Ibid.* 5 March 1881.

70. See *ibid.* 12 March 1881.

71. A forceful letter from Anna to the *Freeman's Journal* of 8 March said: 'I don't wish to be charged with attempting to introduce doubts on religious matters into the minds of the women of Ireland . . . [I said:] "I think if there is another world – and you would not suppose by the way some people act here that there was one – that anyone who helps to turn out starving people onto the roadside will require a great deal of saving". The feeling which stimulated me to say this was a very strong opinion, which I have for a long time held, that it would be perfectly impossible for anyone who really believed in a judgement to come in another world to sanction or tolerate, directly or indirectly, the atrocities which are practised in Ireland under the cover of the law'.

72. *Nation*, 19 March 1881.

73. And were duly thanked for it. See reports of L.L.L. meetings in *ibid.* 26 March, 1881.

74. Speech at Thurles by Anna Parnell on 20 March 1881; reported in *ibid.*

75. *Ibid.*

76. See *ibid.* 2 April 1881.

77. *Ibid.*

78. See *ibid.* 26 March 1881, for a report of her speech at Kilmallock, where she complimented him.

79. *Ibid.*

80. See her speech at Castletown-Kenneigh, Co. Cork, on 1 May 1881 – reported in *ibid.* 7 May 1881.

81. *Ibid.* 28 May 1881.

82. As in her speech at Drumcolliher on 26 June 1881 – see *ibid.* 2 July 1881 – and her letter to the *Freeman's Journal* of 28 June.

83. *Nation*, 11 June 1881.

84. See *ibid.* 14 May 1881.

85. *Ibid.* 13 August 1881.

86. *Ibid*, 20 August 1881. 'She did wonders during the day, journeying across fields and ditches, running and walking alternately for hours in a manner that excited the wonder of all and the admiration of some . . . She skipped over long grass, ditches, and even forded small streams'.

87. *Ibid.*

88. *Ibid.* 27 August 1881.

89. *Ibid.* 23 July 1881.

90. O'Brien, *Parnell*, i, 292.

91. C. S. Parnell to K. O'Shea, 13 October 1881; K. O'Shea, i, 207.

92. *Nation*, 3 September 1881.

93. *Ibid.*

94. A speech on 31 August 1881. See *ibid.* 10 September 1881.

95. On 5 September 1881. See *ibid.*

96. At Leeds, 10 October 1881. See *ibid.* 15 October 1881.

97. 11 November, 13 November and 14 November respectively; see *ibid.* 19 November 1881.

98. Jennie Wyse–Power, 'Anna Parnell', in *Dublin Metropolitan Magazine* (Spring 1935).

99. A. Webb, 'Autobiography', ii, p. 433 (MS to be placed in Society of Friends' Library, Eustace Street, Dublin).

100. *Nation*, 19 November 1881.

101. K. Tynan, *Twenty-five years*, p. 82.

102. A. Webb, 'Autobiography', ii. 434.

103. See *Nation*, 26 November 1881, for especially detailed minutes.

104. See *ibid.*

105. *Ibid.* My italics.

106. K. O'Shea, i, 156. She dates this as 5 November 1880; but Anna was unknown at that time, so it must have been November 1881. Either way, some doubt is cast on Parnell's supposed comment that Anna's 'pride in being burnt as a menace to England would be so drowned in horror at her company that it would put the fire out'; on Guy Fawkes Day 1880 he was in Ireland, and the same day in 1881 he was in Kilmainham.

107. *Nation*, 24 December 1881.

108. *Ibid.* 31 December 1881.

109. *Ibid.* 7 January 1882.

110. See *ibid.* 28 January 1882, for details of their treatment in Mullingar jail.

111. *Ibid.*

112. See *ibid.* 10 June 1882.

113. *Evening Telegraph*, 16 June 1882.

114. Letter dated 15 June, *ibid.*

115. See for instance Davitt, *Fall of feudalism*, p. 356; O'Brien, *Parnell* i, 364–5; W. O'Brien, *Recollections*, p. 463; K. O'Shea, i, 260–1.

116. 'Tale', pp. 191–2.

117. *Ibid.* p. 197.

118. *Ibid.*

119. *Ibid.* p. 227.

120. *Ibid.* p. 235.

121. *Ibid.* p. 238.

122. *Ibid.* p. 239.

123. Published in *Nation,* 29 July 1882.

124. Anna Parnell to Dr Sigerson, 12 December 1907 (N.L.I., Anna Parnell papers, MS 8100 (8) ).

125. Davitt, *Fall of feudalism,* p. 357.

126. Letter to Sigerson (see n. 124 above).

127. K. Tynan *Twenty-five years,* pp. 73, 88. She 'rebuked him because he came in like a conspirator, wrapped in an old coat with capes and a cap drawn over his eyes'.

128. K. Tynan, *Memories,* p. 5.

129. K. Tynan, *Twenty-five years,* p. 88.

130. W. O'Brien, *Recollections,* pp. 462, 464.

131. O'Brien, *Parnell,* i, 364–5.

132. Davitt, *Fall of feudalism,* p. 356.

133. See K. O'Shea, ii, 51.

134. *Ibid.* i, 260.

135. *Ibid.* i, 271.

136. C. S. Parnell to Sir Charles Russell, 6 March 1889 (N.L.I., Parnell letters, MS 5934).

137. W. M. Lomasney to Devoy, 11 February 1881, *Devoy's Post bag,* ii, 36; also a reference in same to same, 18 February 1881, *ibid.* ii, 40.

138. T. M. Healy, *Letters and leaders,* i, 157.

139. Anna Parnell to Helena Molony, 7 July 1910; quoted in T. W. Moody, 'Anna Parnell and the Land League', a lecture given to the Conference on Irish Studies in New York on 20 March 1965. This approach led to her ignoring the very special position of both Parnell and Davitt in her memoir about the Land war.

140. *Nation,* 5 August 1882.

141. See *ibid.* 5 August, 12 August, and 19 August 1882.

142. *Ibid.* 5 August.

143. Leader in *ibid.*

144. See *ibid.* 12 August and 19 August 1882.

145. *Ibid.* 30 December 1882.

146. *Ibid.* 24 March 1883; quoted from *American Celt.*

147. K. Tynan, *Twenty-five years,* pp. 150–1.

148. W. O'Brien, *Evening Memories,* p. 188.

149. See Sullivan Papers in N.L.I. (MS 8237 (7) ). The letter is a rough draft, undated and unaddressed.

150. See T. D. Sullivan, *Recollections of troubled times in Irish politics* (2 vols. Dublin, 1905), pp. 195–6.

151. K. Tynan, *Twenty-five years,* p. 98.

152. 'Tale', p. 46.

153. *Ibid.* p. 5.

154. *Ibid.* p. 241.

155. *Ibid.* p. 256; my italics.

156. K. O'Shea, i, 266.

157. W. O'Brien, *Evening Memories,* p. 188.

158. A. Kettle, *The material for victory,* p. 48.

159. K. Tynan, *Twenty-five years,* p. 90.

160. Quoted in *Wicklow Newsletter,* 31 October 1891.

161. In an addendum about the Parnell Split attached to his unpublished autobiography; see above, n. 99.

## 5. Charles Stewart and John Howard

1. See especially above, part III, chap. 1, pp. 98-100 and chap. 3, pp. 131–5.
2. See J. H. Parnell, pp. 270–6 for a vividly described expedition to the remotest part of the Georgia mountains.
3. See above, part III, chap. 3, p. 135.
4. J. H. Parnell, p. 146.
5. *Ibid.*
6. *Ibid.* p. 156.
7. *Ibid.* p. 277.
8. See contemporary newspaper accounts – above, p. 228.
9. See above, p. 226.
10. J. H. Parnell, pp. 222, 226.
11. *Ibid.* p. 255.
12. See *Wicklow Newsletter*, 26 December 1891.
13. J. H. Parnell, p. 270.
14. *Ibid.* p. 181.
15. See above, part II, chap. 3, p. 70. also above, p. 105.
16. J. H. Parnell, p. 137.
17. See above, part III, chap. 3, p. 135.
18. J. H. Parnell, p. 152.
19. *Ibid.* p. 268.
20. See Bradstreet Press pamphlet, quoted above, chap. 3, n. 13.
21. Speech of 5 April 1881, quoted in *Nation*, 7 May 1881.
22. *Ibid.* 11 March 1882, quoted from *Chicago Citizen*, 18 February 1882.
23. D. T. S. Parnell to T. D. Sullivan, 21 January 1880 (N.L.I., Sullivan Papers, MS 8237), p. 31.
24. See Reg. of Deeds, Mem. for 1882, 13.284; also above, p. 193.
25. *Irish Times*, 12 November, 1885.
26. *Nation*, 25 April 1891.
27. See *Irish Times*, 15 March 1882 – report and editorial.
28. See above, part III, chap. 1, p. 99.
29. See above, part IV, chap. 3, p. 193.
30. Reg. of Deeds, Mem. for 1882, 12.284.
31. J. H. Parnell, pp. 209, 286–8. See above, part IV, chap. 3, p. 193.
32. See W. P. Coyne, *Ireland industrial and agricultural* (Dublin 1902), p. 271; also Mrs Parnell's letter to T. D. Sullivan of 21 January 1880 (N.L.I., Sullivan Papers, MS 8237 (6) ), p. 31.
33. See above, part III, chap. 1, p. 98.
34. J. H. Parnell, p. 103; see above, part III, chap. 2, p. 128.
35. See Epilogue.
36. T. P. O'Connor, *Memories of an old parliamentarian*, ii, 328.
37. *Ibid.*
38. J. Joyce, *Ulysses* (Random House reprint edition, N.Y., 1966), p. 165.
39. J. H. Parnell, p. 277.
40. *Ibid.* p. 177.
41. *Ibid.* p. 179.
42. *Ibid.* p. 277.
43. *Ibid.* p. 172.
44. *Ibid.* pp. 277 *et seq.*
45. *Ibid.* p. 303.
46. *Ibid.* p. 277.
47. W. O'Brien, *Evening memories*, p. 188.

## Epilogue: The Parnells and Avondale after 1891

1. See *Wicklow Newsletter,* 19 December 1893, and *Irish Weekly Independent,* 3 June 1893. He went to America in the summer of 1892 and returned in the autumn, making another visit in March 1893, and writing from Alabama in that month to be entered as an elector for the Rathdrum Board of Guardians.

2. See *Irish Weekly Independent,* 3 June 1893, and an address to the Irish Industrial League quoted in *Wicklow Newsletter,* 10 June 1893.

3. *Wicklow Newsletter,* 4 May 1895: 120,000 furze walking-sticks and 50 wood-wool mattresses.

4. See for instance *ibid.* 27 April 1895, 17 July 1895, 14 May 1898.

5. See *ibid.* 31 October 1896, for a case against the ubiquitous Shiel of Carrignameel; also *ibid.* 19 June 1897. When arbitrary eviction took place at nearby Whaley Abbey, however, John sided with popular opinion; see *ibid.* 25 September 1897 and 22 October 1898.

6. See a long letter from him to the *All Ireland Review,* 11 May 1901, the original of which is in the Redmond Papers (N.L.I., MSS 15, 220). Also a letter of 19 February 1899 to E. O'Flaherty (*ibid.*).

7. See J. H. Parnell to E. O'Flaherty, 19 February 1899 in N.L.I., Redmond Papers, MSS 15, 220; also Reg. of Deeds, Mem. for 1895, 5.204.

8. See *Wicklow Newsletter,* 17 October 1891. At one stage affairs reached the point where it was decided to divide representation on the Harbour Board equally between Parnellites, anti-Parnellites and Conservatives, but the arrangement collapsed.

9. *Ibid.* 3 September 1892.

10. J. H. Parnell to J. Redmond, 2 December 1898 (N.L.I., Redmond Papers, MSS 15, 220).

11. See *Wicklow Newsletter,* 21 November 1891, for one of many references.

12. See Reg. of Deeds, Mem. for 1893, 81.106; 1894, 34.8; 1899, 94.220; 1899, 94.22.

13. J. H. Parnell to J. Redmond, 13 May 1895 (N.L.I., Redmond Papers, MSS 15, 220).

14. Letter to O'Flaherty.

15. J. H. Parnell to J. Redmond, 10 April 1898 (N.L.I., Redmond Papers, MSS 15,220); also see another letter of 2 December 1898. A year later he wrote to Redmond asking him to intercede with another creditor.

16. T. P. O'Connor, *Memories of an old parliamentarian,* ii, 328. The Corporation also placed an order with the quarries when John took them over (*Wicklow Newsletter,* 19 January 1895).

17. See letter to O'Flaherty.

18. J. H. Parnell to P. F. Moran, 4 October 1902 (N.L.I., Redmond Papers, MSS 15,220), also below.

19. Letter to O'Flaherty.

20. Letter to Redmond, 9 July 1901 (N.L.I., Redmond Papers, MSS 15,220).

21. J. H. Parnell to J. Redmond, 12 January 1892 (ibid.) also see *Wicklow Newsletter,* 28 May 1892.

22. See same to same, 30 May 1895 (Redmond Papers, N.L.I., MSS 15,220); also *Irish Weekly Independent,* 15 June 1895, 13 July 1895, 20 July 1895, 27 July 1895.

23. 27 July 1895.

24. 11 July 1896.

25. *Westminster Gazette* interview reprinted in *Irish Weekly Independent,* 26 September and 10 October 1896. This lengthy interview at Avondale vividly conveys the sad hopelessness of both the place and its owner at this time.

26. J. H. Parnell to J. Redmond, 25 November 1903 (Redmond Papers, N.L.I., MSS 15,220).

27. Same to same, 27 May 1900 (*ibid.*)

28. *Ibid.*

29. Particularly John Dillon, who described it as 'a crawling, sneaking . . . outbreak of superabounding snobbery'. See F. S. L. Lyons, *John Dillon* (London, 1968), p. 208.

30. See *Irish Times*, 4 May 1923, *Irish Independent*, 4 May 1923, and J. H. Parnell to P. F. Moran, 4 October 1902 (N.L.I., Redmond Papers, MSS 15,220).

31. David Sheehy.

32. Letter to O'Flaherty.

33. Parnell to J. Redmond, 12 October 1905 (N.L.I., Redmond Papers, MSS 15,220).

34. See *Wicklow Newsletter*, 18 March 1893, and E. Dickinson, p. 195.

35. See a long letter of his to the *Independent*, 25 September 1902.

36. *Wicklow Newsletter*, 4 November 1899.

37. About which John uncharacteristically attacked Dillon in the House of Commons; see *Irish Weekly Independent*, 18 September 1897. See also a letter from Henry Parnell to the same paper, 7 October 1899.

38. *Irish Weekly Independent*, 18 December 1899.

39. See J. H. Parnell to P. F. Moran, 4 October 1902 (N.L.I., Redmond Papers, MSS 15,220), to J. Redmond, 12 October 1900 (*ibid.*), and to the *Irish Weekly Independent*, 25 September 1902.

40. See letters from Samuel Abbott, solicitor, in the *Irish Times*, 10 November 1900, and J. H. Parnell to the *Irish Weekly Independent*, 25 September 1902. Boylan's offer was £1,200 higher than the combined offers of the tenants and the estate was so heavily in debt that it had to go to the highest bidder.

41. See J. H. Parnell to J. Redmond, 17 August 1901 (N.L.I., Redmond Papers, MSS 15,220).

42. See same to same, 4 February 1905 and 1 April 1906 (*ibid.*); also, for the published comment, J. H. Parnell, p. 5 – 'Not only was he [Parnell] flung to the wolves, but his beautiful home of Avondale as well. Little did Charley think . . . to see his home in the hands of the English government under the Board of Agriculture, and the estate worked by English and Scotch labourers.'

43. J. H. Parnell to J. Redmond, 9 February 1892 (N.L.I., Redmond Papers, MSS 15,220).

44. For many letters about all this see the Redmond Papers. In 1905 John initially suggested £100 for the lease, which had 18 years to run; Redmond eventually paid him £40. The go-between was Joseph McCarroll, an old Wicklow Parnellite, who complained to Redmond of John's 'stupidity' and 'unaccountable fits'.

45. Which he could only just keep going. See J. H. Parnell to J. Redmond, 24 October 1905 (N.L.I. Redmond Papers, MSS 15,220).

46. J. Joyce, *Ulysses* (Random House ed., N.Y. 1966) pp. 165, 248.

47. See *Irish Times*, 4 May 1923, *F.J.*, 4 May 1923; *Irish Independent*, 4 May, 5 May, 7 May 1923; *The Times*, 4 May 1923; *Daily Express* (Dublin) 3 May 1923; *Evening Herald* (Dublin), 3 May and 5 May 1923.

48. *Irish Independent*, 5 May 1923, p. 3; *Irish Times*, 4 May 1923.

49. E. Dickinson, p. 203.

50. See *Wicklow Newsletter*, 26 December 1891.

51. *Ibid.* 19 November 1898; she instructed the American Irish to vote for the Democrats and Cleveland.

52. See *ibid.* 3 February 1894, for her departure from the North Wall.

53. See *ibid.* 27 April 1895, and *Irish Weekly Independent*, 27 April 1895; also E. Dickinson, ch. XV.

54. *Irish Weekly Independent*, 18 May 1895.

55. *Ibid.* 14 March 1896.

56. An interview in New York on 28 July 1896, printed in Kansas *Current Remark* and quoted in *Wicklow Newsletter*, 22 August 1896.

57. E. Dickinson, p. 208.

58. *Ibid.* p. 209.

59. *Irish Weekly Independent*, 13 March 1897.

60. E. Dickinson, p. 210.

61. See *ibid.* pp. 212–16 and also almost every contemporary newspaper; the most detailed account being in the *Irish Independent*, 2 April 1898.

62. *Daily Nation*, 1 April 1898.

63. *Freeman's Journal*, 2 April 1898. Maud Gonne wrote a eulogistic article about Parnell in the *Irish Weekly Independent*, 6 October 1894.

64. T. P. O'Connor, *Memories of an old parliamentarian*, ii, 220. He does not give a date, and the book, *Old tales and new*, printed by Sealy, Bryars and Walker, Dublin, does not carry one.

65. *Irish Weekly Independent*, 13 October 1894, excerpts from Anna Parnell's introduction to J. Wyse-Power, *Words of the dead chief*, published that year.

66. *Irish Weekly Independent*, 9 December 1899.

67. This is mentioned in her obituary in *The Times*, 25 September 1911, but I can find no contemporary mention of it.

68. See *Freeman's Journal*, 25 September 1911; also J. Wyse-Power, 'Anna Parnell', in *Dublin Metropolitan Magazine* (Spring 1935), p. 17.

69. Obituary in *Freeman's Journal*, 25 September 1911.

70. See inquest report, *ibid.*; also Theodosia Paget to Helena Molony, 23 November 1911 (N.L.I., Anna Parnell material, MS 12, 144). Anna left Theodosia a little money, with the idea of publishing the 'Tale'.

71. *Freeman's Journal*, 25 September 1911.

72. *Debrett's Peerage.* Of his three children, Captain Mateer tells me that one was mentally retarded and lived with John Howard Parnell; another son died young; and a daughter became mentally unbalanced.

73. Mentioned in *Irish Independent*, 24 May 1918.

74. See Reg. of Deeds, Mem. for 1893, 23.191, 59.81; for 1897, 1.181.

75. *Ibid.* for 1897, 1.181.

76. J. H. Parnell, p. 256.

77. E. Dickinson, p. 237.

78. J. Joyce, *Ulysses*, p. 165.

79. T. P. O'Connor, *Memories of an old parliamentarian*, i, 232.

80. E. Dickinson, p. 238. See above, part III.

81. *Ibid.* p. 240.

82. I am indebted to Captain Mateer, John Howard Parnell's stepson, for some details of what then became of Emily.

83. *Irish Independent*, 24 May 1918.

84. *Irish Times*, 27 May 1918.

85. *Irish Independent*, 24 May 1819.

86. See *Wicklow Newsletter*, 22 April 1893.

87. See report of Anna's inquest, *Freeman's Journal*, 25 September 1911.

88. *Debrett's Peerage.*

# *Index*

Parnells, including Congletons, appear under 'Parnell'; so do wives of Parnells, unless encountered only under their maiden name. Place-names in Wicklow (and elsewhere) only appear if they have a particular importance, or are repeatedly encountered. The same is true for tenants on the Parnell estate. Where John Howard Parnell, Emily Dickinson, etc., are mentioned in the text merely as authorities, their names are not indexed; unless specific reference is made to the nature of the evidence they are presenting. Identifications are kept to a minimum – peers, for instance, appearing under their title, not family name, and distinguished by order of succession only.